The History of Garden Design

Edited by
Monique Mosser
and Georges Teyssot

with 652 illustrations,
129 in colour,
and 51 specially drawn plans

The History of Garden Design

The Western Tradition
from the Renaissance to the Present Day

Thames & Hudson

Committee of Experts
Carmen Añón Feliú, ICOMOS, Madrid
Stephen Bann, University of Kent at Canterbury
Lionello Puppi, University of Padua
Helmut Reinhardt, University of Darmstadt

Executive Editor
Alessandra Ponte

English-Language Editor
Fiona Cowell

Translators
Wendy Dallas
Barbara Mellor
Sebastian Wormell
Anthony Bland
Paul Vincent
(*see facing page*)

Plans
Radames Zaramella
and Silvia Bettini

Special Photography
Giovanni Chiaramonte
Daniele De Lonte
Luigi Ghirri
Fulvio Ventura

First published in the United Kingdom in 1991
by Thames & Hudson Ltd, 181A High Holborn,
London WC1V 7QX
First paperback edition 2000

First published in paperback in the United States
of America in 2000 by Thames & Hudson Inc.,
500 Fifth Avenue, New York, New York 10110

Previously published in the USA under the title
The Architecture of Western Gardens

British Library Cataloguing-in-Publication Data
A catalogue record for this book is available
from the British Library

Library of Congress Catalog card Number 99-67034

ISBN 0-500-28206-4

Printed and bound in Italy

Acknowledgments

A work such as this is the result of a collective effort on the part of many individuals, and it is therefore difficult to make proper acknowledgment for all the assistance received. Special thanks are due to the Department of the History of Architecture (IUAV), Venice, and to the Ministry of Education, Rome, for making research funds available for the collection of illustration material. The editors and publishers would also like to record their indebtedness to the Committee of Experts and all the authors, translators, editors, picture researchers, graphic artists, designers and photographers who have made valuable contributions to the work.

The texts by Georges Teyssot, Lionello Puppi, Luigi Zangheri, Lucia Tongiorgi Tomasi, Paolo Carpeggiani, Gianni Venturi, Bruno Adorni, Margherita Azzi Visentini, Anna Maria Matteucci, Maurizio Gargano, Alessandra Ponte, Paolo Morachiello, Elisabetta Cereghini, Cesare De Seta, Eliana Mauro, Ettore Sessa, Marco De Michelis, Renzo Dubbini, Marco Pogačnik and Sergio Polano and all the captions were translated from the Italian by Wendy Dallas.

The texts by Monique Mosser, Anne-Marie Lecoq, Françoise Boudon, Hélène Vérin, Gérard Mabille, Antoine Schnapper, Marianne Roland Michel, Daniel Rabreau, Anne de Stoop, Antoinette Le Normand Romain, Jean de Cayeux, Thomas von Joest, Annick Brauman, Michel Racine, Catherine Royer and Isabelle Auricoste were translated from the French by Barbara Mellor.

The texts by Reinhard Zimmermann, Dorothee Nehring, Helmut Reinhardt, Dieter Hennebo, Hans-Christoph Dittscheid, Klaus von Krosigk, Vroni Heinrich and Birgit Wahmann were translated from the German by Sebastian Wormell.

The texts by Carmen Añón Feliú, Ignasi de Solà Morales and Fernando Aliata were translated from the Spanish by Anthony Bland.

The texts by Ulbe Martin Mehrtens, Carla S. Oldenburger-Ebbers and Jan van Asbeck were translated from the Dutch by Paul Vincent.

Contents

Introduction:
The Architecture of the Garden and Architecture in the Garden

Monique Mosser and Georges Teyssot

The idea of the garden as a natural space adapted by man to meet his own aesthetic demands grew from the concept that private land could be used to satisfy many human needs, and from the conviction that the beauty of nature could be improved by the work of man (Giulio Carlo Argan). In other words, the garden always has two roles, and it is as inseparable from its utilitarian function as it is from its aesthetic or ideal function. The garden can be seen as the highest form of agriculture or (according to the definition of Erasmus of Rotterdam, which was elaborated by Kant) as a precious sanctuary from the tumult of the city. The garden is, therefore, intended to fulfil private needs for peace and seclusion and at the same time to provide for the common good. As a result of this dual purpose, it has acquired a certain ambiguity, as a place in which nature and culture, work and pleasure meet (Louis Marin). The garden is an external expression of an interior world, a setting for meditation under an open sky and for the revelation of secrets to those worthy of hearing them. 'All that is capricious and extravagant in man, all that there is of the wanderer or the vagabond, can without doubt be contained in these syllables: garden' (Louis Aragon).

The garden is one of the most ephemeral of human creations. Subject to every vagary of the weather, to changes of fashion and changes of ownership, it seems an almost impossible subject for study, let alone for a book whose principal aim is to recount its history from the sixteenth century to the present day.

Other than in Great Britain, no inventory exists of the gardens and parks of Europe and the United States, nor any list of the gardeners, owners, dilettanti, painters, architects and engineers who designed them. Few attempts have been made to compile any sort of comprehensive topographical and bibliographical compendium of the gardens of a single country. Two works have, however, made a significant contribution in this respect: Ray Desmond's *Bibliography of British Gardens* (Winchester 1984) and Ernest de Ganay's *Bibliographie de l'Art des Jardins en France jusqu'en 1945* (Paris 1989), and we hope soon to see further volumes (with a greater emphasis on the history of gardens) in the series on the villas of Italy edited by Pier Fausto Bagatti Valsecchi. On the history of gardens in a wider perspective, Wernersche Verlagsgesellschaft of Worms have published papers on the series of meetings held at Dumbarton Oaks, Washington DC.

It should, however, be remembered that iconographical material on the subject of gardens is to be found in such widely disparate sources as to make research of this kind far from easy: tapestries, miniatures, paintings, memoirs illustrated with drawings, sketches and plans, engravings in treatises, architects' notebooks etc. all provide documentation and new information on gardens and their history. The problem for the curators of archival material of this sort is constantly to update their collections, and not to fall into the trap into which so many books on gardens fall, resorting exclusively to the use of line drawings and engravings, and even nineteenth-century lithographs. This does not, of course, include the wave of opulent coffee-table books full of rather precious and extravagant prose and illustrated with exquisite photo-

graphs of flowerbeds, trees and shrubs, that have appeared in recent years; this is not the place for a discussion of their merits or otherwise. Here the aim is to examine in depth the subject of gardens from the point of view of the spectator, from the camera obscura to the Claude glass and through to the objectivity of photographic recording, from Eugène Atget to Edwin Smith.

In accordance with a current tendency away from vast compilations and *grands récits*, this book is structured chronologically, but proceeds by a series of essays on specific subjects, intended not so much to provide the reader with any comprehensive catalogue of all the gardens laid out in the period under consideration as to demonstrate the wide range of research programmes currently being undertaken. It makes no pretence to be a new and up-to-date Marie Luise Gothein (*Geschichte der Gartenkunst*, 1913, 2nd ed. 1925; English translation, *A History of Garden Art*, London–New York 1928, 2nd ed. 1979), nor does it have the encyclopedic breadth of *The Oxford Companion to Gardens* (Oxford University Press 1986). Any definition of the 'modern age' of western civilization is inevitably contentious, and the scope of knowledge and activity comprising the Art of Gardening, *Gartenkunst, Arte dei giardini* and *Art des jardins* is boundless; but the aim of this book is, nonetheless, without dwelling exclusively on matters concerning the history of botany, to provide an introduction to the architecture of the garden in Europe and the United States in recent times.

The essays, published in chronological order, have been written by specialists from a number of different countries. Some cover aspects of the history of the garden that have already been explored elsewhere – such as the 'humanist gardens' of Tuscany, Rome and the Veneto, or the aesthetic movements that have influenced the evolution of the garden through the ages and inspired, for instance, the English landscape park of the eighteenth century, and fashions for the 'picturesque', the 'pastoral' and the 'sublime'. But these essays shed new important light on the personalities behind such developments, and on the context in which they worked. Other articles present material on historical aspects of the garden that have never previously been explored, such as the *cabinet de curiosités*, the vogues for the 'grotesque' and for labyrinths, the esoteric creations of Bernard Palissy, the technological inventions devised by garden designers, the laying out of public walks in urban environments, the romantic fashion for edifying and poetic inscriptions suspended from trees . . . Also included here, by contrast with many previous books on garden history, are a number of contributions on trends in the development of parks and gardens in the nineteenth and twentieth centuries: the revival of the romantic and classical styles; land art; the ecological movement; problems concerning the restoration and conservation of ancient parks. The essays, arranged in five periods from the sixteenth to the twentieth centuries, are complemented by shorter articles devoted to particular themes (for example, the Masonic gardens of Sicily) or even to individual gardens which can be regarded in some way as paradigms (such as the parks of Wilhelmshöhe and of Leopold in Brussels).

About fifty ground-plans have been meticulously redrawn by Silvia Bettini and Radames Zaramella, using original archive material, much of which consisted of rough sketch plans, of representations of ancient gardens executed in the eighteenth century or later, or of nineteenth- and twentieth-century architectural reconstructions. It should, perhaps, be emphasized here that remarkably few topographical surveys exist of the parks and gardens of Europe, possibly because of the enormous costs and technical difficulties involved in their execution. In spite of this, the wide range of plans reproduced here provide precise and clear information on the scale and the nature of many of the projects discussed.

The garden, one of humanity's finest creations, has always endeavoured to combine the most homogeneous and pleasing aspects of nature, often adapted to the wishes of man, with the highest forms of art. One might say that a nostalgia for the Garden of Eden has provided garden designers throughout history with a model of perfection to aspire to. In recent times archaeologists have, for example, put forward proposals for a reconstruction of the hanging gardens of Babylon. Dating from more than 2500 years ago, and laid out in a country of extreme dry heat, this wonder of the ancient world consisted, it seems, of a vast series of descending terraces overflowing with vegetation – their tranquillity enhanced by the sound of running water and the singing of birds. Against a background of myth and legend, architecture has provided the framework and the context for an art that has been too often ignored or underestimated: there can be few gardens that were not originally laid out to serve or complement a building, whether a temple to the glory of God or a house for the use of man.

The first literary contribution to modern Western culture to be devoted to the art of the garden, the *Hypnerotomachia Poliphili* (Venice 1499), was illustrated with a series of wood engravings which, in various forms, provided the basis for a formula that was perpetuated for more than four centuries: 'the temple with the pyramid', 'the tomb of Adonis'; Priapus under a canopy of foliage; innumerable *treillages* etc. In 1918 Gertrude Jekyll, that beneficent and inspiring influence on the history of the English garden, published a large volume entitled *Garden Ornament* with consisted partly of a history of gardens and partly of a catalogue of decorative garden features. She includes, for instance, items on 'entrance gateways, steps and balustrades; urns, vases and sculptured ornaments; stone-paved courts and paved ways; loggias; orangeries; pergolas and treillage; canals, ponds and water gardens; bridges; fountains and dipping wells; wall gardening . . .' – not forgetting, of course, 'topiary work', the art that transforms living plants into architecture and sculpture.

The representation of gardens would deserve several chapters in any general history of graphic art. It presents a particular problem in that it lies at the junction between architecture and topography, and it is clear that the draughtsmen who drew early garden plans very soon realized the difference between a simple ground-plan and something which expressed the essence of the garden. In effect, the traditional means of conveying the design of a flat, two-dimensional plan reduced it to a series of more or less complex geometric shapes, like the *broderies* of a parterre. From the beginning of the Renaissance, therefore, the technique most frequently adopted for the representation of gardens was that of the bird's-eye-view, by means of which the layout and the details of the garden could be shown in a far more realistic form. In his *Les plus excellents bastiments de France* (1576–9), Jacques Androuet du Cerceau includes an early and remarkable example, and a few years later Just (later known as Giusto) Utens, a painter from Brussels who was living in Tuscany, perfected this method in the views he painted of the Medici villas at Artiminio. He devised a sort of compromise between the techniques of cartographic drawing and the Flemish traditions of landscape painting (in which the horizons appeared very high and extended into the pale blue distance). This style of representation continued in vogue until the end of the seventeenth century. In their innumerable engravings of the great classical parks of the period, Perelle and Silvestre chose to accentuate the central axis in order to achieve a more spectacular effect, with the result that the field of vision became distorted and the viewpoint raised to that of a bird's-eye-view; the very artificiality of this technique did, however, create a sort of heightened reality that was remarkably effective.

Among the great artists of the seventeenth century who illustrated gardens more representationally were painters, garden designers and, particularly, architects. In order to provide a client with a full and realistic idea of a project, and to instruct the team of craftsmen engaged in its execution, it was essential to draw up vast ground-plans to illustrate the overall scheme and also to produce a large number of detailed drawings. From this derived a fashion for 'cartography of gardens and orchards'. The technique employed was that of traditional cartographic relief drawing using shading, but it was combined with an aesthetic approach that gave it a quality of its own. If one studies the plans of Bélanger for the Folie Saint-James or Bagatelle, or of Bergeret for L'Isle-Adam, one is immediately struck by their power to convey, by means of detail, a clear sense of the design of the landscape into which those details fit. The imagination sees beyond the conventions of the technique, and envisages full-grown trees reflected in the waters of a river and the scene complete with beautiful buildings. This romantic cartographic style can, perhaps, be said to have something in common with the Utopian fantasies of contemporary literature, and certainly owed much to a fashion for the exotic in architecture and also in plants, many new botanical species having recently been imported.

In every era garden designers have in their own highly individual ways interpreted the role of architecture in the open spaces of a park or garden. Dezallier d'Argenville, who gathered together and catalogued all the available material on the subject of classical garden design, traditionally symbolized by the great figure of Le Nôtre, wrote in the seventh chapter of his *La théorie et la pratique du jardinage* (1709): 'Arcades, Arbours and Alcoves of greenery are "fragments of architecture" which, when well situated, have a special beauty and

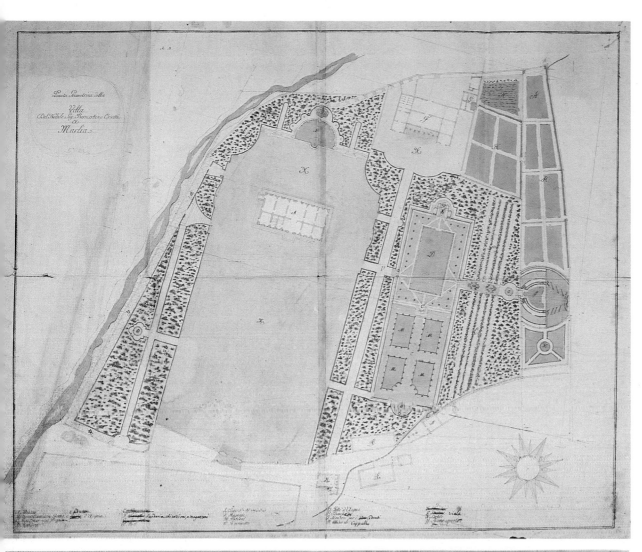

Plan of Villa Orsetti (later Reale, today Pecci-Blunt) at Marlia, Lucca. Anonymous seventeenth-century drawing. Lucca State Archives.

View of Villa Orsetti. Engraving, 1775.

Prospetto della Villa Orsetti a Marlia

13

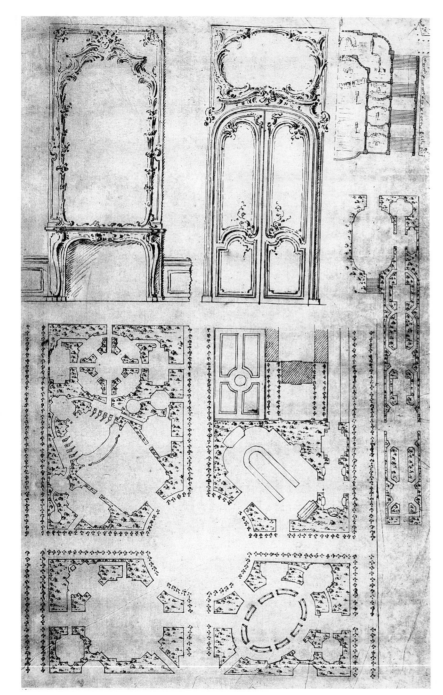

Charles-Albert de Lespilliez (1723?–1796), plan of the garden of a castle with an open-air theatre, and designs for a fireplace and a door. Pencil drawing, 1754. Staatliche Museen Preussischer Kulturbesitz, Berlin.

magnificence that greatly enhances the natural beauty of the garden; it is a pity that, with all the expense and care involved in their construction, they should be so easily destroyed'. The rules of proportion and the search for a sense of harmony with the surrounding landscape, which govern the creation of a garden, are inseparable from a quality of transience. *Treillage*, belvederes and grottoes of rocaille and ornamental shell work were common features in the gardens of the Renaissance and the seventeenth century. Sanssouci, Mon-Plaisir and other such places derive their linear forms and delicate colours from classicism tempered by the influence of the Baroque parks of Piedmont, the Russia of the Tsars and the German principalities.

The creation of parks and gardens in England in the eighteenth century constitutes one of the most important chapters in the history of architecture, engineering and ecology. In a country where the rich were more often aristocratic dilettanti, generals who had exchanged the battlefield for fields of grain, and successful bankers rather than depositories of feudal rights, landowners invested a great deal of money, energy and experience in agriculture and horticulture. By contrast with France, where the state, with few exceptions, was solely responsible for the development of the country, opening up vast tracts of uninhabited land by means of long, straight roads and bridges, the transformation of the English countryside was largely the work of private landowners.

Certainly it is true to say that the classical English garden, in the style of William Kent, was born of the country's particular climatic conditions, but it was also the result of an attitude of mind, of a taste for the irregular and the asymmetric. It was closely related to seventeenth-century English literature, which reflected a new sense of freedom and, in particular, an aversion for an aesthetic based on straight lines, whether classical or Baroque in origin.

The landscape park, although visually extending into the surrounding countryside, in fact consisted of a confined space: outside, in the country, the 'green revolution' slowly brought about a shift in the balance of power; inside, in an area enclosed by invisible fences, the land, the vegetation and the water were controlled and ordered according to the rules governing the styles known as *peigné* or *sauvage* (orderly or wild). A wide range of disciplines contributed to the creation of the English garden of the first half of the eighteenth century, making it in effect a technical and scientific laboratory, a canvas on which to paint an abstract picture, and a place for aesthetic experimentation.

As a technical workshop, the landscape park provided an opportunity for military engineering, hydraulics, surveying and cartography, involving land reclamation and the construction of raised embankments and trenches, ditches and escarpments, canals and watercourses, pools and basins, polygons, rectangles and half moons. The work of Charles Bridgeman and Stephen Switzer offers good examples of the scale of the enterprises undertaken.

As a canvas for an abstract picture, it gave the artist an open space on

14

which to draw geometric patterns consisting of straight, curving or serpentine lines – in the style of Hogarth – circles or spiders' webs, and to lay out a network of intersecting paths and vistas.

As a place for aesthetic experimentation, it offered a setting for references to ancient myth and Arcadian legend through the picturesque and the sublime, in a journey in which all the pictorial, literary and symbolic allusions were made first by means of allegorical quotation (Rousham is an excellent example) and later as a result of the development of the profession of garden designer, thanks largely to the work of Lancelot 'Capability' Brown, which reflected the natural world not only emblematically but also in metaphorical and abstract terms.

At the end of the eighteenth century and the beginning of the nineteenth, with the work of Humphry Repton and the intellectual contributions of Richard Payne Knight and Uvedale Price, the landscape park revived its associations with literature and the picturesque. The theory and realization of the picturesque introduced the modern concept of critical choice in relation to architectural planning, and to the use of montage and 'fragmentation'. At a time when nature was regarded as a complement to the life of the community, the role of the painter, the architect and the garden designer was to select those images from history and the imagination which elicited the desired reaction from the spectator: the various features which comprised the different episodes in the garden – the pavilions, temples, lakes, trees, hills etc. – were chosen and set out in such a way that they made a perfectly composed picture in a frame. Nature was thus created anew and the story of the world rewritten.

As far as France was concerned, one might say that it was with the advent of the landscape garden and the Anglo-Chinese style, that these 'architectural fragments' acquired a new importance. Carmontelle, the bizarre inventor of the *Folie* of the Duc de Chartres, which later became the Parc Monceau in Paris, explained that these microcosmic gardens had to 'unite in a single space all times and all places . . .' by means of their *fabriques* (garden buildings). It is well known that this entertaining man of the world, a painter in his spare time, invented the notion of enormous rolls of transparent paper – some as much as twenty-five metres (eighty-two feet) long – which could be stretched in front of a source of light to illustrate scenes from distant lands and transport the spectator to those 'illusory places' so dear to Jurgis Baltrušaitis.

Architecture therefore became a deviser of drama and display, an enchantress and magician; it was the role of architecture, even more than festivals and the theatre, to provide the scenery for the constantly changing sets of the garden. What, after all, would a 'desert' be without a hermitage, and 'Elysium' without an ancient sepulchre, an 'Arcadian meadow' without a shepherd's hut? This was the kingdom of the *fabriques*, a word which initially referred to 'all the buildings depicted in landscape painting' but which by 1770 embraced 'every construction built in a garden to serve a picturesque or ornamental purpose'. This change in the significance of the word, which marked a shift from two-dimensional pictorial representation to independent architectural

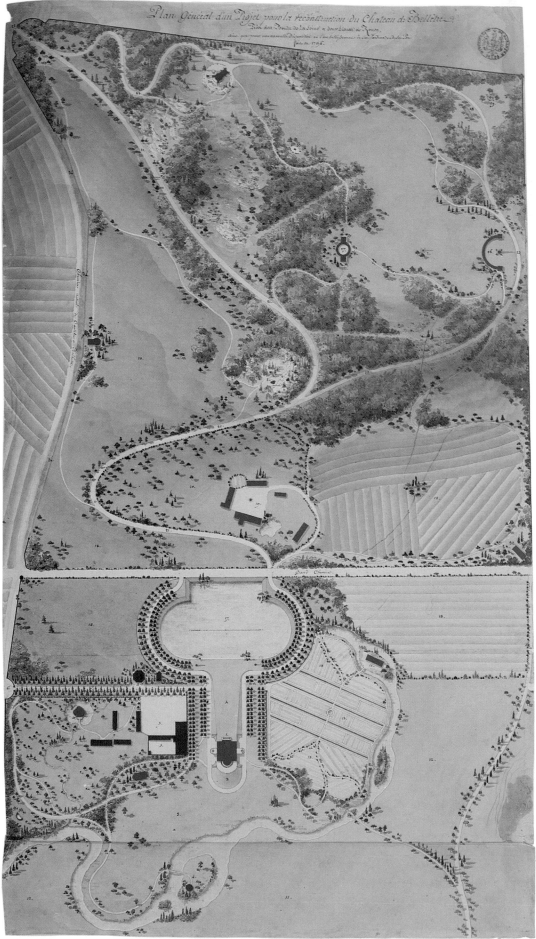

Plan of the park of the château of Bellêtre in Normandy, designed by P.-A. Pâris. Bibliothèque Municipale, Besançon.

16

expression, clearly reveals the factors that at that time linked landscape painting with the art of the informal garden. An example of this new emphasis is provided by the work of the emblematic figure Hubert Robert. According to Morel, another theoretician of the late eighteenth century, the choice of *fabrique* 'depended absolutely on the character of the setting and on the relationship of the surrounding objects'. In effect, it was the task of these 'miniature monuments' to interpret the iconography and symbolism of the garden, to serve as a medium for emotion and sentiment and to express a range of abstract intentions and ideals. From time to time, love, memory or friendship, which inhabit the temples and tombs of the garden, seem to be etched into the rocks themselves, and every element takes on a particular significance. A simple tree trunk can be roughly lopped in such a way as to recall the fundamental debate on the origins of architecture. Further on, a rustic grotto rekindles pagan feelings that are extraordinarily vivid and alive, fostered by the cult of the nymphs. A walk through a garden can sometimes be compared with a lesson in architecture in a park, or even with an initiatory stroll through Mozart's *Magic Flute*.

Gardens, whether they are intended for ruling princes or the general public, for philosophers, scholars or poets, or as the adornment of a suburban villa, whatever the economic and social status of their owner, whatever their situation – the city or the country, an aristocratic residence or a working farm – their purpose is always the same: to provide 'a place of sanctuary in an ancient Arcady or in the Paradise inhabited by early man, a Hermitage, a haven of solitude, a setting for theatre and display' (J. Baltrušaitis). The concept of the garden is inseparable from philosophy, from the idea of the ideal museum, and as such it has developed its own aesthetic doctrines (Lionello Puppi).

As a result of the sort of paradox frequently encountered in history, it was as part of the shift in emphasis from the public to the private sector that policies were formed to provide large cities with public open spaces and to plant gardens to improve the health and living standards of the inhabitants. The most celebrated proponent of this movement was the English philosopher Jeremy Bentham. He was already widely known throughout Europe for having proposed, in around 1790, the sinister but nonetheless ingenious scheme which he called a Panopticon. It consisted basically of a circular plan which could be applied to any building in which a small number of people needed to be able to supervise many others, such as a factory, a prison, a hospital, a school, etc. In his later work, *Chrestomathia* (1816), which was devoted to the educational system, he developed his new theory of eudemonism, based on the Aristotelian concept of the happiness that results from a rational active life. He took as his premise the notion that 'directly or indirectly, *well-being*, in some shape or other, or in several shapes, or all shapes taken together, is the subject of every thought, and object of every action, on the part of every known *Being*, who is, at the same time, a sensitive and thinking Being'. He then transformed this theory into a sort of physico-moral law: 'The quantity or degree of *well-being*, experienced during any given length of time, is directly as the *magnitude*

(i.e. the *intensity* multiplied by the *duration*) of the sum of the pleasures, and inversely as the *magnitude* of the sum of the *pains*, experienced during that same length of time.' It is clear that this rationale could lead only to a quantification of happiness, such as formed the basis of the thinking of the English followers of Utilitarianism, of which Bentham was the founder. They were inspired by the writings of Francis Hutcheson, who, in his *Enquiry into the Original of our Ideas of Beauty and Virtue*, had already established that evil depends on two factors: 'the degree of poverty and the number of those who suffer from it; so that action is best which procures the greatest happiness for the greatest numbers'. On the basis of a similar assumption, the Utilitarians were able to quantify the productivity of every moral and political action.

Throughout the first half of the nineteenth century, the followers of Bentham formed a group whose thinking provided the foundation of the movement for the creation of public parks in Great Britain: among its leaders were the historian James Mill (father of John Stuart Mill) and politicians such as Edwin Chadwick, secretary of the Poor Law Commission, R. A. Slaney and John Arthur Roebuck. They opposed the sale and enclosure of all common lands, a phenomenon which threatened to remove, especially in urban centres, every remaining space suitable for walking, sport and enjoyment of the natural environment. Roebuck was to become one of the most diligent and active editors of the *Report of the Select Committee on Public Walks and Places of Exercise*, published in 1833 by the parliamentary group formed to carry out a programme of research into the need for public open spaces. They recommended the provision of open spaces for walking, so that the working man would be induced to maintain within his family certain standards of 'cleanliness, neatness and personal appearance', because 'a man, walking out with his family among his neighbours of different ranks, will naturally be desirous to be properly clothed, and that his wife and children should be also; but this desire duly directed and controlled, is found by experience to be of the most powerful effect in promoting Civilisation and exciting Industry'. Roebuck fought hard to have the Common Field Enclosures Bill of 1834 adopted by parliament, but with only modest results: from 1837 to 1841, out of 41,420 acres (16,762 hectares) of land sold and enclosed only 222 acres (90 hectares) were turned into public parks. This notwithstanding, it is clear from the parliamentary report already mentioned that this was a constantly recurring political theme in Europe and the United States until the end of the nineteenth century.

John Claudius Loudon, founder of the 'horticultural movement' in England, voiced his view in the *Gardener's Magazine* that when cities and their surroundings are ruled by laws and governing bodies acting in unison, and not, as he felt they were then, in the shoddy and mean-spirited fashion of corporations and parish councils, and when the recreation and the pleasure of the whole of society is taken into consideration by its representatives, public gardens would be laid out, with large and small glasshouses, for the enjoyment of the people and at the expense of the community. This was the basis of the programme for the construction of metropolitan parks in the great urban centres of the nineteenth century. The great difference between the landscape garden of the eighteenth century and the city park of a hundred years later was, in effect, its institutional and urban emphasis.

The 'central park', to use an expression coined by Walter Benjamin, was first and foremost a piece of urban equipment. Its original aim was to raise moral and hygienic standards, as contemporary literature on the subject testifies. The park was an instrument at the service of the city and it functioned along clearly established lines: having provided a well-equipped area of open green space available to all, it demanded that those who used it behaved in a disciplined fashion and conformed with certain standards, and it laid down rules concerning the enclosure of the land, the sale of tickets, the cleaning and sanitation provided and the prohibition of prostitution. Violent activity or sports were confined to designated areas.

For the great garden designers and landscape architects of the nineteenth century (P. J. Lenné, Joseph Paxton, F. L. Olmsted, James Pennethorne, Edward Kemp, Alexander McKenzie and Edouard André, the follower of Adolphe Alphand, who designed – among other things – Sefton Park in Liverpool, for which he produced designs in 1867, the formal ideal governing the design of the public park seems to have consisted of an alternation of concave and convex forms. Without ever conflicting with each other, these shapes allowed the whole scheme to be laid out on a circuit, which was regarded as essential to the enjoyment of walking in the park. In the central park the arabesque became a ubiquitous feature, permitting every element to relate directly to the overall design and extending a curvilinear network over the entire area. The result was that time and space seemed to lose their significance and that an infinite variety of view points and settings was created. The figure of the arabesque had much in common with the impression created by a moving crowd. From 'the man in the crowd' of Edgar Allan Poe to the *flâneur* of Charles Baudelaire, the central park expressed in its labyrinthine forms the 'quality of feeling' aroused by the city itself: 'intensity, sonority, lucidity, agitation, profundity and resonance in time and space' (Baudelaire).

The nineteenth-century notion of walking replaced the classical idea of the *promenade* which had grown up in the seventeenth century, and established a clear link with the idea of a 'cycle' or 'circuit' such as formed the basis of the sinuous lines of the arabesque and serpentine forms of the parks of the period. The philosopher Michel Serres has drawn attention to the fact that the layout of the park, like the construction of a metropolitan organism such as Paris, New York or Berlin, takes as its metaphorical model the working of the motor. Both the park and the city function as two reflective elements which become metaphors in their turn: the *reservoir* as a container of energy (as in Central Park, New York; the Reservoir Botzaris in Buttes-Chaumont, Paris; or the Wasserturm in the park in Hamburg); *circulation* as the principle governing the mobile elements (such as the movement of the crowds and the watercourses); *residues* such as dust and dirt, sewage and

detritus to complete the cycle. By regarding the city as a motor and its technology as beautiful, the central park celebrated the triumph of those skills which were used to exploit that vast reservoir of energy which is nature. In the second half of the nineteenth century, nature and the machine practised the same ritual.

It was in this vein that Friedrich Nietzsche wrote in *Die fröhliche Wissenschaft* (The Gay Science):

It will be necessary sometime, and probably in the not-too-distant future, to realize what above all is lacking in our great cities: peaceful wide-open spaces for undisturbed meditation, long covered areas with ample space for walking in bad weather or hot sunshine, where the noise of cars and the cries of touts cannot penetrate, and in which a respect for others would even prevent the priest from praying out loud: buildings and public gardens that reflect in their conception the sublime nature of contemplation and of solitary walks (Book IV, 280).

The urban park was seen as a temple of meditation in the heart of the metropolis, a perfect setting for secular, contemplative modern life, and it found its most complete expression in Germany in the first half of the present century, in the Volkspark and Kleingarten, Jugendpark and Totengarten, which reflected the principles of Gartensozialismus.

The public park began to decline in the twentieth century, and for certain observers it became a melting pot for new ideas, the anvil on which the theories of modernism were hammered out. It was described as 'a sort of vast shuttlecock that spins in the air and is undirected by any hand'. This was the view of Louis Aragon, who adopted a negatory rather than a merely negative tone in his brilliant comment on the 'natural spirit of Buttes-Chaumont' in the second part of *Le Paysan de Paris* (1926). He visited the place with André Breton one misty night and described it as 'a mad creation born in the head of an architect and inspired by the conflict between Jean-Jacques Rousseau and the economic problems of life in Paris'. It was 'the test tube of human chemistry in which the precipitate speaks and has strange-coloured eyes'.

The park harboured the subconscious of the city. The greatest tragedy was to be aware of the 'modern impossibility of avoiding the ubiquitous influence of the law' and to be unable to control even the 'nature of one's nostalgia'. 'Great cold searchlights surmount all modern machinery, seeking out and subjugating even the rocks, the living plants and the little streams'. The wind of sublime pleasures is easily capable of driving desire towards excess and ultimately death. A significant feature of the park of Buttes-Chaumont is the walk over the great Bridge of the Suicides, 'where people used to kill themselves before a protective grille was provided, as did passers-by who had not even decided on this course of action but who were drawn into the abyss nonetheless'. This sense of desolation, a sort of desperate kiss of love, revolution and death, also took hold of Adrian Stokes in Kensington Gardens:

The startled shorn bodies suggested a touch of extreme 'nature', a nakedness, an exhibitionism, even, a sudden production of the pale body, a child's

amorous game, a suicide, a thousand little boys running nude into the Serpentine on a hot summer evening, allied somehow with the world of correctitude, railings and park-keepers; with parkees and violent dirt, no less. (*Inside Out*, 1947)

In this microcosm of labyrinthine paths and embracing couples, filled with thousands of statues like a cemetery of the imagination, and with lakes lit up by electric moons and painted by Arnold Böcklin, man, says Aragon, rediscovers with some alarm 'the monstrous imprint of his body and the outline of his face. He encounters himself at every step. Here is to be found the mansion of the mind which at last allows him to discover his own identity'. This is perhaps the key to an understanding of Nietzsche's comment on the creation of public gardens: 'when we wander in these arcades and through these gardens it is us that we want to have transformed into stones and plants, it is in ourselves that we want to roam'.

In 1965 John Lindsay, the future mayor of New York, made the creation of parks and playgrounds a priority in his electoral campaign. His later municipal policies were to include both successes and failures. His most notable frustration was of his intention to turn every piece of undeveloped land in the city into a public open space, an initiative which inevitably suffered from the movement away from urban centres which occurred in the Sixties and Seventies. The creation of open spaces fell into two distinct categories: on the one hand the stereotypical structure christened the 'adventure playground', and on the other the squares reserved for those events described by the artistic élite as 'happenings'. Lindsay's equally notable successes include the launching of a policy of conservation: Central Park and Prospect Park were declared 'national historic landmarks'. The results of this endeavour, after more than twenty years of hard work and enormous expense, are exemplary from both the aesthetic and the social points of view.

In the 1940s the public park again gave rise to a debate on its role as a place of active pursuits or of passive contemplation. In order to appreciate the nature of the problem, it is worth returning briefly to the subject of Central Park in its heyday (around 1895). Galen Cranz has stated, in *The Politics of Park Design* (Cambridge, Mass. 1982), that the purpose of the park was to be not so much passive as well structured. Specific areas were set aside for particular activities, such as sports tracks for competitive events; carriage routes, which were linked to the main roads through the park; sandy trails through woodland for horse-riding; polo grounds; cycle tracks; enclosures for children's games, etc.; there were also fountains, watercourses and lakes, open areas to accommodate circus tents or musical bands, grass tennis courts, spaces for political speeches and demonstrations and flat expanses for military manoeuvres. All in all, it was a reflection of a new mentality, a new attitude of mind: the American and European public of the period was, in general, made up of people capable of enjoying a wide range of varied activities. Unlike the sports spectator of today, the people of the time in many respects resembled the television watcher of today who frequently switches programme, reflecting an attitude that is anything but contemplative; on the contrary, it is characteristic of a distracted state of mind.

In conclusion, it should be remembered that a number of sociological research programmes have been carried out in recent times in an attempt to understand the attitude of the public towards the city park, and they have produced the following findings: the first may be defined as the naïve approach ('the park is an uncontaminated corner of nature; it is not an artefact but an oasis of land preserved in its original state'); the second has been described as the aesthetic approach ('the park is an artefact; it has its own style and its own independent process of evolution'); the third, the technocratic approach, is still a powerful force in the development of our European cities today. It is to be seen in the work of the bureaucrats and the town planners who view the world as if from an aeroplane and design 'green spaces' with a bulldozer, of the city councillors who create parks by the simple means of erecting fences around a field, and of the mayors who transform historic parks into abominations filled with all the trappings of urban life, which should be provided in other areas of the city.

There is no question of the philosophy of romanticism or of utilitarianism being applicable to the public parks or gardens of today. But, confronted with the impoverished notions informing the creation of green spaces, and with the contemporary need for access to the natural environment and for an understanding of nature, it is undeniably clear that, at least in Europe, a profound lack of awareness and vision exists on the part both of the public and of the professional planners.

Certainly, the park today is no longer 'central', except perhaps in cases requiring urgent conservation. Indeed, it has been pushed towards the outskirts of the city as metropolitan life is concentrated increasingly in the suburbs. The ancient historical centres are beginning to empty, and soon they will consist only of banks and museums set in pedestrian precincts, populated only by crowds of staring tourists and the convulsive young. Everything is moving to the outskirts because everything forms part of a network, or is tending to do so. Individuals will be seen only on a shining video screen or glimpsed for a fraction of a second through the windscreen of a car. In this era of de-territorialization Jean Baudrillard wrote recently that we have been deprived of that classical sense of natural metamorphosis; even the powerful metaphors created by artists of the nineteenth century in the heart of the metropolis – the real land of the exile – have begun to fade. The exile carries with him at least the knowledge, the memory, even the smells of the shores that he has left behind him for ever. Today, the sense of deprivation has reached both his consciousness and his environment. We believe, therefore, that if we do not think more deeply about the significance of the landscape, the park and the garden today, the future is bleak.

PART ONE

The Humanist Garden:
From Allegory to Mannerism

Part title: *Villa Lante at Bagnaia.*
(Photo Daniele De Lonte)

Garden of the Villa d'Este, Tivoli. From a survey published in C. Lamb, Die Villa d'Este in Tivoli, *Munich 1966.*

The Sacro Bosco of the Villa Orsini, Bomarzo. From a survey published in H. Bredekamp, Vicino Orsini und der Heilige Wald von Bomarzo, *Worms 1985.*

The Garden of Pratolino, Florence. From Pianta dei due Barchi, Viali, Fontane, e Fabbriche della Real Villa di Pratolino *by B. S. Sgrilli (1742) and from a survey carried out in 1962.*

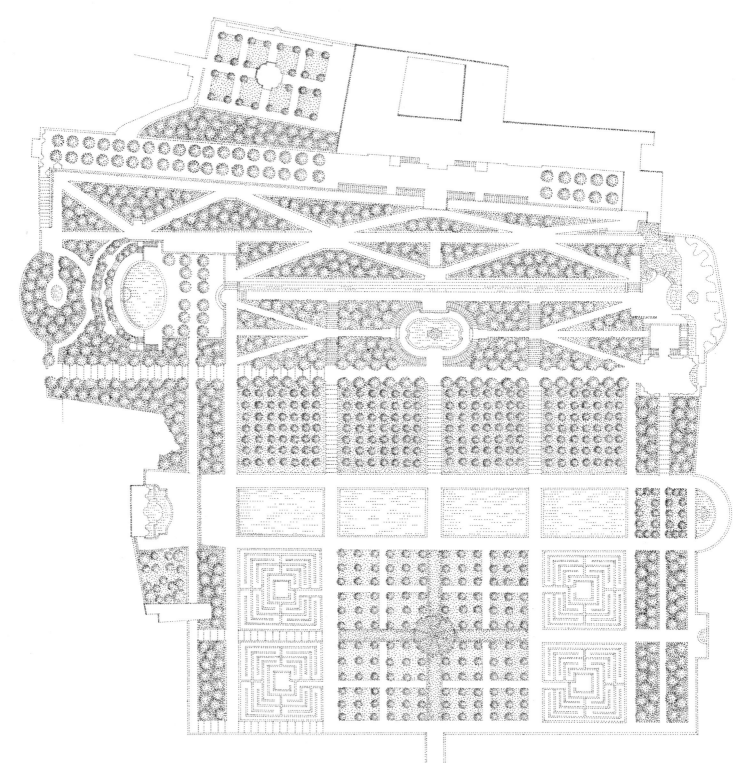

N

0   50m

0   150ft

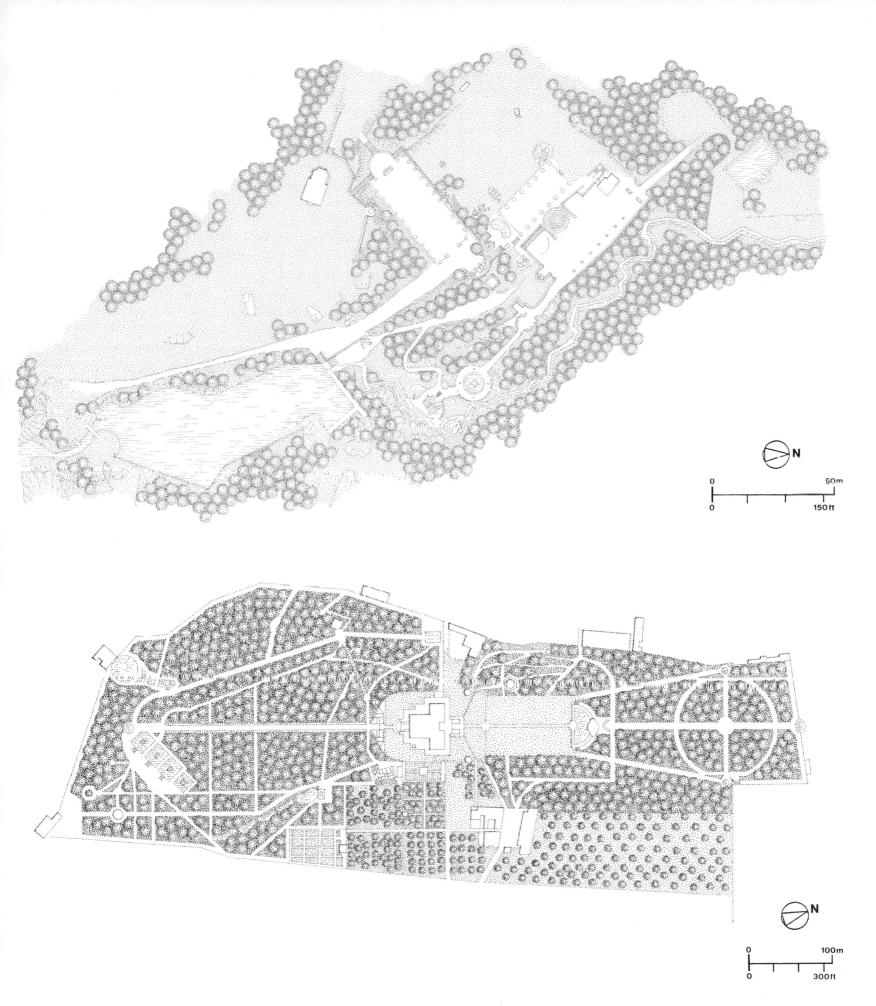

Garden of the Villa Lante, Bagnaia. From a survey published in F. Fariello, Architettura dei giardini, Rome 1985 (reprint).

N

0
50m

0
150 ft

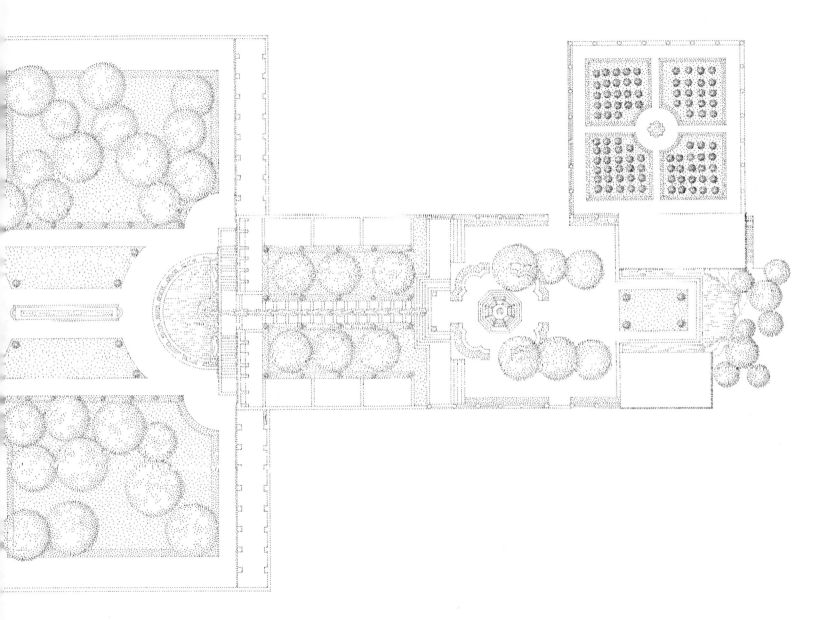

The gardens of the Villa Farnese and of the Casino, Caprarola:

I General plan, after Lebas;

II Plan of the gardens around the villa, from an engraving by G. Vasi, 1746;

III Plan of the gardens around the Casino, from an engraving by G. Vasi, 1746.

0   100m

0   300ft

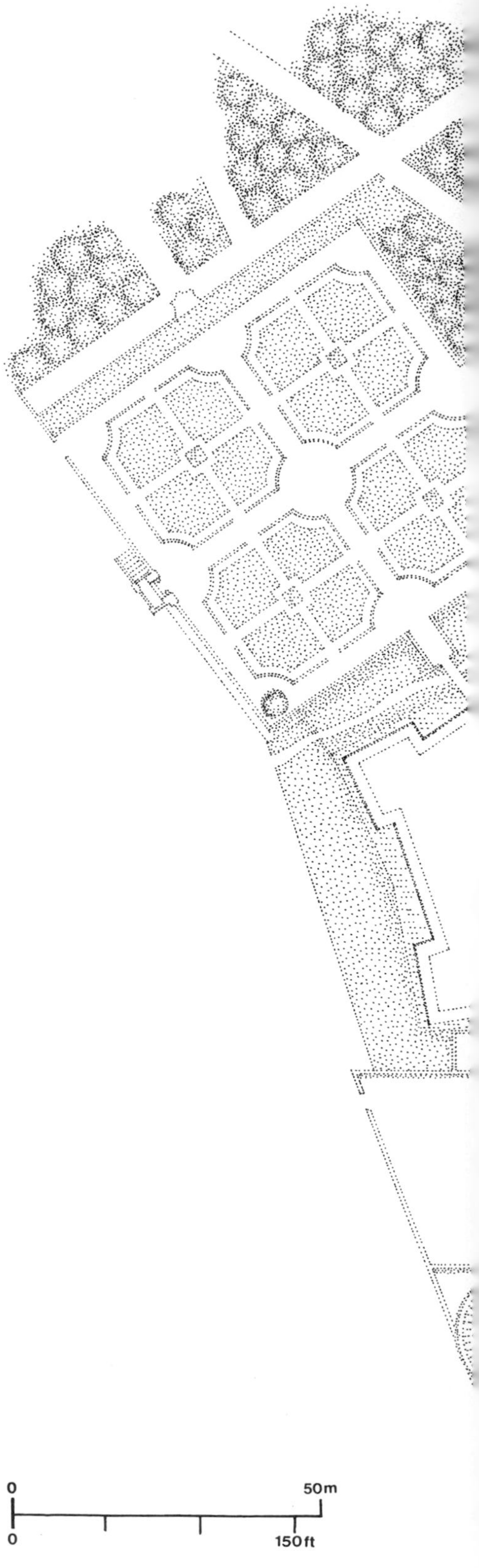

0   50m

0   150ft

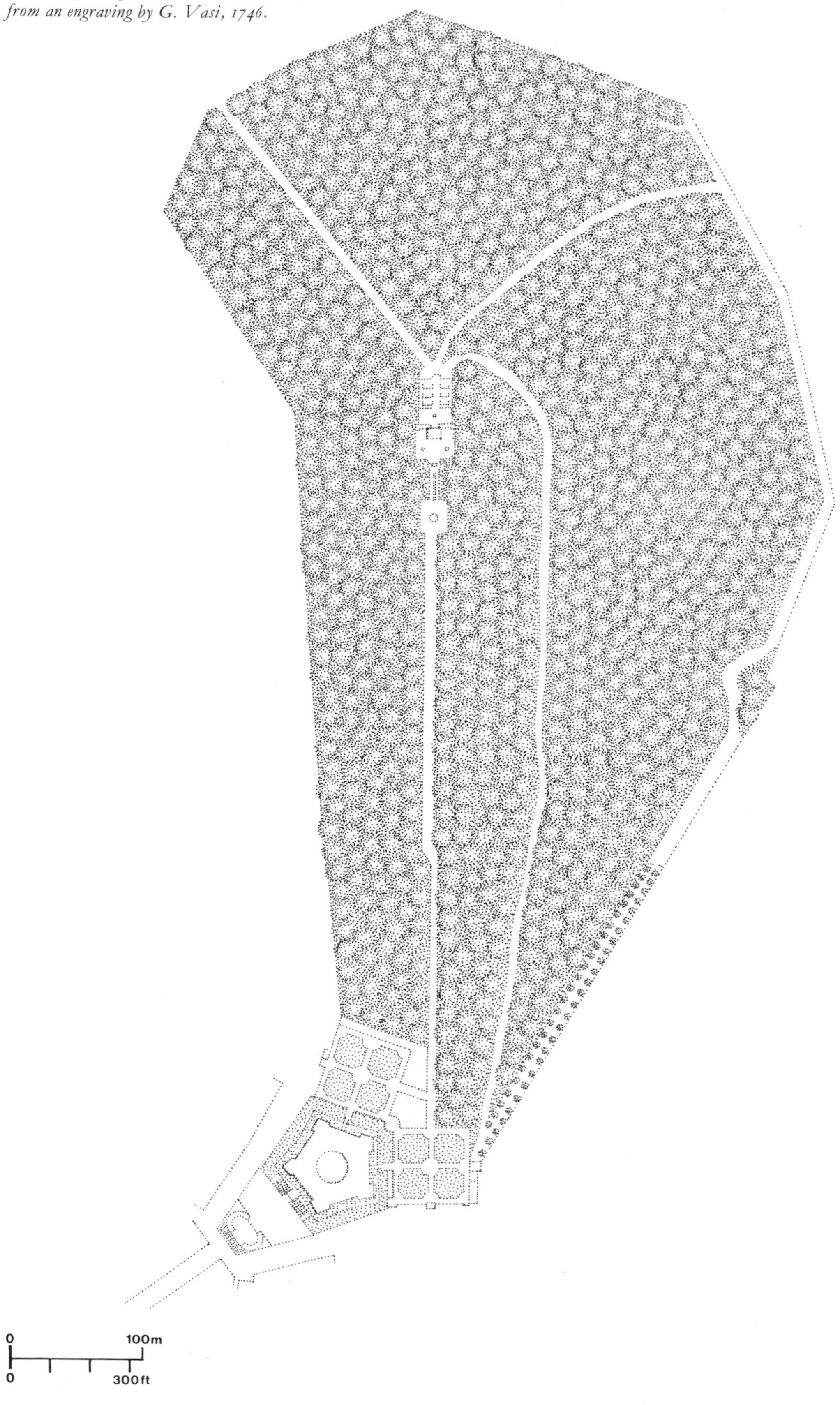

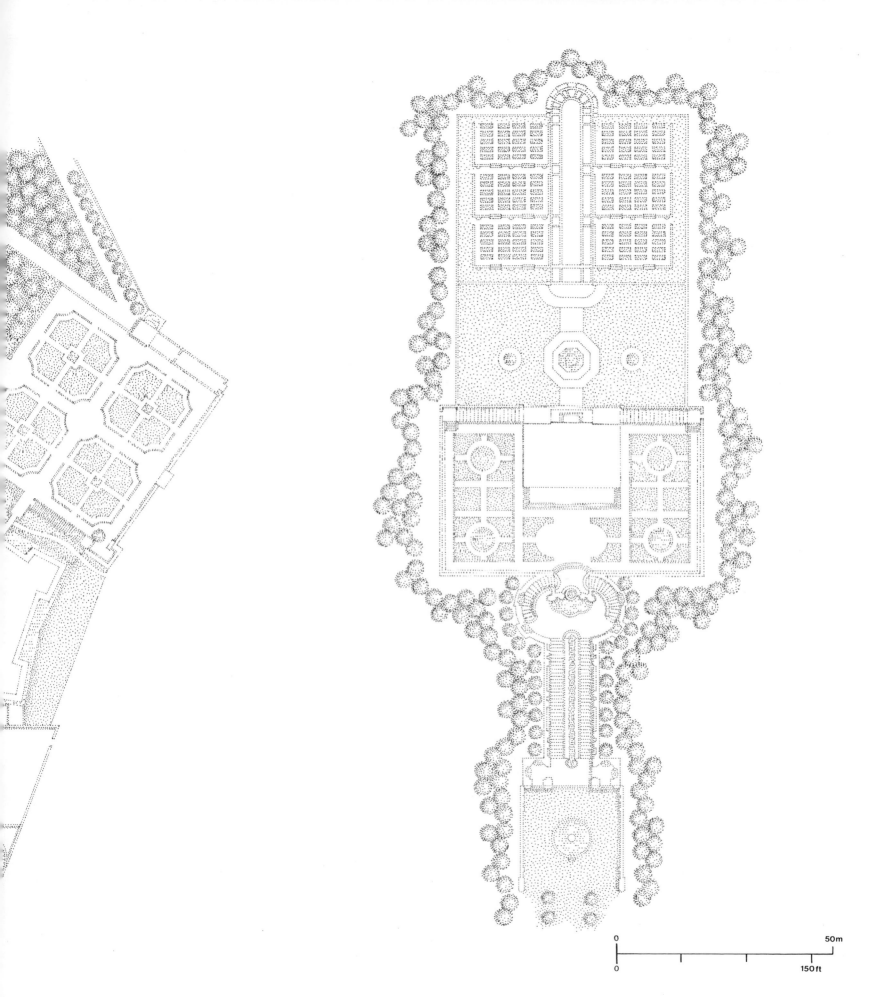

0

50m

0

150 ft

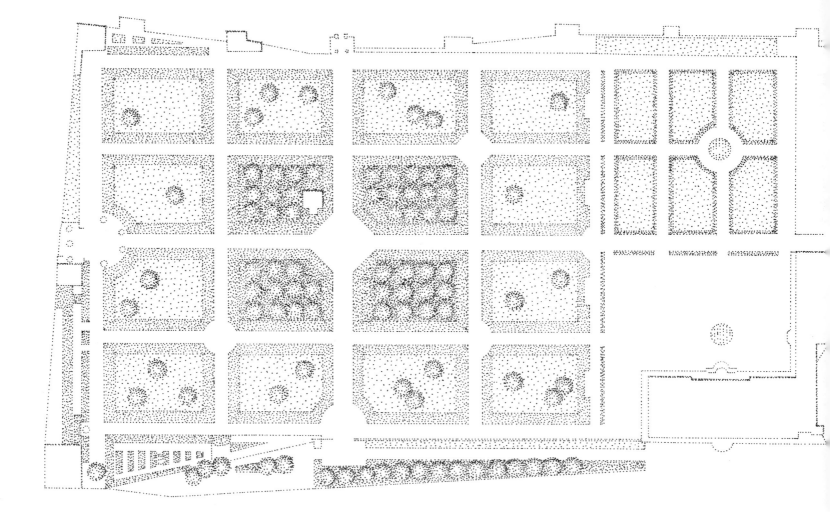

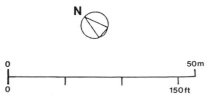

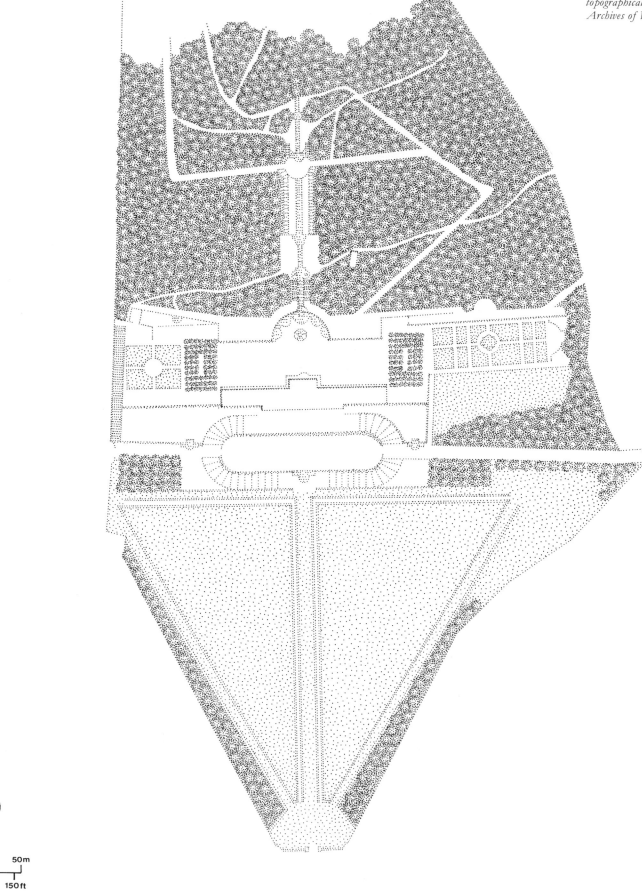

Garden of the Villa Aldobrandini, Frascati. From an engraving published in C. Percier and P. F. L. Fontaine, Choix . . ., Paris 1809, and from a topographical plan (1828) now in the State Archives of Rome.

N

| 0 | | 50m |
| 0 | | 150 ft |

34

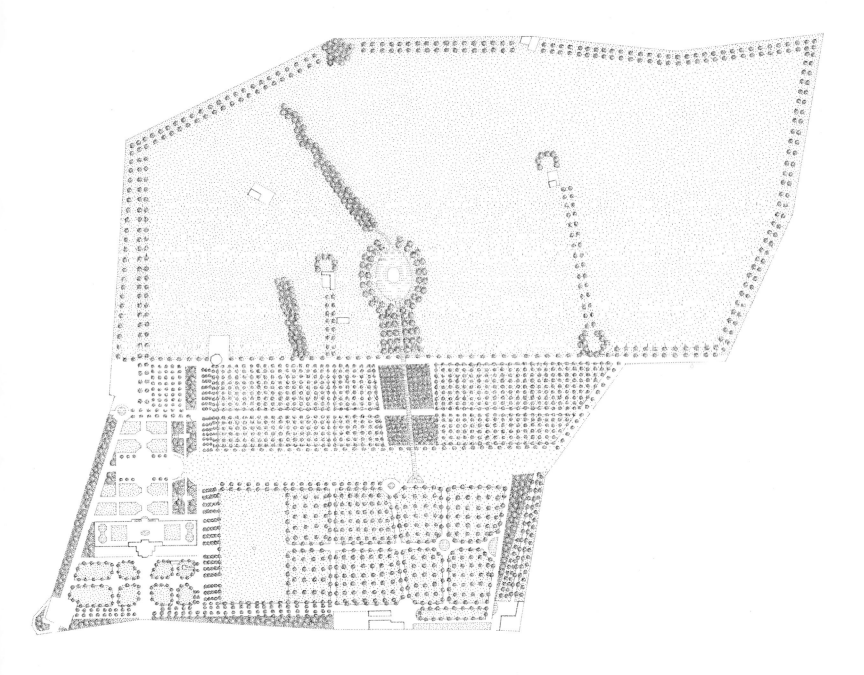

Garden and park of the Villa Doria-Pamphili, Rome. From an engraving by G. B. Falda, Li giardini di Roma, 1683; an engraving by Percier and Fontaine (1809); and a topographical plan of 1852.

N

0   200m

0   600ft

The Humanist Garden

Terry Comito

From Petrarch on, humanists were frequently avid gardeners, inspired equally by a new responsiveness to the seductions of landscape and by the authorizing tradition of classical *otium*. But for the history of gardens, humanists were important less for their own gardens (of which few traces have survived) than for their contribution to Renaissance thought about the nature and importance of gardens. In a sense, most of the great villa gardens were also 'humanist gardens'. Their disposition and iconographical programmes were worked out by humanist advisers, and humanist panegyrics established the terms in which their beauties were to be appreciated. In effect, the humanists provided an ideology that situated the villa garden within the whole project of Renaissance culture and at the same time was not without effect on the evolution of its design.

The characteristic iconography of the Middle Ages located its favoured *auctores* within tightly closed chambers or niches, hunched over their tablets (like the Evangelists on whom their task is modelled) as they take dictation from the Holy Spirit. Erasmus's *Convivium religiosum* offers us a paradigm for a quite different way of conceiving the relation between thought and the world. Constituting themselves a choir of Muses, Eusebius and his friends flee from 'smoky cities' to a rustic retreat whose natural bounty reminds them of the Fortunate Isles. The villa that is to be the site of the mind's feasting is a 'little nest' (*nidulus*) where the self is restored to its original empire over the world, a place where nature is no longer silent or alien but 'speaks to us all the time'. To be sure, the nascent classicism of this vision, with its evocation of Horace, Cicero, and 'St Socrates', is held firmly in place by Erasmus's ideal of learned piety. Not 'Mercury, Centaurs, and other monsters' but St Peter is this garden's porter, and Christ replaces Priapus as its presiding deity. We may find quaintly Gothic the ubiquitous labels and inscriptions with which frescoes and even the garden beds themselves seek to moralize the riches of this better Garden of Alcinous. Nevertheless, Erasmus's vision is not essentially different from that of Ficino and of several generations of Italian humanists who sought to resuscitate classical traditions, Academic and Ciceronian, that brought thought out of the study and found its proper place in leafy bowers or beside the play of water.

We may begin by noticing that the inspiration of Eusebius's 'well cultivated' garden is Georgic, not bucolic. There is 'not a corner' of it that does not 'bear the master's stamp', so efficacious has been his husbandry; and indeed it may finally become 'a place fit for deity'. These are two of the most common *topoi* in Renaissance praises of gardens, and their emphasis explains why those gardens, with their orderly beds and terraces, their disciplined play of water, their extended prospects, could be seen not as evasions of the lord's public responsibilities but – as Pontano, for example, was urging in Naples – as expressions of his splendour. As Ficino was fond of remarking, furthermore, what is cultivated in villa life is the soul as well as the fields. The Ciceronian pun on the two sense of *cultus* runs like a leitmotif through humanist writings, and what it serves to articulate is the conviction that education is only a higher form of husbanding nature's resources. The progress of Eusebius's guests through his villa, from the outer garden to a 'more cultivated' inner one, enclosed in a square and centred on the Fountain of Jesus, enacts the regimen necessary to render the natural world suitable nourishment for the mind as well as the body, to discover the *vera hilaritas* (true mirth) that makes good the (failed) promise of the Garden of Epicurus. (Eusebius's agenda is not far removed from that of Vittorino da Feltre, whose famous school in Mantua occupied the site of a former pleasure garden, La Gioiosa becoming La Giocosa, '*la casa delle gioie lussuriose*' becoming '*la casa di ludi* [*joci*] *letterarie e di delizie spirituali*.'[1] Ficino attributes a similar playfulness, '*platonici ludi atque ioci*,' to the gardens of his Academy at Careggi.) The world becomes a 'green feast' when, through careful cultivation, the claims of mind and body are reconciled, and even the lowly eggs and lettuce Eusebius is able to offer along with scriptural commentary are discovered to taste of Christ.

This sort of appropriation of classical *otium* for Christian purposes had been anticipated by medieval writers on monastic retirement. It is not accidental that so many Renaissance pleasure-gardens (e.g., Villa d'Este, Buen Retiro) inherited both the site and some of the symbolism of monastic gardens. Certainly Eusebius's garden preserves several features of the medieval tradition: the cloister with its central symbolic fountain was also the 'nest' of the soul and a provisional paradise in the wilderness of this world. But for Erasmus – and this is what aligns Eusebius's villa, for all the retardataire elements of its design, with the great gardens of the cinquecento – it is within the world, and not by flight from it, that Edenic perfection is to be cultivated. The emblems in his garden draw upon bestiaries and herbals to celebrate, not the joys of the solitary mind, but the pristine splendour and variety of the original creation. It is a spectacle in which, Eusebius's guests exclaim, the mind is endlessly absorbed: 'A wonderful variety, and nothing that's not doing or saying something'. The actual villa Erasmus evidently had in mind (that of Johannes von Botzheim, the Canon of Constance) was without the hexaemeral splendours of Eusebius's villa, and it spoke to its guests in a rather different way. 'No part of [the villa] fails to offer something splendid and elegant', Erasmus writes to a friend. 'No part is mute but everywhere speaking pictures seduce and hold men's eyes' (*Opus epist.*, ed. Allen, V, 212). By transferring this seductive loquaciousness to nature itself, Erasmus in his dialogue effectively transforms what might seem to a monastic writer an idle *curiositas* into a veritable feast for the intellect. 'Who could possibly be bored in this changing scene?' What is involved is a re-evaluation, fundamental to humanist thought, of the human, or all-too-human, propensity for lifting one's eyes and looking around, for yielding to just that *concupiscentia occulorum* condemned by medieval critics. The kind of 'cosmic piety'[2] that impelled Seneca to exclaim that nature 'has set us in her centre and given us a panoramic view in all directions' (*De otio*, 32) is revived and given tangible expression in the new villa gardens of the Renaissance.

Repertories of villa forms were not readily at hand, but humanists did know Pliny's celebration of the panoramic views of his Laurentine and Tuscan villas. At Poggio a Caiano, and at Poggio Reale in Naples, the form of the medieval French castle with its four corner towers is turned inside out by Lorenzo's architects, opened to light and air, perforated by windows and loggias, brought into relation with the gardens that surround it and the countryside beyond. The new villas turn 'outward toward a landscape rather than inward toward a court',[3] so that the eye, liberated from the restraint of either wall or emblem, may range freely over the prospect of 'pleasant landscapes, flowery meadows, open plains, shady groves, or limpid brooks' in which (according to Alberti) it most delights (*De re aedificatoria*, IX, 2). This establishment of what a later English writer, Henry Wotton, calls the 'royalty of sight' corresponds to a notable shift in the decoration of villas. Responding apparently to the advice of Vitruvius and Alberti, painters were abandoning military exploits and cutting through solid walls with illusionistic landscapes or turning to poetic evocations of the countryside's mysterious potencies. The 'stamp of the master' at places like the Palazzo Schifanoia or the Villa Belvedere or, later, the Farnesina or Poggio a Caiano was evident not in the rigour with which he repulses the world's assaults but the magnanimous openness to the world by which he makes its riches his own. The aspiration implicit in the new gardens is precisely captured in Manetti's *De dignitate et excellentia hominis*. If the eye could grasp in a single glance, *in unu aspectu*, what the mind knows of the landscape's beauty, then man, 'living and looking', would discover a sensible measure of his own greatness.

The *Convivium religiosum* belongs to the tradition of 'villa dialogues' Renaissance writers imitated from Cicero, who in turn was seeking, in his own gardens as well as in his dialogues, to recreate the ambiance and the ethos of Socratic conversations on the bank of the Illissus. What is involved is not merely a literary convention or a social affectation. The association of gardens with dialogue has to do with the nature of humanist thought and of the claims humanists were making, particularly against the scholastics, about their own enterprise. We may risk a rather bald formula. Whereas medieval commentaries or *quaestiones* unfold within a purely logical or textual space, the humanist dialogue, like the Ciceronian, is situated in the real world. And it is *essentially* situated, incarnate, so that an idea cannot validly be torn from the particular individual sensibility, and hence the particular words and cadences, in which it is formulated; or from the particular practices it authorizes and the communities it founds within a particular society (Petrarch's claim that it is better to be good than to understand goodness was often echoed by his successors); or, finally, from the living, 'speaking' cosmos from which it derives its legitimacy and its efficacy. Certainly the avidity with which humanists preface dialogues on the most diverse subjects with an elaborate 'composition of place' suggests a deeply felt, if usually unformulated, sense that the *ubi* or *locus* of thought is one of its essential components. Even tales – the *Decameron* is only the most familiar instance – are not turned loose to sound only in the reader's mind, but are retained within the matrix of the place and time of their telling. Cicero's discussion of the *vis admonitionis* of natural places (*De finibus*, V. 1); Fracastoro's speculation (at the beginning of his dialogue, *Naugerius*) whether character or place is the most fundamental determinant of consciousness; Cardinal Bembo's sense that the laurel trees of the queen's gardens at Asolo, were one sufficiently attentive to their message, would themselves make Love's form manifest: these are not metaphors, figures of speech, so much as attempts to articulate the recovered sense of the potency of space, its pregnancy with meaning, that inspires in Renaissance gardens and gardeners their special self confidence.

Petrarch was at once the first passionate gardener of modern times and the first to conceive his labours, in analogy to his poetic career, as an imitation of the ancients. The link, amounting at times almost to an identification, between his two enthusiasms, for gardens and for antiquity, may serve to remind us that Renaissance *imitatio* was not mere copying. Gardening becomes the privileged model for a species of imitation that seeks not to reproduce its object mechanically but to make it grow: to seize those fruitful principles by which the humanity of the ancients might be cultivated within the space of one's own world and one's own sensibility. For Petrarch, this seems to have been more than a metaphor. His 'transalpine Helicon' at Vaucluse, with its gardens sacred to Apollo and to Bacchus, represents at once an emulation of Cicero's island garden in *De legibus* and an attempt to appropriate the numinous powers of the landscape – powers that lead men (Petrarch remarks, recalling Seneca) to 'erect altars at places where great streams burst suddenly from hidden sources' (*De vita solitaria*). Vaucluse is a *locus plenus*, at once 'patria', 'Helicon', and 'Rome and Athens' (*Exul ab Italia, Fam.* 15.3) – homeland, inspiration, antiquity, grasped *in unu aspectu* – where 'even an inert mind may rise to lofty thoughts' (*Fam.* 13.8). It is in such a place, Petrarch discovers, under the open sky by a 'murmuring stream . . . grateful to the Muses', that the mind's field, *arvum ingenii*, germinates most lavishly (*De vita sol.*). Again and again Petrarch speaks of the way in which the spirit of the place, *ingenium loci*, 'speaks' (*suasere, suggessit, hortata est*) to his own imagination (*Fam.* 10.4; *Posteritati, Var.* 42). Properly to imitate Cicero, either his gardens or his language, is to enter into this fructifying dialogue with the world.

Subsequent humanist gardens continued to pay homage to the classical world, cultivating plants and statues with an equal assiduousness. The humanist Angelo Colocci's garden on the Pincio, with its famous antique nymph reclining in the arch of a Roman aqueduct, was the model for more elaborate displays, like those of the Villa Carpi or the Villa d'Este. The statues and fragments of reliefs with which these gardens were adorned were not curiosities valued for their historical pastness so much as newly uncovered presences, presences that in their restored splendour (their owners did not hesitate to patch and mend, so that their antiquities would match the perfection of the landscapes in which they were displayed) converted their sites into gymnasia and

CASTELLO.

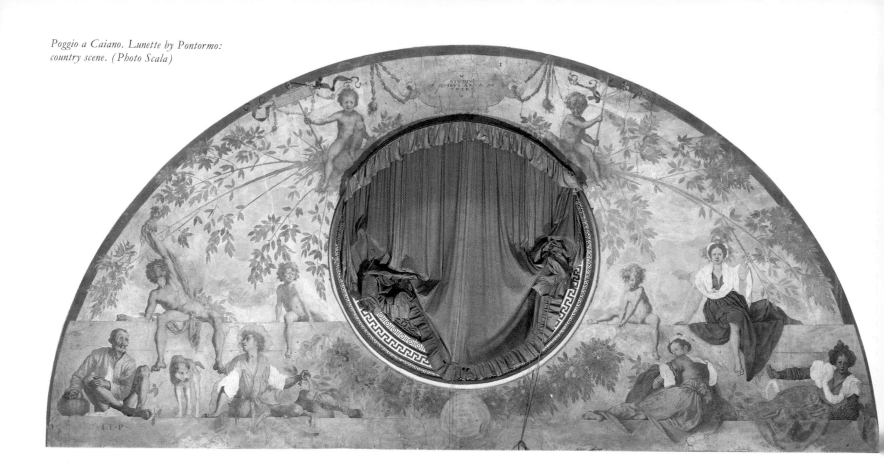

Poggio a Caiano. Lunette by Pontormo: country scene. (Photo Scala)

academies, grottoes of the Muses, sacred groves. In this last aim, Bramante's Belvedere statue court may have succeeded too well. With its great recumbent river gods, its Laocoon and Apollo set in niches painted with arbours full of birds and flowers, its Cleopatra drowsing like a nymph beside her sacred pool in a grotto planted with real foliage, this 'grove of Venus and Cupid' seemed to some visitors little more than a Circean temptation: Pico della Mirandola's nephew, Gianfrancesco, wrote a poem denouncing it, and Pope Hadrian subsequently sealed off the court from impressionable spectators.

It was not merely the decor of ancient villas humanists sought to revive. The growing archeological sophistication of the cinquecento permitted allusions to the actual forms of ancient buildings, as at the Belvedere Court, where echoes of Nero's Golden House, Hadrian's Villa, and the Temple of Fortuna at Palestrina all serve to establish not so much an analogy as a real continuity between the claims of emperors and popes. Elsewhere – at Tivoli, on the Pincio (the ancient 'hill of gardens'), in and around Naples – the very sites of classical villas are resuscitated. In such places, the modern villa does not recreate the past so much as renew and perpetuate a landscape that persists like a concrete instance of the *urbs eterna* itself outside time and history.

The special aura of such places might legitimately associate them with the sacred landscapes that delighted poets and painters as well as gardeners in the Renaissance. Indeed, imitation of this sort seems not far removed from conjuration,[4] a resemblance which might lend some weight to the references to Graces and Muses that come so easily to Eusebius or to Petrarch – or to a multitude of other Renaissance gardeners, even the most modest of whom was apt to boast of a Parnassus Mount or Shrine of Apollo. The Muses figure not simply in poetry but the whole transforming enterprise of humanist *imitatio*: a simultaneous making present of nature and of antiquity. A light-hearted version of this is evident in Mantegna's trip to Lake Garda. The painter and his humanist friends decipher classical inscriptions amid 'wooded gardens so like paradise they might have sprung up as an abode of the most charming of the Muses'; and crowning themselves with the laurel they find growing in these enchanted isles, they play at resurrecting the emperors of Rome. For a philosopher to claim for his discourse the authority of the Muses – as Ficino did, or the 'academy' overseen by Colocci's nymph – is to claim participation in cosmic harmonies beyond the reach of dialectic. 'The Muses do not argue with Apollo', Ficino writes, 'they sing' (*De sole*). And when he seeks to distinguish his thought from that of the scholastics, he does so in terms of the garden at the Villa Careggi, the home of the Graces (he is fond of punning on Careggi = *charitum ager*) and thereby Philosophy's proper homeland. The scholastics, abstracting thought from its seat in the world, have stripped Philosophy of her adornment, left her nude, profaned, and wandering. At Careggi, she will regain her proper sacredness and, as in Plato's Academy, will once again be decked with sweet perfumes and a thousand flowers (*Opera*, Basle, 1576, p. 1129). Central as villa gardens were to the institution of *villeggiatura*, ideologically they presented themselves as sites less of holiday or escape than of homecoming: they were places where thought comes home to itself.

This ideology becomes explicit in the iconography of programmes with which humanist advisers laid out gardens and decorated villas. The myth of the Golden Age was particularly important for Medici propaganda, and it dictated the disposition of both the villa at Poggio a Caiano for Lorenzo and the villa at Castello for Duke Cosimo.[5] More generally, however, some version of the Golden Age, made more resonant by association with Christian notions of paradise and humanistic theories of the *vita contemplativa*, was the fundamental myth of Renaissance gardens.[6] Sometimes, as at the Villa Carpi with its sleeping shepherd, this age seems to promise a sinecure of 'carefree peace' (*secura quies*). But even here, it is the *Georgics* that are cited, not the *Eclogues*. Characteristically, humanist programmes offered not pastoral escape to a realm of the merely picturesque (a pleasure belatedly offered by the English Garden) but, on the contrary, a restoration of cosmic plenitude and perfection that becomes a measure of the greatness of the garden's lord. If the garden is a new Hesperides, its richness is the result of conscious choice, of heroic virtue (as in Tribolo's fountain at Castello) submitting the energies of nature to its will: at the Villa d'Este, it is the visitor who must make the choice, taking at the statue of Hercules either an easy path to the Grotto of Venus or an uphill climb to the Grotto of Diana.[7] Astrological symbolism and references to the seasons and elements indicate not merely the classically mandated salubriousness of the site but also the restoration of cosmic harmony in which contending opposites are reconciled, all realms allowed their proper flourishing. At the Casino of Pius IV at the Vatican, Ligorio's stucco decoration appropriates the sensuous pleasures of the garden – the play of water and light, the sense of pastoral ease – for a humanistic vision of the contemplative life. In the façade facing the rising sun, cosmic and intellectual light, Aurora and Apollo, are assimilated to one another; and the fountains, river gods, and sea creatures that make the Casino a virtual nymphaeum all find their apotheosis in the cup that from the summit of the central façade pours forth the gift of Truth.[8] As in Eusebius's garden, though without the quaintly emblematic promptings, nature speaks to man of his own possibilities.

The cloister garden, with its four-square reticulation and central fountain, already hinted at a cosmic paradigm, and interpreters were often ready to read it as a diagram of the paradise to which the monks' contemplation would admit them. But in the Middle Ages most gardens were no more than a little green space rigidly closed off from the profane world beyond their walls. They signified cosmic harmonies without embodying them, pointing beyond themselves to a perfection grasped by the intellect alone. As I have already suggested, the modernity of Eusebius's garden lies in its readiness to find paradisal harmonies in the created world. In the Renaissance garden cosmic order is not something to be decoded by a process of abstraction. It is realized, made actual, in the stuff of the physical world in sights, sounds, odours, textures. Furthermore, means are found to direct attention to the processes through which this ideal cosmos comes into being. It is seen not as a reproduction of a timeless archetype but, in its contingency, its historicity, as the creation of human power and imagination – an instance, in fact, of that capacity for self creation, self cultivation, that is, according to thinkers like Manetti and Pico, man's special dignity. The harmony of the cloister garden directs the inquiring mind to God; the Renaissance garden testifies to the nobility of its lord, of its city, of humanity in general.

Three design features make this transformation particularly clear: the *bosco*, the use of water, the deployment of space.

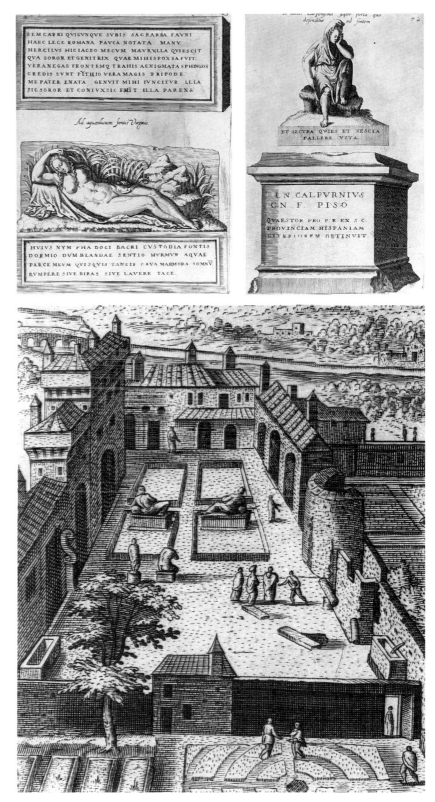

Villa Medici di Castello, Florence: sculpture of Hercules and Antaeus. (Photo Alinari)

The bosco. The formal parterres of the Renaissance garden may owe something to the geometrical rigour of their monastic predecessors. But instead of closing them off from their surroundings, the Renaissance garden juxtaposes them to wooded areas, either providing a continuous transition from the formal beds to the relatively uncultivated *bosco* to the untouched landscape beyond, or, reversing the design, rewarding strollers in the villa's woods with the surprising apparition of cultivated spots – paradise in the midst of wilderness – for dining or discussion. The order of the medieval garden is qualitatively distinct from what lies outside the wall; the order of the villa garden presents itself as the cultivation of potentialities that extend as far as the eye can see. At the Villa Lante in Bagnaia, the progression from uncultivated nature to the triumphs of art is the explicit basis for the garden's iconographical programme, as it is, much later, for the River Road at Caserta.[9]

Water. Within the garden's more uncultivated areas, the fecundity of the natural forces given shape by the garden is often figured by grottoes, fountains, river gods, somnolent nymphs. Rough-hewn stone, tufa, encrusted shells indicate an inchoate source, and the play of water itself makes particularly sensuous and immediate, aurally as well as visually, a sense of potentiality, an Ovidian capacity for transformation – as, for example, when the murmur of streams and canals becomes the exuberant splash of fountains. This trope becomes literal at the Villa d'Este, where a great water organ sounds from behind a figure of the many-breasted goddess of nature, Diana of Ephesus. At the same time, the power to divert and channel these energies, to make them the source at once of astounding displays and fecund life, is regularly cited by visitors and eulogists as a token of princely magnificence. Streams respond to the call of their lord, plants spring up at his bidding – an impression the gardens reinforce by associating *imprese* and heraldry with flowing water. This lordly prowess is no mere technological proficiency, though Roman aqueducts are often brought to mind. A mastery so primordial, it often seems to poets, must draw upon the ancient deities of the place, river nymphs like Ambra at Poggio a Caiano or Parthenope at Poggio Reale, now summoned up for the first time since antiquity.[10]

Perspective. If the prospect seen from the garden is the expression of a kind of royalty of sight, that prospect which constitutes the very form of the garden represents a still more ambitious self aggrandizement, and no merely symbolic one. Bramante's Belvedere court at the Vatican reshapes the natural terrain into three great terraces organized around, not a centre, but an axis. Situated in the papal apartments of which Raphael's frescoes make 'one ideal temple of the human mind',[11] the eye is led by the garden's centre accents through three circles, all concentric to the self, until it comes to rest on an infinity at once spatial and historical: the exedra that is both the vanishing point of parallel lines and the resuscitation of the Temple of Fortuna at Palestrina. The garden is bounded not by walls but by the act of vision itself – by that perspective art which (as Berenson remarked) 'humanizes the void,

Villa d'Este, Tivoli: Avenue of a Hundred Jets. Engraving by G. F. Venturini. Biblioteca Hertziana, Rome.

Villa Carpi, Rome: Diana of Ephesus. From J. J. Boissard, Romanae urbis topographiae, Vol. 4, Frankfurt 1598.

Boboli Gardens, Pitti Palace, Florence: interior of the grotto.

making of it an enclosed Eden'.[12] The Belvedere court was the prototype of such cinquecento gardens as the Villa Lante or the Villa Farnese at Caprarola, but what is involved is a shift not merely in design but in the 'cognitive style'[13] of the gaze with which the world is regarded. This is neatly illustrated by two engravings of the Villa Medici in Rome. The earlier makes sense of the parterre as an agglomeration of nested boxes, whose Procrustean boundaries simply cut out a portion of the world – as do the boundaries of the print itself. The later engraving discovers an axis that binds parterre, *bosco*, and the soft hills beyond into a single perspective, its harmonies achieved without partition (*in unu aspectu*) and in collaboration with the eye of the viewer.

[1] Enrico Paglia, 'La casa Giocosa di Vittorino da Feltre in Mantova,' in *Archivio Storico Lombardo* (1884), p. 153.

[2] Hans Blumenberg, *The Legitimacy of the Modern Age*, trans. Robert Wallace (Cambridge, Mass. 1983).

[3] James S. Ackerman, 'Sources of the Renaissance Villa,' in *The Renaissance and Mannerism* (Princeton 1963), pp. 6–18.

[4] For the hermetic uses of Ficino's garden at Careggi, see Frances Yates, *Giordano Bruno and the Hermetic Tradition* (Chicago 1964) and D. P. Walker, *Spiritual and Demonic Magic from Ficino to Campanella* (London 1958). On Salomon de Caus, see Frances Yates, *The Rosicrucian Enlightenment* (London 1972).

[5] See Janet Cox-Rearick, *Dynasty and Destiny in Medici Art* (Princeton 1984).

[6] See David Coffin, *The Villa in the Life of Renaissance Rome* (Princeton 1979).

[7] Ligorio's intentions were frustrated by subsequent changes in the disposition of the garden's statues, however; see David Coffin, *The Villa d'Este at Tivoli* (Princeton 1960).

[8] See Graham Smith, *The Casino of Pius IV* (Princeton 1977).

[9] See C. Lazzaro-Bruno, 'The Villa Lante at Bagnaia: an Allegory of Art and Nature, in *Art Bulletin*, no. 59 (1977), pp. 553–60; George Hersey, *Architecture, Poetry, and Number in the Royal Palace at Caserta* (Cambridge, Mass. 1983).

[10] See André Chastel, *Art et humanisme à Florence au temps de Laurent le Magnifique* (Paris 1961), pp. 148–57; George Hersey, *Alfonso II and the Artistic Renewal of Naples 1485–1495* (New Haven 1969).

[11] S. J. Freedberg, *Painting of the High Renaissance in Rome and Florence*, 2nd edition (New York 1972), Vol. I, p. 116.

[12] Bernard Berenson, *Italian Painters of the Renaissance* (New York 1957), p. 199.

[13] Michael Baxandall, *Painting and Experience in Fifteenth Century Italy* (London 1972).

Villa Farnese, Caprarola: dolphin cascade near the Casino. (Photo Alinari)

Belvedere Court, Vatican City. Drawing by G. A. Dosio, c. 1558–61 Uffizi, Florence.

DEL SEREN. GRAN DVCA DI TOSCANA PALAZZO ET GIARDINO NEL MONTE PINCIO IN ROMA.

Villa Medici, Rome. From G. Lauro,
Antiquae urbis splendor, *Rome 1612–14.*
Dumbarton Oaks, Washington DC.

Villa Medici, Rome. From G. B. Falda, L[
giardini di Roma, *Rome 1683. Dumbarto[*
Oaks, Washington DC.

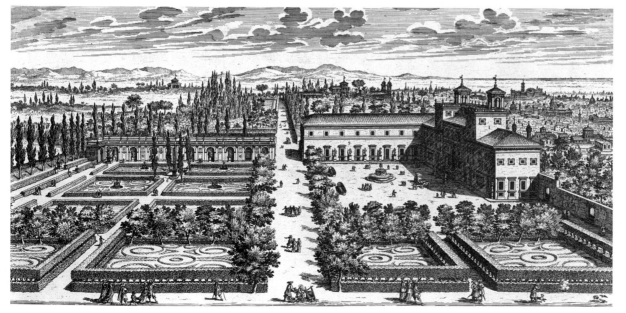

Nature and Artifice in the
Sixteenth-Century Italian Garden

Lionello Puppi

In the most alarming and disturbing of his *Tales of the Grotesque and Arabesque*, Edgar Allan Poe, speculating about the 'land of Arnheim', expresses surprise that 'no-one had ever described the landscape gardener as a poet although the creation of a landscape garden offers to the Muses the perfect opportunity for inspiration'. These words are spoken by Ellison, the main character in the story, who is fired by an intense desire to create a garden of a beauty 'verging on the miraculous', one that would outdo even the wonders of nature itself.

It is clear that in many respects Poe's words encapsulated the essence of an argument at the centre of a contemporary debate (we know that his views were supported by Hirschfeld in *Theorie der Gartenkunst* and by Goethe in *Wilhelm Meister*) and that they formed the basis of new thinking on the part of landscape gardeners of the time. They also provide a means of approaching a problem which still remains something of a mystery today: when, and in what way precisely, did fifteenth-century gardens, whose manifest intention was to imitate and celebrate nature, evolve into creations on a scale of such magnificence and splendour as the gardens of a century later, which were inspired and governed very largely by the imagination, moulding and manipulating natural materials to the point where nature gave way entirely to artifice?[1]

There is of course no conclusive response to a question as complex as this, but I would nevertheless suggest that the circumstances in which this transformation took place yield a plausible explanation. It should be remembered that the *idea* of a garden – the way in which it was conceived and created – in the fourteenth and fifteenth centuries sprang from a recognition of the contrast that existed between *rus* and *urbs*, between the serenity and order of the rural world and the disorder of urban life. The former, full of *iucunditas, salubritas, amoenitas* and *venustas* (pleasure, wholesomeness, loveliness and grace) – in the words of a remarkable essay by Vivit on Platina's *De honesta voluptate et valetudine* (On decent pleasure and well-being) of 1468[2] – was a place set aside for scholarly and erudite conversation, for confidental discussions and for communing with nature; the latter was a background for the confusion, intrigues and passionate political conflicts (*polis – polemos*) of a world that was essentially artificial. The ideological foundations of this argument are well known: the Petrarchian dream of the 'solitary life' – *vere rus illus locus est pacis otii domus, requies laborum; tranquillitati hospitium, solitudinis officina* (Indeed the country is that place of peace where we have a refuge from care, a harbour from our troubles, a calm rest-house, somewhere to work in solitude) (*Ep. Fam.*, XVII, 5, XIII, 8, and XVIII, 8); *linguramus urbem mercatoribus, advocatis, prosenetis, feneratoribus . . . publicanis, architectis, pictoribus . . . non sunt nostri generis* (Let us leave the city to the merchants, the lawyers, the actors, the money-lenders, the tax-collectors, the architects, the painters . . . they are not our kind) (*De vita solitaria*, II, 10): that is to say, 'every inhabited place is a mortal enemy'; 'cities are the enemy'. *Domum parvam sed delectabilem et honestam struxi*, writes the poet, *cumque oliveta et aliquot vineas abunde quidem non magne modestaque familie suffecturas* (The home I have built is small, but it is charming and sound, since when you planted the olives and some vines, you planted plenty but not too much, enough for a modest family) (*Ep. Sen.* XV, 5).[3] Alberti suggests in his *Lapides* that there are two ways of living: *in antiqua ripa . . . per otium et quietem consenescere in libertate* (On an ancient river bank . . . to grow old in peace and quiet and without demands) or *per corruentem amnem agitati nullam inquinissorum laborum . . . requiem* (Beside the running stream the anxious have no rest from their vile burdens).[4] Leonardo echoes these sentiments, warning of the damage and pain to which we expose ourselves if we 'choose to leave the solitary and contemplative life to live in the city among people full of vice and wickedness'.[5] Others, too, supported this belief: Lorenzo the Magnificent wrote 'Seek who will life's glories and high honours, and the city's squares, temples and elegant buildings'; in 1543 Triffon Gabriele described 'the noise and tumult and bustle that surrounds one in the city, and from which one feels the need to flee, content with that which only simple nature offers, a tranquil and restful life. It is solitude that suits me', he went on,' not the life of the Rialto, St Mark's and the squares of Venice . . . .'.[6]

It is apparent that a theoretical and practical definition of the garden as a place of repose and sanctuary was generally accepted among writers and philosophers of the time, such as Varrone; Theophrastus *agricultura digna est homini libero* (agriculture is worthy of the free man); Columella – *nihil agricultura liberalius aut dulcius* (there is nothing sweeter or more fitting for a free man than agriculture); and Pliny the Elder, who wrote of the ten Tables destined to become a *hortus . . . ad voluptatem* (a garden for pleasure) (*Nat. Hist.* XIX, 49–51). This view was adhered to throughout the fourteenth and fifteenth centuries by writers such as Pietro de' Crescenzi in *Ruralia commoda* and Corniolo della Corno in *Divina villa*.[7] After all, according to the scriptures, did Christ not appear to Mary Magdalen dressed as a gardener?[8]

It was generally acknowledged that the layout of a garden was of fundamental importance and that it should be simple in style, like the villa it surrounded. It should be enclosed and orderly, with a pergola, hedges, an orchard and a fountain. In the ideal garden, ' . . . a single arcade runs from the house to the garden, two steps leading up to it from the courtyard; on either side are simple rooms intended for everyday use. The garden has an abundance of fruit trees – apples, pears, pomegranates, damsons – and fertile vines; near the house is a grove of plane trees, with clipped box hedges close by, a beautiful laurel and a spring whose waters, more transparent than glass, are sacred to the muses'[9]. This was a perfect setting for the '*iucunditas et . . . rusticana amoenitas*' of the '*domuncula*' of Leonardo and Bernardo Giustinias at Murano, whose garden was laid out by Triffon Gabriele, with 'a pergola of dense vines surrounded by thick jasmines, which the sun could not penetrate', and a *hortus* by Andrea Navagero.[10] Just as enchanting was Pietro Bembo's garden at Noniano, near Padua, with 'a grove at the top of the garden . . . a charming ornamental bower overhung with roses in full bloom beyond the orchard, and a large and magnificent pavilion'.[11] Other examples are the '*loca plena letitiae*'[12] at

BELVEDER CON PITTI

Pergola and fountain. From F. Colonna,
Hypnerotomachia Poliphili, *Venice 1499.*

Pergola. From F. Colonna,
Hypnerotomachia Poliphili, *Venice 1499.*

Pienza; the Medici gardens at Careggi and those at nearby Quaracchi; the 'paradise' designed by Alberti and furnished with conifers and a large fountain;[13] the *hortus* of Sannazaro at Mergellina; and even more opulent establishments such as the gardens laid out by Pope Nicholas V at the Vatican, Paul II's hanging *viridarium* at the palace of St Mark,[14] and the great Ferrara gardens of Belriguardo and Belfiore.[15] The ideology behind their designs derived from a particular set of elements inherent in the culture of the fifteenth century, which have already been identified here, and it was translated into a style that became synonymous with the gardens of the period. It was of course conditioned by contemporary attitudes,[16] both in the sparing use of such decorative features as topiary, sculpture and architectural ornament, and in the simplicity of its layout, which sought to avoid detracting in any way from the purity of nature, or *rus*. Undoubtedly these gardens conformed to a certain pattern, and defined – through a language of signs and symbolic allusions – the status and function of the property as well as the qualities and aspirations of its aristocratic owner. Specific plants were selected to provide a medium of expression for the underlying symbolism (Theophrastus, Pliny and Crescenzi suggested a number of suitable species), as were stone tablets such as the *lex hortorum*, a particularly explicit example being the vineyards of Cardinal Carafa's property at the Quirinale in Rome, which are known to have been laid out sometime before 1476.[17]

In time, however, intimations of a rejection of this ideology become gradually clearer. Alberti began, tentatively at first, to put forward proposals for the introduction of an element of artifice or deceit into the purity of the natural setting: he wanted 'to deceive the visitor with a playful joke, or better still to amuse him with the charming novelty of surprise'. Similarly, Bernardo Rucellai incorporated ingenious visual tricks into the gardens of Quaracchi by means of the *ars topiaria*, sculpting plants into curious and amazing forms. Similarly Filarete describing the gardens near Plusiapolis hints at a 'fantastic allegorical world'.[18] Francesco di Giorgio unhesitatingly dismissed the ideals of *rus* in favour of artifice: in discussing 'royal and aristocratic houses and their gardens', he underlined the fact that a complementary relationship must exist between the architecture of a villa and the gardens or parkland that surrounds it, and proceeded to list a number of artificial devices that should be employed to this end:

Place a fountain in the centre that is fed by a natural water supply . . . and in the gardens lay out pools, fishponds, loggias and covered and open walkways; set aside areas furnished with watercourses and green spaces, some open and some covered, where animals and birds may be kept. Paths and piazzas must be set out in straight lines, running parallel and at right angles to each other; there must be lawns and glades, with a variety of trees that keep their leaves for most of the year, and other areas where grass and trees are interspersed with temples, labyrinths, loggias, seats and other delights. And the more varied they are, the more pleasing they will be to the eye.[19]

The geometric order and precision of earlier days was still explicit in di Giorgio's recommendations, but it is clear that the principal aim of new

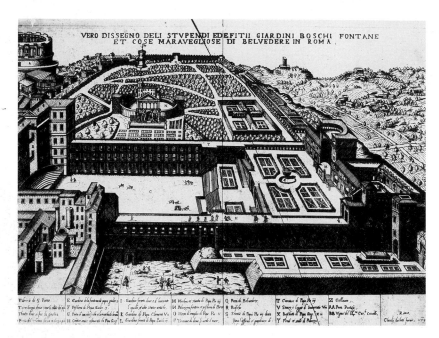

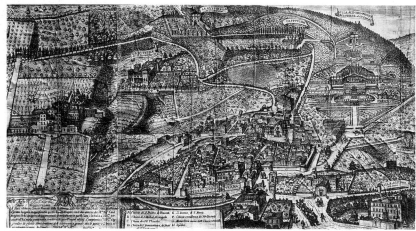

gardens of the period was no longer simply to rule nature with geometry but to create an effect that was 'pleasing and beautiful to the eye'.

In the more culturally sophisticated areas of the Veneto region, the passion for the delights of the rural life, which found expression in the *hortus conclusus*, seems to have freed itself from strict observance of the rigid rules of geometry and obedience to the laws of perspective. The description in *Hypnerotomachia Poliphili* of the gardens of Venus and Polia suggests that they were adorned not only with a profusion of graceful trees and shrubs but also with certain artificial features: 'art and invention is to be employed in the laying of paths defined by apple trees and other plants . . . colourful perennials and ornamental foliage . . . green glades encircled by canals and shimmering rivulets, and a pergola . . . hung with a rich abundance of red roses'. It seems likely that the writer of this description had seen the *barco*, by then almost completed, which was laid out for Caterina Cornaro at Altivole.[20] Wealthy potentates and aristocrats of the period, from kings and princes to church dignitaries and rich patricians, employed every device available in order to emphasize – symbolically and allegorically – their own importance and power. The account, well documented by Coffin and Vivit, of the construction of Francesco Gonzaga's celebrated *viridarium* in Rome, and of the entertaining dialogue that took place in the 1480s and 1490s concerning the layout of the *giardino segreto* there, demonstrate the extent to which artificiality had become an essential element of the symbolic iconography of garden design, and that any attempt to achieve a rural idyll, a return to the Garden of Eden,[21] was doomed to failure; it could produce only a compromise that in no way matched its aspirations. Surviving descriptions of the gardens begun in 1487 for Alfonso of Aragon at Poggio Reale, near Naples, make it very clear (despite the loss of Marcantonio Michiel's account) that they were laid out specifically to celebrate the wealth and privileges of their owner in the most spectacular way possible, and that that entailed the use of artificial elements and ingenious technical devices of every conceivable kind.[22]

Leonardo Giustinian, who worked tirelessly to devise a systematic scheme for the design of the gardens of Charles d'Amboise's magnificent palazzo, next to the church of San Babila in Milan, was responsible for a number of brilliant hydraulic inventions and sound effects, intended to surprise or trick the unsuspecting visitor.[23]

The illusion of the rustic *iucunditas, salubritas, amoenitas, venustas* – the Arcadian dream – evaporated when confronted with a scheme whose Aristotelian aim was to arouse wonder and surprise. Ludovico Sforza had these words inscribed at the entrance to the great Sforzesco Castle in Milan: *Vilis gleba fui nunc sum dignissima tellus/ Cur? Quia Sfortiadum me pia dextra colit./ Mutata est facies, mutataque nomina.* (I, who was a mean piece of land, am now a most noble property. Why? Because the pious hand of a Sforza tends me. My outlook has changed and so has my name.) It is perfectly apparent that the concept defined here is as inseparable from the rejection of the notion of *imitatio naturae* as from

Villa d'Este, Tivoli. Engraving by
E. Dupérac, 1573. Biblioteca Hertziana,
Rome.

Villa d'Este, Tivoli: Rometta fountain.
Engraving by G. F. Venturini. Biblioteca
Hertziana, Rome.

an awareness – deriving from a 'largely ritualistic and symbolic'
attitude – of the political and social significance of an overt display of
wealth and of the 'virtue of magnificence'.

It was no accident that this trend towards opulent theatricality went
hand in hand with the contemporary development of the art of drama
and city festivals, which offered 'as much to content the eye and the
spirit as any material creation or work or art it is possible to imagine', as
Serlio declared.[24] The letter written by Claudio Tolomei to Giambat-
tista Grimaldi on 26 July 1543 is enlightening in this respect in that it
refers to 'the blending of art and nature, so that one cannot discern
whether a thing is the work of one or the other; whether it is a piece of
natural artifice or artificial nature'.[25] It was Grimaldi who, shortly
afterwards, commissioned Galeazzo Alessi to redesign his property
with this concept in mind, and to introduce a series of grottoes (an idea
suggested by the use of volcanic 'magma, a material without
recognizable form', which belonged to the natural world but which
was also recommended by Vitruvius – and by its use in classical times –
as 'a stimulant to new inventions'). *Giochi d'acqua*, which were regarded
as a sort of moving 'life force'[26], were also an essential element of such
artificial schemes, particularly where the surroundings were as ideally
suited to them as those created in 1522 by Perin del Vaga for Andrea
Doria at Fossolo, employing architectural ideas derived from the
Belvedere and Villa Madama in Rome.[27] It is interesting to note that
this work played an important part in defining the relationship of
industry and technology to nature, endorsing the fifteenth-century
concept of 'the pleasure that man derives from the greening of the
earth, from the grace and sweetness of flowers, from the seeding of
plants and the nourishment of fruits', which still, in 1543, underlay the
practical aims of agriculture and the traditional belief that the land was
the inheritance of the rural working people.

In the words of Bonfadio, 'I have done much that nature, combined
with art, has turned into artifice. From the two has emerged a "third
nature", to which I can give no name'. This 'third nature' as Taegio
believed, was the result of certain 'ingenious connections'. Tagliolini,
who has recently published an important work on this subject,[28]
appropriately drawing on the research of Ackerman and Coffin,
identifies in Bramante's plan for the Belvedere in the Vatican
(commissioned in 1504 by Pope Julius II) a seminal influence on the
development of the garden in the sixteenth century, both in Italy and
elsewhere.[29] His complex scheme was carried out on a tract of empty
land that lay between the villa (which was built for Pope Innocent VIII
– work probably began in 1485 – on a hill near the Castello) and the
pontifical palace. A detailed account of the progress of the work is
superfluous here; it is sufficient merely to cite its more remarkable
features, in particular the fact that architecture played an unusually
signficant role in marking the boundaries and the exedra – which was a
focal point – and in linking the different levels of the garden by means
of staircases, which provided a rhythmic counterpoint to the layout of
watercourses and planting schemes. These 'ingenious connections'

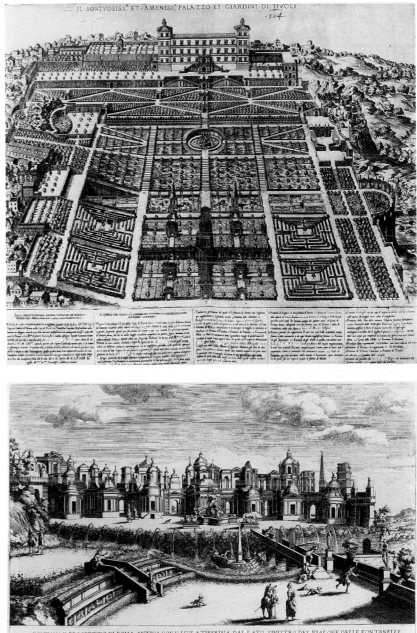

were inspired by the eternal dream of a return to the precepts of the antique world, exemplified by the ruins of the villa and gardens of Nero's Domus Aurea, the Sanctuary at Palestrina and Hadrian's Villa at Tivoli (one is reminded, as was Coffin, of Castiglione's brief essay, written in June 1521, which paraphrases Martial's comments on the villa of Giulio Marziale). That the antique world was the main source of inspiration for these 'ingenious connections' was confirmed by the widespread use of classical relics, and by the clear and deliberate planning of the Belvedere in such a way as to provide an appropriate setting for contemplation and discussion of the philosophy of Humanism by the cultural élite of the period, a pastime which had by then replaced more extravagant entertainments such as banquets, dances and tournaments.

Such artificiality was also to be found in other contemporary gardens (those of the ducal palace of the d'Este family at Ferrara being the only notable exception), where theatrical principles were applied with dazzling originality. The results were sensational and their influence irreversible. Extolling the 'beauty of things made' by the 'judgment and art of the architect', they symbolized the 'liberality of the prince' who had commissioned them. A superb example is the Villa Giulia[30] in Rome, where Ammannati, who refined the work of Vignola, designed the remarkable curvilinear nymphaeum and the series of staircases, loggias and fountains that bring endless variety to every aspect of the garden. The triple terraces of the great Farnese gardens laid out for Pope Paul III by Vignola were approached by a winding road and paths that meandered between colourful beds of flowers overlooked by statues,[31] a plan that may have been influenced by Raphael's designs for the Villa Madama on the slopes of Monte Mario in Rome, which were undoubtedly a response to the current desire for a revival of the villas of Pliny and a reflection of the recent widespread dissemination of the writings of the first-century Latin author Columella.[32] The client for whom the Villa Madama was created was Giulio de'Medici, a cousin of Pope Leo X, who commissioned it specifically in order to promote himself as a man of impeccable virtue and dignity, equal in every respect to the imperial popes.

The popes' lands and possessions were a vast source of wealth, honour and power, which enriched their relations as well as themselves; they and their families were responsible for the creation of some of the most spectacular gardens of the age. The banker Agostino Chigi laid out the magnificent Farnesina gardens, whose gentle slopes were covered with a complex pattern of parterres and glades interwoven with watercourses devised by the great hydraulic engineer Baldassarre Peruzzi; the scheme was so brilliantly conceived and the result so successful that, according to Egidio Gallo in *De viridario Augustini Chisii* (1511) and Blasio Palladio in *Suburbanum Augustini Chisii* (1512), the Farnesina compared with the Belvedere gardens in the Vatican.[33]

Rich cardinals, many of them friends or relations of the pope, also made their mark on the countryside around Rome. There is no doubt

that Alessandro Farnese's choice of the site for the Caprarola gardens – for which Vignola and, later, Giacomo del Duca were largely responsible – had been preceded by an attempt to acquire Villa Madama and also by thorough exploration of alternative sites,[34] while Cardinal Ippolito d'Este's choice of Tivoli was prompted by an existing plan, which Pirro Ligorio was to interpret and realize after (in Zappi's telling phrase) he had 'broken down and transformed the very nature of the place'. The design of the Tivoli gardens, based on an allegorical representation of seigneurial splendour, combines a lucid, linear clarity (the interpretations of Coffin and Madonna are not necessarily contradictory) with the darkness and torment of some esoteric world of the imagination.[35]

In the *sacro bosco* of Bomarzo, which dates from 1552, Vicino Orsini abided by contemporary rules governing the laying out of staircases and watercourses but at the same time he succeeded in creating a world of pure fantasy that has no equal. Looming up among the trees are vast stone monsters, which were intended to give expressions to his innermost feelings and moods (in his own words, to 'offer relief to the heart'). These mysterious, mythical beasts are still there today, though the inscriptions that may once have given some clue to their identity are now for the most part indecipherable.[36] The gardens of Bomarzo take artifice to an extreme in order to deceive and confuse the unwitting visitor, and as a result they are perhaps the ultimate example of the 'third nature' referred to by Bonfadio. If this 'third nature', the incorporation of nature in art, is *de facto* the denial of nature, its historical and cultural links are not easy to define, which perhaps explains why Bonfadio was forced to admit defeat in giving it a name. It is true to say that its origins lie in the civilization of ancient Rome and that its influence extended over a wide, even pan-European sphere; it formed the foundations of what became known as the 'Italian garden', though it was of course interpreted in a variety of ways, according to regional differences in cultural expression. To detail the stages of its development in different areas or enumerate the forms it assumed, particularly in, for example, the great Medici gardens (referred to in various notes), the Palazzo del Te, near Mantua, or the gardens of the House of Savoy is clearly outside the scope of this brief chapter. It

should however be said that the spread of such ideas did not extend to the Veneto region, which resisted any attempt to achieve a marriage of art and nature, preferring to create a setting which complemented the architecture of the villa or palazzo rather than competed with it or even overwhelmed it, as gardens designed according to the Roman formula were apt to do. The notion that a garden should provide pleasures of its own was replaced in the Veneto by a desire that is should serve the building it surrounded and ensure that nature was kept at a safe and respectable distance.

Palladio's rather meagre and terse notes on theory offer ample proof that he supported the Veneto approach, and Scamozzi, while admitting that 'the larger and more spacious a garden is, the more it honours a house', refused to employ any theatrical devices or artifice in solving the problems of terracing, for example. Instead he confined himself, in a series of recommendations on the treatment and relationship of the space devoted to pleasure-gardens, herb gardens and the cultivated landscape, to advocating certain general principles in regard to proportion and balance, though at no time did he suggest that they

should be rigidly adhered to. His attitude did not, therefore, coincide with the firmly held beliefs of his contemporary colleagues in the Veneto, with which he was of course familiar.[37]

Trends in the sixteenth-century Veneto garden were also very much at odds with the spirit of adventure and ingenuity characteristic of Tolomei, and with the ideas of Lomazzo, who firmly believed that time and space should be clearly represented in a garden, enjoining us to 'depict time, the seasons, the months and the years' and to 'extend the arcades and the surrounding walls in such a way as to follow the lines of nature'; a garden should reflect the passage of time, but it should remain a piece of fiction, a work of the imagination,[38] an expression of power, glory and goodness and an outlet for the heart.

We have gone well beyond the point of the extract from Poe quoted in the first paragraph, and in doing so have reached the clear conclusion that the sixteenth-century garden, in which nature was subordinate to artifice, in no way attempted to mirror history in any faithfully represented fashion; yet it was itself an image in which history was obliquely and sometimes disturbingly reflected.

1 See E. Battisti, 'Natura Artificiosa to Natura Artificialis' in *The Italian Garden*, ed. by D. R. Coffin (Dumbarton Oaks 1972), pp. 63–80.

2 A. Vivit, 'L' "insigne viridario" di Francesco Gonzaga in Roma' in *Bollettino del Centro di Studi per la Storia dell'Architectura*, no. 34 (1987), p. 15.

3 B. Rupprecht, 'Villa. Zur Geschichte eines Ideals' in *Wandlungen des Paradiesischen und Utopischen. Studien zum Bild eines Ideals* (Berlin 1966), pp. 210–34.

4 For *Lapides*, see E. Garin, *La città in Leonardo* (Florence 1971), pp. 5–6. But, for an analysis of the attitude of Leonbattista, see *De re aedificatoria*, ed. by P. Portoghesi and G. Orlandi (Milan 1966), bk. 9, 2 (p. 790); bk. 5, 10 (p. 402).

5 See P. Barocchi, *Scritti d'arte del Cinquecento*, III (Milan and Naples 1977), p. 311.

6 *Vita di Triphone Gabriele, nella quale si mostrano apieno le lodi della vita solitaria e contemplativa* (Bologna 1543).

7 See V. Zabughin, *Giulio Pomponio Leto* (Rome 1910–12), Vol. I, pp. 168–9.

8 F. Cardini, 'Il giardino monastico nelle "Sententiae" di Bernardo di Clairvaux' in *Il giardino storico. Protezione e restauro* (Florence 1987), pp. 92–3; 'Il giardino tra filosofia e politica. Il "Paradiso degli Alberti" di Giovanni Gherardi da Prato' in *Il giardino come labirinto della storia* (Palermo 1984), p. 40.

9 F. Zordan, *Poesie inedite di Bartolomeo Pagello celebre umanista, con biografia e note* (Tortona 1984), pp. 54–5.

10 L. Puppi, 'Giardini veneziani del Rinascimento' in *Il Veltro*, Vol. 22, nos. 3–4 (1978), pp. 282–4.

11 L. Puppi, 'Le residenze di Pietro Bembo "in Padoana"' in *L'Arte*, nos. 7–8 (1959), p. 32.

12 Quotation from Vivit, *L'insigne viridario, op. cit.*, p. 18.

13 G. Masson, 'The Gardener's Art in Early Florence' in *Apollo*, 81 (1965), pp. 314–19; A. Perosa, *Giovanni Rucellai e il suo Zibaldone* (London 1960), p. 23; G. Gherardi da Prato, *Il Paradiso degli Alberti*, ed. by A. Laura (Rome 1975).

14 C. W. Westfall, *The Invention of the City; the Urban Strategy of Nicholas V and Alberti in Fifteenth-Century Rome* (1984), p. 261ff.; D. R. Coffin, *The Villa in the Life of Renaissance Rome* (Princeton 1979), pp. 27–34.

15 L. Gundesheimer (ed.), *Art and Life at the Court of Ercole I d'Este* (Geneva 1972), pp. 52–5, 65–6, 68–71.

16 L. Puppi, 'The Villa Garden of the Veneto from the Fifteenth to the Eighteenth Century' in *The Italian Garden, op. cit.*, pp. 89ff.

17 M. Levi d'Ancona, *The Gardens of the Renaissance: Botanical Symbolism in Italian Painting* (Florence 1977), A. Chastel, 'Le jardin et les fleurs' in *Revue de l'Art*, 51 (1981), pp. 42–50; D. R. Coffin, 'The "lex hortorum" and Access to Gardens of Latium during the Renaissance' in *The Journal of Garden History*, Vol. 2, no. 3 (1982), pp. 202ff.

18 A. Tagliolini, *Storia del giardino italiano* (Florence 1988), pp. 58–62.

19 F. di Giorgio Martini, *Trattati d'architettura, ingegneria e arte militare*, edition ed. by C. Maltese and L. Maltese Degrassi, Vol. I (Milan 1967), pp. 245–6.

20 F. Colonna, *Hypnerotomachia Poliphili* (1499), edition ed. by G. Pozzi and L. A. Ciapponi (Padua 1964), pp. 380 and 400 (this is not an appropriate place to enter into the current heated debate on the identity of Colonna). For information on the *barco*, see *Postfazione*, Notebooks of the Benetton Foundation (Treviso 1988).

21 A. Vivit, *L'insigne viridario, op. cit.*, pp. 7–33; D. R. Coffin, *The Villa in the Life of Renaissance Rome, op. cit.*, pp. 182ff.

22 T. Comito, *The Idea of the Garden in the Renaissance* (New Brunswick 1978), pp. 4–7.

23 L. Firpo, *Leonardo, architetto e urbanista* (Turin 1963), p. 107; C. Pedretti, *Leonardo architetto* (Milan 1978), in particular pp. 205–6.

24 R. Pocciani, 'Aspetti dell'imitazione della natura fra Quattrocento e Cinquecento' in *Natura e Artificio*, ed. by M. Fagiolo (Rome 1981), pp. 14–54; R. Strong, *Art and Power: the Feasts of the Renaissance, 1450–1650*, pp. 68–70; P. Marchi, 'Il giardino come "luogo teatrale"' in *Il giardino storico italiano* (Florence 1981), pp. 197–210; A. Chastel, 'Cortile et théâtre' in *Le lieu théâtral à la Renaissance*, ed. by J. Jacquot (Paris 1964), pp. 41–7.

25 C. Tolomei, *Delle lettere libri setti* (Venice 1547) bk. II, no. 1.

26 For an authoritative work on grottoes, see C. Acidini Luchinat, 'Rappresentazione della natura e indagine scientifica nelle grotte cinquecentesche', and, for a study of watercourses, M. Fagiolo, 'Il significato dell'acqua e la dialettica del giardino' in *Natura e Artificio, op. cit.*, pp. 144–53 and 176–89 respectively (an invaluable list of sources on these two subjects can be found on pp. 227–58 of the same publication).

27 G. L. Gorse, 'Genoese Renaissance Villas: a Topological Introduction' in *The Journal of Garden History*, Vol. 3, no. 4 (1983), pp. 255–80, and L. Magnani, 'L'uso d'ornare i fonti': Galeazzo Alessi and the construction of grottoes in the Genoese garden, *ibid.*, Vol. 5, no. 2 (1985), pp. 135–53.

28 A Rinaldi, 'La ricera della "terza natura": artificialia e naturalia nel giardino toscano del '500' in *Natura e Artificio, op. cit.*, pp. 154–75, and A. Tagliolini, *Storia, op. cit.*, pp. 226–8.

29 See J. S. Ackerman, 'The Belvedere as a Classical Villa' in *Journal of the Warburg and Courtauld Institutes*, Vol. 14 (1951), pp. 70–91; D. R. Coffin, *The Villa in the Life of Renaissance Rome, op. cit.*, pp. 80–2.

30 T. Falk, 'Studien zur Topographie und Geschichte der Villa Giulia in Rome' in *Römisches Jahrbuch für Kunstgeschichte*, Vol. 13 (1971), pp. 101–78; D. R. Coffin, *The Villa in the Life of Renaissance Rome, op. cit.*, pp. 150–79 (with later bibliography).

31 See the summary by A. Tagliolini, *Storia, op. cit.*, pp. 185–6.

32 R. Lefevre, *Villa Madama* (Rome 1973); C. L. Frommel in *Raffaello architetto*, ed. by L. Frommel, S. Ray and M. Tafuri; *Raffaello architetto*, exhibition catalogue (Florence 1984), in particular pp. 325–6.

33 C. L. Frommel, *Die Farnesina und Peruzzis architecktonisches Frühwerk* (Berlin 1961); D. R. Coffin, *The Villa in the Life of Renaissance Rome, op. cit.*, pp. 87–109.

34 D. R. Coffin, *The Villa in the Life of Renaissance Rome, op. cit.*, pp. 281–311; A. Tagliolini, 'Il cardinale Alessandro Farnese e il giardino del Cinquecento' in *Ville e parchi del Lazio* (Rome 1984) pp. 17–35.

35 D. R. Coffin, *The Villa d'Este at Tivoli* (Princeton 1960), and *The Villa in the Life of Renaissance Rome, op. cit.*, pp. 311–40; and M. L. Madonna, 'Il Genius Loci di Villa d'Este. Miti e misteri nel sistema di Pirro Ligorio' in *Natura e Artificio, op. cit.*, pp. 190–226.

36 For a study of the *sacro bosco*, see the recent remarkable interpretation by M. J. Darnall and M. S. Weil, 'Il Sacro Bosco di Bomarzo: its 16th-Century Literary and Antiquarian Context' in *The Journal of Garden History*, Vol. 4 (1984), pp. 1–84: but see also the argument put forward by J. B. Bury, *Review Essay: Bomarzo Revisited, ibidem*, Vol. 5, no. 2 (1985), pp. 213–23; For various aspects of the subject, see G. Venturi, *Le scene dell'Eden* (Ferrara 1979), pp. 98–132 and E. Battisti, 'Il ritiro nel giardino monastico come suicidio politico e culturale. La grande tragedia dei protagonisti del '500 romano' in *Il giardino storico, op. cit.*, pp. 97–104.

37 L. Puppi, 'L'ambiente, il paesaggio, il territorio' in *Storia dell'arte italiana*, Vol. 4 (on spatial and technological research) (Turin 1980), pp. 91–3; M. Azzi Visentini and V. Fontana, 'Il giardino veneto dal tardo medioevo a oggi' in *Il giardino veneto*, ed. by M. Azzi Visentini (Milan 1988), pp. 25–50. For a study of the gardens of Venice, see the fascinating work by C. Moldi Ravenna and T. Sammartino, *Giardini segreti a Venezia* (Venice 1988).

38 L. Puppi, 'Il giardino come labirinto della storia' in *Il giardino come labirinto, op. cit.*, pp. 15–20.

Curiosities and Marvels of
the Sixteenth-Century Garden

Luigi Zangheri

In the cultural environment of the sixteenth century, the fashion for collecting works of art and the influence of patronage were to result in the steady erosion of Aristotelian concepts. The Great Cosmic Machine, which had already been the subject of intensive study, particularly in terms of the true relationship between man and nature, the principles of 'symmetry' and the affinity between geometry and reason, gradually began to lose the security of its classical image: the convictions which had helped to define it in the past gradually gave way to uncertainties regarding the role of man in relation to nature. An interest in alchemy, and a passion for strange natural objects and exotic rarities which were being discovered in lands only recently explored, affected the entire cultural development of the sixteenth century.

Gardens offered a means of displaying these wonders to the public in a systematic form, arranging them in an artificial setting that imitated nature – complete with water, rocks, animals and plants – and thereby demonstrated that nature itself was comprehensible and accessible. The fountains, grottoes and labyrinths of which these great gardens consisted nonetheless ensured that the figure of the rich and powerful owner was clearly identifiable behind the display.

One of the earliest of these sixteenth-century gardens was laid out at Mantua for Isabella d'Este. The little garden 'rooms' known as the 'Studio' and the 'Grotto', together with the nearby *giardino segreto*, created a perfect setting for the meetings of intellectuals that took place there to discuss the principles and expression of Humanism, which was the cultural foundation of the Italian courts of the early 1500s.[1]

At the castle built at Liboc, near Prague, by Archduke Ferdinand of the Tyrol shortly after the middle of the sixteenth century, the 'studio' was enlarged to become a building in itself – the Jagdschlosses Stern – which lay inside the royal hunting reserve and served both as a country villa and as a hunting lodge, but it also provided an ideal place from which to study the plant and animal life of the forest. It was laid out in the form of a hexagram or star, like Solomon's seal, though without the connotations of the Star of David, and it enclosed a square courtyard with a gallery on one side. The exterior of the building was as imposing and austere as a mountain face, but the interior was decorated with a rich array of 'grotesque' sculpture like a grotto. Visitors were particularly impressed by the vaulted ceilings of the ground floor, which were ornamented with remarkable stucco work reminiscent of the 'curiosities' commissioned by Archduke Ferdinand for his *wunderkammer*, Schloss Ambras, which ranged from the salt-cellar by Benvenuto Cellino to Montezuma's crown of plumes.[2]

Pratolino, near Florence, is the third and most significant instance of a garden which explored the relationship between open and closed spaces, between areas displaying the wonders of nature itself and those in which 'nature' was imitated or its characteristics reproduced. It was created with the express intention of reflecting the power and virtues of Francesco I de'Medici, who was its inspiration and instigator. After a lengthy tour of Europe in 1565, which included visits to Innsbruck and to the royal courts of Bavaria and Vienna, Francesco had left 'Bohemia,

to call on his Serene Highness Archduke Ferdinand, not wishing to miss such an opportunity to visit his cousin'.[3] This meeting was to lead to a deep friendship between the two men and to inspire in the young Medici prince a desire to become a collector and patron of the arts.[4]

At Pratolino Francesco I outdid all that his cousin Ferdinand had achieved, both at Liboc, with his pavilion-cum-hunting lodge dedicated to the pursuit of nature, and at Schloss Ambras, where he had converted an already existing building to create his masterpiece.

Pratolino was the result of the complete transformation of a large villa into a treasure-house of curiosities and marvels, with a park devoted in part to the glories of the past and in part to the wonders of the present age. Its unique and wholly original character derived from the fact that its gardens consisted of a great labyrinthine open-air display of the miracles of nature.[5] Against a backdrop of Mount Parnassus – with statues of Jupiter, Venus, Apollo and Aesculapius – automata acted out scenes from daily life, representing a knife-grinder, a miller, etc., and the stories of earthly men, such as Narcissus, who became demigods. The walls of the grottoes were painted with scenes depicting the 'mining of silver and every sort of metal imaginable, and the methods by which they were worked'; they were also ornamented with 'corals and other semi-precious stones'. The meadows were thick with 'thousands of varieties of colourful flowers', the aviary contained magnificent birds, the fishponds were full of 'many and various fish' and the woods were inhabited by 'a great quantity of hares, goats and partridges'. Francesco I succeeded in transforming a bare 'mountain slope' into a place of pure delight. Water was brought from springs several kilometres distant and plants were transported from as far away as Trentino, so that 'in the burning heat of summer' one could enjoy 'a sweet and gentle Spring'.[6]

The colossal figure of Appennine by Giambologna, which to Palla Rucellai 'seemed like ice' in the act of melting 'in the scorching rays of the sun'[7], was the greatest of Pratolino's marvels. Reminiscent of the work of Arcimboldo, it combined human and natural forms in a single and incomparably dramatic composition. It was sculpted between 1579 and 1580 and appeared in a number of variations: Costantino de' Servi reproduced it in 1611 for the gardens at Richmond for Henry, Prince of Wales, on a scale 'three times as large as the original at Pratolino, with a number of different rooms inside the body of the statue, a great dovecot in the head, and down below, in the cellars through which the wind blew, two grottoes . . .'.[8] Similarly, Salomon de Caus changed the scale of the figure for '*Les Raisons des forces mouvantes*', planning a '*grand Ciclope dans le corps, du quel sont quelques grottes fort artificiellement fiachtes . . .*'[9] (a great Cyclops in the body, from which are made with great cunning several grottoes).

Visitors to the park were filled with 'great astonishment' and 'wonder' by the 'miraculous inventions', 'ingenious devices' and 'superbly skilful tricks' devised by Bernardo Buontalenti, Bonaventura da Orvieto, Goceramo da Parma, Tommaso Francini and Mastro Lazzaro delle Fontane. The theatre of automata operated by water

View, ground-plan and ceiling detail of the
Jagdschlosses Stern, Liboc, Prague.

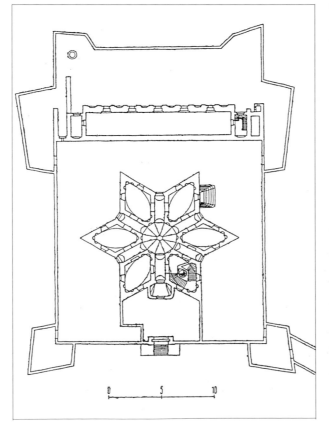

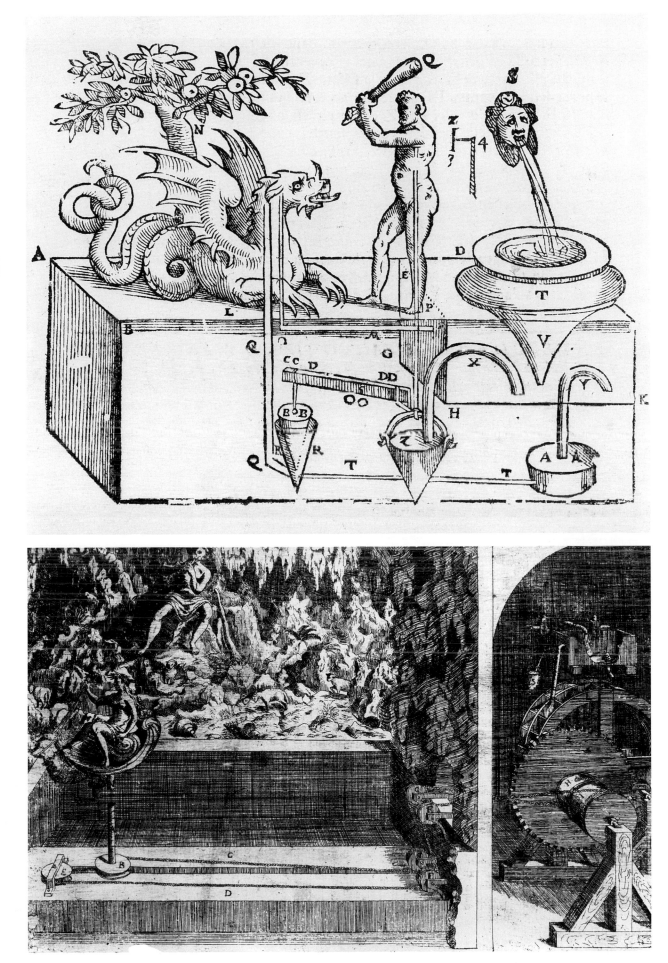

Hercules challenging the dragon that guards the golden apples: design for a mechanical theatre. Engraving by G. B. Aleotti, 1589.

Galatea carried through the water by two dolphins while a Cyclops plays the flute. From S. de Caus, Les raisons des forces mouvantes, *Paris 1624 (1st edition 1615) Bibliothèque Nationale, Cabinet des Estampes, Paris.*

St Germain-en-Laye (Yvelines). Engraving
by A. Francini, 1614. Bibliothèque
Nationale, Cabinet des Estampes, Paris.

power, the hydraulic organs, the mechanisms imitating birdsong and the *giochi d'acqua* combined to create a fairytale world which attracted the attention and admiration of artists and inventors from all over Europe and was described in glowing terms by such illustrious travellers as Montaigne. It was the theatre of automata in particular that aroused the greatest interest among the scientists of the period, who were amazed not so much by the ingenuity of the devices themselves as by the way in which technology seemed to overcome the laws of nature. Agostino del Riccio even declared that if he 'didn't die of some other evil than old age' he was sure to see 'beautiful and unimaginable inventions' in years to come because he was 'a friend of Francini, one of the greatest geniuses of his kind in all Italy . . .'.[10]

The brilliant inventions devised for Pratolino were imitated and reproduced throughout Europe, and they encouraged the creation of a great many new 'gardens of marvels'. Pratolino was responsible for disseminating the most advanced technology of the age, influencing the work of Tommaso and Alessandro Francini, Costantino de' Servi, Cosimo Lotti and Baccio del Bianco, and it was a source of inspiration for artists such as Heinrich Schickhardt and Salomon de Caus. In de Caus's work we find references not only to Appennine but also to Narcissus and Galatea, and to Mount Parnassus, which was reconstructed in the gardens of Somerset House, and was recognized as deriving from Pratolino by the Duke of Saxony in 1613.

Of all these great 'gardens of marvels' only Hellbrunn still exists today. Markus Sittikus von Hohenems, Prince-Archbishop of Salzburg from 1612 to 1619, commissioned Santino Solari to undertake the task of designing it and to supervise its creation. He laid out the castle of Hellbrunn along the lines of an Italian villa and connected it to its adjoining garden by means of a grotto dedicated to Neptune, which was lined in the traditional way with sponges and shells. On the walls of the grotto were groups of ornamental birds which sang – as they do today – by means of pneumatic bellows operated by water power, a device invented by Hero of Alexandria in the first century AD. The grotto was also the setting for a series of theatrical scenes enacted by automata, and for a mask known as the 'Germaul', which swivelled its eyes and stuck out its tongue. Opposite the grotto, and beyond the nearby pools was the 'Roman theatre'; a marble table, with a central water channel to provide a cool storage place for food and drink, stood at the centre, surrounded by marble stools which played water jokes on unsuspecting visitors. Leading to the Grotto of the Crown was a short avenue of water jets, closely resembling an avenue at Pratolino which linked the Medici villa with the pool known as the Vasca della Lavandaia, or Washerwoman's Basin. The knife-grinder, miller and potter automata, together with the Cinghialina, or Little Sow Fountain, representing a mother pig suckling her young, are also reminiscent of features at Pratolino, as indeed is the overall scheme, in which *giochi d'acqua* play an important part.[11]

Sadly, all the other contemporary gardens of this type have now disappeared, though they once included those of Maximilian II at

*t Germain-en-Laye (Yvelines): grotto of
Orpheus. Engraving by A. Francini, 1614.
Bibliothèque Nationale, Cabinet des
Estampes, Paris.*

*St Germain-en-Laye (Yvelines): grotto of
the woman playing the organ. Engraving by
A. Francini, 1614. Bibliothèque Nationale,
Cabinet des Estampes, Paris.*

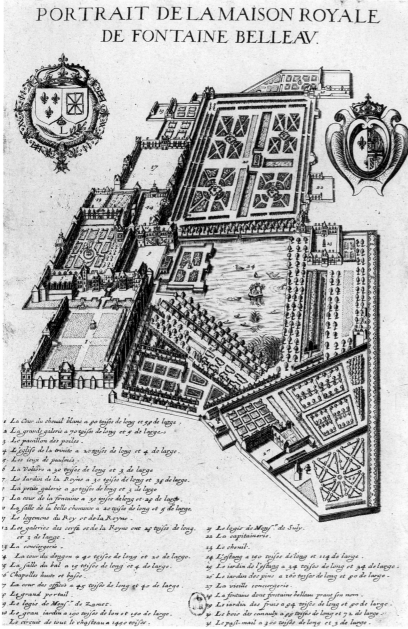

Neugebäude, near Vienna; Rudolf II at Prague; Henry Prince of Wales at Richmond and Henri IV of France at St Germain-en-Laye and Fontainebleau.[12] Historical events, changes in taste and fashion, problems of maintenance and high running costs all contributed to their gradual downfall and dereliction, and all we have left of them now is a few illustrations and enthusiastic accounts by writers who were fortunate enough to visit them. These are enough, however, to tell us that among the most magnificent were undoubtedly the gardens of St Germain-en-Laye, designed in 1594 by Etienne Dupérac, assisted by Claude Mollet, the chief gardener, and Tommaso Francini, who served as hydraulic engineer and deviser of *giochi d'aqua* from 1597. Six great terraces were laid out to link the royal castle with the River Seine, each one provided with grottoes, fountains and pools extending along a central axis. Ornamental stairways and parterres spelling out the initials of the sovereign's name, together with the mottoes and emblems of the royal house, completed the decorative scheme and created the perfect setting for the mechanical marvels laid on by Francini: these included a woman playing an organ, Mercury blowing into a shell, a dragon beating its wings, and elaborate contraptions in the Grotto of Orpheus (all of which had their origins in the automata theatres of Pratolino), and they earned Francini the title of 'Superintendent of the Waters and Fountains of France'.[13]

The celebrated technical inventions to be seen at Pratolino far outdid the curiosity value of its botanical specimens and mineral displays, though these were plentiful and impressive enough to excite the admiration of Aldrovandi, who visited the gardens in 1577 and commented on the horse-chestnuts and conifers, and on species such as *callis praecox, xilobalsamum, altea flore magno*, a type of hibiscus, and *lances ex montibus tridentinis allatis*, describing Pratolino as a botanical garden second only to the Medici gardens of Pisa and Florence. Indeed, as he said, its altitude – 400 metres (1300 feet) above sea level – gave it the climate and the rainfall required to grow 'all those plants well suited to cooler climes'.[14] Cesalpino, Ghini, Mattioli, Benincasa and Clusius, together with Aldrovandi, succeeded in bringing botany to the notice of the ruling houses of sixteenth-century Italy, and ensured that it was regarded as a subject for serious study.[15]

The Emperor Maximilian I described the characteristics and features of his hundred and forty remarkable gardens, and wrote a treatise on gardening inspired by Palladio's *Opus agriculturae*, and Francesco I combined politics and trade with an enjoyment and appreciation of nature: 'When he visited beautiful gardens he took a flower in his hand and contemplated it in all its exquisite colour and beauty with great delight and contentment'[16]. Only botanists, however, initially through the publication of works by Brunfels, Bock and Fuchs,[17] and later as a result of the *ostensio simplicium* and the foundation of the first botanical gardens, succeeded in achieving recognition and respect for this new discipline. By the second half of the sixteenth century, over 1760 species of plants had been identified and classified by European scientists,[18] and could be seen and studied in the botanical gardens of the period.

Villa Medici di Castello, Florence. (Photo Daniele De Lonte)

Villa Medici di Castello, Florence: grotto of animals in stone and marble by Giambologna and his school. (Photo Daniele De Lonte)

An integral part of these gardens were the 'galleries' in which natural curiosities were displayed alongside more conventional exhibits. Protected by a wire fence at the Pisa Botanical Gardens was a collection of extraordinary specimens such as the 'bones of a giant', 'a piece of aloe wood six arms high and as thick as a man's leg' and 'the tail of a sea-snake with the mouth of a serpent', together with 'Turkish boots'; there was also a library consisting of hundreds of rare books, three folders containing three hundred engravings by Dürer and about a thousand tempera illustrations and drawings of natural subjects.[19]

It was this trend towards the establishment of botanical gardens combined with museums that led Francesco I to build a remarkable hanging garden on the Loggia dei Lanzi, next to the Uffizi Gallery in Florence, which he 'planted with evergreen trees and flowers for his delectation'.[20] The grotto became an intrinsic and inevitable part of this garden-gallery concept: an example was La Tribuna, with its dome encrusted with mother-of-pearl and crowned with an elegant weather vane to emphasize its links with the natural world; there objects that seemed closer to art than to nature were displayed in a grotto 'illuminated by the knowledge' that their discovery provided. The Greek philosopher Porphirius would never have dreamt that his *De antro nympharum*, re-published in 1518 with a dedication to Pope Leo X, would become the principal influence and inspiration behind Francesco's magnificent grottoes. Their walls were decorated with shell mosaics and figures made from porous stone, like the walls themselves, the automata, *giochi d'acqua* and the music from hydraulic organs all combined to create an atmosphere in which nature seemed on the point of disclosing its innermost secrets and revealing its ultimate truths. Even Pythagoras had created an artificial grotto in his garden at Samos, 'which was his true philosophical home'.[21]

1 C. M. Brown, 'The Grotto of Isabella d'Este' in *Gazette des Beaux-Arts*, series 6, 89 (1977), pp. 155–71. For a study of the fashion for collecting among sixteenth-century ruling families, see F. Cardini, '. . . un bellissimo ordine di servire' in *Le corti italiane del Rinascimento* (Milan 1985), pp. 77–126, and J. Dixon Hunt, *Garden and Grove: the Italian Renaissance Garden and the English Imagination, 1600–1750* (London 1986), pp. 73–82: chapter entitled 'Cabinets of Curiosity'.

2 J. Krčálová, *Centrální Stavby České Renesance* (Prague 1974), pp. 51–77; *Renaissance Art in Bohemia* (Prague 1979), pp. 52–3. For a study of the collections of Ferdinand of the Tyrol, see *Kunsthistorisches Museum, Sammlungen Schloss Ambras, Die Kunstkammer* (Innsbruck 1977).

3 State Archives of Florence (ASF), *Mediceo*, f. 6377: letter from Cavalier Vinta dated 2 November 1565.

4 Francesco I sent various gifts to Archduke Ferdinand: in 1569, two lions, a leopard and a horse; in 1574, a portrait of Charles V; in 1581, a sallet belonging to Giovanni delle Bande Nere and a suit of armour belonging to Cosimo I. In 1580 he 'lent' him one of the gardeners from the Boboli Gardens for a period of six months. After the death of Francesco I, the Archduke asked Ferdinand I for twenty-six 'small coats of arms and one large one with shield and helmet above' to be made in *pietra dura* for the mausoleum that he was building at Innsbruck: see State Archives of Florence, *Mediceo*, f. 4459, letter of 27 September 1590.

5 On Pratolino, apart from the seminal works of De Vieri (1586), Sgrilli (1742) and Da Prato (1886), important contributions have appeared since 1979: L. Zangheri, *Pratolino, il giardino delle meraviglie* (Florence 1979; re-isssued in 1987 with a revised bibliography); C. Conforti, 'Pratolino, il giardino come mito della conoscenza e alfabeto figurato dell'immaginario' in *La città effimera e l'universo artificiale del giardino*, ed. by M. Fagiolo (Rome 1980), pp. 183–92; A. Rinaldi, 'La ricerca della "terza natura": artificialia e naturalia nel giardino toscano del '500 in *Natura e Artificio* (ed. by M. Fagiolo) (Rome 1981), pp. 154–75. In addition, since 1985, the Province of Florence, the new owners of Pratolino, have organized exhibitions and seminars accompanied by the following publications: *La fonte delle fonti, iconologia degli artifizi d'acqua* – first seminar (Florence 1985); *Il ritorno di Pan; Ricerche e progetti per il futuro di Pratolino* – exhibition catalogue (Florence 1985); *Il concerto di statue* – exhibition catalogue (Florence 1986); *Il giardino romantico* – second seminar (Florence 1986); *Il giardino d'Europa. Pratolino come modello nella cultura europea* – exhibition catalogue (Florence 1986).

6 Vatican Apostolic Library, *Cod. Barb. lat.*, no. 5341, 204–11, transcribed by L. Zangheri, *op. cit.*, pp. 171–7.

7 G. Baccini, *Pratolino capitolo d'Anonimo – Egloga e canzone di Palla Rucellai editata per la prima volta* (Florence 1885), p. 17.

8 State Archives of Florence, *Mediceo*, f. 1348, c. 194r, letter of 16 August 1611.

9 S. de Caus, *Les Raisons des forces mouvantes* (London 1615; Paris 1624), Vol. 2, p. 13.

10 Agostino del Riccio 'Del giardino di un re' ed. by D. Heikamp in *Il giardino storico italiano. Problemi di indagine, fonti letterarie e storiche* (Florence 1981), p. 100. For a study of automata theatres, see L. Zangheri, 'Suggestioni e fortuna dei teatrini di automi. Pratolino come una Broadway manierista' in *Quaderni di Teatro*, Vol. 7, no. 25 (1984), pp. 78–84.

11 F. Czerwenka, *Hellbrunn* (Salzburg 1974).

12 L. Zangheri, 'I giardini d'Europa: una mappa della fortuna medicea nel XVI e XVII secolo' in *Il giardino d'Europa. Pratolino come modello nella cultura europea* – exhibition catalogue (Florence 1986), pp. 82–92.

13 Tommaso Francini was elected 'Superintendent of the Fountains of Pratolino' for a period of two years on 24 October 1594, see State Archives of Florence, *Magistrato dei Nove*, f. 3679, 74. For a study of Francini's activities in France, see P. E. Renard, *Chambourcy-Fontaine Royale 1686–1986* (Chambourcy 1986).

14 Bologna University Library, *MSS. Aldrovandi*, no. 136.XI, c. 73r.

15 Recent publications on the history of the Italian botanical garden include: A. Chiarugi, 'Le date di fondazione dei primi orti botanici del mondo: Pisa (estate 1543), Padova (7 luglio 1545), Firenze (1 dicembre 1545)' in *Nuovo giornale botanico italiano*, Vol. 60 (1953), pp. 785–839; P. Galluzzi, 'La rinascita della scienza' in *Le corti, il mare, i mercanti – La rinascita della scienza – Editoria e società – Astrologia, magia e alchimia* (exhibition catalogue, Florence 1980), pp. 123–243; L. Tongiorgi Tomasi, 'Immagini della natura e collezionismo scientifico nella Pisa medicea' in *Firenze e la Toscana dei Medici nell'Europa del '500* Vol. 1 (Florence 1983), pp. 95–108; M. Azzi Visentini, *L'Orto botanico di Padova e il giardino del Rinascimento* (Milan 1984).

16 L. Berti, *Il principe dello studiolo. Francesco I de'Medici e la fine del rinascimento fiorentino* (Florence 1967), p. 116.

17 See O. Brunfels, *Herbarum vivae eicones* (Strasburg 1530); H. Bock, *New Kreüterbuch* (Strasburg 1539); L. Fuchs, *De historia stirpium* (Basle 1542).

18 G. Moggi, 'Le piante nella pittura italiana dei secoli XV e XVI: problemi e metodi di identificazione botanica' in *Die Kunst und das Studium der Natur vom 14. zum 16. Jahrhundert* (Weinheim 1987), p. 71, quoting P. A. Saccardo, *Cronologia della flora italiana* (Padua 1909), as a reminder that at the beginning of the sixteenth century only 597 botanical species had been classified in Italy.

19 L. Tongiorgi Tomasi, 'Il giardino dei semplici di Pisa', in *Livorno e Pisa: due città e un territorio nella politica dei Medici* – exhibition catalogue (Pisa 1980), p. 516.

20 H. Keutner, 'Der giardino pensile der Loggia dei Lanzi und seine Fontane' in *Kunstgeschichtliche Studien für H. Kauffmann* (1956), pp. 240–51.

21 A. Carcopino, *Etudes Romaines. La Basilique Pythagoricienne de la Porte Majeure* (Paris 1927), pp. 215–16; E. Battisti, *L'antirinascimento* (Milan 1962), p. 184.

Rustic figure representing a river. From S. de Caus, Les raisons des forces mouvantes, *Paris 1624 (1st ed. 1615).*

Hortus Palatinus, Heidelberg: statue of the Rhine.

The Garden of Wisdom of Bernard Palissy

Anne-Marie Lecoq

The world in which, in 1563, Bernard Palissy completed the publication of the *Recepte véritable*...[1] seemed to him a world ruled by Folly. Yet the first war of religion had just ended. The Edict of Amboise, while imposing very severe restrictions on the practices of the reformed church, guaranteed freedom of conscience to the subjects of the French king and granted an amnesty to the Protestants. A few days after the signing of the edict Palissy, one of the founders of the reformed church in Saintes, was set free. He had been arrested and imprisoned at the request of the cathedral chapter who accused him of having taken part in the 'excesses', and particularly in acts of iconoclasm, committed during the occupation of the town by Protestant troops in 1562.[2] For Palissy, however, the much vaunted peace was only a truce. This 'time so troubled and calamitous',[3] this 'time of divorces, plagues, epidemics and other tribulations' was only just beginning. The 'children and chosen of God' would be persecuted until the bitter end by the 'perverts and sinners, simonists, misers and all manner of wicked persons' because they would always revile the two passions most opposed to the teaching of the Gospel – avarice and ambition, the desire for money and for honours which motivates nearly all men. The Protestants, who preached a return to the Gospel, had powerful opponents: young society people and women obsessed by luxury, rapacious and dishonest merchants and above all the Catholic clergy and their myrmidons, royal officers, presidial judges, parliamentary counsellors who, according to Palissy, declared war on the 'new religion' only in order to protect their ecclesiastical benefices. The attitude of these people who amassed worldly possessions was regarded by the world as wise and prudent, but in God's eyes it was mere folly, the acquisition of ephemeral goods at the price of eternal damnation.

Like Erasmus fifty years earlier, Palissy presented this lesson in morality in the form of a fanciful and satirical dream which became the basis of the entire *Recepte véritable*. He employed the well-worn device of a dream experienced by the author in sleep. Palissy could see himself, with the aid of the tools of the architect-geometer and the chemist (or in those days the alchemist) engaged in exposing man's folly. Compasses, ruler, square, plumb-line, level, bevel or false square and astrolabe were all available to him to measure the human head and he had to accept the evidence: 'A fact which Vitruvius and Sebastiano [Serlio] and other architects have been able to pronounce and demonstrate by their diagrams',[4] there is in a man's head no fixed measure or proportion or any straight line, for everything is plunged by madness into a state of flux and imbalance. It therefore remained to analyse the composition of this 'centre of madness' by submitting a number of heads to trial by the furnace, the still and the retort...

Instruments of measuring and 'conduction' (*ducere* = to lead, conduct, bring) were the traditional symbols of the quality opposed to Folly: Prudence or Sapience, uniting wisdom and knowledge. If Palissy, with a nice originality added to them the instruments of analysis, it is because in real life these are what he used. He was very well known as a potter and ceramist, but it is less well known that he had

previously trained as a geometer, designer and surveyor, and had on several occasions been commissioned to draw up plans. He also had some knowledge of architecture and several times in the *Recepte* quotes Vitruvius and Serlio.[5] Moreover he had all his life been a keen naturalist and chemist and his researches into the 'secrets of nature', notably on mineralogy and crystallography, revealed in 1563 in the first part of the *Recepte* and developed in his *Discours admirables*[6] in 1580, brought him the adulation of the nineteenth century.[7] Familiarity with the secrets of nature helped to understand the ways and plans of the Creator, and knowledge in this domain was inseparable from Christian wisdom. Palissy, the man who wielded the instruments of Sapience was therefore in the forefront of the fight against Folly.

His precise role in the fight would consist of putting forward three geometrically designed and architectural projects. One was an impregnable fortified town with streets spiralling up from a squared and octagonal base around a central square, a design inspired by the shell of the murex (tropical whelk). Palissy described the town in an appendix which completed the second part of the *Recepte* in which, through this plan for an impregnable refuge for his co-religionists, he was able to recount the history of the persecutions against the reformed church in Saintonge. Another project was for a 'palace' or 'amphitheatre', doubtless a fortified house built to a centralized, circular or square plan. Palissy only mentions it, promising to return to it in another book, but no more is heard of it. The third, finally, was a garden 'as delectable and useful an invention as was ever seen' which would also serve as a refuge, but this time a moral one, to be a place of retreat and recreation.

This garden, which Palissy dreamed of making and which he described at length, would be entirely devoted to the glorification of Wisdom, that other designation for God. In each of the eight separate areas for visits and for repose would be seen, engraved, carved or formed from cut branches, texts taken from the two sapient books – Proverbs and Ecclesiastes, in which the name of Wisdom would be always present. And at the very heart of the garden the central pavilion would bear words of warning and prohibition: 'Cursed be those who reject Wisdom!' The garden would therefore be the mouthpiece of the enemies of Folly. Above all, however, its very existence would demonstrate the implementation of the virtue of Wisdom, the image of God in the human soul.

In the first place, this would be shown by the practice of an activity worthy above all others – the cultivation of the land. For Palissy, greed and ambition were encouraged in towns inhabited by merchants and law-officers where 'vicious pleasures and wicked trade' were indulged in, to say nothing of the court where luxury and loose living were rife. Life according to God's law was possible only in the countryside. The return to the Gospels necessitated a return to the land and man's first activity, agriculture. This time-honoured sort of sermonizing became popular again in France in the second half of the sixteenth century. The *Recepte* was written at a time when there was a strong movement, in

Proportions of the human head. From L. Pacioli, De divina proportione, *Venice 1509.*

The prudent architect avoids the traps along the way. From Philibert de l'Orme, Le premier tome de l'architecture, *Paris 1567.*

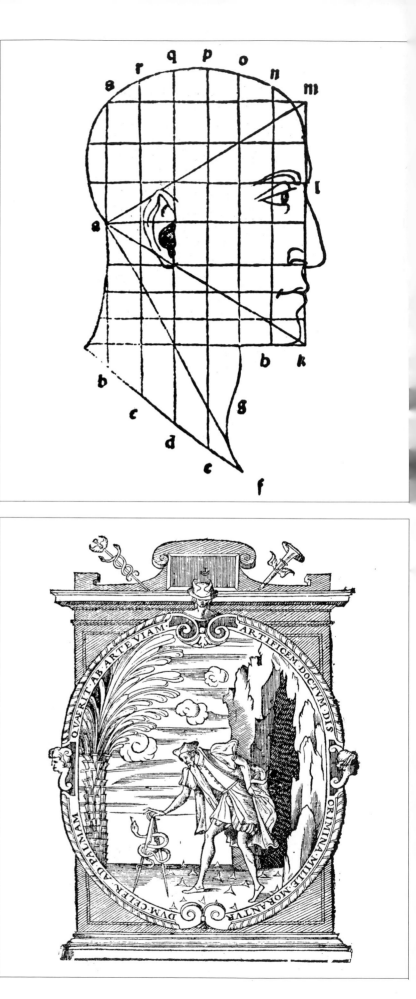

which many Protestants joined, in favour of the pleasures of rustic life in a perfect small country house. This movement, first seen in Charles Etienne's and Jean Liébault's *Agriculture et maison rustique* in 1564 developed by way of the poems of the Sieur de Pibrac, Nicolas Rapin (1575) or Claude Gauchet (1583) to Olivier de Serre's *Théâtre d'agriculture et mesnage des champs* in 1600 in which propaganda in favour of a return to the land became official.

It is folly to despise agriculture. It is also folly to practise it without knowing the laws of nature, thus doing violence to the earth and its produce. This folly is the result of avarice and ambition, since the leading landowners are the Catholic clergy, middle class businessmen and officials, and court nobles who leave to ignorant peasants the cultivation of the land and who, through their desire for money and self-aggrandizement, commit the worst sins, notably the reckless deforestation of the land for their own immediate profit. For Palissy 'there is no art in the world requiring greater use of Philosophy than the art of agriculture', and by philosophy we must understand both moral and natural sciences. The cultivation of the land is impossible without wisdom, and knowledge of the 'secrets of nature'. Two serious and widespread examples of this, the improper storage of manure and the careless pruning of trees, gradually led Palissy the naturalist to propound in the *Recepte* his theory of 'salts', and to discuss the structure of rocks, metals, crystals, plants and the circulation of water. The garden would, in the first place, be a scientifically cultivated agricultural area. Its very situation would obey those natural laws of which Palissy thought he had discovered the secret. For him nature, set in motion by the Creator, was always on the move, destroying here and restoring there. Nothing was lost, nothing created, but everything was in a perpetual state of transformation controlled by two contrary movements – fusion and diffusion. The agents of these changes were various 'salts', called by Palissy 'germinators' or 'generators', which sometimes circulated in water and sometimes settled and 'congealed' to become rocks or metals, but also to transmit their substance to plants, animals and even man.[8] The garden, watered by mountain streams which would feed the vegetation with fertilizing salts accumulated during their course over the crags, would be the universal system in miniature. It would certainly be established near a river or stream, at the foot of a crag, hill, or small wooded mountain from which would gush a spring. The pleasure-garden would be protected by the crag which would give shelter from the wind to the north and west, and walled on the other two sides. To the south, gates would lead to a meadow sloping down to the stream, and to the east there would be gates giving on to plantations of fruit trees, hemp, flax and osiers. Hawthorn hedges would prevent animals grazing in the meadow from escaping, and would also protect the orchards. The spring water would be channelled to circulate throughout the pleasure-garden by forming 'streams' and 'islets', and an ingenious system of perforated elderwood pipes would enable it to water the flowerbeds. Then, it would flow across the meadow between two rows of willows, and down to the stream.

On the northern and western sides the cliff would have 'chambers' hollowed out on two levels. On the lower level, a sort of rustic arcade would serve as orangery, grain store, tool-shed and shelter for the gardeners. Over the arches of these low 'chambers' would be a path, reached from the garden by two flights of steps. The wall forming the frontage of the arcade would be extended to form a parapet along the whole length of this path or gallery, on to which the upper chambers would open. These latter, being reasonably warm and well-ventilated would serve as bookshop and study, shops selling spirits, vinegars, dried fruits and so on, and a laboratory for distilling herbs. Tables, cupboards, shelves as well as doorways and windows, would be carved out of the rock. The purpose of the various cells gives a fairly accurate picture of the master of the place: a man with a deep practical and theoretical interest in nature and who liked to retire, like a hermit, into his cave to read and meditate, or like a magician into his den to watch over his flasks and stills. This sage is nevertheless a lover of nature, enamoured of the pleasures it offers to all the senses. An arbour of hawthorns and fruit-bearing shrubs would shade the path in front of the upper rooms and would attract songbirds. On the parapet, fruits would be set out to dry, there would be flowers and sweet-smelling herbs in glazed earthenware pots, and from here the whole spectacle of the garden could be enjoyed.

This spectacle would have been prepared in the first place with ruler, square and compasses. The garden would be in the form of a square divided by two rectilinear paths into four equal parts. In the four corners, and at the four ends of the cross would be eight 'cabinets'. An amphitheatre, or circular pavilion, would mark the centre of the garden at the intersection of the two paths. The result would be a grid with nine salient points, such as served as a basis for many cosmological, astrological and mnemotechnical ideograms in the Middle Ages and during the Renaissance and the seventeenth century.[9] There is, however, one point of doubt. Did Palissy plan only two rectilinear paths? Or did he omit to mention secondary paths? The latter could, for example, have taken the form of a St Andrew's cross and the plan of the garden would then have resembled the 'carbuncle rays' of the arms of Navarre – a happy coincidence – or even more complex still, a diagram of horoscopes.

The doubt remains, since Palissy provided no illustrations to accompany his text. In the dedications and foreword he claims that he had neither the time nor the money. The fact is, however, that he did not want to, and made no secret of it. This is very evident in the case of his glazes, for which he never gave the recipe even when he described the stages of his discovery in great detail in the *Discours admirables*. Palissy had a great sense of professional secrecy and was wary of competitors who might lay hands on his inventions, damage them, and defraud him of his rightful benefits. So he would provide the 'portrait' of the garden (and of the fortified town) only to those who would ask him to carry out the plans. On the other hand, he made it clear to the reader that the general design of the garden could be adapted to

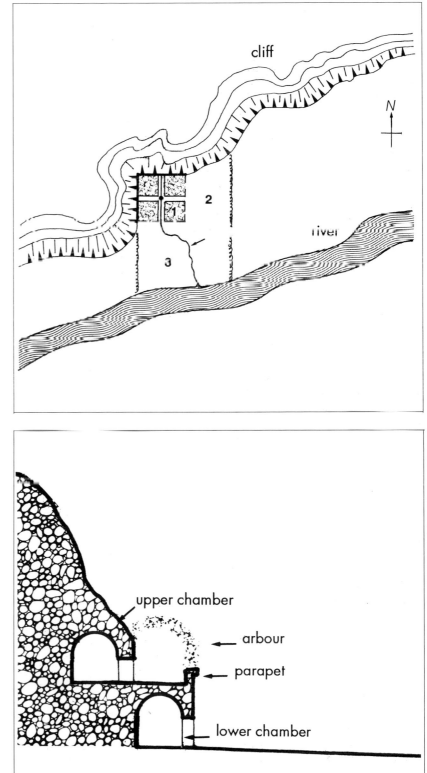

particular geographic and especially financial situations, so the possibility of internal variants on the basic scheme must be acknowledged. There was, finally, one last reason: this design, he said, 'many people are not worthy to view, particularly the enemies of virtue and intelligence'. Palissy was waging war against the opponents of Wisdom, and against folly and foolishness. The garden was a sort of secret weapon, details of which must be revealed only to a small number of initiates, or perhaps conspirators.

The circulation of the water also remained rather vague. A large stream would flow across the garden from north to south, with an island midway. Its connection with the north-south path was not made clear, but it is easy to imagine it flowing down the middle. From each of the peripheral cabinets would emerge 'more than a hundred jets of water' which would form 'streamlets' flowing into the larger one making 'certain circulations which would form pleasant little islands' planted with water-loving plant species. For the twentieth-century reader the 'streams', 'circulations' and 'isles' are more reminiscent of a landscaped garden, but this impression must be resisted – Palissy had not invented the English-style garden. In 1563 the garden of the *Recepte* could not be other than geometric. The 'streams' must therefore be seen as little regular canals and the 'little islands' were probably, like the central one, drawn with compasses. The exact form of the arrangement is not specified but in any case Palissy's garden seems similar to Italian and particularly Roman ones, where there is an abundance of spring water canals.

The 'inventor of rustic earthenware' is much freer with his words when he describes the 'cabinets' around the edges of the garden and in the centre. Here he was able to make simultaneous use of all his talents. He was geometer, architect, mineralogist, tree-pruning specialist, creator of fountains and ceramist. And it was here that, just as the rustic style was becoming popular in France and reached its peak with the grottoes of the Cardinal de Bourbon at Gaillon (from 1550) and of the Cardinal de Lorraine at Meudon (1552–1560), he presented his personal variations on this theme. These variations, which were also to be the manifesto of a 'Protestant' art, engaged in the closest possible dialogue with nature, or in other words, with Creation.

At the corners of the garden were to be placed four stone-faced 'cabinets' or in other words grottoes. Unlike those at Gaillon and Meudon, which concealed classical interiors, their external appearance would be entirely rustic. Each would have a brick frame over which would be placed 'large pieces of rock, uncut and unpolished, so that the exterior of the said cabinet would in no way have the appearance of a building'. On top would grow herbs and shrubs (where birds would sing) and water brought there by concealed pipes would seem to spring naturally between the stones. If the exterior was intended by the fountain-maker to be devoted to the play of water, the interior would be devoted by the potter to fire. The brick structure would in fact act as a furnace, enabling the ceramist to smelt the different coloured enamels he would have placed around the walls and which, as they melted,

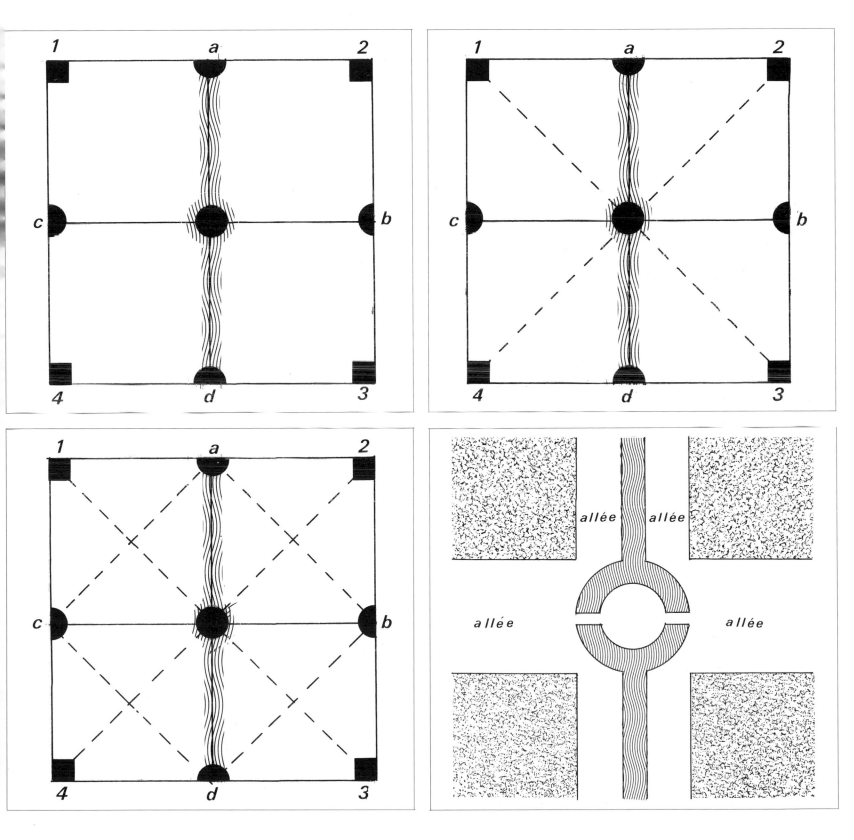

would mingle and 'create very pleasing shapes and ideas' largely because of the effects of fusion. Like the shells Palissy collected and studied all his life, the exterior would thus be rugged, unpolished and irregular, while the interior would be completely covered with smooth, shining colour. Such was the contribution of the 'naturalist' to the contemporary Mannerist taste for bringing together water and fire and for concealing man-made art under the appearance of the work of nature.

The four 'cabinets' would nevertheless not be identical. The brick interior would, before the enamelling, be treated differently in each case. In the one situated in the north-west corner, semicircular recesses would serve as seats between pedestalled columns bearing 'architrave, frieze and cornice'. In the north-eastern one the columns would be replaced by figures making 'strange gestures and grimaces' placed on a continuous base which would serve as a seat, and which would also have architrave, frieze and cornice. In the south-eastern cabinet the only seats would be irregular holes with above them 'a sort or type of architrave, frieze and cornice' which would be carved 'not perfectly' but with heavy hammer blows, with comic effect. Finally, the interior of the south-western cabinet would be full of bumps and holes with everything so askew that there would be 'no appearance or form of sculptural art or of man's labour' and the roof arches would have the appearance of being on the point of crumbling.

The four cabinets would therefore, in a way, serve as samples in a catalogue of grottoes. Provided they were visited in the correct order they would also comprise an accurate illustration of the 'natural' origins of architecture. A passage from Vitruvius had, from the fifteenth century, begun to encourage the theorizing and musings of architects about primitive habitations and the beginning of constructural skills.[10] The visitor to Palissy's garden would penetrate deeper and deeper into 'rusticity', from the full maturity of architecture with its recesses and classical columns back to the natural cave with its bumps and holes, by way of vulgarity symbolized by peculiar grimacing figures and the first comic attempts at architectural language.

The 'green cabinets' at the four cardinal points, and the pavilion on the central island would complete this contemplation of embellishment invented by man, starting from ideas taken from nature. There would have to be indications of the use made, not this time of caves, but of trees, since according to Vitruvius and Serlio 'the ancient inventors of excellent buildings' modelled their columns on 'trees and human forms'. Palissy loved trees, to which he devoted some fine passages of writing. He suffered to see them 'murdered' by ignorant ruffians and like Ronsard he almost heard them cry out. The tree is an image of man, and both provided the model for the column. Playing on these words, as was often done at this time, bringing together man (*homme*) and the elm-tree (*orme*), he imagined four pavilions formed of groves of elms (*homme + orme = (h)ormeaux*). The trunks would be columns and scarification would produce growths imitating bases and capitals. The architrave, frieze, cornice and the whole of the roof would be constructed of branches cut, bent, and woven in the same way as the frontispiece and the tympanum on the three faces of each cabinet. On the 'compass-drawn' island which would mark the centre of the garden a ring of poplars would provide the columns and the entablature of the pavilion. The conical roof would be formed by training the upper branches towards the interior of the ring, and tying their extremities. Between the trunk-columns would be placed screens of woven reeds, and there would be four doors, corresponding to the four paths. The skill of the garden-architect would thus re-create shapes, orginally assumed naturally by certain trees, which were man's first inspiration for architectural decor. Palissy viewed classical architecture in the same way as the eighteenth and nineteenth centuries viewed the Gothic style·[11] an elaboration of forms observed in the forest – in the work, that is, of the 'first and supreme Builder'.

It was to the glorification of this divine work that Palissy's garden would, finally, be entirely dedicated. Everything in it would be disposed for the pleasure of those who could find contentment in the riches and beauty of nature. In the central pavilion there would be a circular table with seats and a 'platform' for crockery, all made of withy. This would be an ideal place for picnics, especially as an arbour built all round the island would also serve as an aviary, and in the pine trees would be placed ingenious weather-vanes with a flageolet through which the wind would make music.

And in this way those who feast below and inside the said pyramid will have the pleasure of bird-song, frogs croaking in the stream, water murmuring as it flows round the feet and legs of the columns sustaining the said pyramid, the freshness of the stream and of the surrounding trees, the cooling breeze from the movement of the leaves of the said poplars. There will also be the pleasure of the music from the summit of the said pyramid.

The four 'green cabinets' would provide comparable delights, but there the sense of sight in particular would be gratified. Inside each cabinet a rustic fountain, in the form of a rock, would be carved against the cliff-face in the north and west and against the enclosing wall in the south and east. The water would be collected in a 'ditch' or basin which would be carefully stocked with animals, fish, tortoises, frogs and so on. The four fountains would be different, but they would all be true marvels of ingenuity, exciting surprise and wonder at the delights and extravagances of nature. The eastern fountain would be made of 'certain white diaphanous stones' which Palissy the collector claimed he had collected in various places. There would be recesses with seats for visitors so that they might conveniently listen to the music of a hydraulic organ placed at the foot of the rock. In the west, stones excavated from the 'mountain' bordering the garden would be used to make the fountain, and it would be decorated with corals and rare stones brought back from various countries: chalcedony, jasper, porphyry, marble, crystal 'and other rich and pleasing stones', 'just as in their natural state' and 'lacking any sign of artifice'. The young elms of

this 'green cabinet' would form seats for the visitor to marvel in at leisure.

In the southern and northern cabinets, to admiration for the works of *artifiziosa Natura* – Nature the artist – would be added almost as much admiration for the works of *naturale artifizio* – 'natural' art.[12] The southern fountain, built of stones from the seashore, especially fossils, would be in the form of a sort of marine grotto, with vaults, over-hanging ledges, crooked pillars and so on; and fragments of enamelled earthenware in the form of snakes, and pieces of turquoise-coloured stone set in the stone-work would complete the illusion. The rim of the pool would be levelled to take various drinking vessels for visitors' refreshment. It was, however, the northern cabinet which would be the triumph of 'natural art'. It would be arranged for banqueting with an oval ceramic table on a foot in the form of a boulder, and the wine could be put to cool in certain crevices in the fountain. This latter would be made entirely of enamelled earthenware, imitating a many-coloured rock full of holes and protuberances, covered with moss, grass and coral and inhabited by a host of small animals: frogs, tortoises, crabs, crayfish, shellfish, snakes, lizards 'carved and enamelled so close to nature' that everyone would be deceived – not only visitors but also the animals in the pool which would also come and perch on the rock beside their ceramic counterparts.

The ceramic animals, shellfish, plants would indeed be exact replicas of the living, just like those which decorate Palissy's famous rustic pottery – the authentic pieces, at least,[13] and those which he had prepared for the Connétable de Montmorency and which later went to Catherine de Médicis' grotto at the Tuileries.[14] Nineteenth-century excavations and especially more recent ones in the Cour Napoléon have brought to light numerous moulds, as well as various enamelled fragments.[15] There can be no doubt (even if Palissy had never mentioned it in his writings) that he modelled his subjects on nature with astonishing precision. At the same time he had succeeded in producing a glaze of extraordinary delicacy and transparency, so that the most minute details, veins, tiny folds, hairs, scales on the original mould are still visible on the finished object.

Palissy did not invent the 'rustic style'[16] but it was he who fully explored the principles of it (and he alone who, thanks to his writings gave the principles precise philosophic justification and poetic value). Contrary to what happened in Italian grottoes and gardens, or those in Italian style, Palissy's style presented no antique statues, fantastic sculptures, paintings or low reliefs of satirical or pastoral subjects from pagan fables, no grotesque murals. Palissy, a Protestant artist, has a dialogue not with Antiquity, but with Nature: his art consists solely in close collaboration with her, for her glorification. As a sculptor, he used Nature's models as he found them, or obtained exact reproduc-tions by precise modelling. As an architect he imitated the effects produced by natural forces which slowly, indiscriminately and irresistibly make and unmake, solidify and dissolve, stabilise and sweep away all things. Or he might perhaps bring them under control and

reveal them according to an idea of order and harmony which belongs only to man. That was his role, as he saw it.

The doubt and difficulty in distinguishing the contribution of one artist from that of another, between Nature and man in the garden, was to be the source of the visitor's pleasure. The 'green cabinets' would have the appearance of being made of stone, the stone cabinets would seem to be heaps of rocks. The way down from the upper walk would be by two flights of steps situated by the north-west and south-west grottoes, the top of which would form a landing. But those walking along the upper level would be 'unaware that there was any building beneath'. The illusion would not stop at the flora and fauna of the rustic fountains. Leaning on the parapet above the concealed portico would be 'certain imitation figures' in ceramic, so lifelike that newcomers would be deceived. Finally, here and there a few mechanical statues would shower those who unwittingly came too close.

The play of surprise and illusion had been an essential part of French and Italian princely gardens since the time of 'international Gothic', and in the garden of the *Hypnerotomachia Poliphili*, cited elsewhere by Palissy, illusions can also be found (mosaic fish in the pools, snakes, lizards, birds, children picking flowers, all in ceramics) and musical weather-vanes. Palissy adopted these apparent trivia, first of all because it was essential to restore the spirits of those who took refuge in the garden from the world's iniquities and persecutions. But, more than that, the production of ceramic figures and lifelike automata would complete the artist's work as an imitation of the Creator. In the *Recepte* God is designated the 'Sovereign Geometer and prime builder', the God with the compasses of medieval imagery. On the other hand, Palissy recalled that God placed the first man in 'a garden, the garden of Eden'. He is therefore the sovereign Gardener. Traditionally the Creator was also presented as a potter working his clay. In realizing his garden Palissy, himself geometer, architect, gardener and potter was acting as the image of the Creator, even to the extent of making creatures of clay.[17]

Nevertheless this second demiurge knew his limitations. He could not instil life or set Nature in movement. That is why, after visiting the enclosed garden, the visitor had to emerge into the meadow, walk through the willow plantations down to the river and traverse the woods on the hillside. And there, it remained only to 'contemplate the marvels of nature', that is to discover in all the detail of plant and animal life the marvellous wisdom and ingenuity of Providence. Then, quite naturally, the Christian would find himself uttering the words of Psalm 104, the hymn of praise to the God of Creation. This was the conclusion Palissy wished to reach, for this had been his starting point. At the beginning of the *Recepte véritable* he recounted how the idea of creating such a garden had come to him. A few days after his release from prison, walking in a meadow along the banks of the Charente, at Saintes, he heard a girls' choir sitting under the willows, singing Psalm 104. He then began to compare the wisdom of the prophet praising God for the works of his creation with the lack of reverence of his contemporaries.

Arbour of greenery. From Hypnerotomachia Poliphili *French translation, Paris 1546.*

The origins of Gothic architecture. From Sir J. Hall, Essays on the Origins, History and Principles of Gothic Architecture, *London 1813.*

To teach them to appreciate the beauty of the world he first had the idea of picturing it as an enormous landscape painting. But 'paintings last only a short time', unlike the ceramics of the Saintongeais 'worker in clay'. And so he preferred to create a garden to impart to his contemporaries respect for and knowledge of nature which is, with the Bible, the Creator's other book.

Thus Palissy dreamed of creating this highly catechismal device, but he dreamed aloud, and wanted his message to be heard. His 'plan' was an offer of service. 'There are in France', he said, 'more than four thousand noble houses' where could be found in one place a hill or mountain with a spring, and open country below, particularly near rivers and streams. This was an appeal to the French nobility, to Protestants in the first place, but also to the Catholic nobility least hostile to the new religion, and even to the royal family. In 1563 the Protestants had by no means lost hope of winning them over to their cause and Palissy, like many of his co-religionists, seemed to have envisaged the possibility of an alliance between the 'very Christian' king and the 'true' believers. The *Recepte* was dedicated to the Connétable de Montmorency, to his son the Maréchal and to Catherine de Médicis. By this gesture Palissy showed his gratitude to them for this release from prison. At the same time he suggested to the Maréchal that he should disclose to him the design of the garden, and declared himself ready to carry it out should the dedicatee so wish. To the queen mother he indicated that she would find in the *Recepte* many things 'which could greatly serve to enhance her garden at Chenonceau' and declared himself ready to work there when it should please her. The 'useful' and 'delectable' garden was therefore by no means a Utopia in Palissy's eyes, and he insisted from the beginning that his garden, unlike that of Polyphilus, was not a dream, but totally practicable. Michel Foucault categorized gardens as 'heterotopian' – places quite other than and different from ordinary life, but nevertheless real places. Referring to Palissy's 'plan' to create in a world of Folly an area dedicated to Wisdom we should therefore speak not of Utopia, but of a heterotopian project.

This plan was never realized, neither at Ecouen for the Connétable de Montmorency, nor at Chenonceau[18] or the Tuileries[19] for the queen mother, nor, as far as is known,[20] anywhere else. The 'pottery' grotto for the Connétable, which Palissy manufactured piece by piece at Saintes between about 1555 and 1565 was apparently never delivered, and the Connétable died in 1567.[21] When Catherine de Médicis in her turn ordered a similar grotto for her new residence in Paris, the potter from Saintes transferred his workshop to the capital and set to work with his sons. As the recent excavations in the Carrousel area seem to indicate, it was a matter of reusing the components of the first grotto and perhaps of completing it.[22] The excavations have also revealed, to the south of the foundations of the palace, the remains of a rock-work fountain with frogs in enamelled earthenware and a system of jets of water similar to those described by Palissy for one of the 'green cabinets' in the *Recepte*.[23] Were the grotto and the fountains ever

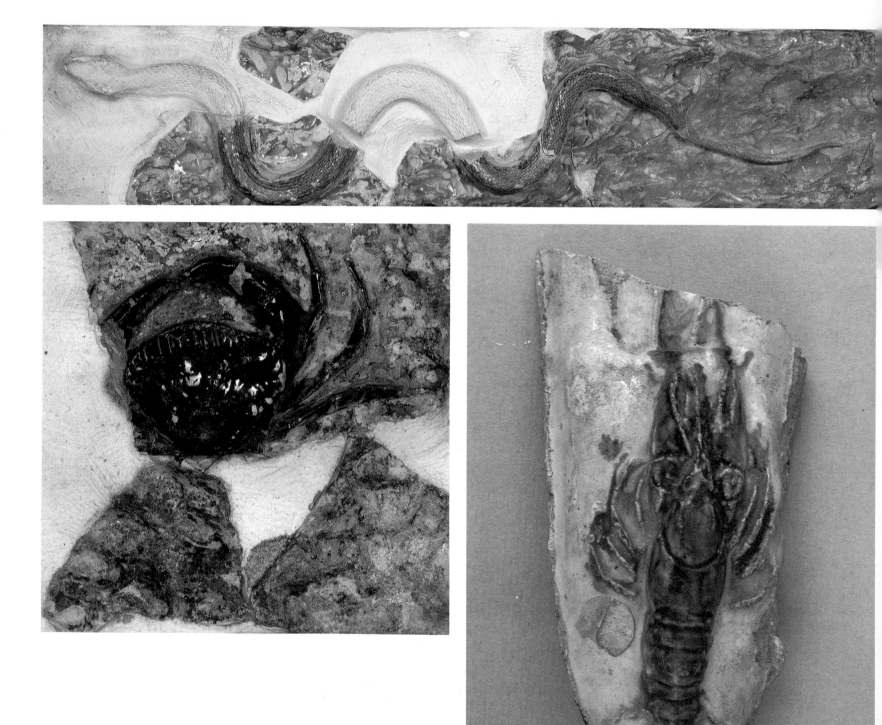

Snake, small crab and crustacean in enamelled earthenware from the grotto of the Tuileries, Paris by B. Palissy. Musée Carnavalet, Paris.

finished? We do not know. We do know that the Palissys were working at the Tuilieries in 1570 and again in 1572 when the Massacre of St Bartholomew's Day took place. Palissy took refuge in Sedan with his family and did not return permanently to Paris until 1576.[24] There is no evidence that he reopened his workshop and resumed work for the Tuileries (where work on the garden, begun in 1564, ended in 1578). His preoccupations from that time were essentially scientific. He gave public lectures on natural history during a brief stay in Paris in 1575 and continued them until 1584. At the same time he was working on the *Discours admirables*, published in 1580.

In 1585 the League was in control in Paris and extracted from the King the Edict of Nemours, which granted the Protestants fifteen days to abjure or to leave the country on pain of imprisonment and confiscation of goods. From 1586 to 1590 Palissy spent time in the prisons of St Germain-des-Prés, the Conciergerie, and the Bastille. And it was there that he died one day in 1590 'of hunger, destitution, and ill-treatment',[25] the man who had written, at the time when the atrocities of the civil war were just starting:

'I have found in this world no greater delight than the possession of a beautiful garden'.[26]

1 *Recepte véritable, par laquelle tous les hommes de la France pourront apprendre à multiplier et augmenter leurs thrésors* (La Rochelle 1563). The most convenient edition is that of P. A. Cap, in *Oeuvres complètes de Bernard Palissy* (Paris 1844). A critical edition by K. Cameron is shortly to be published by Droz.

2 For all the biographical details reference has been made to the chronology of B. Palissy drawn up by Dominique Poulain in the special issue 'Palissy' of the *Revue de l'Art*, no. 78 (1987) pp. 58–60.

3 'Au lecteur', in *Architecture, et ordonnance de la grotte rustique de Monseigneur le Duc de Montmorency, Pair, et Connétable de France* (La Rochelle 1563; facsimile ed. Paris 1919). All other quotations are from the *Recepte véritable*.

4 References to calculations of the proportions of the human body in architectural treatises of the Renaissance period.

5 In 1564 he is called 'Architect and Inventor of the ceramic grottoes of Mgr le Connétable'. The Conciergerie prison register of 1590 describes him as 'architect in earthenware'.

6 *Discours admirables, de la nature des eaux et fontaines, tant naturelles qu'artificielles, des Métaux, des Sels et Salines, des Pierres, des Terres, du Feu e des Emaux. Avec plusieurs autres excellents secrets des choses naturelles. Plus, un traité de la marne, fort utile et nécessaire pour ceux qui se mellent d'agriculture* (Paris 1580; reissued by P. A. Cap, *op. cit.*)

7 On the incredible popularity of Palissy in the nineteenth century, see A-M. Lecoq, 'Mort et résurrections de Bernard Palissy' in *Revue de l'Art*, no. 78 (1987) pp. 26–32.

8 On this matter, and concerning Palissy's connection with certain ideas of the alchemists, see J. Céard, 'Relire Palissy' in *Revue de l'Art*, no. 78 (1987), pp. 77–83.

9 The use of schemes of this sort in the design of parterres during the Renaissance has been emphasized in *La città effimera e l'universo artificiale del giardino*, ed. by M. Fagiolo (Rome 1979).

10 See J. Rykwert, *On Adam's House in Paradise. The idea of the primitive hut in architectural history* (New York 1972).

11 See *ibid.*, and J. Baltrušaitis, 'Le roman de l'architecture gothique', in *Aberrations. Légendes des formes* (Paris 1957), pp. 73–96.

12 The play between two opposing characteristics, essential to rustic style, is explained in these terms by the humanist Claudio Tolomei in a letter dated 26 July 1543, referring to the new fountains in Rome, which show a revival of antique art.

13 On the distinction between authentic pieces, imitations and fakes see the first results of the enquiry conducted by L. N. Amico: 'Les céramiques rustiques authentiques de Bernard Palissy' in *Revue de l'Art*, no. 78 (1987), pp. 61–76.

14 See below, notes 21 and 22.

15 The fragments from the nineteenth-century excavations have been divided between the museums of Sèvres, the Louvre and Carnavalet. There is a good series of illustrations in the early article by L. Dimier, 'Bernard Palissy rocailleur, fontenier et décorateur de jardins' in *Gazette des Beaux-Arts*, Vol. 2 (1934) pp. 8–29. For recent discoveries, see the first evaluation published by the team of archaeologists: B. Dufay, Y. de Kisch, D. Poulain, Y. Roumégoux, P. J. Trombetta, 'L'atelier parisien de Bernard Palissy' in *Revue de l'Art*, no. 78 (1987), pp. 33–57.

16 The best introduction to the 'rustic' style remains that of E. Kris, 'Der Stil "Rustique"', in *Jahrbuch der kunsthistorischen Sammlungen in Wien*, Vol. 1 (1926) pp. 137–208.

17 See references in the article by F. Lestringant, 'Le prince et le potier: introduction à la "Recepte véritable" de Bernard Palissy (1563)', in *Nouvelle Revue du XVIe siècle*, Vol. 3 (1985), pp. 5–24.

18 The nineteenth century, which created a veritable myth around Palissy, attributes to him the creation of the new gardens at Chenonceau, on the left bank of the Cher, in their entirety, and the building of the Fontaine du Rocher on the right bank by the main entrance drive. See in particular C. Chevalier, *Histoire de Chenonceaux* (Paris 1868), which recognizes nevertheless that this attribution is not documented. It is however regularly repeated, as recently as 1977 in N. Miller, *French Renaissance Fountains* (New York and London) pp. 256–60. Palissy's movements can be traced between Saintes, Paris and Sedan, the three towns in which he ever lived. There is no record of him in the Loire valley, where he would have had to stay if he were engaged on important works. The Fontaine du Rocher was a large rock-work standing in a circular basin surrounded by two circular terraces. Neither du Cerceau's description nor the fragments excavated rather before 1868 mention ceramics, an astonishing omission if this were indeed Palissy's work.

19 At the Tuileries, Palissy, as noted by L. Dimier, certainly had no part in the general plan or in the direction of the works as long as Philibert de l'Orme lived – that is until 1570. In his *Discours admirables* in 1580, the Saintongeais did not hesitate to criticize the mistakes in hydraulics made at the Tuileries by 'Monsieur the Queen's architect'. Palissy was therefore not responsible for what happened there. Even when Bullant took over from de l'Orme there is no reason to suspect that Palissy was involved in anything but the building of the grotto.

20 According to C. Chevalier, *op. cit.*, p. 338, 'the park of the castle of Chaulnes in Picardy was made entirely according to the plans of the delectable garden'. I do not know the basis for this affirmation. See A. Arcelin, *Notice sur l'ancien château historique des ducs de Chaulnes* (Amiens 1924).

21 We know of Palissy's project from the booklet entitled *Architecture, et ordonnance . . .* (see note 3). The text was written in 1562 when Palissy, imprisoned in Bordeaux, was trying to obtain from the Connétable his release and the protection of his workshop at Saintes, threatened by Catholic vandalism. The booklet was printed in La Rochelle, a few months before the *Recepte*.

The Connétable's grotto was to be an edifice 13 metres (43 ft) long, 6.50 metres (21 ft) wide and 5.50 metres (18 ft) high as far as the cornice. The whole of the interior was to be in ceramics (nothing is said of the exterior). The front wall was to be decorated with pillars surmounted by statues very 'near life-size' and armorial bearings. The opposite wall would be occupied by a boulder 2.60 metres (8.5 ft) high, and in front of it a 'ditch' filled with water, 30 centimetres (12 ins) wide and deep. This rock would be covered with small animals and plants and at its foot, on a small terrace, tortoises, crabs, frogs, spider-crabs, fish, seals and so on would spout water into the basin which would be filled with fish. On the side walls were to be two superimposed orders: a row of more or less rustic columns with their pilasters linked by garlands of fruit and vegetables and supporting the architrave, frieze (with the Connétable's device) and cornices; between the columns twelve recesses also more or less rustic, above the columns a row of figures 'all rustic and made in strange ways'. On the four walls, the figures were to

form the interspaces between the windows, which were of irregular shape and twisted as if they had been roughly hewn out of the rock with a pickaxe, and support the arches of the roof, also misshapen. On the cornice and in the vaulting various birds and animals usually found in 'rocks and ancient ruins' would take up their abode. The Connétable's grotto was then to combine at least three of the 'cabinet' styles in the *Recepte*.

As L. Dimier (*op. cit.*, p. 17) has already noted, there is no trace or memory of such a grotto at Ecouen, and Peiresc, who visited the château in 1606 (and incidentally attributed to Palissy all sorts of works which were not his) heard not even a mention of it.

22 See B. Dufay *et al*, *op. cit.* (note 15) pp. 40–42. For the restoration of the grotto in the Tuileries it is no longer possible to use the '*Devys d'une grotte pour la Royne, mère du Roy*', published in the *Oeuvres de Bernard Palissy* edn. by B. Fillon and L. Audat, vol. 1 (Niort 1888), pp. 3–8, which very possibly may be a forgery made in the 1860s: see R. H. Bautier and G. Bresc-Bautier, 'Un faux du XIXe siècle: "*Devys d'une grotte pour la Royne, mère du Roy*"', in *Revue de l'Art*, no. 78 (1987), pp. 84–5.

23 In 1585, some Swiss ambassadors described the Tuileries gardens and particularly a fountain 'built in the form of a rock, in which were various pottery animals such as snakes, snails, tortoises, lizards, frogs and other aquatic creatures, which spouted water from their mouths, in addition to that which gushed from the rock itself'. If this was indeed a Palissy fountain, as seems very probable, and the very one of which the remains have just been discovered, it was situated not in the western larger part of the gardens, but in the area between the palace and the ditch which runs the length of the Charles V rampart; see the relevant plans in *Le Louvre et son quartier. 800 ans d'histoire architecturale* (exhibition in the Town Hall annexe in the 13th arrondissement, Paris 1982) catalogue by J. de Fontgalland and L. Guinamard, nos. 26a and 34.

24 Which means that it is not possible, as is often done following L. Dimier, *op. cit.*, p. 24, to attribute to him the rock covered in silver gauze decorated with rustic figures, shells and reptiles which appeared, mounted on a chariot, on the occasion of a fête given for the Polish ambassadors in the Tuileries gardens in 1573.

25 Pierre de l'Estoile, ed., *Journal de Henri IV*.

26 *Recepte véritable*, ed. P. A. Cap, *op. cit.*, p. 83.

Botanical Gardens of the Sixteenth and Seventeenth Centuries

Lucia Tongiorgi Tomasi

Plan of the botanical garden of Padua. From P. Tomasini, Gymnasium Patavinum, *1654.*

Plan of the botanical garden of Leiden. From C. de Passe, Academia sive speculum vitae scolasticae, *1612.*

It should be shown . . . how important and useful is a herb garden as a place for public study . . . so many plants can be raised and studied there by botanical students in a single year. A public garden is a necessity . . . the lack of it would be a serious deprivation. P. Castelli, *Hortus Messanensis,* 1640.

The garden of the sixteenth and seventeenth centuries, correctly defined as a 'complex conception',[1] is not easy to classify because it fulfilled so many different functions: not only was it a place for pleasure and entertainment and for solitary meditation, a setting for sculpture, automata and *giochi d'acqua,* it was also a laboratory for botanical and medical research. As such, the 'scientific garden', or medicinal herb garden, took on an important role in the sixteenth and seventeenth centuries alongside the 'pleasure' garden.

The first botanical gardens were laid out around the same time in many European cities, in about the middle of the sixteenth century, contemporary with advances in science and with a renewal of interest in the classification of plants and natural products used in herbal medicine – the vegetable extracts from which Galenic medicine derived its materials.

Most of the botanical gardens of the period were laid out near the main European universities: Padua[2] and Pisa[3] in 1543, Florence in 1545, Bologna in 1567, Leiden in 1587, Heidelberg and Montpellier in 1593, Oxford in 1621 and Paris in 1626.[4] As a result it was possible to incorporate first-hand observation and study of botanical specimens (a study that came to be known as *ostensio simplicium*) into the university courses offered by the great European botanists of the day, such as Otto Brunfels, Leonart Fuchs, Pietro Andrea Matioli and Charles de l'Ecluse (Clusius), in addition to critical analysis of the works of great classical writers on the subject such as Dioscorides, Theophrastus and Pliny.

Botanical gardens rapidly became the principal centres of scientific experimentation, teaching and study, inevitably sacrificing much of the aesthetic appeal that had been such a feature of late Renaissance and Baroque gardens in order to meet the precise requirements of the cultivation of medicinal herbs. The ingenious devices and artificiality – statuary, fountains, grottoes, *giochi d'acqua* and

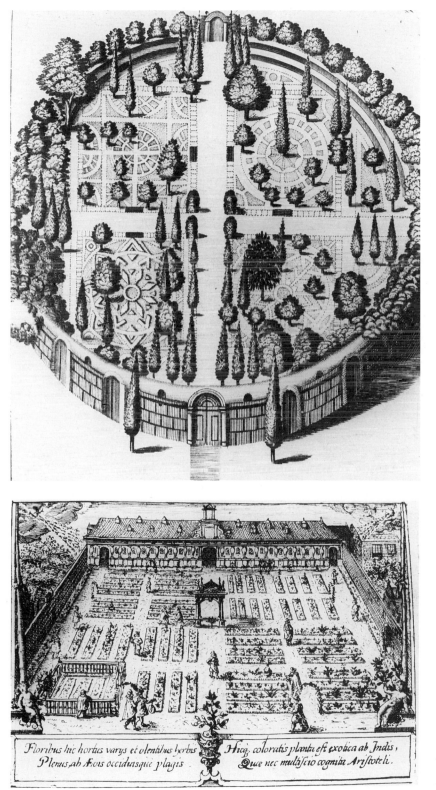

Floribus hic hortus varys et olentibus herbis Plenus, ab Aos occiduasque plagis   Hicq, coloratis plantis est exotica ab Indis, Quæ nec multiscio cognita Aristoteli.

labyrinths – of the pleasure-garden disappeared almost entirely, to be replaced by wonders of a different kind:[5] strange, rare species from the recently discovered New World, such as the sunflower and the agave which had to acclimatize to European conditions, and the many plants collected because of their unusual form or colour. Among the most sought-after varieties, not merely for scientific reasons but also for their visual appeal, were the bulbous species such as the tulip, which became extraordinarily popular throughout Europe, the tuberose, the fritillary, the narcissus and the iris.

Even the flowerbed, one of the fundamental elements of the garden, underwent a change: complex polygonal and other geometric shapes gave way, in a gradual process of simplification, to rectangles laid out on a plan based on the cardinal points of the compass, often with a well at the centre, very much in the way monastic gardens – also devoted largely to the cultivation of medicinal herbs – had been designed in medieval times. The square plan, subdivided into various sections, could be doubled in size, turning it into a rectangle if required, and was therefore easily adapted and extended. Gardens of this type were laid out around the same time in places as far apart as Florence, Paris, Leiden and Oxford. (In the botanical garden at Padua the rectangular plan was contained within a circle.) The geometrical designs of these gardens not only facilitated the organization of their medicinal species but also reflected the arcane traditions and beliefs associated with astrology, which played an important role at that time in the development of the natural sciences. The shapes of the flowerbeds and the precise positioning of the plants took on an esoteric and almost magical significance, the garden eventually becoming to all intents and purposes a *pentacolo* (a short of magic charm, often in the shape of a star) in which the gardener-herbalist-magician practised a 'natural magic' by means of which medicinal herbs were influenced by the power of the stars. It was no coincidence that the design of the botanical garden at Mantua, which was laid out at the beginning of the seventeenth century by the Florentine herbalist Zanobi Bocchi, was based on a square within a square, reflecting the relative positions of the stars and planets at that time.[6]

Plan of the botanical garden of Florence. From P. A. Micheli, Catalogus plantarum, *1748.*

Garden implements. Sixteenth-century drawing. Biblioteca Universitaria, Pisa.

Obscurity and extensive use of allusion make most astrological writings of the period inaccessible to all but the well-informed on the subject, although many writers and garden designers, such as Claude Mollet and Jacques Boyceau de la Baraudière make explicit references to them in their work.

Plants in the botanical garden were arranged strictly according to species and genus, as is clear from Pietro Castelli's *Hortus Messanensis* (Messina 1640) and from Guy de la Brosse, who laid out the Jardin du Roy in Paris and wrote: '*Les plantes sont tellement disposées en leurs quarreaux . . . qu'elles y sont ordonnées en leurs espèces selon leurs genres, de sorte que quiconque connoist une espèce peut assurément dire que le genre connu est là dedans.*'[7] (The plants are arranged in their beds in their species according to their genus, so that anyone familiar with a certain species can be sure that all the known genus is there.)

The arrangement of the plants in the beds was not always, however, a simple matter of classification: often they were laid out in such a way that their identification required a feat of memory. In various European botanical gardens, such as Padua, Pisa and Leiden, flowerbeds were distinguished by letters of the alphabet and the plants by numbers. The *Indice* and *Catalogi plantarum* manuscripts, and the earliest descriptions of botanical gardens printed in publications such as the *Horto de i semplici* of Padua (published by G. Porro in 1591) and the *Hortus publicus academiae Lugdunum-Batavae* (by P. Paaw, 1691) provided perfect opportunities for memory training, while the arrangement of the plants themselves took on the function of a *locus mnemonicus*.

Right from the earliest days of the botanical garden, a natural history museum was frequently established alongside it – similar in principle perhaps to the *Wunderkammern* and the *Raritatenkammern* – providing an occasion for general scientific research as well as for the study of specimens in the garden itself.

These museums, which included an *exsiccata* or 'dry garden' (the modern herbarium), displayed not only collections of paintings depicting the plants grown in the garden or those sent on an exchange basis for scientific research, but also stuffed animals, bones, minerals, shells and a variety of strange or unusual objects produced either by nature or by man. As a result, the three branches of the natural world – the animal, mineral and plant kingdoms – were brought together and the sixteenth- and seventeenth-century botanical garden became a sort of microcosm of the world outside, a reflection of what was then referred to as 'the great book of nature'.

1 E. Battisti, 'Natura Artificiosa to Natura Artificialis' in *The Italian Garden*, ed. by D. R. Coffin (Dumbarton Oaks 1972), pp. 1–36.

2 M. Azzi Visentini, *L'Orto botanico di Padova e il giardino del Rinascimento* (Milan 1984).

3 L. Tongiorgi Tomasi (ed.) 'Il giardino dei semplici di Pisa' in *Livorno e Pisa. Due città e un territorio nella politica dei Medici* (Exhibition catalogue, Pisa 1980), pp. 513–598.

4 J. Prest, *The Garden of Eden: The Botanic Garden and the Recreation of Paradise* (New Haven and London 1981).

5 L. Tongiorgi Tomasi, '"Extra" e "Intus": progettualità degli orti botanici e collezionismo eclettico tra XVI e XVII secolo' in *Il giardino come labirinto della storia*, International Convention (Palermo 1984), pp. 48–57.

6 A. Zanca, 'Il giardino dei semplici di Mantova' in *Kos*, no. 18 (1985), pp. 90–2.

7 G. de la Brosse, *Description du jardin des plantes medicinales estably par le Roy Louis le Juste* (Paris 1636), p. 21.

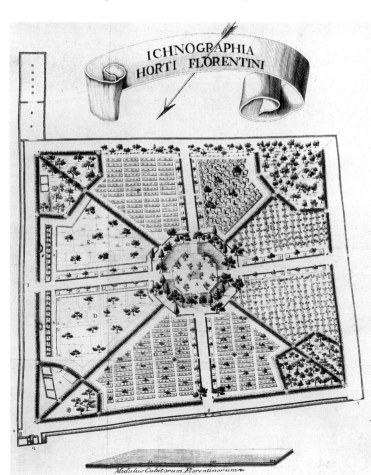

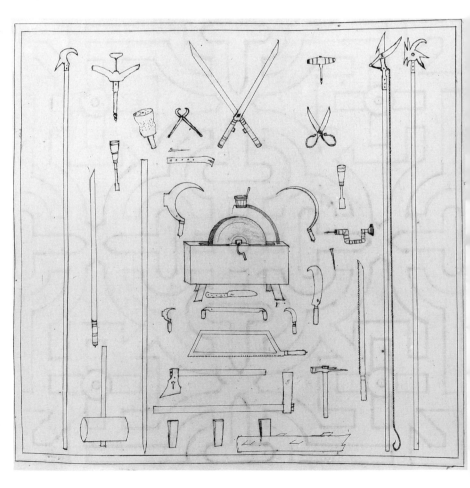

Designs for flowerbeds. Sixteenth-century
watercolour. Biblioteca Universitaria, Pisa.

Labyrinths in the Gardens of the Renaissance

Paolo Carpeggiani

Irrgarten *in the courtyard of the Palazzo del Te, Mantua. Drawing by M. van Heemskerck, Staatliche Museen Preussischer Kulturbesitz, Berlin. (Photo Jörg P. Anders)*

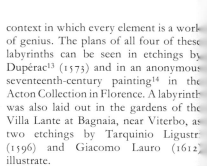

In the complex gardens of the Renaissance the labyrinth acquired the identity of a *topos* as much in a practical as in a conceptual and theoretical sense. But first one must specify precisely what is meant by the term labyrinth, which can after all be applied to a wide variety of forms and therefore convey a number of different meanings. H. Kern, in his exhaustive and stimulating study of the labyrinth,[1] distinguishes it in its real sense from the *Irrgarten*. The true labyrinth consists of a single winding path that leads eventually to a central point, while the *Irrgarten* is made up of a maze in which one can only too easily lose one's way while searching for the one path that leads ultimately to the centre. Although the labyrinth follows a complicated route, its outcome is certain;[2] the *Irrgarten*, on the other hand, is a celebration of irrationality, overturning the concept that 'virtue brings good fortune', which was one of the fundamental doctrines of Humanism. Alberti makes no mention of the labyrinth in his *De re aedificatoria*:[3] the gardens he discusses – comprised of 'circles, semicircles and other geometric figures' – are based on a strict rationale that allows for no extravagances or deviations from the path of discipline. In fact Filarete was the first to put forward a scheme for a labyrinth, in his *Trattato di architettura*,[4] in which he devised plans for one in King Zogalia's royal park. Later, Sebastiano Serlio included two designs for labyrinths, among other garden features, in *Il quarto libro* (Venice, 1537).

Although since classical times frequent references[5] had been made to 'the labyrinth in which one could lose one's way', actual representations of it only appeared quite late: the first notable examples were in fact referred to in the codex written by Giovanni Fontana (Munich, Bayerische Staatsbibliothek, Cod. Icon. 242, fol. 9v, 10r) in the third decade of the fifteenth century, but Fontana's schemes – as Battisti[6] has correctly indicated (by contrast with Kern[7]) – do not refer to gardens. It was only in the sixteenth century that the terms became almost interchangeable and the *Irrgarten*/labyrinth really became established: the apparently accidental nature of its complex and tortuous design, combined with the fact that it repeatedly posed the problem of choosing the right path from a number of alternatives, made it a game

of chance with all the ingredients calculated to appeal to the spirit of the age; it was the perfect entertainment for pleasure-seekers at the hedonistic courts of the period, who found its unpredictability endlessly fascinating. An *Irrgarten* was laid out at the Alcazar in Seville[8] by Charles V in about 1540 – the remains of the floor of the pavilion can still be seen there – and another, probably designed for the amusement of the guests at a series of festivities, once occupied the courtyard of the Palazzo del Te near Mantua, according to a plan in the notebook of its architect, known as the Anonymous Mantovano A (Berlin, Staatliche Museen Preussischer Kulturbesitz, Kupferstichkabinett, 79 D2a, fol. 23v); it is perfectly possible that this *Irrgarten* formed part of a scheme devised by Giulio Romano,[9] who died in 1546. It should be remembered, in connection with both the significance and the purpose of the *Irrgarten* at the Palazzo del Te, that since the time of Isabella d'Este a tradition of music and poetry had existed at the ducal court in Mantua in which the image of the 'labyrinth of love'[10] frequently recurred: the

Palazzo del Te itself was intended essentially as a celebration of the love of Federico II Gonzaga and Isabella Boschetti, and the *Irrgarten* became the setting for a sort of symbolic game in which fortune and misfortune, joy and suffering, all played a part in the attainment of love.

Another *Irrgarten*, this time on an enormous scale, was laid out at Mantua in 1607, a little to the south of the Palazzo del Te, by Gabriele Bertazzolo,[11] who left a description and drawings of it in his *Urbis Mantuae descriptio* (1628): '. . . it is of such great size that in order to reach the centre one must follow a road for more than two miles, but if one strays from the correct path the distance could be much increased. The roads are wide enough for horses and carriages . . . .'

Not all labyrinths took the form of an *Irrgarten* however: four were planned by Pirro Ligorio in the 1560s for the gardens of the Villa d'Este[12] at Tivoli, though only two – which lie beyond the fishpool, next to the Giardino dei Semplici – were ever completed; they are superb examples of formal design, the ingenuity and skill of their conception conspicuous even in a

context in which every element is a work of genius. The plans of all four of these labyrinths can be seen in etchings by Dupérac[13] (1573) and in an anonymous seventeenth-century painting[14] in the Acton Collection in Florence. A labyrinth was also laid out in the gardens of the Villa Lante at Bagnaia, near Viterbo, as two etchings by Tarquinio Ligustri (1596) and Giacomo Lauro (1612) illustrate.

Labyrinths also became popular in the gardens of France, not surprisingly perhaps if one thinks of the frequency with which the image of the labyrinth appears as a decorative motif in the floors of French Gothic cathedrals.[15] Its religious significance – as a representation of a sinful world through which one path alone leads us on to purity and righteousness – was transformed, however, in the great French gardens of the period, into a secular device offering entertainment and little more. Jacques Androuet du Cerceau, in the most ambitious of his published works,[16] provides evidence of two French labyrinths, one rectangular and the other circular, at the Château de Montargis, and of an *Irrgarten* at the Château de Charleval in Normandy, which he himself designed for Charles IX of France in about 1560.

Later on the labyrinth also made an appearance in the gardens of Germany: between 1613 and 1618 the French architect Salomon de Caus designed the Hortus Palatinus at Heidelberg for Friedrich V of Bohemia, though work on it was interrupted by the Thirty Years' War and never completed. He left a description of it,[17] illustrated with copper engravings. A labyrinth also appears in a painting dating from 1620 by the Flemish landscape artist Jacques Fouquières, which now hangs in the Kurpfalzisches Museum in Heidelberg.[18]

A German wood-engraving from the mid-sixteenth century depicts an extremely complex *Irrgarten*, which Kern[19] regards as a model of its type. It was copied some decades later by D. Loris in his treaty on gardens,[20] in which he included some twenty-three schemes for labyrinths.

By this time, however, the theoretical concept of the labyrinth had already been discussed by Thomas Hill,[21] Johan Vredeman de Vries,[22] Hans Puec[23] and Lelio Pittoni,[24] and towards the end of the

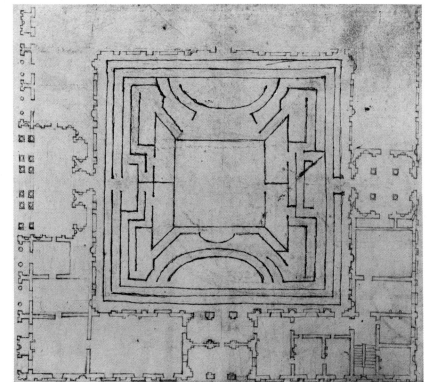

Labyrinth of Love. *Painting, school of Tintoretto, c. 1550–60. H.M. The Queen, Hampton Court Palace.*

Hortus Palatinus, Heidelberg. *Painting by J. Fouquières, Kurpfalzisches Museum, Heidelberg.*

sixteenth century Agostino del Riccio[25] proposed a scheme for a royal garden. This he suggested should contain four labyrinths, each with eight grottoes filled with automata, fountains and *giochi d'acqua*, each labyrinth to be laid out in the form of a large *Irrgarten*: 'If you do not wish to lose yourself', warns del Riccio, 'you must do as the lover of the wandering maiden did; he took a ball of string and tied the end of it to the beginning of the labyrinth so that he could retrace his steps from the centre of the maze and thus escape death; if you do this every time you

will find your way out of every labyrinth'. The game, deprived of its symbolic significance, becomes an explicit reference to the myth of Theseus and Ariadne, and to the love that underlies it.

The extent to which labyrinths became an intrinsic feature of the gardens of the Renaissance is clear from the many illustrations of them that still exist,[26] among them Lucas van Gassel's painting *David and Bathsheba* (*c.*1540) in the Summer Collection of the Wadsworth Atheneum gallery, Hartford, Connecticut; an etching by Hieronymous Cock, *Labyrinthi*

mirabiles ambages, dated 1558; and *Spring Landscape*, 1587, by Lucas van Valckenborch in the Kunsthistorisches Museum in Vienna. The most remarkable and emblematic work of all, however, is undoubtedly a painting from the studio of Tintoretto, dating from *c.* 1550–60 and now at Hampton Court.[27] It depicts an island labyrinth with lovers embracing behind its high hedges and chasing each other along its winding paths, symbolic of the games and traditions associated with the labyrinth of love.

[1] H. Kern, *Labirinti. Forme e interpretazioni. 5000 anni di presenza di un archetipo. Manuale e filo conduttore* (Milan 1981). But ideally one should consult the revised German edition (Munich 1982).
[2] *Ibid.*, pp. 13ff.
[3] Leon Battista Alberti, *De re aedificatoria*, Book 9, chapter 4 (1447–52).
[4] Antonio Filarete, *Trattato di architettura*, Book 15, f. 121 (1460–65).
[5] H. Kern *op. cit.*, p.13.
[6] E. Battisti and G. Saccaro Battisti, *Le macchine cifrate di Giovanni Fontana* (Milan 1984), p. 61.
[7] H. Kern, *op. cit.*, pp. 202–3.
[8] *Ibid.*, p. 386.

9 P. Carpeggiani, 'Labyrinthos. Metafora e
mito nella corte dei Gonzaga', in Quaderni di
Palazzo Te, no. 2 (1985), pp. 62–3.
10 C. Gallico, 'Forsè che si forsè che no' fra poesia e
musica (Mantua 1961).
11 P. Carpeggiani, op. cit., p. 65.
12 D.R. Coffin, The Villa d'Este at Tivoli
(Princeton 1960).
13 H. Kern, op. cit., p. 388.
14 Reproduced in I. Belli Barsali and M.G.
Branchetti, Ville della campagna romana. Lazio, 2
(Milan 1975), p. 133.
15 H. Kern, op. cit., pp. 219ff.
16 J. Androuet du Cerceau, Les plus excellents
bastiments de France, Vol. I (Paris 1576).
17 S. de Caus, Hortus Palatinus a Friderico Rege
Boemiae Electore Palatino Heidelbergae extructus
(Frankfurt 1620).
18 H. Kern, op. cit., p. 581.
19 Ibid., pp. 260–2.
20 D. Loris, Le Thrésor des parterres de l'univers,
contenant les figures et pourtraits des plus beaux
compartiments, cabanes et labyrinthes des jardinages .
. . (Geneva 1629).
21 T. Hill, The Profitable Arte of Gardening
(London 1568).
22 J. Vredeman de Vries, Hortorum viridariorumque elegantes et multiplicis formae . . . (Antwerp
1583, reprinted Cologne 1615).
23 Pucc's treatise on gardens is in manuscript
form and is now in the care of the museum of
Dumbarton Oaks, Washington (G.a.a. three
labyrinth gardens appear respectively on folios
2, 32 and 55).
24 L. Pittoni, Gli artifitiosi, varii, et intricati
quatro libri di laberinti . . . ; manuscript, dated
1611, is housed in the Biblioteca Nazionale
Centrale, Florence, Ms II.I, 279 (CL. XVIII,
no. 13).
25 A. del Riccio, 'Del giardino di un re', ed. by
D. Heikamp, in Il giardino storico italiano.
Problemi di indagine. Fonti letterarie e storiche
(Florence 1981), pp. 59ff.
26 H. Kern, op. cit., pp. 328ff.
27 Ibid., pp. 332–3; J. Shearman, The Early
Italian Pictures in the Collection of Her Majesty The
Queen (Cambridge 1963) p. 248.

The *Giardino Segreto* of the Renaissance

Gianni Venturi

The *giardino segreto*, or 'secret garden', has played an important role in the history of gardening, but its origins are hard to trace and its significance hard to quantify. Neither is it easy to specify precisely what is meant by the term *giardino segreto*, or even to find written references to it in Renaissance works. In order to form any clear idea of its identity, it is necessary to return to the original purpose of a garden and to imagine oneself transported – through drawings and plans dating from any period from the Renaissance to the nineteenth century – to an ideal garden.

Every garden is 'secret' in the sense that the very essence of a garden is to provide solitude and seclusion. The analytical work by McClung (1987)[1] demonstrates this point. The Garden of Eden before the fall of Adam, as described in the Book of Genesis, was not enclosed by walls nor contained by barriers of any kind and was not, therefore, a 'secret' garden. Later references to Eden, from Genesis to the Book of Psalms and beyond, however, suggest that the garden was indeed enclosed and therefore in some way 'secret', close to, and yet distinct from, that other archetype, the Heavenly Jerusalem.

The traditionally accepted notion of the garden according to Christian religious teaching (and later reflected in the courtly gardens of the medieval period) is of a spiritual, sacred space enclosed by walls that suggest both the physical detachment of the garden itself from the world outside and the exclusion of society by means of secular defences such as towers and castellations, as if to imply that religion and history are inseparable. The classical tradition, derived from Vitruvius rather than from the Stoics – a view firmly upheld and propounded by Leon Battista Alberti and by Colonna in the *Hypnerotomachia Poliphili* – refers to the garden in mathematical-philosophical terms that stress rather than exclude the metaphorical and metaphysical aspects of the garden, describing it as a place in which the human spirit can commune with God.

A fascinating theory has recently been advanced in connection with a remarkable new study of the possible links between the fresco known as *The Triumph of Death* in the Camposanto in Pisa and the work of Boccaccio.[2] This theory, turning upside down the chronology of all pre-

vious analyses, puts forward the hypothesis that Boccaccio may have studied the fresco and suggests that it may indeed signify a reaffirmation of the idea of a garden as a place of joy and a sanctuary from the evils of the world, which seem to be symbolically rejected by the representation in the fresco of the young revellers in a garden which is threatened by the scythe of Death. The dual perception in the medieval period of a garden as a place of spiritual harmony, and as the symbol *ante litteram* of Milton's Pandemonium, actually underlines the idea of secrecy and isolation: the *paradisum voluptatis*, by which the Vulgate Bible means the Garden of Eden, contains two differing interpretations of seclusion – secular and religious – according to the context and to the influence on the late medieval imagination of the *hortus conclusus*.

Partly in response to different demands for privacy and partly as a result of the different purposes it was intended to serve, the Renaissance garden took a variety of forms: for example, it was customary for an area to be set aside for private use in the garden of a duke or prince, and excluded from the iconography and symbolism underlying the over-

all scheme. If, as was generally the case with the great Renaissance gardens, the owner was a member of the ruling aristocracy – Belvedere at Ferrara,[3] Castello at Florence,[4] and many other examples come to mind – and his property was an expression of his power, it was essential to retain a secluded space for the exclusive use of the family and for the enjoyment of a truly private life. This custom became more firmly established with time, especially in the royal palaces of the seventeenth century, but it was already widespread in Italian gardens of the Renaissance period, such as the Villa Barbaro at Maser, where, as Puppi has suggested,[5] the nymphacum may well have served this purpose.

If one considers the evolution of the garden as an enclosed space, according to the medieval tradition, it is apparent that there may be a link between the purpose of a *giardino segreto* and its interpretation as a setting for erotic love, as it came to be regarded in its secular guise as a *hortus conclusus*. The *De Sphaera* miniature depicts a secluded space around which courtly life revolved, and it is clear that this garden had close connections with the medieval *fontaine de juvances* (fountain of youth) and *jardin de loisir* (garden of leisure) of the *Roman de la Rose* and with a number of scenes in Boccaccio's *Decameron*, which were the principal European prototypes of the *giardino segreto*. Here again seclusion is provided by encircling walls, which exclude the sophisticated pleasures to be enjoyed in the city's streets and monumental buildings, both secular and religious, which can be seen in the background.

The *giardino segreto* as a setting for love is illustrated explicitly in two expressions of Renaissance culture: one is that great crucible of contemporary philosophy on the art of the garden, the *Hypnerotomachia Poliphili*; the other, the upper section of the fresco representing the month of April in the magnificent cycle of fifteenth-century frescoes in the saloon at Schifanoia, the palazzo built at Ferrara for Alberto V d'Este in the fourteenth century.

Of all the books written in the Renaissance, the *Hypnerotomachia Poliphili*[6] was the most powerful in its influence on the architectural, symbolic and ideological development of the sixteenth-century garden: one has only to think of its

detailed descriptions of the garden of
Venus, though its strange magical quality
belonged unmistakably to the culture of
the time and was impossible to translate
accurately into another context, just as
Vitruvius interpreted by Leon Battista
Alberti was to some extent at odds with
the *sensus abditus* (hidden meaning) of
the neo-Platonic philosophy at the root of the
iter ad sapientiam (journey to wisdom) of
Poliphilus.

The last woodcut in the first book
depicts the young hero in a garden,
surrounded by nymphs telling him that it
is a place sacred to the goddess Venus,
who every year on May Day relives the
sad death of Adonis. Here, in this
supreme example of the *giardino segreto*,
and at a time conducive to love, Poliphilus comes to embrace his beloved Polia.

The garden is protected from the
outside world by the trelliswork enclosing it, excluding all intruders and all
contact with the natural landscape surrounding it. The architectural style and

the pool, to be seen at the centre of the
illustration, are clear allusions to the
ancient world, thereby emphasizing the
sacred aspect of the act of love, but the
most striking feature of the scene is the
sense of secrecy and initiation, which is
explicit in the words of the nymphs:
'Know that this place is mysterious and
that it is venerated and of great renown'.

One might deduce that the *giardino
segreto* is an intrinsic feature of the Renaissance garden, but it should be stressed
that the very idea of a garden suggests a
place withdrawn from the world, a concept inherited from the medieval tradition and applied in a general sense both
to gardens of delight and to gardens of
love. The *giardino segreto* was only to find
full expression in England in the nineteenth century, but it undoubtedly played
an ideological and philosophical role of
great importance in the Renaissance garden. In this sense it is possible to relate it
to the wilderness, examples of which are
to be found in many great gardens laid

out for ruling families of the time, to the
secluded corners reserved for family conversation, and particularly to the gardens
set aside for private meetings, intimate
discussion and amorous dalliance.

It is perhaps not unreasonable, therefore, to interpret the upper section of the
Schifanoia fresco depicting the month of
April as an expression of 'ideological
secrecy'. Here too the pursuit of love,
which is reserved to members of the
court, takes place, as in the *Hypnerotomachia*, in the presence of Venus, whose head
is crowned with a wreath of roses, and the
nymphs, replaced here by the Graces,
preside over arcane and erotic rituals
associated with the act of love: the two
aspects of Venus exert their influence
over the assembled company, those to the
left behaving with all the traditional
elegance and refinement associated with
the court (and with late Gothic representations of it), while those to the right have
the knowing, disenchanted air of the
practised love-maker.

One factor, clearly inseparable from
the fundamental idea of the garden, is
essential to a celebration of the act and the
spirit of love: a seclusion and secrecy
which is obtained not by building high
walls to exclude the outside world but by
returning to the peace and solitude of
Eden before the fall of Adam.

1 William Alexander McClung, *Dimore celesti.
L'architettura del paradiso* (Bologna 1987).
2 Lucia Battaglia Ricci, *Ragionare nel giardino.
Boccaccio e i cicli pittorici del 'Trionfo della morte'*
(Rome 1987).
3 Gianni Venturi, 'Un'isola tra utopia e realtà'
in *Torquato Tasso* (Bologna 1985), pp. 173–8.
4 Claudia Conforti, 'Il giardino di Castello e le
tematiche spaziali del Manierismo' in *Il giardino
storico italiano* (Florence 1981), pp. 147–64.
5 Lionello Puppi, 'The Villa Garden of the
Veneto from the Fifteenth to the Eighteenth
Century' in *The Italian Garden* (Dumbarton
Oaks 1972), pp. 81–114.
6 Gianni Venturi, 'Picta poesis: ricerche sulla
poesia e il giardino dalle origini al Seicento' in
Storia d'Italia, Part 5, Il *Paesaggio* (Turin 1982),
pp. 665–749.

The Villa Lante at Bagnaia
Bruno Adorni

Villa Lante, Bagnaia: plan of the garden.

Key: 1 Fountain of the Deluge; 2 Houses of the Muses; 3 Fountain of the Dolphins; 4 Water Chain; 5 Fountain of the Giants (or of the Rivers or the Sirens); 6 Cardinal's Table; 7 Fountain of the Cave (or the Lights); 8 Grotto of Venus; 9 Grotto of Neptune; 10 Palazzina Gambara; 11 Palazzina Montalto; 12 Fountain of the Moors (or the Square).

In 1202 the small town of Bagnaia in Lazio became part of the feudal property of the nearby city of Viterbo, and in the course of the fifteenth century it was used as a summer residence by the Bishop of Viterbo. In the early years of the sixteenth century Cardinal Raffaele Riario (Bishop of Viterbo from 1498 to 1505), assisted by his nephew Ottaviano – who succeeded him as Bishop in 1505 and held the post until 1523 – embarked on the creation of a *barco* at Bagnaia.

Enclosed by a high wall, which was built around 1514, it covered about twenty-five hectares (sixty-two acres) and was filled with game, hunting being extremely fashionable at the time of Pope Leo X; the *casino* built in the park in about 1521 was in all probability intended originally as a hunting-box. In 1523 Cardinal Nicolò Ridolfi had water brought to the park from two springs donated to him by the town council of Bagnaia, and in 1538 a straight new road, leading from Bagnaia to the sanctuary of Sta Maria della Quercia, was laid out according to plans devised by Tommaso Ghinucci, a priest of Sienese origin, who worked as a sort of factotum for the Cardinal. (In his capacity as architect, he was also responsible for the enlargements

and changes made to the Bishop's Palace at Bagnaia and for the hospital which was built outside the town in 1542.) A new aqueduct, designed by Ghinucci for Balduino del Monte, was begun in 1553 and finished two years later.

From the beginning of the del Monte period, in the mid-sixteenth century, the rapid expansion of the medieval town of Bagnaia, which had at that time about a thousand inhabitants, began to cause considerable problems, with the result that the local council decided to call on the advice of Ghinucci, who had by then been the local 'town-planning consultant' for many years. He was asked to devise a scheme for the development of the outer town, between the castle and the great park laid out by Cardinal Raffaele Riario. Accordingly, on 13 February 1567, Ghinucci presented two alternative plans to the council for the building of a piazza and surrounding streets.[1]

Ghinucci continued to work under Cardinal Gambara, and in 1574 received confirmation of certain privileges conferred on him by the del Monte family for the great services he had rendered '*in architectura palatii et barci non sine magno eius labore*' (for the architecture of the palace and park, sparing no pains). In 1584 the

town council even allowed him to erect a few unauthorized buildings 'as the Cardinal had said he should be allowed to do as he liked'.[2]

Cardinal Giovan Francesco Gambara, who had become Bishop of Viterbo in 1566, had taken personal possession of Bagnaia on 2 September 1568. A letter written to him by Cardinal Alessandro Farnese from Caprarola on 18 September 1568 reads, '. . . as Vignola has already been to see Your Holiness and will do whatever you command of him, there is nothing further for me to add in response to your letter'.[3] Even though there were other problems to solve and other schemes under way at Viterbo (Vignola had produced designs for the della Rocca fountain in 1566 and was currently engaged in the building of Porta Faul, and Gambara himself was considering rebuilding the façade of the cathedral), it was nonetheless at this period that the Cardinal began to devote himself to his property at Bagnaia and to concentrate on plans for its development. Prompted most likely by a wish to redesign and enlarge the *barco*, he decided to engage the services of Vignola, who was by then the undisputed chief architect of Viterbo, where the Farnese family owned feudal

estates and where Alessandro Farnese was Papal Legate. Vignola was then working nearby at Caprarola, involved in concerns very similar to those at Bagnaia: why not at least ask his advice?

Work on the new terraced garden probably began soon afterwards, perhaps in the year of Barozzi's death in 1573–4,[4] and, as is stated in the concession of privileges granted to Ghinucci in 1574, Ghinucci himself was certainly employed at the *barco* at that time as well as at the Bishop's Palace in the town. Montaigne, who visited the place in 1581, presumably accompanied by Ghinucci, who had no doubt exaggerated a little in describing his role at Bagnaia and at Tivoli, wrote: 'The same Messer Tomaso of Siena, who organized the major undertakings at Tivoli, is also in charge of the work here, which is not yet complete: by continuously adding new inventions to the old, he has given to this, his latest endeavour, more art, beauty and elegance than ever'.

A letter from Cardinal Gambara to the Duke of Parma and Piacenza, Ottavio Farnese, dated 7 October 1576 reads: 'I am levelling my garden and planting a grove of plane trees in the *barco* on the advice of Yr Excellency, but I doubt if

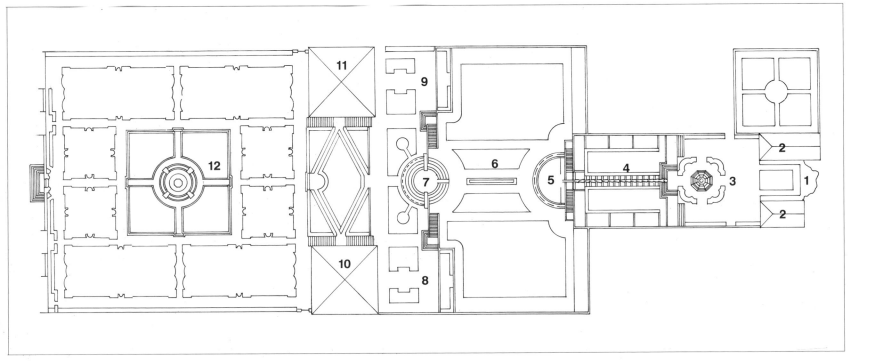

*Villa Lante, Bagnaia. Engraving from
G. Lauro,* Antiquae urbis splendor,
*Rome 1612–14. Dumbarton Oaks,
Washington DC.*

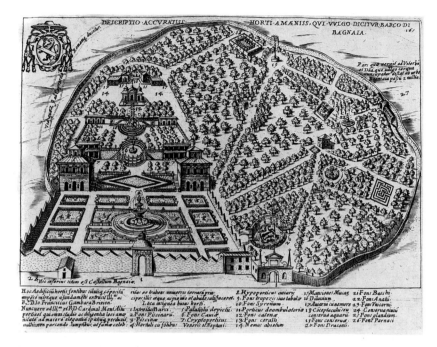

I shall embark on building a *casino*'!5 In 1576 the terraces of the Italian-style garden were still being completed, and the construction of the Palazzina Gambara was still in doubt; it was possibly built rather hurriedly as a result of rumours of a visit by Pope Gregory XIII, which in fact occurred on 14 September 1578, the year inscribed on the stone mouldings of the *palazzina* itself.

The Cardinal's friendship with the Duke of Parma must have been a close one for we know that Duke Ottavio Farnese acted as intermediary in a dispute between Cardinal Gambara and Cardinal Santafiora, and that in May 1573 he visited Bagnaia as a result of a letter he received from Vicino Orsini of Bomarzo.[6] Mythological stories appear on the ceiling of the villa, and carved in the metope of the Doric trabeation under the eaves are a series of heraldic devices, including references to Cardinal Gambara's own name, such as crayfish (*gambero* in Italian) and scorpions, and between two-headed eagles, flaming torches with the words '*Sol Aliis*' and falling stars are inscribed strange superimposed letters surmounted by a crown, which appears to be a tribute to Ottavio Farnese. All this reminds us that the Palazzina Gambara, with its living space on the upper floor, a blind loggia supported by a sort of rhythmic

framework of beams, and a little turret crowning the roof, has more in common with the garden palace of the Duke of Parma, designed by Vignola in 1561,[7] than with the *casino* in the *barco* at Caprarola. And in fact, in spite of a few minor inconsistencies in terms of chronology and style, which may well be attributed to a certain carelessness on the part of the architects then working for Gambara, such as Giovanni Malanca and Ghinucci, it seems to bear the stamp of Vignola, perhaps as a result of a visit to Bagnaia by Duke Ottavio in May 1573.

It is therefore difficult to reject the traditional attribution of the Villa Lante to Vignola, which has recently been confirmed by Coffin and by Fagiolo,[8] and there is little doubt that he was also responsible for the alterations made to Ghinucci's work in the town of Bagnaia, it being perfectly apparent that the three roads from the piazza (or, rather, from the villa) that converge on the tower of the bishop's palace form an essential part of the integrated scheme of the rectangular garden of the villa: Via Palla Corda leads to the entrance of the *barco*, constituting almost a watershed between 'wild nature' in the park and 'artificial nature' in the formal garden; the middle road lies on an exact axis with the central gateway to the garden; Via dei Condotti runs along the

east side of the garden to meet the road from Caprarola.

The clarity and almost rigidly architectural nature of the scheme, based on a series of squares, with terraces positioned in a precisely calculated arrangement, united by slopes, staircases, fountains, loggias, balustrades and colonnades, recalls the famous prototype gardens of the Vatican Belvedere. But they are even more strongly reminiscent of the perspective effects created by the drives, terraces and staircases of the two rectangular gardens of the villa at Caprarola, which are depicted, together with the Villa d'Este at Tivoli, in the painted loggia of the Palazzina Gambara. The vaulted roof of this loggia is filled with emblematic and heraldic references to Gambara himself, and to Cardinals Farnese and d'Este, and, as also in the villas of these two, Hercules is represented performing four of his great labours, including of course his fight with the dragon guarding the entrance to the garden of the Hesperides. The artists responsible for these paintings were probably Raffaellino da Reggio and Giovanni de' Vecchi, who worked for Cardinal Gambara at Sta Maria della Quercia in 1576; and Antonio Tempesta frescoed the hunting scenes, an allusion to the *barco*, in two of the rooms near the loggia. Clearly, Cardinal Gambara availed himself of the artists employed at that time at Caprarola.

In view of Gambara's strong links with Alessandro and Ottavio Farnese, it is possible that he took advantage not only of their architect and painters but also of certain scholars and men of letters employed by them, in order to help him in planning the iconography of the villa and its garden. One such scholar was Fulvio Orsini, librarian to Cardinal Alessandro Farnese, who – encouraged by Angelo Colocci, the owner of a famous antiquarian garden in Rome – had become an important authority on Greek and Latin, numismatics and archaeology, and had also made an extensive study of epigraphy. He was frequently in contact with Gambara, and was much respected by a close relation of the Cardinal, the erudite Brescian poet Lorenzo Gambara, who contributed one of his poems to Orsini's *Imagines et elogia virorum illustrium*, published in Rome by Antonio Lafreri in 1570.

The second *palazzina* at Bagnaia was

begun in Gambara's time, as we know from Ardizio's description of Pope Gregory XIII's visit in 1578,[9] and it was completed with the collaboration of Carlo Maderno in about 1590 for Gambara's successor, Cardinal Montalto, the nephew of Sixtus V. Maderno also rebuilt many of the fountains in the park and altered the central fountain in the rectangular garden (Fountain of the Moors), adding four naked figures holding aloft the mounts and star of the Montalto coat of arms; this new composition replaced what Montaigne had described as 'a high pyramid throwing water in every direction, rising and falling, with four beautiful pools around it full of clear, limpid water. In the centre of each one is a small stone boat containing a trumpeter and two musketeers who discharge jets of water in the direction of the pyramid'. Maderno left unchanged the four stone boats in the pools around the central fountain, and they are still there today, but it is a little hard to relate Montaigne's description of 'a high pyramid' to the circular construction represented in the fresco of the garden in the loggia of the Palazzina Gambara.

The Palazzina Montalto was frescoed in the second decade of the seventeenth century by Agostino Tassi and Cavalier d'Arpino.

In 1653, under Ottavio Acquaviva, a second great aqueduct was built to provide water for the fountains and for the irrigation of the park. In 1656 the villa passed to the Lante family. It was Cardinal Federico Lante who made the side entrances to the two *palazzine* in 1745; the parterre of the rectangular fountain garden was redesigned in the French style between the end of the seventeenth century and the beginning of the eighteenth, when the two de la Trémouille sisters, who married a Lante and an Orsini respectively, often stayed there.

Despite the changes that took place over the years, above all Montalto's transformation of the fountains, it is clear from the inventory taken in 1588 after Gambara's death, together with Ardizio's description of the visit of Pope Gregory XIII in 1578, Montaigne's writings, the frescoes in the loggia of the Palazzina Gambara, the engravings of the Viterbo artist Ligustri, printed in 1596, and the sketches by Giovanni Guerra dating from 1600, that the original iconographic

*Villa Lante, Bagnaia. Fresco in the loggia
of the Palazzina Gambara. (Photo Ente
Provinciale Turismo, Viterbo)*

where Deucalion and Pyrrha were saved from drowning, and thus secured the future of humanity. The peaks are represented here by two pavilions ornamented with the crayfish of the Gambara coat of arms and the grille of San Lorenzo, the saint to whom the cathedral at Viterbo is dedicated (a room in the *palazzina* celebrates the life and work of this saint). Nearby is the Fountain of the Dolphins, which was once enclosed by an octagonal temple in imitation coral, possibly to symbolize the sea, the Kingdom of Neptune, or more simply to serve as a reminder of the dolphins that darted between the branches of the oak trees at the time of the Flood (*Metamorphoses* I, 302–3).

At the end of a long flight of steps the water reappears as if by magic, running down a central channel between yew hedges and enclosed on either side by scrollwork modelled on the articulated claw of a crayfish (the Water Chain). The foot of the slope is guarded by an enormous crayfish which was once surmounted by a siren playing a Roman bugle, perhaps as a reminder that sensual pleasure is illusory, or more likely to suggest that worldly music offers only sensual enchantment in comparison to the perfection of the heavenly music played by the Muses. Through the mouth and claws of the crayfish, water pours into the Fountain of the Giants, where the 'sea water' of the Dolphin Fountain is transformed into the 'fresh water' of the Arno and the Tiber, a reference to the two spirits of the ancient region of Etruria.

On the same terrace the water rises from the serene semicircular basin at the foot of the Fountain of the Giants to run the length of a narrow stone channel cut along the centre of a long stone table, whose surface it may once have covered like a sheet of crystal. In the Fountain of the Lights below it is transformed into fire by masses of little jets which glow 'like silver candles in a chandelier', as Ardizio described them. This delightful fountain recalls the double concave-convex staircase of Bramante's exedra in the Belvedere gardens.

The water finally comes to rest in the four pools forming a rectangle around the Fountain of the Moors, which was redisigned by Maderno for Cardinal Montalto. In this large symmetrical space, which occupies the lowest terrace, Nature is

scheme for the park and garden conceived by Cardinal Gambara has survived to this day.[10]

The Pegasus Fountain, with busts of the Muses supported on corbels projecting from its oval wall, which lies at the entrance to the park, suggests that the entire hillside was intended to represent Mount Parnassus, the home of the Muses. The great evergreen holm-oaks, which

according to Ovid ran with honey in the Golden Age (*Metamorphoses* I, 112), the acorns they produce, the Acorn Fountain sacred to Jupiter, and the Fountain of Bacchus, which alludes to the flowing stream of wine recorded by Virgil (*Georgics* I, 132), all seem to give a metaphorical meaning to the park, linking it to the *aetas felicior*, in contrast to the Age of Jupiter, which is symbolized by the archetypal

Italian-style garden in which Man triumphs over Nature.

With this interpretation in mind, a visit to the garden should begin at the Fountain of the Deluge, which lies at the apex of the perspective view from the two *palazzine* and signifies the dramatic conclusion of the Golden Age. On either side of the fountain are the two Houses of the Muses, the twin peaks of Parnassus,

Villa Lante, Bagnaia: Water Chain.
(Photo Daniele De Lonte)

finally subdued by Art, but so peacefully and decisively that it is not easy to suggest convincingly that it symbolizes the Age of Jupiter, or at least a more dramatic era than the Golden Age personified by the park: an age in which, to quote Virgil, '*Labor omnia vicit improbus et duris urgens in rebus egestas*' (Work conquered all, relentless work and harsh necesssity) (*Georgics* I, 145–6). It is reminiscent of such visions of Eden as the *Fountain of the Evangelists*, depicting the last vision of an earthly paradise, which can be seen in the main cloister of the Escorial Palace near Madrid. Perhaps the four boats can be said to relate to this interpretation, and to the *naumachia* – the ancient representations of naval battles – of which Montaigne wrote, because they may well have alluded to the recent great Christian victory at Lepanto, which is also depicted in the entrance hall of the Palazzina Gambara in homage to Pope Pius V.

Any lack of a continuous narrative thread in the route we have taken can perhaps be justified, if not on literary grounds, at least by the arched entrance to the great rectangular garden of the Fountain of the Moors. Its principal Doric façade faces the two *palazzine*, suggesting that it is an exit from the garden, but it can also be regarded as an entrance to the town, rather in the spirit of the crayfish, which moves forward across the ground and backs into the water.

When Carlo Borromeo visited the villa he was clearly irritated by what he saw, showing all the usual intolerance of the zealous Counter-Reformationist towards the principles of Humanism. To make matters worse, Gambara proceeded to explain the garden's iconography by means of quotations from Ovid and Virgil, and then allowed his visitor to be soaked by unexpected jets of water from the House of the Muses and the Fountain of the Dolphins which, according to Tolomei, caused everyone to 'laugh and create confusion, to the delight of all'.[11] Instead, he should have talked to him of Holy Jerusalem, saying that the water was the water of baptism, that his evergreen oaks were the sons of the tree from which Christ's cross was cut, and that their acorns, like those of the Fountain of the Acorns, were not physical but spiritual food because they were a reminder of the nearby sanctuary of Sta Maria della Quercia, where he wished most devoutly

to be buried. As it was, his severe friend and colleague reproved him, along with Cardinal Farnese, for the enormous expense he had incurred in order to give shelter to birds and animals instead of 'those poor Hungarian, Bohemian and Flemish Catholics, wickedly driven out of their houses by the enemies of the Holy Church'.[12]

1 V. Fritelli, *Bagnaia, Cronache di una terra del patrimonio* (Viterbo 1977), p. 59.
2 *Ibid.*, pp. 63 and 68.
3 D.R. Coffin, 'Some aspects of the Villa Lante at Bagnaia' in *Scritti di storia dell'arte in onore di E. Arslan*, Vol. 1 (1966), p. 570.

4 A few areas were expropriated in 1574 to allow for the creation of a new garden outside the park; see F. Fagliari Zeni Buchicchio, 'G. A. Garzoni da Viggiù, the architect of the Farnese property at Caprarola after Vignola', in *Biblioteca e Società* (Viterbo 1985–6), note 53, p. 14.
5 See the research of Dr V. Lena, c/o the Friends of Bagnaia Association, Bagnaia.
6 H. Bredekamp, *Vicino Orsini und der Heilige Wald von Bomarzo* (Worms 1985).
7 B. Adorni, *L'Architettura farnesiana a Parma 1545–1622* (Parma 1974) p. 36; *idem* 'I giardini farnesiani di Parma e di Piacenza' in *Gli Horti Farnesiani sul Palatino* (Rome 1988).
8 Coffin, *op. cit.*; M. Fagioli, 'Le due anime nelle ville della Tuscia' in *Il giardino d'Europa: Pratolino come modello nella cultura europea* (Florence 1986), p. 77.

9 A.F. Orbaan, 'Viaggio di Gregorio XIII alla Madonna della Quercia' in *Documenti del Barocco in Roma* (Rome 1920), p. 388.
10 The most comprehensive interpretation of the garden at Bagnaia appears in C. Lazzaro-Bruno's 'The Villa Lante at Bagnaia: An Allegory of Art and Nature' in *The Art Bulletin* (1977) 4, 59, pp. 553–60, based largely on Coffin, *The Villa in the Life of Renaissance Rome* (Princeton 1979); interpretative notes by M. Fagiolo, *op. cit.*
11 Letter describing the fountain quoted in E. Battisti, *L'antirinascimento* (Milan 1962), pp. 162–4.
12 Letter of 30 January 1580 to Gambara in G. Signorelli, 'La Villa di Bagnaia' in *Bolletino Municipale di Viterbo* (March 1929).

The Gardens of Buontalenti
Luigi Zangheri

Villa di Pratolino, Florence: plan of the hydraulic system. Reconstruction by the author.

Villa di Pratolino, Florence: Giambologna's Appennine. *(Photo Daniele De Lonte)*

Bernardo Buontalenti interpreted more faithfully than any of his contemporaries the aims and principles of the Florentine culture of the second half of the sixteenth century, and was so highly regarded in his own time as to be described in 1586 as 'a most excellent architect; in his work as engineer and mathematician among other things he ranks with the practitioners of the ancient world'.[1]

Nearly twenty years earlier, on 1 March 1568, he was appointed 'Engineer of Rivers' for the Magistrature of the Guelph Party,[2] and from that time on his reputation stood so high that he was offered official appointments by the Grand Duchy of Tuscany over the head of artists of the calibre of Vasari and Ammannati. He was engaged to build the villas of Pratolino, Artimino and Poggiofrancoli, and to enlarge or renovate a number of existing country residences such as Castello, La Petraia, Lappeggi, La Magia and Cerreto Guidi, where he was also involved in improvements to the gardens, either in a general sense – in redesigning the layout and instituting new planting schemes – or in making

technical alterations such as laying on new water supplies.

His interest in the art of garden design was greatly stimulated by the creation of the magnificent Boboli Gardens in Florence. Eleanor of Toledo, the consort of Cosimo I de'Medici, had acquired the Pitti Palace and its adjoining gardens on 3 February 1550 (1549 according to the Florentine calendar of the time), and entrusted the task of redesigning the gardens to Niccolò Tribolo. Work began on 12 May 1550,[3] and in spite of Tribolo's premature death in September of the same year, it proceeded as he had planned, 'the hill being divided up . . . and everything given its rightful place'.[4] Other artists, such as Vasari and Bandinelli, also contributed to the Boboli Gardens, responsibility for the work passing to Bartolomeo Ammannati in June 1560. We also know that Buontalenti, then in the service of the ducal court, took sufficient part in the transformation of the gardens to write to Gherardo Silvani: 'I devote a great deal of my time to the redesigning of the Boboli Gardens'.[5]

Buontalenti created the Grotta Grande, which can still be seen there, between 1583 and 1593, adapting and covering over a fishpond designed by Vasari; he also redesigned the small grotto adjoining it and added a third one. His principal aim here was to create a suitable setting for four sculptures of 'prisoners' by Michelangelo, which had been given to Francesco I by Leonardo Buonarroti. 'These roughly-hewn figures in the act of lifting up great boulders of travertine were placed in the four corners of the grotto, the texture of the porous rock of the walls around them blending so well with the coarseness of the figures themselves that it seemed as if the whole creation was the work of nature and not of man'.[6]

Buontalenti's grotto, particularly the first and third chamber – the second still has Vasari's wall decorations – appears to have been inspired by Anguillara's translation (1566) of Ovid's *Metamorphoses*, and especially by the story of Deucalion and Pyrrha.[7] The walls were decorated with landscapes and pastoral scenes in stucco and travertine by Pietro Mati,

based on frescoes by Bernardino Poccetti. Water was fed through a network of pipes to provide moisture for the maidenhair ferns that grew in the crevices between the figures and the rocks. Buontalenti also conceived the idea of lighting the grotto in a highly original way, by means of a crystal fish bowl fixed into the circular opening of the vaulted roof: the movements of the fish filtered the light unevenly, creating a shimmering, flickering effect which was further enhanced by the luminescent reflections of pieces of crystal set into the travertine boulders held up by the figures and kept constantly wet by jets of water. It was a complex, ever-changing kaleidoscope of light, which showed off superbly the expressive and disturbing power of the Michelangelo figures.

Buontalenti's major undertaking as a garden architect, however, was the work he carried out at Pratolino. It occupied him from 1568 to 1586, and embraced every detail of an elaborate scheme for the garden park of Francesco I de'Medici's new country house north-east of Florence. Pratolino was divided into two

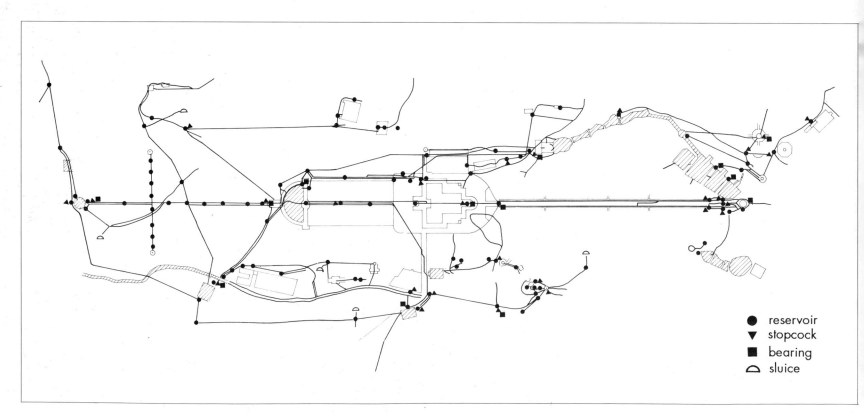

● reservoir
▼ stopcock
■ bearing
◠ sluice

MONTE PARNASO DI PRATOLINO

THEATRO COMMODO A LI SPETTATORI COSI PER VISTA COME PER VDIRE L'ARMONIA

The villa and its park were admired by scholars such as Algarotti and de Vieri; they were illustrated by artists like Schickhardt, Salomon de Caus and Stefano della Bella; and they were described with rapturous enthusiasm by illustrious visitors such as Montaigne and Evelyn. Throughout early seventeenth-century Europe the inventions to be seen in this 'garden of marvels' were wondered at and copied, and they continued to be remembered long after the park was completely transformed in 1819, according to the fashion of the day, into a *giardino inglese*. It was Pratolino above all that caused Buontalenti to be regarded as 'the precursor of surrealism in the art of the garden'.[9]

1 B. de'Rossi, *Descrizione del Magnificentiss. Apparato e de'maravigliosi Intermedij fatti per la Commedia Rappresentata in Firenze nelle felicissime Nozze degl'Illustrissimi ed Eccellentissimi Signori il Signor Don Cesare d'Este e la Signora Donna Virginia Medici* (Florence 1586), p. iv.

2 State Archives of Florence, *Capitani di Parte*, t. 721, cc. 197, 199.

3 A. Lapini, *Diario fiorentino* (Florence 1900), p. 20.

4 G. Vasari, *Le vite de'più eccellenti pittori scultori e architettori* (Florence 1964), Vol. 5, p. 482.

5 F. Baldinucci (ed. by P. Barocchi) *Notizie dei professori del disegno* (Florence 1975), Vol. 7, p. 13. For a recent bibliography on the Boboli Gardens, see F. Gurrieri and J. Chatfield, *Boboli Gardens* (Florence 1972); M. Forlani Conti, 'Il giardino di Boboli' in *Il giardino storico italiano. Problemi di indagine, fonti letterarie e storiche* (Florence 1981), pp. 165–72; P. Marchi, 'Il giardino di Boboli e il suo anfiteatro' in *La città effimera e l'universo artificiale del giardino* ed. by M. Fagiolo (Rome 1980), pp. 162–82; F. Gurrieri, *La grotta del Buontalenti nel giardino di Boboli* (Florence 1980); R. Bencini, 'Il giardino di Boboli nel Cinquecento' in *Il Potere e lo spazio*, exhibition catalogue (Florence 1980), pp. 47–8.

6 F. Baldinucci, *op. cit.*, Vol. 2, p. 499.

7 See D. Heikamp, 'La grotta grande del Giardino di Boboli' in *Antichità Viva*, Vol. 4, no. 4 (1965), p. 30.

8 For a bibliography of works on Pratolino, see note 5 of author's essay 'Curiosities and Marvels of the Sixteenth-Century Garden', p. 67 of this volume.

9 *The Oxford Companion to Gardens* (Oxford 1986), p. 83.

distinct areas: the north park, known as the Parco degli Antichi, and the south park, the Parco dei Moderni. At the centre stood the great Medici villa. At the highest point of the garden, on the axis with the villa itself, stood a figure of Jupiter by Baldinelli, which overlooked a circular labyrinth and, below that, a colossal statue of Appennine by Giambologna and the Field of the Ancients, which contained twenty-six sculptures of antique heroes. At the lowest point of the park was a sculpture by Valerio Cioli – *La Lavandaia* (washerwoman) – depicting a woman washing clothes at a fountain, from which water fell into a large *bassin*. Along the main axis linking this fountain with the villa was a long avenue lined with water jets, their arching sprays creating a spectacular irridescent pergola. Two alternative routes led back from the Cioli fountain to the villa, the left hand path running past Cupid's Grotto, the

Mask Pool, the Red Cockerels' Fountain and the Frog Pool; the right hand one linking a series of ponds for the breeding of crayfish and running on past the Oak Fountain, the Fountain of Ammannati, a mound known as Mount Parnassus and, lastly, a large aviary.[8]

A plentiful supply of water was brought to the garden by an aqueduct five kilometres long, and Buontalenti used all the most advanced technology available to exploit it in every conceivable way: he filled toy theatres with little automata which moved in response to the movements of the water, and set them in grottoes near the villa, by the statue of Appennine and in Cupid's Grotto. Hydraulic organs were placed on Mount Parnassus, and around the garden were scattered dozens of boxes containing bellows operated by water and fitted with whistles which imitated the calls of a wide variety of different species of birds.

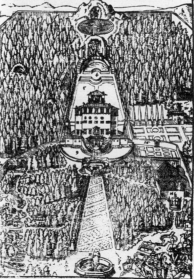

Pratolinum Magni Ducis Hetruriæ.

Illustrations of Gardens in the Sixteenth Century: 'The Most Excellent Buildings in France'

Françoise Boudon

Designs for the château of Chenonceaux (Indre-et-Loire), by J. A. du Cerceau. British Museum, London. Proposal for enlargement, (1576); the garden on the right bank 'as it is today' (1565); proposal for 'enlargement of the two gardens' (1565).

In the 1560s, the master of a large copper engraving workshop, Jacques Androuet du Cerceau,[1] embarked in his studio on a collection of engravings of the finest châteaux in the kingdom of France. A draughtsman of repute, expert in relief decoration, an architect who was also knowledgeable about the reproduction of illustrations, du Cerceau had no difficulty in carrying out his project: the publication in Paris in 1576 of the *Premier volume des plus excellents bastiments de France* (First volume of the most excellent buildings in France), and in 1579 of the second volume, was the publishing event of the latter part of the century.[2] In order to illustrate these unique buildings, du Cerceau uses an unusual technique of view-taking, unknown in the history of architectural presentation, the equivalent of a film-maker's zoom lens. In 120 large engravings (35 × 47.5 cm; 14 × 19 ins) in a carefully arranged progression from the whole to the particular, he skilfully involves the reader in a fairy tale tour of thirty 'exquisite buildings of this kingdom'; this genius with wings takes his spectator on a flight over the roofs of Coucy, Amboise or Bury: as an architect he familiarizes him with the blueprints for Anet and Fontainebleau; as a courtier familiar with the daily round of the court he accompanies him through the halls of the Château de Madrid and the Louvre, and takes him to wander through the arbours of the gardens of Montargis.

Certainly, Montargis was dear to him: he probably drew these wooden galleries during the time he lived in the town as a refugee when it was a Protestant area. As much for his own sake as for his patron Renée de France, he had a deep interest in publicizing the beauty of these gardens. But this was not his only concern. Du Cerceau depicted each château with its garden, using the same technique of magnification from the whole to the detail for the grounds as for the buildings. This approach was no accident; he had his reasons. The first was cultural. Familiar with the sophisticated society of his great clients, du Cerceau knew the importance to them of the garden, for many years as essential a part of the noble residence as the great hall or tennis court. The second reason was personal: du Cerceau loved the countryside; the way in which he speaks of it in the introductory notes to each volume is the best proof of this. His

annotations on the peculiarities of the relief, the nature of the vegetation, the quality of the air are those of an enthusiast. The gardens could not therefore be omitted from the descriptions of the châteaux. Hence *The most excellent buildings* offers a collection of exceptional pictures of some of the most beautiful French gardens of the sixteenth century.[3] The printed collection is not without fault, however. The documentation is neither complete nor uniform from one collection to the next. Compared with the excellent accounts of Montargis, Gaillon or Valléry, many are slight. The famous Tuileries garden merits only one plan and a terse account. These gaps are partly offset by a series of 140 related drawings preserved principally in London,[4] a series parallel to the prints, but constituting only a first draft. Indeed, shortly before or while working on the plates of his 'most excellent buildings' du Cerceau was doing beautiful drawings on the same theme, traced in ink on vellum, grey-washed, with some coloured highlights, including yellow, for the garden. These plates were probably intended to serve as gifts to prospective patrons.[5] For the drawings and the prints the artist used the same documentation, the same sources, the same plans, the same models,[6] all of which explains the similarity between the two groups of documents. However, striking differences separate them. Not only are certain drawings often set within a wider background than the prints, embracing a greater part of the landscape, but in particular several take a viewpoint, give a picture of the garden, lost in the engraving. For Anet, du Cerceau drew two bird's-eye views: one, which was later engraved, looks S-N and shows the château and the garden enclosed by a wall with recesses and projections designed by Philibert de l'Orme; the other, without accompanying engraving, looks SE-NW and is more elevated, prolonging the views as far as the walls of the park and giving useful detail of the watercourses of the river Vesgre which flows along its circumference. The dossier of drawings of Chenonceaux contains, in addition to the grand extension project of 1576 shown in the engraving, two important views of about 1565: a plan of the garden 'as it is today' with the two flowerbeds recently marked out on the left bank of the Cher, and an accompanying plan of a

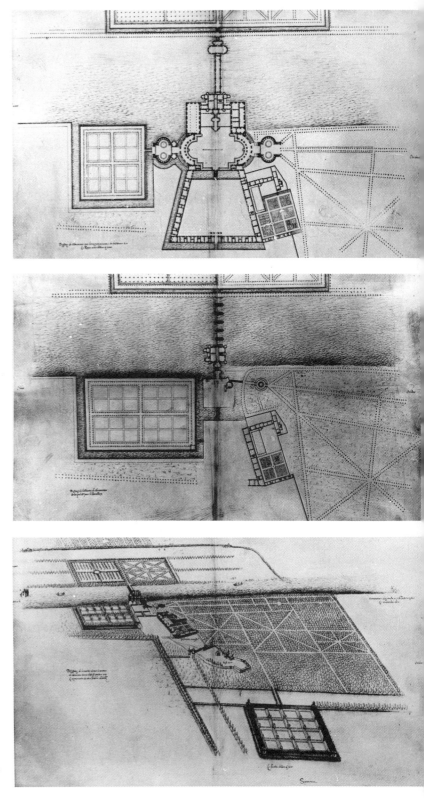

Plans for the château of Verneuil (Oise):
Bird's-eye view, drawn by J. A. du Cerceau.
British Museum, London.
Ground-plan drawn by J. A. du Cerceau.
British Museum, London.

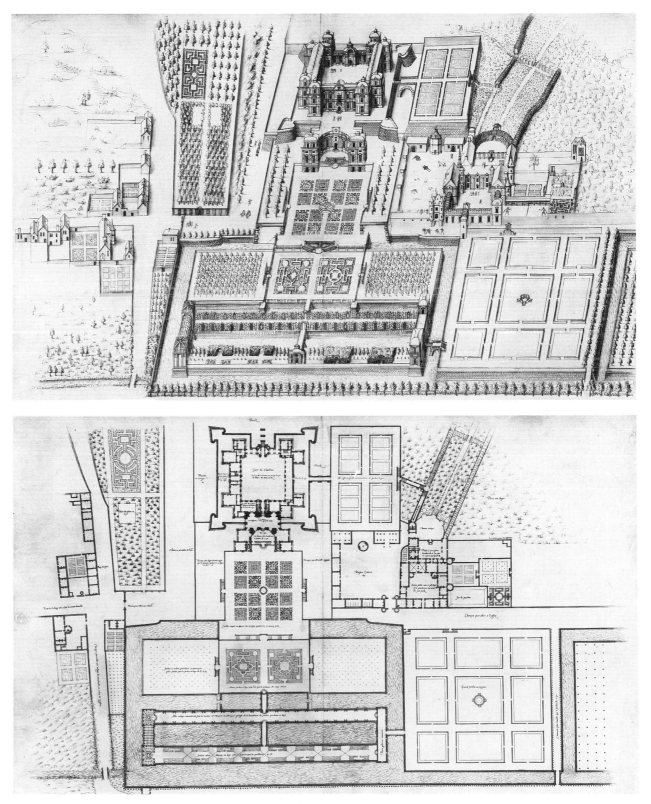

bird's-eye view giving 'the addition of the two gardens which it has been thought good to make' on the right bank. A marvellous progressive sequence of sketches drawn specifically to illustrate Queen Catherine's plan to make of Chenonceaux 'a little house to carry on gardening and other delights'.[7] The drawings also have the advantage over the engravings of being carefully captioned: instead of mysterious alphabetic letters which uselessly clutter the engraving, du Cerceau has, in very legible script, punctuated the drawing with words, even phrases, which give precise information. Thus we learn that at the northern extremity of the park at Valléry the trees were 'planted in line', that the square at the foot of the ancient castle of Verneuil – indicated on the engraving by a terse 'O' – is a 'large kitchen garden'. All these details are valuable: they tend to lead one to believe that consulting the collections of engravings would be useless unless supported by the page of commentary which precedes each of them, and assumes the role of documentary source material. As we have seen, these texts are not only useful for placing the garden in its setting, for showing details of the relief (very sketchily shown in a few rare drawings and indecipherable in the engravings) but also for their historical accuracy.[8] What do we know of the gardens at Charleval, planted even before the immense royal château was begun, apart from what du Cerceau tells us? We have considerable evidence that these commentaries are carefully written from meticulous notes: what he says about the northern garden at Ecouen, unfinished when he was there, confirms what we know from elsewhere: in about 1560, the date of the artist's visit to Ecouen, the fortification of the castle was a much more important concern than the planning of a garden on a perilous site outside the walls and on poor sloping ground.

It remains only to consider the illustrations. It seems unreasonable to attempt to criticize in detail: it is unlikely that we will ever establish the extent of planning involved in the layout of the beds, which seems as advanced in the drawings as in the engravings (for this workshop production, subject to economic constraints, recourse to stereotypes was necessary). On the other hand, it is not difficult to establish the accuracy of the illustrations, once the distortions of the drawings as a whole have been corrected. It is obvious that du Cerceau worked in an ordered and geometric manner in defiance of topography: the pool at Dampierre, constrained to a winding course between two hills, becomes in du Cerceau's drawing a perfectly rectangular stretch of water. The artist conceals reality and its unfortunate irregularities: in the name of the rules of symmetry, the site at Verneuil, in truth so tortuous, is straightened and aligned, the lower gardens are misleadingly placed on an axis with the new castle, and the access to the château of St Maur is irritatingly moved to one side. But – apart from a few obvious cases like the park at St Germain – the picture on the whole seems good and accurate. His evidence is essential since it gives actual shape to the garden area so suggestively evoked by other documentary sources.[9] When a full study – essential but yet to be done – is undertaken of the illustrations of gardens of the *Plus excellents bastiments de France* there is no doubt that du Cerceau will emerge with an enhanced reputation.

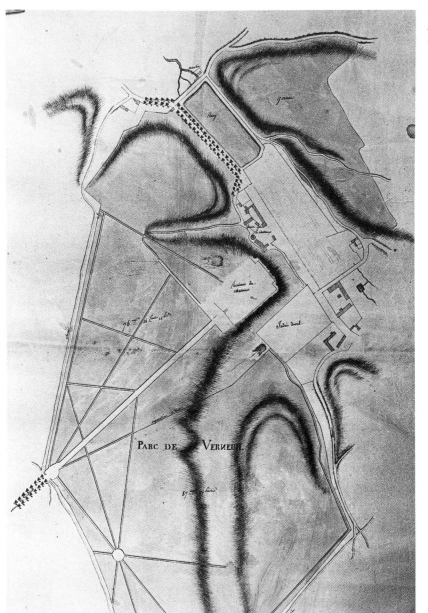

The site of Verneuil, as seen in a map of the mid-eighteenth century. Musée Condé, Chantilly.

PARC DE VERNEUIL

[1] On Jacques Androuet du Cerceau (1520?–1585 or 86), consult H. de Geymuller, *Les du Cerceau* (Paris 1887) and the unpublished thesis of D. Thomson, 1978 Courtauld Institute, London.

[2] *Les plus excellents bastiments de France* has been re-edited by H. Destailleur (Paris 1870). Gregg International published a facsimile in 1970. A new edition under the direction of D. Thomson is in preparation with Editions Sand: Paris. The drawings have been published in part by W-H. Ward, *French Châteaux and Gardens in the XVIth century* (London 1909). For a critical edition of the collection see F. Boudon and H. Couzy 'Les Plus Excellents Bastiments de France: une anthologie de châteaux à la fin du XVIe siècle' in *L'Information d'Histoire de l'Art* (1974).

[3] Confining himself to the 'most excellent buildings' du Cerceau has not included in this selection the country houses of the king's secretaries, often endowed with splendid gardens such as those of Picard at St Cloud; of Neufville or Spifame at Conflans. Sylvie le Clech brings much new information to the subject in her thesis for the Ecole de Chartres: *Chancellerie et culture au XVIe siècle: les notaires et secrétaires de François Ier* (1988, not published).

[4] British Museum, London. Drawings can also be seen in Paris (Bibliothèque Nationale), Rome (Vatican Library), and New York (Pierpont Morgan Library).

[5] The volume of drawings preserved in the Vatican Library was probably presented by du Cerceau to cardinal Francesco Barberini in about 1570.

[6] Du Cerceau makes particular mention of the importance in his documentation of the models of buildings and gardens. In the notes on St Maur he states 'I saw the model made of it . . . in which are contained not only the buildings but also the gardens . . .'. J. Androuet du Cerceau *op. cit.* vol. 2, 1579. On the role of models in du Cerceau's drawings see W. Prinz and R.G. Kecks, *Das französische Schloss der Renaissance* (Berlin 1985) pp. 360–3.

[7] Letter from Chantonay to the Duchess of Parma, 23 March 1560 in *Revue Historique*, 1880, p. 334, quoted in F. Gebelin, *Les Châteaux de la Renaissance* (Paris 1927) p. 85.

[8] Certain dossiers are incomplete on both counts because the château never had a garden, as is the case for instance with hunting boxes in the heart of the forest, such as St-Léger or Madrid. Of Chambord, du Cerceau notes, 'As for the garden, it is nothing and in no way equals the magnificence of the building: nevertheless if anyone wished to add to it, there is room to extend it'. (J. A. du Cerceau, *op. cit.*, Vol. 1, 1576).

[9] Recent research into archives has considerably increased our knowledge of sixteenth-century gardens. See in particular C. Grodecki, *Documents du minutier central des notaires de Paris. Histoire de l'art du XVIe siècle 1540–1600* (Paris 1985) pp. 329–44.

Johan Vredeman de Vries and the *Hortorum Formae*

Ulbe Martin Mehrtens

One constant element in the wayward career of Johan [Hans] Vredeman de Vries (1526–1606?) was the publication of pattern books. From 1555 until 1605 there appear with great regularity, sometimes several times a year, books containing designs for grotesques, cartouches, tombstones, furniture, mantlepieces, architectural façades, vases, caryatids, fountains, trophies, pageant decorations, so that a total of approximately five hundred engravings by him have been preserved.[1] Only twenty-eight of these designs are devoted to gardens.

With the exception of eight designs for gardens which appeared in Antwerp in 1587,[2] this stream of publications was interrupted from 1584 until the beginning of the seventeenth century. The probable reason for this was Vredeman de Vries's departure from Antwerp, where he had been employed from 1571 until 1584 as an engineer on the fortifications. Via Frankfurt he travelled to Wolfenbüttel, where he served as an architect and engineer at the court of Duke Julius until the latter's death in 1589. In Wolfenbüttel he completed several projects; in 1588 he built the new Chancellery, the only surviving building by him, although restored several times over the centuries.[3] He also supervised the execution of a garden design for Duke Julius in 1588, the only design known as yet which was probably carried out to Vredeman de Vries's specifications. Duke Julius made the following note: 'In the new Pleasure-Garden grass banks will be constructed along the cloisters with all kinds of ingenious episodes illustrating reason and virtues, vices, etc. cast in lead'.[4] After the death of the duke, Vredeman de Vries settled for a short time in Hamburg, where he made paintings for Jacob Moor's burial chapel, and in Danzig. Next, after a second stay in Hamburg, he travelled to Prague to join his son, the artist Paul Vredeman de Vries (1567–1630?) who was employed there at the court of Emperor Rudolf II. In Prague he was paid for a plan to extend the castle and for a design for a fountain.[5] In 1601 he settled permanently in the Dutch Republic.

There are grounds for believing that Vredeman de Vries's Antwerp period was of great importance in the production of his graphic work. The overwhelming majority of his pattern books

appeared in Antwerp.[6] Foreign pattern books, from which, as Hans Mielke has shown in his dissertation, Vredeman de Vries drew inspiration in producing his architectural designs, probably first came to his attention in the city, which at that period was the most important economic and cultural centre in northern Europe.

As early as 1549 he stayed at Antwerp and worked with Pieter Coecke van Aelst (1502–1550) on the triumphal arch and chariots which the city had ordered from him for the formal visit of Charles V.

Vredeman's designs were a crucial innovative influence at the end of the sixteenth and the beginning of the seventeenth century, especially in the fields of painting and interior decoration. Amid the great diversity of designs published in Vredeman's books there are two characteristic features discernible in them all, including those of gardens. His designs were modern, in the sense that they were a Southern Netherlands interpretation of a rediscovery of classical antiquity by Serlio, and via Serlio in Vitruvius by Pieter Coecke van Aelst. The development of this interpretation in Vredeman de Vries's oeuvre took place on a seed bed presumably rich in the sixteenth-century emblematic moralism of the Southern Netherlands.[8] Moreover, Vredeman de Vries's designs were put into perspective by what was for the period a very advanced method.

According to Carel van Mander, Vre-

deman de Vries studied in depth Pieter Coecke's edition of Vitruvius, *Die Inventie der Colommen* (The Invention of Columns) and his translation of Serlio's fourth book (1537), *Generale Reglen der Architecturen* (General Rules of Architecture), both published in Antwerp in 1539.[9] In comparison to the *Generale Reglen* the *Inventie*, which appeared first and is an elaboration of among other things Cesarino's Italian edition of Vitruvius of 1521,[10] is much shorter, less technical and more speculative. In addition the *Inventie* contains a historical survey of what Coecke van Aelst regarded as the oldest sources of architecture, in which he mentions Amasis as the builder of the first pyramid, the city of Moses and the building mentioned in the travelogues of Peter Martyr d'Anghiera (Egypt, Russia), Marco Polo and Ferdinand Cortez (China). Coecke van Aelst also mentions the first strange maze, built in Egypt. The author was probably basing himself partly on the *Novus orbis*, published in Paris and Basle in 1532.[11]

For Vredeman de Vries it was probably not only the technical part of the *Inventie* and the *Generale Reglen* which was important: his designs, drawings and paintings were also influenced by Coecke van Aelst's historical survey of the roots of architecture in the *Inventie*. For example, in the preface to his *Architectura*, first published in Antwerp in 1577, almost the whole text of folio 5 and the section on the origin of architecture is included.[12]

Perhaps the pyramids, obelisks and exotic-looking structures in the background to innumerable designs should be seen as a reference to the origin of architecture.

Vredeman de Vries developed his own method for the presentation of his designs, which enabled him to achieve a realism in perspective unusual for his time. In 1604, at the end of his career, the seventy-seven year old de Vries gave a simple exposition of this method, which lay at the root of his success, in his *Perspective*, which was followed a year later by a second volume.[13] The influence of the *Perspective* can be gauged from the many reprints which appeared after 1605.[14] In 1615 the work was included in its entirety in Samuel Marelois's authoritative study on perspective.[15]

Although Vredeman de Vries used perspective in his designs with what was by North European standards great virtuosity, his method was not entirely correct when judged by modern criteria. As Mielke describes, de Vries drew both vanishing points on the horizon without being aware of their function as distance indicators. As a result the perspective of the foreground and especially of the edges of the picture was distorted and there was excessive lengthening when he underestimated the distance between the eye of the observer and the object.[16] Not until the publication of J. H. Lambert's *Die freye Perspektive oder Anweisung jeden Perpsektivischen Aufriss von freyen Stücken und ohne Grundriss zu verfertigen* (Free Perspective, or Method of making any Freehand perspective Sketch without a preliminary Plan), Zürich 1759, was it possible to create the illusion of perspective on a flat surface perfectly enough to meet our standards.[17] In de Vries's time the linear effect of a line construction put into perspective was greatly appreciated, with perspective functioning as a stylistic device and distortion being taken for granted.[18]

1583 saw the appearance of Vredeman de Vries's first book in which the designs were entirely devoted to views of gardens. To these twenty models which made up the *Hortorum viridariorumque elegantes et multiplicis formae, ad architectonicae artis normam affabrè delineatae* there were added a further fourteen in a new edition of *c.* 1600, like its predecessor published in Antwerp. Research has shown that the last six of these fourteen gardenscapes

Gardens from J. Vredeman de Vries,
Hortorum viridariorumque elegantes et
multiplicis formae, *1583.*

were executed from designs by Peter van der Borcht, so that they fall outside the scope of the present study.[19] The other eight designs in the *Hortorum*, by the hand of de Vries, had meanwhile appeared without a title in Antwerp in 1587,[20] but may have already been completed in 1585 when he moved to Wolfenbüttel.

Although unusual, a presentation of designs of gardens was not new in its time. In England Thomas Hill's *The Profitable Arte of Gardening* and *The Gardener's Labyrinth* had appeared in 1568 and 1577 respectively; the latter work contains several garden plans, including mazes. Similar plans are also found in Estienne's *Agriculture et la maison rustique* of 1570. It is not inconceivable that Vredeman de Vries, who as was said above lived in Antwerp from 1571 to 1585 came across these works. Partly because of the virtuoso use of perspective and also because of the subject, the appearance of the *Hortorum* in 1583, 1587 and around 1600 must have made a considerable impact. In addition the designs contain a novelty in garden design, the so-called *parterres de pièces coupées*, a number of sections of a bed grouped into a pattern for the display of exotic plants.[21]

The components of the compositions in the *Hortorum*, such as covered walks, fountains, railings, beds and mazes, are not themselves new. What is modern is the composition of the parterres and the layout of the gardens, which are the result of Vredeman de Vries's interpretation of classical architecture via Serlio and Vitruvius. The first twenty designs in the *Hortorum* are divided into Doric, Ionic and Corinthian orders, added as captions below the drawings. The beds in the Doric models are geometric, those of the Ionic circular in construction. The Corinthian models have beds in the form of labyrinths, but a number of them are indistinguishable in construction from the Ionic models, making the difference between the captions Ionic and Corinthian obscure.

More 'classical' than the captions is the composition of the gardens and the spatial unity of the gardens and their surroundings. The composition of most of the gardens, which are made up of rectangular beds, is hierarchic. The eye of the observer is drawn either forwards to the nearest area, whose centre is accentuated by a fountain, pavilion or tree, or towards the centre of the framework containing the different areas. In some designs this hierarchical structure is less emphatic and the accents are spread rhythmically through the geometrical complex of areas. In yet other models no formal connection can be discerned; these compositions, however, are given unity by their surroundings. In most cases the gardens are bordered at right angles on two or three sides by architecture which though indicated fairly schematically, should probably be imagined as that of a castle or country house. In nineteen designs a gallery or loggia is included in the architectural frame as a link between house and garden. Only sheets two, four and eleven, bearing the captions Dorica, Dorica and Ionica respectively, represent garden views in perspective, without any architectural framework.[22] In most designs the composition of the gardens and their architectural surroundings is given unity by having the axes of geometrical layout end with the gate or door of the main building of the architectural setting.

The concept of spatial unity in a garden design or of the composition of house and garden had never been taken this far in Vredeman de Vries's designs, drawings or paintings. In his dissertation on de Vries, Mielke gives a survey of the designs in various books including garden views.[23] He rightly observes that these views, in contrast to the *Hortorum*, function as a backdrop within a larger whole. In the garden views in de Vries's drawings and paintings the viewer is uncertain about the relation between the composition of the garden and the accompanying architecture and often about the structure of the garden composition itself.

It is probable that Vredeman de Vries, who in compiling his pattern books took his cue in most if not in all cases from existing designs, conceived the compositions in the *Hortorum* partly under the influence of those of the French architect Jacques Androuet du Cerceau (*c.*1520 – *c.*1585). Without wishing to detract from the originality of the *Hortorum*, it must be pointed out that the concept of formal unity between house and garden had already been explored by du Cerceau in his *Les plus excellents bastiments de France*, which appeared in 1576 and 1579, and was presumably available for consultation in Antwerp. Indeed, it has been shown that du Cerceau's designs left their mark on various other model books by Vredeman de Vries.[24]

It is likely that the *Hortorum* had a great influence on European garden design. Particularly de Vries's complex views of flowerbeds, mazes, fountains, arbours and pavilions can be recognized in many designs, from those of Hans Puec (1592) who worked at the court of Rudolf II in Prague,[25] to Jan van der Groen's *Den Nederlandtsen Hovenier* of 1669.[26] According to Roy Strong, a portion of Theobald's Park between London and Ware was probably inspired by Vredeman de Vries's garden models,[27] and the Hortus

Plan for the garden of Gaillon (Eure). From J. A. du Cerceau, Les plus excellents bastiments de France, *1576 and 1579.*

The Buitenhof of Prince Maurits. From H. Hondius, Institutio artis perspectivae, *1622.*

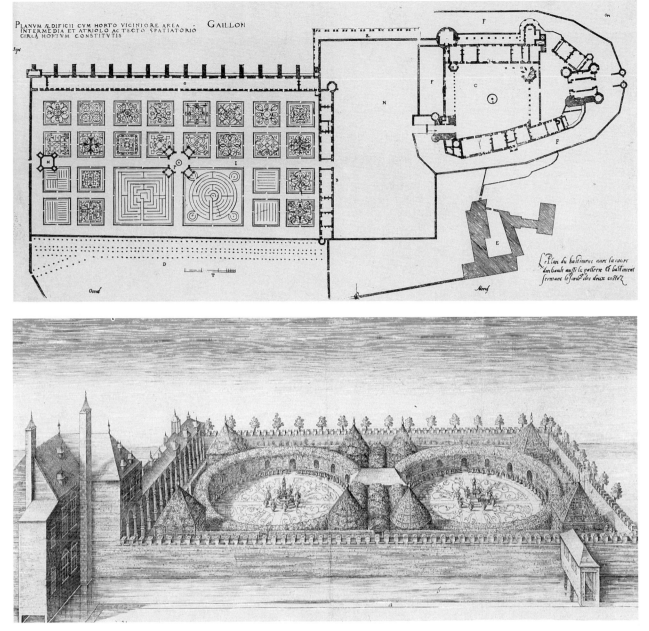

Palatinus in Heidelberg recalls Vredeman de Vries's models both in its layout and in its flowerbeds.

The book also influenced the development of the Dutch classical garden, which it is incorrect to present as breaking with garden design in the style of Vredeman de Vries.[28]

One can see in the *Hortorum* a first attempt to develop a model in which the architecture of the house and the garden become a formal unity. In the plan for the Buitenhof of Prince Maurits in the Stadholder's Quarter in The Hague, which dates from about 1620 and is regarded as the first example of a Dutch classical garden,[29] the unity between the design of the garden and the architecture of the house is achieved in a manner similar to that in the models in the *Hortorum* and the plans of Androuet du Cerceau. An engraving in Hendrick Hondius's *Institutio artis perspectivae* of 1622 shows a bird's-eye view of the garden. Divided roughly in two, it adjoined the house at right angles. It was completely walled, and the brickwork of the wall was integrated with that of the house. There was a gallery or loggia linking house and garden.

In the course of the planning of the garden, probably carried out by Jacques de Gheyn II in conjunction with Prince Maurits,[30] the *Hortorum* may well at least have been consulted, if it was not designed under the direct influence of the plans of Androuet du Cerceau.

1 For the bibliographical history of the pattern books, see Hans Mielke, *Hans Vredeman de Vries . . .* (Berlin 1967).

2 *Ibid.*, p. 59.

3 On this and on Vredeman de Vries's other activities in Wolfenbüttel, see F. Thöne, 'Hans Vredeman de Vries in Wolfenbüttel', in *Braunschweigisches Jahrbuch*, vol. 41 (1960), pp. 47–68.

4 *Ibid.*, p. 53.

5 On Vredeman de Vries's period in Prague, see Hans Mielke, 'Hans Vredeman de Vries', in *Fünf Architekten aus fünf Jahrhunderten*, exhibition catalogue, Staatliche Museen Preussischer Kulturbesitz (1976), p. 7.

6 See note 1.

7 See R. Hotke, 'Hans Vredeman de Vries en zijn invloed op de architectuur in de Nederlanden', in *Bouw*, no. 9 (March 1961), p. 264.

8 On this subject, see for example the influence of Erasmus's *Convivium religiosum*, 1522, which according to Florence Hopper in her essay 'The Erasmian Garden' in *The Oxford Companion to Gardens* (Oxford 1986), pp. 390–1, persists in sixteenth-century architecture and in Vredeman de Vries's work. His interpre-

tation of the Classical orders of columns as symbols of the phases of human life in his *Theatrum vitae humanae Aeneis Tabulis per Ioa Phrys Exaratum* (Antwerp 1577) can also be seen in this context.

9 Carel van Mander, *Het Schilder-Boeck* (Haarlem 1604), fol. 226r. For a bibliographical study, see Rudi Rolf, *Pieter Coecke van Aelst en zijn architectuuruitgaven van 1539* (Amsterdam 1978), which contains facsimile editions of both works.

10 On the influence of Cesarino's *Di Lucio Vitruvio Pollione de Architectura Libri dece traducti . . . opera* (Como 1521), the first Italian translation of Jucundus's illustrated edition of Vitruvius of 1511, see Rudi Rolf, *op. cit.*, pp. 10ff.

11 *Ibid.*, pp. 22–3.

12 *Ibid.*, p. 29.

13 On the use of perspective in de Vries's work, see Uwe M. Schneede, 'Interieurs von Hans und Paul Vredeman', in *Nederlands Kunsthistorisch Jaarboek*, No. 8 (1967) pp. 125ff.

14 Mielke, *op. cit.*, pp. 65–73.

15 The *Perspective* appeared as volumes 5 and 6 in Marelois's *Ars perspectivae quae continet theoram et practicam* (The Hague 1615). Mare-

lois added two models to Vredeman de Vries's *Perspective* (cf. Mielke, *op. cit.* (note 1), p. 68).

16 See Mielke, *op. cit.* (note 5), p. 9.

17 Schneede, *op. cit.*, p. 130.

18 *Ibid.* and Mielke, *op. cit.* (note 5), p. 59 refer to E. Panofsky, 'Die Perspektive als symbolische Form', in *Aufsätze zu Grundfragen der Kunstwissenschaft* (Berlin 1964) pp. 99–168.

19 Mielke, *op. cit.* (note 1), pp. 139–40.

20 *Ibid.*, p. 59. On the bibliographical history of the *Hortorum*, see *ibid.*, pp. 56–7, 59–60, 185–6. It should be mentioned that Mielke did not consult either the Bibliothèque Nationale in Paris or the British Library in London. The possibility cannot be ruled out that if further collections were visited in addition to the libraries on which Mielke's fieldwork was based, the bibliographical history of the *Hortorum* as proposed by him might have to be modified. In this connection it is remarkable that Auguste Schoy, in his *Hans Vredeman de Vries* (Brussels 1876) p. 13, should date the first edition of the *Hortorum* as 1565, calling it '*assez rare*' and regard the 1583 edition as a second edition. Schoy was consulted by Mielke, who, however, omits to mention this detail. Should a first edition of the *Hortorum* of

1565 indeed come to light, then the thesis put forward in this study will need adjustment.

21 See Florence Hopper's article on 'Vredeman de Vries' in *op. cit.* (note 8), pp. 141–2.

22 For this research use was made of the facsimile edition of the *Hortorum* published in 1982 by Van Hoeve, Amsterdam.

23 Mielke, *op. cit.* (note 1), pp. 138–40.

24 *Ibid.*, pp. 141–55.

25 Elisabeth B. MacDougall (ed.), *Fons sapientiae; Garden Fountains in Illustrated Books, Sixteenth-Eighteenth Centuries* (Dumbarton Oaks 1977).

26 See Florence Hopper, *op. cit.* (note 25), p. 42.

27 Roy Strong, *The Renaissance Garden in England* (London 1979) p. 52.

28 Florence Hopper, in 'The Dutch Classical Garden and André Mollet', in *Journal of Garden History*, vol. 2, no. 1 (1982), p. 25, argues that the development of the Dutch classical garden represented a break with Mannerist garden design in the style of Vredeman de Vries, and derived partly from Italian architectural theory, especially that of Alberti.

29 *Ibid.*, pp. 25–6.

30 *Ibid.*, p. 22.

A Model Humanist Garden: Villa Brenzone at Punta San Vigilio

Margherita Azzi Visentini

Concert in a Garden. *Painting by L. Toeput, c. 1590. Museo Civico, Treviso. (Photo Giuseppe Fini)*

Among the most fascinating, best-maintained and least studied of the Renaissance gardens of the Veneto is that of the Villa Brenzone at Punta San Vigilio; it occupies the western portion of a promontory formed by a spur of the foothills of Monte Baldo, which stretches out into the waters of Lake Garda and encloses the bay of Bardolino to the north. Its climate is exceptionally mild. At the centre of the promontory stands the great villa itself, designed by the Mannerist architect Michele Sanmicheli (who took over the project from da Persico), an attribution which is widely accepted today by architectural scholars and confirmed by documentation.

Villa Brenzone is a superb example of a country residence intended as a welcoming retreat from city life, from the pressures of business and from the humid heat of summer. There its owner could enjoy the peace and quiet of rural life and devote himself to cultural pursuits, either alone or in the company of a few select friends, engaging in erudite conversation and convivial pleasures, like the sages of Ancient Rome.[1]

A number of houses, intended to fulfil a similar purpose, had already been built in the Veneto by the early sixteenth century, although many were later destroyed or radically altered. Among them were the villa designed by Pietro Bembo at Sta Maria di Non, near Padua; those by Fracastoro and Verità at Incaffi and San Pietro di Lavagno respectively, in the country near Verona; the villa by Bartolomeo Pagello near Vicenza; and those by Navagero and Ramusio at Murano.

The brilliant philosopher and scholar Agostino Brenzone was a leading member of the circle of humanists at the centre of cultural life in the Veneto at this time. On 13 December 1538 Brenzone bought the property at San Vigilio[2] from Nicolò Barbaro. Next to the chapel (dedicated to the martyr bishop who had converted the people of the Trentino district) was a building that can be seen marked on maps dating from the 1300s. It seems to have stood near the shore of the lake, alongside the landing stage, on the site of an inn which had been granted permission to sell wine, a right that passed to Agostino Brenzone and to his descendants.

The new owner immediately set about the work of building a new villa, and

within a few years it was sufficiently complete for him to invite a number of illustrious guests to come and admire. Sadly, the eulogy dedicated to it by Francesco Zorzi in *Heroic Verses* has been lost, though it was referred to by Brenzone himself in his work *In Praise of Building* sometime before 1553.[3] In about 1542 Pietro Aretino also described the house and the delights that it offered.[4] The most illuminating description of the property, and of the appearance of the villa at the time, is to be found in Brenzone's own account of it, listing the plants under their botanical names and giving details of the statuary and ornament, and of the inscriptions that he himself had written. The sculpture and the inscriptions are still there today, though not all in their original positions.

The first part of the garden to be laid out was the area to the left of the drive, which leads from the main gate and rises in a gradual incline to the villa itself. A double colonnade was built on the slope of the promontory facing the lake. Following the route laid out by Brenzone, the visitor was welcomed at the gate by a series of sculptures in high relief, placed on the wall of the original inn, one representing the marriage of St Mark and the lake of Benacus (Garda) – a legend based on the traditional belief in the association of the Evangelist with the Adriatic – the other depicting Neptune with his trident and, in place of the usual dolphin, two carp from the waters of Lake Garda.[5] This relief was placed on the front of the building, which by Brenzone's time had become a storeroom for tools and equipment used in the nearby olive groves; it was mentioned by Brenzone in his description of the property in his wills.[6]

A little further on is the walled Garden of Venus, 'full of myrtles and citrons'; in its far wall, which forms part of the boundary wall of the property, is a door inscribed with a reference to the four fundamental qualities of heat and cold, sweetness and bitterness, which – according to Pliny and Dioscorides – are to be found both in the lemon and in the pain of love. At the far end of the walled garden, opposite the entrance, stands a magnificent piece of antique marble statuary depicting the goddess Venus; in place of 'Cupid, who urinates to water the garden', as Brenzone records, she is accom-

panied by a pair of lovers, who are seated on the edge of the stone water basin. The inscription beneath the figure of Venus refers to personal events in Brenzone's life, such as the moving tribute to a lost love – '*mortuus obliviscar Flaviae*' (only when dead will he forget Flavia). The luxuriant lemon trees here are protected by eighteenth-century hothouses.

Linked to the Garden of Venus,

there is another garden known as the Garden of Apollo, which is full of orange and cedar trees, and an enormous laurel, tall and wide, the most beautiful to be seen in the whole of the Venetian Riviera. From the pierced eyes of a stone head of Petrarch on one side of the garden flow the waters of a fountain, which

bathes the feet of the laurel so that the water penetrates to its roots; on the other side is a large figure of Apollo carved in the finest marble. Between the two stands the laurel.

Perhaps Brenzone was referring to the sixteenth-century carved marble slab depicting Apollo, Daphne and Laura (which recalls either the muse of Petrarch or Laura Brenzone), where the god is represented in the clothes of a Roman warrior. Today this marble relief is fixed to the external wall of the Garden of Venus, facing the villa.

Further up the slope is 'another Garden, which is full of the fruits of Adam, and for this reason it is known as the

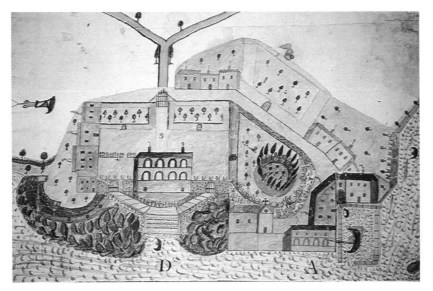

Garden of Adam'. It has two entrances, leading respectively to the main drive and to the villa, with inscriptions alluding to an earthly paradise recreated here. But here, in contrast to Eden, the presiding spirit is protective: life reigns over death, and the fruits of the trees can be freely enjoyed without any fear of serpents or retribution. Originally the marble relief depicting the figures of the garden's progenitors must have been located here, but, probably in the course of alterations in the eighteenth century, it was moved to the Rotunda of the Ancients, which houses a superb collection of antique statuary.

The sculptures representing the marriage of Benacus, and the figures of Apollo and Adam have never been thoroughly researched but they are traditionally attributed to Girolomo Campagna; their dates, however, suggest that this attribution cannot be accurate and that it is far more likely they are the work of the great Veronese sculptor Danese Cattaneo.

These three gardens, which allude to Parnassus, the Garden of Eden and the Garden of Love, are all laid out on the intimate scale of a *hortus conclusus*. They seem to have been conceived as individual and quite distinct sections of the garden rather than as part of an integrated scheme, and certainly they have no clear connection with the nearby villa. In fact the house stands in an isolated position beyond the chapel, where Brenzone wished to be buried: 'One can still see there the tomb of the great poet Catullus; his effigy seems to be looking across the lake towards the town of Sirmione [where he was living at the time of his death in 54 BC]'. A link undoubtedly exists between the splendid ruins of Catullus's villa and the classical sixteenth-century house in whose gardens the poet found a new resting place. It was as if Brenzone had inherited the spirit of Catullus, just as contemporary Venice had wished to accept the mantle of Rome both ancient and modern, and to be seen as its heir since the sacking of Rome by Charles V in 1527.

The feature that perhaps best represents the garden is the Rotunda of the Ancients, which was built in the mid-1550s. The cypresses that now encircle it are not the same varieties as those that were planted there originally, which

Brenzone and, before him, Aretino, methodically listed. In referring to 'that hilly height, where lively groups of rabbits dug out their hollow cells', Brenzone was describing the rocky outcrop between the chapel and the side of the villa, which was transformed to make way for the Rotunda. According to a note relating to expenses, work was still continuing on the site in the late 1550s: it refers to 'certain figures sent to San Vilio . . . sometime after the year 1557', for which 'the boatman, who brought them from Venice, was paid 6 ducats'.[7] The figures in question could well have been the antique heads of the Caesars, which were placed on modern busts and distributed around the various niches of the internal wall of the Rotunda.

The Rotonda itself measures twelve metres (thirty-nine feet) in diameter and has low curving walls forming a sort of parapet overlooking the surrounding countryside. Here too there are a number of inscriptions on plaques set into the walls: over the entrance an epigraph reads '*Carthago Italiam contra*', while others,

some only fragmentary, are discernible on the plinths and niches of the statuary. Among the sculptures are caryatids, which support the remains of Ionic capitals around the outer wall and gaze out over the landscape.

The custom of exhibiting collections of antique relics in a garden dates back to early Roman times. Here, however, the archaeological finds, rather than being simply a random display, seem to form part of a carefully planned and integrated scheme. The twelve heads of the Caesars very likely refer to the twelve months of the year and to the signs of the zodiac, while twelve 'articles' are inscribed on the façade of the villa itself, beneath the bust of Brenzone, to welcome guests to the house. Apart from serving as a belvedere, the Rotunda was also intended as a theatre and as a temple dedicated to the memory of the ancient world. It is clear that its inspiration had much in common with the Botanical Gardens of Padua whose circular plan was based on the cosmos. (They were laid out by Daniele Barbaro, who was also responsible for

producing an edition of Vitruvius in 1556, in which a reconstruction by Palladio of a classical theatre was illustrated.) The Rotonda also evokes the idea of a small reading room, here open to the sky, but nevertheless based on the small chamber with circular plan and domed ceiling to be found in the palaces of the Veneto – as for instance in the Palazzo Thiene in Vicenza, where it is decorated with busts of emperors.

Sculptures of illustrious figures from antiquity were eagerly sought by sixteenth century collectors, who displayed them in pavilions or antique temples in their gardens. The caption to a plan by Lauro of the garden of the Villa Mattei in Rome refers to a 'Bust of Cicero, along with other antique busts, numbering 53 in all', while at the centre of the exedra that terminated one side of the hippodrome in the same garden was a large recess containing a bust of Alexander the Great, who presided over the magnificent spectacle laid out before him. A rotunda on an elevation surrounded by cypresses is a recurrent theme in the Italian garden, but there is no doubt that the Rotunda of the Ancients at San Vigilio is an incomparable example.

Botany, astrology, mythology, the culture of the classical world, references to the Bible and the Christian faith all combine to make the gardens of the Villa Brenzone a microcosm of a perfect world, a dream world in which their owner, the author of the poem *De vita solitaria*, could find refuge. It was a dream that had much in common with that described by Francesco Colonna in the *Hypnerotomachia Poliphili*. Inside the villa Brenzone placed two epigraphs, or 'enigmas in marble', as a conclusion to the series of inscriptions in the garden: they allude to his unquenchable desire to enjoy the place that he maintained was 'the most beautiful in the world'.[8]

Towards the end of the eighteenth century, Agostino Vincenzo Brenzone, who had acquired the title of Conte di San Vigilio in 1786, instigated a number of changes to the villa and the gardens and bought more land to add to the family's estates in the area. In this connection it is perhaps appropriate to mention Trezza's contribution (which has been discussed in detail by Cavattoni) in expanding and developing a scheme to extract from the lake sufficient water to feed the fountains

Villa Brenzone, Punta San Vigilio: the Rotunda of the Ancients. (Photo Cesare Gerolimetto)

Villa Brenzone, Punta San Vigilio: antique statue of Venus. (Photo Cesare Gerolimetto)

Ancients. We do not yet know for certain if the influence of San Vigilio was direct or indirect, but further research into the cultural inheritance left by this great garden will no doubt resolve this point and many others still in question.

in the neo-Gothic loggia behind the chapel. The Conte di San Vigilio was also responsible for commissioning the Gothicization of various features of the garden, such as the windows in the wall of the Garden of Adam, and a number of Gothic additions such as the crenellations on the perimeter wall and the balustrading on the terrace, which add a note of picturesque romanticism to the garden, especially when seen from the lake, creating an effective contrast with the severity of the square and uncompromising mass of the villa. The crenellations appear on the previously unpublished relief plan of the property, drawn up in 1788, in which the garden is only sketchily represented and seems to be entirely dominated by the Rotunda; behind the villa can be seen the steps, not yet lined with espaliered cypresses, running down to the shore of the lake. The straight avenue that today leads up to the villa was evidently a later addition.

If in one respect the garden of the Villa Brenzone belongs to the medieval tradition of the *hortus conclusus*, in another, in terms of the articulation of its design and the juxtaposition of its various elements, in the use of inscriptions, sculptures and ornamental details to convey a personal message, and of tombs, altars and other monuments to suggest a high moral tone, in its relationship with the surrounding landscape and its exploitation of its natural site, it was clearly a forerunner of the English gardening tradition of the early Georgian period.

Critical studies have recently confirmed the close links that exist between the birth of the landscape garden and the Italian garden of preceding centuries. For example, the row of illustrious characters represented in the Temple of British Worthies at Stowe, an idea that had already been proposed by William Kent for Chiswick House, seems to have much in common with the Rotunda of the

[1] A. Palladio, *I quattro libri dell'architettura* (Venice 1570) bk 2, p. 45.

[2] R. Brenzoni, 'Agostino Brenzone, umanista, giureconsulto, ricostruttore di San Vigilio del Garda' in *Atti e Memorie dell' Accademia di Agricoltura, Scienze e Lettere di Verona* (1960) Vol. 13, p. 14.

[3] 'Lettera di Agostino Brenzon . . . per la descrizione del suo luogo a San Vigilio sul lago di Benaco', in S. Cattaneo and B. Grattarolo, *Salo, e sua Riviera* (Venice 1745) Vol. 1, pp. XXXIX–XLII, 78–80. The dedication to M. A. da Mula dates from 1553.

[4] P. Aretino, *Lettere sull'arte* (ed. by E. Camesasca and F. Pertile) (Milan 1957–60) Vol. 1, p. 250.

[5] Thrown in the lake in 1857 as an act of vandalism, it remains there to this day.

[6] Redated to 1 January 1562 and 21 November 1563. See State Archives, Venice: notarial deed and last will, M. Cavanis, 193.52; 197.67 and 71t. See also Brenzoni, *op. cit.*, pp. 8–10. Brenzone died in Venice in 1567.

[7] *Cermison Archive*, Proceeding no. 471, c.2, State Archives, Verona.

[8] 'Lettera', *op. cit.*, p. XLII.

Bibliography

S. Cattaneo and B. Grattarolo, *op. cit.* (note 3).

G. D. Marai, *San Vigilio sopra il Lago di Garda* (Verona 1807).

G. B. da Persico, *Descrizione di Verona e della sua provincia* (Verona 1820–21), pp. 11, 198–202.

H. Thode, *Somnii Explanatio. Traumbilder vom Gardasee in S. Vigilio* (Berlin 1909).

M. L. Gothein, *Geschichte der Gartenkunst* (Jena 1914), Vol. 1, pp. 255–8.

L. Eccheli, *Punta San Vigilio* (Verona 1957).

P. Aretino, *op. cit.* (note 4) Vol. 1, pp. 249–52, 482–3.

R. Brenzoni, *op. cit.* (note 2) pp. 37–52.

G. F. Viviani (ed.), *La villa nel Veronese* (Verona 1975), pp. 237–8, 329–3.

M. Azzi Visentini (ed.), *Il giardino veneto* (Milan 1988), pp. 90–92.

M. Azzi Visentini, *Il giardino veneto tra Sette e Ottocento e le sue fonti* (Milan 1988), pp. 14–15, 19.

PART TWO

The Straight Line and the Arabesque:
From the Baroque Garden to the Classical Park

Park of the château of Rueil (Hauts-de-
Seine). From a reconstruction by Launay
and a cadastral map of 1818, re-drawn by
K. Woodbridge.

N

Island garden, Aranjuez, Madrid. From a
survey carried out by the Servicio de Jardines,
Parques y Montes, Madrid 1985.

N

| 0 | 100m |
| 0 | 300ft |

N

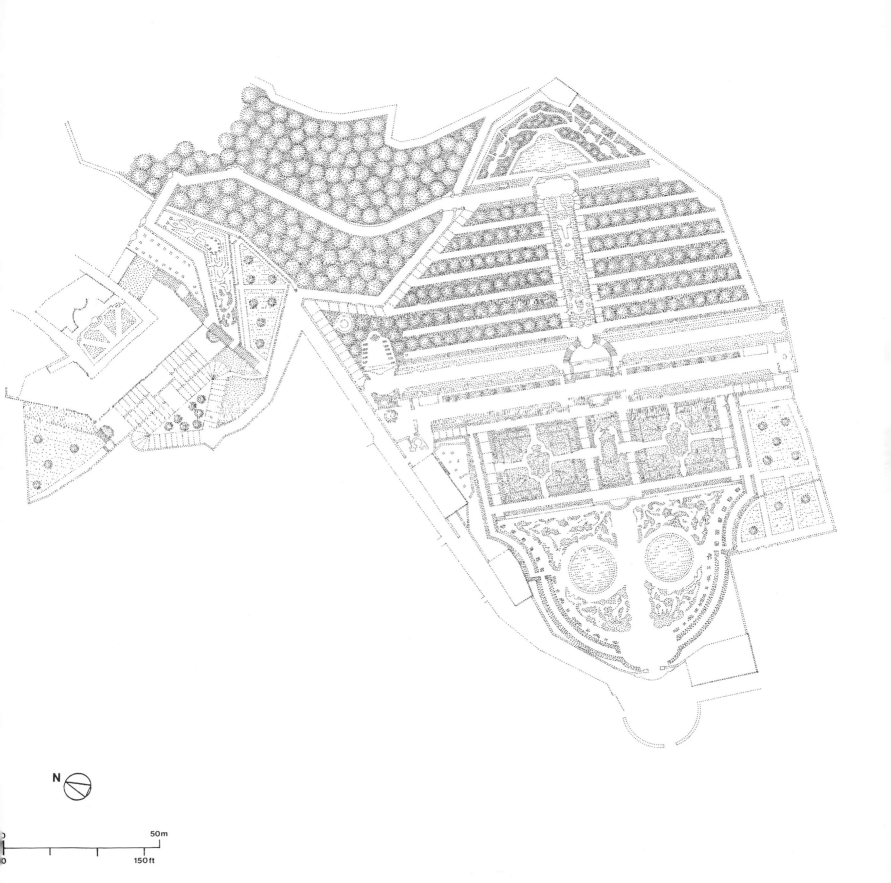

N

50m

150 ft

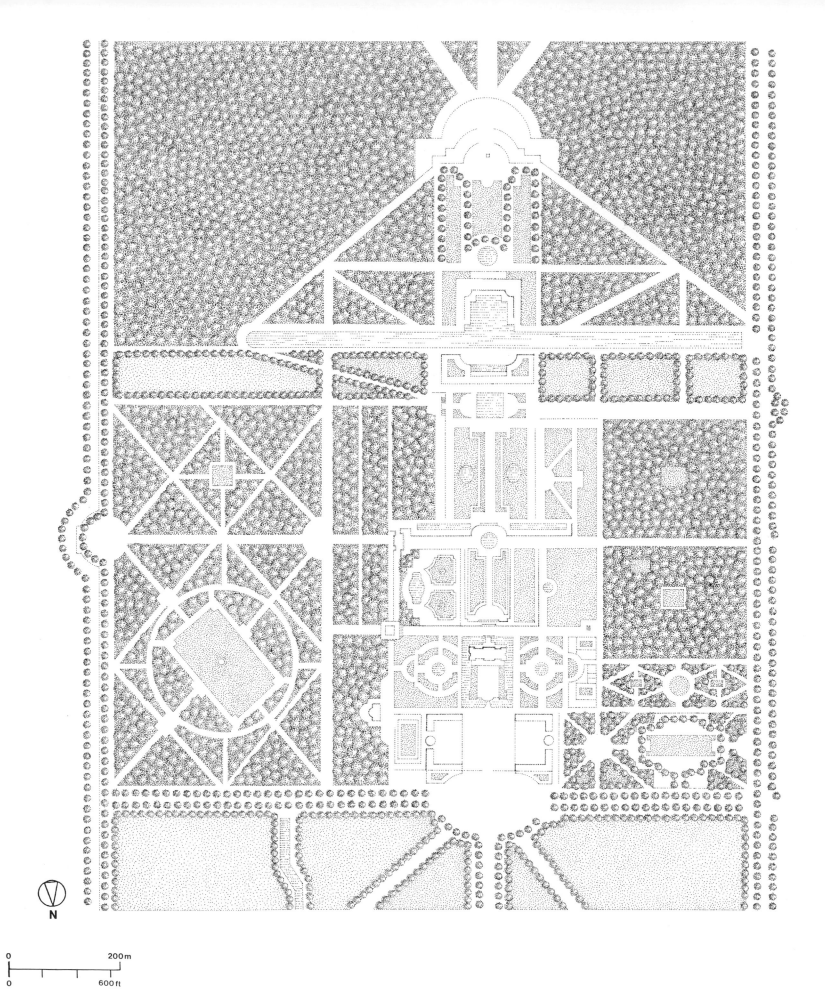

N

0   200m

0   600 ft

114

Garden of Vaux-le-Vicomte (Seine-et-
Marne). From a plan by I. Silvestre.

The Petit Parc at Versailles (Yvelines).
From a plan engraved by Le Pautre (1710)
and a modern survey.

N

0
100m

0
300ft

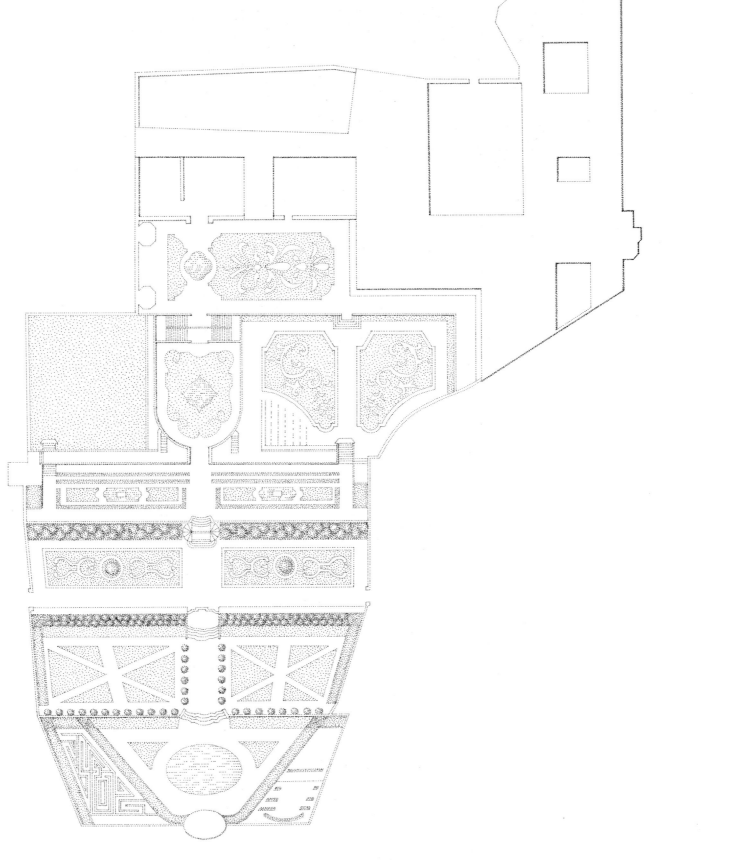

Garden of the Villa Villani-Novati (later Belgioioso, now Brivio-Sforza), Merate, Como. From M. dal Re, Ville di delizia, eighteenth century.

0   50m

0   150ft

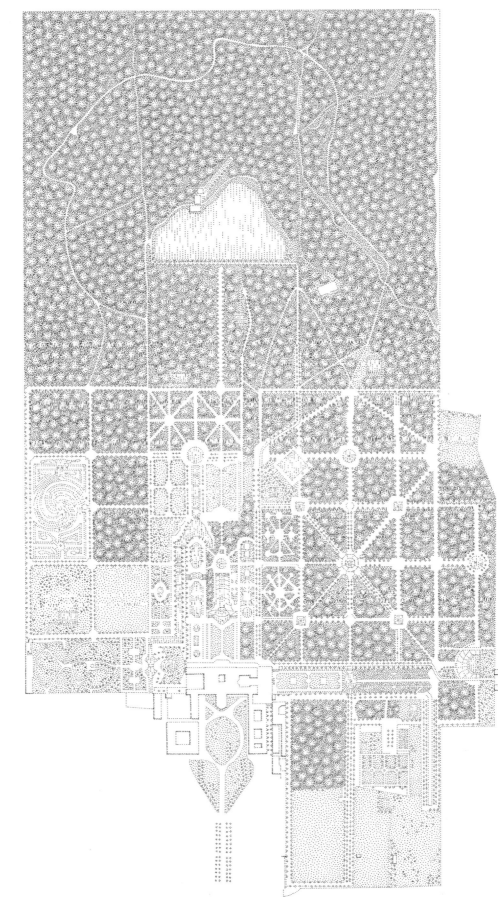

Royal Gardens of La Granja, San Ildefonso,
Segovia. From a survey carried out by the
Servicio de Jardines, Parques y Montes,
Madrid 1985.

N

| 0 | | 200 m |
| 0 | | 600 ft |

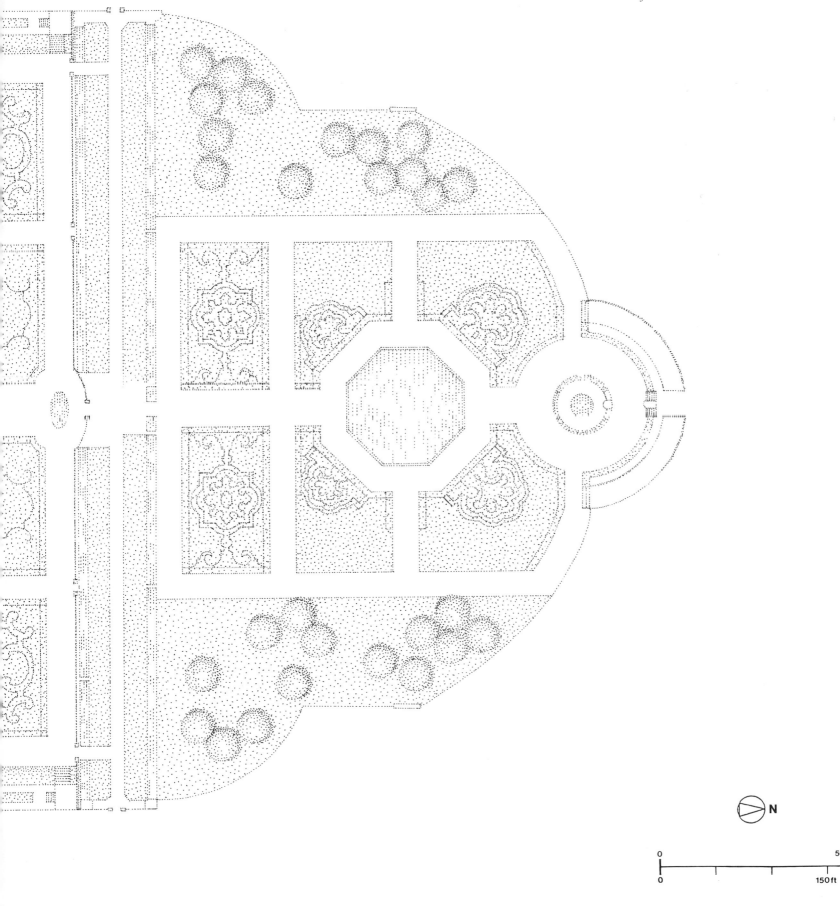

Garden of the Royal Palace of Het Loo, Apeldoorn, Gelderland, Holland. From an aerial photograph and plans for the restoration of the garden drawn up by Baron Jan van Asbeck.

N

0   50m

0   150ft

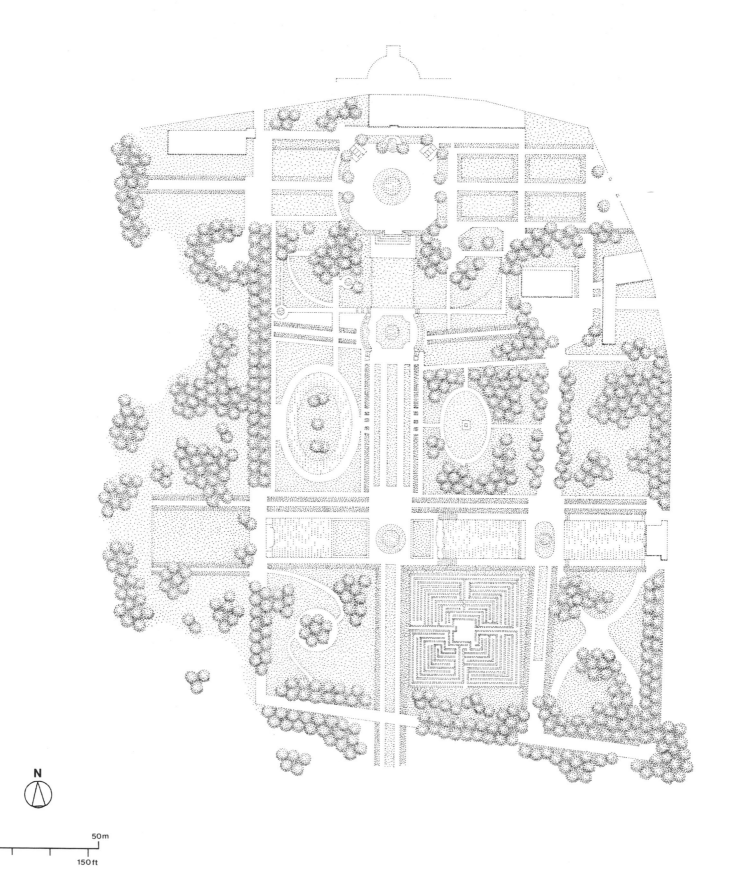

Garden of Villa Barbarigo, Valsanzibio,
Padua. From F. Fariello, Architettura dei
giardini, *Rome 1985 (reprint).*

The Great Garden of Herrenhausen,
Hanover, Lower Saxony. From the plan by
Charbonnier, early eighteenth century.

N

0
0

50m

150ft

N

0   100m

0   300ft

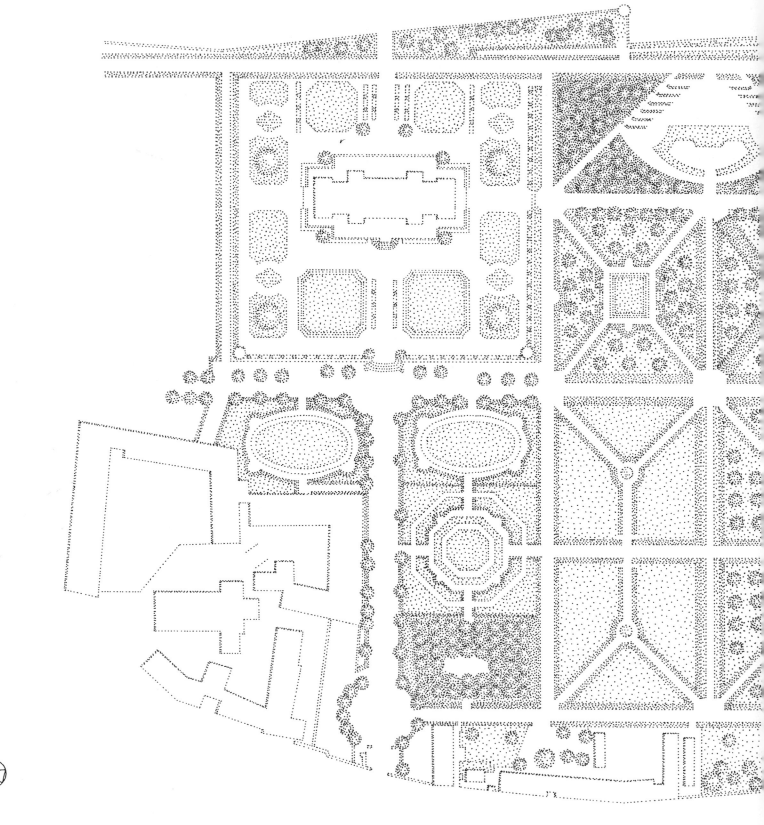

*Court Garden, Veitshöchheim, Bavaria.
From the plan drawn up by J. A. Oth
(c. 1780) and from a modern survey carried
out by the Bayerische Verwaltung der
Staatlichen Schlösser, Gärten und Seen,
Munich 1986.*

N

0   50m

0   150 ft

Garden History and Cartography

Françoise Boudon

If a new history of gardens is to be written, the basis of the study must be defined. Is it to be based on the remaining open spaces, the authenticity of which requires careful examination, or on spaces now disappeared which will have to be rediscovered? For each of these delicate tasks, what instruments should be used? Recent outstanding research into the great princely gardens of the seventeenth century,[1] lavishly illustrated with unpublished plans taken from famous collections, with colourful aerial views, beautifully written texts and clearly explained extracts from archives, have considerably enlarged our field of knowledge. But as for discussion of documentary methods, systems of restoration or analytical procedures, there is very little. The beauty of these remarkable gardens, their luxuriance, the qualities of those who commissioned them, the importance of the published documents – all these encourage us to lose sight, temporarily, of this weakness. It will inevitably reappear when, bowing at last to scientific necessity and determined on carrying out a study in depth, we leave the enchanted paths of a few great princely parks to undertake the more mundane, but nevertheless significant, history of the great number of gardens designed for small or relatively modest residences.

If when a garden is established, as K. Woodbridge usefully reminds us, practicality often prevails over idealism,[2] it must then be admitted that the prerequisite to any study of the garden – that is, of the nature of the vegetation, and the arrangement of plants, colours and perfumes – must include not only the history of its boundaries, but also the choice of position, its long-term relation to the topography of the site with its not necessarily immutable natural features, its relief, its watercourses, its sometimes surprisingly permanent man-made features, the roads, the village, the château and its outbuildings. In other words, one of the essential keys to the history of gardens is historical cartography: indeed this must be the paramount source, since it reveals a wealth of relevant documentation which leads inevitably to a method of investigation, analysis and explanation which, on present evidence, this field currently lacks.

A new style of imagery

Gardens and parks have an important place in cartographic imagery. Few maps, however diagrammatic, fail to indicate by a sign the presence of a garden. If a garden is marked, it is primarily because the surrounding walls make it a part of the building, but also doubtless because few areas of land are so aesthetically and symbolically important. We have, moreover, proof of the cartographers' latent interest in parks: as soon as the scale of the map allows it, the cartographer immediately seizes the opportunity to give a detailed picture of the garden, defining the contours of the park, the direction of the paths, the position of the beds.[3] If, therefore, the garden is one of the constituent elements of the map, the corollary is obvious: maps are one of the fundamental documentary sources of the history of gardens.

Nevertheless, however rich it may be, this material must be carefully sifted.[4] Not all cartographic images are of equal interest. The quality of the imagery is very varied, differing according to the scale of the document, the date of its completion and the purpose – administrative, fiscal, legal, or topographical – for which it was intended.

For reasons which are easily understood, the chronological series of *plans terriers** (land registers) for any single property – and associated plans giving boundaries (*plans de bornage*)* – intended to show the territorial limits of seignorial authority, contain for a single garden a wealth of practical information that is accurately dated, very legible, and of inestimable importance in piecing together the history of the estate. The centre of the seigneurial world, the château and its immediate surroundings, are very often meticulously drawn, coloured, detailed and sometimes even captioned. As far as the garden is concerned we know not only its size and shape, but also the nature of the plantations, at least of the main ones which are obviously in most cases for practical use – a bed planted with sainfoin, vines, vegetables, fruit trees in quincunxes, melon beds etc.

Rich in information and complete as these land registers are, however, they sometimes reveal too many chronological lacunae – details are particularly abundant for the late eighteenth century – and, since they are concerned only with the seigneurial estate, also too many geographical lacunae. Reference to more general sources, topographical or administrative maps, is therefore also required. These maps, intended to give an exact picture of a certain area – the boundaries of a parish, the extent of a forest or of hunting rights, the course of a river, the line of a road, the proposed route of a canal – are unsurpassed as collections of garden plans, and provide valuable pictures of the parks included in the particular area. Situating a garden in its topographical context allows us to study it in its widest implications and smallest details, to appreciate the layout of the cultivated areas, to make a proper evaluation of the position of the lake or the canal in relation to the local hydrographic system and thus to assess the scale and importance of any landscaping.

Topographical maps reveal the types of development on a particular site, and the uniformity or diversity of the solutions to similar problems, by showing to some extent the different attitudes, in different eras, of the landowner and the gardener. Of all these topographical theme maps the most famous is without doubt the *Atlas de Trudaine* (1740)[5] with its meticulous, but not always strictly factual, catalogue of the entire length of the vast network of royal roads, the parks it avoids, the ones it skirts, the avenues it connects. Other series still remain to be investigated: there can be no better iconographic source than hydrographic maps (maps of canals and marshes) to begin the comparative study of waterside gardens. The maps of the water system at Versailles, drawn up in the 1670s at the time of the excavation of the Grand Canal and the construction of the lakes, carefully record the configuration of the neighbouring parklands which were variously affected by these gigantic water works. Even a brief examination of these documents gives more information about the gardens to the west

The garden of Lorrez-le-Bocage (Seine-et-Marne) depicted on seigneurial maps: the garden before 1610, engraving from Claude Chastillon, La Topographie française. (Photo Bibliothèque Doucet).

The garden in 1768, drawing on land register. Archives Départementales, E207. (Service photographique des archives départementales de Seine-et-Marne).

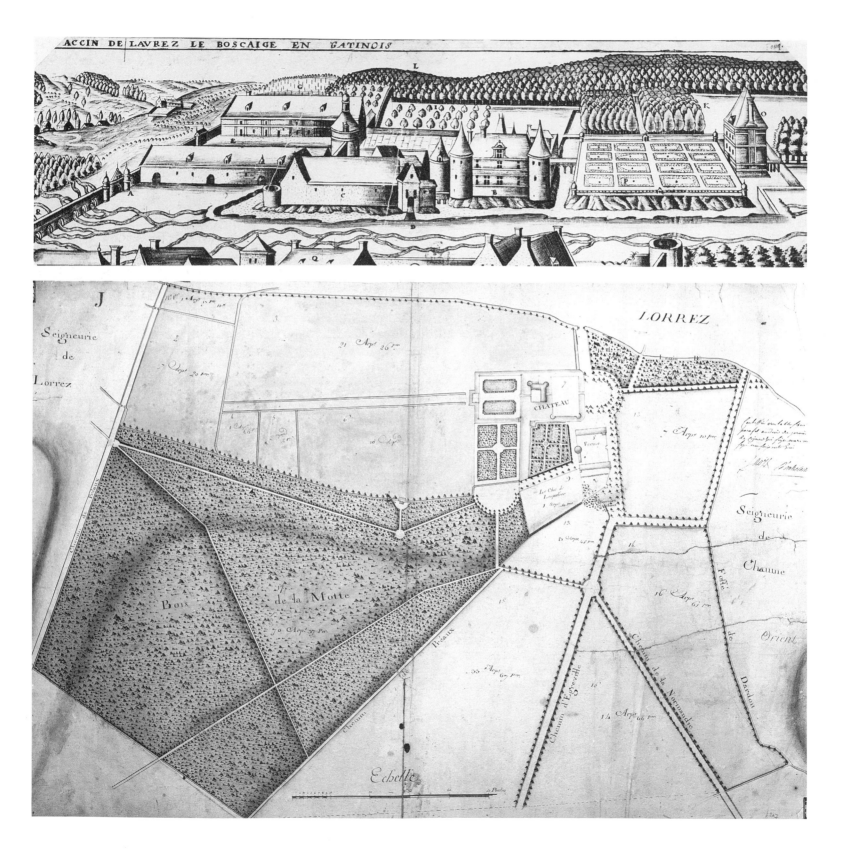

Developments in the creation of the garden:
Bonnelles (Yvelines). The garden and the old
château on its medieval platform, early
eighteenth century; detail of the seigneurial
plan. Bibl.Nat.Ms. n.a.fr.5901–02.
Bibliothèque Nationale, Paris.

The garden after the reconstruction of the
château and the filling in of the moat, late
eighteenth century; detail of map of royal
hunting reserves. Engraving. (Photo
CRHAM)

of Paris in the late seventeenth century than several months of research into bundles of archives.

But, until the mid-eighteenth century at least, not all maps are of the same quality. Before topographical engineers had completely mastered the technique of surveying and draughtsmanship – that is before the formation of the Ecole des Ponts et Chaussées in 1747 – they limited their work to the essentials. Parks are rarely indicated on the maps of the 1660s relating to the reorganization of forests (*cartes de réformation des forêts*)*, but almost always on those showing seigneurial and royal privileges (*cartes de gruerie*)* at the end of the eighteenth century. In all cases, exceptions to the rule are not unusual: even a clumsily-drawn map from the end of the seventeenth century may provide more information than another, more recent, drawn by a careless or hasty topographer. It is therefore wise never to neglect documents of ancient origin. Topographical maps act as cross-checks, overlapping and complementing each other, but are also sometimes contradictory. The garden historian is relatively well qualified to fill in the gaps, to correct incorrect or fanciful plans, where topographical engineers have given free rein to their imagination by indicating imaginary gardens along straight royal roads. The stewardship plans (*plans d'intendance*)* of the late eighteenth century – each covering the extent of a parish – and the national cadastral survey (*cadastre national*)* started at the beginning of the nineteenth century, provide a basic tool for the garden historian, a complete inventory of the parks and gardens of France. The Napoleonic register (not completed until 1830–40) is an essential documentary landmark in the history of gardens. The completion dates for this plan coincided, for large rural estates, with a time of crucial importance in the history of the French countryside. The château, its relationship to the outbuildings and the village, the main outline of the garden, the boundaries of the park, the layout of the avenues: all these features – often soon to disappear – are nevertheless preserved more or less as they were at the end of the eighteenth century. The picture of gardens given in the Napoleonic land register is far from attractive: it is perfunctory and dull, lacking virtually any colour, as unattractive as the glowing watercolour maps of the Age of Enlightenment are entrancing. But it provides a sound basis for fundamental research, because here at last are the correctly drawn source maps essential for any proper reconstruction work.[6]

Picture of garden evolution

Garden history is still generally written according to the 'stop the camera' technique, starting at the moment when a distinguished gardener or patron steps on to the scene, with no regard for the earlier state of the site. Thorough research, based on maps, encourages a more prudent approach. *Ex nihilo* creations are rare. Gardens, like houses, nearly always reappear in the same place.[7] From reading the description of the garden of the king's secretary, Gaillard Spifame, at Conflans (Val de Marne) as given in an account of a visit in 1532,[8] it becomes clear that

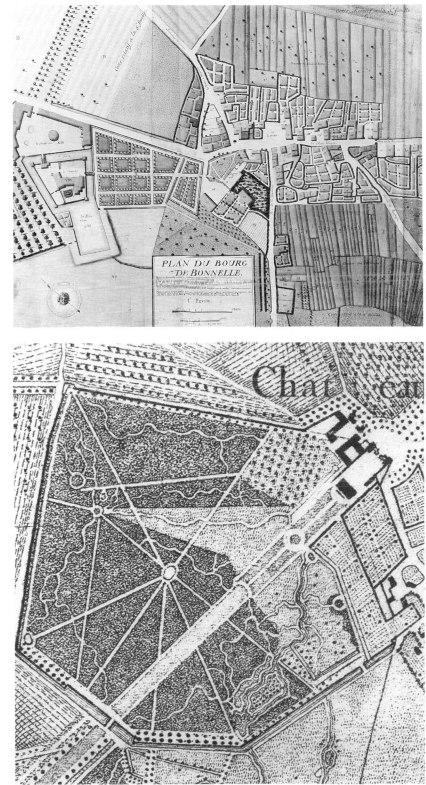

Comparison of evidence from maps and drawings:
Les Bergeries, Draveil (Essonne). The plan of the forest of Sénart in 1708 (below) confirms the testimony of Gaignières of 1707 (above) and the existence at Bergeries of a zig-zag avenue inspired by that at Meudon.

Drawing. Cabinet des Estampes Va 416. Bibliothèque Nationale, Paris. Detail of engraving. Archives Nationales Estampes NI Seine-et-Oise 24. (Photo CRHAM)

what historians celebrate as the perfection of the art of gardening at the beginning of the seventeenth century is to a large extent a creation of the age of François I. The garden at Berny (Hauts-de-Seine) was modified in 1622–3 at the same time as François Mansart was altering the château; the watercourses were canalized but the cultivated areas, planted earlier as can be seen in an engraving by Claude Chastillon, were left untouched. If a garden is rarely new, it is on the other hand never static. A recent theory of the gradual evolution of gardens[9] is a dangerous methodology if it leads – as is unwisely propounded by the author – to the anachronistic use of a late eighteenth-century map to compile a history of gardens of the early seventeenth century. The history of gardens requires patient and well-documented investigation of reality, relying to a very large extent on the study of maps, rather than on theories about the perpetual re-creation or permanence of gardens, which tend instead to slow down the progress of knowledge.

The extraordinary amount of cartographic documentation accumulated since the seventeenth century, well catalogued[10] and so available to garden historians, should encourage them initially to adopt a proven method, used successfully for a long time by historians of towns: the diachronic study of maps, achieved by superimposing successive records of the topography of an area. It is not difficult to see how, by adjusting the scales and superimposing garden plans reconstructed in accordance with illustrations provided by maps produced over a period of time, it is possible to re-create the essential elements in the development of a garden or gardens in a particular area, from the first stages to completion, as can be seen in the region of Paris. Such reconstructions may be accomplished with minimal uncertainty provided the fundamental rule is respected: to proceed from the precise to the imprecise and so work backwards in time, starting from contemporary maps and reconstructing the garden plan chronologically, layer by layer, from contemporary map sources, cadastral maps and relief maps.

By giving priority to topochronological research, translated into cartographic diagrams drawn to the same scale and therefore instantly comprehensible and comparable, we can properly relate the history of the evolution of the shapes to the circumstances of that evolution. The indispensable documentary evidence is available to us. The precision with which small parcels of land are shown on terriers enables us to make an exact assessment of the obstacles encountered by château owners in rearranging the lands around their residences and in extending their parks. A comparative map is the best means of tracing the evolution of shapes, from the most common to the most unusual, and of discovering traces of earlier layouts in new developments. The superimposition of maps offers the opportunity to discover the history of the extension or reduction of landed property following the whims of fortune or the fashions of the time, of the political background to sales and acquisitions, and to deduce from the positioning of a path, a lake or a parterre whether it was the result of invention or necessity. At Bonnelles (Yvelines), created in the mid-eighteenth century, the

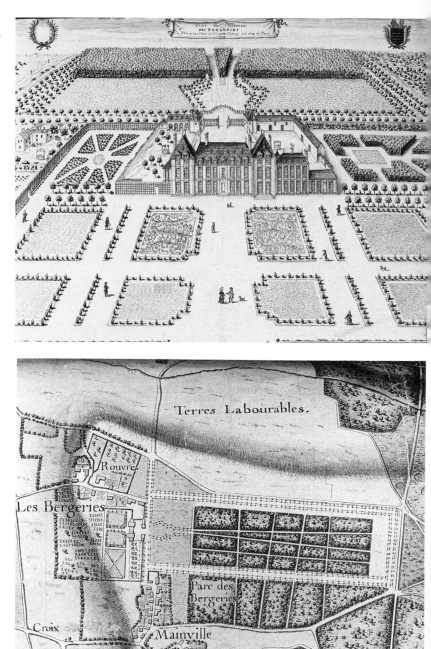

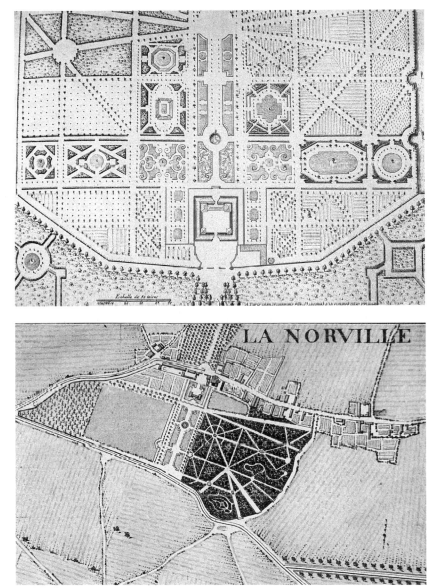

La Norville (Essonne). Above: engraving by Langlois, eighteenth century. Below: drawing from an atlas of the royal roads, mid-eighteenth century, Archives Nationales F/14, 8447, plate 13. (Photos CRHAM)

The engraving is a formalized representation, while the map (which includes the same area turned through rather more than 180°) shows the actual form of the garden as built.

arrangement of the quincunx is not arbitrary, but follows the line of the ditch round the medieval plateau, a line preserved even after the demolition and reconstruction of the old château. The superimposed map allows us to determine finally how much of the development is the result of personal idiosyncrasy and how much reflects general tendencies. It reveals, for instance, the disappearance in the first half of the seventeenth century of the succession of walled gardens which until then characterized French gardens; or, at Brunoy (Val-de-Marne) efforts by landowners on both sides of the river to acquire gently sloping terrain on the nearby hills, thus creating gardens with a dual outlook safely above the river Yerres and its flood plain. Topochronological maps also help to fix the date of appearance and extent of minor changes to buildings and gardens: thus, for instance, from the end of the seventeenth century the enclosed, closely overlapping farmyards which hitherto had prevented access to the plateau on which stood the château, began to disappear, giving way to broad forecourts covered in turf or ornamental flowerbeds.

A critique of illustrations

The history of gardens, which until now has rarely concerned itself with maps, can still be written by relying on unchallenged iconographic documentation. Views of gardens are used as illustrations to support more or less *a priori* arguments, but rarely as instruments of discovery or as sources of investigation, which would assume some kind of check of their veracity. They are simply declared good or bad, and accepted as valid proof or rejected outright without argument. The same significance is accorded to an incorrectly drawn-up plan of the park of La Norville (Essonne) as to the probably very accurate bird's-eye view of the garden at Liancourt (Oise). These exterior views are accepted without taking into account that in most cases they are part of a series done by one artist or one studio with its own method of presentation, interpretation and distortion. A Silvestre engraving or a Lapointe drawing with an empty area round a château does not imply the absence of a garden, but merely an artistic whim or convention – there will be plenty of pictures of the garden on other plates. On the other hand, the same picture drawn by a topographer as captious as Chastillon makes us wonder if this particular château really was devoid of cultivated areas. And the use of illustrated documentation often has to stop when the anachronisms begin. Perelle's illustrations, obviously fanciful but obeying the best rules of perspective, are held in high esteem. Those of Chastillon, badly drawn but rich in authentic detail are neglected. And if du Cerceau's bird's-eye views are highly valued, it is as much for their pleasing appearance as for their content.

Too often the garden historian exploits the content of the drawings without any attempt at topographical investigation to situate them in their surroundings. No one has taken the trouble to find out exactly what Silvestre shows of the park at St Cloud, at what date and from what angle he made these apparently very disparate engravings. From

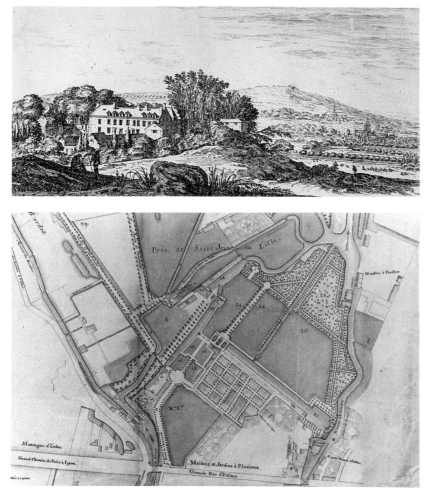

the views of Chantemerle (Essonne) – and from Duchesne's enthusiastic descriptions of this enchanting spot – we can glean nothing about the history of the gardens in the mid-seventeenth century without recourse to a map of this strange place.

A critical reading of illustrated documents of the sixteenth and seventeenth centuries is essential especially since – pending archival discoveries – they are still, for many small gardens, the only sources which give some idea of their appearance. A study has been made of Claude Chastillon's *Topographie française* engraved in 1640 from drawings made before 1610.[11] Historically, the collection is of prime importance. Coming between Jacques Androuet du Cerceau's *Les plus excellents bastiments de France* (1576–1579) and the superabundance of the late seventeenth-century series, Chastillon is almost the only witness to a still inadequately studied period. But is it not paradoxical, and perhaps even unwarranted, to accord the rigid, rough images of the *Topographie* a place among the source works for the history of gardens? Obviously, Chastillon's aim was the representation of architectural objects, châteaux or towns. But as a topographer, used to considering the landscape as a whole, he was incapable of presenting architecture out of its natural setting. In his engravings, with a wide viewpoint, gardens and landscapes play an important part and are depicted with a precision rarely achieved by succeeding generations. Moreover, Chastillon gives implicit proof of his interest in gardens by adapting the size of the plate and the focus of the view to the importance and fame of the cultivated areas. Double plates are reserved for châteaux endowed with gardens which harmonize particularly well with the landscapes, such as Berny, a long garden following the royal Paris-Orléans road, Lorrez-le-Bocage (Seine-et-Marne) which skilfully utilizes the branches of the Loing to display its many plateaux, and Le Pouty (Loiret) with its hanging terraces over the Loire. This is not the general rule. In most cases, Chastillon makes do with standard format copper plates, being prepared to reproduce only a part of the château as in the case of Villepreux (Yvelines) and Montceaux (Seine-et-Marne), in order to do justice to the garden. A checklist of the large plates and special viewpoints in the *Topographie* provides an initial list of the outstanding gardens in the Ile de France, Champagne and Poitou – regions which Chastillon had visited in the years 1600–10.

Chastillon's concern for the natural setting – the concern, as has been said, of a craftsman trained to evaluate the characteristics of an area – has until now been totally neglected. We give more or less serious consideration to the documentary interest of the *Topographie française* for architecture, but never for landscape. And yet, as a professional land-surveyor, would he have been able to present an artificial, stereotyped picture of the landscape? It is not easy to verify such a hypothesis without a sound knowledge of the micro-history of the landscape, each engraving requiring a topochronological reconstruction of the relevant area, and consequently a very precise study of the cartographic documentation, together with exploration on the ground. In the present state of our research it seems certain that Chastillon

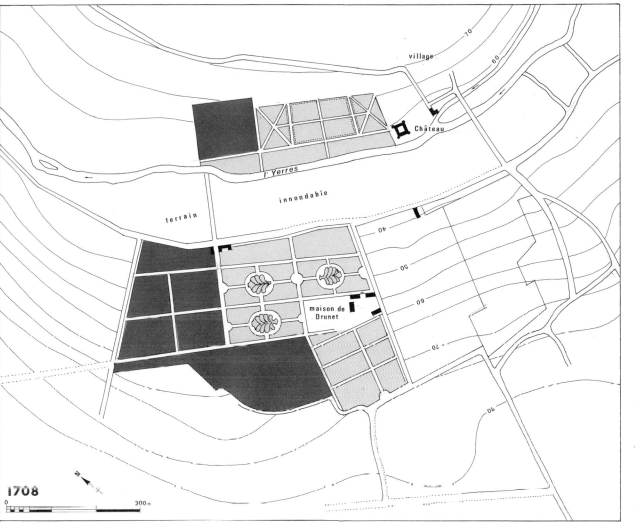

Five maps of the park of Brunoy (Val-de-Marne), from the beginning of the eighteenth century to 1983 (continued on following pages). Based on map IGN 1:5000. Drawn by J. Blécon.

1708

0 ____ 300 m

Late seventeenth/early eighteenth century: two unconnected gardens. State as in 1708, from the Map of the Forest of Sénart and District, *surveyed by Bourgault and Matis, surveyors to the king, 1708. Archives Nationales, NI Seine et Oise 24. On the northern bank of the Yerres, the garden of the old château of Brunoy (fifteenth century, altered in the seventeenth century); on the southern bank, separated from the château by an area of uncultivated land subject to flooding, the great garden covers the gentle slope below the house of the king's councillor, Brunet. Laid out before 1650, the design of the parterres, roughly indicated by the surveyors, does not agree with what we know of the Brunet garden from the work of Silvestre.*

represented the landscape exactly as he saw it: the bare ground in the lower part of the engraving of Montceaux is not a foreground 'effect', but an exact picture of an area of sterile land, a *mauvais pré*, confirmed on eighteenth-century plans of the park. Such attention to detail is not without interest for the garden historian.

As we have said, an evaluation of Chastillon's work cannot be undertaken without an exact correlation between the engraving and the map. This approach demands a preliminary retrospective reconstruction of the gardens from maps, reaching as far back as possible into the seventeenth century if the analysis is to be carried out correctly. This combined study of maps and engravings gives rise to fresh information: not only can gardens which have disappeared be reconstructed through the careful interpretation of traces preserved and recorded by the cartographer, as in the case of Chilly (Essonne), but it is also possible to document alterations in the aspect of building façades and their position in relation to the gardens,[12] as at Villepreux, where the great sixteenth-century garden – engraved by Chastillon – is to the north-east, at the foot of a narrow terrace running the length of the main building, while at the end of the seventeenth century the hierarchy of gardens and façades was reversed – the main garden being henceforth in the south-west, on an axis with a canal. Sometimes, however, the cartographic link breaks too early and it is impossible to reach any definite conclusions about certain illustrations, as, for instance, is the case with the garden of the château at Tresmes.

At almost every stage in the creation of a garden, at nearly every moment of its evolution, there is a relevant map. The collection, comparison and analysis of these documents is an essential preliminary task in the compilation of a new history of gardens.

Glossary

Land register (plan terrier) – map of the fiscal acquisition of a domain, giving details of the lord's possessions and parcels of land outside his domain for which he received rent.

Boundary plan (plan de bornage) – detailed plan of the boundaries between two properties with positioning of boundary marks serving as bench marks.

Map of revision of forests (carte de réformation des forêts) – map of the extent of a forest: these maps date from the late seventeenth century. They follow the revision of royal forests ordered by Colbert.

Map of captaincy (carte de capitainerie) – an administrative map indicating to the captain of hunts the extent of the territory under his surveillance: this map is not limited, like those previously mentioned, to forests but covers large areas of the countryside.

Map of 'gruerie' (carte de gruerie) – map showing the rights of the king and certain lords over woodlands.

Fiscal plan (plan d'intendance) – plan of a parish drawn up at the request of the steward of a fiscal area.

Cadastral register (matrice cadastrale) – in which are briefly described properties constructed and not constructed.

131

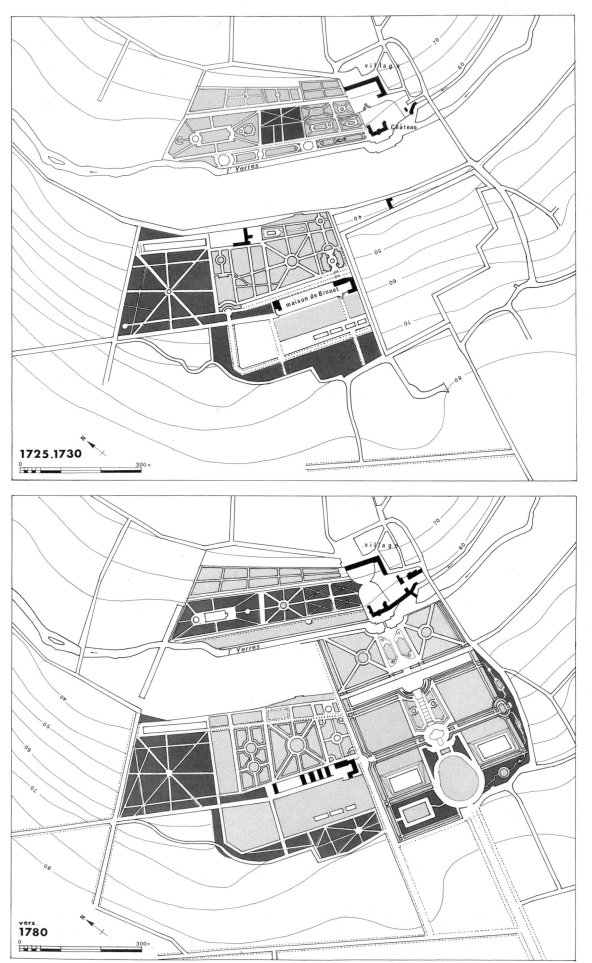

1725.1730

N

0   300 m

Mid-eighteenth century: two gardens facing each other. Appearance c. 1730, from the atlas of the seigneurial domain of Brunoy, 1725–30. Archives Départementales, A711. The Brunet property is unchanged; the apparent transformation of the garden is perhaps an illusion resulting simply from the quality of the map. At all events this confirms the skilful exploitation of the sloping land to construct terraces linked by flights of steps. From 1722 the château belonged to the financier Pâris de Marmontel, who left it unaltered, devoting his attentions solely to the garden. Since the village lay to the east, it was extended westwards along the river and largely redesigned.

vers 1780

N

0   300 m

Late eighteenth century: two merging gardens. Appearance in c. 1780, from the map of the royal hunting reserves (Vincennes, Service Historique des Armées de Terre) and a plan of the watercourses of Brunoy, eighteenth century. Archives Nationales N II Seine-et-Oise 118. In 1774 the Comte d'Artois bought the two properties, joined them together and laid out an elaborate garden on an axis with the old castle and the 'maison Brunet'. The steep slope of the left bank allowed the creation of a waterfall, built by Laurent (Dulaure, Dictionnaire des environs de Paris, Paris 1786, Vol. I, p. 37); it flows into a canal, which corresponds with another canal beside the Yerres at the foot of the old castle, on the other side of the parterre laid out in the area subject to flooding.

Beginning of the nineteenth century: an abandoned park, as seen in 1810–20. From the old land register and map IGN 1:10000 (St-Mandé, IGN). The basic outlines are still visible, but the details of the garden have been lost.

Condition in 1983, from the revised land register and from map IGN 1:5000. A few traces of the avenues are still visible.

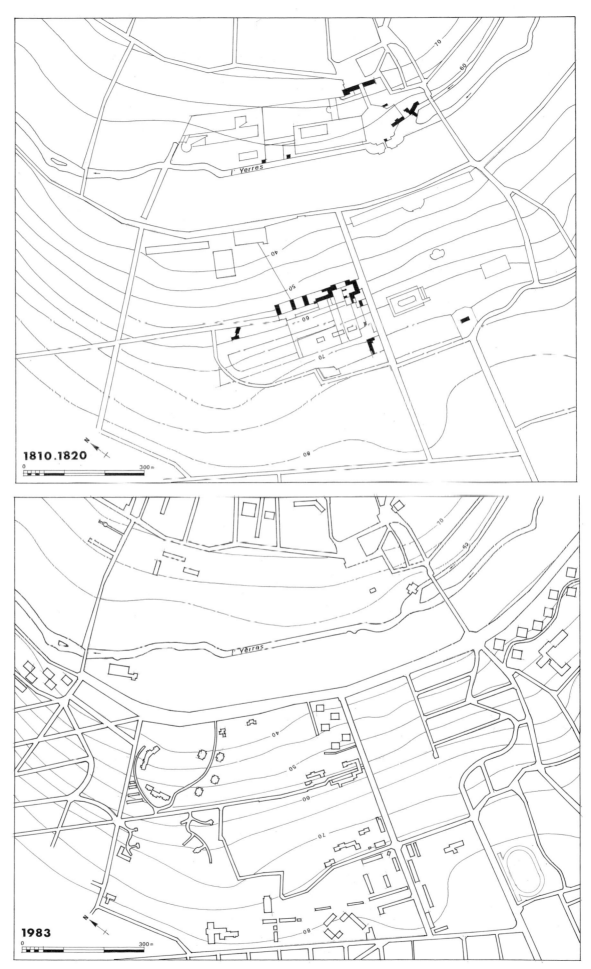

133

1 F. Hamilton Hazlehurst, *Gardens of Illusion, The Genius of André le Nôtre* (Nashville 1980); K. Woodbrige, *Princely Gardens* (London 1986).

2 K. Woodbridge, *op. cit.*, p. 56.

3 Cassini's map of France (drawn up from 1748, engraved about 1815) provides a superb example of the importance given to the representation of a garden. Given the scale of the map (1/86,400) the castle and the garden should have appeared as an initial letter. But from 1756 Cassini's business, having become insolvent, solicited contributions. With the obvious intention of flattering the donors, representations of parks were then done with particular care and given greater importance than the scale of the map required, with detailed research not found in previous drawings. (Colonel Berthaut, *La carte de Cassini 1750-1890. Etude Historique*, Paris 1898).

4 Similarly, some ten years ago, on the use of maps in research into the history of châteaux, F. Boudon and H. Couzy, 'Le château et son site. L'histoire de l'architecture et la cartographie', in *Revue de l'Art*, no. 38 (1977) pp. 7–22. Since châteaux and gardens are closely related, the conclusions reached refer also to gardens.

5 G. Arbellot, 'La grande mutation des routes de France', in *Annales. Economies. Sociétés. Civilisations*, no. 2 (1973), pp. 755ff.

6 In addition to the stewardship maps, it is advisable to consult the additional administrative documents, the cadastral originals which detail exactly the nature of the planting on each piece of land.

The condition of the different versions of the ancient survey gives cause for alarm. Architectural and garden historians should concern themselves with the problem before this irreplaceable document is lost forever.

7 F. Boudon and others, *Le site et ses châteaux, la modernisation du château et le choix d'un nouvel emplacement*, CNRS research/Bureau de la recherche architecturale (Paris 1980 unpublished).

8 S. Le Clech, *Chancellerie et culture au XVIe Siècle: les notaires et secrétaires de Francois 1°*, thesis from l'Ecole des Chartes (1988 unpublished).

9 Thierry Mariage, *L'Univers de le Nostre et les Origines de l'Aménagement du Territoire* (Paris 1980).

10 See, in particular, the invaluable *Catalogue général des cartes, plans et dessins d'architecture* published by the Archives Nationales from 1958. This documentation, particularly rich from the eighteenth century on, is not uniform for the whole of France: the Ile de France undoubtedly receives special treatment.

11 J. Blécon, F. Boudon, J. Bourdu and M. Herme-Renault. *L'archéologie du paysage au 17° siècle. La 'Topographie française' de Claude Chastillon. La région parisienne*. CNRS research/Bureau de la recherche architecturale (Paris 1984 unpublished); summary by F. Boudon, '"La Topographie Française" de Claude Chastillon. Proposition pour une grille d'analyse' in *Les Cahiers de la recherche architecturale* no. 18 (1985) pp. 54–73.

12 Recent studies on the gardens of the sixteenth century tend to reconsider the theory that before the seventeenth century there was no connection between the landscaping and architecture. On this subject, see J. Guillaume and C. Grodecki's 'Le jardin des pins à Fontainebleau', in *Bulletin de la Société de l'histoire de l'art français* (1978) pp. 43–51 and J. Guillaume 'Fontainebleau 1530. Le pavillon des armes et sa porte égyptienne', in *Bulletin Monumental* (1979), pp. 225–40.

Technology in the Park:
Engineers and Gardeners in
Seventeenth-Century France

Hélène Vérin

If the charm of a garden lies in the arrangement of its parts, it is by inviting the gaze to wander, the step to linger. It must use all its skill to lure the visitor.[1] Dezallier tells us that it must not 'weary the sight', but stimulate it,[2] 'not shock it,[3] 'not prevent the eye from looking around',[4] but suggest that it should 'suddenly espy'[5] 'a fine open view'[6] knowing, however, how to 'bring it skilfully to a halt'.[7] In order to encourage walking, the garden must be arranged in such a way as to avoid those slopes which 'weary and fatigue unduly'[8] and terraces, slopes and banks must be created 'sympathetically'.[9] Thus, those 'twenty considerable gardens around Paris which it is not necessary to visit, as they can be viewed in a single glance from the entrance hall of the building without unnecessary fatigue'[10] are the embodiment of failure: the fact is that there can be no pleasure without effort.[11]

Every action, mechanically speaking, can be analysed in terms of shape, size and movement. Whether it is agreed or not, this doctrine demands and imposes certain practices of construction. A garden is an artifice, and every artifice is characterized by a certain arrangement of its parts in relation to the whole, bearing in mind the desired end result. There is of course its 'quality of attraction' which must not only be capable of explanation, but must also be constructed. This is what gardeners work towards when putting together the causes which can produce this effect, which in its turn will generate movement. Physical impressions become spiritual emotions.

It would certainly be unreasonable to see in the design of the great seventeenth-century gardens the immediate application of the flourishing 'new sciences' and the underlying philosophical doctrines. Architects, engineers and gardeners do not need to delve into conflicting contemporary theories of vision in order to align avenues or position lakes and canals. The optical theories of Descartes and his adversary Bourdin are equally acceptable. On the other hand, the physical and geometric analysis of the interaction of bodies, and of body and mind, inspired comment not only from Dezallier, but also from Boyceau and Mollet: to a greater or lesser extent every gardener makes use of a 'natural philosophy' from the moment when he puts his mind to the plan until it is realized and *in situ*. The considerable development of gardens in the seventeenth century made this essential. It was impossible to work from sight only, helped by simple mason's tools, once the distances exceeded a certain limit. And geometry and geometric methods of measurement become especially indispensable when the aim is to make one simple garden where 'everything harmonizes' in one large open space. In these circumstances gardeners faced the same problems as military engineers, who had been facing them and solving them as best they could for almost a century. In the construction of bastioned fortresses in areas of war the same principle applied – all parts must harmonize. The greatest difficulties, according to the engineer Fabre in 1629, concerned 'continuous lines' which 'exceed 100 or 120 even to the extent of 200 *toises* [365 m; 400 yards] for a certain proportion must be observed between the place defended and the distance of the places from which comes their defence'[12] – or

equally, from which they could be attacked. To regulate these proportions, engineers had a standard measure: the range of the firearms which can or could be used in that situation, the angle of sight, direction of fire, and favourable or unfavourable disposition of buildings and apertures. The gardener, too, had at his disposal the range of the eye and its characteristics and possible movement. Doubtless he was also mindful of fortification works – this prestigious example of geometrically controlled space.

One does not have to be a historian to know that the construction of the great pleasure-gardens coincided with the destruction of fortified towns and residences in the French interior. If it would be foolish to see in this some sort of retaliation – entirely geometric – by landowners, there is no doubt that the techniques used by the engineers of the strongholds were also used for these showplaces. Equally, the same 'natural philosophy' is revealed in these two types of works, and further, they have a parallel evolution.

In 1563, when Bernard Palissy, in order to plan his stronghold, sought 'an example from the fortified towns' he turned his attention 'to contemplating the portraits of the sections and other shapes made by Maistres Jacques du Cerceau and several other artists'.[13] The palace of Daedalus was well defended by parterres and a labyrinth. Palissy's stronghold observed in effect the same principle: the assailant would lose himself and his forces in a system of defensive walls fitted one inside the other right into the heart of the town. But above all Palissy's model conforms with one major preoccupation – to avoid large apertures which could facilitate slaughter by cannon fire. It is deliberately conceived as the opposite of the bastioned systems princes were beginning to build throughout continental Europe, and it was also opposed to the concern of the state: protect the frontiers, certainly, but equally, avoid sedition.[14] Like his walled garden, Palissy's stronghold offers the people inside protection from external danger.

A century later another Palissy, visiting 'all the most excellent gardens it would be possible to discover' to help him in his design for a fortress,[15] would have discovered quite contrary theories, aimed at giving slopes in the land the visual appearance of a fortification; at assuming command by having an uninterrupted view over open space; and, for this reason at regulating the proportions and distances of the buildings erected, retaining vistas by means of axes of a length proportionate to the surrounding mass. All these are rules and regulations appropriate to the art of bastioned fortifications. Moreover, the parallel can be taken further – in the seventeenth century the design of gardens owes much to warfare.

When Colbert, concerned about the king's enthusiasm for Versailles, pointed out to him 'that in default of glorious deeds of war, nothing adds more to the glory of princes than buildings'[16] it could only be taken as an invitation to him to proceed with the architectural embellishment of his gardens. Indeed not only is the art of gardens inseparable from science and architecture[17] but it is also a contest between art and nature,[18] as can be seen, according to Charles de Sercy,

in the superb gardens of Vaux-le-Vicomte. In its nobility, this art is comparable to a tactical exercise.[19] It becomes not a botanical but a constructional problem, and rhetorical grandiloquence must be taken into account. Nevertheless, the 'natural philosophy' which guided engineers and master-craftsmen in the seventeenth century was guided by one principle: 'the world is composed of opposing parts, without which nothing can survive'.[20] Everything endures by means of this contradiction, this 'jealousy'. Trees and plants are jealous one of the other, as are rational and animal creatures,[21] in the same way as the parts of a machine or of a system of fortification.[22] This vital principle, if we are to believe A. de Ville,[23] this 'contrariety', this 'discord' must not be suppressed, but rather regulated by art. Only then will it be an imitation of nature and its wonders. The gardener must work like God, 'who has ordered and arranged things quite contrary to their qualities in such proportion that they continue without destroying each other'.[24] It is advisable to maintain proportional discord, without which harmony gives way to monotony. Variety and composition, diversity and disposition, ordered distribution, all these repeated injunctions in treatises on gardening make no appeal to inventive imagination, unless one remains constantly aware of the idea of conflict, ordered, certainly, but very active. Just as in music, where 'four good voices of different pitch are even more melodious and harmonious than if they were all in the same key: in like manner the harmony of the four simple bodies we call Elements is more perfect, their connection closer, as their qualities are at variance or even hostile: for their equal strengths are so admirably in proportion that no one can destroy another'.[25]

Balancing strengths to achieve proportion means introducing disparate qualities into the mass. Boulenger, author of a practical geometry reissued throughout the seventeenth century, and intended for architects, engineers, masons, surveyors and other geometricians including gardeners, supports and amends Claude Mollet's theories on music and the elements. They can indeed be found in Euclid, but this follower of Pythagoras was attempting to define a doctrine. Since it was a question of establishing the basis of a practical geometry, it was important to 'consider rather similarity of shape than exactitude: these shapes being only a symbol or indication of movement and rest'.[26] A 'positive science', according to the elder Nicéron, which 'prescribes rules and gives precepts for practice'[27] thus becomes an art. Desargues summarizes its uses: 'as far as the arts of handicraft are concerned, if you would have a thorough understanding of them there are three matters to be carefully distinguished: first, what is to be done; second, the method of doing it; and third, to do it effectively'.[28] After which, Desargues can proclaim the positive doctrine: there are cognitive processes leading to action, and they are infallible. Of these processes, some are easier to learn than others, but above all, those more easily understood are normally also more expeditious in action.

The confidence inspired by this method arises from the idea that an art is well conceived if it imitates, in its application, a design of nature which could be attributed to the Creator. 'Man sets himself up as a little

Perspective view of the castle of Meudon (Hauts-de-Seine). Engraving after I. Silvestre, 1700. Bibliothèque Nationale, Cabinet des Estampes, Paris.

View of the canal and the great cascades at Vaux-le-Vicomte. Engraving by Aveline. Bibliothèque Nationale, Cabinet des Estampes, Paris.

god'[29] when he applies himself to redesigning in his garden a 'nature' symphathetic to him because he has conceived it, and he understands it according to his rules and his principles. It is an idealistic concept in which tacticians and gardeners are united in utterances such as: 'As it is not the mass of men who draw up battle orders, but the commander-in-chief, so in Nature matter does not run wild, but moves according to rules of form which mould and move the mass at will. Whence comes the shape'.[30] With nature and artifice under one command a new ideal emerges which would allow what is to be done, the means and the execution to be under one sole control with a single purpose in mind. Desargues is too intelligent to venture further, and it is generally agreed that, since there is a choice, success is not infallible and there are no inviolable rules.[31] Nevertheless such an ideal is not easily ignored. The reasoning, moreover, is simple: the theory exists, it is merely giving guidance about the form of the desired object. Now form derives from the idea of the object. The best course – and this distinguishes the good architect – is to conceive simultaneously the idea and the shape. This is what we expect from the design. It is not an intermediary shape between conception and realization or between the survey of the available land and the completed garden, it is the consideration of what has to be done, deliberation, consideration and reconsideration, and then effective execution. The geometric design, the supply of mathematical instruments, ensure control of the scheme and of the raw material, this 'examination' of nature and its secrets, to return to Boyceau's formula.[32]

If, then, we are to follow Desargues's division – what is to be done, the means and the realization – it is from the second premise that we must start. When Boyceau appeals to the 'science of portraiture, base and foundation of all mechanical skills'[33] and makes 'the ordering and disposition of gardens and their embellishment' dependent on knowledge of it, he determines the systematic discipline to which pleasure-gardens will henceforth be subject. It is worth noting that at the same time he justifies his statement: proposing forms and models is meaningless unless the gardeners are familiar with the rules and the instruments required. The manipulation of scale is essential. This will enable the gardener to enlarge or diminish shapes without spoiling the proportions 'making them suit his plan and the situation'.[34] Claude Mollet insists that what is essential for the gardener is 'not to omit taking measurements following the scale'.[35] When he has mastered this skill, all he will need to do when faced with a space too large or too small is to alter the scale – 'he must make the gauge marked on the scale greater or lesser'.[36] In this way he will be able to produce models as in the *Théâtre de plans et jardinages*. This will not be without repercussions on the principles of the trade. The master-gardener will have to give up 'boasting that he is indebted to no-one'.[37] He must get rid of all the preconceived ideas which obstruct good workmanship and exercise his inventive wisdom when confronted by new schemes. The gardener ignorant of design will lack 'any imagination or judgement concerning ornaments and their disposition' over such a wide area.[38] The

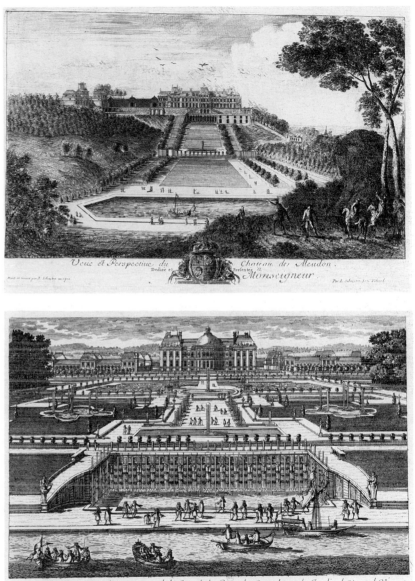

Le Petit Parc, Versailles: bosquet *of the Three Fountains, by Cotelle. Musée de Versailles.*

Frontispiece, with a portrait of Claude Mollet, author of Théâtre des plans et jardinages, *Paris 1652.*

'construction' of the space to be managed operates, therefore, in each of its phases: it is advisable to know how to 'decide on the form' of the terrain and of the watercourses by means of surveying and contouring, 'to draw up plans and elevations' in order to decide 'whether the arrangement is pleasing, if the different parts are suited one to another', and to appraise 'the work before it is undertaken'.[39] The ability to transfer the design from paper to work on the ground is a very delicate task which requires surveying methods and instruments; then the preparation of the terrain, ordering the contours by using a gauge and by the construction of terraces, slopes and banks, is a process borrowed directly from military engineers. All these processes, because of the considerable theoretical work involved – even if the operator uses the instruments without being aware of the underlying principles – make an uncultivated area very 'sensitive' to instruments of measurement.

The proliferation of mathematical instruments throughout the seventeenth century should not obscure the fact that the principle observed in the most elaborate – the ratio between lengths and angles – could be seen in many instruments already in existence in the mid-sixteenth century. When Palissy lists those used in the construction of his garden – compass, ruler, set square, plumb-line, bevel and astrolabe – he is more meticulous than Dezallier in 1709. Indeed, at the end of the seventeenth century each of these instruments had been perfected in precision and suitability for the required tasks. The rules required different sorts of proportional divisions, which differed according to their usage. D'Aviler lists nine types of compass. The bevel was fitted with a gauge and became a pantometer. The set square increased the number of its sight-vanes to eight instead of four and thus served 'gardeners to align and plant avenues of trees in star-form'.[40] It no longer resembled the mason's square.[41] The use of the board became more common and made it possible to draw horizontal angles directly, on sight. (But this was an English sixteenth-century invention). On the other hand levels – different sorts of levels – were considerably improved, not least by the use of field glasses instead of simple sight-vanes.

All these instruments would have been useless without experience in using them. A study of the numerous treatises on practical geometry throws light on the difficulties: the use of them must be 'facilitated', they must be 'simplified', the 'memory' must be considerably 're-freshed' as regards the rules of arithmetic. Obviously precision is particularly necessary when the works, often political, military or economic, are important. The management of land in constructing a garden always incurs considerable expense. In order to level the ground, and prepare the sloping areas the 'winding' of the hillside must be precisely measured, and the outline surveyed and drawn, so as to place the terraces economically and prudently. The chief concern is to avoid removing a great deal of earth.[42] Only an architect or an engineer can have sufficient knowledge, both practical and theoretical, of the pressures of the earth and, in different soils, of the amount of gradient necessary to construct slopes and banks. Terraces faced with stone

resemble bastions, and when Dezallier defines what is known as *pleinpied* he feels obliged to state that it is 'what is called a *terreplein* (earth platform) as a term of fortification'.[43] Treatises on fortification are indeed more detailed about these practices, the instruments and methods more exactly described, and the theory justifying the choice indicated. And always, as with our gardens, there is a question of economy. Adapting a hillside as naturally as possible is not so much a question of aesthetics, as of good works management.[44]

Again, it must be emphasized that work of political and military importance requires precision. This is assured in the 'science of surveying' whose methods were used by gardeners in the second half of the seventeenth century for on-the-spot planning. Even if this science improved greatly with a view to levying taxes and for sales of property,[45] the development in topographical methods is above all due to new military practices: and war is often a question of siege and the advance reconnaissance of the outskirts of a town under attack – by longstanding tradition the work of an engineer.[46] If de Ville protests about the use of these 'mathematical instruments which serve no purpose in capturing places'[47] engineers must nevertheless use them to plan their trenches and dispose their guns in good range. As for the artillery, the quadrant and the square are as much part of its equipment as the transport. Precision in measurement is essential in a war which pits artifice against artifice. Machines such as cannon must be regulated, the range of the missiles being dependent on the angle of fire. The height and depth of space can be measured mechanically, and it is no longer only visible space which can be measured, but also areas covered by the planned trajectory of missiles.

There is one area where precision in measuring requires a different, if not more profound, appreciation of space, and this is in surveying. It is doubtless also in the practice of this art that the delicacy of the artifice and the high degree of skill required in its proper usage are, surprisingly, contrary to conventional practices.

Certainly gardeners' levels generally lack the precision of those developed by members of the Academy of Science. These latter were used for surveying the Grand Canal at Versailles, carried out, Charles Perrault records, by these gentlemen, who attained such a degree of precision that over nearly 900 *toises* (1650 m; 1800 yards) surveyed there was an error of only two to three inches (five to eight centimetres). Nothing gives a better understanding of the difficulties of these procedures than Perrault's explanation of the advantages of the instruments then in use.

This great precision was achieved not only by the skill of the surveyors but also by the superiority of the level, hitherto unequalled. This superiority had three principal features; first, instead of the string which masons usually attach to the level, the academicians introduced a very long female hair which makes the plumb-line infinitely more exact; secondly this hair is enclosed in a metal tube to prevent movement by the wind. There is an opening in the tube at the spot where the hair indicates the perpendicular: this opening is covered with glass to keep out the wind and permit readings. Thirdly, a field glass is fixed to the cross-member of the level. This field glass stabilizes the view to such an extent that it is possible to measure exactly distances of one to two hundred *toises* [up to 365 m; 400 yards] without a hairsbreadth of inaccuracy. None of the workmen could understand how this accuracy could be achieved, for with their ordinary levels they could not survey thirty *toises* [55 m; 60 yards] without an error of three or four inches [eight to ten cms].[48]

Many canals had been surveyed without these refinements, by means of levels with coarser and less supple 'hairs' which swayed in the wind and gave an unsteady view, and sightings subject to changing refraction whose effects were not known, carried out by surveyors who were often only village masons. For assistant helpers it was essential, according to the treatises, to choose men adept enough to learn and remember the coded signals needed to convey orders when beyond call. It is easy to imagine the scene, which emphasizes Picard's methodical strictness in his survey of the heights and slopes of the Seine and the Loire.[49] His meticulous approach gives credence to two normally contradictory ideas about perceived space: that the line of sight is no longer straight beyond a certain distance, since refractions make it curve; and that the apparent level must be corrected. This latter makes 'a right angle with the perpendicular which is a line which leads to the centre of the earth, marks the horizontal.' But this line 'rises above the true level just as a tangent withdraws from the circumference of a circle as it leaves the point at which it touches'.[50] Beyond one hundred *toises*, the surveyor is out in space.[51]

All these geometric practices, writes Nicéron in 1638, owe their instruments to perspective.[52] The architecture of buildings and gardens takes 'order from it for their symmetry and grace' and they are considered beautiful only 'in so far as they please the eye by their proportions'.[53] These practices, and the experiments connected with them, make an important contribution to new classifications of knowledge concerning the visible world. Perspective is assimilated into an application of optics which is further elaborated in the three types: geometric optics, dioptrics (refraction), and catoptrics (reflection),[54] 'new sciences' which were undoubtedly developing, while the natural philosophy of theories of vision and light was beset by Cartesian mechanism which was attempting, less confidently than in optics, research into causes according to the physics of movement and rest. However, the doctrine of opposites generally prevailed among supporters of the art. Certainly it became clarified in appraisals carried out as a result of experiments. But whether these were purely tentative, or influenced by hasty analogical induction, they very often served only to support previous theories, sometimes even favouring a return to theoretical, even 'theological' geometry (to come back to Boulenger's formula) in search of some 'divine proportion'.

It was in the midst of all this ferment of learning and activity that the great gardens were conceived. That they own much to the science of perspective is obvious. Boyceau and Claude Mollet bear witness to this, as do Olivier de Serres, Salomon de Caus, du Breuil, Binet, Desargues, Nicéron, and later Dezallier, d'Aviler, Ozanam – there are few works

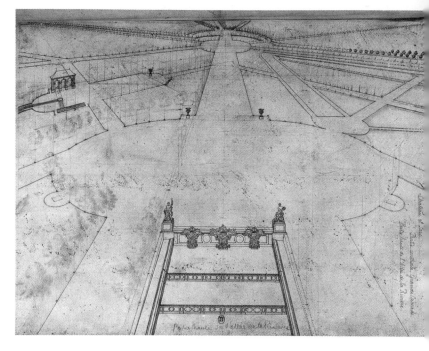

on perspective which do not give gardens as examples of its application, and everything in these gardens is arranged, from the beginning of the century, according to the art of perspective. It prevails above all in the symmetry, axial or otherwise[55] and in the arrangement of the terraces from which the range of vision dominates the whole.[56] According to the laws of optics, visual imperfections become its 'natural state' and can be exploited for simulation. Objects are brought closer; lengthy avenues discourage the walker, so the length is reduced by narrowing or concealing the extremity, by hiding part of it from sight.[57] To lengthen the avenues one can, if the garden is large enough, open it on to the surrounding countryside. If, on the other hand, it is small, care must be taken 'not to make all the avenues go from one end to the other';[58] and even – the best device of all – 'shortcomings' in proportions, due to some wall or displeasing angle, could be remedied by 'adjusting' with edgings of trees against the walls 'to make an agreeable deceit by the considerable extent which makes it appear an enclosure',[59] or 'by remedying it with the brush' by painting in perspectives[60] 'in such a way', wrote Salomon de Caus in 1612, 'that when one is at a distance of a hundred feet from the said wall, at a window thirty-five feet from the ground, it will seem that the said painted garden is natural and contingent with the one which is natural.'[61]

Where is the 'natural' when the space is broken up into obviously variable spaces according to all sorts of possible 'projections', the eye being held close to, or drawn afar, fixed, or in movement?[62] When the 'true spaces' are increased according to the scales of different practices? What is to be done about the tricks of perspective in these gardens when the visitor, leaving his place at the window, the hall or the terrace, sets out to visit them?

From 1642 any architect, engineer or master-craftsman in charge of the design and controlling the scale could plan a perspective garden suited to the area he was to develop. Since the whole of his work consisted in the arrangement of the different parts, it was enough for him to follow the models offered by Boyceau, Mollet and others such as the Abbé du Breuil. 'Plans', he wrote, 'must be made as on sheet 35, 38, or 113 which may be divided into sections as one pleases'.[63] There was no lack of patterns, and shapes could even be taken from Turkish embroideries or tapestries.[64] 'If you desire arbours', continues du Breuil, 'you will find instructions on sheets 60 or 61. If you prefer fencing to arbours, or avenues of trees, sheet 112 gives several examples of procedure'.[65] Similarly for fountains, there is a choice. To assist this choice du Breuil gives virtually no other guide than attractiveness, proportion and symmetry, avoiding confusion and giving the whole an air of grandeur. Nothing gives a better idea of the tedium which this sort of garden can generate than that which one suspects in the architect producing these compositions. It is the professional art of design. With form systematized, 'the idea' is lost in conformity.

When Dezallier points out the shortcomings of these plans and arrangements he finds it difficult to explain them other than by lack of 'the necessary intelligence' which comes, he says, 'from further off than one thinks'. To succeed, in addition to some knowledge one needs 'intelligence and natural good taste which must have been formed by the sight of beautiful objects, by criticizing the bad and by diligent practice in the art of gardening'.[66] We have returned to Desargues, to the first of the three considerations in manual work: what has to be done 'when there is a choice; I cannot see that, to ensure success, there must be certain established and inviolable rules'.[67] Yet Dezallier has one imperative guiding rule which orders these dispositions: the same rule which controls the different areas of a system of fortifications. We could be reading Vauban, or the fortification engineers who were his contemporaries. The doctrine of opposites has given way to a meticulous evaluation of the advantages, and the skill consists in an ordering of normal and artifical elements in which reason prevails over the impetuosity of genius, the nobility of nature over artificial affectations.[68] The perfection of the plan can be measured by the economy of the means to execute it: the three principles Desargues selected depend on each other according to the rules of a sort of technocracy.[69] Herein it may be that we are trying to defend ourselves against a platitude, currently repeated everywhere, that architects, unlike engineers, are unable to justify the reasons for their choice, or explain the thinking behind it.

This is also the criticism levelled against mechanistic philosophy. Bayle used to say, not without a certain malice, that when Cartesians recite the list of principles of their physics, they begin with 'intellect', and then forget it.[70] The whole of practical geometry would not compose a science of mechanics, nor would the whole of mechanics constitute a body of physics, were it not inspired by intelligence – that of God in nature, that of the craftsman in his design. Thus, when La Fontaine praised the beauty of Versailles, he 'took the opportunity to speak of intelligence, which is the essence of these marvels'.[71] In the realm of le Nôtre, 'man sets himself up as a little god'.

[1] In *La Promenade de Versailles* Mlle de Scudéry emphasizes Louis XIV's obvious pleasure in showing visitors his gardens; see too Félibien: the gardens at Versailles which are the great king's delight, are 'visited by all the important people in France', *Description sommaire du château de Versailles* (Paris 1674), p. 5.
[2] Dezallier d'Argenville, *La théorie et la pratique du jardinage . . .* (Paris, edn of 1713), p. 61.
[3] *Ibid.*, p. 24.
[4] *Ibid.*, p. 19.
[5] *Ibid.*
[6] *Ibid.*, p. 37.
[7] *Ibid.*, p. 20.
[8] *Ibid.*, pp. 24–5.
[9] Charles d'Aviler, *Cours d'architecture* (Paris, 1696) Vol. 2, article: *Glacis*.
[10] Dezallier, *op. cit.*, p. 19.
[11] Through a quasi-mechanical training, the idea of arrangement immediately implies that of action. Speaking of the Allée d'Eau at Versailles, Félibien says, 'what is worthy of note is the pleasing arrangement of all these children and their different attitudes', *op. cit.*, p. 64.
[12] Fabre, *Les pratiques du Sr Fabre . . .* (1629).
[13] Bernard Palissy, *Recepte véritable par laquelle tous les hommes de la France pourront apprendre à multiplier et augmenter leurs thrésors* (La Rochelle 1563): ed. *Oeuvres complètes* (Paris 1961), p. 214.
[14] Whence the importance of the citadel, erected as a precaution against possible uprisings. In the seventeenth century squares were classed as small, medium or large according to the proportion of soldiers to inhabitants.
[15] Bernard Palissy, *op. cit.*, p. 214.
[16] P. Clément, *Lettres . . . de Colbert*, Vol. 2 (Paris 1886). Letter of 20 September 1663.
[17] See for example Charles d'Aviler, *Cours d'architecture* (Paris 1696), article: *Jardins*.
[18] Charles de Sercy. The dedication to Nicolas Fouquet of *Théâtres des plans et jardinages* by Claude Mollet (Paris 1652) p. iii.
[19] 'In the past the greatest kings of the realm . . . took as much care in the arrangement of an orchard as of an Army; and we have seen a Diocletian . . . taking more account of planting trees in a row than of drawing up his squadrons in battle', *ibid*. p. iii.
[20] Antoine de Ville, *La fortification du chevalier A. de Ville* (Lyon, edn. of 1666), p. 211.
[21] Claude Mollet, *op. cit.*, p. 119.
[22] Ozanam, for example, speaks of the 'jealousy' between different parts of a system of fortifications in his *Dictionnaire de mathématiques* (Paris 1689), article: *Fortifications*.
[23] 'The immortality of species is perpetuated by the corruption of individuals who taint each other by an excess of qualities . . . one form pursues another, and all is conflict'. *op. cit.*, p. 211.
[24] Claude Mollet, *op. cit.*, p. 229.
[25] *Ibid.*
[26] *La géométrie pratique du Sr Boulenger*, Ozanam's edn (Paris 1691) p. 268. (1st edn 1624).
[27] P. J. F. Nicéron, *La perspective curieuse* (Paris 1638), p. 11.
[28] A. Bosse, *Manière universelle de Mr Desargues, pour pratiquer la perspective par petit-pied, comme le géométral* (Paris 1648), p. 7.
[29] R. P. Etienne Binet, *Essay des merveilles de nature et des plus nobles artifices* (Rouen 1629), p. 456.
[30] Fleurance-Rivault, *Les elemens de l'artillerie* (Paris 1612), p. 3.
[31] Bosse, *op. cit.*, preface.
[32] Jacques Boyceau de la Baraudière, *Traité du jardinage selon les raisons de la nature et de l'art* (Paris 1638), p. 31 (1st edn 1636).
[33] Boyceau, *op. cit.*, p. 68.
[34] *Ibid.*
[35] Claude Mollet, *op. cit.*, p. 192.
[36] *Ibid.*
[37] *Ibid.*, p. 201.
[38] *Ibid.*, p. 201.
[39] Boyceau, *op. cit.*, p. 68.
[40] Nicolas Bion, *Traité de la construction et des principaux usages des instrumens de mathématiques*, 3rd edn (Paris 1723), p. 110.
[41] Dezallier, *op. cit.*, p. 97.
[42] *Ibid.*, p. 133.
[43] *Ibid.*, p. 139.
[44] Claude Mollet gives details of the method of measuring the draining of land by means of a marker 'on which he will make a sign with a seal and Spanish wax so that it cannot be moved', *op. cit.*, pp. 317–8. This was current practice and inevitable when it was necessary

System of water distribution in the park. From A.-J. Dezallier d'Argenville, La Théorie et la pratique du jardinage, Paris 1713.

Method of laying out the design of a parterre. From A.-J. Dezallier d'Argenville, La Théorie et la pratique du jardinage, Paris 1713.

Method of levelling land for the laying out of terraces. From A.-J. Dezallier d'Argenville, La Théorie et la pratique du jardinage, Paris 1713.

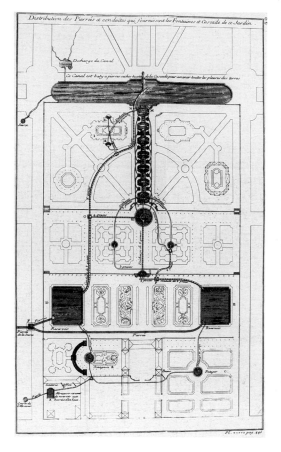

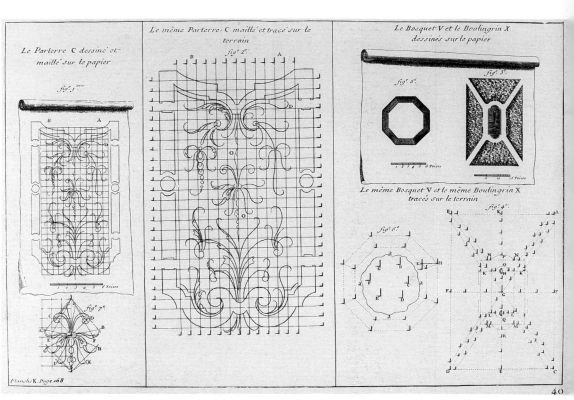

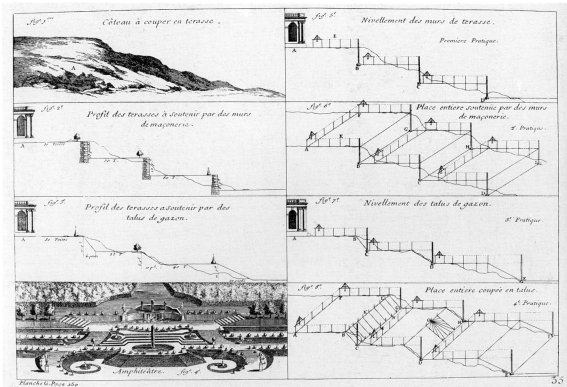

*Levels and methods of levelling. From
N. Bion,* Traité de la construction . . .
des instrumens mathématiques,
Paris 1709.

not only to excavate foundations, but to level large surfaces, as in the case of gardens and fortifications; see A. Manesson-Mallet, *Les travaux de Mars* (Paris 1672), p. 316, 'of the transport of earth with the means of these leaning indicators'.

45 According to Claude Flamand who claims that of geometric surveying he 'found nothing written, except in the Maison Rustique': *La pratique et usage d'arpenter* (Montbéliard 1611).

46 Even if we confine ourselves to medieval Europe see for example: in *Floir et Blanceflor* (twelfth century), 'Vassal, are you an engineer, that you are here measuring our land?'

47 A. de Ville, *op. cit.*, p. 292.

48 Charles Perrault, *Mémoires* . . . (Avignon 1759), pp. 167–8.

49 To provide Versailles with water, it was a question of diverting part of the river Loire as far as the hills of Satory near Versailles. Riquet, relying on the survey he had had done, was very anxious to achieve this. Colbert was in favour of the project. The agreement was prepared. Perrault recounts that 'M. le Nostre said two days ago to the King, when he was accompanying him along the banks of the canal at Versailles, that it would be a fine thing to see the masts and sails of the Loire vessels coming down past the mountain', *op. cit.*, p. 417. Picard, after an intervention by Perrault – if the latter is to be believed – was instructed to check Riquet's allegations. 'Since the matter in question was a very great enterprise, he made his observations with all possible precision'. La Hire, preface to Picard's *Traité du nivellement* (Paris 1684) p. a ii v°.

50 Jean Picard, *op. cit.*, p. 3.

51 The correction was made by means of a table drawn up by Picard. At 100 *toises* the rise is 1⅓ lines; at 600, 4 in.; at 4000, 14 ft 8 in.; see Picard *op. cit.*, p. 4 (1 *toise* = 1.949 m; 6 ft or 1 fathom).

52 'His quadrants, Jacob's staffs and other instruments for measuring length, width, height and depth', Nicéron, *op. cit.*, preface.

53 *Ibid.*, preface.

54 *Ibid.*, p. 11.

55 There is a view 'from the entrance hall', Dezallier *op. cit.* p. 19 and the great central avenue is obligatory. It is from here that the surveying of the terrain and the alignments begins, see Claude Mollet: 'I advise him [the gardener] to establish the true centre of the building: after that he can set up his compass or his square . . .', *op. cit.* p. 326.

56 'It being a question of looking from a distance at the different parts of the establishment of the garden, it is better to place the rows of these further from rather than nearer to each other . . . reducing the size of each object in relation to the distance because of perspective

. . . for which reason it is desirable that gardens should be viewed from above, or from neighbouring buildings or raised terraces around the parterre'. Olivier de Serres, *Théâtre d'agriculture ou mesnage des champs* (Paris 1600), p. 581.

57 Concerning these practices, see M. Charageat 'André le Nostre et l'optique de son temps' in *Bulletin de la Société de l'histoire de l'art français* (1955) pp. 66ff. M. Charageat sees in P. le Muet's plan of the canal at Tanlay an application of Boyceau's doctrine concerning the conjunction of lines of perspective. Le Nôtre at Vaux, Chantilly, the Tuileries, St Germain and Versailles made a different use of perspective to obtain effects of foreshortening with the help of the proportional arrangement of successive lakes.

58 Dezallier, *op. cit.*, p. 36.

59 *Ibid.* p. 20.

60 Du Breuil, *La perspective pratique*, Vol. 3, part 3. Introduction to the third treatise.

61 Saloman de Caus, *La perspective avec la raison des ombres et miroirs* (London 1612).

62 P. P. Bourdin, *Le dessein ou la perspective militaire* (Paris 1655) p. 10.

63 Du Breuil *op. cit.* Vol. 3, p. ii.

64 Claude Mollet, *op. cit.*, p. 190.

65 Du Breuil, *op. cit.*, p. ii.

66 Dezallier, *op. cit.*, p. 16.

67 Bosse, *op. cit.*, preface p. 1.

68 Dezallier, *op. cit.*, p. 15, 'for the greatest skill in planning a garden is a thorough knowledge and examination of the natural advantages and drawbacks of the situation, in order to profit from the one and correct the other'; 'when he wants to conceive a fine plan, making skilful and economical use of the advantages of the site and industriously correcting the drawbacks, slopes and unevennesses in the terrain'. Almost word for word these passages could be part of any contemporary treatise on fortification. This concern to adapt to the site and the terrain within economic limits has always been of prime importance, and has directed research in methods of fortification. The change that took place at the end of the seventeenth century was the establishment of criteria: quantified proportions which permit corresponding variations.

69 It would be wise to make a closer examination of arguments put forward in Dezallier's work which is complex and often contradictory: it should be noted that here he makes an explicit attack on the *nouveaux riches* who imagine that the more costly a garden, the more beautiful it is.

70 Bayle, *Dictionnaire historique et critique* (Amsterdam, edn of 1740) Vol. 2, p. 70, article: *Caïnites*.

71 La Fontaine, *Les Amours de Psyché et de Cupidon* (Paris, edn of 1795) p. 97.

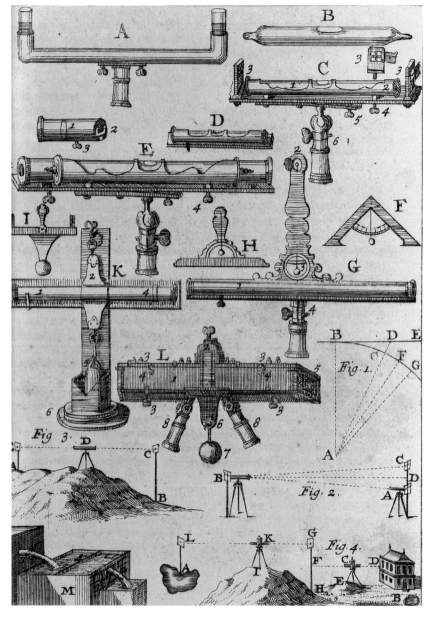

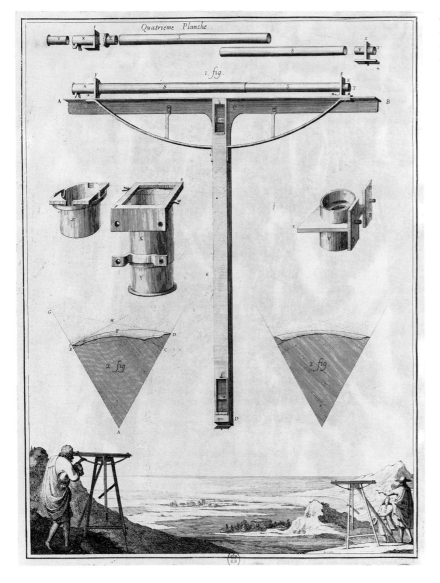

Instrument for calculating levels. From Jean Picard, Traité du nivellement, *Paris 1684. Bibliothèque Nationale, Cabinet des Estampes, Paris.*

The Italian Baroque and Rococo Garden

Anna Maria Matteucci

On 11 September 1714, the day of the marriage of Isabella Farnese to Philip V of Spain, an anonymous chronicler recorded the presence of a number of illustrious visitors to the garden of the ducal palace at Colorno, near Parma. His description is particularly valuable because it documents the appearance of the place just six years after the departure of Ferdinando Bibiena from the Farnese court, where he had spent more than twenty-five years – though not uninterruptedly – in the service of the duke, and had been appointed chief architect. At that time, 'every building, and even every vista, whether in Parma, in Piacenza, or in the delightful garden at Colorno, employed the ideas and the services of Bibiena, who was undoubtedly without equal'[1]

The *Delizie farnesiane* of 1726, the celebrated series of engravings of Colorno, show the park at a more advanced stage, however. By then the hydraulic engineer Jean Baillieul had already been at work there for some time, and seems to have played an important role above all in developing the watercourses and in designing automata for the grottoes. But in 1714 the guests at the royal wedding could already admire 'the three great drives leading from the garden to the wood . . . [and] the orderly division of the wood, vast as it is, into equal sections by means of an infinite number of neat paths, which . . . form perfectly circular open spaces where they intersect'.

It was indubitably, as the engravings of the *Delizie farnesiane* illustrate, a splendid and extremely well-ordered park. In the accompanying text, eulogies are devoted to the 'beautiful fountains' built around 1712, mostly by the architect-sculptor Giuliano Mozani, who had taken over the task of directing operations after the departure of Ferdinando Bibiena. By the time the engravings were made, the Trianon Fountain had already been built, proof of the widespread fame of the original at Versailles.

The early assimilation of French ideas and influences makes it difficult to identify at Colorno essentially Italian characteristics, or rather features typical of the work of Bibiena. Scenes depicting early designs for the garden – for example the water-colour *The Royal Palace of Diana* in the Metropolitan Museum in New York – show plans for great avenues of cypresses and poplars, and for four rows of trees radiating like the spokes of a fan, very much in harmony with the ideas emerging at that time from the French school of garden design. But it is also true to say that the use of the diagonal line inspired schemes in which angles played an important part, as they did in Bibiena's scenic and decorative work. It should be remembered too that the 'garden landscape' of Emilia Romagna is based on the planting of poplar trees in long straight rows stretching out across the fields from the villas (the work of the young Guercino is reminiscent of it), and that this must have influenced Bibiena considerably. His genius can perhaps be seen most clearly in the 'vast expanse of the Orangery', whose elliptical plan, with its five rows of containers, recalls the colonnade of St Peter's Square in Rome; it is laid out on two levels, which enables each tree to be seen individually and creates an uninterrupted view from the centre of the great staircase with which it is aligned. The difference in height between the levels is minimal but enough to be extremely effective, and visitors to this 'great theatre of citrus trees' are always impressed.[2]

The presence in Italy of French gardeners, and above all of French hydraulic engineers, was soon well documented, and much was also being written on the subject of gardens themselves by writers on the other side of the Alps. Among the books in the library of the wealthy Sorra family of Modena were '*Il Giardino francese* by M. René Dahavron, Venice 1704, *Le jardinier solitaire*, Rigud, Paris 1704 . . . *Instruzione per il giardino*, Paris 1678, . . . *Labirinto di Versailles* . . . *Plans and designs of gardens and other views* by S. Bouteux, two volumes . . . manuscripts', all dating from the end of the seventeenth century[3] or the beginning of the eighteenth, and possibly acquired in connection with plans for the villa at Panzano, which in all probability date from the first decade of the eighteenth century.

One must remember, after all, that it was Le Nôtre who laid out the great park of the castle at Racconigi,[4] and there one can clearly see the extent to which the French style influenced Baroque traditions that were typically Italian. It is well known that Guarino Guarini produced a fascinating series of drawings which included not only plans for the transformation of the castle but also a meticulous record of the layout of the park. Among his carefully devised and extremely ingenious designs for the great staircase leading to the *piano nobile* is one based on a lozenge or diamond shape similar to that later used by Bibiena at Colorno; other drawings underline the close relationship between the ducal residence and the service buildings, some of them screened by colonnades, that surround it. Indeed, it should be stressed at this point that above and beyond the undeniably strong influence of French developments on the Italian garden of the period, the placing of the villa in relation to the outbuildings and the garden was very often quintessentially Italian and generally Rococo in character, its origins lying in the great architectural lessons taught by Borromeo and Guarini. The extraordinary villa at Bagheria, near Palermo, which was built by Tommaso Maria Napoli, is a fine example of this relationship in that the lines of the main house are accentuated and complemented by the range of low buildings surrounding it, and by the long series of walks on hanging terraces[5] running close to the villa.

The terrace became a sort of *topos* in the villas of the eighteenth century, where very often it culminated in an elegant group of statuary: for instance, in the gardens of the Villa della Rovere at Albissola, designed by Girolamo Brusca,[6] where mirror-like pools were laid out along the terraces, which were connected by ornamental flights of steps; at the Palazzo Tarsia in Naples,[7] designed by Domenico Antonio Vaccaro, with 'a glazed floor painted with arabesques, *putti* and festoons of flowers . . .'; and the hanging terrace walks of the Villa Trissino (now Marzotto), which link the *piano nobile* with the slope of the nearby hillside and thus enclose the great courtyard.[8] At the Portici Royal Palace near Naples, built by Antonio Canevari, two great terraces extend like outstretched wings along the splendid garden laid out by Francesco Geri.[9]

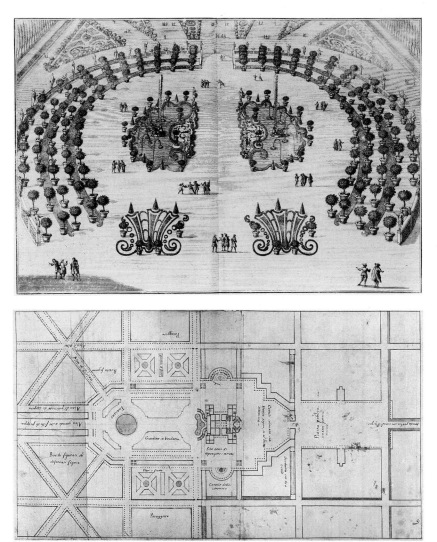

In order to appreciate the variety to be found in the eighteenth-century Baroque gardens of Italy, it is necessary to bear in mind the purpose of the buildings they were designed to serve, the social and economic status of the owner, and of course the extent of the land available. Ever since the days of the Arcadian gardens of ancient Rome, the ruling families, major and minor nobility, scholars, doctors and merchants had all created gardens which in some way reflected their position in society and their economic standing as well as their personal tastes.[10]

The invention of the terrace and of long raised walks derived not only from a desire to integrate the fabric of the building into the land surrounding it but also from a wish to create a variety of viewpoints and theatrical perspectives. In this connection too, the influence of Bibiena and the concepts of theatrical design were strongly in evidence in the great gardens of Italy: in Lombardy, for instance, villa architects such as Federico Pietrasanta were responsible for a number of important and highly dramatic projects. Many of the parks that appear in *Ville di delizia*, particularly those illustrated with engravings by Marc'Antonio dal Re, demonstrate the desire both to extend the variety of the views and to lift the curtain on them only gradually, as it were, by screening vistas in such a way that their revelation introduced an element of surprise and drama, such as can be found in the contemporaneous work of Galliari or Pietro Righini for example.

Features such as delicate wrought-iron gates, or pillars placed at oblique angles and surmounted by lively sculptures, served as highly effective devices in masking a distant view. In neglected gardens, where much of the planting scheme has been lost, one is sometimes even more sharply aware of how carefully such features were originally placed in order to accentuate a perspective, enclose a space or screen a vista. An instance in which gates and groups of statuary were used to highly dramatic effect can be seen in the designs of Massari for the Villa Cordellina, where the garden perfectly counterbalances the severity of the house.[11]

Marc'Antonio dal Re's description of the Villa Brentano di Corbetta indicates very clearly the scheme carried out there by Francesco Croce in 1737, in which much emphasis was placed on 'fleeting glimpses' and 'sudden views'. Dal Re dwells at length on the fact that the windows of the garden front of the villa were designed in such a way that 'with bizarre inventiveness Croce has ensured that each one corresponds with a particular avenue ... running either at right angles or diagonally, creating a precisely calculated and highly individual artistic effect'.[12] The trapezoidal shape of the garden and the layout of the villa itself – based on the traditional Lombardy U-plan – lent themselves perfectly to this concept: the forecourt was enclosed by lower service buildings which shielded the villa from the adjoining farmyard, while openings at intervals offered glimpses of wider views beyond. Croce was much influenced in his designs for the villa by the work of the Roman architect Giovanni Ruggeri, who led the way to important new developments in the design of the villa in Lombardy in the eighteenth

Park of the Villa Pisani (now Nazionale) at Stra, Venice: the orangery and the casino. (Photo Luigi Ghirri)

149

Garden of Isola Bella, Lake Maggiore: the amphitheatre and the terraces. (Photos Daniele De Lonte)

150

View of Isola Bella on Lake Maggiore.
Engraving from M. dal Re, Ville di
delizia, *eighteenth century.*

century. He was also responsible for the introduction of some spectacular garden features: just as Rococo designers loved, for example, to transform balusters into strange asymmetrical scrolls like stylized waves, following Ruggeri's lead, pavilions, fountains and staircases were created in the most bizarre and extravagant forms.

Strong similarities can be seen to exist between these Italian Rococo inventions and those to be found in some of the gardens of the German-speaking Catholic countries; the group of sculpture designed by Ferdinando Tietz for the park at Seehof is a good example, though of a slightly later date.

As part of his modernization of the Visconti castle of Brignano d'Adda (1710), Ruggeri converted the ancient bastions into raised walks ornamented in a style that was perfectly in keeping with his decorative scheme for the interior of the building. And it was with this desire for a truly Rococo plasticity of form that he embellished the balusters and enclosing wall of the park of Villa Arconati at Castellazzo in Lombardy (which dal Re claims were designed by the Frenchman Jean Janda, though a similar scheme, perhaps even more Rococo in style, can still be seen in what remains of the eighteenth-century garden of the Villa Belgioioso).[13]

Another name that should be mentioned in this connection is that of Francesco Muttoni, an architect active in the Vicenza area in the eighteenth century and involved in the creation of the famous garden of the Villa Trissino.[14] The imaginative culmination of the whole scheme in a sort of exedra from which four openings give access to walks and to a balcony-belvedere would be hard to appreciate fully without some knowledge of the work of Ruggeri which inspired it. So many of the most splendid examples of the Italian Rococo garden have unfortunately been irretrievably lost that it is virtually impossible now to set this complex design into its proper context.

It is also difficult to date precisely many of the parks – or the fountains, statuary and other features they contained – that were laid out in the seventeenth century, even when the date of the villa is known. There is no doubt, however, that they were practically all preceded by that fascinating series of schemes devised by Juvara for the gardens of Lucca.[15]

In order to comprehend the nature of the Italian Rococo garden, it is helpful to study in detail the plans signed by Muttoni and probably drawn up before 1718, though only partially carried out, for the transformation of the gardens of Trissino. In the very first part of the list of work to be undertaken, which included the enlargement of the villa itself, reference is made to the plans for 'intersections' and 'vistas', indicating their priority over every aspect of the scheme.[16] The vistas were not directed exclusively to one particular point in the park but were intended to lead the eye in various directions towards the surrounding landscape. Lines marked in yellow on the plans linked the new entrance at the front of the building in a straight perspective with the atrium at the back, where pairs of double columns followed the line on towards a belvedere. The design included a scheme for six linear

axes and meticulously devised plans for the various vistas: only at carefully calculated intervals was the continuous curtain of cypresses, a dense protective wall enclosing the garden, broken to make way for balustrades and belvederes from which to admire the views. This layout well demonstrates the willingness of the Italian school of garden design to accept French ideas and influences without ever losing sight of its own traditions or of the importance of the garden's relationship with the natural landscape around it. Typically, the Italian Rococo garden exploited to the full the potential of its site (very often it was set among gently undulating hills), and it used vistas, statuary and *giochi d'acqua* to emphasize the delights of its situation. Of all the many examples, perhaps Marc'Antonio dal Re's descriptions and engravings of the Villa Pertusati at Comazzo, particularly his illustrations of the tall, sinuous fastigiate hornbeams, define most sharply the spirit of the style that belonged exclusively to the Italian Rococo garden.

1 L. Crespi, *Felsina pittrice, Vita de' pittori bolognesi* (Rome 1769), p. 66.
2 For Colorno and its garden, see V. Comoli Mandracci, 'Le delizie farnesiane di Colorno' in *Arte Lombarda*, Vol. 10, no. 2 (1965), Vol. 11 (1966); and M. Pellegri, *Colorno Villa Ducale* (Parma 1981) and, for the reference cited, p. 54. For Ferdinando Bibiena see D. Lenzi, 'La "veduta per angolo" nella scenografia' in *Architettura, scenografia, pittura del paesaggio* (Bologna 1980) p. 170.
3 See M. Armandi, 'Eden alla moda: il

giardino Sorra' in *Villa Sorra* (Modena 1983) p. 91.
4 For Racconigi and its park, see A. Lange, 'Disegni e documenti di Guarino Guarini' in *Guarino Guarini e l'internazionalità del barocco*, Vol. 1 (Turin 1970). For the development of the park in the eighteenth century, see A. M. Matteucci, 'Scenografia e architettura nell'opera di Pelagio Palagi' in *Pelagio Palagi, artista e collezionista* (Bologna 1976).
5 For the villas of Palermo designed by Tommaso Maria Napoli and for the relevant

Villa Belgioioso at Belgioioso, Pavia: entrance to the garden.

bibliography, see S. Boscarino, *Sicilia barocca* (Rome 1981) pp. 206ff. The engraving of Villa Valguarnera illustrates the garden and the turn in direction of the approach road taking the form of an oval space that reflects the shape of the great terraced courtyard; see M. de Simone, *Ville palermitane* (Genoa 1968).

6   A reproduction of the famous terrace of the Villa della Rovere (later Gavotti) appears in the invaluable guide by B. Marta Nobile, *I giardini d'Italia* (Bologna 1984), and in the volume edited by F. Borsi and G. Pampaloni, *Monumenti d'Italia: ville e giardini* (Novara 1984) p. 251. For the gardens of Genoa not dealt with here, see L. Magni, *Il tempio di Venere: giardini e ville nella cultura genovese* (Genoa 1987).

7   See F. Mormone, 'Domenico Antonio Vaccaro, architetto: Il Palazzo Tarsia' in *Napoli nobilissima* (1961–2) Vol I.

8   For the Villa Trissino (now Marzotto) and its park, see M. Tafuri, 'Il parco della Villa Trissino a Trissino e l'opera di Francesco Muttoni' in *L'Architettura*, no. 114 (April 1965) and R. Cevese, *Ville della provincia di Vicenza* (Milan 1971), Vol. I, pp. 223ff., where the hanging walks mentioned are attributed to the Veronese architect Girolamo dal Pozzo. The magnificent gate to the lower villa is attributed by Cevese to Girolamo Frigimelica, who designed the park of Villa Pisani, which is the subject of a recent essay by A. Corboz, *Il parco di Stra (1719): pista per una ricerca*, in course of publication.

9   For the Portici Royal Palace and its relevant bibliography, see C. De Seta, L. Di Mauro, M. Perone, *Ville Vesuviane* (Milan 1980) pp. 102ff.

10   For the Arcadian gardens of Rome, and for a complete bibliography on the subject, see D. Predieri, *Bosco Parrasio, un giardino per l'Arcadia*, in course of publication.

11   For the villa La Cordellina and its garden, see Cevese, *op. cit.*, p. 257, and L. Puppi, 'The Villa Garden of the Veneto from the Fifteenth to the Eighteenth Century' in *The Italian Garden* (Dumbarton Oaks 1972).

12   Apart from single prints, M. dal Re published two editions (1726 and 1743) of his work *Ville di delizia o siano palagi camperecci nello Stato di Milano*; see reproductions in *Il Polifilo*, ed. by P. F. Bagatti Valsecchi (Milan 1963), which also provides a historical and critical analysis of the various works.

13   For Giovanni Ruggeri, see in particular G. Mezzanotte, 'Giovanni Ruggeri e le ville di delizia lombarde', in *Bolletino CISA*, Vol. 11 (1969). For information on the villas of Lombardy, and of the other regions of Italy, see the invaluable series edited by P. F. Bagatti Valsecchi, *Ville d'Italia*; in particular, for Castellazzo di Bollate, see S. Lange, *Ville della provincia di Milano* (Milan 1972), p. 135; for Villa Brentano *ibidem*, pp. 175ff; for Villa Alari Visconti by Ruggeri and Villa Archinto by Pietrasanta, see C. Perogalli and P. Favole, *Ville dei navigli lombardi* (Milan 1982), pp. 106ff., 152ff.

14   See note 8.

15   For the designs of Juvara and the relevant bibliography, see S. Boscarino, *Juvarra architetto* (Rome 1973), pp. 120–32, 177ff.

16   See note 8.

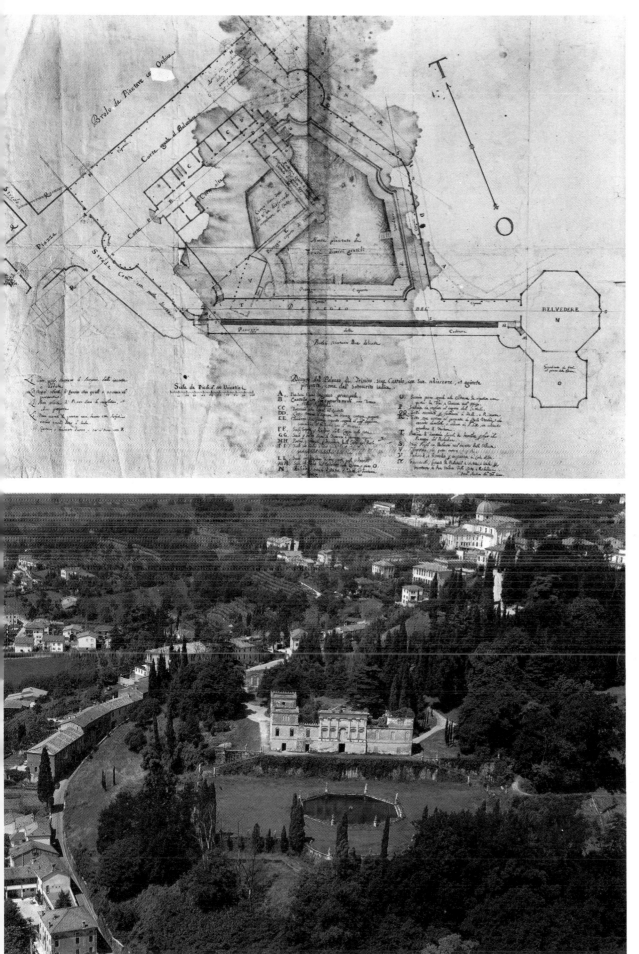

Plan for the redesigning of the gardens and courtyards of the Villa Trissino da Porto (now Marzotto) at Trissino, Vicenza, carried out by F. Muttoni.

Aerial view of the Villa Trissino. (Photo Piero Orlandi)

Villa Pertusati at Comazzo, Milan: view of the cascade. From M. dal Re, Ville di delizia, *eighteenth century.*

View of one of the towers in the garden of Brignano (now Castello Visconti) at Brignano d'Adda. Engraving from M. dal Re, Ville di delizia, *eighteenth century.*

Idea for a Fountain at the Villa Garzoni at Lucca. *Design by F. Juvara, 1714. Biblioteca Nazionale Universitaria, Turin.*

Villa Belgioioso at Merate. Engraving from M. dal Re, Ville di delizia, *eighteenth century.*

Villa Valguarnera at Bagheria, Palermo, designed by Tommaso Maria Napoli. From A. Leanti, Lo stato presente di Sicilia, *vol. II, Palermo 1761.*

The Hortus Palatinus of Salomon de Caus

Reinhard Zimmermann

Simplified version of the Scenographia *by M. Merian of the Hortus Palatinus at Heidelberg. Drawn by Radames Zaramella.*

Key: *1 upper terrace; 2 intermediate terrace; 3 main terrace; 4 lower terrace; 5 castle; 6 entrance to the castle; 7 entrance to the large grotto; 8 great vaulted arch with a statue of Friedrich V; 9 gallery (fish-breeding pools) with small grotto; 10 great arch with pool; 11 water parterre 12 labyrinth; 13 orangery; 14 Bed of the Seasons; 15 belvedere and habitation.*

The history of the Hortus Palatinus begins on 14 July 1614 when the engineer, architect and scholar Salomon de Caus (1576–1626) was commissioned by Elector Palatine Friedrich V (1596–1632, acceded 1614) to work on the new gardens at Heidelberg Castle. De Caus had entered the service of the Elector as an architect and engineer on 1 April 1613 in London, where Friedrich had just married Elizabeth Stuart, the daughter of King James I. De Caus had been working in England since the autumn of 1610 for Henry, Prince of Wales, as well as for other members of the royal family and the higher nobility. He was apparently a Huguenot from Dieppe or its close vicinity, and at some time between 1595 and 1598 had made a tour of Italy in the course of which he is known to have visited the gardens at Pratolino. Then he worked until 1610 in Brussels for Archduke Albert VII as an engineer. Although by far the greater part of the garden at Heidelberg was executed, the scheme was left incomplete. Work on the project was halted after Friedrich's acceptance of the royal crown of Bohemia on 28 September 1619 and the removal of his court to Prague. Its upkeep was neglected and over the years it fell into ruin. In the

nineteenth century it was transformed into an English park. The surviving parts are the terraces (to the extent that they were built) and ruins of most of the stone buildings. In recent years some of the pools, and architectural and sculptural elements have been rebuilt. The original conception of the garden is recorded in de Caus's 1620 book of engravings (see bibliography).

The basic structure of the garden is determined by two long sections of terrace set at right angles to each other along a hollow in the side of the hill on which the castle stands. This relatively broad main terrace, with its two arms, is supported in part by massive substructures, and is at the same level as the main entrance to the castle situated on one side. It is flanked by other narrower and smaller divisions of the garden extending at different levels uphill and downhill. Below, in the corner between the two arms of the main terrace, is a rectangular garden with an extension for a large pyramidal flight of steps. Above the main terrace is the very narrow upper terrace which also has two arms but extends considerably further westwards than the main terrace. Between the east-west arm of the upper terrace and the main terrace

is a long intermediate terrace forming another gradation. The upper terrace is not modelled as a garden (except for a projected but unexecuted extension for a maze, next to the Bed of the Seasons but on a higher level). It was intended primarily as a promenade with views and for access to other areas on the hillside, most of which were purely architectural in character. Apart from the *cabinets* (on a small extension on the eastern edge), the garden is designed on four distinct levels, each different in form and with a different treatment of surface. The main terrace is clearly emphasized by the large area it covers. The garden shows two main themes: one is towards the largest possible areas of level ground, and the other towards stepped terraces in the manner of Italian terraced gardens. There is also the cumulative effect of the juxtaposition of the individual parts, whose difference of shape and size was evidently regarded not as a defect but as a positive aesthetic virtue.

The Hortus Palatinus uses three different forms of parterre: knot parterres with strip patterns; *parterres de pièces coupées* with designs of shaped flowerbeds; and *parterres de broderie* (which were at that time a modern feature) where the pattern

is made of coloured earth or gravel. The relationship of the various compartments to each other is also largely cumulative. Overall structures in the garden are only hinted at: the axes remain latent, and the links between the terraces are treated as of secondary importance. The most important thing was the concept of a gathering of a variety of different structures to be experienced one after another. Among the various designs of parterre three unusual forms should be noted: the (unexecuted) maze; a bed designed as a *parterre de pièces coupées* but with hollows filled with water instead of raised areas; and the Bed of the Seasons in which seventy-two individual beds are arranged in a circle in which the distribution of the plants is determined by the time of year when they are in flower.

The garden contains (or was intended to contain) several lavish works of architecture, including a large grotto, a large tower-like belvedere with apartments in the upper storeys (not completed), a two-aisled gallery leaning against the hillside with ponds for fish-farming, a small grotto and a façade with columns and reliefs showing the story of Hercules in the attic storey, as well as another building, one part of which contained heated

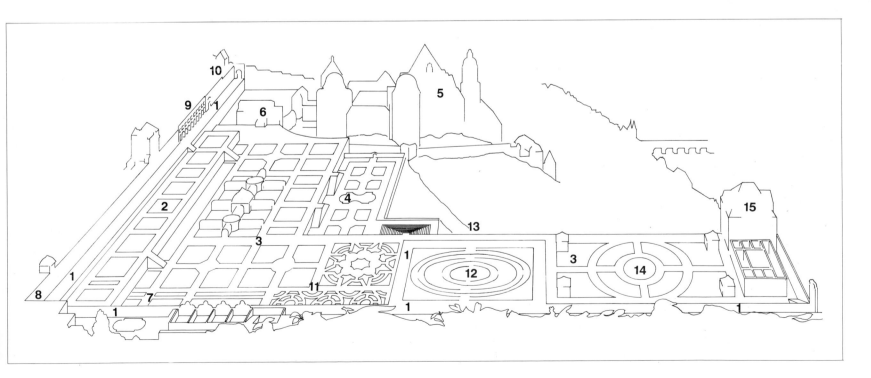

Hortus Palatinus, Heidelberg: the south-eastern section and the Bed of the Seasons. Detail from painting by J. Fouquières, before 1620. Kurpfalzisches Museum, Heidelberg. (Photo Ingeborg Klinger)

bathing facilities and the other was used as an orangery. A separate stone-built orangery was planned but not executed. The predominant order is Ionic; the exterior of the proposed orangery would have been decorated with tree-trunk columns of the Tuscan order. The façade of the *cabinets* included twisted columns. Rustication frequently appears as a decorative element, e.g. in the form of rough-hewn shaft rings on columns and half-columns. The furnishings of the garden also included pools and fountains decorated partly with rocky structures and partly with statues, and mechanical games in the grottoes. The models and inspiration for these were taken from Serlio, Wendel Dietterlin and Philibert de l'Orme, as well as the gardens of the Villa Medici at Pratolino and the Villa d'Este at Tivoli.

The iconography of the Hortus Palatinus is based on two themes: the honouring of the natural elements and the representation of the rule of Friedrich V. Natural elements appear, for example in the statues and reliefs of river gods and the statues of Ceres and Pomona, and the animal figures on the portal of the large grotto. The Bed of the Seasons represents a homage to Vertumnus, the god of the seasons. The iconography of rulership is varied, complex and omnipresent. Above the south-east corner of the uppermost terrace and dominating the garden at its highest point is a statue of the ruler with a tablet bearing an inscription. Inscriptions in other places mention the elector by name. The gods, represented in pictorial or sculptured form, or referred to indirectly, are also allegorical representations of Friedrich: Neptune beneath the statue of the ruler (Virgil in the *Aeneid* had compared the sea god with earthly rulers who knew how to pacify a rebellious people), Hercules, Apollo (in the parterre with the Muses – an indirect representation), Vertumnus (Bed of the Seasons – an indirect representation), as well as the lion, the heraldic beast of the Palatinate, on the portal of the large grotto. Even the Narcissus in the bath-house may refer to rulership – either negatively, as a warning, or positively, as a symbol of self-knowledge. The statues of the river gods of the Rhine, Neckar and Main make the Hortus Palatinus a symbolic depiction of the territory of the Palatinate. Their distribution follows a strict hierarchy: the

Hortus Palatinus, Heidelberg: the large grotto. From S. de Caus, Hortus Palatinus, *Frankfurt 1620.*

Hortus Palatinus, Heidelberg, portal of the large grotto.

tributaries of the Rhine (Main and Neckar) are situated on the lowest terrace, the Rhine itself on the main terrace, while on the uppermost terrace is Neptune with his trident – and above even him stands the statue of Friedrich.

A basic message, clearly expressed in the garden as a whole, is that nature has been subjugated by art. Friedrich V has rivalled the achievements of Roman antiquity by drastically remodelling the terrain, arranging the vegetation as he thinks fit, and subjecting the watery element to his will – in the orangery he has even vanquished the changes of the seasons. The representation of political power is thus equated with power over Nature, indeed they are reflected in each other, just as Friedrich V – with mythological hyperbole – is reflected in Neptune. Because Friedrich has conquered the watery element by art, in the garden he is the real Neptune, who again embodies the image of ideal rulership. Ideal political power as conveyed in ancient mythology is expressed as a form of the control of Nature which rivals and indeed surpasses Roman antiquity. The Hortus Palatinus is at once a symbol of the order of the state, an image of the territory of the Palatinate, and the successor to the ancient Roman practice of controlling Nature. It radically asserts the difference between art and Nature, interprets their relationship in terms of military conquest: Nature is vanquished, made obedient, altered, and even replaced by the achievements of mechanical engineering. Thus the Heidelberg garden provides evidence of a strategy for the control of Nature which has remained influential up to the present day, but has since been recognized as in effect a strategy for the destruction of Nature.

Bibliography

Salomon de Caus, *Hortus Palatinus a Friderico Rege Boemiae Electore Palatino Heidelbergae extructus. Salomone de Caus Architecto* (Frankfurt 1620, published simultaneously in French and German editions).

Salomon de Caus, *Hortus Palatinus. Die Entwürfe zum Heidelberger Schlossgarten*; Part I, facsimile of the 1620 Frankfurt edition [German edition] (Worms 1980); Part II, commentary by Reinhard Zimmermann (Worms 1986, with further bibliography).

Salomon de Caus, *Le Jardin Palatin. Hortus Palatinus*, ed. by Michel Conan (Paris 1981, facsimile of the 1620 Frankfurt edition, French version).

The Garden Designs of Joseph Furttenbach the Elder

Dorothee Nehring

'Schul-Paradeiss-Gärtlin'. From J. Furttenbach, Mannhafter Kunst-Spiegel, *Augsburg 1663. Bayerische Staatsbibliothek, Munich.*

Joseph Furttenbach (1591 Leutkirch – 1667 Ulm) was born into a respectable Protestant family from the Allgäu. After a thorough schooling and a time working in commerce, he spent some years in Italy from 1607 onwards.[1]

It was particularly his studies at Giulio Parigi's Academy of War and Art at Florence that equipped him to become a theoretician and practitioner of the construction of fortifications, engineering and artillery, fireworks and stage design, as well as ballistics. During his lifelong work for the city of Ulm from 1621 onwards, as Stadtbaumeister (City Architect) from 1631, and as Ratsherr (Councillor) from 1636, his designs were concerned with civil, technical and social buildings (palaces and dwellings, waterworks, schools, orphanages, hospitals, ships and artillery) as well as with ideas of reform in this field. Because of him the city of Ulm became the first German city to have a theatre with movable wings in the Italian manner.[2]

Furttenbach's treatises on architecture[3] were intended to aid the architectural work of aristocratic and bourgeois dilettanti. His extensive education in the *artes liberales* and the *artes mechanicae*, and his activity as a collector for the famous cabinet of art and rarities in his house in Ulm, were typical of this period and set the trend for the educational ideals of the aristocracy and bourgeoisie of the early Baroque period in Germany after the Thirty Years' War. Reconstruction and general renewal after the end of the war was the subject of his treatise *Architectura recreationis* (1640) which contains most of his garden designs. Furttenbach is regarded as the first German-speaking architectural writer to deal with garden design on an equal footing with architecture. His significance lies both in the increased importance he attached to garden design and in his introduction of the Italian style of garden.[4] He did not provide any particular theory for the cultivation of nature as an art form, nor are original stylistic innovations or startling iconographical programmes to be found in his work. He incorporated elements that he knew from Italian gardens into his designs, and thus introduced Italian garden design to Germany. What was new about his designs is that they were expressly intended for all social classes, both the aristocracy and the bourgeoisie. In this he may have been following the ideas of Pietro de' Crescenzi, but he was also aiming at the new aristocratic and bourgeois patricians who were very soon to emerge as connoisseurs of the 'new' garden design.

Also noteworthy are Furttenbach's garden designs for educational and social institutions, for example, the 'Schul-Paradeiss-Gärtlin' in the *Mannhafter Kunst-Spiegel* for the recreation of schoolchildren, or the hospital building in the *Architectura civilis*.

He took certain elements, in particular pergolas, galleries, aviaries and grottoes, from Italian garden design,[5] which he praised in his *Itinerarium*, particularly in his description of the gardens of Prince Doria in Genoa, but also in the Roman gardens of the Villas Medici, Farnese, Borghese and Almonte Cavallo. These features constantly recur in his designs in variations depending on the size of the garden and the wealth of the owner.

Unlike the gardens of the later Middle Ages which were still usually laid out without any relation to the associated building, Furttenbach's smaller bourgeois garden was moved right up to the house and enclosed within walls like a courtyard. In front of the house or palace, usually on its central axis, he placed a large pleasure-garden on a long rectangular ground plan. It consisted of a central area with decorative beds, followed by a kitchen garden and orchard or even by a menagerie after the Italian model. The 'Sixth Pleasure-Garden' is unusual in having the garden quarters and the courtyard arranged separately around the four sides of the palace.

Unlike the terraced landscape of most Italian Renaissance gardens – and perhaps because he knew the extensive flat French gardens from contemporary engravings (for instance, those of du Cerceau) – Furttenbach's gardens are designed on a level landscape. The relationship between building and garden is emphasized by enclosing it, often within monumental, star-shaped, fortified constructions, with walls, rows of trees or canals. These are ideal gardens planned in isolation and usually with no relation to the surrounding landscape – neither to 'wild' nature, which was deliberately used in Italian gardens as a counterpart to the cultivated garden landscape, nor to the urban environment. Only in the case of the menagerie is there landscaped terrain within the flat, severely symmetrical composition of the garden – a piece of 'real' nature which is a motif taken from Italian gardens and a particular favourite of Furttenbach in his designs.

The plans of all Furttenbach's gardens are dominated by a cross shape. The parterre in front of the dwelling is arranged in a group of four around a central pool. Its plan is based on asymmetrical ornaments or square beds, as found in contemporary designs and earlier in the designs of Vredeman de Vries,[6] forming a symmetrical overall pattern.

Furttenbach linked the individual sections of the garden by using the principal path as an axis of symmetry, which, together with eye-catchers such as grottoes, urns, and views through arbours, serve to heighten the effect of perspective. But the individual sections of garden are still separated from each other by transverse galleries, pergolas and water courses; they are not subject to a hierarchically ordered overall design as in a Baroque garden, and the accumulative arrangement of the sections of garden is emphasized by the asymmetrical distribution of statues, obelisks, pools, aviaries, ponds with islands, and broad paths, all of which are given equal importance. Furttenbach produced separate designs for the oval maze and the grove garden with its thirty-six gates. Italian models can be found for his designs for a richly ornamental fountain and a grotto.[7]

Furttenbach's great interest was the creation of grottoes and shellwork, the 'rocks' and 'marine forms', which, like the water machines in his *Itinerarium* recall his special admiration for the Genoese gardens. Grottoes with 'sea plants' were not only an important

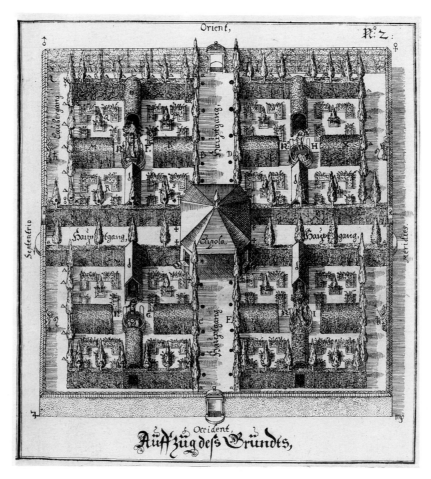

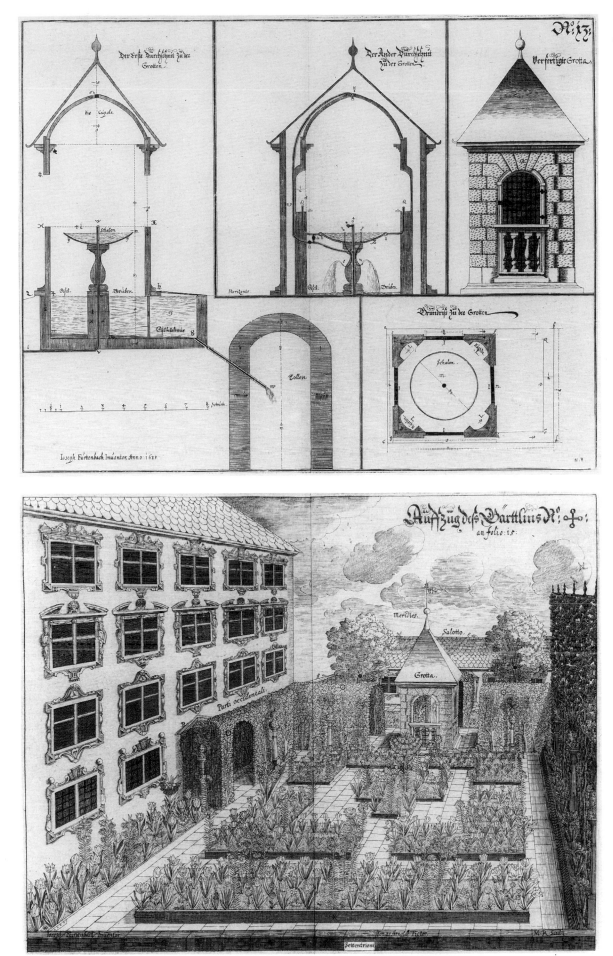

Designs for grotto pavilions. From J. Furttenbach, Architectura privata, *Augsburg 1641. Bayerische Staatsbibliothek, Munich.*

Design for Furttenbach's garden in Ulm. From J. Furttenbach, Architectura privata, *Ausgsburg 1641. Bayerische Staatsbibliothek, Munich.*

feature of Mannerism in the age of Rudolph II, they also enjoyed great popularity in garden design into the nineteenth century.

Furttenbach wrote little about the planting of the gardens; he himself was clearly not particularly knowledgeable about plants. However, an interesting source for south German garden plants of the seventeenth century is the list of plants in the garden of his own house at Ulm – probably his only executed garden – drawn up by his brother, Abraham, who was more versed in botany, which is included in his *Architectura privata*. More than a hundred tulips are mentioned, a particularly valuable collection in view of the price of tulip bulbs at the time.

In the designs for large pleasure-gardens Furttenbach left the planting to the gardeners. The beds are merely represented with single upright plants and clearly defined borders in keeping with the taste of the time. In the Sixth Pleasure-Garden he recommends an oak wood, and in the First Pleasure-Garden the planting of firs in place of cypresses which were rarely found in the north. In his use of deciduous trees cut into domed shapes with windows in the foliage, and viewing platforms in round mounts, Furttenbach was taking up a favourite motif from ancient garden design which had been handed down through medieval garden design to the Baroque period. Generally he recommended 'subtle' plants in the fruit gardens, and besides fig and pomegranate trees, there should be bitter oranges, lemons and lime trees. This accorded with the passion for collecting plants and exotic fruits of the typical garden-owner of the period, who was proud of controlling nature and new methods of cultivation.

Also connected with a dilettante observation of nature was the fact that the gardens could be viewed from above, for example from galleries or from a roof pavilion in the centre of the house for a view over the ornamental part of the garden, or from a pavilion in the garden to view the wild animals in the menagerie; the broad paths for strolling, looking and being seen, also contributed to this, and then there is the bird's-eye perspective itself, in which Furttenbach presented a clear aerial view of his garden designs.

Furttenbach not only gave a considerable boost to the development of garden

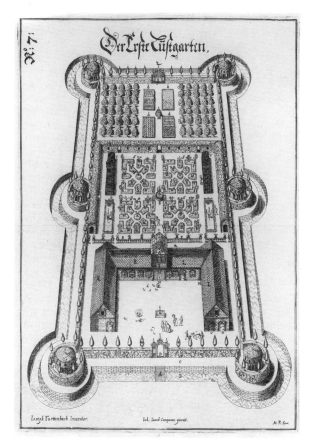

'The First Pleasure-Garden'. From J. Furttenbach, Architectura recreationis, Augsburg 1640. Bayerische Staatsbibliothek, Munich.

Grotto in Furttenbach's private garden in Ulm. From J. Furttenbach, Architectura privata, Augsburg 1641.

design as an autonomous art in the second half of the seventeenth century, he also explicitly addressed a new sort of garden-owner. Knowledgeable about Italian Renaissance gardens and an educated observer of the processes of nature, we shall see this new garden-owner in the garden of the early Baroque period.

1 Joseph Furttenbach, *Newes Itinerarium Italiae* (Ulm 1627). This was one of the most widely read travel handbooks in Germany in the seventeenth century.
2 For Furttenbach's biography see Margot Berthold, *Joseph Furttenbach (1591–1667). Architekturtheoretiker und Stadtbaumeister in Ulm. Ein Beitrag zur Theater- und Kunstgeschichte* (doctoral thesis, Munich 1951), pp. 1–16. A shortened version of this is in 'Ulm und Oberschwaben. Zeitschrift für Geschichte und Kunst' in *Mitteilungen des Vereins für Kunst und Altertum in Ulm und Oberschwaben*, no. 32 (1951).
3 Joseph Furttenbach, *Architectura civilis* (Ulm 1628); *Architectura universalis* (Ulm 1635); *Architectura recreationis* (Ulm 1640); *Architectura privata* (Ulm 1641); *Mannhafter Kunst-Spiegel* (Augsburg 1663).
4 For an assessment of Furttenbach's work see Berthold, *op. cit.*, pp. 170ff., who rejects Dientzel's opinion that even before French garden design, Furttenbach had laid the foundations for Baroque garden design in Germany; see Senta Dientzel, *Furttenbachs Gartenentwürfe* (Nuremberg 1928), pp. 70–6. Hennebo largely follows Berthold's ideas: Dieter Hennebo and Alfred Hoffmann, *Der architektonische Garten. Renaissance und Barock* (Hamburg 1965): Vol. 2, *Geschichte der Gartenkunst*.
5 See Günther Mader and Laila Neubert-Mader, *Italian Gardens* (Stuttgart 1987), pp. 58ff., 82ff.
6 E.g. the garden of the 'Corinthian order' in Hans Vredeman de Vries, *Hortorum viridariorumque* (Antwerp 1583), no pagination.
7 Elisabeth B. MacDougall (ed.), *Fons sapientiae: Garden Fountains in Illustrated Books, Sixteenth-Eighteenth Centuries* (Dumbarton Oaks, 1977), pp. 36ff.

Garden Design in The Netherlands in the Seventeenth Century

Carla S. Oldenburger-Ebbers

The young Dutch Republic soon gained considerably in power and wealth, thanks partly to the setting up of the East and West India Companies. Influential Netherlanders visited France and Italy and their discovery of the Italian Renaissance was an undeniable influence on the development of garden design in the Low Countries. Constantijn Huygens, for example, is known to have been a member of a Dutch delegation to Venice in 1619 and to have admired the villas along the Brenta.

All through the seventeenth century, particularly in the province of Holland, new gardens were laid out in accordance with the Dutch interpretation of classical principles, as found in the translated architectural studies of Italians like Serlio, Scamozzi and Palladio. Applied to Dutch gardens this resulted in a rectangular ground plan, divided into two equal halves by the axis of symmetry, usually the longitudinal axis. This axis runs at right angles to the centre of the house and the rectangular garden is essentially enclosed, by groves of trees and/or a system of canals – the latter being very frequently found in the polder landscape of Holland. The whole is divided into sub-plots, frequently square, which are adorned with French foliage and Dutch flowerbeds. In the view of the French architect André Mollet the gaps in the foliage were intended to be filled in with low edging plants in a single colour. The ideal length-to-breadth ratio of the sides of the rectangle is the harmonious classical proportion of 4:3. However, the Dutch architect Philip Vingboons places his ideal villa within an inner garden, in an overall plan whose length-to-breadth ratio is 2:1. The function of the Dutch classical garden is to proclaim the owner's social status, beautify his environment and provide him with useful produce.

The structural elements which characterize such a garden are: an enclosing wall, harking back to an earlier age, or (at a later date) hedges and rows of trees; moats; woods with avenues radiating from a central point; mazes; arbours and bowers; wooden fencing; low box hedges with decorative borders of, for example, thyme, carnations, camomile; and flowerbeds with pots placed on tiles.

Water plays a more modest role than in Italian gardens, though fountains and waterworks are found at this period. As yet there is little garden statuary, though sundials are already quite frequent.

The plants grown in such gardens in the seventeenth century are described in Jan van der Groen's *Den Nederlandtsen Hovenier* (The Dutch Gardener, 1669). Van der Groen (*c.* 1635–1672) was gardener to the Prince of Orange, working from 1659 to 1665 at the Oude Hof, now the Palace of Noordeinde, and possibly also at Huis ten Bosch, Honselaarsdijk (1665–1671) and Huis ter Nieuwburg (1671). Many of the varieties he describes were probably present at Honselaarsdijk, where he was working at the time the book was written. From about 1675 onwards, Hans Willem Bentinck, William III's favourite, began assembling the first great collection of exotic plants at Zorgvliet.[1]

Among designers of Dutch classical gardens are: Jacob van Campen, Constantijn Huygens, Pieter and Maurits Post and Philip Vingboons. The most famous houses and gardens built and laid out in this style are the palaces commissioned by Prince Frederick Henry, namely Honselaarsdijk (1621), Huis ter Nieuwburg (1630) and Huis ten Bosch (1647). These in turn inspired Constantijn Huygens to build his Hofwijck (1640) and Jacob Cats his Zorgvliet (1651), both, like their models, located near The Hague. But elsewhere in the country too, rich bourgeois had manor houses constructed and country estates laid out. In the seventeenth century, old medieval castles in the province of Utrecht, Overijssel and Gelderland were also occasionally restored or rebuilt in classical style, and gardens were laid out to complement the buildings, as at Kruidberg (*c.* 1660).[2]

In the France of Louis XIV Protestants were severely persecuted after the revocation of the Edict of Nantes. From 1685 onwards many French Huguenots fled northwards, among them the engraver and architect Daniel Marot, who on the recommendation of Bentinck (at the time Dutch envoy in France), made his way to the court of William III.

From about 1680 onwards garden design for country houses, estates and castles was influenced by French interpretations of the familiar classical principles. As had happened in the sixteenth century there was an evolution from closed to open gardens. Under the influence of French classical garden design with its elongated central axis of symmetry, which gave a great effect of perspective, the rectangular Dutch garden, moated and enclosed, gave way to very elongated classical designs, whose borders are often no longer clearly discernible. The garden becomes so extensive that it seems to merge into the surrounding countryside, with the main axis often extending into an avenue. As in the previous period the garden is divided up symmetrically along the central axis and the side axes running parallel to it. The middle section of the

163

House and surrounding garden, Boede, Zeeland. From M. Smallegange, Nieuwe cronyk van Zeeland, *Middelburg 1696. Bibliotheek Landbouwuniversiteit, Wageningen.*

Classical Dutch-style garden at Kruidberg. From J. van der Groen, Den Nederlandtsen Hovenier, *Amsterdam 1669. Bibliotheek Landbouwuniversiteit, Wageningen.*

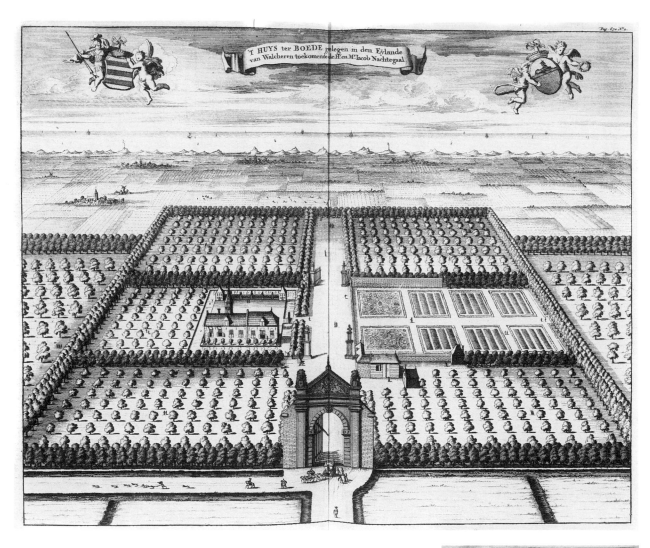

dens, winding walls, pavilions and colonnades. Water gushes from fountains and waterworks, splashes down cascades and has a mirroring function in the moat surrounding the central part of the garden and in the canals affording distant views. Other decorative elements are statues, sundials, shell grottoes, bowers, pergolas, and trellis-work. For added effect there are menageries, aviaries and orangeries.

In the period from 1720 to 1750 the quantity of decorative elements becomes almost excessive. The course of the paths in the bosquets becomes irregular and winding, as a reaction to classical regimentation. Moreover, the central axis sometimes competes with a number of axes radiating from a central point (the main building, the water basin, etc.). At this period too so-called extension gardens and side gardens not included in the original plan are created.

The collections of exotic plants at Zorgvliet, Honselaarsdijk, Gunterstein, Leeuwenhorst and Het Loo enjoyed great celebrity at the time. Among unusual plants prized in this period were citrus trees, pomegranates, olives, oleanders, myrtle, laurel, laurustinus, strawberry trees, mastic trees, Cyprus terebinth trees, lilacs, Judas trees, agave and aloe. The beds surrounding the foliage had to be both symmetrical and diverse in height and variety.[3]

The principal Dutch garden designers of this period are J. Roman, D. Marot, S. Schijnvoet and J. H. Knoop. Some examples of gardens laid out on French classical lines along a long axis of symmetry or those modernized with avenues or canals affording prospects of the centre of the house are: Zeist Castle (1677), Clingendaal (1680), Leeuwenburg (1686), Het Loo (1689), Fraylemaborg (1690), De Voorst (1695), Neercanne (1698) and Heemstede Castle (c. 1700).[4]

Generally speaking, gardens along the Vecht and other rivers were not so deep, so that longitudinal axes at right angles to the house were not as frequent. These gardens were, however, richly furnished with garden ornaments, water basins, topiary and trained trees, etc. At Rosendael and Nienoord Castle in Leek there is still a shell grotto of the period.

garden is enclosed by a semicircular structure in a classical style, derived from the so-called Serlio ordonnance in classical architecture. Daniel Marot, in his *Nouveau livre de parterres* of 1703, is fond of using these semicircular enclosures in the form of an arbour or a colonnade. This Serlian form is also found repeatedly in his flowerbed decorations. The first French-style garden in the Low Countries was probably designed by Jacob Roman; it is not certain whether he knew of the descriptions of the gardens of Pliny the Elder or was inspired by J. Boyceau de la Baraudière's design for the Luxembourg gardens, but there are clear similarities between the Luxembourg gardens and those at Zeist, and later those at Het Loo, De Voorst and Heemstede.

The gardens of the period are characterized by variety and lavish decoration. This is achieved by formal diversity in all the structural elements, and a variety of colours and scents in the garden, water splashing from fountains or over cascades and magnificent garden statuary, representing figures from Greek mythology and often at the same time symbolizing the life of the owner of the garden or his wife. The water in the fountains and waterfalls was pumped by a windmill or by natural springs and by making use of differences in levels on the garden site.

Typical features in the various sections of the garden are mazes, woods with avenues radiating from a central point, arbours of different plants, hedges, bosquets, retreats, orchards, vegetable gar-

Classical French-style garden at Zeist.
Engraving by D. Stoopendaal, c. *1700.*
Bibliotheek Landbouwuniversiteit,
Wageningen.

Huis ten Bosch c. *1660–70 by J. van der*
Heyden. National Gallery, London.

[1] Among contemporary writings on the subject are: P. Vingboons, *Afbeeldsels der voornaamste gebouwen* (1648) (Illustrations of the Principal Mansions); P. Post, *De Sael van Oranje* (1655); J. van der Groen, *Den Nederlandtsen Hovenier* (1669); H. Cause, *De Koninglycke Hovenier* (1676).

[2] In North Holland one finds gardens in this style at Hof te Bergen (1642), De Nijenburg, Frankendael, Trompenburg (1680), Elswout (1645), De Hartenkamp (1691), Het Manpad, Kruidberg (c. 1660), and at Beeckesteijn; in South Holland, gardens of similar design besides those mentioned around The Hague are to be found at Ockenburg (1648), Duivenvoorde, Warmond and Keukenhof (1641); in the province of Utrecht at, for example, Renswoude (1654), Geerestein and Soestdijk (1676); and in Gelderland and Overijssel at among other places De Slangenburg (1675), Oldenaller (1655), Vanenburg (1654), Weldam (1645) and Schoonheten (1640). The subdivisions typical of Dutch classicism can still be clearly seen at Weldam, Beeckesteijn (in the section immediately behind the house) and at Hof te Bergen.

[3] Series of prints of various celebrated houses and gardens were produced by P. Schenk, J. Moucheron, C. Danckerts, C. Allard, L. Scherm, J. Covens, D. Stoopendaal and H. de Leth; slightly later, P. de la Court van den Voort's *Byzondere Aenmerkingen over het aenleggen van pragtige en gemene Landhuizen, Lusthoven, Plantagien en aenklevende cieraden* (Observations on the design of luxurious and modest Country Houses, Pleasure Gardens, Parks and Accompanying Decorations, 1737) became a standard work.

[4] To these may be added Huize Doorn (1701), Oranjewoud (1707), Eerde (1710), Renswoude (1708), Oldengaerde (1717), Duivenvoorde (1717), Keukenhof (1720), Middachten (1725), Twickel (c. 1721), Beeckesteijn (c. 1730), Meerenberg in Heemstede (1732), De Hartenkamp (c. 1735), Borg Welgelegen (1736), Manpad (c. 1740) and Ter Hooge (1751).

Bibliography

'The Anglo-Dutch Garden in the Age of William and Mary', *Journal of Garden History*, Vol. 8, nos. 2–3 (April–September 1988).

D. Jacques and A. J. van der Horst, *The Gardens of William and Mary* (London 1988).

W. Kuyper, *Dutch Classicist Architecture. A Survey of Dutch Architecture, Gardens and Anglo-Dutch Architectural Relations from 1625 to 1700* (Delft 1980).

Villas, Gardens and Fountains of Rome: The Etchings of Giovanni Battista Falda

Maurizio Gargano

View and ground-plan of the papal gardens of the Quirinale, Rome (today the garden of the official residence of the President of the Republic). From G. B. Falda, Li giardini di Roma, Rome 1683.

PROSPETTIVA DEL GIARDINO PONTIFICIO SVL QVIRINALE. *Architettura di Ottauio Mascarini.*

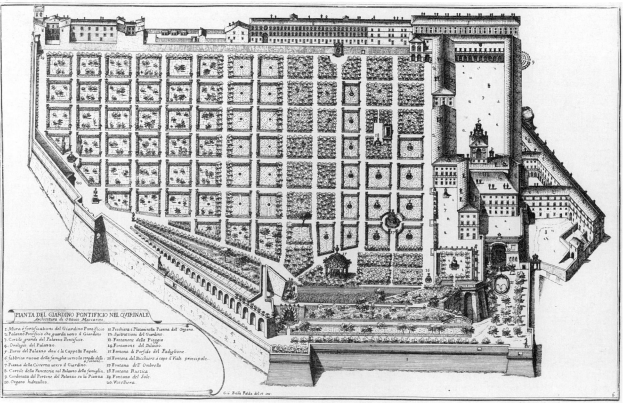

PIANTA DEL GIARDINO PONTIFICIO NEL QUIRINALE *Architettura di Ottauio Mascarini.*

An issue that provoked much heated debate and inspired a mass of printed dissertations in Rome in the second half of the sixteenth century was the question of whether or not the waters of the Tiber were drinkable, and whether they should be celebrated for their therapeutic qualities or regarded with distrust and suspicion. This was a recurrent theme in the work of Alessandro Petroni, Andrea Bacci, Giovan Battista Modio and Agostino Steuco, and they provide clear evidence of the increasing need to resolve the problem of the water shortage in the city, apart from the matter of improving the quality of the water itself.

It was in the 1560s that the first systematic work was undertaken to provide more water for the rapidly expanding population, which could no longer be adequately supplied by water drawn from either the Tiber or the local springs, especially since these two diminishing resources were expected to continue to supply water for fountains and wells in all the piazzas, gardens, cloisters and convents of the city, including those of the private palazzi[1], as they had done since the Middle Ages.

Disregarding occasional efforts on the part of the popes of the fifteenth century (Nicholas V and Sixtus IV), it was only in the course of the sixteenth century that any significant and properly organized attempts were made to repair the city's ancient aqueducts, an endeavour which was to contribute considerably to a shift in the expansion of Rome towards the surrounding hills. Many aristocratic Roman families chose hillside sites around the city for the planting of vineyards and the building of private villas (Pope Julius III's Villa Giulia, which was built in the plain, was one of the few exceptions); it is therefore possible to compare, for example, Villa Madama, Villa Lante, the Farnesina, Villa Medici and Villa Montalto from this point of view, and to appreciate the extent to which the interests of the papal families had become inextricably linked to the concerns of the people since the return of the popes from exile in Avignon. It is apparent that private profit and public need came together at this point in a way which has rarely been identified by historians in attempting to define the characteristics of papal nepotism. The practical needs of the great families of the papal nobility were echoed by the needs of the Roman people, and the building of fountains in public piazzas was a direct result of the water requirements of the vineyards, fountains, elegant nymphaea and *giochi d'acqua* that adorned the palatial hillside gardens of the rich and powerful.

The restoration of the ancient Roman aqueducts continued in the seventeenth century in response to increasing demands for water both in the city and in the countryside around it; much of the old system that had fallen into disuse was strengthened and extended as part of the 'Acqua Felice' campaign encouraged by Sixtus V and the new 'Acqua Paola' scheme promoted by Paul V. It was in the first thirty years of the seventeenth century that, very largely as a result of the increased supply of water, villas such as Ludovisi, Borghese, Pamphili, Patrizi, Corsini, Albani and Giustiniani came into being, contributing considerably to the 'green belt' that was eventually to divide the ancient city, together with its areas of recent urban expansion, from the wilderness of the surrounding landscape. And it was to a detailed study of this aspect of Rome's development that Giovanni Battista Falda devoted his life and work.

'*Anno Domini 1643, die 8 Decembris. Ego Presbiter Io. Petrus Albergantus Parochus Vallisutie baptizavi infantem die antecedenti natum ex Francisco Falda et Catharina filia Bernardi Mazzolae, coniugibus huius Parrociae, cui impositum fuit jomen Joannis Baptistae . . . .*'.[2] This declaration provides documentation of the baptism of Falda, who was born at Valduggia, a small town in the Alta Valsesia, Piedmont, on 7 December 1643. Little is known for certain of his early life, but records certify that at the age of fourteen he was sent by his parents to stay with an uncle in Rome, where his natural talents and inclinations were encouraged and he was launched on his artistic career. A brief but intensely prolific professional life was cut short in Rome, 'after a very long and painful illness': he died on 22 August 1678 at only thirty-five years of age.[3]

The superb quality and highly distinctive character of his draughtsmanship attracted the attention of Giovan Giacomo de Rossi, a well-known publisher and dealer in etchings who was active in Rome at this period. Their meeting was a significant and fortuitous one for the young Falda for it was in de Rossi's studio

and printing works at Sta Maria della Pace that he further refined his technique and learned the art of engraving, which enabled him to transform his drawings into the prints that were soon to become so successful. De Rossi can take the credit for having contributed considerably to Falda's development, and for having given him the opportunity to extend his talents into the fields of architecture and perspective views, which were extremely popular in the Rome of the 1600s.[4]

Falda's artistic energy lay at the root of his enormously successful career. From the publication lists of the Sta Maria della Pace printing works it is clear that he produced a remarkable quantity of etchings and engravings in his short lifetime, an output that is all the more impressive in view of the abundance of detail and the technical precision of everything he did. Economical clarity, strength of line and dramatic contrast of light and shade were the predominant characteristics of his highly individual style. If one considers not only his professional and commercial relationship with de Rossi's printing firm but also his work on the vast and complex undertakings to improve Rome's water system and the urban developments relating to it, together with the new residential villas surrounded by gardens and vineyards, one begins to have some idea of the extent of Falda's energy and versatility, and of the nature of his achievement.

'*The fountains of Rome in piazzas and public places*', '*Fountains in the palazzi and gardens of Rome*', '*The fountains in the villas of Frascati*', '*Villa Pamphili*', '*The Gardens of Rome, their plants and trees*':[5] these subjects, which had all the documentary precision and detail of Falda's city scenes, were repeatedly reproduced in collections of his etchings from the middle of the 1670s. As his popularity grew, he responded to the ever-increasing demands of foreign tourists who were already visiting Italy – and Rome in particular – in vast numbers, and wished to take home a record of the sights. The commercial success of these etchings, which is clear from the numbers of prints produced, is further emphasized by the fact that in the case of *The Gardens of Rome, their plants and trees* his work became a sort of standard reference for everyone – amateurs, architects and planners alike[6] – involved directly or indirectly in the art of garden design.

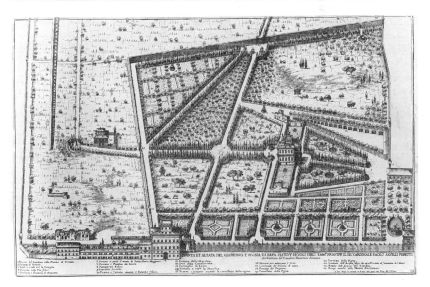

It is not only for his genius as a draughtsman and print-maker that Falda will be remembered, however, but as an artist who left behind an incomparable record of seventeenth-century Rome. His etchings and engravings provide evidence of actual fountains and parks and urban villas that would otherwise have disappeared without leaving a record. He illustrated what he saw around him, and the authenticity of his work is beyond question: in some cases, indeed, what he saw is still there, just as he represented it. The heightened reality of his views contributed greatly to his success both at the papal court and among noble Roman families seeking self-glorification through the palatial magnificence of their villas; it also increased the persistence of the ex-Queen

of Sweden's demands that he should enter her private service.

From historical reports it is apparent that Falda's prints were the first of the period to ensure that depictions of the gardens of Rome were protected from the risks of poor or weak reproduction: the marked contrasts of tone and the strongly architectural quality of his work safeguarded against the problems that frequently beset the reproduction of foliage and vegetation in prints of the period by other artists, where more often than not they served merely as a decorative background to the scene represented. Quality and detail were therefore distinctive features of his garden prints, making them instantly recognizable and highly desirable.

As Rosario Assunto said of Falda's etchings of Villa Mattei, his gardens were 'places in which life and contemplation, nature and history, natural spontaneity and human artificiality all become one in a world of trees and water, hedges and statuary; buildings appear and disappear between the greenery, and they speak among themselves of far-distant times'.[7]

[1] The literature on the subject of Rome's water is extensive. C. d'Onofrio's *Acque e fontane di Roma* (Rome 1977) provides an essential bibliography.

[2] Giovanni Battista Falda's certificate of baptism can be seen in the parish church at Valduggia, Piedmont. The quotation is taken from A. Baudi de Vesme, *Schede Vesme. L'arte in Piemonte dal XVI al XVIII secolo* (Turin 1963–1968), Vol. 2 (1966), p. 451.

[3] A. Rasario, 'Un antico incisore valsesiano: G. B. Falda', in *Bollettino Storico per la Provincia di Novara*' (1932), pp. 196–202, specifically p. 197, and L. A. Cotta, *Museo Novarese* (Milan 1701), pp. 293–95. A bibliography of works devoted to Falda is to be found in P. Bellini's 'Per una definizione dell'opera di G. Battista Falda' in *Arte Cristiana*, Vol. 71, no. 695 (Rome 1983) pp. 81–92, complete with an invaluable chronological catalogue of his works. The essay does not, however, add a great deal to the existing biographical information which appears under numerous entries in biographical dictionaries.

[4] See R. d'Amico, 'La veduta nell'incisione tra '600 e '700: G. B. Falda e G. Vasi' in *Il Seicento. Ricerche di storia dell'arte* (Rome 1976), nos. 1–2, pp. 81–101. The vast output of the printing press at Sta Maria della Pace is documented in the catalogue *Indice delle stampe intagliate in rame, al bulino & all'acquaforte esistente nella Stamperia di Gio. Giacomo De Rossi* (Rome 1677). This catalogue was reprinted and revised in 1705, 1714 and 1735.

[5] See chronological and descriptive details contained in P. Bellini, *op. cit.*, pp. 85–91.

[6] In the absence of specific detailed material on this matter see the short essay, inexact on certain biographical points though it is, by Diane K. McGuire, 'Giovanni Battista Falda and the decorative plan in three Italian gardens', published in *The American Connoisseur*, Vol. 159, no. 639 (May 1965) pp. 59–63. McGuire underlines Falda's success in faithfully documenting his subjects and graphically recording details of vegetation which could be verified by English travellers visiting Italian, and particularly Roman, gardens of the time. R. Assunto provides a fascinating introduction to '*Ville e giardini di Roma' nelle incisioni di Giovan Battista Falda* (Milan 1980), which, through descriptions left by contemporary travellers (John Evelyn had already visited Rome by 1644) and the guides to the city and its environs (for example that of Pietro Rossini in 1776), makes interesting comparisons with the work of Falda, revealing indirectly his accuracy in recording all the various changes and adaptations that took place in the Roman gardens of the period. It should also be remembered that alongside his unemotional factual observations Falda often portrayed slices of daily life, depicting single figures or groups, an aspect of his work which seems to conflict with its more generally recognized characteristics; however, his sensitivity for the human things in life was reflected in these touches and is confirmed by biographical information recording his love of poetry and *belles lettres*, for which – together with painting – he 'demonstrated an excellent disposition' (see A. Rasario, p. 197).

[7] R. Assunto, *op. cit.*, p. 128.

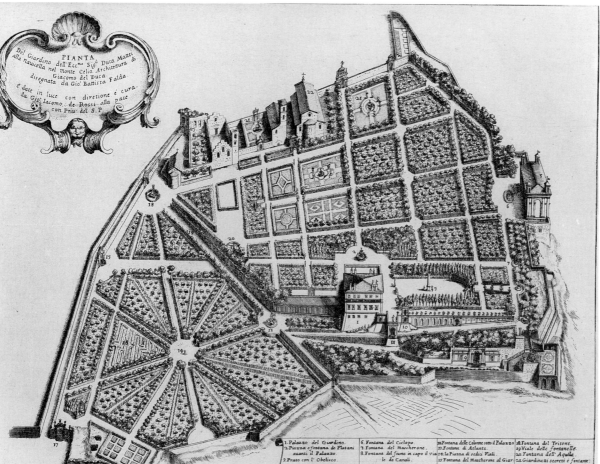

The Architectural Adornment of Cardinal Richelieu's Garden at Rueil

Kenneth Woodbridge

Château de Rueil, near Paris: view of the Vieille Grotte and part of the canal. Engraving by A. Perelle from a drawing by I. Silvestre, 1661. Bibliothèque Nationale, Cabinet des Estampes, Paris.

Cardinal Richelieu's garden at Rueil was celebrated in its time, not only for its architectural features but on account of their picturesque setting. It also embodied Italian influences in more than one respect and it was in complete contrast to his other great garden in Touraine.

Great Italian gardens of the sixteenth century, like the Villa Lante, existed in their own right; often in elevated sites away from the city, cool retreats from the hot Italian summer. The French classical tradition of garden design developed as an architectural setting for the house, which was its most essential feature. This was the character of Jacques Lemercier's Château de Richelieu, which was approached through forecourts extending for some 700 metres (2300 ft), with parterres beyond as the climax to an axial approach. Canals and other parts of the garden were at right angles to this axis. At Rueil however, as John Evelyn wrote in 1644[1]: 'though the house is not of the greatest, the gardens about it are so magnificent that I doubt whether Italy has any exceeding it for all varieties of pleasure.'

The Château de Rueil (or Ruel as it was then called), which Richelieu finally acquired in 1633, had belonged to Jean Moisset (known as Montaubon), a former tailor to Henri IV, who was Fermier Général des Rentes, Aides et Gabelles. He had added twenty acres to a park of sixteen acres, and spent large sums of money on the house and grounds. An English visitor, Peter Heylyn, described Ruel in 1625[2] as

a place so full of retired walks, so sweetly and delicately contrived, that they would even entice a man to melancholy; because in them even melancholy would seem delightful . . . It seemed a grove, an orchard, and a vineyard, so variously enterwoven and mixed together, as if it had been the purpose of the artist to make a man fall in love with confusion. In the middle of the wilderness was seated the house, environed round about with a moat of running water; the house pretty and therefore little, built rather for a banquet than a feast.

The site was a shallow valley, sloping from south to north, parallel to the St-Cloud road. The only ornaments mentioned by Heylyn were 'two fountains of admirable workmanship', one of which was the Fontaine du Dragon, described by Evelyn as 'a basilisk of copper which, managed by the fountainer, casts water near sixty feet high, and will of itself move round so swiftly that one can hardly escape a wetting'.

Jean Héroard wrote[3] that when Louis XIII visited Ruel as a boy in 1624 with his mother Marie de Médicis, '*il va s'asseoir à table avec la compagnie, y mange peu, va aux Grottes, y mouille, y est mouillé.*' [He goes to table with the company, eats little, goes to the grottoes, splashes and is splashed]. One of these was probably the Vieille Grotte illustrated by Israel Silvestre. Although Dr Launay's reconstructed plan[4] sites it in a star-shaped walk on one side of the parterre, Silvestre shows it at the end of a canal, probably that linking two ponds north of the château.

The architectural grotto, illustrated by Perelle and fully described by Elie Brackenhoffer,[5] was probably designed by Richelieu's architect, Jacques Lemercier. It was sited between the upper pond and the canal. Its roof formed a balustraded terrace from which steps led to the entrance of the grotto at the lower level. It was furnished with elaborate water games, described in detail by Brackenhoffer.

It is octagonal, very prettily vaulted with dressed stone, well built and everywhere artistically furnished with fine sculpture and figures, flowers, snails, agates, mirrors, coagulations and other materials. In four of the angles there are satyrs, in the other four nymphs, all life-size, prettily formed of sea shells and snails; each character makes a strange gesture with the hand, sometimes putting a finger on the thigh, sometimes on the mouth, while the other hand directs the *membrum virile* in the air and water spouts from it; on four of the sides there are fountains with fine oval basins; near each stand three marble figures also discharging water from their genitals. In the middle stands an octagonal marble table on which one could do all kinds of amusing things, in that by pressing the instrument or tube coming from the centre, one made all kinds of figures with the water, for example lilies, cups, flowers, glasses, moons, stars, parasols.

When the water was turned on it came from above, below and from the sides so that it was difficult to escape a wetting.

Jacques Lemercier enlarged the house, which overlooked a parterre to the southeast and the upper pond to the northwest. The site of the Orangery, with a *trompe-l'oeil* triumphal arch painted by Nicolas Poussin's friend and collaborator Jean Lemaire, is shown on a cadastral plan of 1818 at right angles to the St-Cloud road. But, like other features such as the Fontaine du Dragon and a circular island with a moat described by Brackenhoffer, the sites are conjectural. Di Launay's reconstructed plan used by Cramail should be accepted with reservations. On the other hand existing roads, which follow the lines of the *allées* of the park shown on the 1818 plan, confirm the position of the Grande Allée, over 800 metres (2600 ft) long, dividing the old gardens from higher irregular ground to the east, incorporated by Richelieu, who enlarged the park by more than half. At its head was the Grande Cascade the first of those monumental French architectural cascades emulating Italian prototypes at Frascati. Water had to be brought from some distance[6]. The lower end of the Grande Allée was closed by the Grotte de Rocaille; also known as the Grotte de la Baleine, described by Brackenhoffer as 'of fine stone, with a great open mouth three or four times the height of a man, with big ears and a powerful throat, frightening from a distance.' The

inside was fashioned like rock, with shells and snails, and contained a fountain. It was probably the work of one of the Francini,[7] who were responsible for all the water-works. A monster's mouth was a widely used symbol for the entrance to the underworld, the point of intersection between Heaven and Hell.[8] There were Italian prototypes; for instance in a garden portal at the Palazzo Zuccari in Rome.[9] There is also an analogy with the gaping mouth in the Orsini garden at Bomarzo, which had the inscription over it, LASCIATE OGNI PENSIERO VOI CH'IN-TRATE (abandon all thought you who enter here): an adaptation of the line from Dante's *Inferno*, LASCIATE OGNI SPERANZA VOI CH'INTRATE (abandon all hope you who enter here).

The French classical tradition represented by Lemercier aimed to display the architecture of the house and its surroundings as a symbol of the status of the owner; his public image as it were. Italian gardens like Bomarzo were not only more private places; they also displayed those fantasies which public dignity did not permit. The obscenities of the Grotto at Rueil and the aggressive water games like the Fontaine du Dragon were a positive incitement to disorder. Louis Huygens[10] wrote in 1655 that people were obliged to leave their swords at the entrance because of the disturbances arising from those who were annoyed at being wetted.

Rueil was in the European tradition which allows the garden to be a proper place for fantasy. This tradition was for a time overshadowed by the rational geometry of the style of Le Nôtre. The Grande Allée at Rueil was a precedent for great sweeping vistas such as Le Nôtre created to dominate the irregular and fragmentary character of the gardens and park at St-Cloud. But at Rueil it led to the mouth of Hell. In fact, fashion in garden design, as in the other arts, fluctuates between the extremes of licence and control, reflecting tensions in the human psyche. In the eighteenth century the romantic movement represented a reaction against rational attitudes and the excessive regularity in garden design which resulted. Somewhere between the two is the balance without which works of art are either arid or anarchic.

1 *The Diary of John Evelyn*, entry for 27 February 1644 (various editions).
2 Peter Heylyn, *The Voyage of France* (1673 edition).
3 *Journal sur l'enfance et de la jeunesse de Louis XIII, 1601–1628*: ed. E. Soulié et E. de Barthelemy (1865).
4 A. Cramail, *Le Château de Rueil et ses jardins* (1888).
5 Elie Brackenhoffer, *Voyage de Paris en Italie 1644–46*, trans. Henry Lehr (1927).
6 The *Mémoires des dépenses* of Richelieu's niece and heiress, the Duchesse d'Aiguillon says '*plus de demie-lieue*'. See Cramail *op. cit.*
7 Thomas and Alexandre Francini, the royal fountainers.
8 There is a medieval example in a choir-stall at the Museum of Valenciennes.
9 Another example is a marble fireplace by Alessandro Vittoria in the Palazzo Thiene, Vicenza, illustrated in John Shearman, *Mannerism* (1967).
10 H. L. Brugmans, 'Châteaux et jardins de l'Ile de France d'après un journal de voyage de 1655,' in *Gazette des Beaux Arts* XVIII (1937).

The Menagerie at Versailles

Gérard Mabille

General plan of the Menagerie at Versailles. Anonymous drawing, eighteenth century. Bibliothèque Nationale, Cabinet des Estampes, Paris.

As it was created in the 1660s, in its broad outlines in virtually definitive form, Versailles, considered with reference to the Petit Parc, revealed a logical, classical and almost timeless design, whose symbolic framework is enhanced by the spatial and functional links between the three main independent areas with their own clear hierarchy. The principal château, though originally very modest, marks the centre at the junction of the axes. It was very soon flanked by two symmetrical 'satellites' each representing one of the aspects of the universe: to the north the Trianon, literally a porcelain palace, was intended as a dreamlike vision of China, while its gardens offer the perpetual luxury of the rarest flowers; to the south the Menagerie, now disappeared, was its obvious

complement, with a fairly complex function and significance. The Menagerie was in fact only a farm, with farmyard, dovecote, cowsheds and dairy, yet it was also a palace at the heart of a strange domain inhabited by exotic animals and rare birds. Thus in its dual role, this architectural creation, the earliest of the personal works of King Louis XIV, immediately reveals its great originality. It is certain that from ancient times the tradition of these collections of rare and wild animals with which royalty liked to surround themselves, even in their everyday life, had been firmly established. The attraction of their exoticism and rarity helped to enhance the power of the monarch. Such was the *Hôtel des lions du roi* created by Philippe VI de Valois at the

Louvre, or again Charles V's comparable establishments at the Hôtel St Pol in Paris. The animals would often engage in ferocious fighting, which barbaric entertainment continued the tradition of the circus games of antiquity: particular examples of this can be found at Amboise at the end of the fifteenth century and in the reign of François I, then at St Germain under Henri II, and lastly at Vincennes in the seventeenth century at the beginning of Louis XIV's reign. It was from 1661 that Louis XIV undertook the transformation of the little château created at Versailles by his father. For almost ten years considerably more work was done on the park than on the château itself, and it is in this connection that it is appropriate to consider the work on the

Menagerie. It was established to the south-west of the park, along the St Cyr road well beyond the perimeter of the gardens, but within the confines of the Petit Parc. It seems probable that the Menagerie was started in 1663, perhaps even in 1662; the main part of the building at least seems already to have been completed in 1664, while the interior decoration was not finished until 1668. The areas intended for the animals were already in use as early as the spring of 1664, on the occasion of the famous festivals of the Plaisirs de l'Ile Enchantée (pleasures of the enchanted isle). The 'maritime' link between the Menagerie and the lower part of the gardens by means of the junction of the Grand Canal, cut between 1668 and 1772, is very clearly later than the original arrangement; this also explains the obvious disparity in the spatial relationship between the two elements, which was immediately put to use: like the Trianon (started in 1670) the Menagerie was henceforth the ideal destination for popular boat trips on the largest ornamental lake in the park. One single great architect dominates the work at Versailles until 1670 – Louis Le Vau. Everything points to the fact that he supplied the plans for the Menagerie, even though we have no longer a single drawing of his relating to this building.

As we have already seen, the Menagerie, designed both to shelter exotic animals and to offer all the advantages of a virtually independent small residence, was a building with a dual function: it is as such that it should be described and examined.

The Menagerie was reached by a long, walled avenue running east-west. In 1670, when it became necessary to create an access to the Canal, a gate was placed in the middle of the north wall; backing on to the south wall was a long building beyond which lay a small kitchen garden together with a large rectangular farmyard, a genuine model farm with dovecote, barn, bakehouse, drinking trough and cowsheds, as well as a dairy where butter was churned for the royal table.

The access avenue led in from the east and terminated in the main courtyard between two symmetrical pavilions, the northern of which housed a chapel. This courtyard was bounded by walls on its northern and southern sides, and closed on the west by a façade of the château.

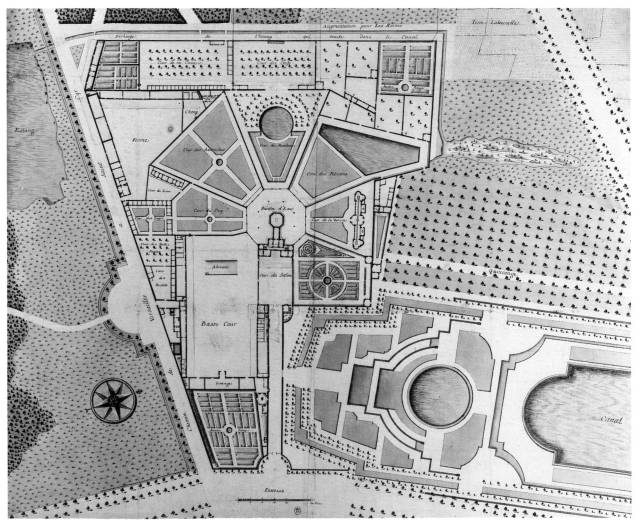

172

Versailles: general view of the entrance front of the Menagerie. Engraving by A. Perelle. Bibliothèque Nationale, Cabinet des Estampes, Paris.

Versailles: general view of the courtyards and pavilions of the Menagerie. Engraving by Aveline. Bibliothèque Nationale, Cabinet des Estampes, Paris.

This latter, because of its reduced proportions, was more on the scale of a pavilion; nevertheless no effort had been spared to give it the appearance of a genuine residence, in which, however, it was hardly possible to spend more than an afternoon, while taking a walk. According to whether it was seen from the east or the west, the château presented two very different aspects, reflecting exactly the complexity of its role and structure. Viewed from the main court, three cuboid pavilions – the centre one set back

comprising a ground floor and first floor surmounted by a loft, constituted a group of buildings of quite traditional appearance; in the centre, a wide opening rising to the full height of the building gave access to the grand staircase, consisting of one central flight. On either side, the ground floor of the pavilions contained kitchens and guardrooms and on the first floor were two complete suites of rooms symmetrically arranged. Much more unusually, in the centre of the convex arrangement of the west façade was the massive projection of an octagonal pavilion surmounted by a dome – a favourite theme of Le Vau – connected to the building behind by a narrow wing at right angles to it, on the same axis.

Internally, this unexpected arrangement was linked on the first floor to a short gallery, accessible from the upper landing of the grand staircase leading to a vast domed octagonal hall, ingeniously placed at the geometric centre of the surrounding area, and reserved for the exotic animals. The octagon, a true belvedere, had seven French windows opening on to a wrought-iron balcony which encircled it and even continued as far as the main building. From it could be observed the meticulous organization of the estate. The immediate surroundings of the octagonal pavilion formed a spacious octagonal courtyard, embellished with parterres and little fountains. Between the paving stones gushed here and there, at random, unpredictable jets of water which soaked passers-by: an unexpected reappearance of those hydraulic surprises so popular in the previous century, a tradition also seen in the rock-work grotto constructed on the lower level of the octagonal pavilion, under the hall. The octagonal courtyard, reserved for strolling, was enclosed by seven iron gates supported by pillars in

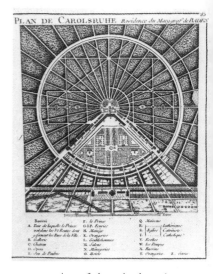

the form of sculpted figures illustrating, very aptly in this zoological situation, Ovid's metamorphoses. Beyond, in six radiating courtyards, lived the livestock and birds. To the north of the main courtyard lay the Cour des Belles Poules (Fine Fowls) where the storks lived adorned with a central ornamental lake. Further west was the Cour de la Volière (aviary) where there was a veritable palace for flying creatures: a gallery with openings protected by a mesh of gilded brass, containing three pavilions, had a little canal with fountains running through its entire length: further west still was the Cour des Pélicans (Pelican Court) or habitat for African birds, with a vast triangular stretch of water, the pelican pool. On the same axis as the château the fourth courtyard, called the Rondeau (rondo) because of its circular *bassin*, which accommodated waders and fish. Further south was the Cour des Autruches (Ostrich Court) with its little circular *bassin*. Finally, between the octagonal pavilion and the St Cyr road, three linked courtyards surrounded by cabins gave shelter to other birds as well as small mammals.

It will have become apparent that at the time of its creation the Menagerie was inhabited only by docile animals, chiefly birds. At the end of the seventeenth century, when the old Menagerie at Vincennes was closed, larger and fiercer animals were introduced at Versailles, where the Cour du Lion (Lion Court), Cour des Chèvres de la Thébaïde (Nubian Goat Court) and Cour des Cerfs (Stag Court) were constructed.

It was not until the eighteenth century that an elephant and a rhinoceros were introduced. It must be emphasized that from its inception in 1662–3 the Menagerie had been conceived as a peaceful, idyllic garden of Eden, far removed from that primitive animal ferocity still seen at Vincennes a few years earlier. At Versailles, the purpose was quite different: the animals kept here offered much more refined pleasures: as well as satisfying to the full the visitors' simple curiosity, everything seemed designed to encourage scientific observation in its most modern sense.

Le Vau's skill is here brilliantly shown in an original plan adapted to a new purpose. Certain details, such as the rock-work grotto and the hydraulic fountains, echo the traditional repertory of the art of garden design; others merely transfer the accepted traditions of civil architecture, as in the case of the château, the plan of which is in essentials only a scaling down of that of Le Vau's great buildings. On the other hand Le Vau showed himself an innovator in setting the octagonal hall in isolation to make it the geometric centre of a radiating arrangement, admirably suited for display purposes.

Thus, in spite of its modest size, the Menagerie is an architectural experiment worthy of note. The novelty and ingenuity of the layout encouraged many later architects to make use of certain elements, which they did not always completely understand; hence other royal or princely menageries were created on this model. The menagerie at Chantilly, established in 1686 under the Prince de Condé, used the idea of radiating courtyards, fountains and a grotto without, however, putting a pavilion in the centre. At Sceaux, from 1710, the architect La Guépière constructed for the Duchesse de Maine an elegant domed pavilion, encircled by a balcony which, although it was placed in the middle of a French garden and called 'The Menagerie', never accommodated any rare animals. The Menagerie established at the Belvedere in Vienna by Eugene of Savoy in 1716 took up again the Versailles arrangement of radiating courtyards. Finally, the one built at Schönbrunn in 1752 by Francis I was even closer to the French model: thirteen enclosures radiate from a central circus in which there stands an octagonal pavilion.

Architects were tempted to adapt Le Vau's plan to the scale of a town, a palace and a park: this was done at Karlsruhe, capital of the Duchy of Baden, founded and laid out in 1715 by the Margrave Karl-Wilhelm. From a central point, marked by a tall octagonal tower linked by a gallery to a palace enclosing a trapezoidal courtyard, radiate thirty-two avenues: nine of these lead to the town and the gardens, the others go deep into the forest. In spite of the enormous difference of scale, this design is indeed a direct development of that of Versailles, and thus an indication of its functional genius.

Bibliography

Gustave Loisel, *Histoire des ménageries de l'antiquité à nos jours*, 3 vols (Paris 1912).

Gérard Mabille, 'La Ménagerie de Versailles', in *Gazette des Beaux-Arts* (Jan. 1974), pp. 5–36.

Gardens and Plant Collections in France and Italy in the Seventeenth Century

Antoine Schnapper

In gardening, making a collection tends to be a paradoxical idea, since flowers and fruits, though they are capable of reappearing the following year, are transient. There is a difference between the scientific sort of collection, herbaria (*hortus siccus*) or botanic gardens, where the purpose is to gather together the greatest possible number of vegetable species, and gardens which aim to collect the greatest possible number of varieties of the same plant or of some particularly valued plants. The second sort of collection may also influence the first.

Private botanic gardens are well documented in Venice from the beginning of the sixteenth century, in relatively favourable climatic conditions which permitted the introduction of some of the numerous exotic plants which were coming into Europe from the Balkans and Turkey and even from Africa and America in the wake of the voyages of discovery. Plants, even more than animals, were valued for their medicinal properties in the ancient world. It was in connection with chairs of botany, linked with schools of medicine, that from 1545 public botanic gardens came into existence in Italy and then throughout Europe. The formation of large collections of plants was all the more attractive since the total number of known plants was remarkably small: three thousand species only are listed in G. Bauhin's *Pinax theatri botanici* (1613), and ten thousand a century later in the time of John Ray, compared with the half million recorded today. Hence, in the mid-seventeenth century it was possible for great botanic gardens such as those in Paris and Blois (Gaston d'Orléans) with their some 2300 plants, to gather together a very large proportion of known plants, even if these figures must be treated with caution, for the distinction between species and variety was still vague.

These botanic gardens doubled as herbaria, the art of which originated with the Italian 'simplicists'. The invention of them is attributed to Giorgio Ghini, and one of the first great herbaria, still preserved and dating from 1563, was that of his pupil Andrea Cesalpino, the first systematic botanist of modern times.[1] These herbaria made it possible to conserve plants which could not be acclimatized or which would be killed by a hard winter in the open. Their largely medical

origin explains the almost ubiquitous presence of herbaria in the countless collections of curiosities belonging to doctors and apothecaries.

Important botanic gardens had printed catalogues which were for a long time arranged alphabetically. These allow us to trace the spread of fashions and tastes among 'florists' or flower-lovers. The word 'simple' was used to denote both exotic plants and flowers; the most famous botanists, such as Clusius, were generally also great lovers of flowers. From the end of the sixteenth century there grew up an international trade in rare flowers, one of the pioneers of which, the Florentine Matteo Caccini, has been the subject of a study by Georgina Masson.[2] The network spread from Italy to the Netherlands by way of Germany, France and England. At the beginning of the seventeenth century the most sought-

175

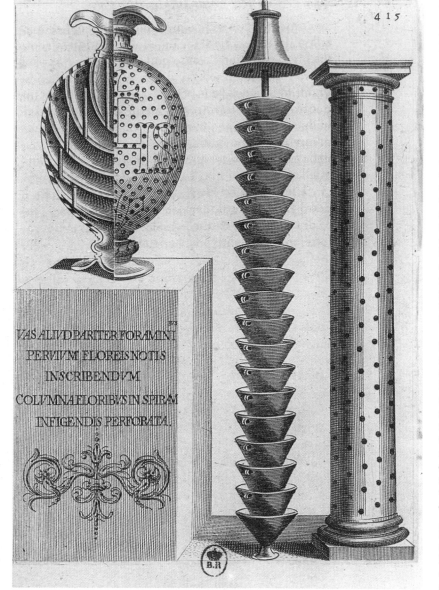

after flowers were varieties of the *Hyacinthus orientalis*, narcissi, iris and especially anemones and tulips (these latter arrived from Turkey about 1560). These fashionable flowers, though of no medicinal value, were particularly well represented in the botanic gardens. In 1636 the first catalogue of the botanic garden in Paris, drawn up according to the classification prescribed by Clusius, lists 108 varieties of narcissus, 60 hyacinths, 47 iris, 44 anemones and 14 special varieties of tulip, apart from unspecified groups of early, late or mid-season varieties.

Anemones and tulips have long interested plantsmen.[3] As early as 1616, in Franeau's *Jardin d'hyver ou cabinet des fleurs* (Winter garden or collection of flowers), 31 varieties of the first and 50 of the second were described, no other species having more than ten. This number of varieties, soon to grow at a remarkable rate, was precisely the reason for the plantsmen's eagerness to acquire new parti-coloured or variegated varieties. Catalogues from French tulip dealers or specialists in the mid-seventeenth century describe from four to five hundred varieties.[4] The fact was that tulips, when grown from seed and not from bulbs, were found to give unexpected combinations of colour and variation, resulting from somewhat unscienti-

fic breeding methods which might be either jealously guarded or on the contrary, given due publicity. Anemones, easier to cultivate, were almost equally sought after, especially the downy variety ('*di velluto*' in Italian) which has now disappeared. Their cultivation, practised in France since 1596, later became much more developed in Italy. Francesco Caetani, Duke of Sermoneta, had in his garden 62,000 plants, including 15,000 tulips and almost 29,000 anemones belonging to 230 different varieties.

These collections of flowers, growing in specialized gardens often at some distance from the house or palace, were not restricted to princes, in spite of the high cost of the rarest varieties. In Paris the obscure painter Roch Voisin possessed, at the time of his death in 1640, two gardens – one containing 6000 and the other 8000 tulips: it is not known how many varieties he had, but he used to exchange his rare specimens with the sculptor Simon Guillain.[5] This passion was nurtured by dealers famous throughout Europe, such as Morin in Paris or Jean-Baptiste Dru in Lyons; and their flower gardens were both collections and commercial stocks for which they published catalogues. The determination to obtain new varieties (described by Alexandre Dumas, along with the research

carried out in Holland in the first part of the century, in *La Tulipe Noire* [The Black Tulip]) and the difficulties of nomenclature (how was it possible to be certain that some bizarre form of tulip, obtained at the cost of so much time and trouble, was really a new strain?) are the reason for the countless plant portraits which interested parties collected, or despatched to each other, and which could be very expensive: the Arenberg-Caccini correspondence tells us that a fine miniature (watercolour on vellum) cost one gold crown. The famous collection of miniatures on vellum in Paris, begun by Gaston d'Orléans, which also includes birds, comes from the same source. These pictures are an unusual example of a very prolific output which also included animals and insects, the fragile and ephemeral models for which were to be found in princely collections in Prague or Florence as well as in simple 'cabinets of curiosities'. Similarly the most prized flowers are to be seen in numerous flower pictures and still lifes produced in France, Italy and particularly in the Netherlands.

As well as flowers there were also collections of fruits, or rather of fruit trees, with the same increase in varieties which no practical value can justify, and which professional gardeners deprecated. Orange and lemon trees were much valued and became luxury items in northern Europe. The number of varieties was smaller, but Peiresc in 1637 boasted of having about twenty different lemons and even more oranges in his gardens at Belgentier. Citrus fruits, to which G. B. Ferrari devoted a famous book[6] were criticized by wise gardeners, who extolled the virtues of indigenous fruits. The favourite was the pear, praised by Claude de Sainte-Estienne.[7] He lists 406 varieties which he himself collected, 'having had them sent from all corners of France'; he also catalogues 157 different plums and 119 peaches. The habit of collecting flowers or fruits, denounced by La Bruyère at the end of the century as the sign of an unhealthy curiosity, has nevertheless persisted to the present day. It spite of the enormous number of known varieties of orchids, do orchid-hunters not still abound?

1 See for example Allan G. Morton, *History of Botanical Science* (London, New York, Toronto, Sydney, San Francisco, 1981).

2 Georgina Masson, 'Italian Flower Collectors' Gardens in Seventeenth-Century Italy', in *The Italian Garden*, ed. David R. Coffin (Dumbarton Oaks 1972), pp. 63–80; see also, by the same author, 'Fiori quali pezzi da collezione nell'Italia del secolo XVII', in *Arte Illustrata*, Vol. 3, no. 30–33 (June–Sept. 1970), pp. 100–9.

3 Antoine Schnapper, '"*Curieux fleuristes.*" Collectioneurs de fleurs dans la France du XVIIᵉ siècle' in *Commentaire* no. 21 (Spring 1983), pp. 171–80.

4 Jean-Baptiste Dru, *Catalogue des plantes, tant des tulipes que des autres fleurs . . .* (Lyons 1649) – also in modern edition; Pierre Morin, *Catalogue de quelques plantes à fleurs, qui sont de présent au jardin de Pierre Morin le jeune* (Paris 1651) – also in modern edition; Charles de La Chesnée-Monstereul, *Le floriste françois, traitant de l'origine des tulipes . . .* (Caen 1654). This is the first work on the subject.

5 Georges Wildenstein, ed., 'Inventaire de Roch Voisin (1640)', in *Gazette des Beaux-Arts* (September 1957), pp. 163–72.

6 Giovanni-Battista Ferrari, *Hesperides, sive de malorum aureorum cultura et usu* (Rome 1646). A great deal of information about the flowers in fashion and their Italian collectors is in the same author's earlier work *Flora, seu de florum cultura libri IV* (Rome 1633).

7 Claude de Saint-Estienne, *Nouvelle instruction pour connoistre les bons fruits selon les mois de l'année* (Paris 1670).

The Formal garden at Het Loo

Jan van Asbeck

Palace and garden of Het Loo. Engraving by R. de Hooghe, c. 1695. (Photo A. Meine Jansen)

Het Loo: the Queen's Garden. Engraving by L. Scherm, c. 1700.

No other historical garden has gained such international celebrity immediately after its construction (*c.* 1693), vanished from the face of the earth after 115 years and finally, 175 years later, been restored in all its former glory as though time had stood still for the intervening three centuries. This sunken Baroque garden was constructed in two stages simultaneously with the hunting lodge of Het Loo, with which it formed a single entity, by William of Orange (1650–1702) and Mary Stuart (1662–1694). Between 1807 and 1809 the sunken garden was buried in sand by Louis Napoleon (1778–1846), King of Holland, and together with all its raised terraces levelled for the construction of a landscape garden.

In 1979, after extensive historical research and minute excavations, the garden was prepared for reconstruction in its original form, and at the same time the house itself was converted into a museum. The restoration and conversion were completed in 1984.

In November 1684 the stadholder Prince William III decided to build a new hunting lodge near Apeldoorn. Via his ambassador in Paris a request was submitted to the Académie Royale d'Architecture for the preparation of a plan. The minutes of its meeting of 15 December show that he requested '*un corps de logis sur caves voûtées composé d'un vestibule, d'un escalier et de deux appartements et leurs dépendances*' (a main block over vaulted cellars, comprising a vestibule, staircase, two apartments and their offices), while those of 6 April 1685 record a visit by the Dutch ambassador to thank the Académie for the drawing prepared for the Prince of Orange. The plans in question have not been traced, either in France or in the Low Countries, but may be regarded as the basis upon which the Dutch architect Jacob Roman (1640–1716) and Daniel Marot (1663–1752), of French origin, developed their design for Het Loo. Marot especially, who had fled to Holland as a Huguenot refugee in 1685, was responsible for the design not only of the house's interior, but also of the formal gardens, garden urns, wrought-iron railings, coaches and a great variety of objects. It is safe to assume that he also designed the *parterres de broderie*.

Het Loo was constructed in two stages, which succeeded each other quite

De Koninginne Tuin met 't Groene Kabinet, en de Oranjerie, van Achteren te zien

C. Allard exc   *cum Privilegio*

quickly. The first of these began in the spring of 1685. By 1687 the palace looked more or less as follows: living quarters, with two quadrant colonnades which, true to Palladian principles, linked the main buildings with the wings. The colonnade was measured and precisely described in 1687 by the well-known Swedish architect Nicodemus Tessin who visited Het Loo on his way to Paris. The garden was for the moment restricted to the so-called Lower Garden and the two side gardens which from 1689 onwards became known as the King's and the Queen's Gardens. The form is characterized by a strict geometrical ground plan, consistent symmetry, and Renaissance elements in the design. In the planning of the garden the following formal parameters of the site had to be observed: on the north side the existing avenue leading to the Het Oude Loo, henceforward to be called the Dwarslaan or Transverse Avenue; on the south side adjoining the front forecourt the King's Avenue; the Het Oude Loo to the west and the boundary of the estate to the east. The area between the two avenues is divided exactly in two, with the lodge buildings, the two colonnades, the wings, the King's Garden and the Queen's Garden situated to the south of the central axis. North of this line is the Lower Garden, designed as a lavish *salle de dehors*, reached by the wide terrace with fan-shaped steps leading down to the central avenue. Unique in the Low Countries are the raised promenades surrounding the Lower Garden in a U-shape, bounded to the north by the Transverse Avenue with its four rows of oaks.

Looking down at the garden from these terraces one had a view of eight square beds, of which the middle four were *parterres de broderie*. In addition there were cascades, basins, fountains and borders, bushes and topiary. At the main intersecting points of the geometric design there were statues, either in white marble or in whitewashed sandstone or gilded lead, and finally stone, lead and terracotta urns. All in all a colourfully decorated, imposing outdoor space. Looking west from the side terrace one had a view of the Het Oude Loo – a moated medieval hunting-lodge – and in addition a number of features added after 1684 which have since disappeared, such as the maze and the menagerie, the side gardens with basins, fountains and statuary, and finally in the distance the formal park behind the Het Oude Loo.

Both the King's Garden and the Queen's Garden were accessible from the raised terrace via the brick steps at either end by the garden wall. The King's Garden was in two sections. The part directly adjoining the house had box trees clipped into all kinds of shapes. There were two beds with borders filled with plants and flowers, and at regular intervals pyramid-shaped juniper bushes or box trees. At the heart of the design was an octagonal white marble basin with a gilt spouting triton in the centre and at the edges eight gilt sea dragons. In the other part, on a level with the stables, was the sunken mall with a wide gravel path on all four sides. The King's Garden was connected to the maze by a wrought iron gate in the garden wall and also to a complex of gardens, waterworks and a menagerie at the side of Het Oude Loo.

The Queen's Garden was situated to the east of the lodge and could be reached from the queen's apartment on the first floor by means of a separate staircase leading down to the basement. Here the staircase ended in a space adjoining the shell grotto, so that the queen could enter the garden through it. This garden was also in two parts. The first, adjoining the Lower Garden, had three beds, two of which were surrounded with borders. Between the clipped box trees in these borders were juniper bushes trimmed into pyramids and between them plants and flowers. In the middle was the octagonal white marble basin by Arion. On the white marble edge of the basin were eight gilt sea-horse waterjets. The second part of the garden was four steps higher and consisted entirely of a number of arbours of hornbeam. It contained five fountains with spouting gilt tritons seated on rocks in stone and shells in basins of carved rock and pebble mosaic. There were also a number of tall alcoves cut out of the intertwined branches to rest in. One could leave the Queen's Garden and walk in the adjoining gardens with their high hedges, footpaths, fountains, waterfalls, rock gardens, trellises, statues, urns and benches and take one's ease. These side gardens also disappeared.

After the coronation of William and Mary as king and queen of England in 1689, Het Loo was expanded. It was

Het Loo: plan for landscaping the upper part of the garden. Drawing by P. W. Schonck, 1781. (Photo A. Meine Jansen)

Het Loo in Gelderland: map dating from c. 1760. (Photo A. Meine Jansen)

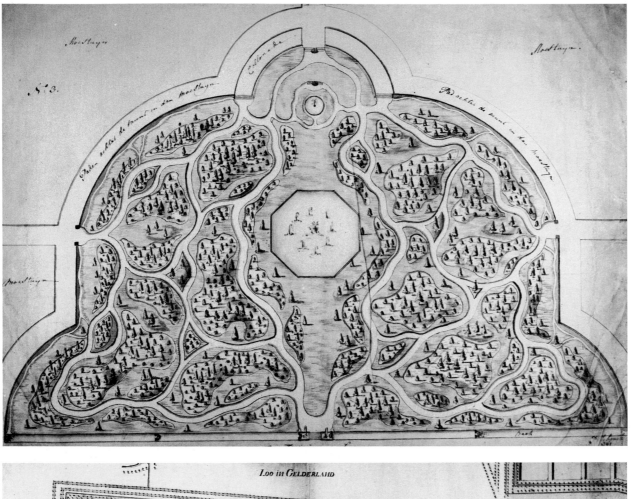

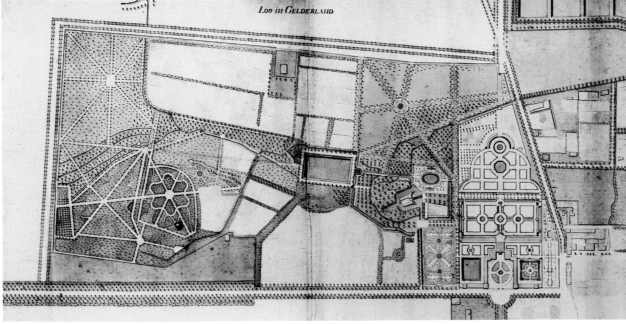

decided to build four new pavilions in place of the quadrant colonnades and to resite these in the garden, to serve as the crowning feature of the slightly raised Upper Garden. The oak-lined Transverse Avenue linking the Lower and Upper Gardens assumed the character of a 'green colonnade' between the two formal gardens.

The *pièce de résistance* in the Upper Garden was the octagonal basin, 32.5 metres (106 ft) in diameter with the 13-metre (42.5 ft) high King's Fountain, which was fed by a natural spring and hence operated day and night. Standing between the two colonnades on the axis of the whole garden one's eye fell on the obelisk 800 metres (2,600 ft) away, a classical eye-catching device suited to a royal Baroque garden.

When Walter Harris, William III's personal physician, published his detailed description of the garden in 1699 (*A Description of the King's Royal Palace and Gardens at Het Loo* by Walter Harris M.D. Physician in Ordinary to His Majesty, and Fellow of the College of Physicians, London, 1699) Het Loo and especially the garden was at its most beautiful and its fame had already spread far and wide. In the eighteenth century the gardens were maintained as well as possible. The oaks in the Transverse Avenue were replaced with beeches and the formal layout of the Upper Garden gave way to a landscape garden designed by Philip W. Schonck (1735–1823).

After the departure of the Orange family at the time of the Batavian Republic, Het Loo was plundered and the gardens fell into complete neglect. During the short reign of Louis Napoleon, using plans by the Frenchman Alexandre Dufour (1750–1835), the remains of the formal garden were removed, the ground was levelled and a picturesque garden was laid out in the landscape style then in vogue, without, however, including the ponds originally designed because of Louis Napoleon's fear of water. In the nineteenth and twentieth centuries the trees planted in 1807 were allowed to grow and areas of rhododendron added. Fortunately the ponds Dufour intended were not dug even after Louis Napoleon's departure, for if they had been the reconstruction of the formal garden would have been an even greater problem.

The Garden of Villa Garzoni at Collodi

Alessandra Ponte

Villa Garzoni (now Gardi), Collodi, Pistoia. Plan of 1692. Fondo Garzoni, n. 198 c. 13. State Archives of Lucca.

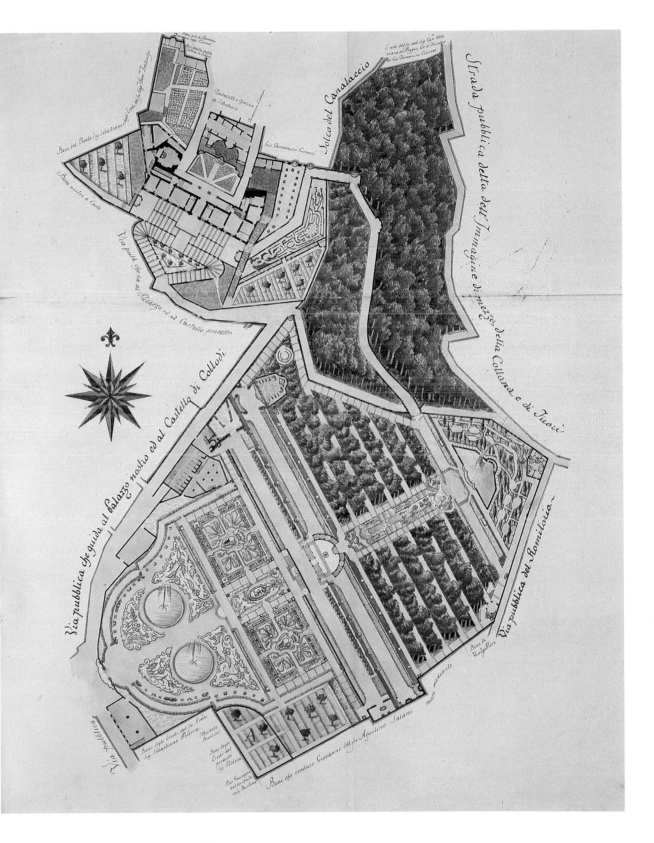

The garden of Villa Garzoni (now known as Villa Gardi), at Collodi in Tuscany, is perhaps the most spectacular and certainly the best conserved example of any of the seventeenth-century gardens of the province of Lucca.

The existence of a garden at Collodi is documented in a sixteenth-century survey (the property of the Gardi family) and in a drawing dating from 1633 (now in the State Archives of Lucca). From both it is clear that the garden then occupied a very small area, running east from the villa and extending as far as the bank of the river. It appears to have been divided by walls that formed a series of irregular enclosures, and it was accessible by means of staircases descending at various points from the side of the building. The drawing of 1633 also shows a bridge built to link the villa with the large new garden that was laid out shortly afterwards.

A poem entitled *Le Pompe di Collodi* by Francesco Sbarra, published in 1652, describes in minute detail the delights of the garden created at Collodi by Romano Garzoni. The situation of the garden was unusual in that it was laid out to the side of the villa rather than directly in front of and behind it, and it seems to have been conceived as a self-contained entity, with a separate entrance from the public road outside.

At the time of Sbarra's poem, most of the major excavation work required to transform the steep slope beyond the river (referred to by Sbarra as a 'craggy, vertiginous precipice') into a formal and orderly succession of terraces had been completed. It is not clear whether an attempt was made from the start to achieve the illusion of height that makes the view of the garden from below so dramatic, the arrangement of dividing walls accentuating the verticality of the plan and concealing the depth of the terraces. From above, on the other hand, the descent from one level to the next is disguised by the width of the terraces, which seem to unfold like a carpet in a single continuous slope.

From Sbarra's poem it is apparent that in this first phase of work the earth around the great semicircular entrance to the garden was 'glazed with highly polished stones', the labyrinth was laid out in the hollow between the terraced hillside and the villa, and the garden was planted with ornamental trees and shrubs

181

which were clipped into strange, mythological and symbolic shapes:

In mille guise so contorce e stende
Il bel cipresso hora scherzante, hor grave,
Hor esprime una Torre, hor una Nave,
Hor di Pera, Hor d'angel sembianze prende
(In a thousand guises the fair cypress twists and stretches, now jesting, now serious. Now it forms a tower, now a ship, now it takes the semblance of a pear, now that of an angel.)

In 1662, the year in which Ferdinand of Austria and Anna de'Medici visited Collodi, the fountains and statues were not yet *in situ*, though they are mentioned in a survey of 1692. This document describes the garden as being surrounded by walls, and refers to a 'small painted chapel and the rooms of a hermitage' in the upper reaches of the property; it also describes avenues of

clipped laurels and cypresses, with wide openings cut out of them, the foliage of the cypresses cut into spheres . . . sandstone steps, walls covered with espaliered citrus trees, with niches for statues and grottoes for pools and fountains, compartments made up of myrtles with figures of birds and other creatures, a kitchen garden for the growing of vegetables and herbs, rows of fruit trees divided by espaliered roses and, in the valley below, a meadow with a beautiful theatre enclosed by clipped cypresses, and twin avenues . . .

All this is illustrated on the detailed plan of the property made the same year, which shows the garden very much as it is today. It also depicts a number of other features: the elaborate parterres and the two great circular pools – from each of which rises a single jet of water – near the entrance gate from the road; the three partitions of the first terrace, decorated with the Garzoni coat of arms; the three transverse terraces known today as the Avenues of the Palms; of the Emperors; and of the Turk; the walled semicircular arena enclosing the statue of Neptune; the theatre; the water staircase at the top of the final ascent, overlooked from above by two statues representing the two divisions of the commune of Pescia (the lion for Tuscany and the panther for Lucca, referring to the two city states of Florence and Lucca); and, lastly, the irregularly-shaped basin at the summit, spurting a great jet of water which sprays on to the stone shells ornamenting the base of the statue of Fame. A winding

Villa Garzoni, Collodi: statue of Lucca with a panther; in the foreground the lion that accompanies the statue of Florence. (Photo Daniele De Lonte)

avenue, known today as the Avenue of the Camellias, links the upper part of the garden with the villa by means of the bridge illustrated in the drawing of 1633.

Equally interesting if rather more mysterious is a document published in its entirety in a guide to the villa and gardens of Collodi by N. Andreini Galli and F. Gurrieri (1975). This document (now in the possession of the Arnolfini Foundation and housed in the Lucca State Archives) contains a description of the garden which has been interpreted by the authors of the guide to date from the seventeenth century. It lists the works completed 'from 1670 onwards' in a logical topographical order, descending from the villa at the top to the entrance to the garden from the road. It is devoted principally to a description of the 'little garden' immediately next to the main house and to the avenue (now known as the Avenue of the Poor), which divides it from the labyrinth, where 'five clay statues were placed in niches encrusted with tufa'. It also refers to two niches built near the bridge, the first containing a sculpture of Hercules fighting the Hydra (which still stands there today), and the second a statue of Samson victorious after his defeat of the Philistine. The major hydraulic works undertaken around this time are then described in some detail, in particular the 'great mill-pond' which contained 'about twenty thousand barrels of water' and supplied all the fountains, *giochi d'acqua* and pools in the garden. A new bathing area was constructed, with three individual pools, a podium for an orchestra and changing rooms, which replaced the hermitage at the top of the garden. The text relating to ornamental features in the upper part of the garden corresponds precisely with the plan of 1692, but even more fascinating is the account of the work carried out on Neptune's Grotto, which was described as 'admirable':

built with great skill and artistry, it has a mosaic floor and is entirely encrusted with tufa and a mixture of other materials; at the top is an eye . . . which allows enough light to enter to create a suitably mysterious atmosphere; around it are niches of varying sizes containing statues representing Neptune, with sea-horses pulling his chariot, and a series of sea-creatures spouting water. Endless entertainment is provided by *giochi d'acqua*, among them a gate and stone seats which eject sudden spurts of

Villa Garzoni, Collodi: view of the garden from below; the villa can be seen on the left-hand side. (Photo Daniele Da Lonte)

water at the unsuspecting visitor. This grotto leads on to two rooms that may serve for the preparation of refreshments.

The document then goes on to list other statues sited in various corners of the garden: a rough peasant with a barrel on his shoulder, who stands at the edge of a pool; the Muses of Tragedy and Comedy in the theatre; the 'wild boar that spurts water'; figures representing the seasons; Pomona; the satyrs; the 'twelve monkeys playing with a ball'. There is also mention of a 'bosquet cleared to make space for recitations of Arcadian poetry, with little enclaves and secret tracks that lead to the far corners of the wood'.

The existence of this bosquet (which seems from the description to have been 'informal') and of the theatre, together with the suggestion by the anonymous author of the document that the statues represented 'a variety of mythological fables', indicates that the garden was laid out according to an iconographical scheme of some complexity, comprising a number of different themes. Unfortunately, no thorough study of its iconography has yet been carried out, though a number of different theories have been advanced which at least partially explain its significance in relation to other gardens of the period in Tuscany and Rome. It would be revealing, for example, to examine the relationship of Collodi to Pratolino and the Boboli Gardens, where, it seems, certain features were influenced by if not actually copied from Collodi: the sculptures of the wild boar and the peasant with a barrel, for instance, and above all the use of statuary inspired by the myths of Ancient Greece and Rome in combination with figures specifically associated with country life.

During the last phase of work at Collodi the name of an architect, Ottaviano Diodati, is associated for the first time with the transformation of the gardens. Employed by the last Romano Garzoni (1721–86), he worked there in the two-year period from 1786 to 1787. He was very probably responsible for the plantation of new trees in the lowest part of the garden, the addition of a number of statues and other ornaments and the installation of a new hydraulic system.

It was shortly after his time, at the end of the eighteenth century, that the garden's fame and magnificence reached their zenith. Charles VII of Naples commissioned Diodati to draw up plans for the royal park at Caserta (though his scheme was not eventually carried out), and Stanislas Poniatowski, King of Poland, requested from Paolo Lodovico Garzoni, the owner of Collodi at that time, a drawing of the villa, which was duly executed in 1793 by the Luccan artist F. A. Cerchi. By then, however, attitudes were changing, as is confirmed by the verses written by Cerati and Franceschi, describing the beauty of the garden in the 1780s.

Bibliography

F. Sbarra, *Le Pompe di Collodi, deliziosissima villa del Signor Cavalier Roman Garzoni* (Lucca 1652).

G. C. Martini, called Il Sassone (The Saxon), *Viaggio in Toscana 1728–1745* (Massa 1969).

A. Cerati, *Le Ville Lucchesi con altri opuscoli in versi ed in prosa* (Parma 1783).

F. Franceschi, 'Descrizione delle Ville Lucchesi al principe di Kaunitz. Ode III' in *Odi e Prose del dottore Francesco Franceschi* (Lucca 1788).

N. Andreini Galli, F. Gurrieri, *Il giardino e il castello Garzoni a Collodi* (Florence 1975; reprinted Pisa 1985).

I. Belli Barsali, *Ville e committenti dello Stato di Lucca* (Lucca 1980).

'Hell and Paradise Are Here': The Garden of Villa Barbarigo at Valsanzibio, Padua

Lionello Puppi

Villa Barbarigo, Valsanzibio, Padua. Plan of the garden drawn by A. Gornizai, 1717. State Archives of Venice.

Villa Barbarigo, Valsanzibio, Padua. Painting by anonymous artist, late seventeenth century. Private collection.

Reduced to the abstract lines of its geometric plan, the garden of the Villa Barbarigo seems surprisingly simple in concept. It consists of two great intersecting axes, the longitudinal axis – the more dominant of the two – running north-south and rising almost imperceptibly from the main entrance gate to a wide flight of steps. It is then carried up to a terrace running the length of the simple, uncluttered façade of the villa itself, which is silhouetted against a backdrop of the gently undulating Euganean Hills. This perspective line is taken up again in the centre of the rear elevation, where a rustic exedra opens on to another flight of steps; climbing steeply upwards, it finally loses direction in a series of paths winding up the hillside behind. The east-west axis links two pools, which are overlooked respectively by a pavilion and an artificial rocky outcrop; running parallel to this axis are a number of shorter paths, which cut across the main north-south line, interrupting its flow.

The garden's extraordinarily rich visual imagery is given cohesion and unity by the gridiron plan of its design, emphasized by fine topiary work, which provides a framework for an iconological scheme of great complexity. Among its principal features are the pavilion dedicated to Diana the Huntress, and a triumphal statue of Aeolus which looms over the rocky crag, both reflected in the waters of the pools below them. *Putti* watch over the fountains and sculpted figures mark the crossing points of the main route to the villa, while other sculptures line the approach to the terrace and the balustrade of the terrace itself; the disturbing presence of Chronos dominates the intersection of the two axes. Two of the smaller paths lead to a labyrinth and a 'rabbitry'. Inscribed stones, still partly legible (and all of them recorded and reproduced by Salomonio[1]), mark the individual features of the garden, suggesting that they are all related and form part of a coherent scheme whose meaning is about to become clear; any such confidence is quickly dispelled, however, by a strange, enigmatic inscription that seems inconsistent with the rest and succeeds only in veiling the light of reason and logic.

Apart from Valsanzibio's complex iconography, to which we shall return later, one of the most remarkable features of

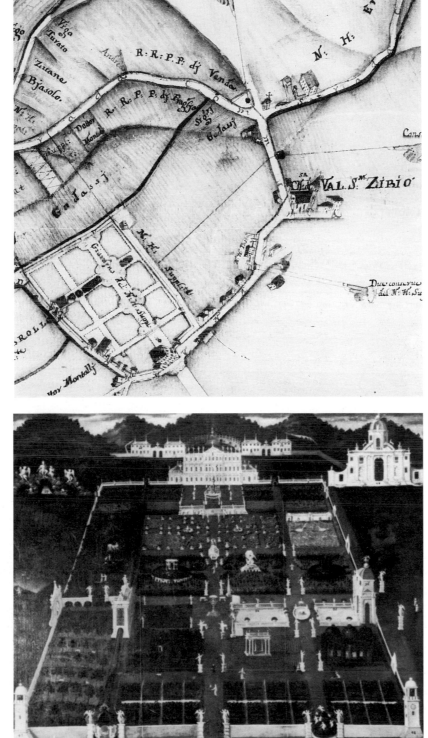

this great garden is its state of preservation, and fortunately enough documentation of the original garden exists today to ensure that any damage that may occur in future years as a result of neglect or changes in design need not be irreparable. Apart from the evidence accumulated by Salomonio, descriptions of Valsanzibio – with etchings by G. Campana – were published by Rossetti in 1702,[2] and reproductions of a painting are still available (the original is in a private collection in Turin), which is datable to the same period, though it appears to represent a project for the garden rather than the completed scheme.[3]

Today the property belongs to the Pizzoni Ardemani family, but it was very largely the seventeenth-century creation of the Barbarigos, wealthy patricians who came originally from Venice. The major part of the land on which the villa and its garden were laid out seems to have come into the hands of Gianfrancesco Barbarigo, who bought it from the Contarini family, on 30 August 1627, further acquisitions of land having been made by 1650.[4] A map of 1570 shows that the property then consisted of an area of fields bordered by marshland.[5] There is no doubt that soon after buying the land Barbarigo began to build himself a house, which forms the nucleus of the villa today. Documents dating from as early as September 1628 refer to this building, and the following year the astronomer Andrea Piccolomini stayed as a guest there: in a letter of 10 August 1629 he recalled not only 'the perfect sweetness of the air' but also 'the various comforts available throughout the day'.[6]

In 1661 the Venetian magistracy registered the existence of 'a domicile with an outbuilding and two enclosed fields'.[7] Alterations to the original house cannot yet have begun because we know that the outbuilding was demolished in order to make way for the garden, which must have been planned and laid out shortly afterwards. In fact a contract was drawn up on 1 June 1665 with two stonemasons, Pio and Domenico, for columns to flank the entrance doors and for a series of stone fountains. Work also began on vases and obelisks to ornament the gardens.[8]

By 22 January 1670, only five years later, so much progress had been made that the great Nicolò Ratti was called in to

*Villa Barbarigo, Valsanzibio, Padua:
fishpool with pavilion dedicated to Diana.
(Photo Luigi Ghirri)*

*Villa Barbarigo, Valsanzibio, Padua:
aviary. (Photo Luigi Ghirri)*

186

*Villa Barbarigo, Valsanzibio: 'Rabbitry
with an aviary for small birds'. From
D. Rossetti, Le fabbriche e i giardini
dell'Ecc. Casa Barbariga a Valsanzibio,
Verona 1702. Museo Civico, Padua.*

appraise 'the work carried out . . . at Valsanzibio'.[9] There can be no doubt that by then the scheme was largely complete: indeed this is confirmed by a dated map by Jacopo Cuman of 10 September 1678 and by a letter written by Gregorio Barbarigo (the future saint) three months later describing 'the delights to be enjoyed in yonder garden'.[10]

All that was lacking by that stage were a few 'iron supports for the statuary' (which were ordered and paid for in 1678), heraldic devices (expenses for a coat of arms were settled in 1688), the rabbitry (which was built in 1693) and finishing touches to the villa, which had by then been partially reconstructed, as documents of 1694 confirm.[11]

Responsibility for this great undertaking had now passed to Antonio Barbarigo, the son of Gianfrancesco and the brother of Gregorio. He was to die on 5 June 1702, at about the time of the publication of Rossetti's work on Valsanzibio, which describes every detail of the garden as it must have looked since at least 1696, when Salomonio gathered together and published his collection of inscriptions. Antonio Barbarigo had been actively engaged in politics and had held a number of important official posts, including that of Procurator of St Mark's in Venice. Attempts have been made to interpret Valsanzibio as a celebration of Antonio Barbarigo, and to establish a direct relationship between his *cursus honorum* and the plan of the garden, but efforts to do so have proved largely fruitless. Similarly, endeavours to trace the designer of the garden layout and the author of the iconographical scheme have met with no success, though it is perfectly possible that both were the work of Barbarigo himself. It seems likely that Valsanzibio was intended not as a celebration of its owner but rather as a representation, through metaphor and allegory, of the superiority of the harmony of nature over the confusion of political life, a retreat from the artificiality and pressures of the city. 'Here activity gives way to extreme idleness and peace', as one inscription reads, and others declare that 'this is no place for tears but the seat of laughter' and that 'the Graces reign where pleasure rules':

Here the sun's rays shine more brightly;
Here Venus rises more lovely from the sea;

The phases of the moon are clearer here;
Here nothing arouses the passions of Mars;
Here Jupiter plays with carefree smile
And Mercury sets aside all clever deceits.

Most important of all, however, the 'charms' of the garden are 'the work of nature and not of art'. The references to the presiding divinities over the world of nature, Diana and Aeolus, in the temple and on the rocky crag, dominate the Villa Barbarigo. The water of the pools and fountains (which have 'the world for a cradle and the sea for a tomb') can be identified with *natura generosa*, affirming its image as a mirror of the world in its most primitive form. Is the garden therefore intended as a sanctuary – a place of salvation – or as the essence of nature in its pure original state, untouched by 'art'? In the rabbitry and the labyrinth, tricks and illusions undoubtedly play an important part, and the figure of Chronos, bent under the weight that he carries on his back, seems to suggest that a spirit

of transience ('the hours fly past and the years vanish') rules the garden, which is nothing more than an illusion created by art. 'Hell and paradise are here', reads another inscription, which may provide a key to Valsanzibio, though there are as many interpretations of the symbolism as there are visitors who wander there, either accepting without reserve the dream it offers and living it as if it were reality or rejecting it as invention and falsehood, refusing its ironical invitation to follow the paths which, at the top of the steps from the exedra, seem to lose themselves among the rocks and streams in the dense, mysterious woods that lie beyond.

1   J. Salomonio, *Inscriptiones patavinae sacrae et prophanae* (Padua 1696).
2   D. Rossetti, *Le fabbriche e i giardini dell'Ecc [ellentissima] Casa Barbariga a Valsanzibio* (Verona 1702).
3   L. Puppi, 'The Giardino Barbarigo at Val-

sanzibio' in *The Journal of Garden History*, no. 3 (1983), p. 281 and fig. 1.
4   Bibl. Correr, Venice (BCV), MS PD *c.* 2485/7 and MSS PD *c.*2486/6, PD *c.*2485/22, PD *c.* 2485/43 respectively.
5   BCV, MS PD *c.*2359/I.
6   BCV, MS PD *c.*2472/23, B. Brunelli & A. Callegari, *Ville del Brenta e degli Euganei* (Milan 1931), p. 220.
7   BCV, MS PD *c.*2403/4.
8   BCV, MS PD *c.*2392/6.
9   BCV, MS PD *c.*2392/6.
10   State Archives of Venice. Superintendent of Works, Drawings Department, Padua and Polesine region, Roll 19. See also B. Aikema, 'A French Garden and the Venetian Tradition' in *Arte Veneta*, no. 35 (1981), pp. 121–31, and S. Serena, *San Gregorio Barbarigo e la vita spirituale e culturale del suo Seminario* (Padua 1963) Vol. 2, p. 479.
11   BCV, MS PD *c.*2392/6. It is worth emphasizing that the first illustrative document representing the garden in its final and complete form is a ground-plan drawn by A. Gornizai in 1717, now housed with the State Archives in Venice, and published by M. Azzi Visentini, 'Note sul giardino veneto: aggiunte e precisazioni' in *Arte Veneta*, no. 37 (1983) p. 87, n. 25 and fig. 9.

The Garden of the Prince-Bishop at Veitshöchheim

Helmut Reinhardt

Garden of the prince-bishop at Veitshöchheim, near Würzburg. Plan, anonymous drawing, c. 1725. Bayerische Verwaltung der Staatlichen Schlösser, Gärten und Seen, Munich.

Situated a few miles north of Würzburg, the former summer residence of the Prince-Bishops of Würzburg at Veitshöchheim has a garden unique in the German-speaking world – it is regarded as the Rococo garden *par excellence*.

Its beginnings date back far into the seventeenth century, when the cathedral of Würzburg acquired two small lodges on the site of what was later to be the Hofgarten. About the time that the summerhouse or pavilion was built in 1680–82, extensive estates were purchased south of what had hitherto been a relatively small garden. In 1686 further adjustments of the boundaries gave the estate its present orientation and form. There was a pleasure-garden extending as far as the village street and a wooded park to the south for pheasants and game – its average length was 475 m (520 yd) and width 270 m (295 yd).

During the reign of Prince-Bishop Johann Philipp von Greiffenclau (1699–1719) major works were carried out, which affected the future layout of the garden: a high wall was built around it, the square area around the schloss was separated from its surroundings by retaining walls like a terrace, and four artificial lakes were dug.

However, it was not a layout which followed the ideal pattern of the time, which was a single axis radiating from the schloss through parterre, bosquet area and woodland. Instead there were two parallel gardens and two main axes, an untypical arrangement presumably due to the different functions as pleasure-garden and hunting ground.

Around the middle of the eighteenth century the prince-bishops turned what had been a temporary hunting lodge into a summer residence, and in the following years they extended and enlarged the schloss and estate buildings.

The garden too was to be remodelled. In 1752 the sculptor Johann Wolfgang von Auvera was commissioned to make a group of Olympian gods and Muses for the schloss terrace, but the outbreak of the Seven Years' War in 1756 interrupted all further plans. It was not until the reign of Prince-Bishop Adam Friedrich von Seinsheim (1755–79) that Veitshöchheim took its final form.

A few days before the Peace of Hubertusberg in the spring of 1763 brought to an end the war that was devastating Germany, an order was issued to the court for the remodelling of the garden. The pheasantry was finally to be done away with and its whole area was to be included in an overall composition.

Besides the prince-bishop himself, a number of artists worked on the scheme: the architect Johann Philipp Geigel, the sculptors Ferdinand Tietz and Peter Wagner, the plasterer Materno Bossi, the painter Christoph Fesel, and as garden designers, probably Johann Prokop Mayer as well as the court gardener Georg Joseph Oth and his son Johann Anton.

The two gardens, which had been formally unrelated to each other for more than eighty years, were to remain independent entities, and were just linked together loosely by visual axes, avenues and steps.

The former pheasantry was already divided into three long strips of different widths. At its centre was the Grosser See (Great Lake), from which avenues and paths extended to the edges of the garden. In 1753 there had been plans for a sculptural group for the lake representing Hercules binding Cerberus, the hound of hell, but Adam Friedrich von Seinsheim decided against the Hercules episode. Instead he built the Parnassus Rock, surmounted by Pegasus, in the middle of the lake, a sculpture which evoked far more complex associations with contemporary events. The spruces planted around the lake in the 1750s were

removed and replaced by a hedge border with niches and cabinets which Ferdinand Tietz filled with statues of the Olympian gods, allegories of the arts and the seasons.

At the same time the remodelling of the adjoining bosquet area was begun. At the intersection of its transverse and longitudinal axes a circular space was left open, with corridors, *salons* and *cabinets* to the north and south forming an enfilade. On the open grassy area a circle of topiary niches was laid out and furnished with an extravagant wealth of sculptures: allegories of the four continents, dancers with shepherd musicians, vases with animal groups, trophies with hunting weapons and musical instruments, and stone seats. Variations on the themes of nature, poetry, music and dance were continued in the *salons* and *cabinets*.

In 1767/68 work began on the neighbouring wooded area. This part of the garden had always been the most densely overgrown and now its woodland character was intensified by reafforesting with spruce. Three rectangular areas of equal size accommodated various functions. In the northern part a hedge theatre was formed, with sandstone *commedia dell'arte* figures painted in colour set in front of the wings. In two symmetrical zones left and right of the main axis in the central section, the fountains were adorned with groups from La Fontaine's *Fables* with bizarre Chinese pavilions built next to them. Lastly, in the south part labyrinthine paths within the gloomy spruce plantations led through an octagonal space to the brightly lit Lindensaal (Linden Hall).

Immediately after this the remaining parts of the garden were modernized. Smaller elegant *parterres de broderie* were made to take the place of the four old-fashioned angular parterres around the schloss. Figures of Muses and gods by Auvera were placed on the balustrade of the retaining walls to the west and south.

The works came to an end with the inclusion in 1773 of the long thin triangular area situated between the wooded area and the edge of the garden. The central axis of the lake which ran through the Festsaal (Banqueting Hall) was given a focus by the building of a cascade here in 1772/73: the Parnassus Rock and Neptune Grotto were thus set in contrapuntal relationship to each other.

To the south was a Belvedere with a grotto-like lower storey from which stepped ramps led to the octagonal *salon* above. The sculptures for this part of the garden were made by Peter Wagner following the departure of Ferdinand Tietz in 1768.

The garden's decline began soon after its completion. After it was opened to the public in 1776 complaints began to be made about losses and damage to the works of art and buildings. It was saved from conversion into a landscape garden by King Max I Joseph of Bavaria, a true Romantic who appreciated the elegiac atmosphere of the decayed and long unfashionable Rococo garden, and in 1823 ordered that 'the symmetrical forms of this royal garden' be preserved.

In spring 1945 the garden was damaged by bombing and the cascade destroyed, with the result that an important element for understanding the composition is now missing.

Veitshöchheim's importance for garden design, apart from its relatively good state of preservation, lies in the successful way it combines the styles of two distinct periods. The early eighteenth-century garden with its small-scale, grid-like division reminiscent of early Baroque gardens, and its long, narrow strips intersected by diagonals reminiscent of Italian terrace gardens, was filled with a new spirit after 1763. Within a mere ten years, and without disturbing the earlier arrangement, Adam Friedrich von Seinsheim introduced intimate spaces in the Rococo taste and decorated the garden with a wealth of sculpture.

The three zones – lake, bosquet area and woodland – are filled with a chorus of messages expressed in the plants, statues and architecture. Seen from the Parnassus in the Grosser See, the symbolic centre of the garden at the intersection of its main axes, the iconographic programme becomes clear. The nine Muses are gathered together here under the leadership of Apollo. Corresponding to them around the lake is a cycle of gods with allegories of the seasons and arts. The legend of the deluge in Ovid's *Metamorphoses* recounts how after the destruction of the world Parnassus would rise above the waters and from it would come a new cosmic order, ruled by the Olympian gods. The end of the Seven Years' War is thus reflected in a striking manner by the choice of this programme.

In the Golden Age which was dawning Apollo, the leader of the Muses, would help bring about a new resurgence of the arts. The axial paths radiating from Parnassus in the garden clearly demonstrate the subordination of nature to divine authority and order. Since Apollo is also the sun god at the centre of the planetary gods arranged in a circle around him, there is also a reference here to the sun symbolism of the prince's absolute rule, a symbolism for which Louis XIV had already provided a model in the *Parnassus* at Versailles.

At the end of the main axis which runs through the Parnassus Rock at Veitshöchheim is Neptune in his grotto surrounded by nymphs and tritons. He is to

Garden of the prince-bishop at Veitshöchheim: the Parnassus Rock by F. Tietz.

be seen here both as the god of water and as god of the underworld in opposition to Apollo. Between these two poles are distributed the various figures carrying the message of the garden in a variety of guises. In the woodland, bosquet and lake zones the primeval forms of human life are depicted. Neptune and his cascade filling the garden with water and life, are at the starting point of the path that must be followed. The wooded area with its labyrinthine paths and spaces populated by natural creatures represents purely natural existence. From there the brighter bosquet area is reached, where the dominant theme of festivity with a fanciful variety of music, dancing and masquerade, symbolizes the cultural-social development of man. In the spacious, light-filled lake area the legend of the deluge and the triumph of Apollo represent intellectual resurgence and striving for order and beauty as the highest aims of earthly existence.

Even if the means used were already well tried, the creators of this garden succeeded in producing a distinctive work of art, which, with its interplay of refashioned nature, sculpture and architecture, still retains its original charm today.

Bibliography

Georg Karch, *Der königliche Garten zu Veitshöchheim* (Würzburg 1855).

Georg Karch, *Der königliche Garten mit dem Schloss in Veitshöchheim nach Platons Schule* (Würzburg 1881).

Heinrich Kreisel, 'Die Entwicklungsgeschichte des Veitshöchheimer Hofgartens', in *Münchner Jahrbuch der bildenden Kunst*, new series III (Munich 1926).

Heinrich Kreisel, *Schloss und Garten Veitshöchheim* (Munich 1932).

Heinrich Kreisel, *Der Rokokogarten zu Veitshöchheim* (Munich 1953).

Felix Mader (ed.), *Die Kunstdenkmäler des Königreichs Bayern*, Vol. 3 (Munich 1911).

H. K. Röthel, 'Der Figurenschmuck des Parks von Veitshöchheim', in *Der Kunstbrief*, No. 7 (Berlin 1943).

Walter Tunk, *Veitshöchheim, Schloss und Garten* (Munich 1977).

*Garden of the prince-bishop at
Veitshöchheim: view from the pavilion.*

The Grosser Garten at Herrenhausen near Hanover
Dieter Hennebo

Design for the gardens of Herrenhausen, near Hanover, by M. Charbonnier; early eighteenth century. Hanover State Archives.

The development of garden design in the Baroque period did not really begin in Germany until about 1680, because of the aftermath of the Thirty Years' War.

With the territorial fragmentation of the Holy Roman Empire the various political and dynastic connections between the princely families, as well as the personal preferences of individual rulers, played a considerable role, and individual and regional differences are on the whole more apparent than in other countries. Thus, for instance, the increasing influence of French garden design everywhere was often combined with other continuing influences – in the south these came from Italy and in the north from the Netherlands. Occasionally – and this is true of the Grosser Garten at Herrenhausen near Hanover – with the change of patrons over the various phases of construction of a park the artistic orientation also changed.

When Duke Johann Friedrich of Brunswick-Lüneberg, who was a connoisseur of art, decided in 1665 immediately after his accession to transform into a summer residence his father's estate, then situated a long way outside the gates of Hanover, he was no doubt also inspired by memories of the villas of the Venetian mainland which he had visited on his Italian travels.

A site plan made about 1666 shows the outlines of the first, very modest park. Beside the 'Prince's Summerhouse, called Herrenhausen', which had wings flanking a courtyard at the front which opened (surprisingly) on to the garden, was an orchard. The almost square area of the pleasure-garden proper was divided by a central path leading towards the centre of the *corps de logis* and was bordered by two fish ponds. To the south of these, beyond the edges of the garden, an avenue continued the line of the central axis as far as the bank of the River Leine.

During a second phase of construction beginning around 1673 the house and garden were enlarged under the direction of the court architect, Hieronymo Sartorio, who was of Venetian origin, and the French gardener, Henri Perronet, who was working in Celle at that time. Who was responsible for the garden designs that were submitted and which of them was executed are not known. The evidence is only that the parterre, which until then occupied the area of the first pleasure-garden, was rearranged and more richly ornamented. It was also given surroundings with regular plantations of fruit trees and bosquets. Two important and characteristic features from this phase, the Haute Cascade and the grotto, still exist today.

Significantly it was not until after 1680 that the summer residence of the Guelfs was given its final form and decoration, characteristic of the apogee of the culture of absolutist courts in Germany, by the Duke (and later Elector) Ernst August (ruled 1679–1698) and his wife Sophie. It was she in particular who strove for the improvement and enlargement of the park. In 1713 she described it as '*Le jardin de Herrenhausen, qui est ma vie*' (the garden of Herrenhausen, which is my life). It was not surprising that she sought inspiration not only in French garden design, as was usual at the time, but also in the gardens of the house of Orange. Throughout her life she maintained close contacts with the Netherlands where she had been born and had spent her youth (she was the daughter of the Elector Palatine Friedrich V who was living in exile there).

Sophie probably intended from the very outset to extend the Herrenhausen gardens, and it was largely for this reason that in 1682 she summoned the gifted gardener Martin Charbonnier to Hanover from Osnabrück, where he had been working for her since 1677. However, the first fifteen years of her work there – which can be seen as the third phase of construction at Herrenhausen – were concerned with the completion of the existing design, for example the setting up of new sculptures and the erection of the Garden Theatre (1689–93), which immediately became famous. There were also continual efforts – though with little success – to improve the fountains. Because the schloss no longer satisfied increasing social demands, the Gallery Building was built next to it between 1694 and 1700. This was a banqueting hall flanked by habitable pavilions, which until the building of the new Orangery also served as winter quarters for the tub-plants.

In 1695 Martin Charbonnier once more visited the Orange residences in Holland. A year later the fourth and final phase of construction at Herrenhausen began under his direction. This concluded with the completion of the Grosser Garten.

This was when the Nouveau Jardin was added to the existing, orthogonally articulated layout (with its newly formed parterres and hedge bosquets). It was almost the same size but quite different in form. These two parts, each almost square, now formed a rectangle of approximately 50 hectares (123 acres) surrounded by a wide ditch (called the Graft). The central axis opened out into an apse at the junction of the two gardens, and then continued as a broader, tree-lined avenue leading to an oval *bassin*. Two round pavilions built in 1708 from designs by Louis Rémy de la Fosse mark the southern corners.

When the Electress Sophie died on 8 June 1714 in her beloved garden, it must have looked as it appears in most early eighteenth-century plans and views. These show the schloss with its three wings, the semi-circular *cour d'honneur* to the north and the compartments situated to the side of the gallery wing: to one side – behind the Haute Cascade – the Electress's private garden and to the other – behind, near the grotto – a 'fruit and melon garden'. Still further to the side is the Gallery Building with the Orangery Garden, which the Garden Theatre adjoins to the south in axial alignment. The parterre area is surrounded by further hedge bosquets with *salons* and *cabinets*, two quincunxes and four pools created out of the former fishponds. The four inner fields of the parterre area, forming a unified pattern with a central fountain, are marked on almost all plans and illustrations as *parterres à l'Angloise*, i.e. pieces of lawn ornamentally divided by a pattern of paths and framed by *plates-bandes coupées en compartiments* (beds divided into compartments). The four outer fields are set within very similar borders, but in keeping with the compositional principles of the time (which demanded that furnishings and decoration decrease the further away they are, or the greater their distance from the castle and the central axis), they are not subdivided.

The Nouveau Jardin is divided by crossed avenues with the great fountain in the centre, to form four square areas occupied by star-shaped gardens. At the centre of each of these are round open spaces with octagonal fountain pools forming another square around the great fountain. Most of the triangular compart-

193

Gardens of Herrenhausen: the Garden
Theatre with trees and clipped hedges.
Engraving by J. van Sasse after J. J. Müller,
c. 1720. Historisches Museum am Hohen
Ufer, Hanover.

Gardens of Herrenhausen: the Haute
Cascade. Engraving by J. van Sasse after
J. J. Müller, c. 1720. Historisches Museum
am Hohen Ufer, Hanover.

ments (Triangeln) created by this system of articulation contained fruit-trees planted in a regular pattern.

The Grosser Garten at Herrenhausen is one of the few Baroque gardens to have survived in its essentials. However, a comparison with its original form and furnishings, which are recorded in numerous sources, shows that the comprehensive and highly commendable restorations in 1936/37 and 1960–66 did not always follow the historical evidence. This is particularly true of the planting of the Triangeln in the Nouveau Jardin and the structure of the parterres.

Bibliography

Udo von Alvensleben and Hans Reuther, *Herrenhausen, die Sommerresidenz der Welfen* (Hanover 1966).

Wolfgang Fiedler and Martin Heinzberger, 'Der Pflanzenbestand des Barockgartens zu Herrenhausen im frühen 18. Jahrhundert und heute', *Niedersächsisches Jahrbuch für Landesgeschichte*, Vol. 55 (1983), pp. 207–42

Wilfried Hausmann, *Gartenkunst der Renaissance und des Barock* (Cologne 1983), pp. 252–5.

Dieter Hennebo and Alfred Hoffmann, *Geschichte der deutschen Gartenkunst*, Vol. 2: *Der architektonische Garten – Renaissance und Barock* (Hamburg 1965), pp. 162–5.

Dieter Hennebo and Erika Schmidt, 'Das Theaterboskett. Zu Bedeutung und Zweckbestimmung des Herrenhäuser Heckentheaters', in *Niedersächsisches Jahrbuch für Landesgeschichte*, Vol. 50 (1978), pp. 213–74.

Karl H. Meyer, *Königliche Gärten* (Hanover 1966).

Kurt Morawietz, *Glanzvolles Herrenhausen* (Hanover 1981).

Herrenhausen 1666–1966. Catalogue of the Jubilee Exhibition in Hanover 1966.

Schönbrunn:
A Theatre of Fragments

Paolo Morachiello

In 1569 a farm belonging to the monastery of Klosterneuberg stood at Katterburg, about ten kilometres (six miles) from the centre of Vienna. There the waters of the Wein-Fluss operated a mill and irrigated the vineyards and orchards of the surrounding plain, which extended to the Katterhölzel woods covering the slopes of the woods beyond. Maximilian II bought the farm, the mill and the land around it and turned the property into a game reserve. With the help of a bird-breeder, Domenico Weiner, and a gardener, Martin Gutta, he enclosed the house and the woods, populated the land with birds, planted a garden and created a fishpond.

In 1622 a spring was discovered and the emperor requested that the gardener of the day, Christopher Strauss, should devise a way of bringing the outflow closer to the house. The newly located water source gave the reserve the name of Schön Brun (beautiful spring). By 1660 four large lime trees and the spring itself made a natural enough setting, without any need of additional scenery, for a production of *The Springs of Boeotia*, an operetta with music by the Italian composer Pederzuoli.

In 1682–3 the Turks interrupted both the old life of the hunting-box and the new Arcadian idyll of Schönbrunn, and during these years of siege both the stamping of the horses' hooves and the voices of the singers remained silent.

The Habsburg victory in 1683 led to a change both in the appearance and significance of the imperial game reserve, transforming it from a place of private refuge into an emblem of Habsburg power.

Ten years after the war, in 1693, Hieronymus von Scalvinoni was supervising the restoration of the hunting box when Fischer von Erlach was ordered by Leopold I to design a new palace fit for the imperial house. Accordingly, he produced a scheme for a magnificent edifice with allusions to Versailles, the temple of Praeneste and Bramante's Belvedere, to be built on a five-sided plan made up of rectangles and curves. Surrounded by terraces ornamented with pools and fountains, from which a series of paths would lead away in various directions down wide ramps, the castle itself was to stand high on a hill, specially created by means of Titanic earth-moving operations, in order to provide the House of Austria with a site suitable for a revival of the glorious days of the Caesars. From the summit the building would dominate literally and metaphorically both the city and the plain, as far as the Hungarian border. It would serve as the emblem of a land and a people to which peace and prosperity had been restored, and it would act as a symbol of a Christian Europe freed for ever from the bondage of Ottoman rule.

The project was monumental in scale – perhaps too monumental – and as work progressed a sense of proportion and moderation began to prevail, influenced no doubt by economic motives: a stretch of land behind the palace was in the process of being flattened to make a park, and a chessboard of parterres and avenues laid out in the direction of Hetzendorf, where it would blend with the woods and countryside, when caution prompted the Emperor to commission a second, more modest, version of the scheme. Fischer von Erlach responded by simplifying the building and setting it in the plain, in front of the main entrance gates to the property, in order to create a large flat area at the back of the building, extending

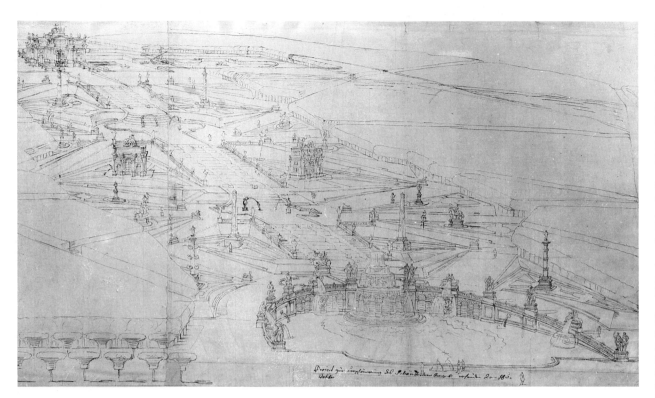

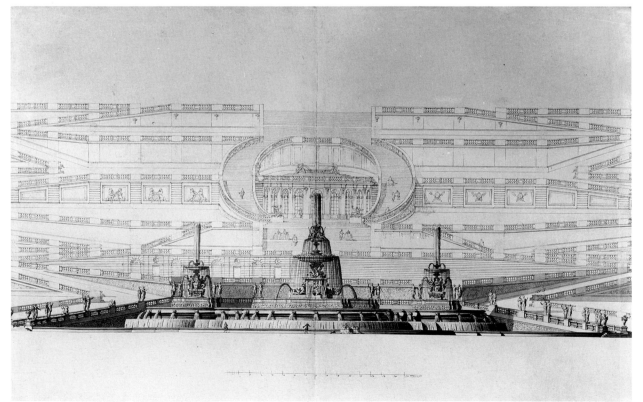

as far as the lower slopes of the hills behind. He also laid out a navigable canal for pleasure-boating and redesigned the avenues and parterres. Following the symmetrical balance of the new plan, whose main axis ran from the entrance gates to the main façade of the palace, he placed a loggia at the far end of an avenue which ran across the flat expanse at the back and continued up the slope of the hill beyond.

With modifications at various stages, this second plan was successfully carried out, with Fischer himself, followed by Anton Erhard Martinelli and Nicola Pacassi, directing operations until the completion of the work in 1750.

From 1695 the engineer Johann Trehet was engaged almost exclusively in work on the park. Having studied the parks of France, he returned to Schönbrunn in 1698 and devoted his energies to the laying out of reservoirs, tanks and channels in order to provide water for the fountains required by the architect. He ordered twenty thousand beech trees to add density to the woodland, and he imported flowers from Holland and yews from France for the parterres.

All these pains were to some extent wasted, however, as Charles VI had little affection for Schönbrunn, and under his sovereignty it suffered years of virtual abandonment. Its fortunes were restored on the accession of Maria Theresa, who left unaltered the broad outlines of the garden but introduced a number of changes to its internal design. Among the maps in the Albertina are two unsigned plans of the park in its final form, as completed by the Dutch garden designer Adrian van Steckoven, who most probably worked with Pacassi. One shows the twin rows of trees as a simple avenue extending up the hillside, the other illustrates the transformation of the area between the trees into a series of cascades starting at the foot of the loggia at the top. The concept of long, straight paths and unlimited vistas, which seemed to lose themselves in the plain or the forest, was set aside: hedges and trees were planted to create small enclosures which were shielded from the avenues running parallel or at right angles to the castle. These little enclaves, set apart from the rest of the garden, were full of surprises and discoveries: in one was an sculpture of Diana, in others representations of

Avenue in the gardens of Schönbrunn. (Photo Daniele De Lonte)

Avenue in the gardens of Schönbrunn. (Photo Daniele De Lonte)

Plan of the gardens of Schönbrunn, with a proposal for a scheme laid out on a central axis with the hill. Anonymous drawing, after 1756. Albertina, Vienna.

Apollo and Hercules, in yet another the 'nymph of Schön Brun' in her grotto. The enclosures were laid out in a range of geometric and free shapes – a trapezium, a circle, a trefoil, a half-moon and a star, a labyrinth, a serpentine and an open-air panopticon (the Menagerie). Maria Theresa's gardeners abandoned the unity of the original plan, with its vast sense of scale, heroic proportions and triumphal gestures, in favour of something better suited to a sober and enlightened monarchy which had no wish to perpetuate the cult of the individual sovereign but rather to magnify the importance of the monarch's official function.

The gardens at Schönbrunn are made up of a series of artistic and theatrical scenes which are neither heroic nor grandiloquent in concept but act as an extension into the outside world of the many literary references to be found in the castle itself. For the Austrian archdukes and archduchesses, as indeed for Maria Theresa, it was a favourite setting for recitations of the works of the highly regarded court poet Metastasio. Against a background of 'extravagant masses of intertwined greenery' (*Alcide al Bivio*, 1760), celebrated actors expressed in endlessly repetitious phrases the limited range of emotional states – pleasure, melancholy, nostalgia, loneliness, oblivion – aroused by the delights of nature.

In 1770 Maria Theresa's chief minister, Prince Kaunitz, commissioned the architect Ferdinand Hetzendorf von Hohenburg to complete the park. To counterbalance the Menagerie which terminated the diagonal axis to the right, he placed an obelisk and a ruin at the end of the left-hand axis, introducing into the garden the universal symbols of time passing and of the immortality of the ruling dynasty. He then turned his attention to redesigning the ascent of the hillside, where the thick woodland was already intersected by paths at various levels. He conceived a plan for a series of cascades and for a ramp climbing up the slope of the hill between flowerbeds, with columns carved with historical scenes and classical references, obelisks and equestrian statues at suitable intervals, triumphal arches beside the loggia on the ridge of the hill, and a belvedere in the form of a Greek cross with a cupola and pronaos. It was in many ways a revival of Fischer von Erlach's monumental scheme, but it was not a

success. Largely abandoned, it was replaced by a simplified version: a still pool dedicated to Neptune and his retinue was carved out at the foot of the hill, and a loggia (known as the Gloriette) ornamented with inscriptions and trophies was built on the summit.

In 1773, at the express wish of Maria Theresa, Kaunitz ordered the garden designer Bayer to complete the parterres of the great avenue, placing a row of statues in front of the hedges, which served as a backdrop. Tranquil images taken from mythology and history were contrasted with the drama of emblematic references to the victories of the Caesars and the glory of the Habsburgs. The Empress, more modestly, and with greater awareness of the moment and its place in history, found it easier to admire the Gloriette and the grassy slopes of the hill.

Bibliography

Darstellung historische topographische Schönbrunn (Vienna 1824).
E. M. Kronfeld, *Park und Garten von Schönbrunn* (Vienna 1923).
K. Kobald, *Schloss Schönbrunn* (Vienna and Leipzig 1924).
P. Morachiello, 'Schönbrunn: una serie di progetti mancati' in *Storia dell'Arte*, No. 22 (1974) pp. 277–90.
D. Raschauer, *Schönbrunn* (Vienna 1960).

La Granja:
Castilian Baroque and
European Classicism

Carmen Añón Feliú

La Granja, San Ildefonso, Segovia: the Carrera de Caballos. (Photo G. Careaga)

La Granja, San Ildefonso, Segovia: view down La Cascada to the façade of the palace. (Photo G. Careaga)

Early La Granja sources refer to a rustic refuge built by the King of Castile, Henry III (1390–1406). It was also visited often by Henry IV (1454–74) who founded a hermitage dedicated to San Ildefonso, and next to it built a house of refuge which the Catholic Monarchs gave to the Hieronymite monks. Philip II (1556–98) built nearby the palace of Valsaín, frequently used by later Spanish kings.

Philip V (1700–24) the first of the Bourbons, brought with him to Spain the images and memories from the years he spent at the magnificent court of Louis XIV. During a stay at Valsaín, he visited the hermitage and *granja* (farm) of the Hieronymites, and decided to build a new palace, retaining as its central part the friars' hospice whose cloister is now found at the very nucleus of the building, as the Patio de la Fuente.

Building began immediately. The king made Teodoro Ardemans responsible for the design of the central part of the palace, the chapel, later changed into a collegiate church, and the main altar of San Ildefonso. However he was later replaced, probably on the advice of the queen, by Felipe Juvara, then considered one of the finest architects in Europe, and he redesigned the façade. The replacement may also have been a result of the influence brought to bear by the foreign artists employed to design the garden statuary, or because Ardemans' taste proved too sober for the king, who kept an eagle eye on the progress of the works. However Juvara, who had also received the commission for the new Palacio Real, died shortly after his appointment and in the event the project was executed by Giovanni-Battista Sacchetti, a pupil of Juvara's. In 1729 Procaccini was put in charge of the decoration.

The building works, encouraged by the presence of the king and queen, proceeded apace, and the main body of the palace and the chapel were built in just three years. Philip V wanted to take up residence as early as possible, so work on the gardens, which had been proceeding more slowly than the building works, took precedence, especially the creation of the Cascada Nueva: the king's apartments looked on to it. On 27 July 1723 the king moved in.

The building designed by Ardemans only went as far as surrounding the Hieronymite cloister, with the chapel

adjoining the rear façade. This arrangement, placing the church at the centre and entrances at the sides, shows as much concern for traditional Spanish architecture as did the king's interest in the gardens.

The arrival of Procaccini spelt the end of this plan. The Italian architect made the façade three times as long, adding two parallel wings, resulting in an H-shaped

building with two sets of royal apartments. Procaccini collaborated with Sempronio Subisati on the design of the Patio de la Herradura, a 'delicately Rococo' courtyard, and 'one of the most delightful corners of the palace'.

The façade, designed by Juvara, was not completed until the reign of Charles III (1759–88). It is an extraordinary architectural work, achieving 'a degree of

elegance, simplicity and grandeur rarely seen elsewhere'. Its 'exceptional total beauty' is 'thanks to the pink granite of Segovia which is used for the columns and the Italian white marble used for decorative motifs. This combination results in a lively and elegant colouration which gives the façade a particular animation'.

Pickaxes and gunpowder were used to hack the garden from solid rock. Earth had to brought for each tree. Limes were brought from Holland in record time, chestnuts, hornbeams and yews from France. The elms of the Hieronymites were left standing, and the box came from Alcarria and from the hills of Cuenca.

More than five thousand men worked on the construction of the gardens. But if the ground was hard and construction enormously difficult, at least there was no shortage of water. There was a great difference in altitude between the highest hill at 1325 m (4347 ft) and the palace, which made possible fantastic jets and *giochi d'acqua*, which were arranged in a series of skilfully contrived fountains, canals, cascades etc. Foreign travellers who visited the palace in the past marvelled at this delightful place. 'The king employed an engineer called Marchand to set out the gardens and avenues which we see today. . . . The planting of the gardens was left to a certain Solis and to Don Esteban Boutelou, father of the renowned Don Esteban Boutelou II, head gardener at Aranjuez. The fountains, statues and other sculptures were the work of Master Masons Frémin and Thierry, both of whom were highly esteemed in Paris, and the first of whom studied in Rome'.

Notwithstanding this account by Ponz, it appears that work in the gardens began under the direction of René Carlier, a pupil of Robert de Cotte.

On Carlier's death in 1722, Esteban Boutelou took charge, assisted by Joly, Basani and Lemmi, who later became the first of a long line of head gardeners at La Granja. It seems that it is to Carlier that we owe the parterre and the Cascada Nueva beyond it, and perhaps also the Bosquete de Las Ocho Calles. Carlier, who was also a draughtsman, directed the first sculpture workshop; twenty-six lead fountains, fifty-four white marble statues, sixty-seven marble benches, about forty groups comprising one hundred and

La Granja, San Ildefonso, Segovia: the nymph and huntress Clio, by the sculptor Pitué. (Photo G. Careaga)

forty-eight sculptures and fifty urns were made in the workshop which was set up at Valsain. Most of the fountains were installed between 1722 and 1739.

After Carlier's death it was decided to have another sculptor as Garden Director. Frémin was the most important of these, followed by Bousseau and Dumandré. All of them used Le Brun's unexecuted designs for Versailles as models. Feminine themes were taken from mythology, in keeping with the taste of the eighteenth century, and chaste Diana, the great huntress, goddess of the woods and of nature was taken as the dominant theme in the garden.

The three stages of the purchase of land mark very clearly three distinct periods in the creation of the garden and explain perhaps the lack of an overall plan which would have given it greater unity of design. Despite the disparities of its planned parts, the sculpture gives it an aesthetic unity. There is no point from which the whole garden can be seen. Views either disappear or cross each other. They are like small theatrical sets, one following the other within the same framework.

The main sculptors were René Carlier, René Frémin, Jean Thierry, the brothers Dumandré, Pierre Pitué, Jacques Bousseau, pupils of the great sculptors of the time, Girardon, Coysevox and the brothers Coustou. They were all inspired by Le Brun and had worked at Versailles and Marly.

Except for the statues of the Canastillo and the faun in the Andromeda group, the statues and pedestals are of marble. The original intention was to cast the figures for the fountains in bronze, and the Roman bronze worker Fernando Rey was summoned for this purpose. However disagreements arose with the sculptors, and the figures were finally cast in lead, painted green and white and gilded, misleading many visitors.

Even today, two and a half centuries after they were made, the statues continue to fill visitors with admiration. The waters are collected in the pools known as the Mar and the Estanque Cuadrado. Apart from these there are numerous natural springs in the park and even in years of drought water has never been lacking at La Granja.

To the right of the palace, across the Patio de la Herradura, at a lower level is

200

La Granja, San Ildefonso, Segovia: the bridge over the canal. (Photo G. Careaga)

Rafael Breñosa, and Joaquín María Castellarnau, *Guía y descripción del Real Sitio de San Ildefonso* (Madrid 1884).

Campau: 'Residencias reales de España. Los jardines de La Granja' in *La Esfera* (Madrid 1914).

Candido: 'Cartas descriptivas del Real Sitio de San Ildefonso, de sus jardines, fuentes y otras preciosidades' in *La Epoca* (Madrid 1856).

Ramón Carnicer, *Gracia y desgracias de Castilla la Vieja* (Barcelona 1976).

Colegio Oficial de Arquitectos de Madrid, *Patrimonio arquitectónico y urbanístico de Segovia* (Madrid 1979).

Joaquín María De Castellarnau, *Recuerdos de mi vida* (Burgos 1942).

Juan De Contreras, Lopez De Ayala (Marqués de Lozoya) and Angel Oliveras Guart, *Palacios reales de La Granja de San Ildefonso, Riofrío y Museo de Caza.* Patrimonio Nacional, 7th edn (Madrid 1976).

De la Cruz y Bahamonde (Conde de Maule): *Viaje a Valsaín y San Ildefonso* (Cádiz 1812).

Carlos De Lecea, *La Comunidad y Tierra de Segovia* (Segovia 1894).

De Rouvroy, Louis (Duc de Saint-Simon), *Mémoires. Voyage à Valsaín . . .* [1722]

Jeanne Digard, *Les jardins de La Granja et leurs sculptures décoratives* (Paris 1934).

Cayetano Enriquez de Salamanca, *Por la Sierra de Guadarrama* (Madrid 1981).

José de Faroaga and Tomás Muñico, *Descripción de los Reales Sitios de San Ildefonso, Valsaín y Riofrío* (Segovia 1845).

F. O. and V., *Nueva guía de La Granja (San Ildefonso)* (c. 1890).

Mariano Grau, 'Notas sobre la venta de los pinares de Valsaín, Riofrío y Matas robledales', in *Estudios Segovianos*, Vol. 21 (Segovia 1969).

Pascual Madoz, 'Valsaín' in *Diccionario geográfico y estadístico* (Madrid 1850).

Estanislao Maestre, *San Ildefonso. La Granja. Valsaín-Riofrío. Segovia.* Notes for a guide. (Madrid 1936).

Marquesa de Casa Valdes, *Jardines de España* (Madrid 1973; Eng. edn 1987).

Santos Martin Sedeño, *Descripción del Real Sitio de San Ildefonso y de sus jardines y fuentes* (Madrid 1825).

Peñacitores 'La Granja y el Valsaín', in *El Campo* (Madrid 1884).

Antonio Ponz, *Viaje a España* Vol. 10 (Madrid 1781).

Antonio Prast, and Rodriguez del Llano, *Bosquejo histórico del palacio de Valsaín y de los jardines de San Ildefonso* (Madrid 1925).

R. Rosillo Abillo, 'Tres árboles distinguidos del pinar del Valsaín', in *Universidad y Tierra* (Segovia 1934).

Juan Manuel Santamaria, *El Bosque de Valsaín y los jardines de La Granja* (Segovia, n.d.).

Carlos Sarthou Carreres, *Jardines de España* (Valencia 1949).

the Parterre of Fame, at the end of which stands the fountain which gives it its name. This is renowned for its enormous jet (at one time the highest in Europe) which can be seen from the city of Segovia on a clear day. It is almost 50 m (160 ft) high, is fed directly from the Mar, and spouts forth from the trumpet of Fame riding on Pegasus.

Opposite the main façade of the palace is the Parterre of La Cascada, over which stands a pavilion of delicate architecture. It is built of pink stone, with four doors. In front of it stands the Fountain of the Three Graces from which springs a veil of water which covers the polychromed marbles of the ten stepped pools down to the Fountain of Amphitrite.

The whole of the cascade is enlivened by putti, dolphins, tritons and sea creatures. Two venerable old men represent the rivers Guadiana and Guadalquivir. The parterre that separates it from the palace is also decorated with numerous statues. The whole cascade is a *trompe l'oeil* which lengthens, by successive optical effects in a rhythmic succession of planes, the short distance between the palace and the mountain, the huge natural barrier which shuts out the horizon. The cascade was completely restored during the reign of Isabella II in about 1835.

In another avenue parallel to La Cascada run a series of pools from the Fountain of Andromeda, where she appears with Perseus, to the pool of Neptune, in which the god is in his element surrounded by sea horses. This series is called the Carrera de Caballos and has 114 jets. Its five pools are graded to form a series of cascades which pour into a larger one called the Media Luna, emptying into the Ria which takes the waters out of the park.

Three less important fountains, one called the Fan because of shape of its jets, and the other two called the Caracolas complete this parterre which runs up to the main façade of the palace. Lateral to the Cascada Nueva, a new vista is opened up framed by noble trees, and at its end the dark green mass of the Silla del Rey. The delicacy, finesse and grace of the composition, together with its statuary and water-jets, make this one of the finest examples of European Baroque garden vistas.

The well-known classical repertory of the eighteenth-century world extends throughout the garden. The Fountain of Latona, the Three Graces, the Canastillo, the labyrinth (a copy of the one which appears in the work of Dezallier d'Argenville and one of his many proposals which are noticeable in the design of the garden) are illustrative of the absence of a predetermined overall plan for the garden. Nonetheless the sense and measure of space, the originality of the landscape, the beauty of the building, the rhythm and movement of the statuary make the garden complete and give it a definite personality of its own.

Bibliography

F. Arias de Verastegni, *Costumbre de Segovia y sus preheminencias y jurisdicción* (Segovia 1611). Manuscript. Archivo Municipal de Segovia.

Yves Bottineau, *L'art de cour dans l'Espagne de Phillipe V, 1700–1746* (Bordeaux 1960).

PART THREE

Picturesque, Arcadian and Sublime:
The Age of Enlightenment

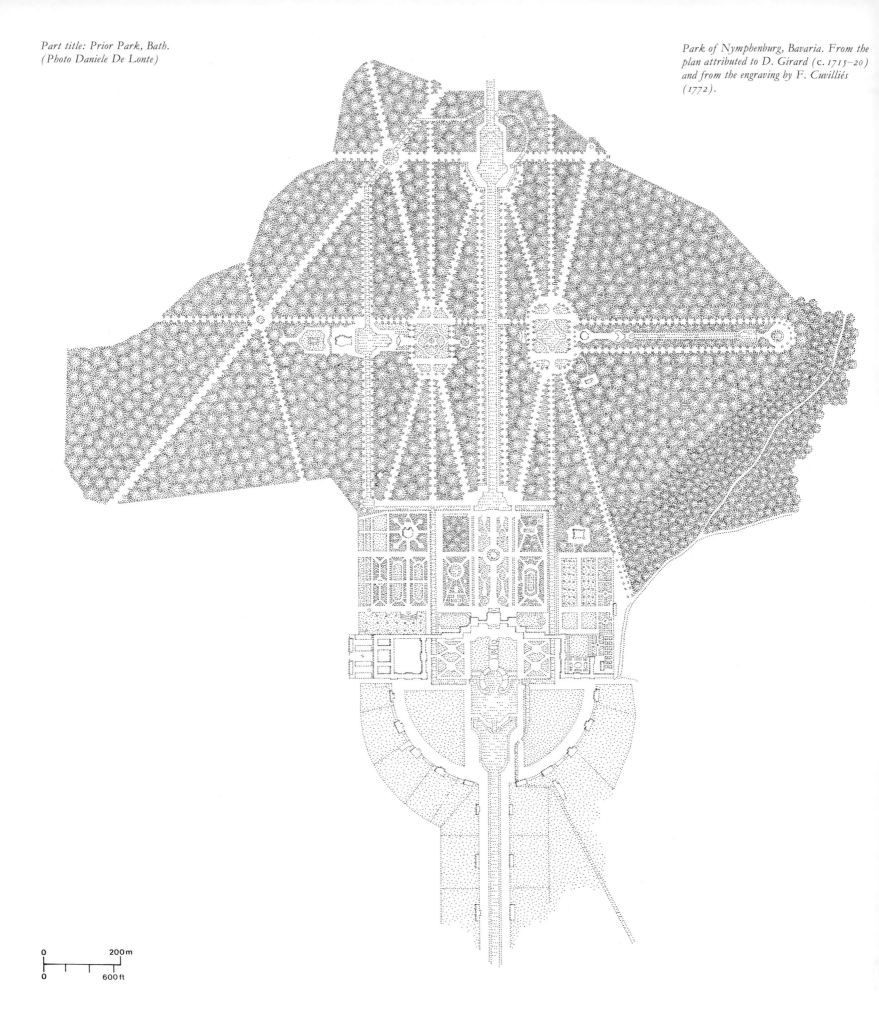

*Park of Nymphenburg, Bavaria. From the
plan attributed to D. Girard (c. 1715–20)
and from the engraving by F. Cuvilliés
(1772).*

0

200 m

0

600 ft

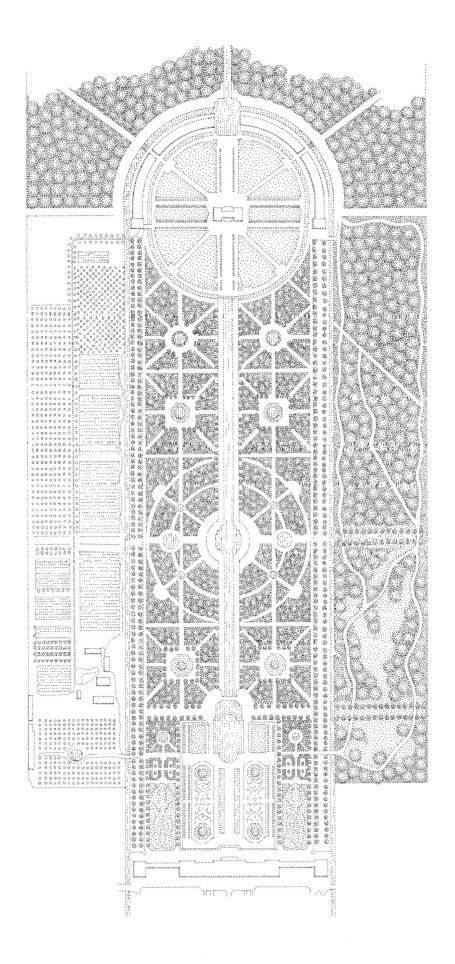

Garden of Schleissheim, Bavaria. From the
plan drawn by D. Girard (1715–17) and
from a modern survey by B. Ringholz
and E. Götz.

N

200 m

600 ft

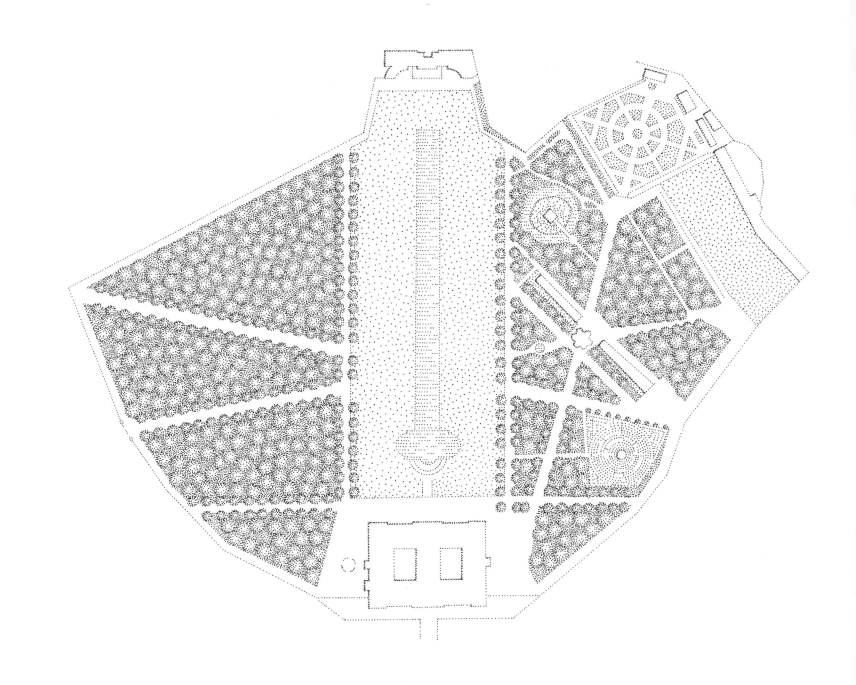

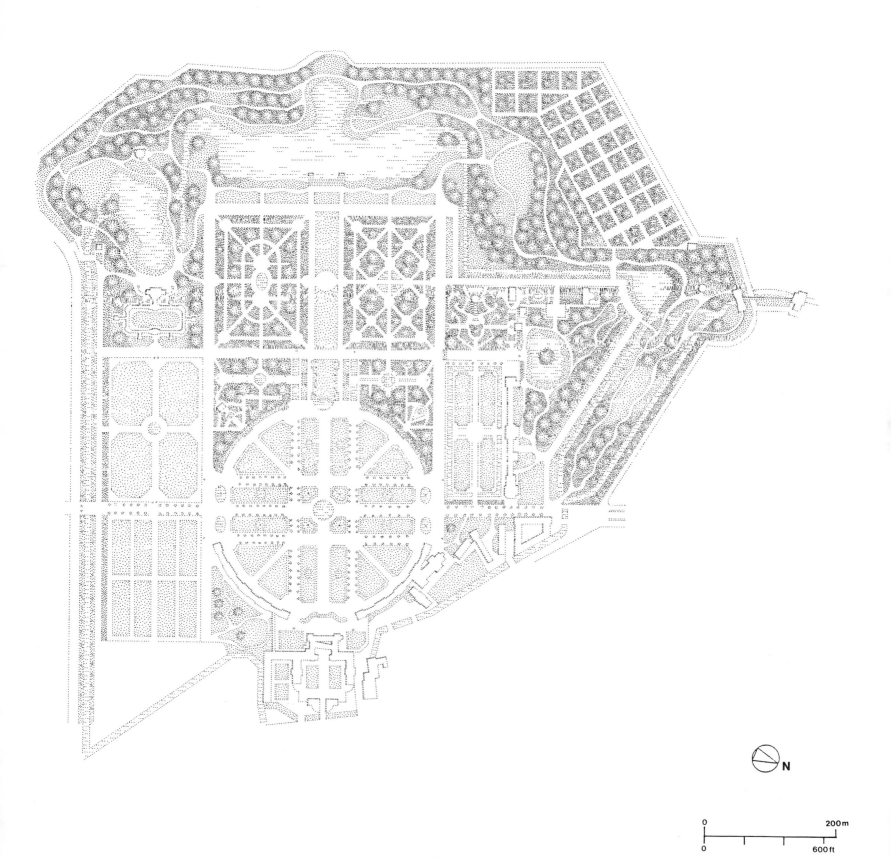

Schwetzingen Park, Baden-Württemberg.
From the plan by Johann Ludwig Petri
(1773) and, for the landscape extension,
from a plan engraved in 1834.

N

0   200 m

0   600 ft

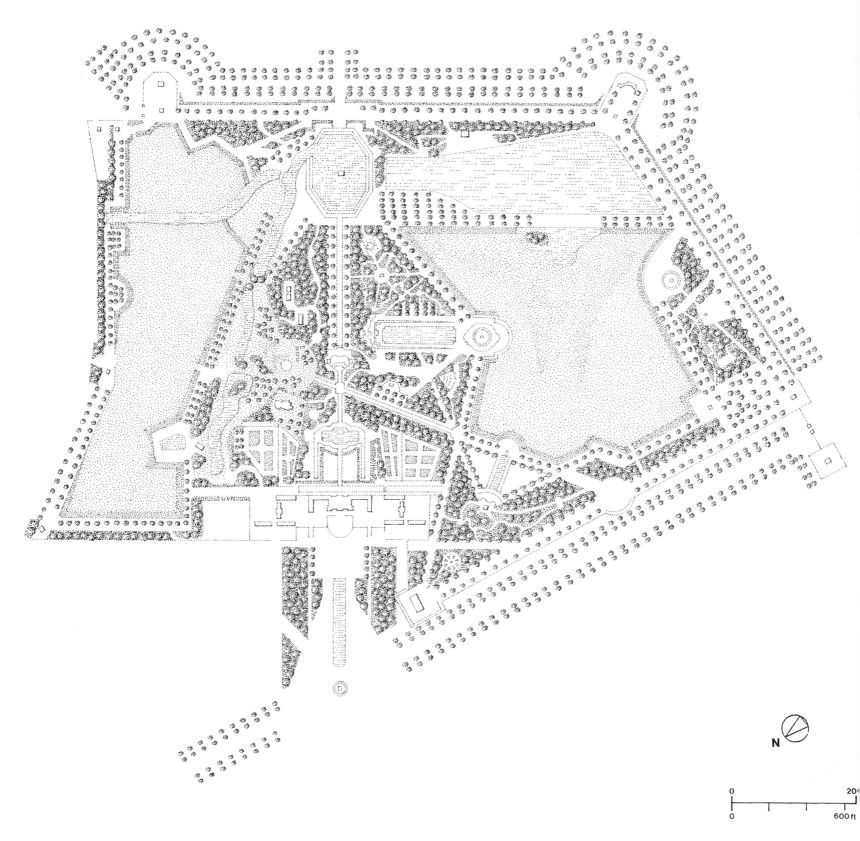

N

| 0 | 20 |
| 0 | 600 ft |

The garden of Lord Burlington's villa at
Chiswick, Twickenham, London. From
. Rocque's plan, 1736.

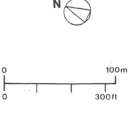

I In the version drawn up by Charles Bridgeman (c. 1715–20), from a survey carried out by the Historic Buildings and Monuments Commission for England.

II In the version drawn up by William Kent, from a survey carried out by the Historic Buildings and Monuments Commission for England.

N

| 0 | | | | 50m |
| 0 | | | 150 ft | |

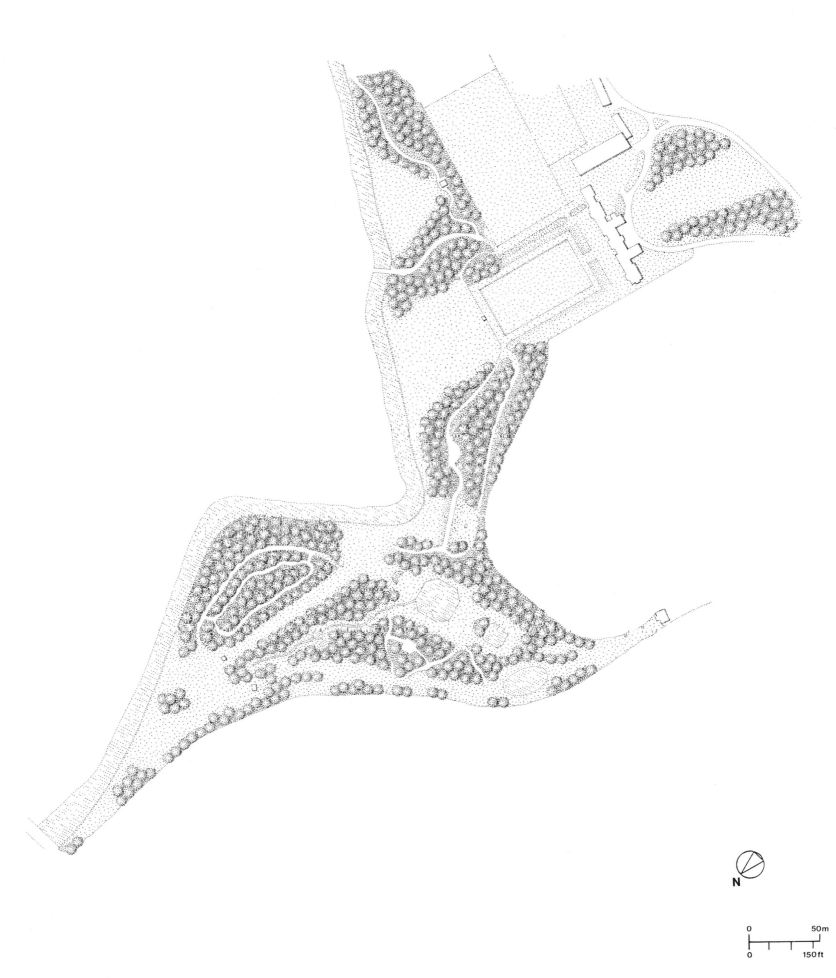

The park of the villa of Claremont, Surrey, shown after the involvement of William Kent. From J. Rocque's plan (1738) and from a modern survey.

N

0
200m
0
600 ft

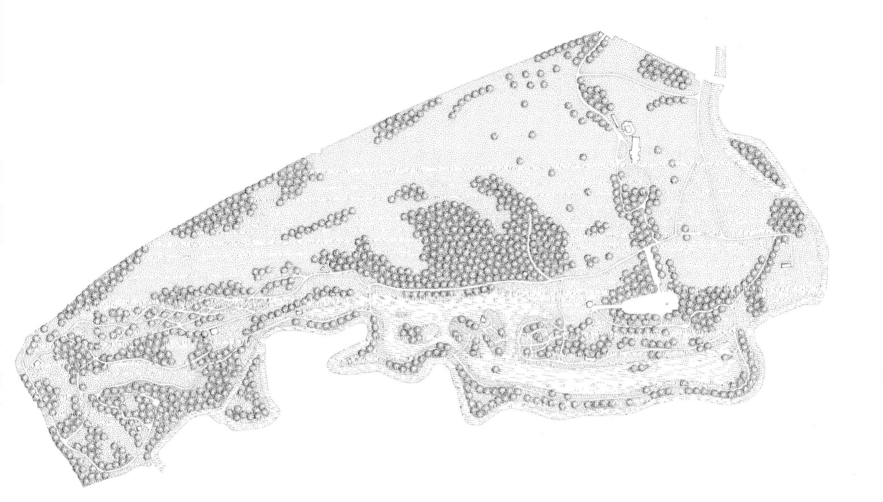

Painshill Park, Surrey. From a survey made by the Painshill Park Trust.

N

0		200 m
0		600 ft

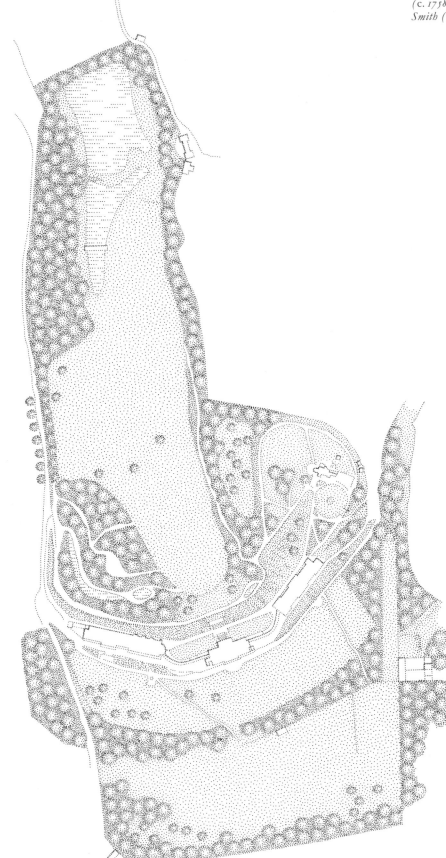

Estate of Prior Park, Bath, Somerset.
From the survey by Thorp and Overton
(c. 1758–63) and from a plan by Daniel
Smith (1856).

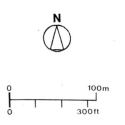

N

0   100m

0   300ft

Stourhead, Wiltshire. From the plan drawn by Piper (1779) and from a plan made for The Conservation of the Garden at Stourhead, *National Trust (1978).*

N

| 0 | | 100m |
| 0 | | 300ft |

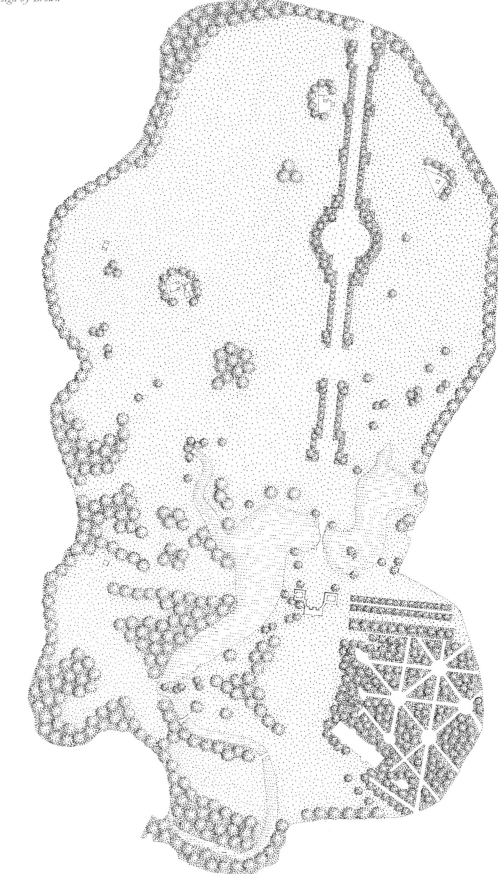

Blenheim Park, Oxfordshire. Plan of the park after the alterations made by Lancelot 'Capability' Brown. From a design by Brown (1764) and a modern survey.

N

0   500m

0   1500ft

Court Garden of the Eremitage, Bayreuth, Bavaria. From a plan engraved by Johann Gottlieb Riedel (c. 1765–70) and from a modern survey by the Bayerische Verwaltung der Staatlichen Schlösser, Gärten und Seen, Munich 1984.

N

0   100m
0   300ft

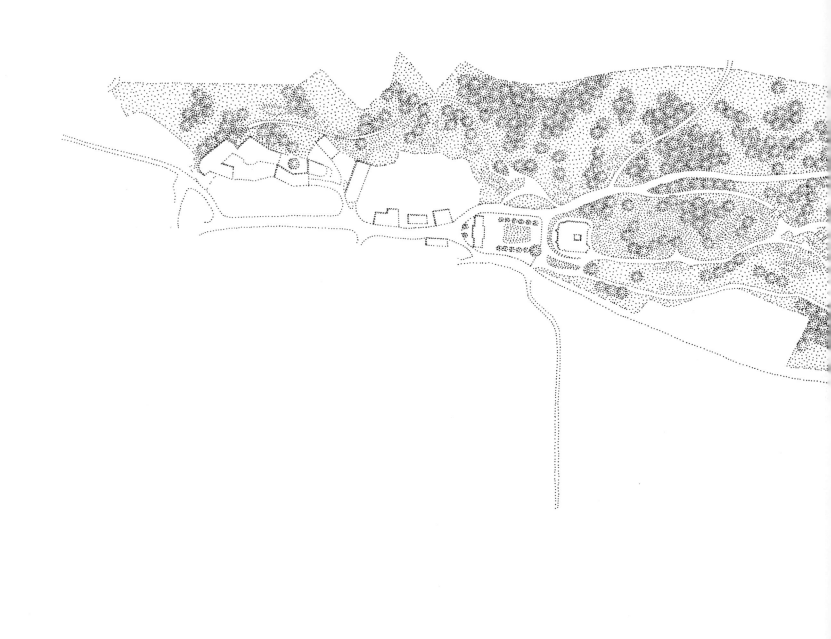

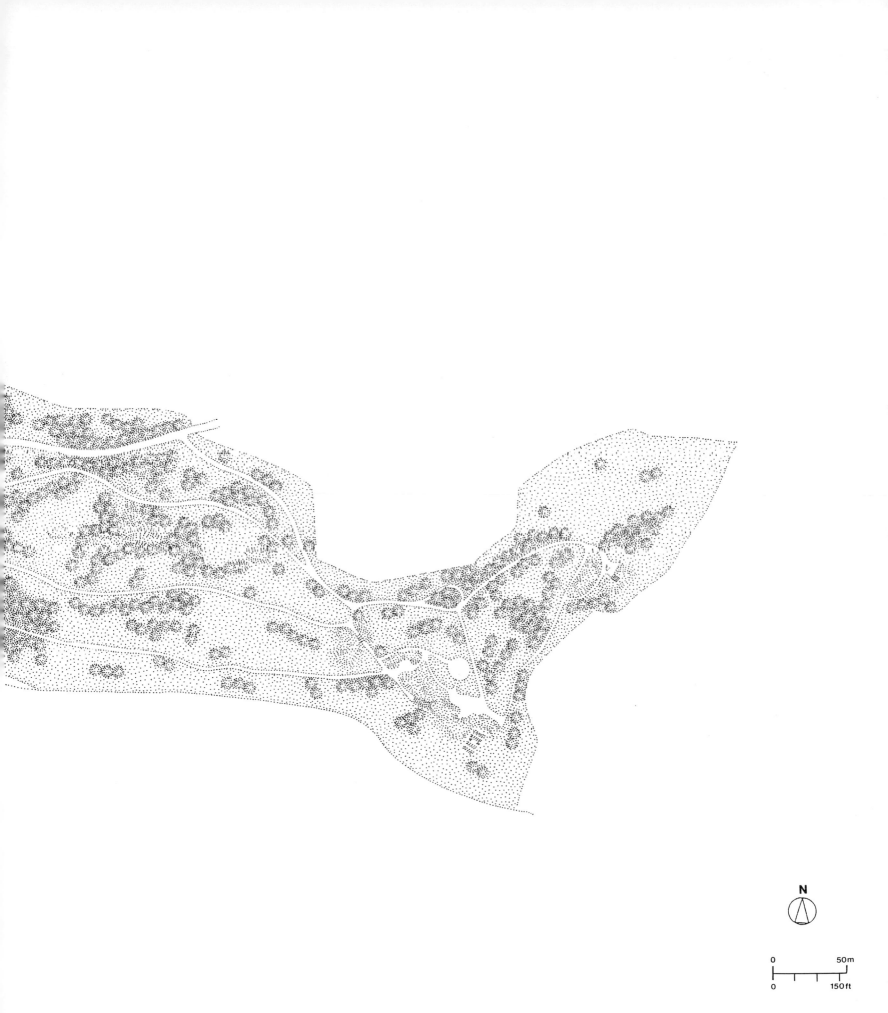

N

0 ——— 50m
0 ——— 150 ft

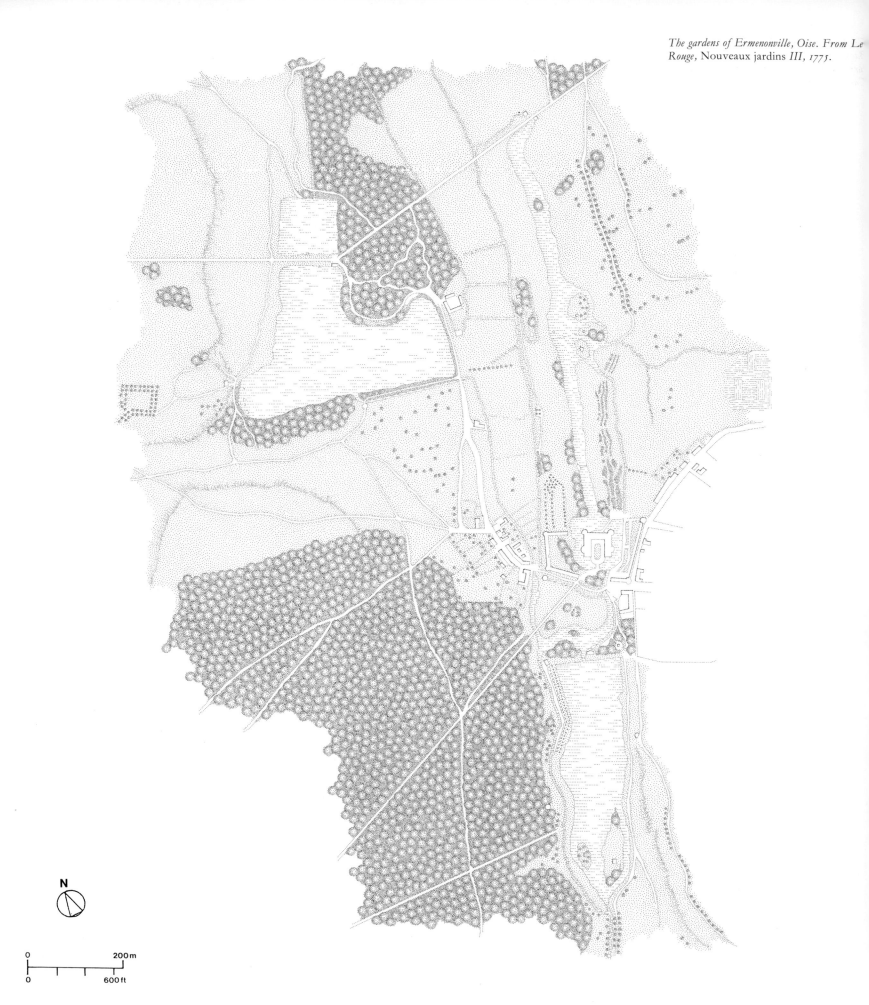

N

0   200 m

0   600 ft

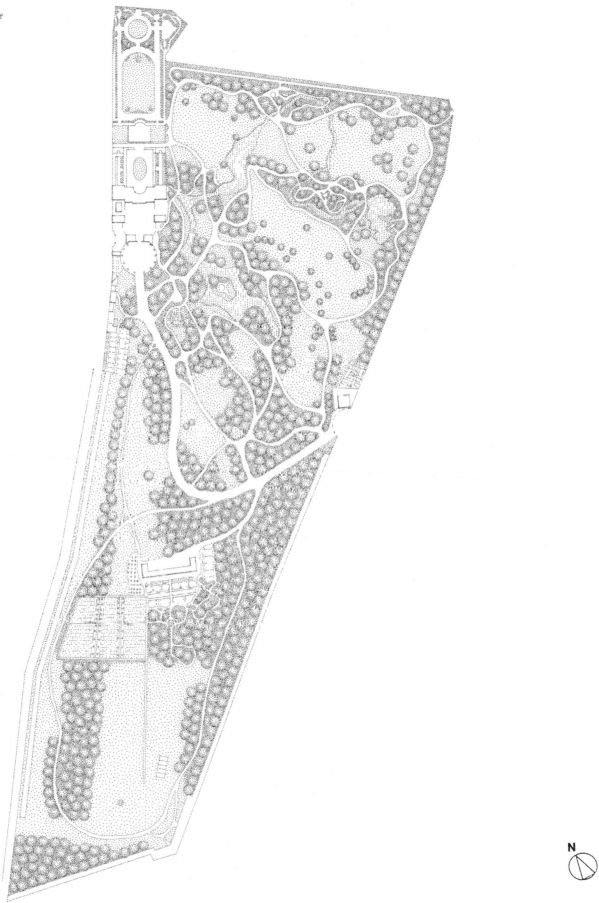

Garden of the Folie d' Artois, known as
Bagatelle, Bois de Boulogne, Paris. From the
survey by Boucher and Nicolas, 1814. Musée
Carnavalet, Paris.

N

0   100m

0   300ft

Plan of the Folie de Chartres, known as the garden of Monceau, Paris:

I in the version drawn up by Carmontelle, from the plan by Le Rouge (1783);

II in the version by Thomas Blaikie, from Plan d'un Jardin à Mouceau [sic], c. 1788, and from a survey by Lauly of 1803.

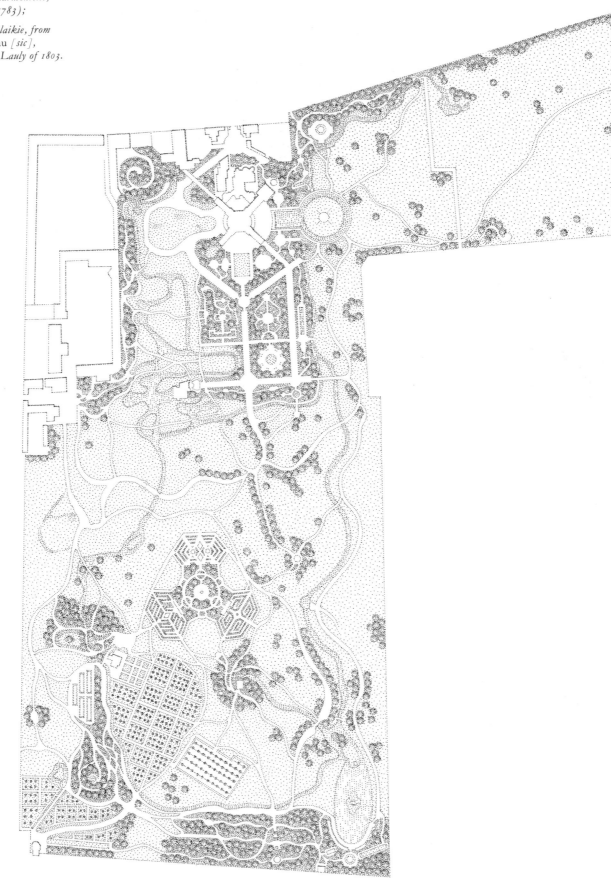

N

0   50
0   150 ft

N

0   50m
0   150ft

The Désert de Retz, Chambourcy, Yvelines.
From the plan by Collet Duclos (1 April
1811, Versailles, Arch. Dép. des Yvelines)
and from a recent survey carried out under the
direction of Olivier Choppin de Janvry.

N

0   100m

0   300ft

Park of Wörlitz, Halle. From the plan by
Rohde and from a modern survey published in
R. R. M. Borchard, Elysische Felder.
Berlin 1987.

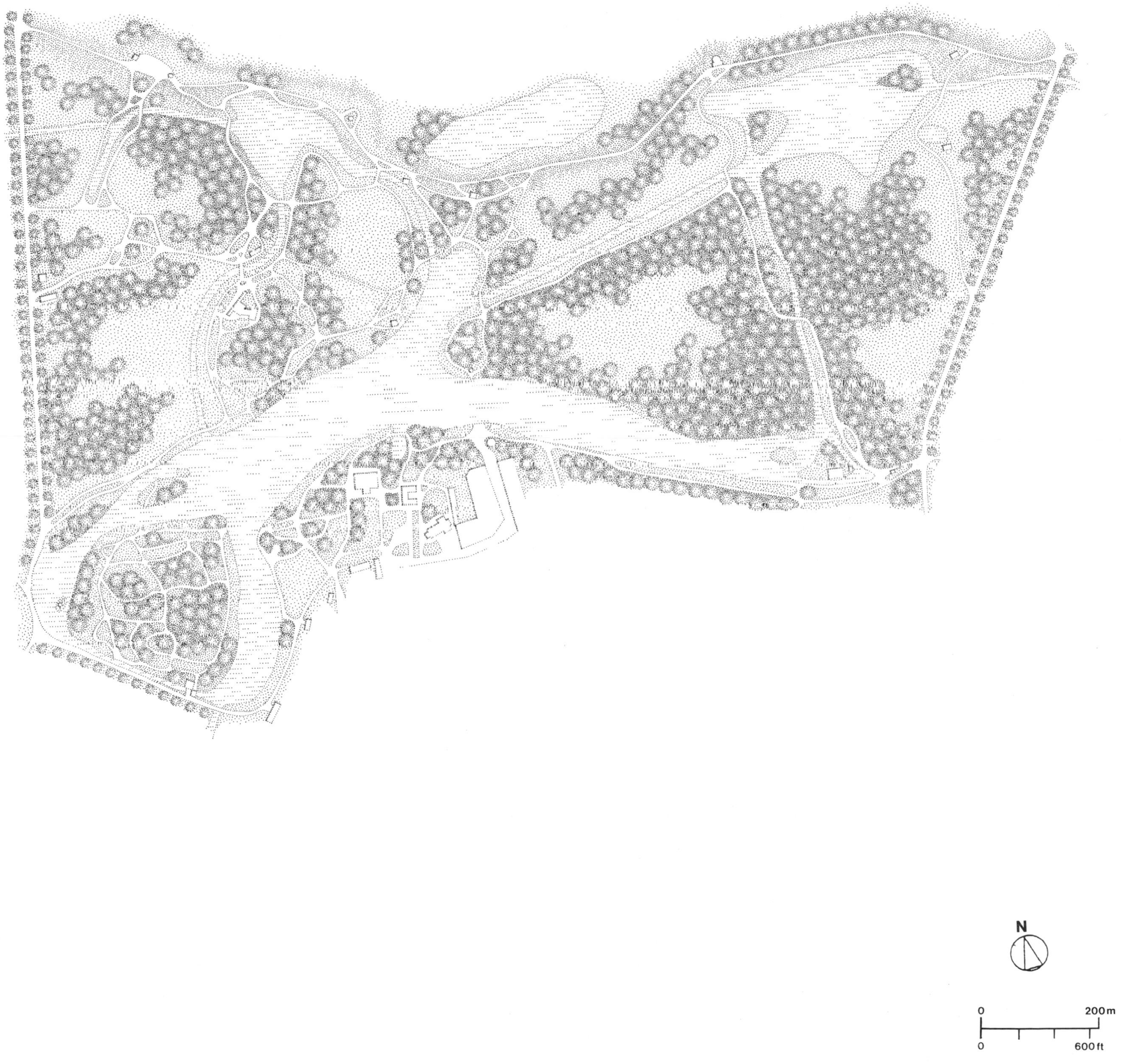

N

0   200 m

0   600 ft

*Park of Schönbusch, Hessen. From a
drawing by E. J. d'Herigoyen (1788) and a
modern survey.*

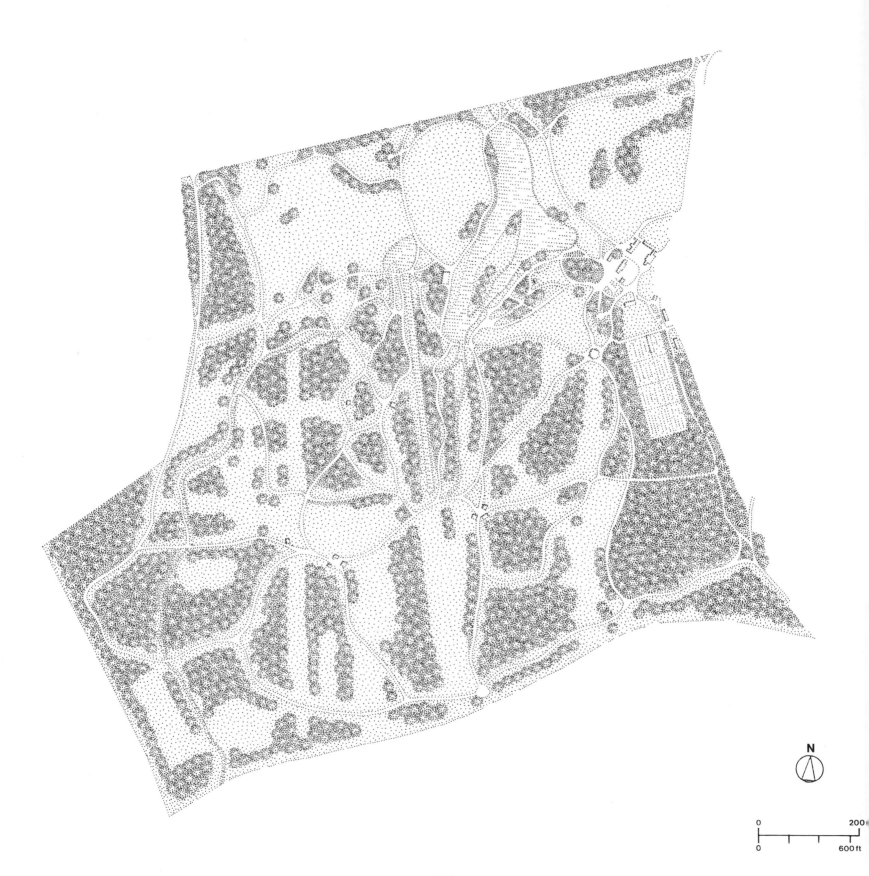

N

0   200
0   600 ft

Park of Wilhelmshöhe, Kassel.
From an engraving by
G. W. Weise from C. C. Chaeffer (1800).

N

The Prince's Garden, Aranjuez, Madrid.
From a survey carried out by the Servicio de
Jardines, Parques y Montes, Madrid 1985.

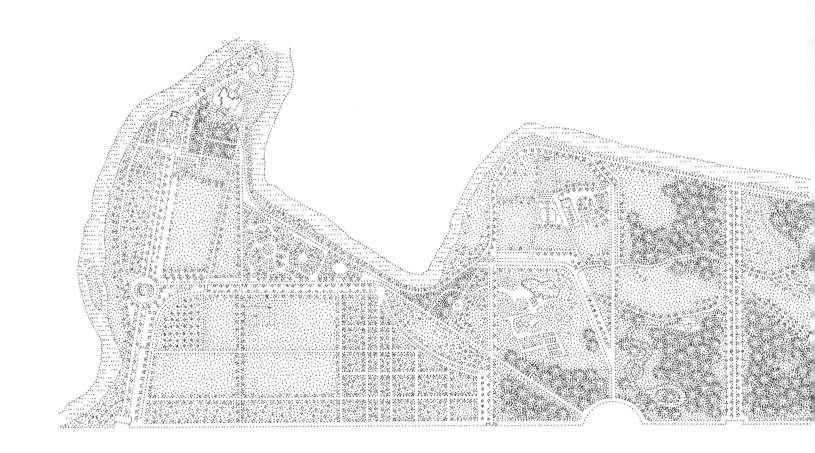

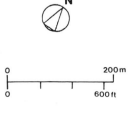

N

0   200 m

0   600 ft

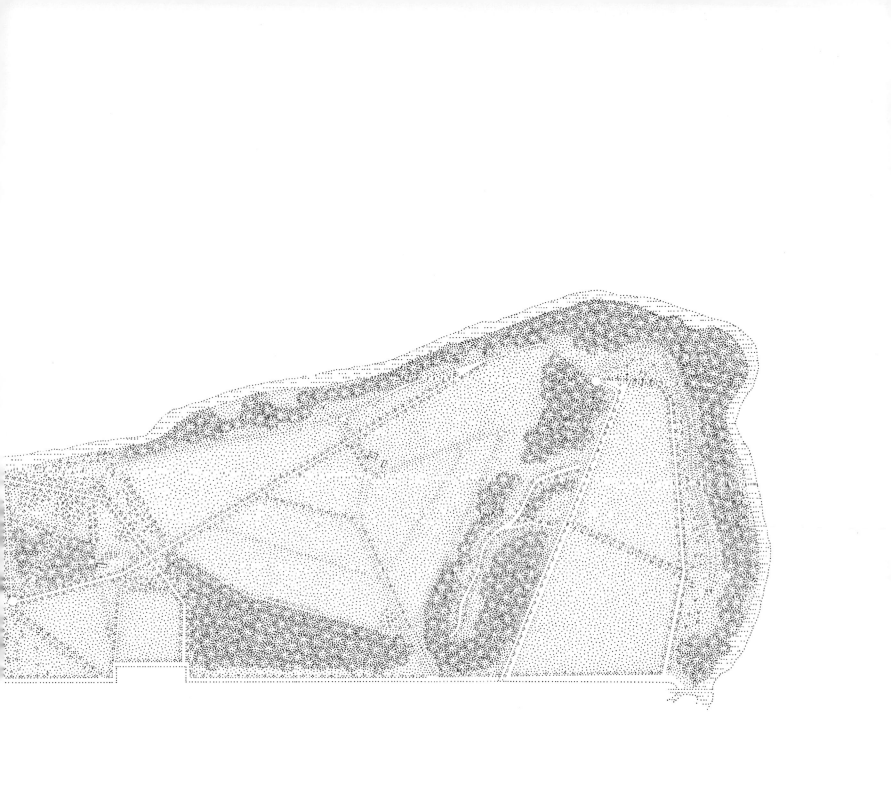

'Ut Pictura Poesis':
The Garden and the Picturesque
in England (1710–1750)

John Dixon Hunt

The picturesque vogue of the eighteenth century has come to be seen as a phenomenon of garden and landscape taste. While this may be true of its later phase, such an emphasis distorts its earlier history, with the consequence that much discussion of the beginnings of landscape gardening in the first fifty years of the eighteenth century has been skewed by an unnecessarily teleological bias. The term 'picturesque' in English (as its equivalents in French and Italian) was originally used to refer to material that was suitable for inclusion in a painting or, by extension, material in the actual world that could be conceived or viewed as if it were already part of a picture. As late as Tobias Smollett's novel *Humphry Clinker* one character describes the scene of Clinker in prison preaching to the inmates and other visitors as 'strongly picturesque':[1] the orator and his variously attentive congregation are deemed to be similar to, or apt for, a history painting such as perhaps Guido Reni or Nicolas Poussin might execute. That the term picturesque did not, therefore, necessarily adduce an experience of *landscape* is crucial to the history of the early landscape garden.

Among the earliest theorists of the so-called English garden, Addison, Pope and Shaftesbury all invoked painting directly or indirectly as a model for garden design:

Fields of Corn make a pleasant Prospect, and if the Walks were a little taken care of that lie between them, if the natural Embroidery of the Meadows were helpt and improved by some small Additions of Art, and the several Rows of Hedges set off by Trees and Flowers . . . a Man might make a pretty Landskip [a Dutch term meaning a painted representation of landscape] of his own Possessions.[2]

All gardening is landscape-painting. Just like a landscape hung up.

You may distance things by darkening them and by narrowing the plantation more and more toward the end, in the same manner as they do in painting . . .[3]

And Shaftesbury's attempt to discriminate between art and nature in garden design has been shown to invoke perspective,[4] as Pope does in that third quotation. It should be noted that none of these writers uses the term 'picturesque'; and even when they do, as on other occasions (as we shall see) Pope invokes it, the meaning cannot be that of a merely formal arrangement of rough or 'busy' (the term is Gainsborough's) texture, which would become the central connotation by the end of the century. For these early theorists of landscape, paintings were models for garden organization because they gave to a relatively new art of garden layout the *imprimatur* of a more established and distinguished sister.

Neither Addison, Pope nor Shaftesbury sees the garden as anything but an artificial creation, so they seize upon analogies with painting to signal that assumption. And beyond – or even before – matters of simply formal composition, what gardens could learn from pictures was a deployment of themes and meaning. This is clear from one of Pope's invocations of 'picturesque' in his Homer commentaries, written during the 1720s. He tells readers of *The Iliad* XVI that the attitude of Patroclus, prostrated before Achilles and pointing to the burning Greek fleet, is 'lively and Picturesque'. Whatever landscape element Pope admits into this Homeric picture ('the Rocks or Sea which lay in prospect before them') is wholly subservient to the human action which takes place in the foreground. Homer's readers are invited to read his scenes as if they were paintings in the manner of, say, Raphael, Poussin or the Carracci; texts like Homer's offered subjects to history painters who expected in their turn that viewers would invoke the literary texts to gloss (literally: give a tongue to) the action: hence *ut pictura poesis*, as in a picture, so in a poem, and vice versa.[5]

The way to understand Pope's uses of picturesque, then, is in the light of contemporary commentary upon interchanges between the arts: such a text as Dryden's *Parallel of Poetry and Painting*, which was reissued in 1719 with Pope's own *Epistle to Jervas*, Jervas being a painter friend of Pope's. At the centre of Dryden's parallel is the affirmation of both arts' imitation of some significant and unified human action. The decorum and invention with which painters and poets treat such subjects would be, by extension, what the garden designer also had to master. So the *Postscript to the Odyssey*, focusing upon the diction of natural description in the 'imaging and picturesque parts', states that their 'character' is 'simplicity and purity'; in other words, they do not distract from, but rather give support to, the actions for which the descriptions provide the appropriate background. Hence the 'Circumstances the most Picturesque imaginable' in Homer's famous night scene in *The Iliad* X are praised by Pope because of their contribution to the ensemble of another Homeric painting, in which the 'human Figures . . . are excellent, and disposed in the properest Actions'.[6]

Just as in that Homeric 'prospect' the action is central and the expressive scenery, though prominent, is secondary, so in the gardens of these early landscapists: *ut pictura hortus*. Pope never seems to have lost sight of the need to attend to some significant action or meaning in garden design (just as, more obviously, he never did in his poetry, beginning with the early 'Ode on Solitude'). At Twickenham he so arranged an obelisk, temple, urn or statue, with attendant inscriptions that glossed the action, that his garden may be, indeed should be, seen 'in the Great Light of a History Painting'.[7] Two projects which he never executed, for a pair of river gods beside the Thames, accompanied by quotations from Virgil and Poliziano, and a statue of a nymph in his grotto (later realized by Henry Hoare at Stourhead) both show his dedication to meaning at the centre of the garden experience.

The circle of gardenists in which Pope moved – especially Lord Burlington and his protegé, William Kent – all seemed to have shared this concern for a garden landscape in which meaning was carefully encoded. Today, looking back from our perspective this side of the enormously popular picturesque movement of the later eighteenth and nineteenth centuries we ignore this encoding as well as the significance of the privileged visitor able to decode the gardens at Twickenham, Chiswick, Stowe or Rousham. We are not helped in recovering this essential historical attitude by our failure also to register the proximity of garden and theatre design. Pope and his friends also thought of

gardens as composed of 'scenes', and his response to landscapes outside gardens was also to read them as stage scenery (the Avon Gorge at Bristol was like 'the broken Scenes behind one another in a Playhouse').[8] And what links stage scenery to the 'picturesque' landscapes of history painting is that both are backgrounds in front of which some action unrolls. Thus when Félibien discussed the Poussin painting now known as *Landscape with a Man Killed by a Snake*, he stressed how all its effort was directed, via expressive contrasts between its foreground tragedy and surrounding landscape and via the eloquent gestures of the humans involved, to represent '*des passions que peu d'autres Peintres scû figurer*'.[9]

If we look at William Kent's garden drawings, we shall see this same concern with human presence and action vis-à-vis a given scenery. And the significance of this is that Kent, we know (even if few examples survive), worked in the theatre as well as in landscape design.[10] But Kent's drawings also highlight a crucial problem with this early eighteenth-century determination to transfer thematic as well as formal characteristics from painting to garden design. For what in a garden takes the place of actors on the stage or of figures in history painting? First, the scenery itself begins to take responsibility for the action. Second, garden visitors, in these most learned of English Palladian or Augustan gardens, are required to become actors as well as spectators.

A drawing like that for the Chatsworth hillside shows a group of people who are both observing and participating in a gardenist history painting: the cascade begins its descent at a classical temple, the so called Sybil's Temple from Tivoli, flows through rustic arches, modelled on those on the hillside of Kent's favourite Villa Aldobrandini, and falls into a pool between two capricciesque Roman pavilions. This progress of gardening – from classical times, through modern Italian to the present, Derbyshire location – is both watched by and understood by the garden visitors; inasmuch as their comprehension is crucial to Kent's scheme, they are actors, participants in that meaning.

Not all of Kent's drawings display this central human action, but it seems clear that he expected his scenery to be completed by and with it. Another drawing, not for a garden design but rather for an imaginary landscape, actually has the 'text' of the action written down the margin. Kent is here illustrating another progress of culture: from ancient Rome, represented by both the sea-god driving his team of horses down river and the classical temple in the distance which is modelled upon Palladio's reconstruction of the Temple of Fortune at Palestrina (the classical Praeneste), to 'medieval' England, represented by Hampton Court at the left and 'Wolsey's Tower' at Esher in the far right, and finally to the present day, represented in its turn by the figures watching this progress and by Kent's own work at Hampton Court and Esher. The significant action at the very centre of this scene involves the landscape itself as part of that action; the text which Kent has inscribed in the margins is from Michael Drayton's *Poly-Olbion* and constitutes the scenario, as Ovid or Virgil would for a painting by Claude Lorrain. The English verses celebrate the meeting of the Rivers

Thames and Mole, shown by Kent in his drawing, and are part of Drayton's praise of England's cultural descent and inheritance of classical culture (the Greek title means 'having many blessings').

Now gardens do not easily incorporate such literary texts to sustain and shape their cultural history paintings (any more than do pictures themselves, in this being different from the theatre where, ballet excepted, there is a spoken text). Of course, gardens may invoke inscriptions, as is done in such crucial places as the Elysian Fields at Stowe, or name garden features like the Praeneste Terrace at Rousham and so inscribe meaning. And one of the major pronouncements of the early garden landscape movement, Joseph Addison's description of the imaginary territory of the goddess Liberty, relies upon a full range of conventional iconography to make its significance palpable.[11] That at least some garden visitors were happy to accept the responsibility to get involved in reading such garden 'texts' is perfectly clear from the various drawings of Stowe and Chiswick executed by Jacques Rigaud.

If we compare the activity depicted by Rigaud and the seriousness or centrality to garden experience which his scenes suggest was given to this intelligent response to garden meanings and action with a later drawing by Rowlandson, we can immediately grasp the declensions through which picturesque went by the second half of the century. Rowlandson mocks the interest of his garden visitors in the herm before which they have paused; they are interested in its priapic member less (it is implied) for some sense that Priapus was the god of gardens than for its relevance to their own amorous involvements. The technique of the drawing emphasizes a merely formal interest in shape, line and texture, exactly the ingredients of the picturesque taste contemporary with Rowlandson. A similarly crucial moment of picturesque taste may be studied in William Gilpin's *Dialogue upon the Gardens . . . at Stow* of 1748. Primed by the local and rather old-fashioned guidebook Gilpin's visitors discuss the meaning and significant history paintings of the gardens; but left to their own devices, it is the formal visual properties of the scenery that delight them. If pictures helped to structure experience of the natural world, as William Gilpin's later writings all show readers how to do, it was their formal not thematic contribution that was prominent. Countless tourists exploring the British and European countryside were encouraged to frame views, to graduate prospects from foreground to background, and above all to ensure variety of painted, drawn or engraved texture, which mimicked similar qualities in the natural world. Even the antiquarian interest in British landscape, originally promoted by the Royal Society as part of its empirical enquiry into history, devolved from considering how the past was inscribed in ruins and topography to relishing 'deep Caverns, remarkable Rocks, uncommon Echos or picturesque Views' for their own sakes.[12]

Several factors were responsible for this declension in picturesque

values; they need to be briefly surveyed so that the earlier picturesque
which this essay is concerned to address may be more sharply
registered. First, there was a decline in iconographical expertise. This
was noted by Joseph Spence in his *Polymetis* of 1747, where he tried to
rescue the nomenclature and attributes of classical deities for an age that
was quickly forgetting them; its popularity as a text book – two
editions in 1755 and 1774, plus a school version of 1764 that went
through six editions – suggests how much such an encyclopaedia was
needed. Spence's eponymous character arranges this memory theatre in
the form of a landscaped park with temples dedicated to different
groups of classical gods and goddesses, a mode of gardening that
would soon surrender to the unlearned forms of 'Capability' Brown
who promoted a landscape generally stripped of allusion and meaning.
Even before Brown, a poet like Joseph Warton had in 1744 promoted
an escape from 'gardens deck't with art's vain pomps', from Stowe's
'attic fanes . . . obelisks and urns' to 'the thrush haunted copse'.[13]

Second, as Spence's own garden design work shows, the taste for
gardens was spreading to smaller gentry without either the education
(they had perhaps not been on a Grand Tour) or the means to afford
gardens with statuary, inscriptions and temples – the essential syntax of
history paintings. This decline in the incidence of items which would
stimulate ideas in garden visitors, pre-coded messages to be interpreted
by those who had the skill and wit to do so, coincided with the gradual
influence of Lockean epistemology, with its insistence upon how each
individual constructs his/her own mental world. This undoubtedly
privileged the private sensibility, the local and personal rather than the
public and general. Gardens, as perhaps Rowlandson's drawing
reminds us, were then places where visitors were left to their own
devices, and what significant actions took place were inward and
private.

As far as garden history is concerned, these developments are
codified in Thomas Whately's *Observations on Modern Gardening* of 1770.
In a now famous passage[14] he distinguishes between emblematic and
expressive gardening, in effect between the syntax and grammar of
history painting and the freer, personal meanings which visitors fed
into the scenery around them without the stimulus of statuary and
inscriptions. Whately is simply reformulating for a far less learned
readership Spence's remark in *Polymetis* that 'the figures of things
themselves speak . . . the clearest language', which is therefore to be
preferred to allegorical devices.[15]

The picturesque that was based upon the learned parallels to which
the tag *ut pictura poesis* gestured and that sustained the early landscape
movement had surrendered by the last quarter of the eighteenth century
to a concern with visual excitement and texture. This surrender is
actually registered by a writer in the *Analytical Review* of 1794,
significantly in the course of reviewing Uvedale Price's *Essay on the
Picturesque*. He scorns the 'futility of such mutual inroads of poetry and
painting on each other' that had led poetry to attempt description and
painting to depict emotions and narrative.[16] Instead, as Price was

235

View of the park at Esher Place with a temple and a bridge; drawing by William Kent. Victoria and Albert Museum, London.

Two artists painting a ruin; anonymous, late eighteenth century. British Library, London.

expounding, the picturesque would attend to the visual satisfactions of a scenery viewed in the light of engraving, busy with the texture of incised line, or of painting's translation of the natural world into shape and colour.

We have tended to read this later picturesque into our accounts of early landscape gardening. Pope is thus misread as a latterday picturesque gardener, prophetic of developments he could never have known,[17] and Kent is seen as, so to speak, a John the Baptist to 'Capability' Brown's Christ.[18] But Horace Walpole, who was largely responsible for promoting this teleological history of landscape gardening, was not only a Whig, writing with full confidence in the progressive potential of cultural politics, but somebody writing with hindsight in the 1760s. Yet sometimes even Walpole's garden observations mark, as do more conspicuously the designs of his hero William Kent, the watershed that it has been the business of this essay to survey. In Kent's park at Esher in May 1763 he saw a 'Parnassus as Watteau would have painted it'; what he found was both a *fête champêtre* that harked back to the garden as theatre, a local of human action, however trivialized, and a scenery (he uses the word 'scene') of supreme formal delights – 'the beauty of the landscape, a rainbow on a dark cloud falling precisely behind the tower of a neighbouring church, between another tower, and the building of Claremont . . . the trees, lawns, concaves, all in the perfection in which the ghost of Kent would joy to see them'.[19]

Walpole considered Esher Place Kent's supreme achievement (there he was 'Kentissime') and Thomas Whately, too, accorded it high praise:

The groups [of trees] are few and small; there was not room for larger or for more: there were no opportunities to form continued narrow glades between opposite lines; the vacant spaces are therefore chiefly irregular openings spreading every way, and great differences of distance between the trees are the principal variety; but the grove winds along the bank of a large river, on the side and at the foot of a very sudden ascent, the upper part of which is covered with wood. In one place it presses close to the covert; retires from it in another; and stretches in a third across a bold recess, which runs up high into the thicket. The trees sometimes overspread the flat below, sometimes leave an open space to the river; at other times crown the brow of a large knole, climb up a steep, or hang on a gentle declivity. These varieties in the situation more than compensate for the want of variety in the disposition of the trees . . .[20]

But that account is wholly devoted to the 'picturesque' qualities of Esher, its 'variety', 'form', irregularity, and disposition of natural forms. It is significant, then, that Whately does not consider Kent's Rousham. This garden, with something of that ambivalence already noticed, Walpole also rated highly; but his praise, though signalling a meaningful garden of classical associations, does so in the broadest terms – 'elegant and antique as if the emperor Julian had selected the most pleasing solitude about Daphne to enjoy a philosophical retirement'; or, on another occasion, 'the sweetest little groves, streams, glades, porticoes, cascades . . . all the scenes are perfectly

Rousham, Oxfordshire: lion attacking a
horse, by Scheemaker.

View of the park at Castle Howard,
Yorkshire. (Photo Daniele De Lonte)

classic'.[21] What Walpole does not even begin to do is respond to the elaborate meanings which Kent seems to have engineered at Rousham: the sculpture of the lion attacking the horse, with its allusion to the Fountain of Ancient Rome at the Villa d'Este; the eloquent Praeneste Terrace, a diminished rendition of the ruined classical temple at Palestrina, aptly miniaturized in its translation to Hanoverian England; the Vale of Venus, with its echo of Frascati; the Georgic emphases – the many views out into agrarian landscapes, a Temple of the Mill; or, finally, the eyecatcher, both Roman triumphal arch *and* Gothic screen.

Kent's creation, surely his *chef d'oeuvre* (at least it survives, unlike Esher), elaborates a witty version of that progress of the art of gardening that we have seen him negotiating in the illustration to Michael Drayton's *Poly-Olbion*. In the small scale of this garden, created in 1739–40, Kent presents visitors with a series of history paintings in which England's place in the declensions of gardening from Rome to Oxfordshire is canvassed.[22] Yet its concept of garden picturesque was already beginning to be outmoded; Kent himself, trained as history painter as well as being a practised theatre designer, was nevertheless as much tempted by the merely formal delights of Esher's groves as by the learned compositions of his friend Alexander Pope. Kent's career marks a crucial moment in the fortunes of the picturesque, as it transformed itself from a limited and erudite mode of representation into a popular, aesthetic appreciation of scenery's visual splendours and opportunities.

[1] *Humphry Clinker* (1771), ed. A Ross (Harmondsworth 1967), p. 184.
[2] Addison, *The Spectator*, No. 414, 25 June 1712.
[3] Pope, recorded by Joseph Spence, *Observations, Anecdotes and Characters of Books and Men*, ed. James M. Osborn (Oxford 1966), Vol. 1, pp. 252–3.
[4] David Leatherbarrow, 'Character, Geometry and Perspective: the Third Earl of Shaftesbury's principles of garden design', in *Journal of Garden History*, Vol. 4 (1984), pp. 332–58.
[5] For a typical example of the expected connections between visual image and literature see Jonathan Richardson's considerations of Michelangelo's paintings in terms of texts by Dante and Villani in *Two Discourses* (London 1719), pp. 26ff.
[6] These Pope passages are most easily consulted in the modern Twickenham edition of his poetry (London and New Haven, 1967). I have considered them in somewhat more detail in my essay, 'Ut pictura poesis, ut pictura hortus, and the picturesque', in *Word & Image. A journal of visual/verbal enquiry*, Vol. 1 (1985), pp. 87–107.
[7] David Jacques, quoting Dryden's translation of Dufresnoy's treatise on painting, 'The art and sense of the Scriblerus Club in England 1715–35', in *Garden History*, Vol. 4, No. 1 (1976), p. 42. For other considerations of Pope's gardening see Peter Martin, *'Pursuing Innocent Pleasures'. The gardening world of Alex-*

Stourhead, Wiltshire: the Temple of Apollo.
(Photo Daniele De Lonte)

ander Pope (Hamden, Conn. 1984), Maynard Mack, *The Garden and the City* (Toronto, Buffalo and London 1969), and John Dixon Hunt, *Garden and Grove* (London 1986), chapter 11.

[8] *The Correspondence of Alexander Pope*, ed. George Sherburn (Oxford 1956), Vol. 4, p. 201.

[9] André Félibien, *Entretiens* (Trevoux 1725), p. 150.

[10] See John Dixon Hunt, *William Kent. Landscape Garden Designer. An assessment and catalogue of his designs* (London 1987).

[11] Addison, *The Tatler*, No. 115 (1705).

[12] The phrase, from a 1795 Welsh Literary Society questionnaire about 'observables' in the landscape, is cited by Graham Walters in his essay in the 'Maps and Mapping' issue of *Word & Image*, Vol. 4, no. 2 (1988).

[13] Warton, *The Enthusiast* (1744), in *The Genius of the Place*, ed. John Dixon Hunt and Peter Willis (new, revised edition, Cambridge, Mass. 1988), p. 241. On the decline of iconographic knowledge see the seminal essay by D. J. Gordon, 'Ripa's Fate', in *The Renaissance Imagination*, ed. Stephen Orgel (Berkeley and Los Angeles 1975), pp. 51–74.

[14] Whately, *Observations* (1770), pp. 146–51.

[15] Spence, *Polymetis*, p. 290.

[16] *Analytical Review*, No. 20 (1794), p. 259; the writer signs himself 'R.R.'.

[17] See Morris Brownell, *Alexander Pope and the arts of Georgian England* (Oxford 1978), and my review of this in *Review*, No. 3 (1981), pp. 155–64.

[18] This is Walpole's thesis in his *History of the Modern Taste in Gardening*, ed. Isabel W. U. Chase, *Horace Walpole: Gardenist* (Princeton 1943).

[19] Walpole, *Correspondence*, ed. W. S. Lewis *et al.* (New Haven and London 1937 *et seq.*), Vol. 10, pp. 72–3.

[20] Whately, *op. cit.*, p. 52.

[21] Walpole, *History, ed. cit.*, p. 29, and *Correspondence*, Vol. 10, p. 72.

[22] Rousham is discussed fully in Simon Pugh, *Garden-Nature-Language* (Manchester 1988) and in John Dixon Hunt, *op. cit.* (see note 10).

Garden of Chiswick House, London: view of the Pantheon in winter. (Photo Daniele De Lonte)

Scenography and Perspective in Eighteenth-Century French Gardens

Marianne Roland Michel

Among the arabesques engraved by Huquier in the style of Watteau some years after the latter's death are two matching plates. Both depict figures in ornamental gardens: a bacchante in a wild landscape where trees and reeds border a deep ravine, and 'gallants' in a French-style garden of symmetrical design with clipped yews and statues linked by a colonnade rising above cascades. The first, no doubt because of its canopy of foliage, is entitled *Le Berceau* (the bower), a term evocative of classical gardens, while the second is *Le Théâtre*, an allusion to the arrangement of the foreground, to the perfect symmetry, and also to the steps which make this garden a sort of concave stage set; garlands hang from scrolls and little monkey musicians confer an additional note of theatricality to the composition.

There are other similarly ambiguous, thematically linked plates: *Les Jardins de Cythère* and *Les Jardins de Bacchus* which depict scenes symmetrically arranged around a fountain and a bacchic statue. On the horizon is a line of trees, while a flight of steps slopes down towards the foreground. The whole is surrounded by draperies, garlands, festoons, trophies and masks and flanked by pillars, which further emphasize the stage-set aspect of these gardens, where static couples, intended to give them life, only stress their theatricality. One last arabesque, also engraved by Huquier and entitled *La Grotte* offers once again, this time on a dais, a garden setting where a curving arcade frames a grotesque statue surrounded by static figures. Even if the titles of these engravings are Huquier's rather than Watteau's[1] they are nonetheless explicitly linked to the garden vocabulary of the first half of the eighteenth century, and are undoubtedly used in these arabesques to give a scenographic impression. The theatrical aspect of Watteau's work, rightly considered as fundamental to his art, is usually referred to in connection with the paintings depicting French or Italian players or the theme of the isle of Cythera inspired by Dancourt's *Trois Cousines*, but it is rarely considered in relation to the arabesques.

Little attention has been paid, it is true, to Watteau's truly scenographic imagination[2] of which these engravings are the proof. Yet d'Aviler's definition of 'garden theatre' is of a 'sort of raised terrace with ornamentation, vistas of avenues of trees or arbours wherein to enact pastorals. The amphitheatre opposite has several steps of stone or turf.'[3] This definition, perfectly illustrated by Watteau's arabesques, is reproduced textually in the *Encyclopédie* under the article 'theatre' and not 'garden'. This is an important consideration at a time when there is much ambiguity about these two terms, which are either closely associated or, on the contrary, carefully separated.

We come back to Watteau by way of his gardens. Some of them are places of entertainment referring directly to ballet or plays. Thus the *Fêtes Vénitiennes* (Venetian fêtes) (Edinburgh, National Gallery of Scotland) whose name, deliberately or otherwise, recalls a Campra ballet, take place on a 'stage' enclosed by a curved wall. A spectator, perhaps Watteau himself, conducts a couple (the man none other than the painter Vleughels) in a minuet. The painting, which is thus a combination of *fête galante* and reality, of theatre and social entertain-

ment, appears to be one half of a scene which is lacking its other half on the right. The complete picture would show a true stage setting with a row of trees on either side meeting in the background so as to form a semicircle behind a fountain. A similar composition can be seen in the *Summer* and *Autumn* of the Jullienne Seasons. In these engravings, reconstructions of lost paintings, characters make music in a dream garden, half of which is taken up by an arcaded wall, fountains and statues, and even some rather theatrical grape-picking takes place before a fountain, mounted on a platform in a trellis-work pavilion.

La Perspective is a choice example, were it only for its title,[4] with its scenographic implications. This 'perspective' leads in the middle ground to a vaguely Palladian façade whose transparency seems to translate into a setting without depth; to this leads a central tree-lined avenue, enlivened by a few figures. Tradition has it that this is Crozat's house and garden in Montmorency, but the general impression of the composition is more reminiscent of an opera backcloth, such as the gypsy scene in the *Fragments de M. de Lully*, presented at the Opéra in 1702, or perhaps the set designed by Torelli for the *Noces de Thétis et Pelée*. Once more there is a confusion, as in the *Fêtes Vénitiennes* or perhaps even more so, of real locations and stage sets, characters taken from life and actors playing a part, truth and fiction. Walpole, who criticized the artificiality of Watteau's gardens, accounted for it by what he saw in Parisian gardens: 'there I saw the originals of those tufts of plumes and fans, and trimmed-up groves that nod to one another like the scenes of an opera'.[5]

This iconographic confusion continues in contemporary texts, with a curious mixture of gardens reminiscent of some stage set or, on the other hand, of stage sets inspired by real gardens. Thus the article on 'theatre' in the *Encyclopédie* ascribes to this word the meaning, among others, of 'a collection of several buildings which by their elevation and happy disposition present an agreeable scene to the spectator. Such are most of the buildings in Roman vineyards . . . and in France the riverside aspect of the château of St Germain-en-Laye'.[6] It is further stated in this same article that in Greek and Roman times the theatre 'was accompanied by long colonnades, covered galleries and fine tree-lined avenues'. Dezallier d'Argenville, on the other hand, describes and illustrates in 1747 a 'portico and arbour of greenery' comprising rows of seats, amphitheatres etc., while Neufforge shows a plan for a grotto, temple or belvedere 'suitable for ornamenting a garden, or other usage', the other 'usage' being evidently a stage. And so we have two contemporary texts which on the one hand compare the garden to a theatre, and on the other describe the theatre by reference to the garden. The ambiguity of this dual attitude is constantly to be seen at this period.

The garden on stage

Referring to various *pièces de verdure* (spaces left within plantations) Blondel gives examples such as '*les salles de bal, les salles des antiques, les*

LA GROTTE

amphithéâtres', etc.[7] Blondel also, in *L'homme du monde*, describes the gardens at Marly in terms similar to those used in commenting on a dramatic entertainment: we are 'astonished', we experience 'a sort of enchantment' before the fountains, gentle slopes, 'natural and artificial porticoes and marble staircases'. The enclosures, groves, arbours, amphitheatres, statues are described as though they were theatrical props.[8]

Again, these are theatrical contrivances and illusions, tricks of perspective which produce dramatic vistas in urban gardens in spite of their unremarkable size: porticoes, colonnades, arbours, statues are disposed, or even feigned, to give the illusion of unlimited space. Painters such as Jean Daret, Jacques Rousseau, and Philippe Meusnier specialized in this sort of illusion. Even when the area available was vast, as at Versailles, optical illusions were not despised, being used to create a succession of perspectives which provided constant surprises for the astonished stroller. Cotelle, who placed nymphs and deities in his illustrations of the gardens of Versailles, understood this very well. A century later Watelet rightly terms 'theatrical scenes, these *deliberate arrangements* used to embellish new parks'.[9] The avowed aim was indeed the transposition into the garden of the effects produced by the painter on his canvas or the designer on the stage. Carmontelle insists that his garden of Monceau is a land of illusion. He claims that we should 'change the scenes in a garden like the stage sets at the Opéra: let us show as reality what the most skilful painters offer as decoration, at all times and in all places'.[10]

The garden is thus conceived as a place of dreams and illusions, but also as the practical realization of those dreams. By its very conception, by the effects created within it, the *fabriques* placed in it, the vistas contrived, it becomes more or less dramatic, more or less charming. Nature is invoked and used according to the required effect. Shaftesbury describes 'the rude Rocks, the mossy Caverns, the irregular unwrought Grotto's, and broken Falls of Waters, with all the horrid Graces of the Wilderness it-self' as so many examples of real nature.[11] Similarly Chambers notes that the Chinese in their gardens make a distinction between scenes of enchantment, horror and pleasure,[12] which enabled J. Baltrušáitis in his turn to speak of the 'theatrical art' of Chinese gardens, where one is both spectator and player.[13] Moreover, is it not possible to compare theatrical exoticism with that of gardens, whether Chinese, English or Italian, and is it not the function of pagodas, Gothic towers and Chinese bridges to embody the literary and imaginary world of the beholder?

Artists themselves reflect this constant ambiguity, and in their representations of gardens, painters and designers maintain the topographical enigma, in such a way that it is impossible to tell whether we are in a garden aping a theatre or on a stage in the form of a garden. Oudry gives the most surprising example of this since in his many drawings of the gardens at Arcueil[14] – of which Natoire, Boucher and Portail also produced many versions of drawings and paintings at this time – he manages to give the colouring of a stage set to the aqueduct,

La Perspective, *by J. A. Watteau. Boston Museum of Art.*

Le Parnasse français, *engraving by Maisonneuve, from a painting by Lajoue. Bibliothèque Nationale, Cabinet des Estampes, Paris.*

The Garden of Arcueil: *drawing by J. B. Oudry. Courtauld Institute of Art, London.*

flights of steps and arbours of these neglected gardens. Lajoue, similarly, when he stages Titon du Tillet's *Parnasse français*, or places extravagant sculptures and no less extravagant people in the gardens he paints, produces the same effect. It is true that he has the advantage over Oudry of total invention, even if his Parnassus is situated in a place deliberately reminiscent of Versailles. And when Lancret chooses to depict La Camargo dancing, or the actor Grandval,[15] he places them in gardens which serve as a backcloth but which are, as in the theatre, complete fantasy.

On the other hand, when Huet, Boucher and Fragonard undertook the decoration of the Demarteau salon[16] they recreated the carefree atmosphere of a garden ornamented with statues, birds, groves, fountains and flowers. So vivid is the impression that we find ourselves wondering if Vivant Denon was not thinking of a similar place when he described the lovers' boudoir in *Point de Lendemain*.

I saw only an airy grove, quite enclosed, which seemed to float supported by nothing. The side by which we entered was composed of trellis-work porticoes decked with flowers, with bowers in every alcove; on another side could be seen the statue of Love distributing garlands. In front of this statue was an altar on which gleamed a flame, . . . a graceful temple completed the decoration on this side, opposite was a shady grotto watched over by the god of mystery at the entrance; the floor, covered with a velvety carpet, looked like turf.

This text clearly illustrates the erotic role of the garden, since the bower destined for the young lovers has deliberately been given the appearance of a garden; at the same time this is a theatrical scene of sensual pleasure, pleasure increased by a deliberately planned stage set as if the lovers needed this precise setting of colonnades, flowers and lawns. This was undoubtedly the effect sought by Fragonard in his painting for Louveciennes of the four large canvasses of the *Progrès de l'Amour*,[17] four moments in a love story, four couples set in an atmosphere of wonder created by enormous trees, flowers, orange trees in pots and all the trappings of a 'green paradise'. This lyrical aspect of the garden is perhaps even more obvious in his *Fête à Rambouillet*, a mysterious painting in which an omnipresent garden serves as the backcloth to a romantic embarkation.[18] In spite of the wild nature of the site, we are indeed in a garden, as can be seen from the statue on the left from which the waterfall flows; the trees (yews?) clipped into grottoes and passages; the steps and the clumps of flowers.

The stage-set as a garden

In the *Fête à Rambouillet* the mystery lies in the leafy grotto, in the people who do not emerge from its shade. We are no longer in a real garden: we are setting out with the elegant ladies and their escorts for some shady Cythera. Is this then some festival? What time of day is it, and what season? Does the astonishing ray of light which encircles the swaying tree-tops come from the setting sun, or from an approaching storm, or is it to be seen as artificial stage lighting?

So many questions are posed by this garden which in reality is not a garden at all but, like Watteau's isle, a stage set for romantic dalliance.

If gardens were often conceived as stage sets, the reverse was also true. There are countless examples in theatre and opera of stage sets representing a garden. Just as the panoply of a garden included amphitheatres, terraces and ballrooms, so Frézier included among the theatrical accessories he used 'pyramids, statues, obelisks, fountains, gardens, forests, landscapes, vistas'.[19] An artist such as Lajoue makes much use of this almost unlimited vocabulary so that we are never sure whether we are on a stage or in a garden. His contemporaries were so confused by his ambiguity that an engraving by Huquier of one of his compositions under the title of *The Fountain*, which showed a statue of the Graces in a garden of flowers, was incorporated for its visual effect in a series of stage sets. The new title, *The Fountain of the Graces* marks the transition from a design for a garden to one for the stage, and emphasizes the unity of decorative purpose. This practice accords with theory, if we are to believe the remarks of Grimm or Gougenot on stage sets by Servandoni and Boucher. 'The talent of a stage-designer', writes the first, 'no longer lies in the re-creation of miracles or even of nature in action: it is nature in tranquillity which will provide a thousand wondrous scenes for the designer who has the genius to see them;'[20] and Gougenot, comparing Boucher with Servandoni, declares 'Who can depict better than M. Boucher these beautiful gardens, grottoes and landscapes where one recognizes with pleasure a happy mixture of views of Rome and Tivoli, Sceaux and Arcueil?'[21] Rome and Tivoli provide a picturesque palm tree or ruin, but Sceaux and Arcueil contribute the theatricality of their gardens. This curious mixture was in fact used with delight by all the stage-designers, and the stage gardens differed but little from those in which people strolled and disported themselves.

There are numerous other examples: for the *Fragments de M. de Lully*, already mentioned, a set designed in 1702 in Bérain's workshop for the *Triumph of Venus* was revived, with gardens leading towards a palace.[22] Rameau's *Hippolyte et Aricie* was created in 1733: for the revival, nine years later, Servandoni designed a set for Hippolytus' garden which, according to Pellegrin, 'depicts a delightful garden forming the avenues of the forest where Aricia can be seen reclining on a bed of verdure.' Again, it was Servandoni who designed the set for the flower scene in the *Indes galantes* in 1735: the magnificent garden of Ali's palace offers 'an avenue of trees intermingled with yews leading to a spacious bower'; in the background, an arbour; on either side a five-arched colonnade; these meet in the foreground at a fountain, and a rose-bush marks the centre of the stage.[23]

Michel-Ange Slodtz was also commissioned to design sets for Rameau's operas. For *Anacréon* he designed a 'trellis-work arbour decorated with columns forming latticed balusters' in addition to other arbours.[24] For the production at the Versailles theatre of Bury's *Hilas et Zélie* in 1763 he devised 'the setting of a pleasing country scene preceded by a small wood', and for the revival of the *Eléments* in the

same year he designed 'the orchards of Pomona' for the fourth entry of the ballet.[25]

When Mondonville's heroic ballet *Les Fêtes à Paphos* was presented in 1758 the setting for the second act provided for a small wood where Bacchus enjoys the 'soft murmur of the stream which bathes its banks and the thousand burgeoning flowers scintillating all around', and the lateral flats figured flowers, trees, waterfalls and a fountain.

All these settings, described, conceived and realized, derive from a common, almost banal, topography, but it is nevertheless of interest to note that there is scarcely a theatrical production which does not have its garden. An example of the choice available is given in the description of the little mechanical opera produced by Magny for Bonnier de la Mosson.[26] The constructor provided the traditional succession of sets for the prologue and each of the five acts: 'The subject of the last act is formed by a delightful Garden and ornamented on all sides with Statues, Alcoves and verdant arches. In the centre springs a fountain, and in the distance can be discerned a magnificent colonnade leading to a splendid palace.'

By the time Pierre-Adrien Pâris came to design his numerous sets for the court, it was extremely difficult to distinguish reality or travel sketches from true theatrical invention. In the *Jardins de Cythère*, for example, a grotto, a statue of Venus, and various trees compose a convincing landscape, which we nevertheless know the designer created for this particular purpose. At the same time these elements are interchangeable, as in a garden, and a different arrangement would enable them to be used in a variety of other ballets.[27]

This multi-purpose aspect of a set based on real elements is particularly well illustrated in a series of scale models which were for a long time attributed to Servandoni, but have recently been ascribed by J. de la Gorce to Algieri. This designer, who in fact worked with Servandoni as well as with Boucher, invented a dozen multi-purpose sets, which are today preserved at the Château de Chambord. These universal sets can be combined and their elements used at will in any of the models. The backcloth is sometimes replaced by an engraving: the gardens at Marly engraved by Rigaud or the groves at Versailles by Silvestre. These authentic representations of famous gardens placed in settings adorned with all the elements of traditional stage-craft – garlands, extravagant fountains, trellises breaking up the space at regular intervals – show the deliberate confusion between the reality of gardens and the fantasy of stage sets conceived for Rameau's *Surprises de l'Amour* or Mouret's *Amours des Dieux*.

Stroller and spectator are finally reunited in a common framework. Caught in the trap of a carefully created and sustained illusion they abandon themselves to this particular pleasure, the ultimate aim of garden and theatre.

[1] It should be remembered that the plates of *Le Recueil Jullienne* were engraved after Watteau's death and that apparently none of the titles of the paintings were the invention of the artist. It was probably Jean de Jullienne who was responsible for them, and perhaps Huquier for the arabesques.

[2] See on this subject M. Roland Michel, *Watteau, un artiste au XVIIIe siècle* (Paris 1984) and J. de La Gorce, 'Watteau à l'Opéra (1702?)', in *Antoine Watteau, le peintre, son temps et sa légende* (Paris and Geneva 1987).

[3] A. C. d'Aviler, *Dictionnaire d'architecture civile et hydraulique et des arts qui en dépendent* (Paris 1696 and later editions).

[4] Boston Museum of Art. Regarding the title, see note 1.

[5] H. Walpole, *Anecdotes of Painting in England* (1762–71) Vol. 4, 'Antoine Watteau'.

[6] Is it for this reason that Natoire, Director of the Académie de France in Rome, enlivened the drawings that he made in the 1760s of the gardens around Rome, Frascati and the Villa Madama with Biblical or mythological figures, transforming pure landscapes into painted scenes?

[7] J. F. Blondel, *De la distribution des maisons de plaisance et de la décoration des édifices en général*, Vol. 2 (Paris 1738).

[8] J. F. Blondel, *L'Homme du monde éclairé par les arts* (Paris 1774).

[9] Watelet, *Essai sur les jardins* (Paris 1774).

[10] Carmontelle, *Le jardin de Monceau près de Paris* (Paris 1779).

[11] Shaftesbury, *The Moralist* (London 1711).

[12] Chambers, *Designs of Chinese Buildings* (London 1757).

[13] Catalogue of the exhibition *Jardins en France 1760–1820, Pays d'illusion. Terre d'expériences* (Paris 1977).

[14] See H. Opperman, in catalogue of exhibition *J. B. Oudry*, nos. 129–38 (Paris 1982–83).

[15] Several versions of Lancret's *Camargo Dancing* are known, notably in Leningrad (Hermitage), London (Wallace Collection) and Nantes (Musée des Beaux-Arts). *The Actor Grandval in a Garden* is in the Indianapolis Museum of Art.

[16] Paris, Musée Carnavalet.

[17] New York, Frick Collection.

[18] Lisbon, Calouste Gulbenkian Foundation.

[19] Frézier, *Traité des feux d'artifices* (Paris 1706)

[20] Grimm, *Correspondance littéraire* (April 1754).

[21] Abbé Gougenot, *Lettres sur la peinture . . .* (1748).

[22] J. de La Gorce, *op. cit.* (Note 2).

[23] J. de La Gorce, 'Un grand décorateur à l'Opéra au temps de Rameau: Jean-Nicolas Servandoni', in proceedings of the *Colloque Rameau* (Dijon 1983).

[24] F. Souchal, *Les Slodtz, sculpteurs et décorateurs du roi* (Paris 1967) p. 475.

[25] F. Souchal, *op. cit.*, p. 478.

[26] This mechanical opera was described in detail by Gersaint in the catalogue of the Bonnier de la Mosson sale in 1745. It was bought by Scheffer on behalf of Queen Louisa Ulrica of Sweden and transported to Stockholm. It has since disappeared.

[27] Besançon, Musée des Beaux-Arts. See catalogue cited in Note 13, no. 62.

The Gardens of Cythera: *stage set for a ballet, by P.-A. Pâris. Musée des Beaux-Arts, Besançon.*

Cupids in an Arbour of Greenery: *stage set attributed to J.-N. Servandoni. Château de Chambord.*

Received Ideas on Pastoral*

Simon Pugh

Artificial

Like sex, dexterously managed, can be taken as natural. Like love, the natural is fortunate when decidedly artificial. Sexual relationships, a palimpsest, are effaced and rewritten in landscape form. (17)

Beauty

As 'the beautiful in nature', a critique of absolutism's arboreal phalanxes and flattened earth. Supposedly a repudiation of dominated nature. Replicated as art, 'natural beauty' is a tautology. Needs novelty: intimacy with the beautiful leads to its neglect. (3, 17)

Citizen

Term of contempt, a stylist without substance. Gilds his balls, squirts up his rivulets in jetteaus, admires no part of nature but her ductility (penetrating imagery without 'elegant turns'). The peasant is his admirer. (17)

Deception

Sophism. Metaphorically, the art of transposing, distancing and approximating. Nature decoyed.
(i) Tivoli. Cascade of tin, water, from the bung-hole of a hogshead.
(ii) *Hic Frigida Tempe*. Dripping fountain, a small rill trickles down a rude niche of rock work through fern, liverwort and aquatic weeds. (17, 5, 9)

Eye

The mark of fine taste but easily bored. Distances, commands, shuts out the view. Must have balance and a plain space near to, abjures repetition of the same object. Foot and eye must not travel over the same ground. Can be easily controlled by looking away or shutting the eyes. (17)

Farm

Indolent amusement. An apparent attention to produce obliterates the idea of the farm as a category of garden. What has farming to do with Temples, Mock Priories and Artificial Cascades? Without them, who would visit? The plastic configuration of pastoral poetry. Signifies a place of retirement from splendour and constraint of rank in favour of pastoral simplicity. Distinguish from the working country as landowner from tenants,

> Nor let Ambition e'er invade
> The tenants of this leafy bower. (13, 19, 5)

Garden

Intended to walk or to sit in. (19)

History

A circumstance, an event, that 'furnishes' an object. (17)

Inscriptions

Imported mood. Should be well known, admired, apt. Applied to a farm, raises it above the ordinary level. (19)

Jokes

Double-edge, ironic.
(i) To the 'common people' the ha-ha is a sudden and unperceived check to a walk.
(ii) To Columella, the ha-ha he dispensed with would have prevented his 'farm' from being overrun by pigs. (18, 7)

Knowledge

The perpetuation of accepted beauties by associating a garden or landscape with some classical site or text. Knowledge is an accretion of 'freedom' (*to* not *from*): freedom to transpose sites, to control random promiscuous nature. *The* Knowledge:** of designated routes, a circuit usually marked by seats with classical inscriptions. This accretion of 'freedom' anticipates the automobile and comes with new regulations: speed limits (inscriptions, 'stay awhile'), instructions to stay in lane (guide books), diagrams showing the shape of the road ahead (maps), and the need to keep eyes on the road ahead ('objects' to run the eye over). (10)

Leasowes

Discovered and improved by Shenstone, a principal place to be seen. A perfect picture of Shenstone's mind, simple, elegant and amiable, unaffected and unadorned as a common field. (5, 19)

Mistresses

Venus (*semi-reducta*), rural fays and faeries in cool grot (rarely seen by mortal eye), naiads and dryads (beloved mistresses, naked and exposed by that ruffian winter to universal observation), Maria Dolman (*Ah Maria Puellarum Elegantissima*) who died of small-pox at twenty-eight years of age. Naiads must not be invited by inscriptions to bathe their beauteous limbs in crystal pools impregnated with all the filth which generates from stagnation. Mistresses are pure nature under a different guise, objects of venal veneration. (5, 17, 6)

Nature

Appearance only, never the stuff of work or material reproduction. Culled, collected and epitomized by art which accomplishes what nature strives for in vain. Best when anticipates skill of the artist. Female, impulsive, without care can be violated. What thwarts nature is treason yet as model she implies bestiality and deceit; taken in (in both senses of the phrase) by culture, she is absorbed. If art sets foot in nature this must be done clandestinely and by night, an assignation. In pastoral form, nature is not much depraved. (15, 17, 3, 14, 5, 1, 2, 8)

Stowe, Buckinghamshire: the Rotunda by Vanbrugh, c. 1719. (Photo Daniele De Lonte)

Stowe, Buckinghamshire: the Gothic Temple by Gibbs, 1741. (Photo Daniele De Lonte)

Frontispiece by Copleston Warre Bampfylde for R. Graves's Columella or the Spiritual Anchorite, *Vol. 1, London 1779.*

Portrait of William Shenstone from R. & J. Dodsley, The Works in Verse and Prose of William Shenstone, *Vol. 1, London 1764.*

One-Way Paths

Simple circulation, the carefully controlled itinerary, the scenic route (sign posts, direction indicators, shifts of mood, travel notes, guide books). End up at the beginning having seen everything.***

Pastoral

Modern mode in ersatz ancient style, using shepherd as paradigm of rural simplicity. A form of illusion, concealing miseries, not a description of shepherds as they really are. Shows the beauties without the grossness of country life, hiding the meanness of it, its misery. The Pastoral is not the whole truth but only that part which is delightful. Misfortune is a thorn in the foot. An utter disregard both of life and nature. A stylized recollection of a non-repressive condition that never existed. (4, 12, 8, 11, 3)

Quaff

Diction. 'Elegant turn' on *drink*, preferably limpid springs from a beechen bowl by one contented in a russet stole who had previously bathed in courtly bliss and toiled in fortune's giddy sphere. (5)

Rural Elegance

Stratagem for pastoralist to sidestep agriculture: (i) tedious; (ii) bliss without alloy. *Divina Gloria Ruris!* (16, 5)

Shenstone

Columella of Halesowen. His pleasure all in the eye (the splinter in the eye is the best magnifying glass). He pointed his prospects, diversified his surface, entangled his walks, and winded his waters. He had, said Dr Johnson, an obsessive need for fresh entertainment. Clumsy, negligent of his clothes. Caught between doing *too much* (improper decorations) and *not enough* (cleaning his grounds). Poetry lacks substance. Blind alley off circuitous path from Pope to Wordsworth. (2, 12, 6)

Travel

Largely metaphysical or by proxy. Tempe becomes a grotto, Virgil's Grove a thicket and a stream. Minor cultural appropriations destroy Otherness, a dry run for colonization (palpable, profitable travel).

Ugly

Disagreeable. (17)

Variety

Fine configuration of parts, frequent comparisons of agreeable objects, beautiful digressions, elegant turns on words. Novelty without excess. (5, 4, 17)

Wood

Condemn those who have neither planted a tree nor begot a child. Trees analogous to men: the oak a manly character, British, not

Virgil's Grove: engraving by C. Grignion for R. & J. Dodsley, The Works in Verse and Prose of William Shenstone, *Vol. 2, London 1764.*

Frontispiece by R. Graves, Recollections of Some Particulars in the Life of the late William Shenstone, Esq., *London 1788.*

Plan of The Leasowes, Warwickshire. From R. & J. Dodsley, The Works in Verse and Prose of William Shenstone, *Vol. 2, London 1764.*

suddenly elated by prosperity or depressed by adversity, the rough grandeur of its bark and the wide protection of its branches, venerable, overarching, noble, magnificent. Tall stately oaks . . . their satisfaction, their happiness in their life, their growth and their blossoming . . . an infinite multitude of tiny creatures in the meadows . . . (or so says the 'intimate confessions of a true socialist' – 'Man', says Marx, could observe a quantity of other things in nature, e.g. the bitterest competition among plants and animals . . . in his 'forest of tall and stately oaks' how these tall and stately capitalists consume the nutriment of the tiny shrubs . . .)**** (17, 5)

Yeoman
Pejorative term, a yahoo. A lower degree than the (polished) shepherd. Character conforms to cultivation which has encroached on the wild not subdued it. (19)

Xystus
Extremely disgusting unless free from weeds. (9)

Zig-Zag
Troublesome. An exact serpentine is a foolish affectation. At the Leasowes, the proprietor took the naiad by the hand and led her a (irregular) dance. Preference for irregularity and randomness is akin to the spirit of nominalism. Zig-zagging between worship and domination, the spirit and the name. (6, 9, 5, 3)

*With apologies to Gustave Flaubert (*Bouvard and Pécuchet*, translated by A. J. Krailsheimer, Harmondsworth, 1976, pp. 293–330) and Julian Barnes (*Flaubert's Parrot*, London, 1985, pp. 153–9). Numbers at the end of each letter entry refer to the following bibliographic references:

(1) Theodor W. Adorno, and Max Horkheimer, *Dielectic of Enlightenment*, trans. by John Cumming (London 1973).
(2) Theodor W. Adorno, *Minima Moralia, Reflections from a Damaged Life* trans. by E. F. N. Jephcott (London 1974).
(3) Theodor W. Adorno, *Aesthetic Theory*, trans. by C. Lenhardt (London 1984).
(4) John Butt (ed.), *The Poems of Alexander Pope* (London 1963).
(5) [R. & J. Dodsley], 'A Description of The Leasowes', in *The Works in Verse and Prose of William Shenstone* (London, 2nd edn 1765) Vol. 2, pp. 287–320.
(6) William Gilpin, *Observations relating chiefly to Picturesque Beauty, made in the Year 1772, on . . . the Mountains and Lakes of Cumberland and Westmorland* (London, 2nd edn 1788).
(7) Richard Graves, *Columella or the Spiritual Anchorite*, 2 vols (London 1779).
(8) *The Guardian* (1713), 23, 30.
(9) James Heely, *Letters on the Beauties of Hagley, Envil, and the Leasowes*, 2 vols (London 1777).
(10) Max Horkheimer, 'The revolt of nature', from *The Eclipse of Reason* (New York 1974) pp. 92–127.
(11) Samuel Johnson, *The Rambler* (1750) 36–7.
(12) Samuel Johnson, 'William Shenstone', in 'The Lives of the English Poets', from *The Works of Samuel Johnson* (London 1792) Vol. 11, pp. 276–85.
(13) [William Marshall], *Planting and Rural Ornament* (London 2nd edn 1796) 2 vols.
(14) George Mason, 'Discussion . . . on

Prior Park, Bath. (Photo Daniele De Lonte)

Blaise Hamlet, Gloucestershire. Group of cottages designed by John Nash in collaboration with G. S. Repton and completed around 1811. (Photo Daniele De Lonte)

Shenstone', from *An Essay on Design in Gardening* (London 1768).

(15) William Mason, *The English Garden: A Poem in Four Books*, a new edn (Dublin 1786).

(16) William Shenstone, 'Rural Elegance, An Ode . . . 1750', from R. & J. Dodsley, *op. cit.*, Vol. 1, pp. 111–22.

(17) William Shenstone, 'Unconnected Thoughts on Gardening' from R. & J. Dodsley, *op. cit.*, Vol. 2, pp. 111–31.

(18) Horace Walpole, 'History of modern gardening', from *The Works* (London 1798) Vol. 2, pp. 517–45.

(19) Thomas Whately, *Observations on Modern Gardening* (London 1770).

**'The Knowledge' is the designation given to the defined routes through London that the London taxi-driver must learn before 'graduation'. The garden circuit, pathfinder for the picturesque guide, makes the random ramble through nature redundant.

***It is clear from the various guides that there was an accepted way round The Leasowes, a circular route that begins and ends in the valley beneath Virgil's Grove. See 5; 9; 19; *A Companion to the Leasowes, Hagley and Enville with a sketch of Fisherwick* (Birmingham 1789); *A Description of Hagley, Envil and the Leasowes, wherein all the Latin Inscriptions are translated, and every particular Beauty described* (Birmingham *c.*1800). Such defined circuits were not uncommon in eighteenth-century gardens, such as Rousham, Hagley and Stourhead.

****Quoted from *The German Ideology*, in Alfred Schmidt, *The Concept of Nature in Marx* (London 1971) pp. 129–30.

Bowood, Wiltshire: park designed by
Capability Brown with waterfall by Charles
Hamilton of Painshill, 1785.

Paradox in the Garden:
A Brief Account of *Fabriques*

Monique Mosser

It was the Frenchman Jean-Marie Morel who, in his *Théories des jardins* (1776), provided one of the best studies of garden *fabriques*:

It is particularly this relation of character to site which I call seemliness in the art of gardens. When I have made this known, when I have discussed the location best suited to each sort of building, to its nature, shape and size as well as its style, and the colour which best accords with the landscape of which it will be part, my work will be done: the architect's task will be to add solidity to the plan, to give the buildings the external appearance the gardener expects in order to lend charm and authenticity to the pictures he creates. . . . Buildings planned from this point of view are what in painting are called *fabriques*, a term I shall use to describe all the 'show' buildings and all the constructions with which human industry supplements the works of nature for the adornment of gardens, and if architecture adopts the term as such, it will form a new branch of that valuable art.[1]

It is to these 'miniature monuments' that he returns thereafter to explain the iconographic, and therefore symbolic, design of the garden. Being in close relationship with the whole range of human emotions and feelings, these garden buildings must express the most secret parts of them. And so, in turn, love, remembrance or friendship inhabit these temples, hover over the cenotaphs or are engraved on the stones. Every object takes on a special meaning. The simple, roughly hewn tree trunks forming a cabin take us back to the fundamental debate on the origins of architecture. Further on, a rustic grotto revives a curiously vivid paganism, filled with memories of the ancient cult of the nymphs.[2]

Beyond their intrinsic poetry is the essentially cultural role of the *fabriques*. Whether it be an antique tholos, a Chinese bridge or a Gothic keep, all are perceived as emblematic objects which speak of a distant country, of a past era. They are the outward signs of some new architectural alphabet, and weave together the chronicle of these gardens, so closely linked in other respects to the history of literature. In so far as they are the constituent elements of these microcosmic landscapes, it is easy to understand the desire to collect them, to amass them, to make learned associations between them for spiritual satisfaction and to add to the pleasure of the walk. The garden becomes an encyclopaedia; a walk round it is like turning over the pages of the book of the world. The rapid growth in popularity of this 'new branch of architecture' explains the proliferation of collections of models and the astonishingly large circulation of certain works such as Le Rouge's *Les jardins anglo-chinois* and Grohmann's *Ideenmagazin*.[3] Many landowners were anxious to possess a great variety of *fabriques*, from druid menhirs to Egyptian pyramids, from Turkish mosques to primitive huts. The garden was no longer merely a succession of pictures; it became at once a cabinet of curiosities and an open-air library, for literary quotations abounded.[4] We must be careful not to belittle this practice which was much more than a 'fad', for the greatest European architects followed it, often with some passion. *Fabriques*, standing halfway between idea and reality, provided the opportunity to experiment with shapes, to carry into effect a sort of experimental

architecture, to create the vocabulary of a new style – Paestum Doric, neo-Gothic or oriental. Consequently, the phenomenon must be studied according to both series and type in order to reveal innovations as well as repetitions. Finally, every symbol has some philosophical, even ideological content. The exact meaning of these small buildings, so rarely spared the ravages of time, is sometimes forgotten. Thus, at Ermenonville the Temple of Modern Philosophy, far from being a ruin in the antique style, as was once thought, is on the contrary revealed as a sort of hymn of praise to human progress, a monument which only future generations will be able to complete, according to the man who himself began the work, the Marquis de Girardin, a fervent admirer of the Enlightenment and follower of an esoteric order with Masonic connotations.

Every extravagance has its critics, and the verses of the Abbé Delille in his poem *L'Art d'embellir les paysages*, written in 1782, are well known: 'Banish from gardens all this confused mass of different buildings showered on us by fashion. Obelisks, rotundas, kiosks and pagodas; Roman, Greek, Arab, Chinese buildings; pointless, tasteless architectural chaos whose sterile fecundity encloses the four corners of the world in a garden. . . .'[5]

All these characteristics of the very special world of *fabriques* have for a long time attracted the attention of historians, and we now have detailed studies and virtually comprehensive inventories. Grottoes, nymphaea and other fountains constitute the group which, in its development from ancient times, has without doubt interested the greatest number of scholars.[6] In the more limited period which concerns us the importance of ruins, of the Gothic revival and oriental models, among many others, has given rise to a great deal of literature of variable quality.[7] On the occasion of a recent exhibition, the Georgian Group attempted an interesting typological study for England, and identified no fewer than twenty-two categories.[8] Throughout Europe other research is being carried out on specific topics, for instance bath houses or hermitages. Since much light is therefore being shed on the subject, it is acceptable here to discuss only what may be called 'borderline cases'. Each in its way demonstrates to what extent the art of garden *fabriques* constituted at that time an entirely separate branch of architecture – a branch in which, as it will be seen, obsession may verge on mania; where the taste for concealment (and for revelation) may inspire many curious contrivances; where excess, pure and simple, is adequate proof that it was in gardens that these cherished 'visionaries' were able to realize their finest fantasies. Finally, the very real links between literature and garden art in the eighteenth century cannot be over-emphasized. We have perhaps too often examined images out of their literary context, when this is precisely where their inspiration and explanation may be found. This, then has guided our methodological approach: a concern to establish parallels which may act as mutual agents of enlightenment, or of development in the photographic sense, constantly suggesting disquieting connections.

Carmontelle Presenting the Keys of the
Garden of Monceau to the Duc de
Chartres. *Painting by Carmontelle. Musée
Carnavalet, Paris. (Photo E. Revault)*

Charles-Joseph de Ligne – the prince of fabriques

If we had to chose from among the numbers of garden writers, garden-lovers and other theorists the person who has best celebrated *fabriques*, the prize would undoubtedly go to the Prince de Ligne. His short autobiography, *Coup d'oeil sur Beloeil et sur une grande partie des jardins de l'Europe*, a curious collection of ideas on the art of informal gardens, abounds in descriptions, aphorisms and comical asides on the subject.[9] We know the Prince de Ligne was typical of the enlightened, truly cosmopolitan thinking of the late eighteenth century: a writer of great elegance on many subjects, he moved effortlessly from military strategy to erotic tales. This distinguished garden-lover made of his estate at Beloeil, in the former Austrian low countries, a vast allegorical garden after his own heart, which traced life from 'the cradle of childhood' to the 'chamber of death': 'I have sometimes been reproached for the names and walks in my allegory. Visitors who do not wish to be provoked to thought have only to accept the entire garden as groves and paths amid shrubs and flowers.'[10] Brimming with ideas, this man, whose advice was sought by his peers in all the courts of Europe, amused himself by drawing up a typological inventory of the different buildings which could ornament a garden. After the 'Residence' and the 'Palace', he dwelt at length on *fabriques*, even though he challenged the correctness of the term.[11] The 'Château' must have four towers, the 'Country house' was characterized by an Italianate balustrade, a 'Rural residence' could be 'covered in mellow brick', a 'Hunting lodge' calls for 'white rough-cast' to 'contrast with the trees', while the 'Farm' should be distinguished by a roof 'half thatch and half tiles'. Then come the 'Vineyard House', the 'Hut' and the 'Cottage.' After these more or less 'vernacular' types, the Prince moves into the realm of exoticism. 'Chinese houses' smack of the streets and fairground, 'Gothic houses,' also, are becoming too common. Only 'Moldavian houses', still quite unknown, deserve to be 'more widely seen' according to this devotee of the wildest sort of originality.

Indeed the Prince, like many other protagonists of this movement – especially architects – views the art of *fabriques* as a kind of anti-classical 'war-machine':

I see no great merit in copying, for a hundred thousand crowns, an engraving of a great Monument. I hold in greater esteem the man who, ignoring the orders of Vitruvius and the five orders of architecture, makes one for himself: it may be that his unusual structure will give more pleasure than a dozen Doric columns that we know by heart. Unusual buildings, not necessarily baubles (which I abhor) or childish (which I scorn), make a wonderful contrast on a lawn, and savages' tree-trunk encampments, Peruvian huts, Laplanders' shelters, little palaces from the Caucasus are more striking than eternal parodies of the gods of the Sun, War and Wine, and of Heroes of antiquity less worthy than those under whom I have served. At present everything is so predictable, so familiar, that we need a new approach. English monotony, driving out French monotony, has become so unvarying that modern gardens need to be modernised still further, without following any model. Look at the engravings of London and Yorkshire to be seen in every washroom and

265

corridor. They are all the same – a Greek temple, surrounded by a few trees, on a hill-top. They bore me.

And indeed the Prince was always an innovator, as can be seen in Baudour, one of the most original parts of his immense estate, which we also know from a series of plates by Le Rouge. The truly panoramic appearance of the arrangement, like the formal syncretism and the polychrome buildings, remind one irresistibly of the most outrageous fantasies of the draughtsman Jean-Jacques Lequeu, many of whose plates seem to echo the repertory of *fabriques* in a vast fantasy park.[12]

Half a league from there, towards the East, in the heart of the woods which do not entirely prevent the enjoyment of one of the finest views in the world – an amphitheatre adorned with towns, convents, châteaux, villages – stands a château, seven hundred years old, called BAUDOUR, formerly BOIS D'OURS since many bears were found there. Inside, I preserved its air of nobility, antiquity and respectability. Outside, I demolished the gables and filled in the ditches, except on the south side where I planted vines. To make the shape regular, I had to build on the right to conform with the projecting angles on the left, and the whole represents Hannibal's first battle order at Cannae. There is an Italianate roof, hunting trophies of all kinds and some trophies of war, love and the wine-harvest. All this is painted in fresco, green on one side, as are the two pavilions at the entrance, the gates, the Chinese lanterns and the regularly spaced wooden posts which surround the courtyard. The inner courtyard is in the Chinese taste, one side in blue and white porcelain and the other in Egyptian marble. The garden is also an aviary. The whole of the other façade is covered by a portico in trellis-work. Some of the columns are painted pink, others yellow, and there is an even more gaily-coloured staircase. The stable roof is like an artist's palette. Finally, inside this house, which I wanted to rid of its pompous air, can be found all that is strange, extravagant and even mad, but with the elegance that should always attend the hunt, since stags, boars and wolves come right up to the windows of this lively and extraordinary house.

The scope of this visionary imagination and boundless creativity reveals profound, almost organic, links with the world of literature. Indeed many pages of the *Coup d'oeil* seem to be directly inspired by detailed descriptions of settings in fairy tales, such as those of Madame d'Aulnoy.[13] The profusion of riches, the sense of surprise, the taste for monkey figures inherited from the Rococo style, are found almost unchanged in these informal gardens. And this is not the least of the paradoxes. The Prince de Ligne, by a simple association of ideas, let his imagination follow in the wake of the monkey princess, Madame d'Aulnoy's 'Babiole':

That gave me the idea of an island and a town inhabited by monkeys. I already know where I shall put this establishment. Already I can see them in their dresses and uniforms. Every day I meet some who are not nearly as merry as mine will be, and which I would not wish to have. Already I feel I can see them receiving visits. Long, light chains will partly restrain their attentiveness. Only their politeness will be difficult to control.

It must be said that humour and irony were an essential aspect of the contemporary view of gardens. Furthermore, nothing in this style is

Detail of a Turkish tent in copper at Haga in Sweden. From designs by L.-J. Desprez, 1787.

more amusing than one of the *Hieroglyphic Tales* of Horace Walpole, the 'Gothick' creator of Strawberry Hill and the author of *The Castle of Otranto*.[14] The story in question is *Mi-li. A Chinese Fairy Tale*, and in it we follow the peregrinations of a 'true' prince of the Middle Kingdom in search of his promised lady in Georgian England, where we witness his growing astonishment before the unfolding vistas of an exorbitantly 'English' garden but not a wholly fictitious one, since the author drew his inspiration directly from Park Place![15]

An interior garden, or the trompe-l'oeil of Eros

In his *Contes immoraux* the Prince de Ligne pays tribute to the scenery he preferred above all, and describes thus the delights of a 'true garden of Semiramis' on the shores of the Baltic in an unnamed Russian country, but one which he knew. Indeed many novellas of this period found in the 'new gardens' a propitious backdrop for the adventures and misadventures of their plots. They deserve therefore, alongside the châteaux, a prominent place in the list of 'Asylums of Libertinage'.[16] But in the works of one author after another a delightful idyllic setting can suddenly give way to the realms of pure fantasy. Then the garden, an ideal place, enclosed and removed from the world, becomes the sole support of the imagination, the shifting and ambiguous setting for a theatre of the mind. Once more the words are as important as the images. No further proof of this is needed than a strange 'garden of love' situated in Poland, which corresponds very closely to a short 'novel' written by Vivant Denon, the future director-general of museums under Napoleon.

A series of drawings preserved in the library of the University of Warsaw re-recreates for us a *trompe-l'oeil* garden, half 'real' scenery, half mural painting, constructed in the basement of the little Mniejszy Palace in Warsaw. The artist, Szymon Bogumil Zug, one of the greatest architects of the Polish Enlightenment,[17] was also responsible for the spread of landscape gardens in Poland. Of the many he created, one was the famous Arkadia, near Nieborów, for Princess Helena Radziwill.[18] Born in Saxony, Zug worked first in Dresden, then doubtless travelled in Italy in 1756 before going to Poland, where he spent the greater part of his career. Exposed to many influences, he was also a theatre set designer and a 'gardener' as well as an architect of 'new towns'. For the Mniejszy Palace, Zug designed in 1775–7 a setting the like of which had never been seen: a secret garden of love, a place unmistakably devoted to the pursuit of pleasure, the access to which seemed very like some sort of initiation ceremony. Here too we are confronted by one of these borderline cases where some explanation is needed. In this project, strangely, the desire to re-create the illusion of a natural setting finds itself confronted by the need to violate the strict rectilinear design of a traditional plan and arrangement. From there we enter the world of artifice and illusion, guided by the architect himself, who with signs written in French has marked out the curious arrangement of this 'garden-apartment', the plan of which is reminiscent of a labyrinth and

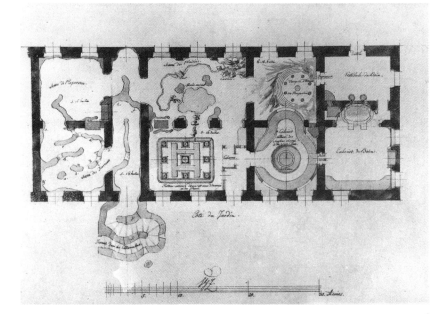

of theatrical stages sets. The entrance stairway, called the 'descent to the catacombs' and twisting in rocky meanders towards the 'scene of horrors', makes a disquieting approach, even though it finally emerges on the 'scene of hope'. In a sort of symbolic hyperbole, Zug's designs for the elevation in this area reveal, like a vast fresco, an Egyptian setting haunted by grimacing divinities, grotesque representations of the god Bes, monumental hieroglyphics and funerary urns. Zug's apparent source is easily identified as Piranesi's impressive engravings of the *Diverse maniere d'adornare i camini*, published in 1769. So by a curious transition from Rome to Warsaw, the entrance to Zug's garden of love recalls even more fancifully the design of the 'Caffè degli Inglesi'. Then the landscape returns to its rightful self, and the 'scene of hope' is like a cave or grotto in the heart of a mountain. After this comes the more rustic site of the 'scene of pleasures', a truly informal garden, crossed by a stream running from a cascade to an open pool. Here a rocky arch leads to the 'view of the temple of love'. Opening on to the 'water parterre decorated with oranges and flowers' is a wooden rustic hut roofed in thatch, an innocent-looking building which serves as a double illusion, since it conceals the entrance to the 'chamber of divans in the Turkish style' a charming rotunda with a murmuring fountain. From there a 'secret door' leads to the 'bath chamber' occupied by a large bath tub and a vast divan.

In Zug's illusionist landscape, certain details of the setting refer directly to a short erotic novel published in 1777 in the *Mélanges littéraires, ou journal des dames* by Dominique Vivant Denon, under the title *Point de lendemain*.[19] In this charming account of a brief amorous encounter the setting, a noble estate in the country, and all its devices, become in a way the main protagonist:

It must be admitted that I did not feel the eagerness, the devotion needed to visit this new temple, but I was very curious: it was no longer madame de T. . . . I desired, it was the chamber. . . . As I was about to enter, I was stopped. 'Remember,' someone said in grave tones, 'that you will be considered never to have seen, nor even to have suspected the existence of the sanctuary to which you are about to be admitted. There must be no foolishness: I am not concerned about anything else.' Discretion is the foremost among virtues, and to it we owe many moments of happiness. All this had the air of an initiation. Held by the hand, I was led along a dark corridor. My heart was pounding like that of a young proselyte before the celebration of the great mysteries. . . . the doors opened. . . . I was astounded, enraptured. I no longer knew what was happening to me. I began in good faith to believe in magic. The door closed behind me, and I could no longer see the way by which I had entered. I saw only an airy grove, quite enclosed, which seemed to float, supported by nothing. At last I found myself in a vast cage of mirrors on which objects were so artistically painted that as they were repeated, they gave the illusion of being exactly what they represented. No light was to be seen inside: a gentle, heavenly glow filtered through according to how much illumination was needed for each object, perfume-burners exhaled delicious fragrances, figures and ornamental groups shaded the eyes from the flame of the lamps which gave a magical light in this delightful place. The side by which we entered was composed of trellis-work porticoes decked with flowers, with bowers in every

270

Garden inside the Mniejszy Palace in Warsaw: scenes depicting Horrors, Pleasures and Hope. Drawing by S. B. Zug, 1775–7. University Library, Print Room, Warsaw.

Plan of the four levels of a fabrique.
Drawing by J. D. Dugourc. Fondation
Claude-Nicolas Ledoux, Arc-et-Senans.

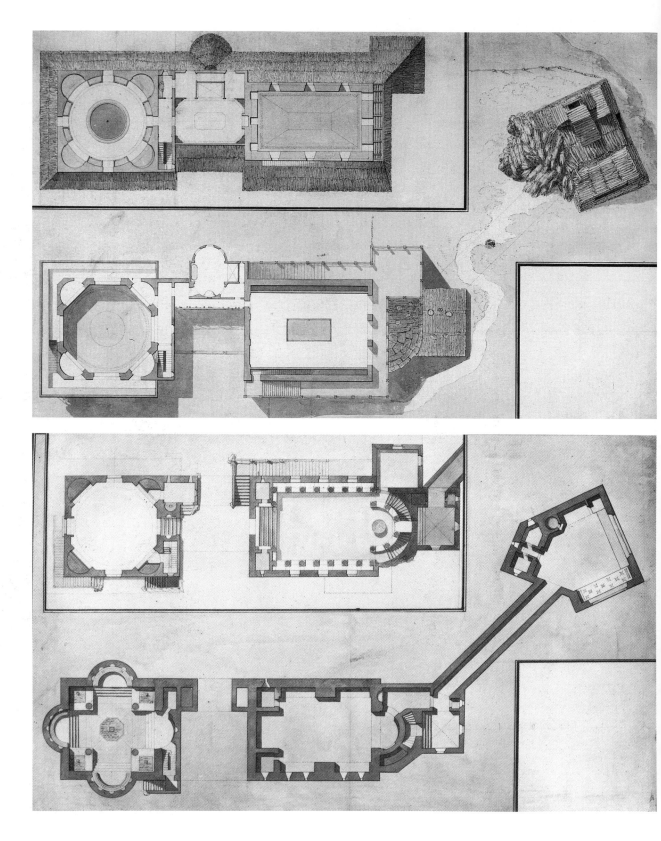

272

alcove; on another side could be seen the statue of Love distributing garlands. In front of this statue was an altar on which gleamed a flame; at the foot of the altar were a chalice, crowns and garlands; a graceful temple completed the decoration on this side; opposite was a shady grotto, watched over by the god of mystery at the entrance; the floor, covered with a velvety carpet, looked like turf. From the ceiling hung garlands held by guardian spirits, and on the side opposite the colonnade was an awning under which was heaped a mound of flat stones with a canopy supported by cupids. Here the queen of this place seated herself with great composure. I fell at her feet; she leaned towards me, held out her arms and, in a moment, since this pose was repeated all around, I saw this island as a place entirely populated by contented lovers. The sight of them inflamed my desires. 'Would you', I said to her, 'leave my head uncrowned? Shall I, so close to the throne, feel such deprivation? Could you refuse?' –'And your vows?' she replied as she rose; 'I was a mortal when I made them, you have made me a god; to adore you is my only vow.' 'Come,' she said, 'the shadow of the mystery must hide my weakness, come....'. Saying this, she approached the grotto. Scarcely had we crossed the entrance when I know not what skilfully contrived force pulled us forward. Impelled by the same motion we fell softly on to a pile of cushions. Darkness reigned in the silence of this new sanctuary. Our sighs spoke for us. Growing more tender, more frequent, more ardent, they interpreted our feelings and were an indication of their intensity; after some time the last sigh of all reminded us that this was our homage to love. . . .

In this highly suggestive description by Vivant Denon, certain material details, like the 'velvet' carpet imitating turf, leave little doubt about the reality of such settings, even though embellished by memory and literature! We are also reminded of the decorative details of Le Camus de Mézières, or of Maillier who, in his poem *L'Architecture* transforms a lady's chamber into the 'groves of Idalia'.[20] Thus gardens and their retinue of *fabriques* so obsessed these times that garden lovers were not satisfied merely to enjoy them in the course of a walk, but also wanted to possess them within their own dwellings, and achieved this end by means of strange subterfuges.[21]

A voyage of initiation in the land of temples and cottages

This endless catalogue of surprise, pleasure and sheer delight sometimes gives way to more complex mysteries, to higher demands. For several years historians have striven to expose the close links that existed, throughout Europe, between the art of landscape gardens and Freemasonry.[22] But it is not easy to relay what was cloaked in silence, or to reveal what was meant to remain hidden. Many explanations, therefore, were too elementary or too obvious to be wholly convincing.[23] There are certain undeniable facts, but others are simply part of that very special late eighteenth-century world of the imagination, when light suddenly gave way to darkness. In a recent study Helmut Reinhardt has attempted to review what, in the motley collection of *fabriques*, could be associated in any way with the initiation ceremony:[24]

What interests us particularly are *fabriques* whose names denote a certain philosophical idea (Elysium; Temples of Friendship, Virtue, Wisdom; Altars of Friendship; Houses and cottages intended for hermits, philosophers, brahmins, and so on). These are followed by the towers, keeps and fortresses whose medieval exterior recalls the days of the Knights Templar, the mythical ancestors of the freemasons. After these comes the range of Egyptian architecture which invaded gardens in the form of pyramids, temples and statues. Add to these the buildings and grottoes where, under Rosicrucian influence, spiritualist séances were held and alchemy was practised.

There were also 'masked buildings' whose mysterious purpose was deliberately concealed.

If we consider only what happened in France, it cannot be denied that many of the great picturesque gardens created between 1770 and 1780 belonged to members of the Masonic aristocracy:[25] the garden of Monceau (which belonged to the Duc de Chartres, Grand Master of the Grand Lodge of France); the park of Canon in the Eure (where Elie de Beaumont had a private lodge built); the park of Castille near Uzès (where the Baron de Castille installed inside the château a Doric temple with a star-spangled vaulted ceiling); Ermenonville (which belonged to the Marquis de Girardin; Mortefontaine (property of the administrator Le Peletier); the Folie Saint-James at Neuilly (owned by the 'rockman', Baudard de Saint-James); Méréville (property of the farmer-general de Laborde); and Maupertuis (owned by the Marquis de Montesquiou). Finally it must be remembered that the Prince de Ligne, a member of several lodges in the Austrian Netherlands, was affiliated in France to the lodge of 'St Jean de Montmorency-Luxembourg'. The prince, who lamented the incomprehension of some visitors before his 'allegory' was, as we have seen, typical of those great nobles who, whether for sport or by conviction, originated a 'cryptic' language of gardens, which came to resemble a vast puzzle made up of *fabriques*.

We should not, however, restrict ourselves solely to the decorative elements without considering the arrangement as a whole. We must remember that from that time every initiation entailed ritual journeys – that is, a succession of specific moves corresponding to the 'ordeals' which symbolize the essential moral and spiritual evolution of the future initiate. Now the space of a garden lends itself ideally to this sort of symbolic circuit, to almost ritual perambulations, in which the *fabriques* became compulsory 'stages' as well as functioning as 'triangulation points' in the landscape. At Wörlitz, the Prince von Anhalt-Dessau's estate, the visitor had to begin his circuit in front of the 'mystagogue's cell' and choose between the 'path of the ignorant uncultured man' and the 'mysterious way of the mystagogue, apprentice in divine knowledge.'[26] More often the 'message' was more difficult to decipher, but just as ambitious. We are reminded of Ermenonville, or again of these curious 'gardens of the Revolution' where philosophical and political discourse mingled.[27] Anthony Vidler, in his essay 'The Architecture of the Lodges',[28] has rightly shown the importance of the specific nature of these initiation areas, and the diagrams he has reconstructed show clearly that there had to be

a 'third dimension'. He analyses at length the visit of the English writer William Beckford, accompanied by the great architect Ledoux, to what seems in every detail a 'lodge' in a park near Paris.[29] Some of Beckford's biographers have been unwilling to see in this long 'letter', clearly written and full of literary 'suspense', anything more than a 'story'. Yet, once more, it seems that apparently romantic fiction here coincides closely with architectural reality, in the domain of the garden.

Indeed, the discovery of the drawings of the French architect-designer Jean-Demosthène Dugourc suggests disturbing parallels with Beckford's account. As in the encounter between Zug and Denon, it is not a matter of alleging a strong influence, but rather of emphasizing that such close analogies tend, as is very understandable, to prove that literary imagination feeds on real facts and places. Michel Gallet gives a resumé of this strange excursion:[30]

On the stated day the architect and the young Englishman left Paris in a cab with lowered blinds. After more than an hour on the road the coachman stopped them in a wooded estate where long rows of huts reminded Beckford of a village in Tartary. They entered a building where there were various successive ill-lit areas: first a barn and the living-room of a cottage opening on to a garden, then a quite impressive entrance hall where a very large cockatoo seemed asleep on a perch. From there they entered a chamber of almost regal magnificence. . . . Here they met a sinister ceremonious old man who invited them to approach a large pool. In the depths of the water appeared cadaverous, moving forms which left our Englishman chilled with fear. Overcoming his anguish, he climbed a staircase, a brilliant copy by Ledoux of Bernini's *scala* in the Vatican. This stage led him into a railed gallery where he could hear strains of impressive chanting. The pious young man recognized some fragments from the Prophets and the verses from the Magnificat which announce the fall of the mighty and the exaltation of the humble. Ledoux then told him that he had just witnessed things which must not be repeated, but he was free not to abide by what had been revealed. When night fell, and the architect had accompanied his return, Beckford was ill for some time before he was able to write the account of this strange excursion.

Beckford himself used the word 'bedevilment' and the future builder of Fonthill Abbey refers to the *Quatre fils Aymon* and the supernatural in *chansons de geste*. What is striking, finally, in this bizarre account, is the amount of 'pragmatic' detail: the zenithal lighting of different areas, the strictly architectural progression from the most cursory or humble (piles of wood) to the most opulent (the grand salon and the chapel), and also the subtlety with which Beckford describes the range of his emotions.

The two drawings by Dugourc, who was the brother-in-law of Bélanger and drew up a number of garden projects, show a development of plans, on four different levels, for a curious building – a large irregular-shaped thatched cottage adjoining an enormous pile of wood.[31] The four plans correspond to an underground level, a semi-basement, a slightly raised ground floor and a first floor. The rusticity of the exterior, as far as one can judge, conceals a strange and sumptuous interior arrangement. The heap of wood, a sort of hidden

entrance, rises above a building like a kitchen, where cooking ranges can be seen. An underground passage, invisible from the outside and lit by a shaft, leads to a rectangular space, like a crypt, and with no apparent connection at this lower level with the 'baths' on the quadrilobe plan. Different staircases allow access to the semi-basement level where there is a 'chapel' bordered by a colonnade, the 'apse' of which encloses a sort of large pool. On the two upper levels, where intercommunication is possible, it is easier to recognize arrangements corresponding to an apartment: an octagonal drawing-room and its mezzanine balcony doubtless lit by a sky-light, a bedroom with four alcoves and a small private bathroom, and a large billiard room. All things considered, one cannot help wondering about the purpose of this 'mysterious building'. The 'pile of wood' with a few faggots falling off is reminiscent of Beckford, but also of other examples, like the one described by the Prince de Ligne at Peterhof near St Petersburg: 'In this new garden which is being created there is a chalet in the form of a haystack. A few trusses block the doors and windows, and have to be removed before you can enter. One always mistakes the truss, but this piece of trickery is easily pardoned when you enter a salon decorated in the best Parisian taste.' On the other hand, what was the purpose of this 'chapel' and these apparently sumptuous 'baths'? Then we remember what Beckford wrote:

I ventured to say to him 'To what convent is the Chapel below annexed, and to what order do the monks I heard ascending from behind the screen of the choir belong?' 'If this were indeed a chapel,' replied the Architect, 'you must pardon my not disclosing its name – remember our agreement. Let it suffice for you to know that this truly sacred edifice is set apart for a high, though not entirely a religious purpose. Let me entreat you to abstain from asking me any more questions.'

In the face of this silence shrouding a mystery scarcely unveiled it is difficult not to make the connection with the end of the passage in *L'Architecture*, where Ledoux 'presents' the entrance to La Saline in Arc-et-Senans, an unusual *fabrique* if ever there was one. Ledoux concludes, 'It was in vain that I informed the traveller that the building in question had no celebratory character, that its nature was entirely different, that it was necessary to go back to the underlying principle. In reply to my reticence he put forward a few insignificant thoughts based on commonplaces of prejudice.' It is indeed difficult to make converts!

Anthony Vidler recalls in his essay that the famous Cagliostro, founder of the 'Egyptian' ritual, built near Basle for the banker Sarasin, in the most secluded part of his estate, a 'Regeneration' lodge, where the candidate was to live in the company of his hierophant for forty days before his initiation. This is not very far from Dugourc's drawings!

The emblems of unreason

Erotic labyrinths, initiation courses: in the minds of garden-lovers and of artists the only rule for the 'game of *fabriques*' lies in the prodigious

276

scope of the imagination. Traditionally, the emphasis has been on the pleasure to be gained by this architecture of amusement, these 'follies'.[32] Their eccentric aspect has also come under scrutiny, especially on English estates.[33] Less often has their 'troubling strangeness' been considered. The word schizophrenia has been used in connection with Castle Goring.[34] Many other examples reveal a strange megalomania, or even other pathological 'fixations'. This very excess is symptomatic of the overwhelming curiosity which seized people at the end of the eighteenth century. With the passage of time, the lighting has changed:

Indeed, black is beginning to invade the landscape, bearing away the drifting islets of light from the idyll and thus causing a panic crystallization. . . . The encounter with nature has not taken place: we have been content to simulate it on the chessboard of artifice. And from one artifice to another, in the belief that we were venturing on to another 'map of Love', we have lost our way on the 'map of Frenzy'.[35]

This 'frenzy', this 'true passion of the soul' can take different forms. For some it takes the form of obsessive hoarding, with the collector-owner unable to rest until he possesses everything he can possibly gather together. The Prince de Ligne, a shrewd connoisseur, criticizes some 'garden maniacs' among his peers; among 'collectors' he finds a special place for the Duke of Württemberg and his estate at Hohenheim,[36] created in 1782 near Stuttgart:

It is a property like few others: from the Château you pass through a succession of small natural gardens to a garden in the best of taste, the most ornate, perhaps the most marvellous there is: there are more than sixty different views treated in the same manner: the Duke, in order to possess in his garden what others are happy to have on engravings in their closets, has there constructed the finest parts of Italy in the proportion of four to one. That is, all the proportions of his building are the same and the columns, for instance, are a fourth part of the size of the ones of which the Romans left us such fine remains, in the hope of persuading us to make a special pilgrimage to that edifying and charming place. I will not recount all that I saw there, I will say only that the first scene is the ruin of Nero's house of gold, then there are three superb half-buried columns (those of the Temple of Jupiter in fact); the tomb of Caius Sextus with funerary urns, the temple of the Sybils, Diocletian's baths above a charming stream. . . . a Roman sepulchre and a score of other similar monuments, all separated by clumps of trees, two more streams, bridges or hedges; never clashing, but harmonizing agreeably when seen together. All the clumps of trees separating these different scenes are plantings from the other three corners of the world, trees by which Heaven seems to have wanted to compensate them for not being as civilized as Europe.'[37]

There are many other examples of such encyclopedic collector-gardens. In England, Shugborough seems to be the three-dimensional embodiment of the plates in the first volume of the *Antiquities of Athens* (published in 1762 by James Stuart and Nicholas Revett), for the park contains one after the other, the 'Tower of the Winds', the 'Lanthorne of Demosthenes' (or Choragic monument of Lysicrates) and a triumphal arch copied directly from that of Hadrian.[38] In Poland, some of the *fabriques* designed by S. B. Zug for Arkadia seem a direct imitation of the well-known drawings of Clérisseau who, moreover, played an important part at Wörlitz. But even if we confine ourselves only to a catalogue of ancient ruins, we should mention the strange collection of Roman-style architecture at the end of the entrance drive at Potsdam, and the magnificent drawings of the Frenchman Charles de Wailly for the 'New Herculaneum' which he dreamed of creating for the Duc d'Arenberg at Enghien, in the former Austrian Netherlands.[39]

But the fascination becomes total when architectural excess equals the patron's megalomania. One remarkable case can be mentioned, not well known, and yet still visible: The Tsaritsyno park near Moscow. For the empress Catherine the Great, Vasily Ivanovitch Bazhenov – who deserves a place in the Pantheon of 'visionaries' as the equal of Ledoux or Boullée – conceived a park in which every building would be a veritable palace. This unfinished work, which brought about the architect's disgrace,[40] had its origins in 1775, on the occasion of the signing of an important peace treaty between Russia and Turkey. Great fêtes were organized, with sumptuous settings created by Bazhenov and Kazakov, on the Khodinka, Moscow's parade ground. This ephemeral architecture representing palaces and fortresses taken from the Turks, mingled classical and oriental elements with traditional Russian architecture. They so pleased the Empress that she expressed the wish that they should be copied on the vast estate she had just bought from prince Antiockh Kantemir, and which occupied a difficult site: the abrupt escarpment of a vast sloping plateau. Bazhenov designed a 'panoramic' arrangement: the group of palace pavilions of different sizes and very different styles would rise in three successive tiers with several monumental entrances and two 'bridges' connecting obvious differences in levels. The construction of this enormous complex started in 1775 and continued amid many difficulties. When Catherine came to visit the works in 1785 she pronounced the buildings too dark, the ceilings too low, the rooms too confined, and dismissed Bazhenov. All the architect's drawings – plans, elevations and general views – have been preserved.[41] This vast documentation gives us the opportunity to consider generally the symbolic function of *fabriques* and their role in the architect's creative process. It could almost be said that every architect has an 'inner garden' thronged with a great catalogue of *fabriques*, in a sense the whole of his potential output. Thus Bazhenov devoted himself wholeheartedly to the art of creating infinite combinations. The plans play upon cellular, geometrically-based models (semicircles, triangles, squares with rounded corners, diagonals) which result in 'self-reproducing', almost 'organic' forms. As for the elevations which make use of every possible contrast in the display of red brick with white stone ornamentation, they appear so very strange as to defy all attempts at description. When work ceased, abandonment and ruin followed. But even today Tsaritsyno remains one of the most eccentric architectural dreams ever imagined.

Generally, our first idea of *fabriques* is their reduced size, their appearance of being 'models' or architects 'toys'. Frequently these

demonstration pieces turned into feats of great technical skill. At
Tsaritsyno the extravagance of the enterprise was marked by a
corresponding excess of scale. The broken column in the Désert de
Retz is an indication of this 'over-scaling', sometimes even beyond the
bounds of science fiction:[42] it has been calculated that, if the correct
Doric convention of eight diameters were to be applied, the unbroken
shaft would have had a height of 120 metres (384 feet). We could
mention many other *fabriques* whose very gigantism has brought about
their irreparable decay. In Waldershare Park in Kent, for instance, Lord
Burlington built for Sir Robert Furness in 1725–27 an immense
Belvedere. Now, the magnificent Palladian bays open only on to a
void.[43] The 'Rocher' at Attre in Belgium, built between 1782 and 1788
for Comte François-Ferdinand de Gomegnies, is a sort of curious
metamorphosis between a ruin and a mountain, concealing a 'volcano,'
where one passes from an underground grotto into delightfully
decorated chambers. 'It was made by the assembling of rough stones,
several of which weighed more than twenty-five thousand pounds,
which were dragged there from a league away by eighteen horses and
raised by the work of forty men for eight years under the personal
supervision of the Count.'[44]

Decidedly, garden enthusiasts form a strange brotherhood, entirely
devoted to creating the impossible. And among their number are to be
found enthusiasts for other 'manias' too. The passion for collecting
leads to a sort of cataloguing so meticulous in its detail that it becomes a
sort of taxonomic mania, a pathological urge for compilation
reminiscent of Sade's *Cent vingt journées*.[45] But mockery, twin sister of
folly, is never far away. Hubert Robert painted an elegant dog kennel in
the form of a little grotto surmounted by an obelisk, and M. A. Carême
published in 1815 *Le pâtissier pittoresque*, containing fabrications of
spun sugar and almond paste copied directly from Durand's *Parallèle*.[46]
Perhaps the absurd is after all merely one of the aspects of the sublime.

[1] Jean–Marie Morel, *Théorie des jardins* (Paris
1776; reprint, Geneva 1973). E. Cereghini is
currently preparing a study of his theories.

See under heading 'Fabriques' (M. Mosser)
in *The Oxford Companion to Gardens* (Oxford
1986) p. 182. For France, Ernest de Ganay has
published a series of articles useful for
reference:

'Le goût du Moyen-Age et des ruines dans
les jardins du XVIIIe siècle', in *Gazette des
Beaux-Arts* (1932) pp. 183–97.

'Fabriques aux jardins du XVIIIe siècle.
Edifices de la Chine et de l'Orient. Temples,
belvédères, pavillons', in *Revue de l'Art Ancien
et Moderne*, Vol. 64 (Jan–Dec, 1933) pp. 49–74.

'Les rochers et les eaux dans les jardins à
l'anglaise', in *Revue de l'Art Ancien et Moderne*
(July 1934) pp. 63–80.

And two further reference titles: Jurgis
Baltrušaitis, *Jardins et pays d'illusion*, in *Aberrations, Quatre essais sur la légende des formes* (Paris
1957; re-issued 1986) pp. 97–126, and also the

catalogue of the exhibition *Jardins en France
1760–1820, Pays d'illusion, terre d'expériences*,
C.N.M.H.S. (Paris, April–June 1977).
[2] On this research subject, among recent
articles are:

Monique Mosser, 'Le rocher et la colonne,
un thème d'iconographie architecturale au
XVIIIe siècle', in *Revue de l'Art*, No. 58–59
(1982–83) pp. 55–74.

Georg Germann, 'Höhle und Hütte', in
*Jagen und Sammeln, Festchrift für H.G. Brandi,
Jahrbuch des Bernischen Historichen Museums,
1983–84)* (Bern 1985) pp. 121–30.

For 'pagan architecture': Johannes
Langner, 'L'architecture pastorale sous Louis
XVI', in *Art de France*, No. 3 (1963) pp. 170–
186, and also Henri Lavagne, 'L'Amalthaeum
de Cicéron et la "laiterie de la Reine" au
château de Rambouillet', in the collection: *La
mythologie, clef de lecture du monde classique* (Tours
1986), pp. 467–74.
[3] Le Rouge, *Jardins anglo-chinois ou détails des*

Design for a cake in the shape of a Chinese pavilion on a rock. From M. A. Carême, Le pâtissier pittoresque, Paris 1815.

nouveaux jardins à la mode (1787), 21 parts carrying 496 plates. Ernest de Ganay (*op. cit.* notice 99): this author notes that the appearance of Le Rouge's work in separate *cahiers* means that there are very few complete collections. These plates had a European distribution just as, later, Johann Christian Grohmann, *Ideenmagazin für Liebhaber von Gärten, englischen Anlagen und für Besitzer von Landgütern*, 5 volumes (Leipzig 1796–1806). The history of these volumes, also frequently translated, is very involved.

[4] The links between gardens and literature in the eighteenth century have been closely studied. For Great Britain see John Dixon Hunt and Peter Willis, *The Genius of Place. The English Landscape Garden 1620–1820* (London 1975).

For Germany, Siegmar Gerndt, *Idealisierte Natur. Die literarische Kontroverse um den Landschaftsgarten des 18. und frühen 19. Jahrhunderts in Deutschland* (Stuttgart 1981).

For France, Denise and Jean-Paul le Dantec, *Le roman des jardins de France, leur histoire* (Paris 1987).

For the more specific subject of inscriptions and quotations see:
M. Mosser, 'Le texte mis en espace ou la littérature dans le jardin', in *Eidos*, No. 4 (1989).

For Italy see E. Balmas, Leo S. Olschki (eds.) *La letteratura e i giardini*, proceedings of the convention, Verona-Garda, 2–5 October 1985 (Florence 1987).

[5] L'Abbé Delille, *Les jardins ou l'art d'embellir les paysages*, poem in four cantos (first edition, Paris 1782). Ernest de Ganay, *op. cit.* notice 502, records ten or more editions in 1782. The first edition was followed, until 1844, by a score of other editions. There are translations in English, Italian and Portuguese.

[6] A whole volume could be written on the bibliography of this subject, but among the more important works are:

for Ancient Times, see Henri Lavagne, *Operosa Antra. Recherches sur la grotte à Rome de Sylla à Hadrien* (Rome 1987).
For the modern period, mainly in France:
ed. Elisabeth B. MacDougall *Fons Sapientiae. Renaissance Garden Fountains* (Dumbarton Oaks 1978).

Naomi Miller, *French Renaissance Fountains* (New York 1977) and *Heavenly Caves* (New York 1982).

Gerold Weber, *Brunnen und Wasserkünste in Frankreich im Zeitalter von Louis XIV* (Worms 1985).

Barbara Reitssch, *Künstliche Grotten des 16. und 17. Jahrhunderts, Formen der Gestaltung von Aussenbau und Innenraum an Beispielen in Italien, Frankreich und Deutschland* (Munich 1987).

Arte delle Grotte, per la conoscenza e la conservazione delle grotte artificiali, convention proceedings, Florence 1985 (Genoa 1987).

[7] For ruins in the period which concerns us see:
Günter Hartmann, *Die Ruine im Landschaftsgarten. Ihre Bedeutung für den frühen Historismus und die Landschaftsmalerei der Romantik* (Worms

1981).

For the growing interest in the East, apart from the two never replaced great classics, Eleanor von Erdberg, *Chinese Influence on European Garden Structures* (Buchram 1936; re-ed. New York 1985) and Oswald Sirén, *China and Gardens of Europe of the Eighteenth Century* (New York 1950) see Patrick Conner, *Oriental Architecture in the West* (London 1979).

[8] *Georgian Arcadia: Architecture for the Parkland Garden*, exhibition catalogue, Colnaghi (London July–Aug. 1987).
The categories listed are: Arches, Banqueting Houses, Bath houses, Boat houses, Bridges and cascades, Churches and chapels, Columns, Eye catchers – Follies – Ruins, Gazebos, Grottoes and shell houses, Hermitages, Lodges and *cottages ornés*, Mausolea, Monuments, Obelisks and pyramids, Orangeries and conservatories, Practical buildings, Rotundas and umbrellos, Seats, Summerhouses and pavilions, Temples, Towers.

[9] There are numerous editions, all private, of the *Coup d'oeil sur Beloeil*, the first dating from 1781. See Ernest de Ganay, *op. cit.* notice 110. Here we have used the annotated re-edition drawn up by Ernest de Ganay 1922, from which all the quotations here from the Prince de Ligne are taken.

[10] The Prince de Ligne has been the subject of many biographical studies. For his specific role as 'lover of gardens' see the preface by Ernest de Ganay to his edition of *Coup d'oeil sur Beloeil*
and also by the same author, 'Le Prince de Ligne et les jardins', in *La Revue de Paris* (15 July 1935) pp. 400–13.

[11] See *Coup d'oeil* p. 275. 'It is sufficient that I have accepted the word *fabrique* which no longer retains the idea behind it. It is all the more ill-chosen because it would be very appropriate, to populate a park, that there should be a real factory (*fabrique*) where it would be pleasing to watch 500 young people of both sexes at play or sleeping on the grass during their time off'.

[12] There is little worthy of notice in the album published under the signature of Philippe Duboy, *Lequeu. An Architectural Enigma* (London 1986). For this particular question see Günter Metken, 'Jean-Jacques Lequeu ou l'architecture rêvée', in *Gazette des Beaux-Arts* (April 1965) pp. 213–30, and Jacques Guillerme, 'L'instance scénique dans l'oeuvre de Lequeu', in *Ligeia*, No. 2 (1988).

[13] *Le cabinet des fées*, Vol. 1: *Contes de Madame d'Aulnoy* (Paris 1988) pp. 77–99; and Laurence Jyl, *Madame d'Aulnoy ou la fée des contes* (Paris 1989).

[14] Horace Walpole, *Hieroglyphic Tales* (1785). For a recent monograph: B. Fothergill, *Beckford of Fonthill* (London 1979).

[15] For bibliography concerning Park Place see Ray Desmond, *Bibliography of British Gardens* (Winchester 1984) p. 211.

[16] A. Vidler, 'Asylums of Libertinage. De Sade, Fourier, Lequeu', essay published in *The Writings of the Walls* (Princeton 1987) pp. 103–24.

[17] Marck Kniatkowski, *Szymon Bogumil Zug,*

P. 15

architekt polskiego oświecenia [S. B. Z. architect of the Polish Enlightenment] (Warsaw 1971). See also a more general account of the period: Stanisław Lorentz and Andrzej Rottermund, *Neoclassicism in Poland* (Warsaw 1986). I should like here to express my gratitude to Mme Wanda M. Rudzínska, Keeper of Drawings in the Warsaw Library, for her scholarly help, and for sending photographs of these drawings.

18 On the question of the spread of English gardens in Poland, in addition to the relevant chapter in Lorentz and Rottermund, see Brian Knox, 'The Arrival of the English Landscape Garden in Poland and Bohemia', in the collection *The Picturesque Garden and its influences outside the British Isles* (Dumbarton Oaks 1974) pp. 101–16. More specifically, J. Wegner, *Arkadia* (Warsaw 1948 – in Polish).

19 Dominique Vivant Denon, *Point de lendemain* (1777); texts, variants and chronology of Denon in *Romanciers du XVIIIe siècle* Vol. 2, 'Bibliothèque de la Pléïade' (Paris 1965), pp. 379–401.

20 Monique Mosser, 'L'Arredamento libertino, ovvero il letto del pittore', in the catalogue of the exhibition *Il progetto domestico. La casa dell'uomo: architipi e prototipi*, XVIIe Triennale di Milano (Milan 1986) pp. 58–73.

21 Similarly, the Prince de Ligne describes 'winter apartments' standing next to greenhouses, which constituted a sort of 'interior garden'. Some existed in the grand palaces in St Petersburg, as in the Tauride palace for Prince Potemkin where there was 'a winter garden so extensive that there were several avenues, and in the centre a temple in which was a statue of the empress'. In the garden of Monceau, on the estate of the Duc de Chartres, there was an 'arbour or winter garden with a drawing-room and dining-room arranged in the rocks'. (See Thierry, *Guide des amateurs et des étrangers . . .*, (Paris 1787) Vol. 1, pp. 64–66.) Later, for less wealthy proprietors, illusion became commonplace, and was the origin of the vast wallpaper panoramas of the early nineteenth century.

22 See, among others, Adrian von Buttlar, *Der englische Landsitz 1715–1760. Symbol eines liberalen Weltentwurfs* (Mittenwald 1982); Günter Hartmann, *op. cit.*; Monique Mosser, 'Le rocher et la colonne . . .', *art. cit.*; Magnus Olausson, 'Freemasonry, occultism and the picturesque garden towards the end of the eighteenth century', in *Art History*, Vol. 8, No. 4 (Dec. 1985), pp. 412–33; Giuliana Ericani, 'La storia e l'utopia nel giardino del senatore Querini ad Altichiero', in *Piranesi e la cultura antiquaria. Gli antecedenti e il contesto*, proceedings of the convention Nov. 1979 (Rome 1983) pp. 171–85; see also, in this volume, the essay by Eliana Mauro and Ettore Sessa, 'Masonic Gardens in Sicily'.

23 As in the case of dubious analyses for the Park in Brussels and the maze in the Jardin des Plantes in Paris.

24 Helmut Reinhardt, 'L'Influence de la franc-maçonnerie dans les jardins du XVIIIe siècle'. To be published in the proceedings of the Conference organized by the Grand Lodge of France, Paris, April 1988.

25 M. Mosser: 'Les Arts' in *Histoire des francs-maçons en France*, under the direction of Daniel Ligou (Toulouse 1981) pp. 127–33. For sources, see Alain Le Bihan, *Francs-Maçons parisiens du Grand Orient de France, fin du XVIIIe siècle* (Paris 1966).

26 Quoted by H. Reinhardt: August Rode, *Beschreibung des Fürstlichen Anhalt-Dessauischen Landhauses und Englischen Gartens zu Wörlitz* (Dresden 1788; reprint Dessau 1928) p. 81.

27 Monique Mosser, 'Le temple et la montagne: généalogie d'un décor de fête révolutionnaire', in *Revue de l'Art*, No. 83 (Jan. 1989) pp. 21–35.

28 Anthony Vidler, 'The Architecture of the Lodges. Ritual and Symbols of Freemasonry', in *The Writings of the Walls* (Princeton 1987) pp. 83–102. This study had appeared originally in *Oppositions*, No. 5 (1976) pp. 75–97.

29 This letter of William Beckford is quoted by J. Oliver, *The Life of William Beckford* (London 1932) pp. 171–82. It has been closely studied by A. Vidler, who was the first to draw attention to the document. See above, note 28.

30 Michel Gallet, in his turn, has published a translation of this document in his book *Claude-Nicolas Ledoux 1736–1806* (Paris 1980) p. 24 and pp. 269–71.

31 See the sale catalogue *Jean-Démosthène Dugourc (1749–1825)*, Paris, Salle Drouot, 3 June 1988, No. 118: 'Plans for two artefacts on four different levels' with reproductions. These drawings belong today to the Claude-Nicolas Ledoux Foundation. For information on Dugourc, see Simone Hartmann 'Fabriques et jardins: dessins de Jean-Démosthène Dugourc dans la collection de Tassinari et Chatel de Lyon', in *Bulletin de la Société d'Histoire de l'Art Français* (1980) pp. 211–18.

32 Traditionally in French the term '*folie*' (folly) is used particularly for a small country house. 'Follies' have been the subject of coffee-table books, not very well done mainly because of the quality of the photographs.

33 For England see Barbara Jones, *Follies and Grottoes* (London 1953). Here the author, among others, stresses the important role of the architect Thomas Wright whose collection *Arbours and Grottoes* (1755 and 1758) has been excellently re-issued by Eileen Harris (London 1988); see also Gwyn Headley and Wim Meulenkamp, *Follies. A National Trust Guide* (London 1986) with a very full bibliography.

34 See Headley and Meulenkamp, *op. cit.* p. 132. The effect of mixing different styles of elevation is another of Lequeu's peculiar inventions.

35 Annie le Brun, *Les châteaux de la subversion* (Paris 1982); see the chapter 'L'interrogation du paysage', p. 110. The same 'black' idea inspired the Canadian philosopher Geoffrey James in his book *Morbid Symptoms. Arcadia and the French Revolution* (Princeton 1986).

36 Adrian von Buttlar, *Der Landschaftsgarten* (Munich 1980) pp. 147–53; and see also E. Nau, *Hohenheim. Schloss und Gärten* (Siegmaringen 1978).

37 Prince de Ligne, *Coup d'oeil . . .*, pp. 123–25.

38 Shugborough, near Stafford, is included in the *Bibliography of British Gardens* by Ray Desmond, *op. cit.* p. 237. In addition, the guide to the garden and its monuments, published by S. E. Pybus in 1984 provides an interesting list of sources, articles and references.

39 See Monique Mosser and Daniel Rabreau, *Charles de Wailly, peintre architecte dans l'Europe des Lumières*, exhibition catalogue of the Caisse Nationale des Monuments Historiques et des Sites. (Paris 1979) p. 87. The drawings for the park at Enghien are divided between the Wrightsman Collection (USA) and the National Archives in Brussels (Belgium).

40 A. I. Mikhailov, *Bazhenov* (Moscow 1951 – in Russian). See also the article on 'The Imperial Gardens of Russia' in this book.

41 These very numerous drawings are preserved in several places. Some large designs are displayed at the Moscow Museum of Architecture (at Donskoï). On the other hand the detailed plans and elevations are shared between the Museum of the Academy of Fine Arts and the Department of Drawings at the Hermitage in Leningrad. See A. I. Mikhailov, *op. cit.*, pp. 111–68.

42 See Olivier Choppin de Janvry, *Réponses à 101 questions sur le Désert de Retz*, catalogue of the exhibition at the Musée-Promenade de Marly-le-Roy-Louveciennes, 1988. Among numerous publications by the same author, 'Avant que disparaisse à jamais le Désert de Retz', in *L'Oeil* (September 1967) pp. 30–40.

43 See G. Headley and W. Meulenkamp, *op. cit.* p. 103 and *Georgian Arcadia (op. cit.)* p. 55.

44 Benoît Fondu, *Le Val de Beaulieu-Attre*, final-year thesis for the 'Conservation of Historic Landscapes, Parks and Gardens' department, Architectural Association School (London 1988). Typewritten copy.

45 See Anthony Vidler, 'Asylums of Libertinage', *supra* and Annie Le Brun, *supra*. Some of Sade's novels contain interesting descriptions of gardens, as in the *Marquise de Gange* in which a labyrinth recalls very precisely the arrangement in the Bois des Tombeaux of Castille, near Uzès.

46 See the catalogue of the exhibition, *L'Art culinaire au XIXe siècle. Antonin Carême* (Paris 1984) chapter written by Daniel Rabreau: 'Le citoyen-architecte'.

Nature and the Idea of Gardening in Eighteenth-Century Spain

Carmen Añón Feliú

At the start of the eighteenth century the Bourbons came to the throne in Spain, supplanting the Habsburg dynasty. This was a time when the whole of Europe followed French sources in the field of garden design. Versailles and its glories were still a source for inspiration and imitation, though the latter was achieved with limited success despite an endless series of gardening tracts on the gardens at Versailles. Spain not surprisingly followed these stylistic tendencies, not least in seeking to gain some of Versailles' glory through emulation: this aspect was still more significant when it came to designing gardens than creating art.

Gardening treatises of the period reflect this. By and large they consisted of lists of academic principles based on Le Nôtre's empirical rules, rather than seeking to encourage new ideas in design. They were manuals for the craftsman rather than for the artistic creator; the patterns and directions followed theories which sought to achieve 'a noble simplicity allied to a diversity of forms'. Manuals and treatises, however, can be dangerous in hands without talent, and the result in Spain was an endless repetition of clichés with which able gardeners, rather than inspired designers, hid their lack of creativity. Architects stepped in where the gardeners had failed, taking a new interest in gardens, and many achieving renown as a result.[1]

From this tradition emerged the new figure of the landscape garden designer. Although his role was loosely defined, his aims were complex:

What we need is a good-natured, optimistic young lad, and of good working stock. He should not be delicate, but should give the promise of growing up strong. Before then we will teach him to read, write, draw, and plan on paper, as good design springs from a knowledge of what is beautiful . . . He should also learn geometry, arithmetic, and if he shows himself able enough, architecture . . . He should be made to sketch on the ground both his own designs and those which his instructor suggests. He should be taught to plant and tend parterres, and with the long-handled sickle, palisades. He should learn the properties of fertilizers, the nature of winds, and the movements of the moon, so that from this knowledge he will be able to predict the weather, and also become familiar with plants and the methods for separating or transplanting them . . . [and] he should then teach those around him.[2]

Morel had already suggested that:

From the moment the architects took over the design of gardens the inevitable happened, they applied the same principles to gardening as to architecture. Used for too long to successfully adapting regular forms for the creation of architecture, they sought to link the garden to the building, the focus of attention, in such a way that the garden was reduced to an accessory.[3]

Dezallier d'Argenville described the ideal gardener as

a geometrician, a draughtsman who knows the art of architecture. He must have an understanding of decoration, know the qualities of all the plants typically found in great gardens, and know the effects they can achieve. He should be inventive, and as well as all this be intelligent with good natural taste, which should be trained by the observing of good things and by criticizing the bad, and have a consummate understanding of the art of gardening.[4]

The *Encyclopaedia of Gardening* of John Claudius Loudon (1783–1843), gives 'the different conditions of men engaged in the practice or pursuit of gardening':

'labourer, apprentice, journeyman, foreman, master gardener, head gardener, nursery foreman, travelling gardener, botanic gardener, and royal gardener.' The 'Mansion Residence' is run by 'the gardener, who manages the garden-scenery, including the park . . . [and who] has under him a forester for the demesne woods and park trees; a pleasure-ground foreman for the lawns and shrubbery; a flower-garden foreman; a forcing-department foreman, and a kitchen-garden foreman.' Tree specialists used to be common in Spain, and though they no longer exist, their work remains as proof of their achievements.

However in seeking to draw up the blueprints for those great gardens and in the absence of many true creators, the gardening manuals – splendid in other respects – became the gardeners' bibles, and Europe drowned in clichés repeated by those who sought to cover up their lack of originality. This led to architects becoming involved in gardens, amongst whom Robert de Cotte, Mansart, Lassurance, Gabriel, Vanvitelli, Sacchetti, Sabatini, Ribera, Ventura Rodriguez and Villanueva are notable.

But to reduce the French garden to a simple formal expression, however perfect, would be to demean it. We would be led by the sorry attitude which we hear so often now that the art of gardening has been debased or forgotten: 'Are you making a French or an English garden?' What profound ignorance this reveals, and how far removed this type of thinking is from the true meaning of the world of gardens.

The French garden was never that which later critics made of it: cold, geometric, intellectual, symmetrical, all formality and correctness. On the contrary it was a place for life, light, movement, colour, noise, games and music. . . . as Taine was to say in his evocation of the *ancien régime*: 'Its parks and parterres are open-air salons; there is nothing natural about nature there, she is entirely organized and adjusted to the service of society; it is not a place for solitary relaxation, but somewhere to walk in company and exchange greetings.'[5] It was a manifestation of the sublime, with its own poetry, literature and music, befitting its style. It had a perfect or 'ideal' nature, the expression of the Good, the True and the Beautiful. Its naturalness was cogently defined by Batteux:

If the arts are the imitators of nature, they must imitate wisely and clear-sightedly, without servility. They should rather take objects and traits from nature, and present them as perfectly as possible. In a word, where nature is imitated one sees not nature as she really is, but as she could be, and what one detects is her spirit.[6]

C. Kintzler has also clearly expressed it:

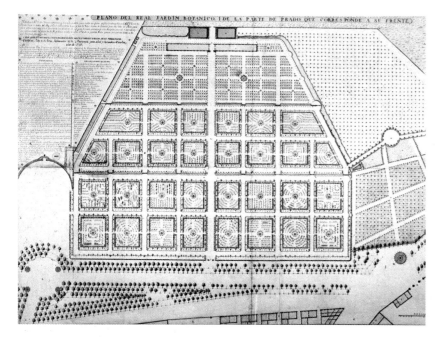

Aesthetic Cartesianism does exist, in the form of a theory of pleasure. It allows one to understand the French garden, the geometric spot where the classical arts take their places. The essence of the French garden has a precise definition; it is not the detached coldness which banality suggests. Going beyond an expression of worldly phenomena, the French garden expresses a paradoxical aesthetic, where reality and truth are in opposition, and where, by mastering illusion, artifice becomes the revealer of nature.[7]

What did the French garden, introduced by the Bourbons, find in Spain? A complex and diverse situation, which prevented it from having a common character throughout the kingdom. The regional differences of soil and climate, and the variety of traditions and development made Spanish gardens both individual and different.

There was a strange symbiosis between the universality of an empire which had led Charles I to spend more than two-thirds of his life outside Spain, visiting his lands with a sense of Europe now difficult to understand – strange though this may seem – and the rule of a dynasty from the courts of France and Naples; they met a blinkered provincialism, the result both of the poverty of the ordinary people and of the unrepresentative attitude of the wealthy upper bourgeoisie. At high level, planning was done on a European scale, but its implementation and the use of techniques was based on inherited regional traditions, and the climate led to changes in the planting schemes.

On a Roman culture, common to almost all of Europe, the Arabs in Spain had left a profound mark of their special understanding of the garden. The interior garden, more typical of the oriental and Roman worlds, had brought about a special way of gardening in all the south and a great part of the centre of the peninsula. Notwithstanding the continuous fighting of the reconquest, the reality of daily life imposed itself among the Moors, Jews and Christians resulting in an enriching interchange of cultures and traditions.

Allah specified firm tenets for the next life; the wealthy Muslim sought to advance them in this life through literary and architectural exercises inspired by the ideals of *suras* in the Koran, together with traditions derived from ancient cultures (Persian and Yemeni), and also from Jewish and Christian legends ... one can detect two cultural strands to which Islam would become heir, with many other characteristics, on the one hand the *badiya* or romantic wish for anti-urban liberty, typical of the Bedouin, and on the other seigneurial and economic models, which from the time of the Republic had been a constant feature of Roman life, and which, reborn in the Veneto of the sixteenth century, were to become commonplace in certain European cultures.[8]

The oriental luxury and refinement of pavilions among clouds of water, palm trees with copper-covered trunks, lakes of mercury, were to link with the spirit of gardens from the misty north: a luxurious courtly chamber, small in scale and refined in detail, as in the splendid Brussels tapestries which adorn royal palaces.

The Spanish kings were swift to adopt the Moorish manners of dress and to enjoy their newly-conquered palaces. Arab techniques of irrigation and cultivation had succeeded in inspiring a link between

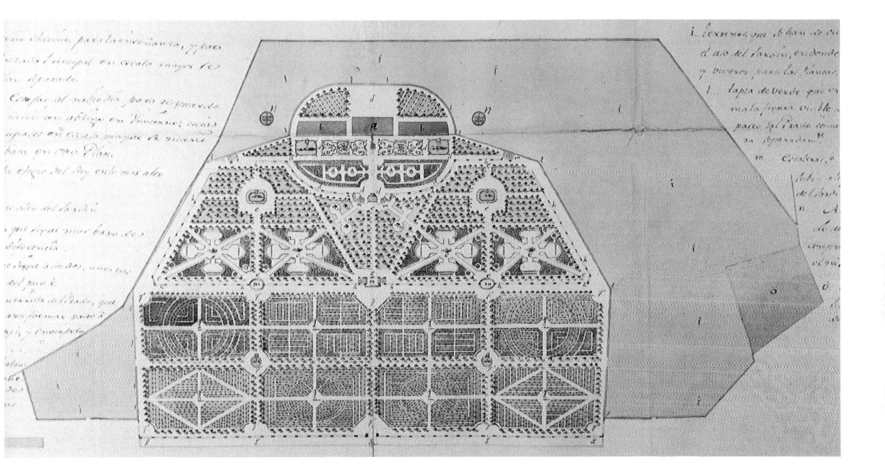

Plan of the island garden at Aranjuez by Cuéllar, 1737. AGP, Madrid.

Plan of the gardens for the Palacio Real in Madrid, designed and drawn by Esteban Boutelou, head gardener at Aranjuez, 1747. AGP, Madrid.

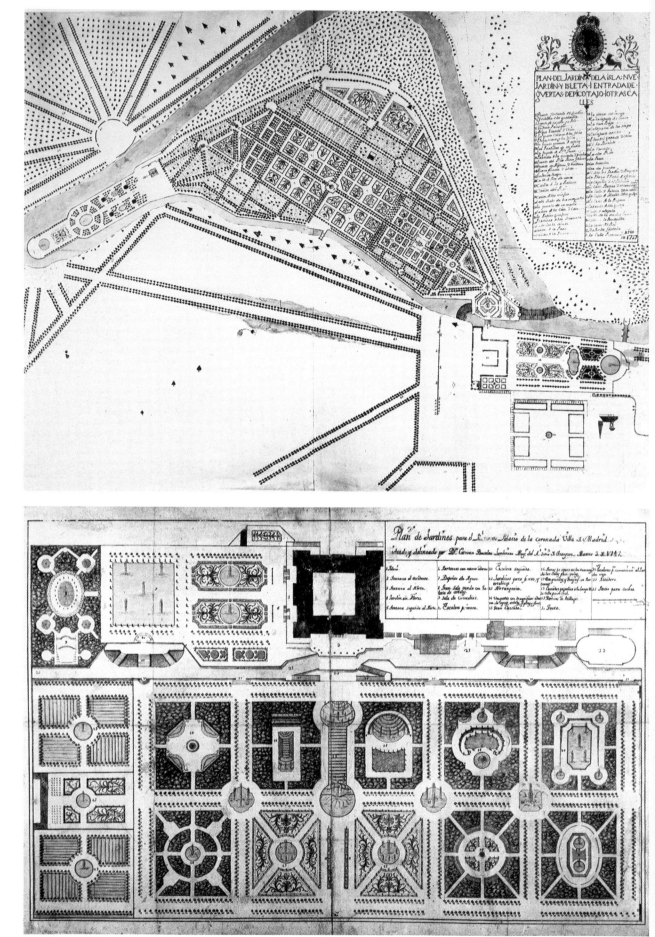

advanced technology and sensuality, and aesthetic symbolisms of great refinement.

Charles V and Philip II both approved of the meeting of Spanish and Islamic traditions. Philip II indeed was a major promoter, thus revealing his great artistic and aesthetic sensibility. This is the immensely attractive side to Philip II which recent research has stressed: his exquisite taste in architecture, gardens and fine arts.[9]

He was responsible for sending gardeners and architects to Flanders, France and Italy, and for inviting Flemish gardeners to Spain. His masterpiece, the Escorial, was the prototype for a complete urban programme. The site of the palace was chosen with great care, and assessed not only in terms of its surroundings, but in terms of its estates, maintenance, vegetable gardens and leisure gardens. At all times the *genius loci* was taken into account. This was clearly shown by the numerous other works undertaken by the architect-king. For example, Moors were released from captivity to help Juan de Herrera in his restoration of the Alhambra, 'as no one knows more about these buildings than they do'. The technical and aesthetic coherence of this garden was thus maintained. But Philip chose a different solution when faced by the Alcázar in Seville; in a state of disrepair which made restoration almost impossible, it became instead the setting for a Mannerist garden.

The Mannerist garden and its profound symbolism was to spread in Spain. Pedro Soto de Rojas provides an example, in an exquisite poem, 'Paradise is closed to many, gardens are open to a few' written whilst constructing his *carmen* (the house and garden typical of Granada), which reflected an intensely individual aesthetic later to appear in poetic form. This deification of gardens was later reflected in the symbolism which flowers and plants acquired, and also in the manner in which the work of the gardener was turned into an art form which would come to be seen to be replete with meaning. The analogy became reality in the writings of Rojas: the poetical garden was thus to last as garden poetry. The difference between this garden and its classical and Islamic predecessors is that it is not only a paradise, but an academy in green. To walk through such a garden is to follow a philosophical path in search of truth; the language of the garden is created and speaks, as does the language of painting.[10]

It was against this backdrop that the eighteenth-century garden was to develop. It also had to adapt itself to varied landscapes and climates, and the result was to be a marked contrast between the misty gardens of the north, those of the central plain and the Mediterranean gardens of the south. The differences were enriching, and would result in a broad iconography, typified by local forms and names of country residences: Galician *pazos*, Catalonian *masias*, Toledan *cigarrales*, Mallorcan *sones*, Granadian *carmenes*, and Andalucian *patios*. The enormous influence of the classical French garden in the tradition of Le Nôtre was nevertheless to continue throughout the century.

The association of nature with the well-springs of liberty was however becoming influential. The philosophical debate also saw

The labyrinth in the gardens of Enghien,
Belgium. G.-L. Le Rouge, Details de
nouveaux jardins à la mode, *1776.*

LABŸRINTHE D'ANGUIEN

Moitié du Théatre
de Pithurin
Tracé par le Rouge
Seig.r du dit Lieu.

Projet de Jardins Publiés par M. Louis Archi.
1200 Toise

artistic expression. To quote with hindsight: 'Towards the end of the eighteenth century love of nature, particularly wild nature became almost a religion.'[11]

Urteaga points out the two directions which the discovery of nature would take, the two traditions conveyed by the term 'landscape':

It is not strictly landscape we see when looking at a landscape, but views; for centuries the only meaning of the word 'landscape' was a territory occupied by man. From the end of the sixteenth century the term became used in Holland and England exclusively for painting. During the seventeenth and eighteenth centuries 'landscape' was the scene encompassed by the onlooker, or to be precise, the view which fell within the gaze of the painter. 'Landscape' thus referred to pictures, but later, rather like the word 'relief', would come to have scientific and geographical meanings also. It is interesting that although the naturalists of the eighteenth century, viewing the lie of the land with a recording eye, did not speak of 'landscape', they nevertheless meant what we mean by the term today.[12]

The Romantics, who were to have such an influence towards the end of the century, were still a long way off from the enlightened dilettante admiring the landscape which he had shaped. An ostensible battle was about to take place between the rational organization, technological developments and the hopes placed in scientific progress on one side, and the new artistic theories on the other. Cavanilles expressed the dilemma with clarity: 'It would be pleasant to find fields left alone in their natural state; but rather than this, I would like to see prosperous agriculture, manufacturing and the progress of the human species.'[13]

It was hardly surprising that, faced with the problems of poverty, misery and helplessness found in the Spanish countryside, as well as in the towns and cities, in this period many considered that the alleviation of these conditions took precedence over aesthetic concerns. This might explain the prevalence of the useful, even in royal gardens, stately homes and public parks: ornament was very much a secondary consideration.

However a very satisfactory compromise was reached from the conflict between utilitarian and pleasure-gardens: 'everything in a garden lives together, without losing its identity, without discord and without fear of extinction. The garden is, like the kitchen-garden, a place of taste as well as cultivation, a living ideal, an image of thoughtfulness, of life itself.'[14] And so in the best gardens of this period, gardens and kitchen-gardens grew and developed side by side.

Though Rousseau was censured in Spain, his ideas had taken root in the loftiest circles. The book of Pedro Montagón y Paret, *Eusebio*, published in 1786 and 1788, received great acclaim as well as condemnation. The education of a castaway landing on the American coast is clearly drawn from Rousseau's *Emile*, with its praise of nature and the simple life and image of 'the blessed life of primitive man'.

Nevertheless one cannot speak only in terms of science or beauty. Paul Vernière tells us how

French classicism is also a cultural manifestation. Weak in Italy and Spain, although less so in Naples and Madrid as a result of the Bourbon connection, it

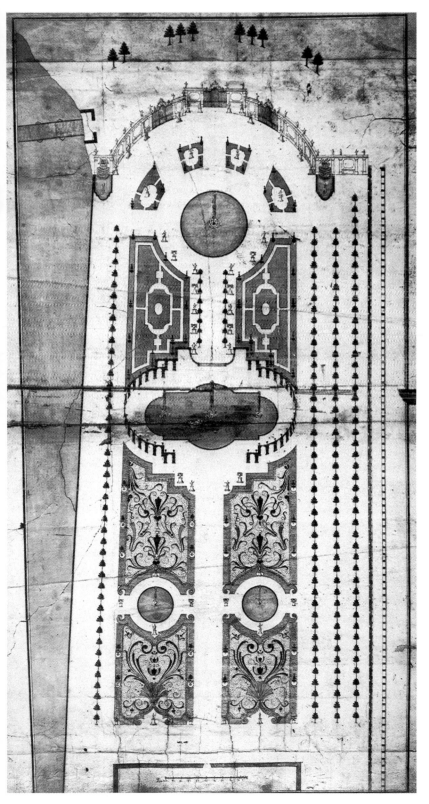

Parterre at Aranjuez: a detail of the pattern in box between the palace and the central fountain. Designed by Marchand, c. 1730. AGP. Madrid.

was most strongly expressed in England. . . . From the reign of William and Mary, however, we can see a more or less concerted and more or less conscious offensive against French fashions and French taste.[15]

To all this we must add the interest generated by the sciences, the resulting innovations being well spelled out by d'Alembert in mid-century:

The science of nature becomes richer by the day; the limits of geometry are stretched, taking its torch to those parts of Physics which are closest to it; the true workings of the world have been revealed, developed and made perfect. . . . From the earth to Saturn, from the history of the skies to that of insects, Physics has changed totally, and with her, almost all the Sciences have taken the necessary new form.[16]

If we consider nature with a broader vision we find

a duality of positions before the natural world and man's use of it. One of these stems from classical culture, crosses the medieval theological tradition and that of the Renaissance, . . the survival of the anthropocentricity of Judeo-Christian culture . . . a criterion of 'ecological triumph' . . . its natural medium over-exploited (or badly applied) . . . is the result of ignorance.[17]

The study of science implied an awareness of man's relationship with nature; geology, climatology, botany and zoology were all established forms of learning through which landscape could be understood and studied in a rational manner. The sciences were to become increasingly important and eventually to take the place of the arts. This was the golden age of Spanish botany, of José Quer, Antonio Palau, Miguel Barnades, Casimiro Gomez Ortega, and of the botanical expeditions of José Celestino Mutis to the kingdom of New Granada (Colombia), of Sessé and Mociño to New Spain (Mexico), and Ruiz and Pavón to the kingdoms of Peru and Chile.

This interest in science took two forms. Firstly the appearance of the first real botanical gardens, which had previously concentrated on the medicinal uses of plants, but which would now perform a scientific function. Secondly, interest in botany increased enormously, so that the history of its horticultural application became inseparable from that of gardening. At the same time there developed a passion for acclimatizing exotic plants which were to have a lasting influence on garden design.

Gardens had previously relied on plans, optical tricks and water to achieve their effects. Crushed brick and slate were often used to enhance their frequently drab colouration. The landscape garden at first also used very little colour, achieving its effects through the grouping of trees and vertical features (which were a throw-back to the time when gardens needed reference points around which the garden was created), or the age-old undulations of the land. Towards the end of the century, however, colour invaded the garden and offered a new world of possibilities. The mania for colour would later degenerate into an obsession with mosaiculture which was typical of the latter part of the nineteenth century, and which sadly still has its attractions.

287

Collections of exotic plants were introduced, some becoming naturalized. Conifers were widely used and gradually the cypress, the incense pine and cedar of Lebanon were introduced, also beech, birch, red cherry, pink acacia, ginkgo, liquidambar, liriodendron, magnolia and ailanthus. Flowering shrubs were imported for their colour, with great success: philadelphus, privet, dogwood, lilac, hazel, potentilla and hydrangea.

During the first half of the century French architects and gardeners were charged with garden design. Robert de Cotte, with his plans for reconstructing the Buen Retiro, of which only the designs for the ornamental gardens were used; Marchand working at La Granja or making important changes at Aranjuez by laying out the ornamental garden in front of the east façade; Carlier, pupil of Robert de Cotte, built, with the help of Boutelou, the fountains at La Granja; Garnier de l'Isle worked at the Palacio Real; Marquet's work for the king and the Dukes of Alba and Piedrahita; Bélanger for the Dukes of Osuna; all giving a strong French flavour to their work. Juvara, Sacchetti and Sabatini left their Italian influence. In the same period Ardemans and Ventura Rodríguez provided a more developed vision, although their most important plans were never realized.

Gradually Sabatini was surpassed. Villanueva's botanical gardens in Madrid had an imposition of rigorous and measured criteria within a framework of formal simplicity. Earlier excesses disappeared, and this attitude to design soon became common practice.

The first landscape gardens, with essential clichés and attendant paraphernalia, made their appearance towards the end of the century. They did not flourish, largely because of the nature of Spain's terrain and contemporary social conditions. Examples of the landscape garden in Spain remain poor and few, with the sole exception of Alameda de Osuna's Capricho.

The meeting of garden and nature in Spain over these three centuries was always conditioned by a subconscious esteem for the land. Agriculture, and the correct cultivation of the soil was seen as its proper use, linked through space and time by a common philosophy. It was a reflection of the wise coupling of leisure and husbandry which is always present in the most refined gardens. This intimate inter-dependence of corresponding dominion was a reflection of complete harmony. The Spanish garden is one which rarely imposes itself, which knows how to fit in with the landscape with a profound sentiment for the earth which it conquers tenderly, so that it is unharmed by change. It is a return to the deep springs of a garden which gives a transcendental meaning to agriculture and the defence of its private existence very close to the romantic desire for solitude.

Perhaps the garden as the selective image of nature is a fitting definition of the desire for heaven which all gardens should possess.

The 'Fresneda', an artificial lake with an island in Philip II's garden in the Escorial.

The garden of the Alcázar, Seville.

289

Fountain in the House of Pilate, Seville.   *Gardens of the Pazo de Oca, Galicia.*

Garden of Mi Capricho, Alameda de Osuna, Madrid: lake and landing stage. (Photo Gonzalo Careaga)

[1] C. Añón, 'El arte del jardín en la España de siglo XVIII', in *El Real Sito de Aranjuez y el Arte Cortesano del siglo XVIII* (Aranjuez 1987).
[2] C. Mollet, *Théâtre des plans et jardinages* (Paris 1652); quoted from M. Conan in *Le jardin de plaisir* (Paris 1981).
[3] J. M. Morel, *Théorie des jardins, ou l'art des jardins de la nature* (Paris 1776).
[4] A. J. Dezallier d'Argenville, *La théorie et la pratique du jardinage* (Paris 1747).
[5] H. Taine, *Les origines de la France contemporaine. L'Ancien Régime* (Paris 1904–7).
[6] C. Batteux, *Les Beaux-Arts réduits à un même principe* (Paris 1746).
[7] J. P. Rameu, C. Kintzler, *Splendeurs et naufrage de l'esthétique du plaisir à l'âge classique* (Paris 1983).
[8] A. Jiminez Martin, 'Los jardines de Medinat Al-zahrà', in *Cuardernos de Medinat Al-zahrà* (1987).
[9] C. Añón, 'L'immagine della natura nel-l'Escorial di Filippo II' in *Restauro-Città*, 5–6 (1987).
[10] P. Soto de Rojas, *Paraiso cerrado para muchos, jardines abiertos para pocos* (Madrid 1981).
[11] T. Keith, *Man and the Natural World. Changing Attitudes in England 1500–1800* (London 1983).
[12] L. Urteaga, *La tierra esquilmada* (Madrid 1987).
[13] Quoted from Urteaga, *ibid.*
[14] R. Gaya, April 1985.
[15] P. Vernière, 'Les incidences philosophiques et politiques de l'art des jardins' in *La letteratura e i giardini* (Florence 1987).
[16] D'Alembert, *Essai sur les éléments de philosophie* Vol. 4 (Amsterdam 1759).
[17] L. Urteaga, *op. cit.*

Garden of Mi Capricho, Alameda de
Osuna: the canal and fort. (Photo Gonzalo
Careaga)

German Gardens in the Eighteenth Century: Classicism, Rococo and Neo-Classicism

Helmut Reinhardt

The limited space available here for a discussion of the development of gardens in Germany over a period of about 150 years means that it is possible to give only a representative selection of those gardens which are artistically most important and outstanding. In this complex subject such incompleteness will necessarily result in some abbreviation and simplification. Gardens are mentioned here only if they stand out among their contemporaries for their quality or if they exerted a crucial influence on further development.

We shall be dealing with only the gardens of the aristocracy because until the end of the eighteenth century the aristocracy was almost alone in having the means to create gardens and parks, which were usually extensive. It was not until the mid-century that the middle classes, grown richer and more self-confident, begin to appear as major patrons. For several decades their gardens continued to follow the models provided by the aristocracy – as had been the case with the bourgeois gardens of the preceding centuries – though on a more modest scale.

The fragmentation of the German Empire into many independent princedoms (around 1700 there were about a hundred princes ruling their own territories under the emperor), the lack of a capital city to provide stylistic direction, the complex interweaving of interests and families with other European countries are among the reasons why, until about the middle of the eighteenth century, German garden design was dominated by foreign influences which varied depending on the political or dynastic orientation of the patron.

The outbreak of the Thirty Years' War in 1618 with its catastrophic consequences for large areas of Germany resulted in a sudden interruption in building activity and made any further artistic development impossible for the time being. In these years, perhaps because of this lack of building commissions, there appeared a number of architectural treatises and pattern books which prepared the intellectual ground for the first new palaces and gardens built from 1650 onwards. Nevertheless it took another thirty years before the material and intellectual foundations had been laid for a new generation of rulers to build palaces and gardens in the forefront of European artistic achievement.

Until well into the seventeenth century, artistic development in Germany was dependent on Italy for its style and direction. After the end of the Thirty Years' War the gentleman of quality still made his tour of Italy, where – among other things – he became acquainted with Tuscan, Roman and Venetian villa gardens. From then on, however, the Grand Tour also took him to France where around Paris he saw gardens in the new style which had reached such perfection in the hands of Le Nôtre and his predecessors that they had begun to overtake Italian gardens in the esteem of contemporaries. Every German prince was fascinated by the splendour of Versailles and attempted to create a similar glittering court on his own territory, and to lay out similar magnificent gardens. Besides Italian and French influence there are also features in German gardens of the seventeenth and eighteenth centuries

which point to the Netherlands. In the practical field of market gardening and land improvement, the influence of the Netherlands had been important in almost all European countries. For pleasure-gardens in Germany Dutch influence was still particularly strong in many north German principalities, where dynastic connections meant that Dutch artists had been brought in. The south German princes on the other hand were more orientated towards France, or, like the imperial court at Vienna, remained committed to Italian traditions. Also, even when formal styles of garden predominated in Germany, there was still the subliminal presence of other influences dating back to the later Middle Ages and never quite relinquished.

Although one should beware an over-simplified division into periods, the gardens discussed here are divided into groups according to shared characteristics, which necessarily results in a chronological sequence.

The first formal gardens, modelled to a greater or lesser degree on Le Nôtre's designs, appeared in Germany from about 1690 onwards. Over the following four decades they gained general acceptance and developed in a number of different forms. However, since this type of garden had been adopted in Germany at a point when it had already passed its artistic zenith in its country of origin, it was not long before the appearance of symptoms of a late stylistic phase formed a transition to the next stage of development. This is the Rococo garden, which is found between 1730 and 1770. This was followed by the arrival of the landscape garden in Germany around 1770, that is after it had already gone through several transformations in England. After beginning with a very literary phase, it reached its greatest maturity between 1800 and 1820, and soon afterwards went into a decline.

The Classical garden 1680–1730

As has already been mentioned, after the end of the Thirty Years' War and a period of transition there followed a time of intense building activity in all parts of the German Empire which lasted until the end of the century. New residences were founded in emulation of Louis XIV and former hunting-lodges and manor houses converted into expensive palaces with extensive gardens. 'The striving after *variété*, which was so fruitful for garden design, drove the court from palace to palace, from festivity to festivity. Once again it must be stressed that these festivities, particularly the garden entertainments, were at the centre of life and endeavour of Baroque courtly society' (Hennebo/Hoffmann, Vol. 2, p. 153).

The main centres of garden design were the courts of Berlin, Hanover and Salzdahlum in the north of Germany; Dresden in the east, Kassel, Bamberg, Würzburg and Mainz in central Germany; Bonn and Brühl in the west; Ludwigsburg and Munich in the south; and lastly Vienna. In all these places, besides the palaces and gardens of the ruling princes, we also find those of the court nobility and the lesser nobility.

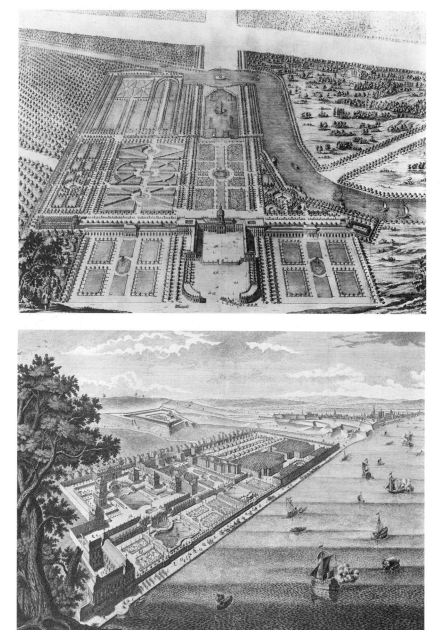

Italian, French and Netherlandish influences soon combined with local conditions and traditions. In the course of the century, particularly after the publication of the standard work *La théorie et la pratique du jardinage* by Dezallier d'Argenville in 1709 (first German edition 1731), the dominance of French gardening ideas considerably reduced Italian and Netherlandish influences. Original works were created which differed in many details from their models, and there were only a few gardens in which the Le Nôtre scheme was taken as law.

One peculiarity of German gardens is the lack of a dominant main axis; in many gardens there are pronounced cross axes, or individual garden zones are arranged parallel to each other. They thus create an impression of greater width and recall Renaissance gardens. Often they are completely enclosed by a wall, hedge or canal so the garden axes do not radiate into the surroundings. The position of the principal building in the garden often does not correspond to the Versailles model; it rarely stands at the highest point or at the entrance of the garden. Sometimes it is located in the centre of the garden, or some of its functions are delegated to other garden buildings, or the main axis of the garden is aligned with a side wing of the building. It can stand on the highest terrace of a garden arranged in several steps (Pommersfelden), or like an Italian mountain villa on a slope (Kassel-Wilhelmshöhe), or at the lowest point (Schönbrunn). If the terrain is quite flat terracing can be completely omitted (Berlin-Charlottenburg), or a change in level can be suggested by means of an optical illusion (Munich-Nymphenburg).

VIENNA

Schönbrunn Palace is discussed elsewhere, but because of the high quality of Viennese garden design a few other examples should be mentioned here.

After the Turkish threat had been averted the first new summer palaces were built outside the walls of the city soon after 1683. The imperial Favorite auf der Wieden (1687–90, the garden 1690–92), the garden palace of Liechtenstein (1691 or 1698–1711); Schönbrunn (first unexecuted project *c.*1690, the garden after 1695); and the most significant of all Viennese gardens, Prince Eugene's Belvedere (essentially created between 1716 and 1721) were followed in the next decades by a series of aristocratic gardens in which a synthesis of Italian and French ideas gave rise to original solutions, usually within restricted areas of land.

BERLIN-CHARLOTTENBURG

In 1694 the future King Friedrich I of Prussia had a palace built and garden laid out for his consort Sophie Charlotte in the village of Lietzenburg west of the capital Berlin. The first plan was drawn up by Simon Godeau, a pupil of Le Nôtre. A proposal commissioned by the princess from Le Nôtre himself in 1696 was rejected by her as 'too simple'.

The basic outlines of the garden were laid out by 1700, and in about 1706 by order of the king the area was doubled in size.

An ideal plan dating from around 1717 represents the desired state of the garden, though it was never quite achieved in this form. The main axis in the form of a *tapis vert* runs from the central saloon of the palace through the parterre, which (in a manner reminiscent of Herrenhausen) is divided in eight parts, then continues across the long lake adjacent, and disappears into the distance as a broad avenue beyond the Spree. The area beside the parterre is formed into bosquets like its French prototypes, while the numerous alleys were taken from Dutch gardens.

KASSEL-WEISSENSTEIN (renamed 'Wilhelmshöhe' in 1798)
The great influence still exerted by Italian ideas of garden design around the turn of the century – forty years after Le Nôtre began work at Versailles – is apparent in the massive project of Landgrave Karl of Hesse-Kassel. He had travelled to Italy in the winter of 1699/1700 and while there had commissioned the architect Giovanni Francesco Guerniero to work out a project for him to transform the whole of a hillside near his seat at Kassel into a terraced garden. In 1705 Guerniero published the final version of this park in a magnificent book of engravings. But when he left Kassel in 1715 only a third of it had been completed because of technical difficulties and the enormous cost.

The original idea envisaged a giant Octagon to be used as a reservoir on the top of the hill, linked by means of a complex stepped waterfall to a villa further down the slope. From this villa axes were to radiate into the adjacent forest areas with the main axis extending for five kilometres to the town of Kassel.

In comparison with French gardens flat beds and parterres are neglected, but like Italian villas great emphasis is given to waterworks and the slope is articulated by means of a system of cross-axes. The villa was not built, but the Octagon 63 metres (200 ft) high was surmounted by a 9.2-metre (30 ft) tall statue of Hercules based on the Farnese *Hercules*. Here he is the victorious ally of the gods in the battle of the giants, the theme of which is taken up in many forms in grottoes, fountains and water effects along the water axis.

MUNICH-SCHLEISSHEIM
The starting point for the garden schemes of the Bavarian Elector Max Emanuel at Schleissheim was Lustheim, the small garden pavilion built in 1684–87 by Enrico Zuccalli.

After his return from Brussels, where he had been Governor of the Spanish Netherlands (1692–1701), the foundation stone for an extensive palace was laid at Schleissheim in 1701, and at the same time the enlargement of the Residenz in Munich and Schloss Nymphenburg was energetically carried forward. The ambitious plans of Max Emanuel can only be understood against the background of his manoeuvring for the Spanish throne. The outbreak of the War of the Spanish Succession in 1701 when he sided against the emperor forced him into exile in France and he could not return again to Bavaria until 1715.

Plan of the gardens of Sanssouci, Potsdam: anonymous drawing, c. 1752.

Garden of Sanspareil, Bayreuth: Diana's Grotto and the Rock of Love. Engraving by J. G. Köppel, 1793. Landesbildstelle Nordbayern, Bayreuth.

Several plans had already been prepared for the garden at Schleissheim before the 1715–17 project of Dominique Girard, a pupil of Le Nôtre, was finally carried out.

Despite the Elector's long stay at the court of Versailles and the fact that his gardener was French, Zuccalli's basic scheme, dating back to 1690, was adopted in the parterre area. As is often the case in Germany, the garden stretches between two buildings, the main schloss and the Lustheim, the earlier garden pavilion. Consequently, only the parterre and bosquet parts of the classical sequence (parterre – bosquets – great park) could be executed. Girard's parterre is only as wide as the *corps de logis* and is slightly sunken. It is a *parterre de pièces coupées pour des fleurs* (cut-work parterre with flowers), a type that had already fallen out of fashion in France according to Dezallier d'Argenville. Each side is closed by a *parterre de broderie mêlée de massifs de gazon* (embroidered parterre mixed with bands of turf). The bosquets contain a series of unusually lavish garden rooms. The whole garden is surrounded by a circular canal, a very un-French practice which the Elector adopted from Dutch gardens.

MUNICH-NYMPHENBURG

Max Emanuel's second great garden was created at Nymphenburg. In 1701 Enrico Zuccalli was asked to produce plans to remodel the summer palace that had been built for the Elector's mother. The designs for both palace and garden were heavily dependent on Dutch models, such as Het Loo.

After the return of the Elector from exile a new plan for the garden was devised by Dominique Girard and Josef Effner in the latest French taste. Yet here too Dutch influences are apparent in the inclusion of many canals in the scheme.

The great parterre is arranged around a gilded fountain of Flora. Nearest the palace are two *parterres de broderie* and, towards the canal, two lawns with floral borders. To the sides the parterre is bordered by four bosquets with a variety of *salons* and *cabinets*. Beyond the canal which marks the end of the garden proper is an extensive wooded area divided by axial waterways and avenues. In the following years various lesser palaces were built following the pattern of the French Trianons.

MAINZ-FAVORITE

Lothar Franz von Schönborn, elected Archbishop of Mainz in 1695, was one of the greatest garden enthusiasts among the princes of his time. He had already remodelled the gardens at Seehof Palace near Bamberg and at his family seat at Gaibach east of Würzburg before creating one of the most original of German garden designs at the Favorite. In 1700 he acquired a garden situated on the Rhine upstream from Mainz and immediately set about enlarging and remodelling it. Although the name Favorite is reminiscent of the imperial summer palace in Vienna, it was specifically to Louis XIV that Lothar Franz referred when he spoke of his new garden as *le petit Marly*.

The garden consists of three completely independent parts descending in a number of terraces down the hillside to the Rhine below. The larger section, on the left, contains the pavilions, the presence of which explains the comparison made with Marly. Around 1722 the garden was as it is shown in the engraving by Salomon Kleiner (it was destroyed without trace during the seige of Mainz in 1792–93).

Its division into three parts, with axes running partly parallel and partly perpendicular, breaking up the strict unity into a multiplicity of delightful individual spaces, already looks forward to the gradual dissolution of the hierarchical scheme of the Classical garden.

BRÜHL-AUGUSTUSBURG

Clemens August, the son of the creator of the gardens at Schleissheim and Nymphenburg, was elected Archbishop of Cologne in 1723. There were already earlier plans for the gardens of the summer residence Augustusburg, but it was not until Dominique Girard, then the leading garden architect in Germany, was summoned to the archbishopric in 1717 that the work there took a decisive turn.

Girard kept the irregular ground plan of the park area. He arranged the main garden in front of the south wing of the palace. In the Classical sequence starting from the viewing terrace, he developed the two-part *parterre de broderie mêlée de massifs de gazon*, bosquets and park which, like Nymphenburg, is intersected by axial waterways and paths and contains lesser palaces. These are the Schneckenhaus (Snail House), 1750–60, and the Indianisches Haus (Indian House) 1745–50, which, with their bizarre architecture and their own separate gardens, belong to the next generation of gardens.

The Rococo garden 1730–1770

Already in some of the gardens mentioned above there is evidence of the dissolution and superseding of the French garden plan. Although Dezallier d'Argenville had demanded more naturalness, the French garden as an art form was at first not questioned on the Continent. However, its over-studied rigidity and unified character gradually diminished, and exotic and bizarre features increasingly found their way into it. Asymmetrical layouts were preferred in which a deliberately planned disorder reigned, and numerous small, intimate garden spaces could reveal the development of a pure, unrestrained delight in play and entertainment. The gardens shut themselves off from the surrounding countryside and turned inwards. They were less easily seen as a whole, and no longer contained a single viewpoint from which the overall scheme could be taken in. On the contrary, the various parts developed a strong individuality, and sometimes seem to split off into autonomous areas, only loosely linked by axes.

POTSDAM-SANSSOUCI

Between 1734 and 1739, when he was crown prince, Friedrich II of Prussia had already had his first experiences of the laying out of a

garden at Rheinsberg. He became king in 1740 and after 1744 he had a new palace built at Potsdam based on his own design. Its name expressed the yearning, typical of many princes of the period, to escape from the oppressive court ceremonial to a more intimate milieu.

The long, single-storey building rises above six terraces which curve back in the centre. In no way does it correspond to contemporary conventions of a royal palace, in fact its fruit-tree plantations and secluded position are rather reminiscent of a hermitage.

Running from the sides of the palace is trellis-work ending in pavilions, an arrangement which establishes the width of the garden. It is framed on either side by avenues of five rows of chestnut and walnut trees, which also enclose the small parterre situated in the level area below the terraces, thus isolating it from its surroundings. Each of the terrace walls has twenty eight niches in which figs and vines grow behind closeable glass doors. Between the niches cherries, apricots and peaches were grown on espaliers. In the four cutwork sections of the parterre, which are arranged around the quatrefoil pool with a fountain, grows an extravagant wealth of flowers.

After 1750 the adjoining forest area (deer park) was remodelled with an avenue running perpendicular to the main axis of the Sanssouci terraces. The garden was again enlarged and altered in 1763 after the end of the Seven Years' War when the Neues Palais was built.

BAYREUTH-EREMITAGE

In 1735 Friedrich II's sister, Wilhelmine, who had been married to the Margrave of Bayreuth since 1731, was given the Eremitage garden which had been in existence for two decades. She immediately set about remodelling it. There was already a palace situated on the ground sloping down on three sides to the Roter Main, and scattered through the forest were a number of wooden hermitages.

In the following years the French architect Joseph Saint-Pierre built an orangery known as the Neues Schloss, with a garden which was only loosely connected to the already existing one. Many statues and waterworks were dispersed among the bosquets and woods.

In the Eremitage there is neither a central garden area nor a dominant axis to tie together the individual zones. Geometric parterres are contrasted with areas kept in a 'natural' state, which also border the whole garden. Here a surrounding path in the manner of an English 'garden belt' draws the surrounding countryside into the garden by artfully arranged vistas. These echoes of the English landscape garden, appearing at Bayreuth for the first time anywhere outside England, must certainly derive from the Margravine, whose close family connections with the English court must have made her familiar with the development of garden design in that country.

BAYREUTH-SANSPAREIL

Another very individual creation by Wilhelmine is the remodelling from 1745 onwards of a natural beech wood at Sanspareil, about 30 km (18 miles) west of Bayreuth. By the introduction of figures she

Garden of Sanssouci, Potsdam: the pavilion.

Garden of the Eremitage, Bayreuth: the Fountain.

transformed the terrain, with its picturesque rock formations, into a magical place, the setting for the adventures of the young Telemachus in Fénelon's novel *Les Aventures de Télémaque* of 1699. Although in this rocky garden Wilhelmine made use of the natural features without any structural alterations (except for a sunken geometric parterre in front of the main building, the Morgenländischer Bau [Oriental Building]), it was not part of her understanding and interpretation of nature to emphasize the beauties of the landscape. She was more concerned with using wild nature as a theatrical setting for scenes from *Télémaque*, with the intention of presenting the visitor with the didactic moral messages contained in the individual episodes – in the spirit of the German Enlightenment. On one hand Sanspareil with its adherence to literary allusions and its light-hearted charm still has close connections with Rococo gardens of the period, while on the other hand it looks forward far into the future. Perhaps because it was so ahead of its time it had no immediate successors.

SCHWETZINGEN

The conversion of an older schloss and garden to the summer residence of the Elector Palatine Carl Theodor began in 1748/49. After only a short period building work ceased in 1750 and did not resume again for three years.

The two circular buildings known as the 'Zirkelhäuser', which were used as an orangery and banqueting rooms, project from both ends of the palace forming quadrants enclosing a semi-circular parterre. The circle is completed by *berceaux* which echo the Zirkelhäuser: it is then extended to form a square by the addition of spandrels, and is finally extended westwards to form a rectangle. This is without parallel in European garden design. The plan by Johann Ludwig Petri dates from 1753, possibly made in collaboration with the French architect Nicolas Pigage. The garden itself was being laid out in the years up to 1758, and was enlarged under the direction of Pigage after 1761. By extending the central axis to form an impressive central perspective, Pigage was able to open up the garden and give it added dynamism. Although his ideal plan of 1762 was only partly executed, he managed to give the garden a pronounced monumental character through the strict axial articulation. Yet in the new bosquet areas between these axes he created numerous intimate garden spaces connected with each other by a subtle *anglo-chinois* network of paths. These garden *salons*, which the Elector furnished with architecture, fountains and sculpture, answered Rococo society's need for diversion, variety and refined play.

STUTTGART-SOLITUDE

After 1763 Carl Eugen, Duke of Württemberg, inspired by a desire for a refuge away from his residence, built a new schloss with a garden to the south-west of Stuttgart.

Work on the garden began in 1764. A change of plan in 1767 and extensions would have made Solitude into a third residence after Stuttgart and Ludwigsburg, had not the duke lost interest in it around

Luisenkloster, Weimar. Drawing by
J. W. Goethe, 1778.

Garden of Sanspareil, Bayreuth: grotto.

1770/71 and turned his attentions to Hohenheim, the last of the gardens he created.

As its plan makes clear, Solitude represents the collision of two contradictory ideas: on one hand, there is the use of axes extending far into the landscape in the Baroque tradition; on the other, the bewildering complexity of the interior planning of the garden with its almost manic attempt to string together small and even smaller garden areas.

This marks the end of an artistic development. The architectural garden, which threatened to become lost in planned confusion, or else – if it sought to return to the forms of the Classical garden of the late seventeenth century – ran the risk of becoming paralysed in academic rigidity, could no longer be renewed from within. It needed a powerful external stimulus from a quite different garden aesthetic.

The landscape garden 1770 – 1800 – 1820

From the late seventeenth century onwards no German prince was immune to the fascination of the French royal court. French culture and French art had entered into a close partnership with local traditions. In garden design Dutch and Italian influences still asserted themselves, but in the course of the century they became less and less important. The almost unrestricted hegemony of France in matters of taste distracted attention from the theory of the English landscape garden with the result that this did not gain a foothold in Germany until the landscape garden had already passed through several stages of development in the land of its origin. Moreover, the Seven Years' War between 1756 and 1763 hindered direct contact with English art. With the exception of the harbingers at Bayreuth, this late appearance of the landscape garden in Germany is all the more surprising when one considers, for example, that since 1714 the electors of Hanover had also been kings of England and stayed regularly in their German principality.

Because the political circumstances were different in England there had developed a feeling for nature which rejected the severity and artificiality fostered by the French garden. A similar consciousness only appeared gradually in the German states under the influence of the writings of the Enlightenment. One result of this was that the formal, geometric gardens were interpreted as the expression of an undesirable absolutist system of government to be contrasted with unfettered nature as the expression of liberty. In this respect the triumph of the landscape garden also has a political aspect – though most of its princely patrons were no doubt unaware of this.

After 1770 descriptions of English gardens became increasingly widespread in Germany. The appearance of the first theoretical treatise on the new style, Johann Georg Sulzer's *Allgemeine Theorie der schönen Künste* (Leipzig, 1771–74), helped the new aesthetic to achieve rapid success. In Rococo gardens there was already a noticeable inclination to

301

isolate the various parts of the garden and separate them from each other; there was also the frequently found use of spaces within bosquets for agricultural purposes. This tendency towards a more natural approach was connected with influences which can be traced back to late medieval gardening ideas, which had never quite been abandoned – as, for example, in the rocky garden and hermits' garden laid out by Count Sporck in his Bohemian estates.

Wörlitz

At the beginning of the 1760s Fürst Leopold Friedrich Franz of Anhalt-Dessau had made two extended journeys through England accompanied by his architect, Friedrich Wilhelm von Erdmannsdorff, and his gardener, Johann Friedrich Eyserbeck, and had visited the most important gardens. After the destruction of his first attempts at garden design when the Elbe flooded, work began in 1770 on the conversion of an already existing hunting-lodge with a small garden. A plan of 1763/64 shows the difficulties experienced in handling the new art form. In 1778 the garden was extended, and between 1790 and 1798, and again after 1800 it was further enlarged.

Wörlitz is important in the development of garden design because for the first time it was not merely an imitation, but followed a new path as a synthesis of foreign concepts and original ideas, suited to the conditions of the locality. Goethe described his impressions in 1778:

Here it is now infinitely beautiful. It moved me very much yesterday evening, as we crept through lakes, canals and woods, how the gods had allowed the prince to create a dream around himself. As one passes through it, it is as if one were being told a fairy tale, and has all the character of the Elysian Fields. In the gentlest multiplicity one thing flows into another, no height draws one's eye and one's yearning towards a single point, one wanders about without asking whence once has gone or where one is coming. (Quoted from Hennebo/Hoffmann, Vol. 3, pp. 79–80.)

Goethe's description reveals that the function of the individual parts of the garden was to carry a meaning. The Wörlitz garden is assembled from a large number of individually-composed main pictures which are disclosed to the visitor in a gradual progress along paths and waterways. The many groups of statuary and the areas assigned them were intended to evoke very particular associations in the wanderer and release carefully calculated emotions. Hirschfeld praised Wörlitz as 'one of the noblest parks in Germany' (*Theorie der Gartenkunst*, Vol. 5. p. 360), presumably because the various categories of sentiment (cheerful, solemn, melancholy etc.), which he strongly advocated, were expressed here in exemplary fashion.

Passing over the rearrangement of the garden at Hohenheim near Stuttgart (from 1774), the partial conversion of Schwetzingen into a landscape garden (also from 1774), and the literary-sentimental remodelling of the landscape of the Seifersdorfer Tal near Dresden (from 1781), we shall turn to Weimar.

WEIMAR

Goethe, who lived in Weimar from 1775 onwards, made various references to gardens in his works. In 1777 in *Der Triumph der Empfindsamkeit* (The Triumph of Sensibility) he makes a biting attack on 'modern' gardens overladen with innumerable miniature figures, and returned to the subject again in 1809 in *Die Wahlverwandtschaften* (Elective Affinities).

The opportunity for the remodelling of the Ilmauen was provided by the *Luisenfest* which he organized on the banks of the river Ilm (this was, incidently, thoroughly in the style of the figures he had ridiculed). The visit Goethe and Duke Karl August of Saxe-Weimar made to Wörlitz in the same year may have inspired them to create a landscape park out of the low-lying land by the river, remembering the idea of the prince at Wörlitz 'to transform the whole land into a garden'. But it was not until the nineteenth century that the garden attained its present form and extent. Like Wörlitz the site is divided up into relatively small, enclosed spaces which were to present the visitor with ever-changing scenes with small buildings, commemorative stones and cultivated areas, and thus touch his emotions.

Almost all German gardens of the last quarter of the century are permeated with strong literary allusions. These give meaning to the individual areas of the garden and stimulate the spectator's powers of imagination either by the sight of a monument, an inscription, or a planted section. Not until the turn of the century did the landscape garden free itself from this sentimental coquetry with nature, and reach its apogee in extensive parks where trees, meadows and water were almost the only elements of the composition. The gardens that were created in this manner up to *c.* 1820, such as the remodelling of Wilhelmshöhe, Kassel (between 1758 and 1793) and Nymphenburg (from 1804 by Friedrich Ludwig Sckell), and the laying out of the Englischer Garten in Munich (also by Sckell from 1804), are the most mature examples of the style.

Bibliography

C.C.L. Hirschfeld, *Theorie der Gartenkunst*, 5 vols (Leipzig 1779–85 – reprinted in 2 vols, Hildesheim, New York 1985).

M. L. Gothein, *Geschichte der Gartenkunst* (Jena 1926 – reprint of 2nd edn, Munich 1988).

P.O. Rave, *Gärten der Goethezeit* (Leipzig 1941).

G. Allinger, *Der deutsche Garten* (Munich 1950).

E. Bachmann, 'Anfänge des Landschaftsgartens in Deutschland' in *Zeitschrift für Kunstwissenschaft*, Vol 5 (1951).

P.O. Rave, *Gärten der Barockzeit* (Stuttgart 1951).

A. Anger, 'Landschaftsstil des Rokoko' in *Euphorion*, Vol 3, no. 51 (1957).

G. Lippold-Hällsig, *Deutsche Gärten* (Dresden 1957).

H. Kreisel, 'Das Rokoko und die Gartenkunst' in *Festschrift für Eberhard Hanfstaengel* (Munich 1961).

E. Berckenhagen, *Deutsche Gärten vor 1800* (Hanover, Berlin, Sarstedt 1962).

D. Hennebo and A. Hoffmann, *Geschichte der deutschen Gartenkunst*, 3 vols (Hamburg 1962–65; reprinted Köningstein 1981).

H. Schuttauf, *Parke und Gärten in der DDR* (Leipzig 1973).

S. Gerndt, *Idealisierte Natur. Die literarische Kontroverse um den Landschaftsgarten des 18. und frühen 19. Jahrhunderts* (Stuttgart 1981).

W. Hansmann, *Gartenkunst der Renaissance und des Barock* (Cologne 1983).

H. Scharf, *Die schönsten Gärten und Parks in Deutschland und Österreich* Düsseldorf 1985.

T. Wengel, *Gartenkunst im Spiegel der Zeit* (Innsbruck, Frankfurt am Main 1985).

Urban Walks in France
in the Seventeenth and Eighteenth Centuries

Daniel Rabreau

Walking: 'Moderate exercise, consisting of alternate movement of legs and feet, by means of which one progresses gently and pleasurably from one place to another . . . If travelling on foot is convenient, travelling by rude conveyance or on horseback is even more so'.[1] Reference to the most modern contemporary ideas or usages is not by any means a regular feature of articles in the *Encyclopédie*; on the other hand the relative length of the commentaries accompanying several definitions of the same word reveals a genuine desire to investigate, to instruct by persuasion or command. This is the importance of the expanded article which treats the medical advantages of walking, compared with the brevity of the definition of the idea; and the reference to this activity in certain articles of a historical nature (for example, 'walks of the Romans'[2]) is a further encouragement to editors who, in dealing with this subject, neglect the study of contemporary manners.

Although still very popular throughout the nineteenth and the early twentieth centuries, the habit of urban walks is no longer today a social characteristic of French towns, except perhaps in certain southern areas where it has survived. Consequently, if the point at issue is to trace its origins and development under the *ancien régime* (before 1789) we must also investigate not only the incidence but also the underlying significance which has been lost to view for more than half a century. Every age in history has practised this 'moderate exercise' – it may be compared to and contrasted with the aristocratic pursuit of hunting – according to a ritual, conscious or otherwise, which has become literally denaturized in the course of time. Novels,[3] theatres, newspapers, memoirs, anecdotes and researches into archives inform us that urban walks in the mid-eighteenth century differ appreciably from the above definition which refers to country walks. In towns, walking formerly meant going out to see, be seen and to show oneself. The game of self-identification, as an individual and as a member of society, acted like a magnet for this display.

The meaning of this activity, noted by all the chroniclers and confirmed by historians[4] overlooks the naturalistic and medical definition of the idea. Perhaps the *Encyclopédie* definition is out of touch with reality. For instance, a carriage ride is no longer in a 'rude' conveyance (except in the country) but, from the mid-seventeenth century, in a comfortable coach. The idea of a conveyance 'from one place to another' is associated rather with the country or the grounds of a château: it had become vague because of the purposelessness of the journey, more of a there-and-back affair, or a circular trip which resulted in the making of particular paths and plantations, even in the seventeenth century.[5] The ritualized 'amusement' prevails: urban walks, a feature of society, become part of the leisure activities of a well-organized community.

The pursuit of happiness[6] in towns becomes part of a controlled and recognizable organization of open spaces, including records of the regulation of the impact of buildings on nature. Nevertheless, if we except the perennial use of private gardens, urban walks historically precede this impact. The movement, finding itself somewhat cramped in this environment, then moved out into the country, around the houses, in holiday areas; and on Sundays and holidays, for lack of anything better, on rustic sites adjoining the towns. In urban localities, the adaptation of nature for public use, whether in easily discernible cultivated areas or by opening up viewpoints, is one of the chief characteristics of urban civilization in modern times. From the time of Louis XIV to that of Napoleon III, by way of the legend of Le Nôtre's French garden transposed into the town, and until the authoritarian enterprises of Haussmann, which derive from them,[7] urban walks and public gardens have for two hundred years been recognized as an essential element of French town planning. It may be that this particular element takes on a dual nature in the mid-eighteenth century, when France was influenced on the one hand by Rousseau's virtuous nature, and on the other was being introduced to the enchantment of the landscape garden, sometimes known as Anglo-Chinese.[8]

The natural kingdom and monarchic order

Another article in the *Encyclopédie* often disappoints historians[9] by the apparently archaic nature of the initial definition of *Town*: 'An enclosure surrounded by walls, containing several districts, streets, public squares and other buildings'.[10] This definition is surprising, for it is purely conventional at a time when Paris had many years previously replaced its ramparts by beautifully planted boulevards, and throughout the country, towns at a safe distance from the frontiers were progressively following this practice. It must nevertheless be remembered that this is correct from the judicial-economic point of view, since the toll levied on produce and merchandise at the barriers and gates required a demarcation of fiscal territory which was no mere symbol – as the Parisians learned to their cost at the end of Louis XIV's reign, with the construction of the notorious wall of the Ferme Générale[11] by Ledoux – and which also had its associations with the problem of walks and leisure.

For Paris (though the centralization typical of France saw the idea spread throughout the country) the development in the seventeenth century of great axes outside the city, impressively tree-lined for walking (as were the great boulevards or ring roads, built shortly afterwards, coincides with the town's increasing awareness of landscape in relation to its surroundings. The exercise of walking is enhanced by the pleasure of viewing the river, the plains and the neighbouring hills: on his return the walker, like a traveller, is filled with pride at the delight of a view leading to the urban agglomeration, following a path which, to all intents and purposes serves the same purpose as rural paths leading directly to the château. Nor is this similarity fortuitous, if we consider the roads leading out of Paris. To the west, one led to the Tuileries palace; to the east another led from the Cours de Vincennes to the château of the same name; and the town of Versailles, created at the junction of the three roads which converge towards the château, remains a perfect example of the influence of royal

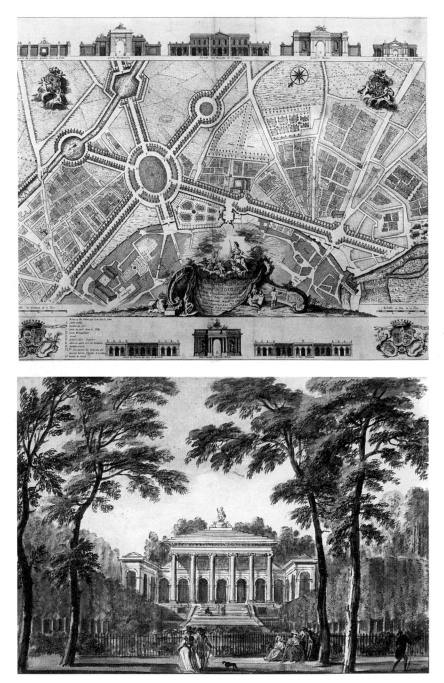

power on the town – a power which created the town here in the wake of its own image. In the seventeenth century there could clearly as yet be no question of rural amusements in the town. But the considerable expansion of the towns in the eighteenth century brought about a rapid integration of these walks into the main part of the town. In Paris this can be seen in the Invalides and Arsenal districts and particularly on the Grands Boulevards, first in the north and then in the Mont-Parnasse district in the south. At this stage, that is from 1760 to 1770, urban walks led towards the natural world from which the town was separated physically and judicially but walking was above all a sort of organized activity, practised according to the laws of fashion. It evolved with the appearance of the public park and later, in the last third of the century, with the introduction of pleasure-gardens.[12] The difference between country walks and the fashionable exercise of walking is clearly revealed in the article *Promenade, Promenoir*: 'The first word is now used to signify a place where one walks, and the second has become obsolete: it should have been retained, for it enriched our language and at the time of Louis XIV these two words, from the same root, differed in meaning. *Promenade* indicated something more natural, *promenoir* was more artificial.'[13] It is for this reason that every programme of urban embellishment entails, in addition to such statuary as is considered necessary, a green setting and quasi-scenographic open spaces – opening on to external nature – suitable to serve this art of the realm of sociability.

This art, as we have said, is part of the search for identity pursued at that time by town dwellers through ways of behaviour which had many forms of expression: the art of conversation refined on the stage by Marivaux, the obsession for *fêtes galantes* after Watteau and for pastoral scenes after Boucher,[14] the play of mirrors in the design of drawing-rooms, the conviviality of emotionally-charged religious services,[15] and so on. The municipal officers of the *ancien régime*, responsible for urban economy and policy, were skilled in taking advantage of this sensitivity – not only to ensure the acceptability of what would extend their power, but also to increase the demand for it. The demographic, architectural and territorial development of the town in the eighteenth century was not an accident of fate: it was the result of politico-economic business management of property ('wealth from the land', as it was then called – inherited property, income from exchange or production) together with a very gradual change of outlook.

The city/country, town/nature relationship was gradually trans-formed, until the role of nature in the communal habitat was defined in terms of planning and development. Promenades, with their views of the surrounding countryside, similar to the view of the town in a chosen situation, were the perfect device to symbolize the relationship of the city to the state, and to locate it in relation to the extent of the territory. 'Open space . . . was a royal privilege: the eighteenth century did not have to invent it, it simply popularized it' writes P. Lavedan.[16] This was also the time (under the Régence, after the court had been initiated into the new delights of Paris) when the Apollonian

View of Place Louis XV in Paris *(now*
Place de la Concorde). Painting attributed to
J.-B. Leprince. Musée des Beaux-Arts,
Besançon.

iconography of the park of the Sun-King spread into the town, like a symbol of the spirit of Enlightenment metamorphosed into stone.[17] The centralism of Versailles, then of Paris, explains the unusual character of France in this respect in the seventeenth and eighteenth centuries: it conjures up the image of a country subject to the new administrative methods of the Ponts et Chaussées (highways department), the military engineers and the bailiffs of the financial districts. 'For the engineer, a tract of land is a sort of garden in which a scheme is realized, in the same way as a *fabrique* in a park'; 'from one map to another one finds the same obsession: Versailles and its avenues', writes A. Picon[18] in a recent study on architects and engineers in the Age of Enlightenment. The construction of promenades, where terracing, pathways, architectural decoration, sculpture and masterpieces of hydraulic art attracted as much public admiration as the planted areas, was evidence of their skill.

The Cours-la-Reine, a 1500-metre (1640-yard) promenade planted with elm trees, which was created in 1616 along the banks of the Seine to the west of the Tuileries gardens and later redesigned by Le Nôtre, is traditionally accepted as the first example of a planted *promenoir*. 'Cours, moreover,' writes Sauval, 'was a new word and a new idea, invented by Marie de Médicis. Until the Régence, walking in France was done on foot and in gardens, but then she brought to Paris the Florentine fashion, practised now in so many places, of taking carriage rides in the cool of the evening.'[19] Old plans of Paris show this 'avenue' with a triple row of trees, broken in the middle by a vast semicircle where carriages could turn. Originally reserved for the royal family and the aristocracy, the Cours-la-Reine was closed by wrought-iron gates at either end. In 1669 an embankment was built along the road to Versailles; in 1723 it was completely replanted; in 1729 lanterns were placed alongside the ditches to deter the often disreputable company. Strangely, in 1766, after several years of free access, entry to the Cours was once again made subject to authorization, in the form of a pass. Meanwhile, a new public promenade had become very popular between the Tuileries gardens and the Etoile, along the slopes of Chaillot – the Champs-Elysées.

From the seventeenth century, on a site similar to that of the Cours de la Reine but to the east of Paris, another promenade had been created – the Mail de l'Arsenal. This extension of the Faubourg St Antoine, linked with the new layout of the Cours de Vincennes which started at the Place du Trône, might have crowned the prosperity of the Marais district, but it was not to be. The Paris–Versailles axis soon definitively directed the urbanization of the capital westwards. The idea of developing a vast pleasure park on the Champs-Elysées can be attributed to Marie de Médicis, but it was not until the aftermath of the Peace of Aix-le-Chapelle (1668) that, at the instigation of Colbert, the Grands Boulevards, with their Triumphal arches at each entrance to the capital, were constructed – together with the plan of the Champs-Elysées (1670–1723). This vast promenade, famous above all others, became a model for lesser ones which, taking the form of an esplanade,

extended the role of planting, which had been confined at first to the boulevards and to the slopes of the ramparts in provincial towns.

One of the more ambitious plans to be partially realized in imitation of the layout of roads in Paris was that of Louis de Mondran in Toulouse (1752). More clearly even than in Bordeaux, which also had imposing squares and extended boulevards laid out in the first half of the eighteenth century, the Toulouse plan gave pride of place to facilities for walking, to public health and to uninterrupted views.[20] Axial roads radiated out from the Grand Rond, between the Garonne and the Canal du Midi, and gave access to the Botanical Gardens and the Royal Garden. As in Paris, these peripheral radiating roads, which within a few decades became part of the urban agglomeration, foreshadowed the recommendations of the theorist Laugier in his *Essai sur l'architecture*, one of the bestsellers of architectural literature in the Age of Enlightenment:

A town must be considered in the same way as a forest. The streets of the former are the paths of the latter; they must be driven through in the same way. The essential beauty of a park lies in the multiplicity of the paths, their size and arrangement; but that is not all – the plans must be drawn up by a Le Nôtre.... Let this concept be applied, and let the design of our parks serve as a plan for our towns.[21]

We know the extent to which this idea prevailed in France, until the urbanization of the centre of Paris under Baron Haussmann[22] in the latter part of the nineteenth century.

Another idea inspired by the achievements of the Grand Siècle (the age of Louis XIV), that of the Place Royale, a vast, level open space providing the setting for the bronze statues of the monarch,[23] became in the eighteenth century a perfect opportunity to reclaim for new ceremonial occasions the walking areas which had been set aside for urban leisure. Following the construction of the Place Bellecour in Lyons and the Promenade du Peyrou in Montpellier (two esplanades planted and 'architecturalized' in honour of Louis XIV), came the Place Louis XV (Place de la Concorde) in Paris, said to have been built 'in the fields' between 1755 and 1763, which was to become the true starting point of the Champs-Elysées in the city. In Louis XVI's reign the square and the avenues became completely integrated into the town.[24]

All the tree-lined promenades in the provinces in the seventeenth century also originated from royal influence, particularly through the medium of military governors – under Louis XV administrators had more influence. These promenades were the consequence of a remarkable event linking local urban life to the history of central power. In every case, the policy of appeasement followed by Louis XIV (internal after the Fronde, external following his conquests) and developed in the eighteenth century lies at the origin of this urban strategy: the opening up and planting with trees of towns whose ramparts were now unnecessary had as their corollary the proliferation of fortified towns and citadels devised by Vauban as components of the national defence system.

View of the Port of Bordeaux from
Château-Trompette. *Painting by
C. J. Vernet. Musée du Louvre, Paris.*

*Elevation of river front buildings along the
Loire, showing the Bourse and public walks,
Nantes. Drawing by M. Crucy, 1790.
Archives Municipales, Nantes.*

*Plan of the Cours in Nantes. Drawing by
J.-B. Ceineray, 1763. Archives Municipales,
Nantes.*

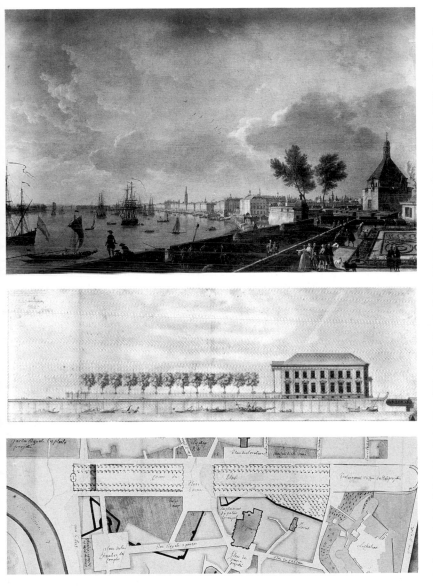

These promenades also appeared in the large provincial capitals, even before the impact of classical town planning; their presence moreover contributed to this new definition of the urban entity.[25] As early as 1676 Caen had a Cours-la-Reine; in Bordeaux the paths of the Chartreuse were used for carriage rides and the town had a square planted with elm trees, the Ormée, which curiously gave its name to the Bordeaux Fronde, whose instigators met here (1651–3). It is not surprising that the creation of promenades should follow the return of peace to the kingdom, or that, in the case of recently conquered towns, should serve as a mark of allegiance to Versailles. In Lille, the promenade and public parks developed throughout the eighteenth-century extend over the open land between the town and the citadel. In Strasbourg, Maréchal Duxelles was already in 1692 suggesting to the Magistrate a scheme for avenues of lime trees – the Allée des Pêcheurs, which became the Allée de Robertson (a reminder of the annexation of the town in 1681). A historical study published in 1931 still notes the legend which attributes these paths to Le Nôtre![26] In Bordeaux the glacis of the Château-Trompette were the birthplace of the grandiose design of the *cours*, of the plant nursery and soon after the public park, which enabled the town to double its area in a few decades and to expand towards the river and the suburbs where the wine-trade was carried on.[27] The king's architect, Ange-Jacques Gabriel, who was in charge of the Place Royale workshop started by his father, drew up the plan for this garden (1746). The great administrator and town planner Tourny defined in these words the programme for this very practical enterprise: 'In a commercial town, one should deem it necessary, or least most useful, to this commerce to have a garden where merchants, who must often meet together, may do more business. It is in some respects a second Stock Exchange, an evening market.'[28] The idea of a promenade-cum-business area should be borne in mind: we find it again half a century later in Nantes, where by extending the open portico of the new stock exchange, the architect Mathurin Crucy designed along the banks of the Loire a tree-lined square called the open-air exchange.[29] As well as taking the air, merchants, slave-traders and shipowners could indulge in the pleasure of a view of the harbour traffic. The construction of walks along quaysides is clearly one of the main themes of town planning in the eighteenth century. Magnificent examples are to be found in Brest, Bayonne, Tours, Toulouse, and elsewhere.

The tree-lined promenade in urban areas hardly exists before 1700–1720, but there are earlier promenades, planted when new communities were extended in the second half of the seventeenth century, and which found themselves in a central position well before the end of the eighteenth. The three best examples are undoubtedly the Cours Mirabeau in Aix-en-Provence (1649–58: the road, originally exclusively for carriages, was first planted with elms before being embellished in the nineteenth century with the beautiful plane trees which are still there today), the Allées de Meilhan and the Grand Cours at right angles to the Canebière in Marseilles (part of the plan for extending the town at

View of the Promenade du Peyrou,
Montpellier, 1765–76.

View of the Place de la Carrière, Nancy.

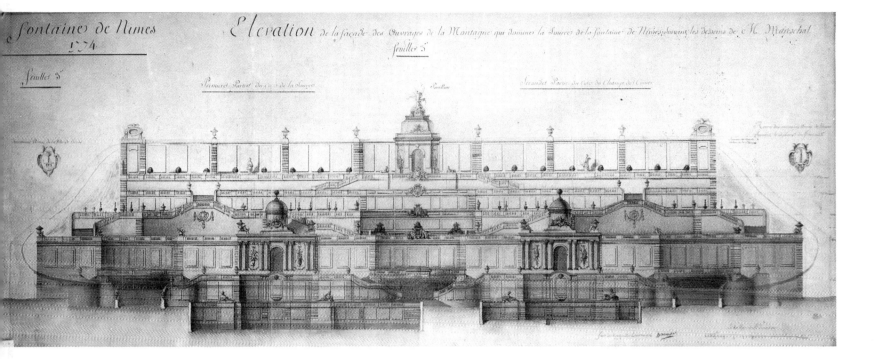

the behest of Louis XIV in 1666), and the Place de la Carrière in Nancy, chosen by Duke Léopold – recently reinstated by Louis XIV – to give access to the sumptuous palace which Boffrand was to build for him. In this latter instance, the idea of the transparency of open spaces and the mobility of the glance is intensified by the genius of the architect who, by using the device of a free-standing portico to open up the entire ground floor of the building, permits communication between the public promenade and the garden of the ducal palace. Here, the demolition of the ramparts encouraged a move towards integrating the new districts into the old town. For King Stanislas Leszczynski, father-in-law of Louis XV, Boffrand's successor E. Héré, was to extend this network of throughfares and urban perspectives by placing on either side of the tree-lined Carrière two magnificent open spaces – the Hemicycle and the Place Royale. At the eastern end of the latter the gilded wrought-iron railings of the fountain stand out against the foliage of the Parc de Pépinière established by Stanislas in 1766, the year of his death.[30]

These illustrious examples should not make us lose sight of the rapid evolution which was also transforming small towns, even in the least favoured provincial areas. H. F. Buffet's study of Brittany records no fewer than fifty-four promenades created between 1675 and 1791 in twenty-eight towns in this province.[31] From Guérande to Dinan, from Fougères to Quimper, by way of Josselin and Ploërmel, there are small fortified medieval towns where, very often, the open slopes of the ramparts were planted with elms or lime trees. These new promenades, in areas traditionally used for leisure pursuits such as shooting and boules, are the type most often found in small towns. But the nomenclature of the places which have become promenades is astonishingly diverse. In more important towns or where the site is by the sea, a river or an escarpment, the name reflects the type of associated activity. Only in large towns are there cours reserved, as we have seen, for carriages: elsewhere there are mails (malls) – from the name of a game of boules played there; boulingrins (lawns/bowling greens) – often in the public gardens of religious communities; promenades with panoramic views (as for example the Mail de Guérande, overlooking the distant salt-marshes of the Croisic peninsula); quais-promenade (riverside or harbour walks); tree-lined champs de foire (fairgrounds); avenues; champs de bataille (battlefields); esplanades; places d'armes or champs de Mars (parade grounds). Today there is no chief departmental town without some tangible souvenir of this urban improvement, this embellishment inherited from the Age of Enlightenment, to which we do not always acknowledge our debt.

From entertainment to an appreciation of nature – an urban theatre?

'I am greatly astonished that the finest towns I have yet seen in this country have no public walks to equal those in our smallest towns', wrote Président de Brosse[32] on the occasion of his travels in Italy in 1739, thus confirming the general impression current at the time. Carriage riding, imported from Italy by Marie de Médicis, took place beyond the Alps on a corso – a square, avenue or road without any particular planting arrangements. Walking on foot took place under

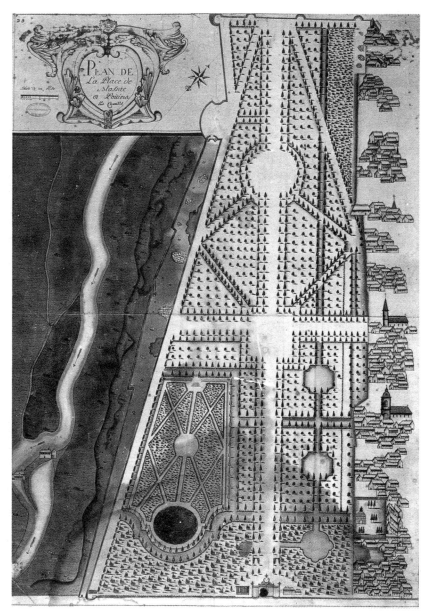

*Plan of the Parc de Blossac and promenade,
Poitiers. Bibliothèque Municipale, Poitiers.*

arcades or porticoes in streets and squares, in the shade. Nature, accessible in private gardens, was certainly also the aim of a walk, but it was found outside the walls, along unspoilt roads which knew nothing of the art of the French *promenoir*. With the exception of Lucca, where the ramparts were planted in the sixteenth century, it was not until the second half of the eighteenth century that tree-lined promenades were introduced to Italy; in Turin, but especially in Parma (the Stradone created by E. Petitot in 1767) and in Naples, where, as in Madrid[33] the Bourbon influence explains the French-style beautification. We know that around 1800 Napoleon Bonaparte systematically exploited this device, which was to become typical of French *préfectures* in the 'Sister Republics'.[34]

While Arthur Young records his admiration for all the provincial promenades during his three sojourns in France at the end of Louis XVI's reign, philosophers and other environmental theorists agree with him in his severe criticism of the artificial aspect of Parisian promenades.[35] This admitted difference between urban life in the capital and in the large provincial towns in about 1780 arises from two complementary causes. The first is from an established fact: a large conurbation is synonymous with harmful consequences – it is contrary to human progress and to the logical contentment it should engender. The second is a yearning for the truth and wisdom to be found in a state of nature, a quest discernible in all aspects of the Enlightenment, and which ultimately brought about unlimited variation in forms of plant life and the different ways of enjoying it in the very heart of the city.

The idea of progress, cherished by philosophers, encyclopaedists, artists and enlightened officials, seemed to flourish particularly in provincial capitals, where recent town planning had resulted in a complete change of appearance. It was a question of scale: Paris was overpopulated and too vast; but, specifically, the officials in charge of the transformation had come up against an economic and political situation so complex that it was difficult to beautify Paris in other than a piecemeal fashion. Walking in the city, a purely social diversion, created a wide social mix on the Champs-Elysées and the Grands Boulevards, and as a consequence fashionable outings on horseback, or in a carriage, gig or coach moved further afield to Longchamp, in the Bois de Boulogne.[36] Chroniclers reported the unrestrained behaviour of high society parading along the old road which led to the religious retreat of the abbey at Longchamp.[37] Dancers, singers, actresses and well-known women of doubtful virtue vied with each other in extravagant spending, and foreigners, especially the British whose horseracing habits were imitated,[38] did not hesitate to join in the spectacle. 'An Englishman appeared at Longchamp in a silver coach, the wheels inset with precious stones and the horses shod with the same metal. It was a question of who could display the most opulent turnout, the most elegant trappings, the most ostentatious livery. Elegant mummers, representing theatrical personages in vogue at the time, wandered through the crowd.'[39]

Against the frenzied luxury of the capital, and the corruption of

Entrance to the Parc de Blossac, Poitiers.
Drawing by Duché de Vancy, c. 1780.
Bibliothèque Municipale, Poitiers.

View of the Palais-Royal, Paris. Drawing
by Lespinasse, 1791. Musée Carnavalet,
Paris. (Photo Bulloz)

manners which, as we shall see, found in public gardens a convenient hiding-place, provincial towns displayed middle class affluence, a rare and short-lived luxury which epitomized the advantages to health – both physical and moral – and to the municipal economy to be derived from such embellishments. Two promenades, impressive examples both of architecture and of the art of terracing, have indeed lent the cachet of nobility to two Languedoc towns, Montpellier and Nîmes, whose resources were by no means comparable with those of the great ports and trading cities such as Bordeaux, Nantes and Lyons.

In Montpellier, writes Arthur Young,

the great object for a stranger to view is the promenade or square, for it partakes of both, called the Perou [sic]. There is a magnificent aqueduct on three tiers of arches for supplying the city with water, from a hill at a considerable distance; a very noble work. A *château d'eau* receives the water in a circular basin, from which it falls into an external reservoir, to supply the city, and the *jets d'eau* that cool the air of a garden below; the whole in a fine square considerably elevated above the surrounding ground, walled in with a balustrade, and other mural decorations, and in the centre a good equestrian statue of Louis XIV. There is an air of real grandeur and magnificence in this useful work, that struck me more than anything at Versailles. The view is also singularly beautiful. To the south the eye wanders with delight over a rich vale, spread with villas, and terminated by the sea. To the north a series of cultivated hills. On one side, the vast range of the Pyrenees trend away till lost in remoteness. On the other, the eternal snows of the Alps pierce the clouds. The whole view one of the most stupendous to be seen, when a clear sky approximates these distant objects.[40]

Arthur Young did not describe the Jardin de la Fontaine in Nîmes, which is nevertheless equal in beauty, grandeur and convenience to the wondrous Peyrou. In addition, this multiform open space, both promenade and garden, has a distinguished history of which the men of the *ancien régime* were particularly aware. The site, between the Tour Magne and the canal supplying the fountain, had been revered since ancient times. The population growth in Nîmes in the eighteenth century, along with the development of the textile industry, required a better water supply obtainable only by regulating the erratic flow of the Fountain which gushed from a hill overlooking the town. The initial work, undertaken in 1738, uncovered the superb remains of a Roman temple which were preserved as part of a wide terraced walk laid out on the hillside and along the banks of the canal. Triumphing over several rival projects – some of which proposed building a Place Louis XV in conjunction with the promenade[41] – the engineer J.-P. Mareschal carried out his own plan between 1745 and 1760. The Fountain of Nîmes became a vast garden, architecturally designed round the pool in which the spring water collected, together with a nymphaeum, terraced balustraded walks, bridges over the canal and a profusion of statues and sculpted vases. In 1819 the planting of trees on the hill was completed, while plans to extend the town were realized as a continuation of Mareschal's scheme of 1774: the main road through the centre of the new town led to the Fountain.

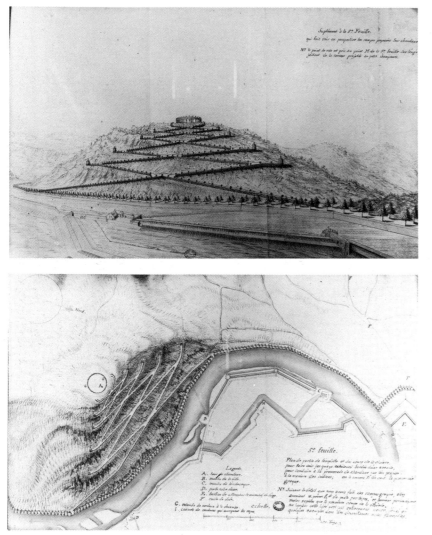

Arthur Young praises the promenade in Bayonne for the delights of its shade; that in Reims for the beauty of its wrought-iron gates; those of Montauban and Poitiers for their views; the one in Besançon for its unusual character – a vast promenade achieved within the walls of the military area[42] – and observes that in their 'public decorations, promenades etc, French towns are much beyond English ones'.[43] He was referring not only to their recreational aspect. Public health, convenience, economic and industrial benefit – some promenades served as plant nurseries, others as areas for rearing silkworms on mulberry trees[44] – also influenced the traveller-cum-economist. The fact was that in the provinces promenades set aside areas of controlled nature for the use of the inhabitants, and not merely selected nature, as at Versailles, or degraded nature as in Paris resulting from the decline in standards of behaviour.

All observers of the reign of Louis XVI deplored it: the pedestrian in Paris risked his health and sometimes his life in the perpetual, confused onslaught of carriages and vehicles of all types. The promenades themselves, according to Arthur Young, had become veritable racetracks, highly dangerous, where were encouraged an 'infinity of one horse cabriolets, which are driven by young men of fashion and their imitators, alike fools, with such rapidity as to be real nuisances.[45] In summer, 'walking in the Champs-Elysées,' relates Mme d'Oberkirch, 'is unbearable. There is not a single drop of water, the monotony is tedious and above all the dust is tiresome because of the proximity of the Versailles road.'[46] Because of this discomfort, and the licentiousness of the public walks near the city centre, well-bred people wishing to stroll on foot under the shade of trees without the trouble of going further afield in a carriage, crowded into the older public gardens in the capital, the Tuileries, Luxembourg and especially the Palais-Royal, which were all enjoying public favour at this time.

In his *Parallèle de Paris et de Londres* L. S. Mercier drew attention to the difference between the two traditions of public walks and planted areas; the legendary English respect for nature, their stay-at-home love of comfort and their good citizenship encouraged the building of their famous squares whose virtues are unknown to the French. These squares – a private version of the public square – are embellished with lawns, fountains and shrubberies, 'the whole well-maintained and providing the local people with a place for walking: these squares are large and very beautiful; they are many and frequent. New dwellings are built only round the sides of the square, thus forming four rows of houses.'[47] Two different forms of social contact emerge from the comparison between the two cities – in London it is concerned with health and real nature, in Paris with spectacle and social rivalry. There are similarly two contrasting forms of town-planning – in England, neighbourhood autonomy and a controlled environment; and in France beautiful views and the opening up of the countryside. For in spite of his preference for London urban life, Mercier cannot help admiring the beauty of a good vista: 'Paris has its tree-lined boulevards, an adornment not seen in London.[48] With the exception of the

antiquated quarters of the medieval centre, which he dislikes, the ugliness of Paris seems to him less physical than moral, and lies in the degeneration in behaviour: 'In London,' he writes, 'one does not see as in Paris fat women or little rouged mistresses carrying their little dogs to the public park, and leaving their children in the care of a servant-girl.'[49]

The harmony of the plan of Paris, taking into account that this was after all an urban plan, was not criticized for the role, design, or arrangement of its cultivated areas – gardens, avenues, boulevards. 'Paris is effectively cut into two by the Seine, with the advantage of the Tuileries on one side, the Luxembourg on the other, and in addition the Palais-Royal, the king's garden, that of the Arsenal and others such as the Soubise and the Infanta's garden.'[50] Mercier draws a parallel with the time when the garden of the Palais-Royal, newly developed as an area for walks under arcades by Victor Louis, became, as a square, one of the finest enclosed areas in Paris. But a public square! For what purpose? To become this Pandora's box, this brothel where gaming and other vices were arrogantly paraded. Mercier, who deplored the fact that the entrance to the Tuileries gardens was guarded by an official who checked that those entering were correctly dressed[51] described in his Utopia, L'an 2440, rêve s'il en fut jamais, a healthy improvement in behaviour in the capital.[52]

In reality, as we have seen, practical administration concentrated in the first place on satisfying the accepted leisure needs of good society. Its abuses, together with attacks by philosophers and artists influenced by Rousseauism and Anglomania, gave rise to fresh invasions of nature into the town, and saw finally, around 1770–80, the introduction of the landscape garden to replace the regular parterres and lawns of private houses.[53] Opened up to the public just before the Revolution, which deprived Marie-Antoinette of her sheep at Versailles, these were eventually to become the pleasure gardens of the Directoire and the Empire, the Tivolis, Idalies and Frascatis of the urban imagination[54] – quite different from the promenades of the Grand Siècle or the provinces.

1 Encyclopédie ou Dictionnaire raisonné . . . , Vol. 13 (1765) p. 444.
2 Ibid., p. 150 (by the Chevalier de Jaucourt).
3 See La ville au XVIIIe siècle, proceedings of the Aix-en-Provence conference (1973).
4 M. Poëte, Promenade dans Paris au XVIIe siècle (Paris 1913); and Au Jardin des Tuileries. L'art des jardins. La promenade publique (Paris 1924).
5 P. Lavedan, Histoire de l'urbanisme, Vol. 1: Renaissance et temps modernes (Paris 1959).
6 R. Mauzi, L'idée du bonheur au XVIIIe siècle (Paris 1969).
7 H. Haussmann, Mémoires du Baron Haussmann. Grands travaux de Paris, 1853–1870 (Paris, reprinted 1979).
8 Jardins en France 1760–1820. Pays d'illusion, terre d'expérience, Catalogue of the C.N.M.H.S. exhibition (Paris 1977).
9 P. Lelièvre, 'Expansion et morphologie', in La ville au XVIIIe siècle, op. cit. (note 3) pp. 135–43.
10 Encyclopédie, op. cit., Vol. 17, article Ville.
11 M. Gallet, Claude-Nicolas Ledoux (Paris 1980).
12 Jardins en France, op. cit. (note 8).
13 Encyclopédie, op. cit., Vol. 13, p. 444.
14 R. Tomlinson, La fête galante: Watteau et Marivaux (Geneva-Paris 1981).
15 Introduction to the exhibition catalogue Les arts du théâtre de Watteau à Fragonard (Bordeaux 1980).

16 P. Lavedan, op. cit. (note 5) p. 200.
17 D. Rabreau, Apollon dans la ville. Essai sur le théâtre et l'urbanisme en France au XVIIIe siècle (in preparation).
18 A. Picon, Architectes et ingénieurs au Siècle des Lumières (Paris 1988) pp. 202–5.
19 Quoted by P. Lavedan, op. cit. (note 5) p. 200.
20 G. Costa, 'Louis de Mondran, économiste et urbaniste (1699–1792)', in La vie urbaine, no. 1 (1955). On air and health see R. Etlin, 'L'air dans l'urbanisme des Lumières' and R. Favre, 'Du "médico-topographique" à Lyon en 1783', in Dix-huitième siècle, no. 9 (1977).
21 M. A. Laugier, Essai sur l'architecture (Paris, 1753; re-ed. 1755) p. 209.
22 Op. cit. (note 7).
23 P. Patte, Les Monuments érigés en France sous le règne de Louis XV (Paris 1765). See also Monuments Historiques, No. 120 (Mar.-Apr. 1982).
24 Les Champs-Elysées et leur quartier, exhibition catalogue (Paris 1988) and S. Granet, La Place de la Concorde (Paris, 1963).
25 P. Lavedan, op. cit. (note 5).
26 G. Delahache, Strasbourg (Paris 1931).
27 J. P. Bériac, Jardins en Aquitaine (Aix-en-Provence) – in preparation.
28 Quoted in L. Desgraves, Evocation du vieux Bordeaux (Paris 1960) p. 353.
29 C. Cosneau, Mathurin Crucy, architecte nantais néoclassique, exhibition catalogue (Nantes 1986); and P. Lelièvre, Nantes au XVIIIe siècle. Architecture et urbanisme – new revised edition (Paris 1988).
30 W. Ostrowski, 'Stanislas Lesczynski urbaniste', in La vie urbaine, no. 4 (Oct.-Dec. 1957).
31 H. F. Buffet, 'Les promenades urbaines en Bretagne au XVIIIe siècle', in Mémoires de la Société d'Histoire et d'Archéologie de Bretagne, Vol. 35 (1955) pp. 11–30.
32 Cited by F. Boyer in 'Les promenades publiques en Italie du nord au XVIIIe siècle' in La vie urbaine, no. 3 (July-Sept. 1959). Also F. Boyer 'Les promenades publiques en Italie du centre et du sud au XVIIIe siècle', in La vie urbaine, no. 4 (Oct.-Dec. 1960).
33 Jardines classicos madrileños, exhibition catalogue (Madrid 1981). Mainly about the Prado Paseo.
34 F. Boyer, 'Napoléon Ier et les jardins publics en Italie', in La vie urbaine, no. 1 (Jan.-Mar. 1954).
35 La ville au XVIIIe siècle, op. cit. (note 3).
36 V. Fournel, Le Vieux Paris (Paris 1887).
37 Ibid., p. 151.
38 Ibid., p. 421.
39 Ibid., p. 162.
40 A. Young, Travels in France in 1787 to 90 (1792). Journal for 25 July 1787. See also Projets et dessins pour la Place du Peyrou à Montpellier, exhibition catalogue (Montpellier 1980).
41 V. Lasalle, La fontaine de Nîmes de l'antiquité à nos jours (Paris 1967) and M. Raphel, Les comptes de la Fontaine de Nîmes (Nîmes 1920).
42 On Besançon, see E. de Ganay, 'La promenade de Chamars à Besançon', in Le Figaro artistique, no. 166–8 (1927) and L. Estavoyer, Besançon au Siècle des Lumières (Besançon 1978).
43 A. Young, op. cit. (note 40).
44 Notably in Toulouse, Perpignan and Poitiers (for this town see M. E. Pilotelle's study of the Promenade de Blossac, in Mémoires de la Société des Antiquaires de l'Ouest, Vol. 22 (1855, edn. of 1856).
45 A. Young, op. cit. (note 40).
46 Baronne d'Oberkirch, Mémoires (Paris 1970). p. 302.
47 L. S. Mercier, Parallèle de Paris et de Londres (c. 1781), ed. by C. Bruneteau and B. Cottret (Paris 1892) p. 60.
48 Ibid., p. 57.
49 Ibid., p. 76.
50 Ibid., p. 60.
51 M. Poëte, Au jardin des Tuileries, op. cit. (note 4).
52 L. S. Mercier, L'an 2440, rêve s'il en fut jamais (Paris, edn. of 1786), Vol. 1, p. 50 'To refuse entry to the garden to the common people seems to me a gratuitous insult, the more so since they are not aware of it.'
53 M. Mosser, 'Il pittoresco nella città – Giardini privati a Parigi nel XVIII secolo', in Lotus International, no. 30 (1981/1), pp. 28–37.
54 Jardins en France, op. cit. (note 8).

The Park of Wilhelmshöhe:
From the Baroque *Delineatio Montis* to the Heroic Landscape

Hans-Christoph Dittscheid

Plan of the garden of Weissenstein (later Wilhelmshöhe), near Kassel. Drawing by the court gardener Fuchs, c. 1780. Staatliche Kunstsammlungen, Kassel.

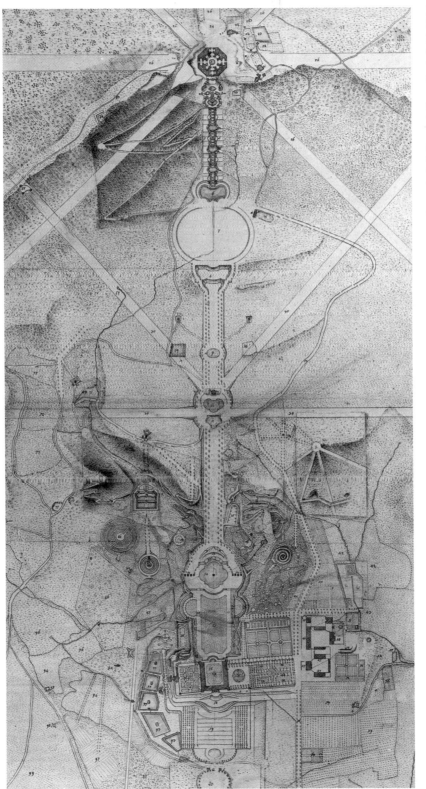

The landscape garden of Wilhelmshöhe has a prominent place in the history of European garden design. The natural features of the site were in themselves exceptionally suited for the creation of an extensive park: the broad hillside of the Karlsberg which rises above Kassel, the seat of the Landgraves of Hesse-Kassel seven kilometres away, has a plentiful supply of water and a volcanic soil, a combination which ensures the lush growth even of exotic plants.

The park sprang from a combination of three eighteenth-century developments, each with a distinct stylistic orientation: the Italian-inspired Baroque of the beginning of the century was countered in the second half of the century, when the sources of inspiration came from England, by the sensibility of the Rococo style, and finally by Romanticism. In the first (Baroque) phase and the third (Romantic) phase the achievements were intended to surpass those of the countries where they originated.

Landgrave Moritz the Wise at the beginning of the seventeenth century was the first to recognize the advantages of the site and built Schloss Weissenstein half way up the slope, a modest house with three wings facing eastward towards the town. Behind the schloss Moritz laid out a garden ending in the Moritzgrotte, the precursor of the later Plutogrotte. But it was not until the reign of Landgrave Karl, from about 1700, that there were any particularly ambitious plans for the garden. Karl, who both politically and through his personality was the most significant of the eighteenth-century Landgraves of Hesse, decided to extend the park up to the summit of the Karlsberg, where in 1696 he erected the first building, to the south of what was later to be the axis.

The turning point in the conception of the design of the garden was a journey to Italy in 1699/1700, when Karl visited Rome and the villas of the Roman Campagna and probably met the artist whom he commissioned to produce the designs for his park (at that time called Weissenstein). Giovanni Francesco Guerniero, who signed himself 'Architectus Romanus', was originally a '*stuccatore*', and there is no evidence that he practised as an architect before his work at Kassel. Only about a third of his designs for Weissenstein were executed,

but the whole project is known from a lavish series of engravings published in Rome in 1705, and at Kassel in 1706, under the title *Delineatio montis . . .*, on which the celebrated engraver Alessandro Specchi from Rome collaborated.

The bird's-eye view in the *Delineatio* makes it clear that the terrain of the park was largely to be left in its natural state. The remodelling was restricted to the great geometric axis formed by a cascade of water linking the schloss to the east with the Octagon on the Karlsberg to the west. The park was probably intended to retain its character as a hunting ground, as it had been in the reign of Landgrave Moritz. The cascade is interrupted at two points. In front of the Moritzgrotte it is crossed by a great avenue with parterres and fountains. The mid-point of the cascade is occupied by a plateau with a central tempietto from which six paths radiate from the sides of the cascade to the wooded garden. Two triumphal columns with garlands wound round them lead to the upper part of the cascade. The cascade springs from two grotto courtyards placed axially one in front of the other before the Octagon on the summit of the hill. The fountain in the lower grotto springs from the head of the giant Enceladus, who fought against Hercules. Among the sculptures in the niches of the grotto are a centaur and Pan playing a flute. This lower grotto courtyard is based on the Mannerist *teatro d'acqua* of the Villa Aldobrandini at Frascati built a century earlier, where the Hercules theme, the *gigantomachia*, and the triumphal columns, which should be interpreted as the Columns of Hercules, all appear. Thus the Villa Aldobrandini, which Karl admired, can be seen to be the most important inspiration behind Guerniero's design. As if to confirm this, two dragons have slipped in above the grotto in Guerniero's engraving – they are the heraldic beasts of the Borghese family making an unexpected appearance on the Karlsberg.

The Octagon itself, begun in 1701, is a stronghold reserved entirely for the world of the gods, a sort of Olympus in stone. The lower one-and-a-half storeys are in rough-hewn masonry imitating rocks, for which the easily eroded basalt tufa found on the site was used. The principal storey has wide arched openings above rusticated piers – this stronghold

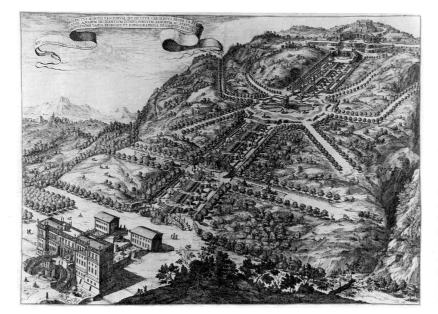

still not built. The three projects by the Paris architect Charles de Wailly did not arrive in Kassel until 1785, the year of Friedrich's death.

Friedrich's son, Wilhelm IX (Elector Wilhelm I), who reigned from 1785, completed the park, which since 1798 has been called Wilhelmshöhe after him. Wilhelm had been brought up by his mother in the spirit of English culture, and his court architect, Heinrich Christoph Jussow, also embraced the ideal of the landscape garden in its mature form as developed by 'Capability' Brown. At the same time, however, the schloss, a relic of absolutism typical of continental Europe, still had to be presented in a suitable manner. Jussow created an heroic naturalistic landscape with wildly cleft rocks artificially piled up, the ruins of a Roman aqueduct, torrential waterfalls and a Devil's Bridge. The Roman aqueduct

with its long fall of water and the fountain shooting up more than thirty feet above the bowling green in front of the schloss give the elemental force of water full rein, and this stage-managed representation of the omnipotence of nature produces a threatening effect. The quest for the sublime was also evident when the Octagon was for the first time made habitable for Landgrave Wilhelm. The creation of 'terrible scenes' showed the influence of William Chambers's theories at the court of Kassel. Broad avenues, easily passible in a coach, with pictorially composed views superseded Friedrich's small-scale, playful scenes. To the south-east, in front of the schloss, Jussow amalgamated five small ponds to form a lake in which the whole park was reflected by the light of the setting sun. Work on the new building began in 1786. It was divided into two complexes in divergent styles. The main

of the gods was never intended for living in! It is probably the most monumental architectural structure of the time to be designed purely as a monument. The most important model for it was the Mannerist Villa Farnese in Caprarola, built by Vignola in 1559–75 in the shape of a pentagon on the foundations for a castle, on a site that also dominated the landscape around it. In the first plan the Octagon was to have been surmounted by an accessible platform, and it was only during construction that the desire was felt to give prominence to one of the sides. From 1713 a slender obelisk-like pyramid was erected above the east side of the Octagon closest to the cascade, bearing a colossal copper statue of Hercules of the Farnese type, chosen as an idealized figure of the absolutism of the all-powerful ruler of Weissenstein.

The powerful effect of the Octagon is the result of the typical Baroque contrast between the natural substructure and the artificially sublime superstructure. Guerniero himself pointed out this characteristic in his commentary in the *Delineatio* when he described the Octagon as 'raised up on the hill not only by art but as it were by nature'. This conceit shows Guerniero to be a direct follower of Gianlorenzo Bernini. By basing himself on Bernini's style Guerniero moved beyond the Mannerism of earlier Italianate gardens.

Guerniero had planned a building halfway down the hill, based on Bernini's third project for the Louvre but transformed into a villa with open arcades in the centre. This part remained unexecuted because the Octagon and the cascade had exhausted all available funds. Moreover, the form of the projected villa was still undecided. The entrants in the design competition even included Filippo Juvara.

Even before his accession Landgrave Friedrich II had already set new standards in European garden design by surrounding his Schloss Bellevue at Kassel with an Anglo-Chinese garden, the earliest example of this style on the continent. The English influence at Kassel came from Friedrich's wife Mary, daughter of King George II of England. The garden designs were published in 1781 in Georges-Louis Le Rouge's *Jardins anglochinois* (cah. 9). After the Seven Years' War Weissenstein was remodelled in the same style, breaking up the area immediately around the schloss into numerous sentimental scenes. The garden architecture was inspired by the buildings in Kew Gardens, of which the neoclassical temple and Turkish Mosque were copied at Kassel. William Chambers and Simon Louis du Ry, the architect to the court of Kassel, had studied together in Paris with J. F. Blondel. The villa, however, was

View of Wilhelmshöhe. *Painting by J. E. Hummel, c. 1800. Staatliche Kunstsammlungen, Kassel.*

Idealized View of the Octagon. *Painting by J. van Nickel. Staatliche Kunstsammlungen, Kassel.*

part, which was split into three separate wings and presented itself to the public in classical garb, was balanced by a private pseudo-ruin, the neo-Gothic Löwenburg, which represented a return to nature. Landscape garden and schloss park were now in equilibrium.

The idealized view by Johann Erdmann Hummel shows Wilhelmshöhe in about 1800 as a happy synthesis of three generations, each in its own way remaining faithful to the heroic *genius loci* which culminates in the figure of Hercules. It can still be experienced today.

Bibliography

P. Heidelbach, *Die Geschichte der Wilhelmshöhe* (1909).

A. Holtmeyer, *Die Bau- und Kunstdenkmäler im Regierungsbezirk Cassel*, Vol. 4: Kreis Cassel Land (Marburg 1910).

A. Holtmeyer, 'Giovanni Francesco Guerniero', in *Zeitschrift für Geschichte der Architektur*, Vol. 3 (1909/1910), pp. 249–57.

A. Holtmeyer, *W. Strieder's Wilhelmshöhe* (Marburg 1913).

K. Paetow, *Klassizismus und Romantik auf Wilhelmshöhe* (Kassel 1929).

H. Vogel, 'Englische Einflüsse am Kasseler Hof des späteren 18. Jahrhunderts', in *Hessisches Jahrbuch für Landesgeschichte*, Vol. 6 (1956) pp. 218–31.

H. Vogel, *Heinrich Christoph Jussow, Baumeister in Kassel und Wilhelmshöhe*, exhibition catalogue (Kassel 1958).

E. Berckenhagen, *Barock in Deutschland. Residenzen*, exhibition catalogue (Berlin 1966).

H. Reuther, 'Der Carlsberg bei Kassel – Ein Idealprojekt barocker Gartenarchitektur', in *Architectura*, Vol. 6 (1976) pp. 47–65.

Aufklärung und Klassizismus in Hessen-Kassel unter Landgraf Friedrich II. 1760–1785, exhibition catalogue (Kassel 1979).

A. v. Buttlar, *Der Landschaftsgarten* (Munich 1980).

H.C. Dittscheid, 'Charles de Wailly in den Diensten des Landgrafen Friedrich II von Hessen-Kassel', in *Kunst in Hessen und am Mittelrhein*, Vol. 20 (1980) pp. 21–77.

H.C. Dittscheid, *Kassel-Wilhelmshöhe und die Krise des Schlossbaues am Ende des Ancien Régime. Charles de Wailly, Simon Louis du Ry und Heinrich Christoph Jussow als Architekten von Schloss und Löwenburg in Wilhelmshöhe (1785–1800)* (Worms 1987).

The Italian Origins of Rousham

Elisabetta Cereghini

Half-way through the ten years (1709–19) that William Kent spent visiting the major artistic centres of Italy, he kept a sort of diary (1714–15).[1] This precious manuscript, whose true value has not been fully recognized until now, contains a remarkable quantity of information on all the most important events and personalities of the decade; it also comprises a comprehensive record of Kent's researches and preparatory work for the projects he later undertook. In laying out his landscape gardens he referred constantly to this diary, as has become clear from the extensive studies carried out to establish the origins and influences behind his work at Rousham (the property of General Dormer), which he designed between 1737 and 1741.

A superficial examination of the garden reveals the principal elements of the plan: the various architectural and sculptural features, such as the Praeneste, the fountain and grotto of Venus' Vale, Townesend's Building, the colossal statue and the three statues arranged in a semicircle to form a theatre. Around them Kent devised his overall scheme for the garden and its individual 'scenes'. One such is composed round Townesend's Building, (The Temple of Echo), its main façade ornamented with a portico, which is approached by a gently sloping lawn and enclosed at the back by a screen of trees. The essential element of this composition is its architectural use of space, which was derived from the work of the *quadratura*[2] painters. The *quadraturisti*, as they were known, used geometric devices and perspectives in order to represent the spatial effects of architecture on a flat surface.

In Italy, Kent worked closely with one of the major exponents of the school of *quadratura*, Giovanni Paolo Pannini (1691–1765),[3] who was celebrated for his landscape views. They met in the studio of Benedetto Luti (1666–1724)[4] after Pannini moved to Rome in 1711,[5] having studied under the architect-scenographer Ferdinando Galli Bibiena (1657–1743).[6] During this initial study period Pannini concentrated on the theory of technical perspective and its application, not only to the field of painting but also to scenography: for the *quadraturisti*, painting, architecture and scenography were complementary and of equal importance. It was after this that Pannini achieved a

sort of synthesis between the compositional principles of landscape painting and those of *quadratura*, adapting them to the new theories of spatial composition. The aim of these theories was to use perspective as a means of relating real space to the space represented.

According to Kent, the various 'scenes' comprising the garden of Rousham needed to be correlated in such a way that the overall scheme had a homogeneity of design as well as variety and naturalness. These two latter characteristics – which for Pope were the result of certain specific aesthetic judgements – were for Kent the effects of a technique calculated to create a sense of 'real' space. They became the basis of the perspective principles to which Kent, while still in Italy, devoted most of his studies, as sketches at the end of his diary testify. (These sketches are the subject of a treatise by Giulio Troili,[7] on which Pannini was also to work.[8]) Instead of devising a space based on a central perspective line,

along which the eye of the spectator travelled from a fixed viewpoint in a formally organized scheme (as in the Baroque garden), Kent adopted a technique based on the use of oblique perspectives comprised of two or more axial lines converging from points outside the 'scene', which no longer corresponded with the line of vision of the spectator. This prompted the spectator to seek out viewpoints independently rather than be confined to any single perspective prescribed by the architect.

The rules and principles of oblique perspective were laid down and illustrated in the treatise by Ferdinando Bibiena *L'Architettura civile*[9] (Parma 1711), in which the author demonstrated the effects achieved by the use of multiple perspectives. A perfect example was provided by the spatial structure of Venus' Vale, the Praeneste and the theatre, which together form the nucleus of the garden of Rousham; from the end of the Elm Walk (now the Lime Walk)

which begins with the statue of Colossus, it is impossible to take in these three features at a single glance because they are set at oblique angles to the viewpoint of the spectator. This spatial device involves the choice of at least three different points of view from which to frame the scene. And it now becomes clear in what way the various features are interrelated: a scene viewed in a direct line is comprised also of aspects of those scenes placed at the margins of the spectator's vision, in which the architectural focus is set at an oblique angle to the straight perspective. Such an arrangement creates a natural transition from one area of the garden to another, and ensures that the various features are revealed in turn, as they are in nature. Returning to the point above, one can of course choose to allow one's glance to be led in the direction of the surrounding landscape, the background for the architectural elements of the garden: at Rousham the Oxfordshire countryside is an essential feature of every view.

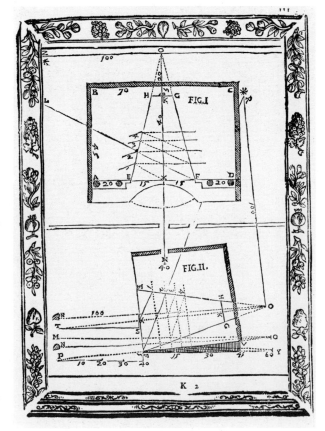

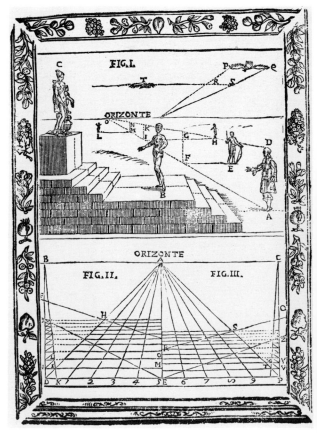

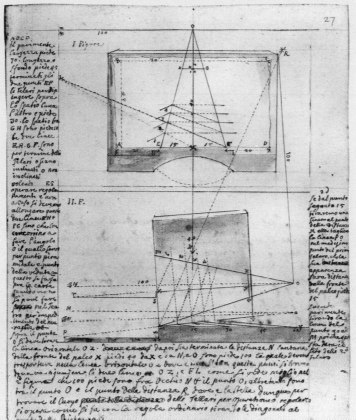

As in the schemes created by Bibiena, Kent devised a system based on multiple perspectives which resulted in a spatial dynamic in which created spaces and natural spaces contributed equally to the design of the landscape garden. He chose the device of the oblique perspective in order to unify the various 'scenes' of the garden, demonstrating for the first time his ability to manipulate natural spaces without destroying their natural order, and actually to establish an alternative order based on the same principles of variety and freedom.

The spiritual values of the age, those reflected especially in the theories of Lord Shaftesbury, were clearly mirrored in the gardens of William Kent. The decision to employ certain techniques derived from a desire for a particular means of expression, and was based, as Panofsky[10] confirms, not only on a specific vision of the world but also on a specific conception of the world.

1 William Kent, *Italian Diary (1714–1715)*, in the possession of the Bodleian Library, Oxford (MS Rawl. D.L. 1162).

2 *Quadraturismo* developed in the sixteenth and seventeenth centuries in Milan, Rome and Venice, but above all in Bologna. See: *Architettura, scenografia e pittura di paesaggio. L'arte nel settecento emiliano* – exhibition catalogue (Bologna 1980); A. Negri, 'Prospettici e quadraturisti' in *Enciclopedia universale dell'arte*, Vol. 11, pp. 100–15; R. Bossaglia, 'Riflessioni sui quadraturisti nel settecento lombardo' in *Arte*, Vol. 7, (1980), pp. 377–98.

3 An impressive monograph on all aspects of the art of Pannini is that of F. Arisi, *Giovan Paolo Pannini* (Bologna 1961).

4 Luti was a pupil of the artist Carlo Maratti, after whose death (in 1713) he became one of the best known painters in Rome. Kent worked at his studio and left only after the Clementino competition of 1713 and his travels of 1714–15. Little exists in the way of biographical material on Luti; see instead historical sources such as L. Pascoli, 'Vita di Benedetto Luti' in *Vite de' pittori, scultori e architetti* (Rome 1730); M. Missirini, 'Il principato di Benedetto Luti' in *Memorie per servire all storia della romana Accademia di S. Luca* (Rome 1823); and the essay by V. Moschini, 'Benedetto Luti' in *Arte* (1923).

5 See F. Arisi, *op. cit.* According to Wittkower, Pannini went to Rome only in 1713; see *Arte e architettura in Italia 1600–1750* (Turin 1972).

6 On Bibiena's work as scenographer and architect both in Italy and in the European courts, and on the Bibiena family in general, see: M. Mayor, *The Bibiena Family* (New York

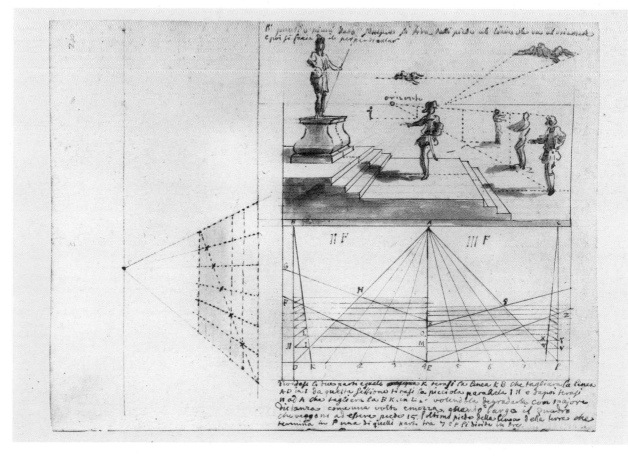

Rousham, Oxfordshire: Venus' Vale.
(Photo Daniele De Lonte)

1954); 'Four Centuries of Theater Design' in *The Italian Source of European Stage Design* (Yale University Art Gallery 1964); J. Sullivan Hatfield, *The Relationship between Late Baroque Architecture and Scenography 1703–1778* (Philadelphia 1981).

[7] Painter and essayist, born in Bologna in 1613. His treatise *Paradossi per praticare la prospettiva senza saperla* (Bologna 1683) was used by many artist-scenographers, among them Ferdinando Bibiena. Troili's treatise was included in L. Vagnetti's 'De naturali et artificiali perspectiva' in *Studio di Prospettiva*, No. 9 (Florence 1979).

[8] Indicated by a sketchbook of perspective drawings dated 1708, now in the Biblioteca Comunale di Piacenza (MS Pallastrelli 256); see F. Arisi, *op. cit.*

[9] The Bibiena treatise of 1711 was expanded by the author in 1753, the date of publication of *Direzioni della prospettiva teorica* (Bologna). For an analysis of these two treatises, see: F. Ruffini, 'Per un'epistemologia del teatro del Settecento. Lo spazio scenico in Ferdinando Bibiena' in *Biblioteca Teatrale*, No. 3 (1972); F. Maratti, *Lo spazio scenico in Italia dall'età Barocca al Settecento* (Rome 1974).

[10] E. Panofsky, *La prospettiva come 'forma simbolica'* (Milan 1966).

Bibliography

C. Hussey, 'A Georgian Arcady, William Kent's Gardens at Rousham, Oxfordshire' in *Country Life*, Vol. 99 (1946) pp. 1083–1133; M.

Jourdain, *The Work of William Kent* (London 1948); E. Croft Murray, 'William Kent in Rome' in *English Miscellany*, Vol. 1 (1950) pp. 221–9; H. Hugh, 'John Talman and William Kent in Italy' in *Connoisseur*, Vol. 134 (1954) pp. 3–7; J. Fleming, 'William Kent at Rousham. An 18th-Century Elysium' in *Connoisseur*, Vol. 153 (1963) p. 158; S. Pugh, 'Nature as a Garden: a Conceptual Tour of Rousham' in *Studio International*, Vol. 186 (1973) p. 121; K. Woodbridge, 'William Kent as a Landscape Gardener' in *Apollo*, Vol. 90 (1974) p. 126; K. Woodbridge, 'William Kent's Gardening: the Rousham Letters' in *Apollo*, Vol. 100 (1974) p. 282; H. Moggridge, 'Notes on Kent's Garden at Rousham' in *Journal of Garden History*, Vol. 6, No. 3, pp. 187–226.

The Sublime as Paradigm: Hafod and Hawkstone

Malcolm Andrews

Plan of part of the Hafod estate, Dyfed, Wales. Engraving by W. Blake for G. Cumberland, An Attempt to Describe Hafod, *London 1796. National Library of Wales.*

The garden is an arena in which the tensions between artifice and nature, order and wilderness are exercised. Each age establishes what it feels to be the most satisfying compromise between these two extremes, and each age gives a different stress to one or the other. England in the eighteenth century offers a remarkable example of a full pendulum swing from gardens of highly formal design – rectilinear patterns and elaborate topiary – to gardens satisfying the taste for the wild and the sublime in the later decades of the century. In the case of some of these later gardens, one might be forgiven for asking in what useful sense the term 'garden' can be applied at all to an estate consisting of hundreds of acres of rocky terrain, thickly forested, intersected by rough mountain streams, with here and there a clearing for grazing sheep and cattle. For such was the character of Hafod, the estate in mountainous Cardiganshire.

How thin was the dividing line between garden and wild nature can be seen in the response of Arthur Young, the agricultural writer, when one of his investigative tours brought him to Derwentwater in the Cumbrian Lake District:

Winding paths should be cut in the rock, and resting-places made for the weary traveller: Many of these paths must necessarily lead through the hanging woods, openings might be made to let in views of the lake, where the objects, such as islands, etc., were peculiarly beautiful. . . . It is amusing to think of the pains and expense with which the environs of several seats have been ornamented, to produce pretty scenes, it is true, but how very far short of the wonders that might here be held up to the eye in all the rich luxuriance of nature's painting. What are the effects of a *Louis's* magnificence to the sportive play of nature in the vale of Keswick![1]

Young is complaining about the difficulty of access to some of the best viewpoints and is here recommending the development of Derwentwater into a kind of mid-eighteenth-century landscape garden by maximizing its picturesque amenities. The natural wildness is not to be disturbed, but some adjustment is necessary to facilitate the enjoyment of it. The disparaging reference to Versailles ('a *Louis's* magnificence') is characteristic of these late-eighteenth-century tastes in their repudiation of any signs of artifice and formality. Such preferences were

hardly evident at the beginning of the century except in the case of a small articulate minority. 'A spacious horizon is an image of liberty', wrote Joseph Addison in 1712. He argued that open, uncultivated country and mountainous landscapes had a special kind of pleasure: 'that rude kind of magnificence which appears in many of those stupendous works of nature.' Addison's contemporary, the 3rd Earl of Shaftesbury, gave memorable expression to the same relish for nature's 'rude kind of magnificence' in his 'Philosophical Rhapsody':

I shall no longer resist the Passion growing in me for Things of a *natural* kind; where neither *Art* nor the *Conceit* or *Caprice* of Man has spoil'd their *genuine order*, by breaking in upon that *primitive State*. Even the rude *Rocks*, the irregular unwrought *Grotto*'s, and broken Falls of Waters, with all the horrid Graces of the *Wilderness* it-self, as representing NATURE more, will be the more engaging, and appear with a Magnificence beyond the formal Mockery of Princely Gardens.[2]

The intensity of this feeling is remarkable. The wild landscape stimulates a hardly resistible passion in the speaker. This is very different from the mood of so many of the Restoration garden poems, where the formality of design, the carefully contrived opportunities for sweet seclusion, are seen as constituting an escape from the passions. But tumultuous

emotion was to be inseparable from the experience of the sublime garden: sudden terror at finding oneself emerging from a dark cave to within a few feet of a loud waterfall; giddying prospects from selected cliff-top viewpoints; the alarming obscurity of grotto passages. These sensations were incorporated into the idea of the Sublime in Edmund Burke's famous treatise, *A Philosophical Enquiry into the Origin of our Ideas of the Sublime and the Beautiful* (1757: rev. 1759). There he argued that the ideas most likely to make a powerful impression on the mind are 'self-preservation' and 'society'. Anything that threatens the idea of self-preservation is a source of the Sublime: 'that is, it is productive of the strongest emotion, which the mind is capable of feeling.' Terror, which is 'the latent ruling principle' of the Sublime, is excited by the following: obscurity, power, privation (i.e. deprivation – of light, sounds etc.), vastness, infinity. Beauty, on the other hand, stimulates the social 'passions' by presenting alluring forms which, far from threatening self-preservation, encourage gregariousness and sexual companionship. Here are the essential contrasts:

For sublime objects are vast in their dimensions, beautiful ones are comparatively small; beauty should be smooth and polished; the great, rugged and negligent; beauty should

shun the right line, yet deviate from it insensibly; the great in many cases loves the right line, and when it deviates, it often makes a strong deviation; beauty should not be obscure; the great ought to be dark and gloomy; beauty should be light and delicate; the great ought to be solid, and even massive.[3]

The great parks of Hafod and Hawkstone naturally afforded opportunities to indulge the full range of emotions associated with the Sublime. Their appeal depended on their scenic features being precisely 'vast', 'rugged', 'negligent', 'dark', 'gloomy', 'massive'. Both these gardens were developed over the last third of the eighteenth century and it is appropriate now to give some brief account of them, their owners, their history and the opportunities they afforded the visitor to experience the Sublime in landscape terms.

Hafod, the estate in the county of Cardiganshire (now Dyfed) was developed in the 1780s. Its owner was Thomas Johnes, an MP, much of whose family wealth derived from early industrialism. The estate spread upwards and outwards from a narrow valley, through which the river Ystwyth ran, to cover miles of rugged hillside terrain. Although there was a small two-acre garden designed as a shady retreat, with some careful cultivation of shrubs, small trees and flowers, the dominant character of Hafod was that of

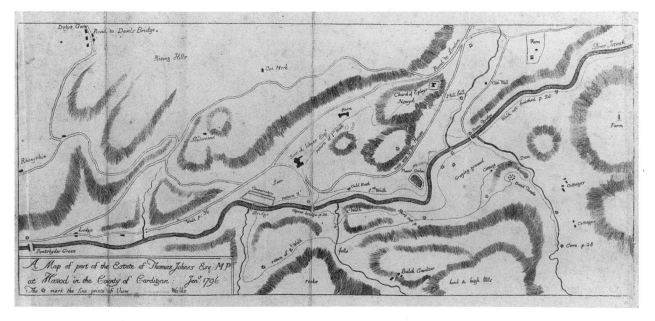

Hafod House, Dyfed. From J. E. Smith,
Fifteen Views Illustrative of a Tour to
Hafod, *London 1810, plate I. National
Library of Wales.*

*The Cavern Cascade at Hafod, Dyfed. From
J. E. Smith*, Fifteen Views Illustrative of
a Tour to Hafod, *London 1810, plate V.
National Library of Wales.*

The garden of Hawkstone, Shropshire.
(*Photo* Country Life)

wildness. It aimed to stimulate in the visitor certain strong sensations. Burke had suggested a particular kind of cathartic, anguished delight as a hallmark of the Sublime:

If the pain and terror are so modified as not to be actually noxious; if the pain is not carried to violence, and the terror is not conversant about the present destruction of the person, as these emotions clear the parts, whether fine, or gross, of a dangerous and troublesome incumbrance, they are capable of producing delight; not pleasure, but a sort of delightful horror, a sort of tranquillity tinged with terror.[4]

Effects productive of exactly this 'delightful horror' were achieved almost effortlessly at Hafod, according to one of its most enthusiastic topographers, George Cumberland:

No language can image out the sublimity of the scenes; which, without quite aiming at a sentiment of aversion, produces, in the empassioned soul, all those thrilling sensations of terror, which ever arise from majestical, yet gloomy exhibitions.[5]

Certain walks and choice viewing points were created as the garden was developed to exploit the stupendous natural advantages of Welsh mountain scenery and its bardic associations. The popularity of Celtic and Gaelic legend was inseparable from its wild Highland and Cambrian settings. This was the period of the Celtic Revival and a widespread interest in Welsh cultural history. Thomas Gray's *The Bard* (1757) imagined the last of the persecuted Bards high on the slopes of Snowdon, denouncing the invading English army. The vogue for impassioned bardic literature also helped to launch the cult of Ossian, the legendary Gaelic bard and warrior. With bardic associations in mind, George Cumberland described the impression on him of one of Hafod's viewpoints, an impression which he thought 'indelible':

Yet I saw it without any advantageous concomitants. What then must be the effect of sunshine – vapours – autumnal foliage – a fine aurora – or a clear moon light! what, in the language of Ossian, 'When the blast has entered the womb of the mountain-cloud and scattered its curling gloom around,' for here, on this globose promontory, a bard might indeed sit, and draw all his fine images from nature![6]

A 'druid' stone-circle was introduced near this spot to enhance the bardic character of the site. Elsewhere on the estate a passage was cut through rock to give the visitor a sudden, unexpectedly close view of a waterfall:

As we creep along the winding and slippery path, a dark hollow in the rock attracts our notice on the right; the din of falling water reverberates through the cave, and makes us hesitate about committing ourselves to its damp and gloomy recesses. By a simple but successful trial of art, the termination of the passage forwards seems to disappoint our hopes, when, on turning suddenly to the left, a rude aperture admits the light, and a sparkling sheet of water, in front of the aperture, urges its perpendicular fall from the rock above, into a deep hole below the cave.[7]

We find many of the same vertiginous delights when we come to consider Hawkstone in Shropshire:

He that mounts the precipices at Hawkstone wonders how he came hither, and doubts how he shall return. . . . He has not the tranquillity, but the horror of solitude, a kind of turbulent pleasure between fright and admiration. The Ideas which it forces upon the mind, are the sublime, the dreadful, and the vast.[8]

This is Dr Johnson describing the same complex sensation of the Sublime as we have already encountered in Burke's treatise and Cumberland's response to Hafod. Hafod's unrelieved mountain sublimity was not to be found at Hawkstone; but in some respects Hawkstone's landscape was even more disconcerting. Its craggy, sheer-sided hills rise very abruptly from the north Shropshire plain and afford extraordinary views over twelve counties. It was these 'precipices' which formed Hawkstone's chief attraction. The estate was owned by the Hill family. In the eighteenth century it was Sir Richard Hill MP (1733–1808) who was mainly responsible for the more bizarre and spectacular scenic initiatives which were displayed on the ten-mile tour of the estate. Hawkstone was peculiarly eclectic in its garden motifs. There was a gothicized farm house, 'Neptune's Whim' (a statue of Neptune sitting between two large ribs of a whale), a Knot-House, a 'Chinese' temple, a 'Scene in Switzerland' with Alpine bridge, the (genuine) ruins of a thirteenth-century castle, a Hermitage, a Menagerie, and a 'Scene at Otaheite' which featured a hut derived in design

Red Castle and the Alpine bridge.
Engraving from A Description of
Hawkstone, the Seat of Sir John Hill,
Shrewsbury 1822.

from illustrations to *Captain Cook's Voyages*.

The most awesome feature was Grotto Hill. Planted with pines and a ruined Gothick arch, this was a triumph of the landscaped Sublime. The hill was partly hollowed, cavernous chambers were scooped out, the darkness mysteriously relieved here and there by circular windows of yellow, blue and green glass. The rough surfaces of the pillars, walls and ceiling were encrusted with appliqué shells and fossils. There were other, more surprising antiquities in the Grotto:

We were next conducted through a dark passage to a window over a wickett, which discovered a Cell with a table and Jug, and presently appeared a Gigantic figure in the dress of a Druid with a Wand in his hand, who in a coarse voice bid us good morning, there was just sufficient light to distinguish the dress and figure, who walked twice in our view bowed & retired, the effect was admirable.

This startling figure was a waxwork effigy of one of Sir Richard Hill's ancestors, its movement operated by a hidden lever to which the gardener-guide had access. The gardener was also the 'coarse voice'. As the visitor emerged from the Grotto into daylight, the relief was short-lived; for he found himself still high above the plain, perched on the 'Awful Precipice' or 'Raven's Shelf'. The descent path looked formidably steep. The great Shropshire plain spread away below. The ravens circled overhead noisily. The whole experience might duplicate a scene or two from one of those Tales of Terror which so dominated the fiction market in the 1790s.

The very idea of a garden involves the sense of man's domestication of wild nature. The estates which I have briefly described challenge this assumption by accentuating and exploiting their naturally Sublime scenery. They provoke the

irrational, sensationist response in ways which must make one wonder about the conventional definition of the word 'garden'. In the heyday of the taste for wild scenery, this teasing problem was put succinctly by Sir Joshua Reynolds in his thirteenth Discourse to the Royal Academy (1786):

Gardening, as far as Gardening is an Art, or entitled to that appellation, is a deviation from Nature; for if the true taste consists, as many hold, in banishing every appearance of Art, or any traces of the footsteps of man, it would then be no longer a Garden.

1 Arthur Young, *A Six Months Tour through the North of England* (1770), pp. 155–6.
2 Anthony Ashley Cooper, 3rd Earl of Shaftesbury, *The Moralists* (1709), from *Characteristicks of Men, Manners, Opinions, Times* (1711) Vol. 2, p. 125.
3 Edmund Burke, *A Philosophical Enquiry* (1759), pp. 237–8.
4 *Ibid.*, p. 257.
5 George Cumberland, *An Attempt to Describe Hafod* (1796), p. 40.
6 *Ibid.*, p. 31.
7 Benjamin Malkin, *The Scenery, Antiquities, and Biography, of South Wales* (1804), pp. 344–5.
8 Samuel Johnson, quoted in A. Oswald, 'Beauties and Wonders of Hawkstone – I' in *Country Life* (3 July 1958), p. 18.

Gardens of the Palazzo Reale at Caserta

Cesare De Seta

Views of the Palazzo Reale and gardens of Caserta. From L. Vanvitelli, Dichiarazione dei Disegni del Real Palazzo di Caserta, *Naples 1756, plates XIV and XIII. (Photo Massimo Velo)*

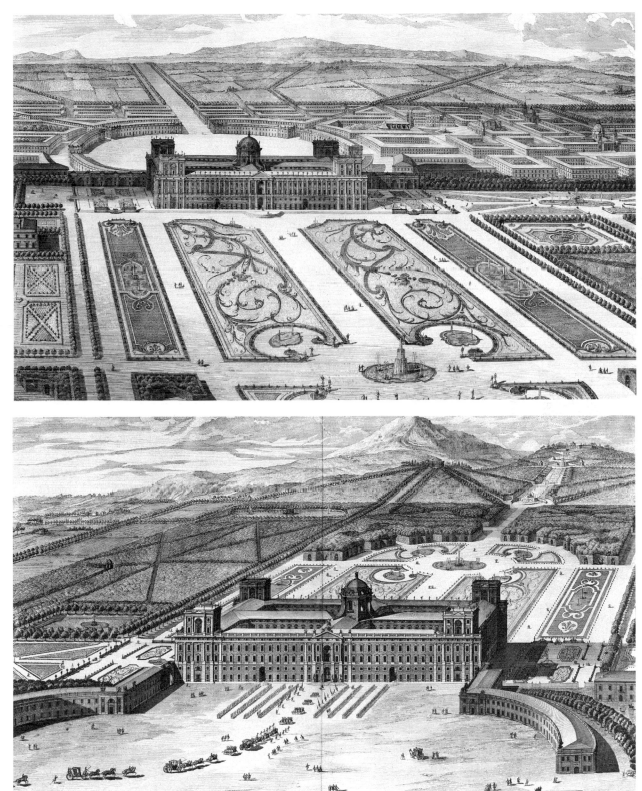

The predominant characteristic of the Palazzo Reale and its park at Caserta is unity, with the natural and the artificial working together and inseparably in a scheme that is as ambitious as it is vast. Its Neapolitan architect, Luigi Vanvitelli, who began his great masterpiece in 1752, was an educated man but far from erudite. His great strength lay in his practicality and his wide range of experience of dealing with matters relating to every aspect of the project. The unfounded accusation that he had taken Versailles as a model for Caserta upset him considerably, and in the *Epistolario* he refuted the allegation in order to silence the slander.

Vanvitelli laid out his great plan for Caserta along an axis about three kilometres (nearly two miles) long, following a tree-lined avenue leading to the palace from the direction of Naples, and running on without interruption to link up with the gallery of the main façade; this perspective was then taken up by the central avenue at the rear of the building and extended as far as the Grand Cascade.

The most reliable sources of information on his original scheme are the drawings (now housed in the Palace) and the etchings taken from them and reproduced in *Dichiarazione dei disegni del Real Palazzo di Caserta . . .* (published by the Stamperia Reale, Naples 1756). As Vanvitelli was unable to follow through in person much of the work on the palace, and the greater part of the work on the gardens (which were largely created by his son Carlo, though to his own design) it is important to study at least three of the plates reproduced in the above volume (the etchings and the original drawings are almost identical, apart from the absence of some insignificant detail from the drawings and the lack of a few captions). Plate I, *The General Plan*, lays out the foundations of his scheme, and it is interesting to note that in the course of the six or seven months that he was engaged on these draft designs he made a number of small changes to his overall plan for the park. From the drawings it is clear that he wanted it to cover a vast area, and to include the long avenue leading to the palace from Naples; it was also to have a great oval piazza (in imitation of Bernini's design for St Peter's Square in Rome), to be approached by three avenues (reminiscent of the design of the Piazza del Popolo) – proof if any were

Plan of the Palazzo Reale and gardens of Caserta. From L. Vanvitelli, Dichiarazione dei Disegni del Real Palazzo di Caserta, *Naples 1756, plate I.*

needed of Vanvitelli's familiarity not only with the great Renaissance buildings and theatrical perspectives of contemporary Rome but also specifically with the architecture of Gianlorenzo Bernini; in fact at Caserta he makes repeated references not only to the work of Bernini, but also to that of Pietro da Cortona and Borromini.

The truly urban character of the park is particularly evident in Plate XIV, *A View of the Great Parterres of the Garden according to the first plan, showing the palace in the distance, the hanging gardens and the New City*, and it is perhaps significant that Vanvitelli refers here to the 'first plan'. In this plate the great avenue leading to Naples can be seen beyond the gardens and the royal palace. Sadly, however, the two rows of plane trees which flank it have been seriously damaged by disease in the course of the past fifteen years, and as a result not only has the approach to the palace lost much of its splendour but the whole scheme has been deprived of one of its most important elements. Now the piazza is also under threat as part of it is having to be adapted in order to provide the public with essential facilities. The other two of the three avenues lead respectively to the new city planned by Vanvitelli (though never built) and to the open countryside at the farthest end of the park, which provides the perfect contrast to the domesticated artificiality of the garden.

Plate XIII shows the view in the opposite direction, looking towards the Grand Cascade: *A View of the Royal Palace from the Great Piazza, with the garden in the distance, showing certain variations between the scheme executed and the general plan*. In referring to 'certain variations' Vanvitelli indicates that here too changes took place in the course of the work. Hanging gardens were to extend to right and left at one end of the building, and there were plans for a parterre and for fountains, dedicated to Flora and Zephyr, ornamented with statues and urns. To the right was to be a riding arena and an open training area, and to the left four paths lined with lime trees enclosing a parterre with a central fountain. In this early conception of the project the great open space beyond the palace rose in a gentle slope towards the background hills, revealing – astonishing though it now seems – that at that time Vanvitelli had no plans to include the Grand Cascade,

which was to be perhaps the most spectacular and celebrated feature of the whole design. (Indeed, the original proposal was strongly reminiscent of the gardens of Vaux-le-Vicomte, particularly in the layout of its terraces and the steps connecting them.) On the other hand, the design of the central pool clearly formed part of the original scheme, as did the approach to it by way of the 'broad main avenue two miles long, running right to the summit of the hill, to a loggia intended as a place of repose and as a belvedere'. The parterres in front of the loggia were undoubtedly inspired by French and Rococo models: illustrations of Versailles and Marly, published in Paris between 1714 and 1715, were quite widely available in the world in which Vanvitelli grew up and learned his craft, and all his completed architectural work (for example the interiors of the Palazzo Sciarra in Rome) testifies, as do many of his drawings, to the influence of the *rocaille* work of the period. The origins of the great parterres laid out in front of the palace, with their boxwood *broderies* and arabesques (letter K on the plan) are unmistakably French in style. At the sides are avenues of limes (letter N) with long, narrow fountain pools down the middle, and at the centre a symbol of the 'royal rivers' enclosed by four symmetrically arranged circular spaces. Following the route leading in the direction of the hillside, one next encounters a 'circular theatre with limes and espaliered hornbeams' (letter M) among woodland ornamented with statues and fountains.

The harmony and unity of this central section of the garden derives largely from the regular pattern of avenues which Vanvitelli used as a framework for his design. The plan of these various avenues – some wide, some narrow, some running diagonally, some axially – and of the open spaces and circular areas at their intersections, is extremely elaborate, yet its mathematical order, combined with a certain uniformity in the style of the ornamentation throughout, gives it a remarkable homogeneity.

A large rectangular pool, the Peschiera Grande (letter X), with rounded projections at the ends, was laid out on the edge of the woodland – the Vecchio Bosco – and at right angles to the main axis. The other main features flanking the central parterres, ranging from the Renaissance

Aerial view of the park of the Palazzo Reale at Caserta. (Photo Piero Orlandi)

The Palazzo Reale at Caserta: the giardino inglese. *(Photo Giovanni Chiaramonte)*

labyrinth to typically Baroque and even English elements (a *giardino inglese* was laid out a few years after Vanvitelli's death), were designed with the express intention of creating an encyclopaedia of references to the European gardening tradition.

Vanvitelli's great vision for Caserta was fully realized with the addition of the famous fountains and, of course, the cascade, which was built after the completion of the aqueduct. The brief descriptions of the plates make it clear that the garden, as his son Carlo created it, was a simplification of the original plan but that in spite of that it remained faithful in essence to the concept of the master.

The fountains, pools and cascades, together with the sculptural groups – most of which represent mythological hunting scenes – are spectacular setpieces of great originality and inventiveness, the most celebrated of them being the highly dramatic fountain at the foot of the Grand Cascade: its superb sculptures depict the legend of the huntsman Actaeon, who unintentionally glimpsed Diana bathing. This powerful composition, with figures by Paolo Persico, Angelo Brunelli, Pietro Solari and others, forms the visual and symbolic heart of Caserta's gardens. On either side of the cascade two flights of steps rise from a grotto from which gushes the water brought by the great arcaded aqueduct to feed the whole magnificent display.

Bibliography

A. Venditti, 'L'opera napoletana di Luigi Vanvitelli' and C. De Seta, 'Disegni di Luigi Vanvitelli, architetto en scenografo' in *Luigi Vanvitelli* (Naples 1973).
C. De Seta, *Architettura, ambiente e società a Napoli nel Settecento* (Turin 1977).
An up-to-date bibliography is to be found in *Civiltà del '700 a Napoli*, – exhibition catalogue (Florence 1979–80).
C. Knight, *Il giardino inglese di Caserta* (Naples 1988).

The Tiled Gardens
of Southern Portugal
Anne de Stoop

Casa de Fresco at the Quinta da Bacalhoa, near Setúbal; mid-sixteenth century. Detail of the Hispano-Arab azulejo.

Quinta da Bacalhoa, near Setúbal; mid-sixteenth century. The Nile, *western loggia.*

The northern gardens of Portugal, with their giant camellias naturalized at the time of the great discoveries, or their granite statues, are highly unusual, but less intriguing than the gardens of the south which, with their *azulejos* (ceramic tiles) are unique in Europe. Portugal is a subtle mixture of east and west, where European influences are always tempered by a fascination for Asia and a longstanding Arab presence.

The women rarely emerge from their houses, but take their walks in extensive gardens enclosed by high walls. The hot climate encourages movement from the very private courtyard to the more open terrace, then to the large ornamental lake with its summer houses, and on towards the groves of orange and lemon trees. Here, in these deliberately unrelated, almost independent, areas perspective exists only as an illusion created by the brilliance and rhythm of the tiles.

Courtyard gardens
These transitional areas are private, and reserved for certain people. As in the rooms next to them, the walls and ground, and even seats, pools and flower pots are covered or lined with tiles. In these oases nature, tamed, becomes almost abstract. In the royal palace at Sintra the 'verdure' of the tiles seems to accentuate that of the foliage. Until the sixteenth century these Arab-inspired tiles, often made in Spain, had a raised surface with a beading to prevent the colours mingling during the firing. The geometric pattern imposed by these technical constraints gives the whole a repetitive, almost spell-binding harmony. Throughout the centuries these walls, in changing colours, evolved according to contemporary taste, and always the air was filled with the fragrance of flowers and orange blossom, and the sounds of birdsong and murmuring water. Walled courtyards, and more open loggias or terraces were all designed as a paradise for the delight of the senses.

Loggias
Loggias, so well adapted to the Portuguese way of life and climate, first appeared during the Renaissance, and like terraces became characteristic of the country's architecture. These enclosed areas, often without an external staircase,

have no view out on to the surrounding countryside, but instead are designed for enjoyment of the gardens. Here too the *azulejos* open the gates of the imagination. Between 1550 and 1570 the loggia of the Quinta da Bacalhoa, near Setúbal, was decorated with allegorical figures representing rivers. The tiles, now smooth and no longer in relief, were manufactured using the same technique as for earthenware, in which tin, by fixing the colours in

the firing, prevents them from spreading. Since only certain metal oxides can withstand the high firing temperature, the range of colours is restricted: green from copper, blue from cobalt, yellow from antimony, purple from manganese. This proved no limitation however, since the skilful use of the bright colours contributed to the creation of something greater than simple painting on earthenware.

These *Rivers*, inspired by engravings, were no longer derived from geometric Hispano-Arab designs. With the new latitude now permitted to painters came a remarkable increase in the production of *azulejos*, in this land so rich in clay, tin and metal oxides. Some hundred years later, at the end of the seventeenth century, the loggia at the Fronteira Palace near Lisbon became a long terrace, a favourite strolling place leading to the chapel. Here the fanciful ceramic decoration is conceived in relation to the architecture. Among the stonework and reliefs in the style of Della Robbia are to be found tiles depicting antique ornaments and large allegorical figures as well as marble busts and statues. Like the Chinese ceramics and Delft tiles imported into Portugal, these new *azulejos* are blue and white, with some violet highlights. As the painter became more skilled in the technique, he was able to produce finer designs, at the same time drawing his inspiration from a new collection of high quality engravings. An independent area like the courtyards, this terrace also has fountains, seats and flower pots all similarly covered with tiles patterned, very aptly, with pictures of oriental gardens.

In the eighteenth century perhaps the most fitting theme for these terrace gardens, which were transitional areas, was that of the four seasons: bucolic images of the transience of time. These figures are treated as sculptures whose attitudes, clothing and backgrounds change according to the decorative fashion of the time. At the Quinta Grande (great estate) at Damaia (about 1740) the seasons are Baroque in style and painted in blue; at the Pinteus Palace at Loures (about 1755) they are Rococo and polychrome; and at the Barão estate in Carcavelos (about 1770) they are already neo-classical. Sometimes the painters also have recourse to more erudite themes, such as the gods of mythology at the National Palace in Belem, or Christian allegories as in the Quinta Grande in Damaia.

The low cost and the shortage of qualified artists was not the only reason for the abundance of these *trompe l'oeil* pottery tiles in a country where marble is plentiful. Rather it is the Arab tradition of wall-covering, which endured for a long time in this country that had been isolated by the Spanish occupation from 1580 to 1640, and weakened for a long time after.

Quinta dos Azulejos, Lumiar, Lisbon,
1745–75.

Fronteira Palace at Benfica, Lisbon; late
seventeenth century. (Photo Andrea Nulli)

Thus these *azulejos*, which tend by the
intensity of their colour to compensate
for lack of space, are also found in
gardens, around pools, and on seats,
flower pots and enclosing walls.

Water in gardens

Water cisterns, much used by the Arabs,
were transformed in the sixteenth century
into large pools ornamented with decorated walls, or surrounded in the Italian
manner by 'Casas de Fresco'. Like the
loggia, the Casa do Lago (by the lake) at
Bacalhoa, is hung with tiles, with panels
depicting historical, mythological, biblical or ornamental subjects. *Suzannah Bathing* is justly famous for the delicacy of the
design, the treatment of colour, and the
unusual addition of a date – 1565. Some
years later in the Fronteira Palace near Lisbon, the chief feature is the water mirror
which reflects a sort of Pantheon to the
glory of Portugal liberated from the Spanish yoke. The tiled panels depict fourteen
life-size knights in blue and white. Portrayed as Atlases symbolically supporting
the Gallery of Kings, rather than as
images of beauty, they are executed in
bright colour and rapid brush strokes,
firmly in the Portuguese tradition.

Throughout the eighteenth and nineteenth centuries *azulejos* continued to be
used to glorify water, to become identified with it, even to deify it. The mythological figures at the Pinteus Palace near
Loures, or the heroes from Ovid's metamorphoses on the Correio-Mor estate in
Loures were particularly apt decorations
for ornamental pools.

But the most famous of these celebrations of water is undoubtedly the Cas-
cata da Taveira on the Marquez de
Pombal's estate at Oeiras. There the
walls, covered with almost 12,000 tiles,
seem to have become limpid streams
where divinities and sea creatures disport
themselves, painted in monochrome blue
after engravings by Claude-Joseph Vernet, about 1770.

The Portuguese seemed nevertheless
to prefer less academic subjects, scenes
from daily life, which came into fashion in
the seventeenth century. A typical group
can be seen in the royal palace at Queluz,
where the water is treated as a mirror,
throwing back an image of life itself.
Along the banks of the Rio Jamor, on
four walls each 115 metres (377 feet) long,
are hung 55,000 tiles by João Antunes.

The Gardens of Benfica. *Painting by
J. Pillement, 1785. Musée des Arts
Décoratifs, Paris.*

They depict, like reflections, the duties and diversions of the courtiers. Such poems of daily life can also be found on innumerable smaller fountains, such as the one on the Arriaga estate at Sintra, dating from about 1780. There are even splendid biblical scenes, such as the Marriage at Cana, painted by Basalisa in about 1920 in blue cameo to resemble frescoes, beside the spring on the Pombal estate at Sintra.

Azulejos are everywhere, unifying unrelated areas – patios, loggias and gardens. They are used to make transitions from terraces down steps and low walls; they become a sort of immovable furnishing on seats and flower troughs, and they make the high enclosing walls throb with colour and life.

*Gardens and groundwork: walls,
seats and flower troughs*

Azulejos on steps and retaining walls helped to lend charm to the many differences in level caused by the problems of terracing at the time. These mounds of earth when suitably arranged became enormous screens where, in blue and white, mythological scenes were enacted, as on the Marquez de Pombal's estate at Oeiras (*c.* 1765). Rustic scenes or even fabulous exotic forests in *trompe l'oeil* also appear, painted by Luis Ferreira, on the estates of São Mateus at Dafundo and the Assunção at Belas (mid-nineteenth century).

Gardens were sometimes designed as green arbours. For the sake of order and easier watering flowers were often grown in troughs, diffusing their scent – essential in Portuguese gardens – over the adjacent seats. The decor of these 'rooms', intended to be contemplated at leisure, was always very carefully conceived. A veritable display of fireworks is to be found at the Quinta dos Azulejos at Lumiar. Here everything seems designed above all to explore the decorative possibilities of the tiles, which have become at the same time powerful polychrome sculptures in circles of relief, and mannered pictures in the style of Watteau (1745–1775).

Differences in level are often emphasized by low walls which require less maintenance than hedges. Highly symbolic figures of the *Labours of the Months* can be seen at the Fronteira Palace; and the Mitra Palace in Loures has equally symbolic *Baskets of Flowers*. Lastly but more rarely, the walls of these arbours may be enlivened by *trompe l'oeil* paintings of characters: dark and light blue for the gods of mythology at the Military College in Carnide (1750–1760) and lively polychrome for the good-natured citizens at Quinta Nova da Assunção.

Behind these high walls, overhung by the occasional orange-tree bough, lies a wealth of hidden beauty.

Bibliography

A. de Stoop, *Stately Homes and Houses in the Vicinity of Lisbon.* (English edn Oporto 1989).

H. Carita and H. Cardoso, *Tratado da Grandesa dos Jardins em Portugal, ou da Originalidade e Desaires desta Arte* (Lisbon 1987).

The Imperial Gardens of Russia

Peter Hayden

While there had been imperial gardens in Moscow since the fifteenth century, there was nothing in Russia to rival the best gardens of western Europe until the reign of Peter the Great. Peter visited gardens in Berlin, Holland and England in 1697–98 and, although he did not visit France until 1717, he learned much about French gardens from books and engravings. In and near his new city, St Petersburg, he was determined to create parks and gardens which would be second to none and he engaged gardeners and architects from abroad to help realize that ambition.

The Summer Garden, begun in 1704, was influenced by the Dutch gardens Peter had seen and by French gardens he had read about. There were many fountains, including a series of fountain statues based on Aesop's fables, and a fine collection of more than two hundred statues from Italy of which about ninety survive. Lines of trees were clipped to form green walls and tunnels, and single trees were shaped into balls, cubes and pyramids.

The palace at Strelna was built on a natural terrace overlooking the Gulf of Finland with an upper and lower park. There were canals, which still survive, and fountains, but the water supply was inadequate and Peter concentrated his attention instead on Peterhof (now Petrodvorets), where the palace was built on the same natural terrace as Strelna with an upper and lower park. An excellent water supply, conducted by canal from the hills near the palace of Ropsha, twenty kilometres (twelve miles) or so away, feeds one of the world's greatest water gardens. The basins in the Upper Park serve as reservoirs for the cascades and the many fountains, including some good trick fountains, in the Lower Park. The most spectacular water feature is the Great Cascade where the water flows from under the palace and down marble steps below its sea-facing façade to the Samson Fountain and then along the canal to the sea. Samson wrestles with the lion and, its jaw having been forced open, a jet of water gushes high into the air. This contest symbolized the war with Sweden which ended in a Russian victory and the recovery of her Baltic lands. J. F. Braunstein was the first architect at Peterhof, but Alexandre Le Blond made the major contribution. He was succeeded by Niccolo Michetti, while Bartolomeo Ras-

trelli later enlarged the palace and the Upper Park for the Empress Elizabeth.

Prince Alexander Menshikov's palace at Oranienbaum (now Lomonosov) was built a few kilometres beyond Peterhof on the same natural terrace overlooking the Gulf of Finland and was also linked by canal to the sea. It became an imperial palace in 1743 as the summer residence of the future Peter III, ill-fated husband of Catherine the Great. The Italian architect Antonio Rinaldi built a palace-fortress complex, Peterstadt, for Peter to house his Holstein regiment. The most impressive building at Oranienbaum is Rinaldi's Sliding Hill Pavilion, which was once associated with an elaborate version of the Russian sliding hill, ancestor of the modern roller coaster.

There are two palaces at Tsarskoe Selo (Pushkin), one remodelled by Rastrelli for the Empress Elizabeth, but called 'Catherine's', and Giacomo Quarenghi's palace for Alexander I. The earlier palace has impressive formal gardens with bosquets, avenues, statues and some notable garden buildings, Rastrelli's Hermitage and Grotto among them. Catherine the Great was a devotee of the English landscaping style, and John Busch, a Hanoverian by birth, was persuaded to sell his nursery in north London and to go to St Petersburg to lay out gardens for her. He worked with Vasily Neelov at Tsarskoe Selo, where the regular basin became an irregular lake, 'natural' watercourses and pools were introduced, a good deal of earth was rearranged and many trees were planted as nature might have disposed them. At the end of the lake Neelov designed a fine Palladian bridge, inspired by the bridge in the park at Wilton in England. Charles Cameron, the Scottish architect, designed a number of buildings here for Catherine, the most important being the Cameron Gallery, a covered promenade attached to the palace, from which Catherine could look out over the formal garden, the landscape park and the model town of Sofia, also by Cameron, the streets of which were aligned with the Cameron Gallery. Among the structures in the park were a number of monuments commemorating victories in the wars against the Turks.

Near to Moscow, at Tsaritsyno, Vasily Bazhenov was engaged to build a palace and various other buildings in the Russian Gothic style for Catherine, but she

Samson Fountain and part of the Great Cascade at Peterhof.

View of a pavilion in the park of Kuskovo: engraving.

General plan of the park of Kuskovo, the property of Prince Ceremetiov, near Moscow. Engraving, 1788.

was offended by his use of Masonic symbols in the ornament of the buildings – Freemasons had plotted to place her son the Grand Duke Paul on the throne in her place – and ordered their demolition. New buildings were designed by Mattei Kazakov, but were left unfinished when she died. They were set in a hilly wooded park with some fine pavilions and artificial ruins.

Pavlovsk, near to Tsarskoe Selo, was the home of the Grand Duke Paul and his wife Maria Fedorovna, a princess from Württemberg. It is with the latter that the park is particularly associated, for she closely supervised its development, and its sentimental pastoral style, with a dairy, a charcoal burner's hut and a hermit's cell, echoed the parks she had known in her youth. Cameron designed the palace, laid out the gardens around it and began the landscaping of the valley of the Slavianka. He also designed some outstanding park buildings including the Temple of Friendship, the Apollo Colonnade, the Monument to the Parents, the Aviary and the Temple of the Three Graces. After Paul became Emperor Vicenzo Brenna laid out areas of the park in a more ceremonial style including the Old Sylvia, a large circular clearing from which twelve paths radiate. A statue of Apollo stands in the centre with statues of the nine Muses and Mercury, Neptune and Flora on the circumference of the circle. After Paul's death Pietro Gonzaga, turning to landscaping towards the end of a distinguished career as a theatre and stage designer, transformed the parade ground into a landscape of meadow, wood and water. He later landscaped the large flat tract known as the White Birches, taking as his model the northern Russian landscape of meadow and forest.

Paul's favourite park was Gatchina, where the heart of the composition is a group of interconnected picturesque lakes with water of exceptional clarity. Their surfaces reflect the architectural features and the trees along the shore and on the skilfully placed islands. The landscaping is attributed to John Busch. His son, Joseph, landscaped Elagin Island, an occasional residence of Maria Fedorovna in the estuary of the Neva, working with Carlo Rossi who remodelled the palace and designed the park buildings.

Five landscape parks were created at Peterhof – the English Park for Catherine

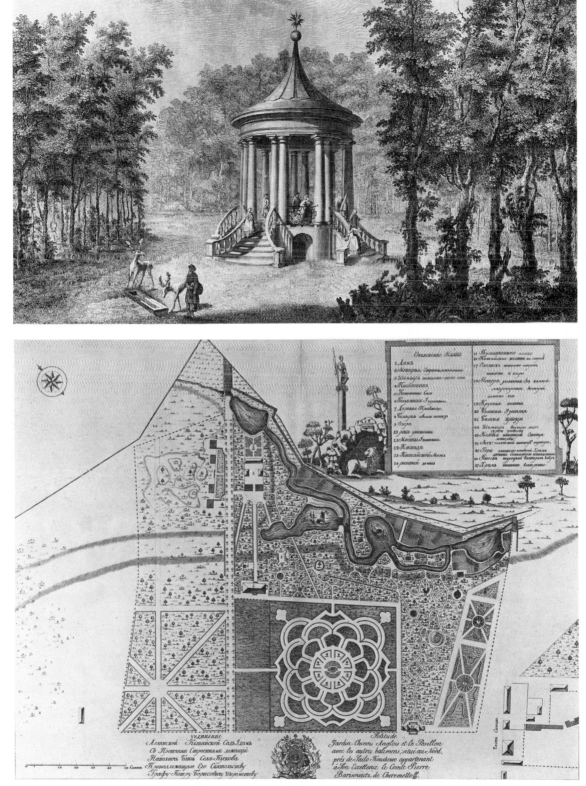

The lake at Tsarskoe Selo, with the grotto by Rastrelli ornamented with masks of Neptune, tritons, nereids, dolphins and sea-horses.

by James Meader, the setting for Quarenghi's English Palace; the Alexandria Park with the Cottage Palace both by Adam Menelaws for Nicholas I; the Aleksandrinskii (now Proletarskii) Park, by Menelaws and others; and the Kolonistkii and Lugovoi Parks, both for Nicholas I. There are also two former imperial parks near Yalta, at Livadia and Oreanda.

Bibliography

V. Ya. Kurbatov, *Sady i parki* (Petrograd 1916).

A. N. Petrov and others, *Pamiatniki arkhitectury prigorodov Leningrada* (Leningrad 1983).

A. S. Elkina, *Gatchina* (Leningrad 1980).

A. Raskin, *Gorod Lomonosov* (Leningrad 1979).

A. Raskin, *Petrodvorets* – in English (Leningrad 1978).

A. Kuchumov, *Pavlovsk: Palace and Park* – in English (Leningrad 1975).

The 'Ideas'
of René de Girardin
at Ermenonville

Antoinette Le Normand Romain

When the Marquis de Girardin (1735–1808) took possession of the Ermenonville estate in 1766, he found at the bottom of a small, marshy valley a château – which cut the terrain in two – consisting of a quadrangle flanked by towers, surrounded by running water. Making the most of the available natural resources, he decided to create a park after the manner of those he had admired in England. Completed in 1779, much visited and often painted, the park reached the peak of its success with the visit and death of Rousseau, who was buried on the Ile des Peupliers (Isle of Poplars) on 4 July 1778.

'*Ajouter et composer*' (increase and integrate) – these were René de Girardin's guiding principles. For although the name of Hubert Robert (whose part has never been clearly defined) has always been mentioned in connection with Ermenonville, and although the landscape architect Morel certainly assisted Girardin, Ermenonville is in all respects, in its conception and its realization, the work of its proprietor. Mayer has left us his portrait, in work clothes, wearing knee-length boots, stick in hand, his face protected by a wide-brimmed hat.[1] It is indeed his personality which is reflected in the park, the lessons of his day-to-day experiences which are set out in his treatise, published in Geneva in 1777, entitled '*Of the composition of landscapes, or ways of embellishing the land surrounding dwellings by bringing together what is pleasurable with what is useful.*'[2]

However, his principal merit lay in the flair which enabled him to recognize instinctively, as a true artist, the essential 'pictures' which together would constitute the park. He began, it seems, by creating the one in the north: in this area, by demolishing a French-style parterre, he devised an artificial stream which also drained the land. Along its banks *fabriques* of Italian (Moulin Neuf) or medieval inspiration (Tour Gabrielle) were skilfully placed, adding considerable depth to the perspective. To the south, the work was on a larger scale. Girardin wanted to make the great hall, which formed the central part of the château, a viewpoint from which all the different aspects of the park could be seen. He therefore began by demolishing the south wing in order that the courtyard, which he dug up and planted, should open on to the park. In

front of the château, the busy road from Senlis to Meaux was incorporated into the landscape to enliven the scene, while the kitchen garden beyond became an ornamental lake fed by the Petit Etang (small pool) which cascaded into it over the former retaining wall. The stark lines of the wall were softened, and the design of the upper pool and the undulations of the ground altered in their turn. This was doubtless done with the help of Mayer, who was familiar with Ermenonville, of which he left several views in addition to the Marquis' portrait. *Fabriques* were erected on the slopes of this natural hollow: the Ice House and the Temple of Modern Philosophy, built about 1775 and left unfinished rather than 'ruined', unlike its model the Temple of Tivoli, since philosophy was *nondum perfectae* (not yet brought to perfection): unfinished or

rough-hewn stones wait to this day to be lifted on to the six columns already raised to the glory of six philosophers who had advanced the progress of the human race – Descartes, Newton, Penn, Montesquieu, Voltaire and Rousseau.

In 1780 Rousseau's tomb was erected in its final form, as designed by Hubert Robert (or d'Aubert?)[3] and with reliefs by Lesueur, and Girardin put the finishing touches to the tableau. Fortunately it has come down to us virtually unaltered, as has the Désert, an expanse of sandy wasteland, strewn with rocks and

covered with pine, heather and broom – hardly touched by the Marquis, who did no more than build a hermitage here, on which he placed inscriptions chosen to emphasize the natural solitude of the place.

This multiplicity of inscriptions in French, Latin, English and Italian, designed to guide the mind of the visitor, reflected Girardin's own tastes, ideas and beliefs. They made it easier to understand the meaning of the 'pictures', over which the owner had pondered both as philosopher and as artist, by making preparatory drawings – 'the only way to write down one's idea in order to know exactly what it is before putting it into practice.'[4]

By chance, more than eighty drawings have come down to us. They were collected in an album[5] by René de Girardin's great-grandson, who doubtless found them in portfolios grouped by subjects: plans for *fabriques* (to which Girardin confusingly applied the mistranslation 'factories'), 'sketches of views of Ermenonville as they were composed before they were carried out on site', plans for altering the château.[6] They are in no way architectural drawings, but are mostly quite small and done in pencil or ink on cream or bluish paper in a rather unsophisticated and precise manner – the inscriptions are still legible – like small pictures, with plans carefully shown, and enlivened with drawings of individuals engaged in various activities. They make up a collection of 'ideas' which sheds light on Girardin's sources of inspiration, particularly with reference to England, which he had visited before undertaking the transformation of the park. They are also of interest for the evidence they give of his twin concerns – to please the eye and to 'speak to the heart and the imagination.'[7] Sometimes he is concerned with the fundamental arrangement of a picture – in the Bois du Rossignol (Nightingale Wood), where he was planning the layout of an uneven area, should he make a bower of greenery and a waterfall, or perhaps a more formal composition inspired by the fountain of the nymph Egeria, which he had visited in Rome with his son in 1775? 'It is at present only a great arcade fallen into decay, with six recesses where formerly there were statues, one of which still lies there broken (. . . .) water still flows there abundantly'.[8] Sometimes he hesitates about how to present a view: for instance, he thought at first of placing, in the foreground of the Prairie Arcadienne (Arcadian Meadow), a sarcophagus bearing the famous inscription '*Et in Arcadia ego*' (I too have lived in Arcady), but his natural optimism led him to prefer something less melancholy, and it was a reed hut, the Cabane de Philémon et Baucis, which he finally placed there, recalling the golden age he believed might return.

The plans for the transformation of the château make a particularly interesting series. Girardin had no thought of rebuilding, but rather of restoring it, and while he often follows the French tradition, he is sometimes carried away by his admiration for English castles and Italian villas: monumental staircases sweep down to the water, and a loggia based unmistakably on the one at the Villa Medici, spans the ground floor.

Elsewhere, Italian and medieval references mingle in a plan which consequently is reminiscent, in its eclecticism and its proportions, of England: windows divided by slender columns are let into the far ends of two short wings which flank a massive portico with a triangular pediment; a series of flat roofs is surmounted by a belvedere; and the château is linked to the surrounding countryside by a covered bridge in the Renaissance style.

The Egeria fountain was never built nor was the château altered. Very soon the gardens began to deteriorate: on the night of 7 December 1787 a violent storm devastated the Prairie Arcadienne and burst the embankment of the Petit Etang – neither of them was restored, and by that time Girardin had left France. After the fall of the Bastille the inscriptions, condemned as 'feudal', were destroyed. Finally it was decided to transfer Rousseau's ashes to the Panthéon, and this was done on 9 October 1794. Throughout the nineteenth century the park remained more or less abandoned, but in shedding some of its trappings which belonged to a very precise period in the history of taste, it has only become more beautiful. In revealing Girardin's talent for 'composing landscapes' it helps us to recognize 'nature understood and managed by a great artist.'[9]

[1] Former Girardin collection – Abbaye de Chaalis, Musée Jacquemart-André.
[2] R. de Girardin, *De la composition des paysages ou des moyens d'embellir la nature autour des habitations en joignant l'agréable à l'utile.*
[3] Louis Gillet, 'La collection Girardin à Chaalis. Le reliquaire de Jean-Jacques', in *Revue des Deux Mondes* (1 September 1925), pp. 134–59.
[4] R. de Girardin, *op. cit.*, p. 21.
[5] *Dessins originaux. Croquis au crayon et à l'encre du marquis René de Girardin, vicomte d'Ermenonville, concernant sa terre d'Ermenonville, comté de

The park of Ermenonville (Oise): the Ile des Peupliers. (Photo Fulvio Ventura)

Senlis, Isle de France. Projets et exécution définitive. Le tout recueilli et classé par le comte Fernand de Girardin. Private collection.
6 The existence of the portfolios, possibly simple paper packets, can be deduced from their headings handwritten by René de Girardin (note the use of English words – factories, prospect) cut out and stuck on one of the first pages of the album.
7 R. de Girardin, op. cit., p. 44.
8 Stanislas de Girardin to his mother, 9 November 1775. Letters from Switzerland and Italy written by René de Girardin and his son, 1775–1776, manuscripts. Private collection.
9 Louis Gillet, Abbaye de Chaalis et musée Jacquemart-André. Notice et guide sommaire des Monuments, des Collections et de la Promenade du Désert (1933) p. 184.

Bibliography

René de Girardin, *De la composition . . .* (Paris and Geneva 1777). New edition with postscript by M. H. Conan (Paris 1979).
Promenade et itinéraire des jardins d'Ermenonville (Paris 1786 and 1811). May have been edited by Stanislas de Girardin. With 25 engraved plates by Mérigot after the Girardin family drawings.
André Martin-Decaen, *Le dernier ami de J. J. Rousseau. Le marquis René de Girardin d'après des documents inédits* (Paris 1912). With full bibliography.
Antoinette Le Normand, *Ermenonville 1766–1794*. Notes for thesis, University of Paris – Nanterre, 1974. Typescript.

The Gardens
of Hubert Robert

Jean de Cayeux

The Landing: *painting by H. Robert (1733–1808). The Fine Arts Museums of San Francisco.*

In an important but as yet unpublished text the architect Pierre-Adrien Pâris (1745–1819), who was responsible for Louis XVI's *Menus Plaisirs* or 'Amusements', reveals his *Réflexions sur le caractère particulier des jardins romains*.[1]

It is an abuse of our capacity for comparison to attempt to find a similarity between objects which are too unlike. I have often heard parallels drawn between Roman and English gardens in an attempt to decide which are preferable. It seems to me that such discussion is a waste of time. Each style has its own particular attractions, not found in the other, resulting from climate and situation, and it would be as difficult to create English gardens in Rome as it is to create Roman gardens anywhere else . . .

What adds further to the great charm of Roman gardens is the impression of dignity imposed by the hand of time. Created in times of great wealth, with all forms of art readily available, they have suffered neglect owing to changes in the water table and other natural causes. Nature has in a way reclaimed her rights, triumphing over art, and the two have combined to produce the most picturesque of effects. This neglect, this decay, this rampant vegetation make wonderful pictures. . . . Roman gardens excite in me an enthusiasm for the Arts, evoke the memory of great ideas and lead me to meditate on events which have changed the world physically and morally. These antique noble marbles seem to me to have been placed there by those famous Romans whose features are traced on the statues all around me.

These *Réflexions* seem a perfect commentary on the greater part of the work of the greatest French landscape painter of all time Hubert Robert, who was moreover a friend of Pâris.[2] Antique ruins overrun by vegetation and haunted by shepherds, the picturesque intrusion of everyday life into the heart of ruins of former grandeur, parasol pines casting their shade on tombs and statues; such images penetrated so deep into the spirit of the artist from the days of his apprenticeship, that they were to haunt the whole of his work. Atmosphere, memories, variations on an imagination always ready to merge the real with the fanciful: Hubert Robert appears, indeed, as an 'inventor', a 'composer' of landscapes, whence this special taste for gardens.

We know that the young painter, whose patron was the Comte de Stainville, future Duc de Choiseul, spent eleven years in Rome during which time he familiarized himself not only with the

ruins and monuments of antiquity and the Renaissance, but also with famous gardens, both urban and suburban. He sketched and painted abandoned gardens as well as the more or less well-maintained ones of the most famous villas: Albani, Borghese, Farnese, Madama, Mattei or Sacchetti.[3] While in Naples he sketched the gardens of Portici and, at nearby Pozzuoli, the ruins of the temple of Serapis, reminiscent of a vast wild garden. But the most interesting group concerns the estates on the outskirts of Rome. Thus in Tivoli he stayed at the Villa d'Este, which the Abbé de St-Non had rented, and where he found himself in the company of another famous painter, Fragonard. He was also inspired by the

diverse charms of the gardens of the Farnese palace at Caprarola, and perhaps even more by that of Frascati, a summer refuge from the unhealthy climate in Rome; there he made further sketches of the Pamphili, Aldobrandini and Conti gardens. When he returned to France, Hubert Robert made the most of his rich harvest. From his sketches he painted a whole series of pictures which were regularly included at the Salon between 1767 and 1775. But the memory of his wanderings in Rome was to remain with him for the rest of his life: thus *La Fontaine* and *Le Jet d'Eau* (Baltimore, U.S.A.) were doubtless painted in 1793 while he was imprisoned in St Lazare during the Revolution!

The same mixture of 'wild' and 'tamed', of grandeur and neglect, could be found at that time in certain of the great royal estates on the outskirts of Paris, where overgrown foliage had gradually ravaged the original classical order. And so the painter loved to linger at St Cloud, whose fountain of La Gerbe became a sort of leitmotif, on the melancholy terraces of Marly, or in the shady green tunnels of Rambouillet. But the 'painter of gardens', sensitive to the logic of the landscaped garden, was soon to become one of the masters of this style, a quite independent 'gardener'. On the advice of the Comte d'Angiviller, his director of buildings, the young King Louis XVI, who had decided to proceed forthwith with the essential replacement of over-mature trees in the park at Versailles, commissioned Robert to record a 'spectacle which would not be seen again within a century.' Thus in the 1777 Salon were exhibited paintings entitled *La Vue des jardins de Versailles vers le Tapis Vert au moment de l'abattage des arbres* and the *Vue du Bosquet des Bains d'Apollon lors de l'abattage des arbres* (Views of parts of the gardens at Versailles at the time of felling the trees – see illustration p. 529). This latter canvas, on which appears a fragment of the *Chevaux d'Apollon*, can be regarded as a precursor of the first great achievement of the painter as a creator of gardens. That same year he was commissioned to draw up a plan for a new development for the grove of the Bains d'Apollon, which he successfully accomplished in collaboration with Thévenin between 1777 and 1780. He devised a monumental and picturesque, almost operatic, arrangement: the entrance to a vast architectural grotto represents the portals of the palace of Thetis, where stands Apollo surrounded by his nymphs. As a result of this work Robert was appointed 'Designer of the King's Gardens' (1778), an office which had lain vacant since the death of the great Le Nôtre. Subsequently, he collaborated with Mique in creating for Queen Marie-Antoinette the gardens of the Petit Trianon, and in particular the plan for the Hameau with its rustic dwellings. There is more evidence for his role at Rambouillet, an estate acquired by Louis XVI in 1783 from his cousin Penthièvre, where we know that Robert drew up plans for the new gardens. He also worked with

Rocky Landscape with Figures near a
Waterfall: *painting by H. Robert. Private
collection, Paris.*

Thèvenin on the superb Queen's Dairy
where according to the fashion of the
time aristocratic ladies would drink milk
and taste cheese or offer these to their
guests. This complex and extravagant
structure was inspired by Cicero's Amalthaeum at Arpinum.[4]

Parallel with these 'official' projects,
Robert also undertook commissions for
noblemen who were both art collectors
and garden-lovers. Numerous drawings
in red chalk and contemporary accounts
reveal that he was a regular visitor to the
estate of Claude-Henri Watelet, the celebrated Moulin-Joli, situated on an island
in the Seine at Colombes, the truly rustic
charm of which he greatly appreciated.[5]
An interesting correspondence between
the painter and the wealthy farmer-
general de Laborde follows the progress
between 1786 and 1790 of the work he
carried out on the park at Méréville,
where he succeeded the architect
Bélanger. The very numerous works
(drawings and paintings) that survive in
connection with this estate provide an
opportunity to appreciate the full ambiguity of the relationship between gardens
and painting, so difficult is it to distinguish between sketches of the actual
gardens, plans for improvement and purely imaginary views.[6] In many of them the
element of the 'pastoral' or the 'picturesque' gives place to the 'sublime'.

The part that Robert was able to take in
the work at Ermenonville remains uncertain, so jealously did the proprietor, the
Marquis de Girardin, apparently guard
the preservation of his entire inheritance.[7]
Nevertheless, many 'views' of the park
occupy a not inconsiderable place in
Robert's pictorial works: the Temple of
Philosophy, reminiscent of that of the
Sybil in Tivoli, for example, or the
Brasserie (brew-house) with its thatched
roof. We know, moreover, that the actual
tomb – now empty – of Jean-Jacques
Rousseau on the Ile des Peupliers was
carved by Philippe Lesueur after designs
by Hubert Robert. Curiously, fifteen
years later, when the philosopher's
remains were transferred to the Panthéon, the artist was to paint two superb
canvasses of the provisional tomb erected
in the middle of the lake in the Tuileries.[8]
It seems that Hubert Robert, who benefited from the protection and friendship
of the noblest in the land, and who was
often invited to stay in their country

The Rustic Pavilion: *painting by H. Robert. Private collection, Dublin.*

Hornbeam Arbour in a Park: *drawing by H. Robert. Institut Néerlandais, Paris.*

residences, was induced to offer his advice far and wide, if not to produce more developed plans. This was the case particularly for the Maréchal de Noailles at St Germain, an estate which no longer exists. On the other hand, the last garden where he was in charge of the works, as is attested by recently discovered documents, was the one which he designed for Lafayette at the château of Lagrange in Brie (1800–1801).

With his knowledge of Rome and the Ile-de-France and his sound grasp of ideas from across the Channel, Hubert Robert is a perfect example of a 'painter-gardener'. From the 'idea' to the 'created landscape' on the canvas, he came quite naturally to the arranged landscape in nature. Here there was no looking back, no reference to Claude, to Berchem, or to Salvator Rosa, but instead almost unique innovation. Even bearing in mind the dual role of the Englishman William Kent half a century earlier,[9] never has an artist presented with such skill the other side of the picture.

[1] The entire works and archives of the architect Pierre-Adrien Pâris were bequeathed to the municipal library in Besançon (Doubs) where he was born. This text occurs in Volume 480: *Etudes d'architecture, Volume III, Palais.* Pâris also made numerous surveys of the gardens around Rome during his time at the Academy (1771–1774) as well as fine watercolours and drawings in red chalk which have sometimes been mistaken for those of his friend Hubert Robert, some of whose works were in his collections. Until the publication of a monograph, reference can be made to the earlier book of A. Estignard, *P.-A. Pâris, sa vie, ses oeuvres, ses collections* (Paris 1902), and also to E. de Ganay, 'L'architecte P.-A. Pâris' in *Revue de l'Art Ancien et Moderne* (June-Dec. 1924), pp. 249–64.
[2] The bibliography in respect of Hubert Robert is very extensive. Obviously, therefore, reference must be made, for a full and up-to-date account, to Jean de Cayeux's very recent biography, *Hubert Robert* (Paris 1989). Concerning the role of the painter in the sphere of gardens see Jean de Cayeux, *Hubert Robert et les jardins* (Paris 1987).
[3] Very comprehensive sets of these views of Italian villas are preserved in the Louvre in Paris, the Hermitage in Leningrad, the Metropolitan Museum in New York, the Albertina in Vienna and the Musée de Valence (France).
[4] The similarity between the 'rock' of the Bains d'Apollon and the Dairy at Rambouillet has moreover been quite fully explained else-

where. See Henri Lavagne 'L'Amalthaeum de Cicéron et la "Laiterie de la Reine" au château de Rambouillet', in *La Mythologie, Clef de lecture du monde classique, Hommage à R. Chevallier* (Tours 1986) pp. 467–74.
[5] One of the best documentary and historial analyses is to be found in Dora Wiebenson's book *The Picturesque Garden in France* (Princeton 1978).
[6] A certain number of these works, such as those at Sceaux and in the Nationalmuseum in Stockholm are reproduced in J. de Cayeux, *Hubert Robert et les jardins*, pp. 102–12. It is important to note that some of the garden furnishings from the park at Méréville were taken in the nineteenth century to another park on the Essonne, to the south of Paris at Jeurre. In fact the site at Méréville, although very dilapidated, still retains the entire original structure of the park, and it is to be hoped that a way will very soon be found to protect it.
[7] See, in this book, Antoinette Le Normand-Romain's article on René de Girardin and Ermenonville.
[8] These pictures which can be seen, respectively, at the Musée Carnavalet (Paris) and in Dublin, show a Doric pavilion in some way reminiscent of Cook's monument in the park at Méréville. However, it has not so far been proved that Robert was responsible for the project.
[9] See John Dixon Hunt, *William Kent, Landscape Garden Designer* (London 1987); and in this volume, the article by Elisabetta Cereghini.

The Character of the Tree:
from Alexander Cozens
to Richard Payne Knight

Alessandra Ponte

At Downton and Foxley, the parks created at the end of the eighteenth century by the two great leaders of the Picturesque Movement, Richard Payne Knight (1751–1824) and Uvedale Price (1747–1829), there are no temples, columns, statues, inscriptions, rustic cottages, Chinese pavilions or other artificial elements of any kind to interrupt the natural landscape. Knight condemned the temples and pagodas transplanted into eighteenth-century English gardens as 'excrescences without meaning'.[1] An essential characteristic of the Picturesque garden was the concealment of artistry; any artificial features had to be discreet, disguised, with an air of impermanence about them, as if their lifespan was no longer than that of the plants and trees around them. The Alpine Bridge at Downtown, the subject of a painting by Thomas Hearne,[2] was little more than a few boards held up by tree trunks, and not a sign of it now remains. The rough stones depicted by William Owen[3] in his watercolour *The Roman Bath* formed part of three small rooms which looked more like grottoes or Druid caves than pieces of classical architecture; even then they were partially concealed by undergrowth and bushes and now they are completely overgrown.

At Foxley, Uvedale Price was even more restrained. In the drawing by his friend Thomas Gainsborough *Beech Trees in the Wood at Foxley with Yazor Church in the Distance*, the only artificial element to be seen, apart from the church spire in the village, is a fence of entwined branches; the path is a narrow dirt track.[4] A few lithographs of Foxley, dating from about 1830, show only trees, fields and woods, with the house a long way off and almost hidden by vegetation.[5]

If we think of great eighteenth-century gardens in the landscape tradition such as Stowe, Rousham, Stourhead or Chiswick, with their temples, inscriptions, grottoes and obelisks, and their literary and classical allusions, these Picturesque parks and gardens seem mute and inexpressive by comparison. If their architectural and sculptural elements were removed, all that would remain would be rocks, water and trees to stamp them with a character and personality of their own, or to identify them as work of art. If in fact the creation of a park is to be considered art, on an equal footing with

poetry and painting, surely something more is required of them than simply the imitation of nature. As Knight observed in his treatise on taste (first published in 1805), only the ignorant derive pleasure from art that is mere imitation. For the cultured, the pleasures of imitative art are quickly exhausted and cannot hope to offer 'something of character and expression, which may awaken sympathy, excite new ideas, or expand and elevate those already formed.'[6] Knight was a supporter of the principles that motivated the Scottish school and a convinced believer in the theories of Edmund Burke. As he explained in discussion with Price, a picturesque quality is just one of the many characteristics of a landscaped park or garden, and he went on to list some of the others: a classical landscape ornamented with fragments of antique statuary or columns, evocative of classical literature and the ancient world; a wild romantic landscape, full of surprises and excitements to stimulate the imagination; pastoral scenes with shepherds, flocks of

sheep, fields and cottages, reminiscent, to the well-read and educated, of pastoral poetry and paintings. Picturesque landscapes were powerful reminders of the work of the great Venetian and Flemish landscape painters, of Poussin, Claude and Salvator Rosa. Picturesque, Knight firmly maintained, meant 'in the manner of the painters', and a landscaped park laid out in accordance with their view of nature, complete with the elements that were characteristic of their particular vision of the world, was a source of pleasure and satisfaction because, through a knowledge of their work, it seemed familiar and in some way preordained.[7] Apart from their agreement on this question, Knight and Price were also fully in accordance over the use of natural materials in the design of a park or garden, and over the principles of landscaping. Theirs were not the only voices raised in favour of 'nature' and against the introduction of extraneous sculpture and architectural features in order to impose character on the garden. John Dalrymple,

writing in his treatise on the garden in the mid-eighteenth century, underlined the fact that nature herself impresses certain distinct characteristics on the landscape;[8] in *Observations on Modern Gardening* (1765), Whately records in a well-known passage,

. . . even without the assistance of buildings, or other adventitious circumstances, nature alone furnishes materials for scenes, which may be adapted to almost every kind of expression; their operation is general, and their consequences infinite: the mind is elevated, depressed or composed, as gaiety, gloom or tranquillity, prevail in the scene . . .[9]

One must bear in mind of course that the 'nature' Whately refers to here is not nature in its true aspect but a nature that has been re-ordered and re-designed. William Gilpin, the author of a number of guides to the wildest and most picturesque areas of England, intended for amateur painters and for lovers of remote and desolate country, warns that natural scenes only rarely lend themselves to

Languid or Delicate, Penetrating, Engaging, Good-natured, Timid, Cheerful, Artful, and Innocent. These qualities could be variously represented by combining different elements, which Cozens subdivided into the six facial features – the forehead, nose, mouth, chin, eyebrow and eye, each having between two and sixteen variations. He employed the same method in another, much more ambitious, project which was never completed, *The Various Species of . . . Landscape in Nature*. The frontispiece of one of the published sections of this enormous work lists sixteen types of landscape, fourteen categories of 'object' (such as rocks, water, woods, buildings etc.) and twenty-seven 'circumstances' (the times of the day, the seasons, the weather conditions). According to Cozens, different moods and feelings correspond to different types of landscape: surprise, fear and superstition belong to the abyss or ravine; peace, melancholy, terror and alarm to a chain of Alpine peaks; serenity, pleasure, coolness and freshness to lakes and seas; an expansive happiness, freedom and grandeur to a landscape of wide open spaces . . . Two other sections of this project should also be mentioned in this context: *The Shape, Skeleton and Foliage of Thirty-Two Species of Trees* (1771) and the series of 'Skies' which appeared with the famous *New Method*. Cozen's study of trees and clouds corresponded precisely with his analysis of the features of the human face. While the character of a face can be conveyed by combining features in different permutations, that of a landscape results from the combination of different 'objects' and 'circumstances'.[11]

In his poem *The Landscape* (1794), Knight proposed theories similar to those of Cozens, drawing analogies between the methods used by painters and sculptors to express the character of the human face and the means employed in the art of garden design to impose a particular character on the landscape. Knight recounted in verse the eighteenth-century myth of the noble savage who spoke the 'language of action' through his facial expressions and the movements of his limbs. The Greek artists had learned to communicate this language through their sculpture, representing mental impulses and reactions in the expression of a face or the attitude of a body, free from the constraints imposed by rules of aesthetics

being depicted as they are: they need to be adapted and transformed, to have features added or subtracted, in order to convey reality as convincingly as the works of the great masters of landscape painting. In one of his guides he writes that he always sets himself the task 'of not barely examining the face of a country; but of examining it by the rules of picturesque beauty: that of not merely describing; but of adapting the description of natural scenery to the principles of artificial landscape.'[10]

In 1778 Alexander Cozens published a remarkable work entitled *The Principles of Beauty*, in which he set out a complex set of theories outlining the means by which it is possible to create or identify a face of 'simple beauty', in other words 'a beautiful face unmixed with character', and by what means one can identify a 'compound beauty' or 'a beauty to which some character is annexed'. He listed sixteen 'denominations' of beauty: The Majestic, Sensible or Wise, Steady, Spirited, Haughty, Melancholy, Tender, Modest,

them minutely and often reproduced
them in exquisite detail, they became a
favourite subject (as we have seen with
Cozens). Botanists, amateur gardeners
and landowners argued for hours about
the aesthetic merits of the oak tree as if
they were discussing the Belvedere
Apollo.[14] Their passion was undoubtedly
tinged with anthropomorphism, human
qualities and characteristics being attributed as freely to trees as to people, as
William Shenstone, a poet and essayist of
the period, demonstrates:

All trees have a character analogous to that of
men: Oaks are in all respects the perfect image
of the manly character . . . As a brave man is not
suddenly either elated by prosperity, or
depressed by adversity, so the oak displays not
it's verdure on the sun's first approach; nor
drops it, on his first departure. Add to this it's
majestic appearance, the rough grandeur of it's
bark, and the wide protection of it's
branches.[15]

1 R. Payne Knight, *An Analytical Inquiry into
the Principles of Taste* (4th ed. 1808, [1st ed.
1805]; reprinted Farnborough 1972) p. 170.
For a complete biography of Payne Knight, see
M. Clarke and N. Penny (eds.), *The Arrogant
Connoisseur: Richard Payne Knight, 1751–1824*
(Oxford 1982).
2 Thomas Hearne (1744–1817), a minor expo-
nent of the English school of landscape views,
known above all for his 'antiquarian topogra-
phies'; between 1784 and 1785 he executed a
series of views of the park of Downton Castle.
See M. Clarke and N. Penny, *op. cit.*, pp. 156ff.
3 William Owen (1769–1825), a portraitist
patronized by Knight and by the Townley
family. See M. Clarke and N. Penny, *op. cit.*,
p. 159.
4 Gainsborough visited Foxley in the 1760s,
i.e. before the estate was redesigned by Uvedale Price. However, the image left of it by the
artist (who was a close friend of Price's grand-
father and of Price himself, who used to accompany him on expeditions in the neighbourhood
of Bath) does not contradict later descriptions
and pictures of Foxley. On this subject see
D.A. Lambin, 'Foxley: the Prices' Estate in
Herefordshire' in *The Journal of Garden History*,
Vol. 7, no. 2 (1987), pp. 244–70.
5 For a study of the work of Price, see D.
Lambin, 'Uvedale Price and the Picturesque' in
Urbi, No. 8 (Autumn 1983), pp. L–LVII, and
M. Allentuck, 'Sir Uvedale Price and the
Picturesque Garden: the Evidence of the
Coleorton Papers' in *The Picturesque Garden and
its Influence outside the British Isles* (Dumbarton
Oaks 1974).
6 R. Payne Knight, *op. cit.*, p. 102.

or convention, and not yet corrupted by
bad taste or repetition. Thanks to some
'innate sympathy' which gives human
beings an understanding of each other,
the language of these signs is instantly
recognized and universally compre-
hended. The garden designer's duty is to
make the natural objects and materials in
the landscape 'speak', just as Greek
sculptors succeeded in making their statues expressive of thought, mood, emotion and the human condition. The garden designer, like the artist, must be
aware of this universal language but,
unlike the painter or sculptor, he cannot
control what Cozens called the 'circumstances'. He can control the 'objects' only
up to a point, and in fact has complete
freedom only in the choice and distribution of the trees. So it is through the trees
above all that he expresses the character
of the garden and defines its identity.

In his *Essays on the Picturesque* (1810)
Price wrote,

It is in the arrangement and management of
trees, that the great art of improvement
consists; earth is too cumbrous and lumpish
for man to contend much with . . . But trees . . .
they alone, form a canopy over us, and a varied
frame to all other objects; which they admit,
exclude, and group with . . . . Without them,
the most varied inequality of ground is
uninteresting.[12]

Knight devoted the third part of *The
Landscape* exclusively to trees. It was a
passion that he shared with many of his
contemporaries: by the end of the eighteenth century the planting of trees had
become one of the most popular occupa-
tions of the landowning classes, like
hunting and the breeding of dogs and
horses. It represented simultaneously the
mark of good taste, social distinction,
farsightedness and love of one's country.

The Royal Society for the Encouragement of the Arts actually awarded medals
for tree-planting. Thomas Johnes (1748–
1816), a relative of Knight's, ruined
himself financially by planting about five
million trees on his estate at Hafod over a
period of about thirty years. In Scotland,
three generations of the Dukes of Atholl
planted fourteen million larches between
1740 and 1830. Trees become almost a
cult: Dr Johnson maintained that a noble
aim for a rich man was to propagate every
species of tree that grows in the open;[13]
for William Gilpin trees were the greatest
and noblest product of the earth; and Sir
George Beaumont (an amateur painter
and a friend of Price and Knight) bought
a tree when he visited Italy simply to
prevent it from being cut down. Drayton,
Cowper, Wordsworth and Clare were all
to express their love of trees in their
poems, and for painters too, who studied

The Principles of Beauty: Noses and Mouths. *Engraving by F. Bartolozzi after A. Cozens, 1778. The Board of Trustees of the Victoria and Albert Museum, London.*

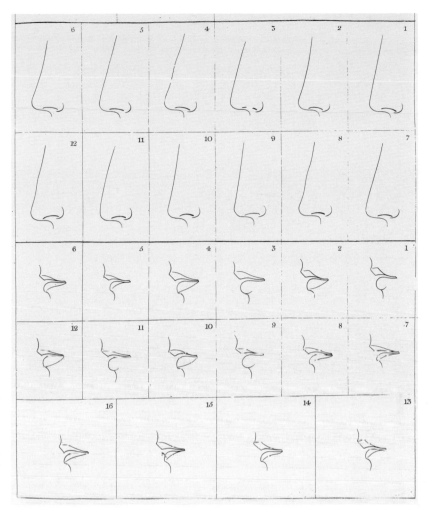

The Various Species of Composition of Landscape in Nature. *Engraving by A. Cozens: four examples from a series of sixteen. The Trustees of the British Museum, London.*

[7] For a comprehensive study of this argument, which has been discussed only superficially here, see W. J. Hipple, *The Beautiful, the Sublime, and the Picturesque in 18th century British Aesthetic Theory* (Carbondale 1957); P. Funnel, 'Visible Appearances' in M. Clarke and N. Penny, *op. cit.*, pp. 82–92; S. Ross, 'The Picturesque: An Eighteenth-Century Debate' in *The Journal of Aesthetics and Art Criticism*, Vol. 46, no. 2 (1987) pp. 271–9.

[8] Dalrymple's text was republished with an introduction by R. Williams under the title of 'Sir John Dalrymple's "An Essay on Landscape Gardening"' in *The Journal of Garden History*, Vol. 3, no. 2 (April-June 1983) pp. 144–56.

[9] Whately's treatise was written in 1765 and published five years later in London and Dublin; it was immediately translated into French and German.

[10] W. Gilpin, *Observations on the River Wye, and several parts of South Wales* (London 1782), pp. 1–2. The best presentation of the debate in England on the perception of the landscape at the end of the eighteenth century is to be found in J. Barrell, *The Idea of Landscape and the Sense of Place, 1730–1840. An Approach to the Poetry of John Clare* (Cambridge 1972).

[11] This paragraph is a summary of the theory put forward by K. Sloan in *Alexander and John Robert Cozens. The Poetry of Landscape* (New Haven and London 1986). Knight most probably knew the work of Alexander Cozens partly as a result of visiting Italy with his son, John Robert Cozens.

[12] U. Price, *Essays on the Picturesque* (1810, reprinted Farnborough 1971) Vol. 1, pp. 259ff.

[13] J. Boswell, *Life of Johnson* (Oxford 1985; original edition 1791), pp. 475–6.

[14] The information contained in this paragraph is largely based on K. Thomas, *Man and the Natural World. Changing Attitudes in England 1500–1800* (London 1983).

[15] W. Shenstone, *Unconnected Thoughts on Gardening* (1764) transcribed in part by J. Dixon Hunt and P. Willis in *The Genius of the Place. The English Landscape Garden 1620–1820* (London and New York 1975) p. 292. This summary is based on research carried out for: A. Ponte, *Il viaggio alle origini. Il diario siciliano di Richard Payne Knight e il Neoclassicismo pittoresco in Inghilterra*, doctoral thesis, I.U.A.V. (Venice 1987). For a seminal analysis of this debate, see C. Hussey, *The Picturesque. Studies on a Point of View* (1st ed. 1927), 3rd ed. London 1983, and the more recent publication, D. Watkin, *The English Vision. The Picturesque in Architecture, Landscape and Garden Design* (London 1982).

Masonic Gardens in Sicily

Eliana Mauro and Ettore Sessa

Topographical map of the Villa Giulia at Palermo (1777–9), designed by Nicolò Palma. Engraving by G. Fortuyn, 1779. Biblioteca Comunale, Palermo.

Between 1700 and 1800 the gardens of the Conca d'Oro around Palermo – the 'gardens of the Hesperides' par excellence – were testaments to an ideal and a culture linked to the continuance of traditional scientific attitudes and beliefs but also consistent with the trends of modern science. A number of gardens of the time combined contrasting tendencies in a similar way: the garden of the dukes of Montelone, for example, with its pyramid, loggia and observatory; the plants and flowers 'never before seen', according to Goethe's description, of the Villa Giulia in 1777; the funerary pyramids of the Masonic Grand Masters and Masters of the Lodge, together with the Chinese garden and frescoes of the Casina Cinese, commissioned in 1799–1800 by the Bourbon King Ferdinand III and Maria Caroline of Austria.

At the end of the 1700s a public botanical garden (with which the Viceroy Francesco d'Aquino – ex-Grand Master of a French Masonic lodge – was connected) was laid out next to the Villa Giulia. Designed in the neoclassical style, it was a perfect example of a 'temple of learning'. The original plan of the garden, which was devised by the Frenchman Léon Dufourney in about 1790, was to have included a hill as a counterpart to the villa, with a spiral path winding up to a temple on the wooded summit; the crown of the hill – like the top of a 'holy mountain' – was a goal that could only be reached by means of a path of initiation through Nature, leading from Botanical Science to Knowledge and a state of spiritual well-being.

With the rediscovery of the 'laws of Nature', scientists engaged in classifying and ordering the species of the natural world found an echo in the hierarchical structure of Freemasonry. The Sicilian prelate Giuseppe Gioeni d'Angio (1717–1798) endorsed this connection in 1785 in drawing up a new codex and in establishing a new Sicilian state, with its capital, surrounded by gardens, at the centre of the territory.

At that time, Sicilians scholars who were followers of Freemasonry often imitated features from the architecture of antiquity in their gardens, thus contributing a new set of symbols to the philosophical imagery of the age and creating opportunities for experimentation with the new neoclassical style. An example of

this was the observatory temple of the Masonic garden laid out by the Pignatellis, dukes of Monteleone, in Palermo in the early years of the nineteenth century. In its original form the garden was an expression of the discipline and linear clarity which characterized the neoclassical movement. Architectural features inspired by the rationalism of the Age of Enlightenment marked the most significant elements of its design, forming part of a scheme which, while adhering to the principles of neoclassicism, did not ignore the ideals of romanticism which

had already given rise to a new vocabulary of metaphor and symbolism. It was thus one of those rare examples of two aesthetic and philosophical extremes coming briefly together in a perfect equilibrium.

The Masonic philosophers active in Palermo between the late 1700s and the first decade of the 1800s, many of them leaders of the constitutional reforms of 1812, gave new life to the notion of a symbolic garden, devising a language of symbolic imagery based on the arcane and secret ideology of their movement. The

Prince of Castelnuovo – Master of the Lodge of St Demetrius in Palermo and Minister of Finance in the government of 1812 – laid out a park and gardens which conformed with the aesthetic principles of rationalism but which were neoclassical in imitating a formal landscape. In this setting he built a house made up of two quite separate but identical villas, the main one for the family, the other for guests; a small 'lodge' supported by two caryatids, at the front of the main building, symbolically faced the entrance gates. (The later Agricultural Institute in Palermo was also built by the Prince of Castelnuovo as a 'temple of learning' in the neoclassical style.)

In the park laid out by the Prince of Belmonte – Foreign Minister in 1812 – the principles of neoclassicism were combined with the ideology of romanticism to produce a result that was remarkable both in stylistic terms (the neoclassical villa by G. V. Marvuglia is complemented by Greek, Roman and Gothic temples) and in the range of its symbolic imagery, which referred to the ideals of Freemasonry throughout history. The Belmonte park is a testament to the widespread dissemination of the theories of Edmund Burke which, since about 1770, had been absorbed into the 'new' culture whose influence was then spreading throughout the intellectual circles of the day.

Contemporary attitudes regarding the treatment of agricultural land, set out in the treatise *Il podere fruttifero e dilettevole* (The profitable and pleasing estate), which was published in Palermo in 1735 by Baron F. Nicosia, favoured an approach not far removed from the principles of Addison and Pope and the English followers of Palladianism. Model farms, with neoclassical and informal gardens, were established in the countryside around Palermo. They were mostly conceived as metaphors for an ideal society with liberal tendencies which no longer bowed to the divine right of the oligarchy but offered a guarantee of social order and general well-being. In its Sicilian form, this ideology was identified with the group of landowners who, like the constitutionalists, were intent on boosting the economic development and productivity of the island, and with those intellectuals involved in science and the arts who were associated with the Acca-

Belvedere with nymphaeum and exedra, with eight niches and sculptures of saints, at the beginning of the walk to the hermitage of the convent of Sta Maria di Gesù dei Frati Minori at Palermo: end of the sixteenth century. (Photo G. Cuttitta)

Villa Giulia at Palermo: tomb of the illustrious Sicilians of antiquity. Early nineteenth century. (Photo G. Cuttitta)

demia di Studi and were open to the influences of more enlightened modern thinking. Among them were the architect G.V. Marvuglia; the astronomer G. Piazzi; the poet, physician and botanist (as well as Freemason) G. Meli and the agronomist P. Balsamo; they also included admirers of the work of Arthur Young and of the experimental methods of George Washington, who believed in combining utilitarianism with human rights.

Around 1780 the archaeologist I. Paternò, Prince of Biscari, laid out a park at Catania according to the principles of utilitarianism, with an adjoining Lodge and a Chinese garden. It was the forerunner of a Mediterranean aesthetic movement which was exemplified by the Butera Wilding garden in Palermo and was characterized by a series of contrasting picturesque effects in a close-knit sequence. For Biscari, a well-ordered park resulting from man's labours was both a pleasure to see and a tangible example of social well-being, an expression of the Masonic belief that the landscape should be 'a reflection of cosmic order'.

This concept was also supported by Baron V. Schininà who, like most eighteenth-century patricians of Catania, was a member of the commission superintending the rebuilding of the city of Ragusa, where he owned a villa and a *giardino segreto*. The Masonic ideal of cosmic order was fundamental to Biscari's humanist interpretation as indeed it had been behind the 'philosophical garden' of the sixteenth century, of which a few significant examples existed in Palermo.

Biscari himself employed certain traditional elements of these earlier gardens in his park at Catania: one was the labyrinth, whose symbolic significance as a path of initiation and learning made it an essential feature of every garden of the aristocratic Sicilian Freemasonry until the middle of the nineteenth century. It frequently appeared in geometric schemes, such as the late eighteenth-century Palermitan garden of Princess M. Christina Gaetani (a member of the Palli family of Lucca, which had connections with the Reform Lodge), but also in romantic settings such as the park laid out at Olivuzza near Palermo between 1810 and 1840 by the statesman-archaeologist and Freemason, the Duke of Serradifalco.

Park of Real Favorita at Palermo, c. 1799:
exedra of cypresses and the Hercules
fountain, early nineteenth century. Early
twentieth-century postcard. Biblioteca
Comunale, Palermo.

Garden of the Duke of Serradifalco,
Olivuzza, Palermo, c. 1825. Late
nineteenth-century photograph. Biblioteca
Comunale, Palermo.

It continued to appear in the more eclectic gardens of the region even after the risings of 1848: one example was the copy in stone of the Hampton Court maze which Baron C. Arezzo de Spuches laid out in his neoclassical garden at Donnafugata.

It was Biscari who began the trend in Sicily for relics from antiquity to be displayed among groups of exotic trees in private parks. Collections of such relics, and of rare botanical specimens, became an integral element of these 'gardens of delight' and a characteristic of the romantic period which survived for so long in Sicily. It was not to die out in fact until about 1870, when the gardens of the Villa Tasca were created on the outskirts of Palermo; their exotic subtropical profusion, combining elements of the aesthetic-scientific philosophy of the botanical garden with a highly individual eclecticism, made them the epitome of romanticism.

At the start of the period in which relic collecting became fashionable, a garden was laid out by the archaeologist Landolina, an elder of a Masonic lodge in Syracuse, in an area of the city where excavations were already taking place. It alluded symbolically to the Masonic theme of the tomb as a place from which the spirit ascended to the Zenith, and to theories on the Egyptian origins of the ancient Sicilian culture. It thus represented the search for the roots of Sicilian Freemasonry which many archaeologist Freemasons of the period were eager to explore. Their endeavours were finally rewarded by the discovery of certain instruments believed to have been used by the 'supersensitive' as a means of achieving more profound awareness and understanding of the human condition in a culture, clearly identifiable with Freemasonry, that dated back to the archaic and classical periods.

The search for cosmic harmony and for a return to man's original state of grace took on even greater symbolic significance in the garden of the Real Casa dei Matti in Palermo. It was made by Baron P. Pisani in three contrasting styles – Greek, Roman and Chinese – with two avenues, in which trees alternated with seats, and two courtyards which served as introductions to the complex historical iconography.

Bibliography

H. Tuzet, *La Sicile au XVIII siècle vue par les voyageurs étrangers* (Strasbourg 1955).

G. Pirrone, 'Palermo e il suo "verde"' in *Quaderno dell' Istituto di Elementi di Architettura e Rilievo dei Monumenti*, No. 5/6 (Palermo 1965).

M. de Simone, *Ville palermitane* (Genoa 1968).

G. La Monica, *Sicilia misterica* (Palermo 1982).

R. Assunto, *Il parterre e i ghiacciai. Tre saggi di estetica sul paesaggio del Settecento* (Palermo 1984).

G. Pirrone and G. G. Cosentini, *Donnafugata, un castello, un giardino* (Palermo 1985).

R. Giuffrida and M. Giuffrè, *La Palazzina Cinese e il Museo Pitrè nel Parco della Favorita a Palermo* (Palermo 1987).

Il giardino come labirinto della storia, First International Convention (Palermo 1987).

E. Mauro, *I giardini di Palermo tra '700 e '800: un itinerario massonico*, in Proceedings of the International Convention 'Freemasonry and Architecture', Florence 1988 – in course of publication.

G. Pirrone, *Palermo una capitale* (Milan 1989).

PART FOUR

*The Eclectic Garden,
and the Town and City Park*

Part title: Philips Park, Manchester.
(Photo Daniele De Lonte)

Plan of Queen's Park, Manchester. From A
Few Pages About Manchester (c. 1849).

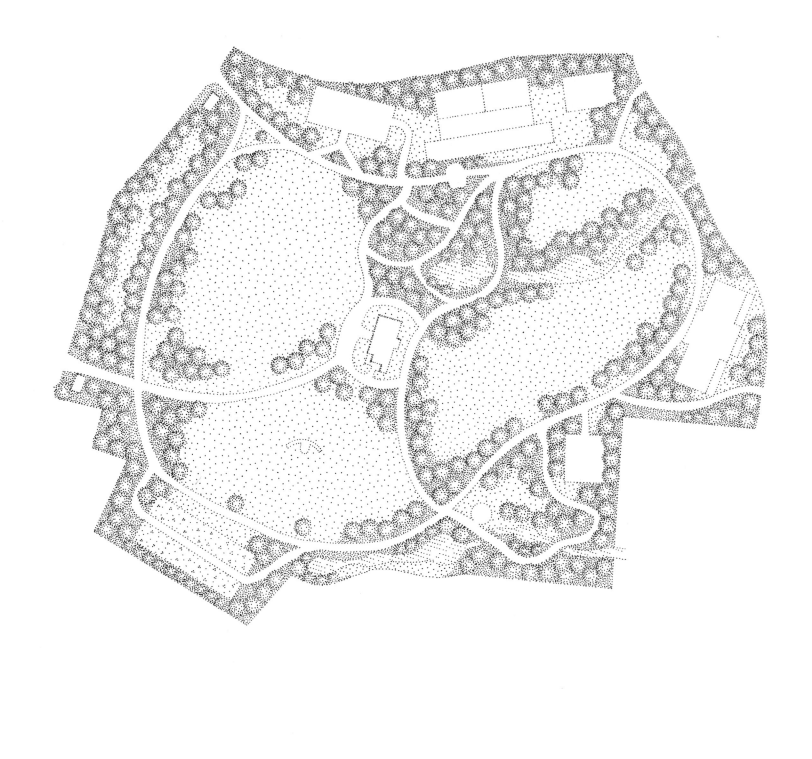

0   50m

0   150ft

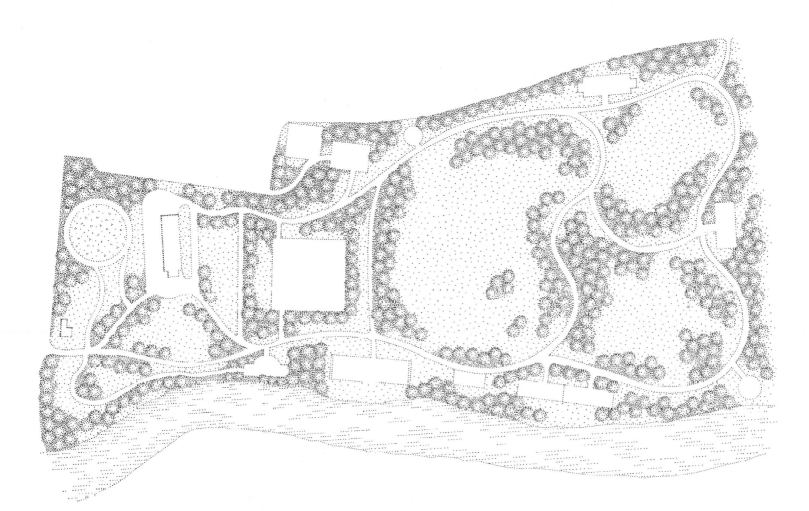

0   50m

0   150ft

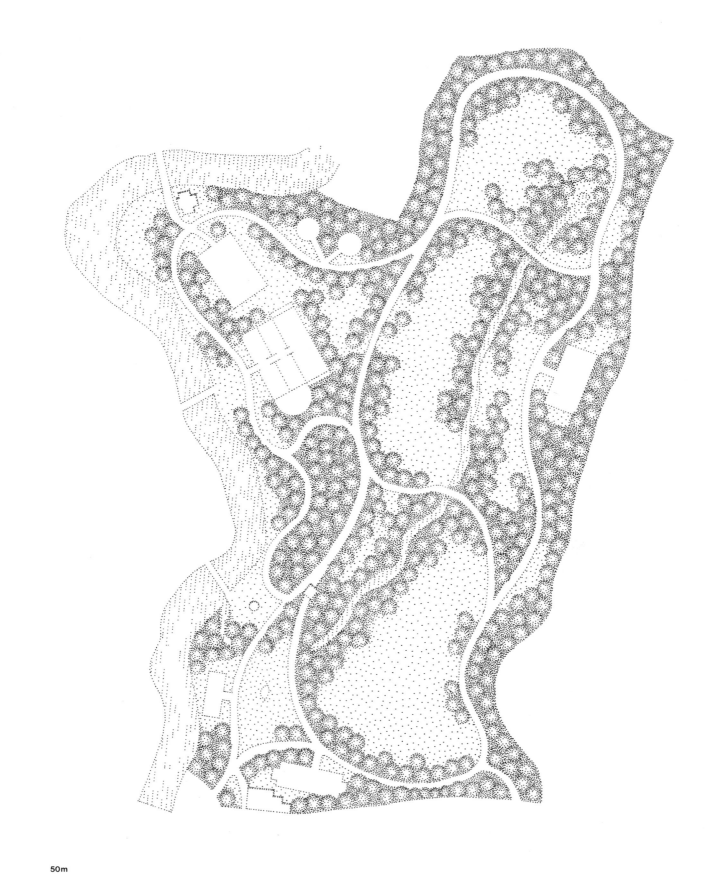

0   50m

0   150ft

Park Güell, Barcelona. From a survey carried out by E. Torres and E. Martinez la Peña (1988).

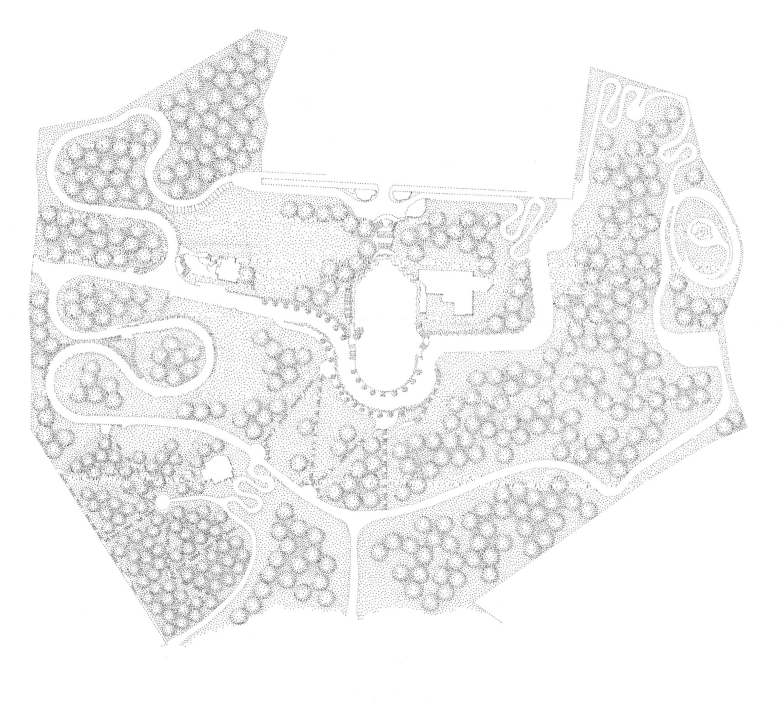

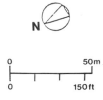

N

| 0 | 50m |
| 0 | 150ft |

Central Park, Manhattan. From a plan by
F. L. Olmsted and C. Vaux for the
Department of Public Parks, and from a
survey of the park today.

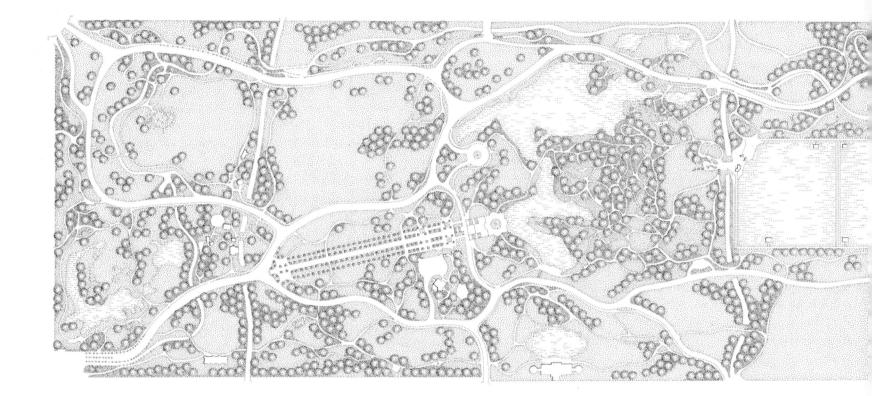

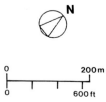

N

| 0 | | 200m |
| 0 | | 600ft |

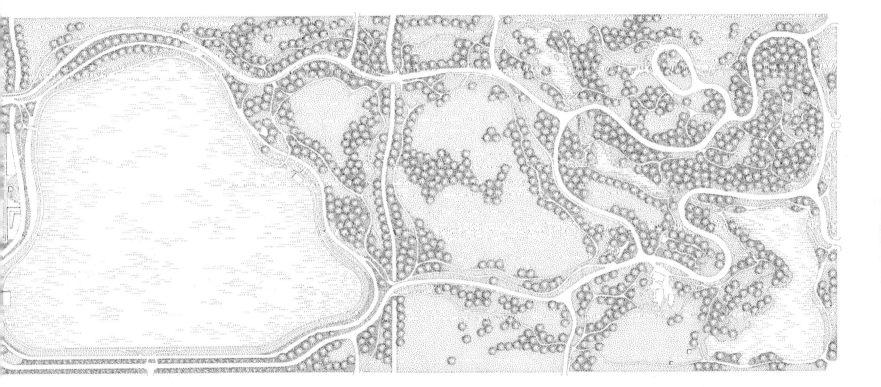

The Eclectic Garden and the Imitation of Nature

Georges Teyssot

The architectural theorist Antoine Chrysostome Quatremère de Quincy, commissioned by the publisher Panckoucke to draw up the architectural volumes of the *Encyclopédie Méthodique* (first volume 1788), is still famous today for having formulated the theory of the 'character' of architecture. It is less well known that he added an article on the 'character' of the garden, applying 'to the art of the garden some of the principles and observations' set out in the earlier work and making two specific points, one in relation to the site, the other in relation to the particular purpose of the garden. The first was based on 'an understanding of nature'; the second 'on the circumstances and social rank of the client, on the nature of the associated buildings, on the factors that governed the layout and facilities, and whether it was intended as a private or a public garden'.

The first series of characteristics were those discussed by many eighteenth-century writers: Thomas Whately, Claude-Henri Watelet, Jean Marie Morel and others. In his *Observations on Modern Gardening*, published in 1770, Whately had established a fundamental distinction between the emblematic (didactic and allegorical) character of the landscape garden and its expressive (metaphorical) character. In Quatremère's writings, the first series related to naturalistic characteristics: 'Nature, following the eternal laws of beauty and variety, which always govern it, has given the landscape an infinite variety of characteristics, and in doing so it seems to have taken into account the diversity of taste and inclination to be found in the men who inhabit it.' In this way an analogy was established between the characteristics reflected in the external features of a site and aspects of the human temperament, in order to 'satisfy our personal tastes in our gardens in as much variety and richness as is possible in painting or poetry'. The garden could therefore be 'pleasing', 'joyful', 'smiling' or 'grave and melancholy'. In the latter category would be included works of architecture, such as mausoleums and ruins; sculpture, such as monuments, urns and columns; and even poetry ('inscriptions intended to suggest a mood, to emphasize the fragility of worldly things or to impart wisdom'), which, if used with discretion, served to create the desired atmosphere or effect. There also existed the 'romantic' character, which owed little to art and almost everything to nature, and depended on the use of such elements as hills, rocks, caverns, grottoes, cascades and waterfalls.

This concept finds echoes in *Essai sur les jardins* (1774) by Watelet, a painter and architect, who was responsible for the enchanting garden of Moulin-Joli on the Seine, near Argenteuil. In his famous chapter on 'modern parks', Watelet singled out three principal 'characters': the picturesque, the poetic (with allusions to mythology and mime) and the romantic (expressed in references to the sublime and to allegory). In his *Théorie des jardins* (1776) Morel also subdivided the 'garden proper' into various classifications: the 'poetic' (including mythology, fable and history); the 'romantic' (inspired by a sense of wonder or alarm, and by the influence of China); the 'pastoral' and the 'imitative' (exotic). Quatremère studied closely Watelet's and Morel's writings, and as a result created the 'majestic' style (ancient forests) and the 'sublime', placing gardens on top of mountains, on promontories or on rocky precipitous slopes.

The second series of characteristics introduced by Quatremère were metaphorical, and related to function and the social standing of the owner of the property: 'There can be no doubt that gardens must be analagous to their owner's rank; and what applies in this connection to buildings applies also to gardens'. It is clear that Quatremère had some difficulty in singling out individual characteristics inherent in the garden, and for this reason referred frequently to the field of architecture; his list of gardens includes 'royal', 'rustic' (for ordinary citizens), 'public gardens' (incorporating several wide symmetrical avenues), 'academic' gardens (with allegorical ornament), convent gardens (melancholic), gardens of spa towns and of hospitals (sunny and salubrious).

In another section Quatremère refers to 'tree gardening', discussing the *verte architecture* of the garden, in which trees were planted according to their characteristics, such as the texture of their trunks, the arrangement of their branches, their habit, form, foliage or colour. 'Trees for water are those with blue-green colouring, such as willows, poplars and certain reeds and rushes, chosen to blend with the blue of the water; those with waving crowns and rippling foliage suggest the waves of the sea.' He also suggested 'composing living pictures whose subtle shades create, as in painting, an infinite variety of effects'.

With Quatremère de Quincy the theory of garden design became inextricably linked with artistic imitation, the Green *mimesis*, as he was later to confirm in his *Essai sur la nature . . . de l'imitation dans les beaux-arts* (1823), which echoed the platonic theories of Cratylus: 'Imitation in the fine arts means reproducing the likeness of a thing, but in another form, which becomes the image of it'. Throughout the eighteenth century theoreticians had clashed on the question posed by architecture: which is the real model to imitate? The French disciple of Winckelmann responded – in the *Encyclopédie Méthodique: Architecture* – that architecture did not deal in models of reality but only in 'analogies', or in 'models which represented metaphysical or indirect imitations'. True imitation did not consist in copying nature but in creating ideas inspired by it. At the base of all architecture is the notion of 'analogical imitation'. Extending this premise into the wider context of the garden, Quatremère introduced a series of analogies. It is worth recording that analogy in art could be described as the sort of harmony that exists between an artistic work and its spectator, and which arouses intellectual and imaginative responses. Using different terminology, the mental process of 'association' was described by the Scottish rationalist Archibald Alison in his *Essays on the Nature and Principles of Taste* (1790). For him beauty was not intrinsic to the object but existed in the mind of the observer. If we now turn to the writings of Quatremère we find that the art of the garden 'can awaken in us the same ideas, and bring to our souls the same sensations as nature does'. It reveals in us something that already exists, reflecting concepts and

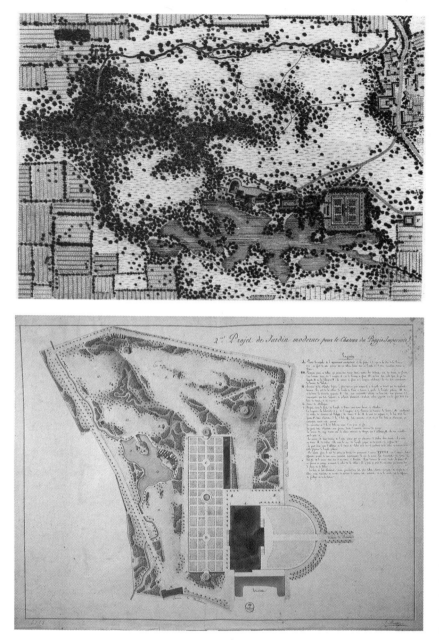

sensations that are already in our minds. However, if this can be said to apply to art in general, it must be more clearly articulated in relation to the aesthetics of the garden: this 'hybrid' art operates through analogy to excite in us those sensations that nature is capable of arousing.

In order to proceed further along this path, the theory of the 'character' of the garden must be examined more thoroughly. Since the end of the seventeenth century it had been represented by classical and neoclassical imitative aesthetics, and for Quatremère and others it provided a medium without which such theoretical principles would have remained pure speculation. To study it in detail, one must turn to the two sister arts of painting ('*composer de véritables tableaux*') and architecture ('*la nature des édifices dont [les jardins] dépendent*'). Such observations offered little that was new: similar statements had already been made by Horace Walpole, for example. However, they formed the basis for a number of propositions put forward towards the end of the eighteenth century and during the first thirty years of the nineteenth century in various parts of Europe. In England the famous debate, in which the two dilettanti Richard Payne Knight and Uvedale Price engaged in battle against the professional landscape designer Humphry Repton, seems to have been based on the nature of the double imitation employed in the art of the garden, the two analogous factors which Quatremère had also discussed: those of painting and architecture. The main difficulty lay, perhaps, in the fact that one medium was two-dimensional, the other three-dimensional.

As Hegel declared in the introduction to the third part of his *Aesthetics*, the art of garden design is an 'incomplete' art, an example of a 'hybrid medium, but one which while falling short of perfection nevertheless does not lack merit or the quality of charm'. The so-called 'combined' arts have always caused problems in studies of eighteenth-century aesthetics: one has only to think of the debates surrounding eloquence and architecture, both of which combined the useful and the beautiful. The garden, which was included relatively late in such theoretical discussions, incorporated – apart from painting and architecture – other disciplines, such as natural history (botany), engineering and hydraulics. Watelet's writings give a strong sense of the uncertainties surrounding its true place in aesthetics, and suggest that its functions can be divided into two categories: 'The architect's task is to bring beauty to every aspect of a vertical plan. The garden designer's talents are employed in bringing beauty to a horizontal scheme.' This division between the two professions corresponds to the division that existed between the visual arts and aesthetics. The architect, according to Watelet, 'must allow the eye to see everything in a single glance' while the garden designer 'must reveal the beauties of the garden only gradually'. This notion was elaborated by C. C. L. Hirschfeld, the Danish professor of aesthetics at the University of Kiel, and author of *Theorie der Gartenkunst* (published in Leipzig in German and French in five volumes, 1779–85). He maintained that this division accounted for the 'failure' of the geometric garden which followed the strict rules of symmetry governing architecture: 'The art of the garden

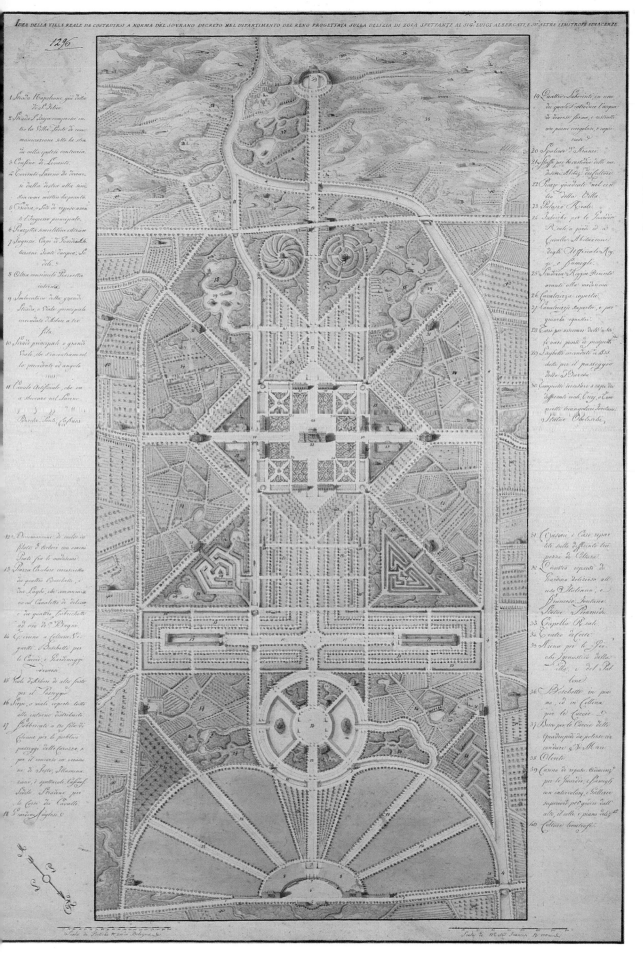

Design for 'A holiday retreat for Napoleon' at the Villa Albergati di Zola Predosa, Bologna. Drawing by Antonio Basoli and Ercole Gasparini, 1805. Biblioteca Comunale dell' Archiginnasio, Bologna.

was no more [if judged by the work of followers of Le Nôtre] than architecture laid out on the ground' (Vol. 1, section 2, p. 138).

These were by no means the only hurdles to be overcome, however. In a desire to imitate nature there was a risk of reproducing its less attractive features as well as its obvious delights. The President of the Royal Academy, Sir Joshua Reynolds, warned against this danger in his *Discourses on Art* (1769–90), in which he advised painters to avoid the temptation to imitate the more bizarre aspects of nature and to concentrate instead on representing its beauty. The concept of 'beauty in nature' informed all contemporary aesthetics and led to the notion of an 'ideal' in the arts. Abbé Batteux had already discussed this view in his book *Les Beaux-Arts réduits à un même principe* (published in 1746 and translated anonymously into English in 1749), recommending artists to produce 'an imitation in which one sees nature not as it is but as it might be if conceived by the imagination and the spirit'. The imitation of nature, though it appears in landscape painting to consist of accurate representation, is not enough in itself: 'It is for this reason that the great painters never omit to include in the barest landscapes a few traces of human presence, if only an ancient sepulchre or the ruins of an old building. This is mainly because they paint for man.' Reynolds observed, more radically perhaps, in his *Thirteenth Discourse*, that the art of the garden was 'a deviation from nature; for if the true taste consists, as many hold, in banishing every appearance of Art, or any traces of the footsteps of man, it would then be no longer a Garden.' Many other eighteenth-century writers were equally conscious of the difficulties created by the imitation of 'pure nature'.

Yet Morel maintained in 1776 that his 'theory was entirely based on Nature: she alone has provided the garden with its precepts, its influences and its materials'. And he added: 'The aim of garden design is not to produce a counterfeit representation but to order the garden in conformity with the rules laid down by Nature.' From 1800 onwards this principle was supported by the majority of theoreticians and architects. The panegyric on Morel written by Savalette de Fortaire in 1813 summarized his beliefs:

Morel conceived both the overall scheme and the details of the garden in relation to its site with such skill and ingenuity, and disguised its artificiality with such artistry that even the far horizon seemed to be part of his plan and his plan to be indispensable to the surrounding landscape. The elements of his design – woodland, torrents, lakes, rocks, shrubs, rivers – were so perfectly arranged as to seem an integral part of the whole, linked in some subtle and indefinable way by means of a scheme which allowed them to reveal themselves in turn in a carefully planned sequence of images and reflections, leading both the eye and the step from one to the other in a series of natural and invisible transitions.

In the notes added to the second edition of his *Théorie des jardins* (1802), Morel defended the cause of 'irregularity'. For example, he criticized those who created artificial mounds on flat ground, and maintained that water should not 'appear as if unnaturally contrived by art'. In fact, it seemed that nothing had changed since the Duc d'Harcourt had written

Plan of the park at Courson (Essonne) c. 1820. Drawing by Louis-Martin Berthault. Private collection.

Plan of the château and park of St-Leu-Taverny (Val d'Oise). From Nicolas Vergnaud, L'art de créer les jardins, Paris 1835.

at the opening of his essay on the landscape, the epigraph: *Ars est celare artem* (Art lies in the concealment of art).

This policy influenced above all the formal French-style garden, but also the first experiments in informality executed elsewhere on the Continent. One of the first examples that springs to mind is the Folie de Chartres, designed by the painter Carmontelle and begun in 1773, which later became the Parc Monceau in Paris. A guide by Dulaure (*Nouvelle Description des Environs de Paris*, third edition, 1790) gives an indication of popular reaction at the time:

It is to the Chinese that the Europeans owe these new gardens; this new fashion spread from China to England, where the architect William Kent was the first to influence his compatriots in its favour; the French adopted it with enthusiasm, but their early endeavours proved unsuccessful. An excessive quantity of objects gathered into a small area made these new gardens ridiculous and unacceptable, and gave them the appearance of a shop full of columns, obelisks and ruins rather than stretches of landscape; but, within a few years such excesses had been moderated, resulting in delightful gardens which enchanted the heart, the spirit and the eye.

Among them were the gardens of Liancourt, the property of the Duc de La Rochefoucauld, which was redesigned in the English style by the architect Louis Villars; Moulin-Joli; Ermenonville; Saint-Leu-Taverny, to which Dufort de Cheverny, the banker Laborde, the Prince de Conti and the Duc de Chartres all contributed in turn.

The first voices raised in protest against the widely disseminated theory of imitation as applied to the design of the garden were those of the cultural circle surrounding Melchiorre Cesarotti, the translator of Ossian, creator of the emblematic garden of Selvazzano – the Italian counterpart of The Leasowes. In 1792, the Veronese poet Ippolito Pindemonte, who had visited England, presented to the Paduan Academy, at the invitation of Cesarotti, a dissertation on the subject of the English garden and its application in Italy (printed in 1817). Comparing the beauty of the countryside with the garden, he denied the possibility of garden design being assimilated into the 'fine arts'. By contrast with the painter or sculptor, who could employ brushes, colours or marble in their work, or the poet, who could use words and verses to evoke the beauties of nature, the garden designer had only nature to call upon, and nature could hardly imitate itself. The work of a landscape painter might allowably be imitative if, 'in a painting of a hamlet he depicts a beautiful landscape, perfecting the scene he has chosen to paint and idealizing the truth in his imagination; but I would never suggest that the imitation should consist of the same elements as the original, that, for example, nature should imitate nature'. What he failed to find in an 'artificial scene' and recognized in the natural landscape was 'that beauty . . . produced by accident', which was an endless source of wonder and delight. It was this realization that produced a renewed appreciation of the formal garden, which was a symbol of nature adapted to the will of man. As a result of this re-evaluation, the traditional Italian garden saw a significant revival.

Pindemonte's thesis was refuted by Mabil, a teacher of classical

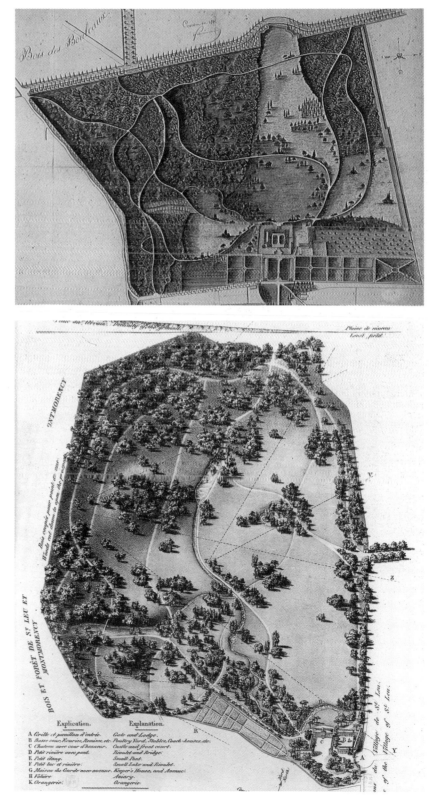

philology and aesthetics at the University of Padua, in his *Saggio sopra
l'indole dei giardini moderni* (1796). Pindemonte attempted to defend the
creations of the 'artist-gardener', who was expected to be an
'agricultural instructor' and to avail himself of 'every aspect of science',
and also a 'designer and decorator' capable of embellishing a piece of
land with imagination and artistry. Mabil, on the other hand,
developed an entirely different theory of imitation. It had nothing to do
with 'imitating nature by nature' but with reproducing the character of
a place. He believed that one should not copy the natural features of a
site but 'rather the mood, the atmosphere, the attitude that [the garden]
evoked, which gave rise to a delightful uncertainty as to whether nature
or art had created the scene, had prepared the surprise, had painted the
picture'. In the end, however, Mabil too placed gardens in two
categories: one the symmetrical, formal garden for the display 'of
collections of nature's most beautiful objects', an idea which anticipated the nineteenth-century fashion for collections of rare and exotic
plants; the other the informal garden.

It was during this period that the informal garden became
widespread in Italy as a result of influences disseminated from Vienna,
London, Germany and Paris. The garden of the Villa Belgioioso (now
the Villa Comunale) in Milan is thought to have been designed by the
architect Leopold Pollack in 1793, and it is very probably his work
although it seems that Count Ercole Silva attributed it, somewhat
remarkably, to Lancelot 'Capability' Brown, who had died ten years
earlier. Silva enjoyed a certain celebrity as a result of transforming his
own Baroque garden of Cinisello Balsamo (today the Villa Silva-
Ghirlanda), to the north of Milan, into a microcosm of the informal
garden, made famous by engravings by Lanzani. In the second edition
(1813) of Hirschfeld's little-known *Dell'arte dei giardini inglesi*, first
published in 1801, reference is made to the changes made to the royal
park at Monza, which was begun by Giuseppe Piermarini and
redesigned in 1805 by the architect Luigi Canonica and the garden
designer Luigi Villoresi, who had previously laid out the panoramic
terraces of the Villa Melzi d'Eril at Bellagio, on Lake Como. Partly in
order to follow the fashion and partly to economize on maintenance
expenses, many European gardens were transformed into landscape
parks around this time. In Italy plans were drawn up by Giuseppe
Manetti in 1811–12 to redesign the gardens of Villa Poggio Imperiale
(which were never realized), and by the Bohemian Joseph Fricks for
Pratolino (which unfortunately were, in 1823), and practically the
entire Baroque design by Giacomo Muttone for the gardens of the Villa
Villani-Novati (later Belgioioso), at Merate on Lake Como, was
irrevocably lost as a result of landscaping.

An exception to the Anglomania of the day was the plan for 'a
holiday retreat for Napoleon' (1805) at the Villa Albergati di Zola
Predosa at Bologna, devised by the eccentric architect and scenographer Antonio Basoli, with the collaboration of Ercole Gasparini. His
scheme for the park consisted of a vast network of tree-lined avenues
intersecting obliquely or at right angles, cutting the ground area into a

Feast given by King Carlo Alberto in the park at Racconigi, Piedmont, in 1842 to celebrate the marriage of Victor Emmanuel. Watercolour drawing. Biblioteca Reale, Turin.

View of the garden and the Jacquard theatre at the Rossi wool mill, Schio, Vicenza. Coloured lithograph by Matschegd, 1864. Biblioteca Bertoliana, Vicenza.

series of small polygonal sections, each of which was laid out in a different style as an individual garden. The plan echoed the patterns to be seen in the landscape of Bologna, where traditional farming divided the land into a patchwork of small plots, but in the originality of its conception it recalled the strange fantasies of Charles Percier and Pierre-Francois Fontaine in restoring the park of Versailles.

There was a new feeling in the air, and an indication of approaching change could be detected in the discussions between Napoleon I and his favourite architect Fontaine. The latter had in fact irritated the Emperor by his references to the new fashion, launching a diatribe 'against the futility of the English-style garden and against the stupidity of those people who waste their fortune making little lakes, little rocks, little rivers, as at Bagatelle, at Mousseau [Monceau] and at Fontaine-bleau. Such expressions of naïvety are the whims of bankers; my own English garden', he declared, 'is in the Forest of Fontainebleau, and I want no other.' (P. Fontaine, *Journal*, 3 March 1813). It is clear that the careers of many garden designers depended on their friendship with high financiers, as was the case with the architect Louis-Martin Berthault, who, under the Directoire, was launched by the banker Récamier and his celebrated wife Juliette, for whom he decorated a house in the Rue du Mont-Blanc; he was later employed by the army supplier Gabriel-Julien Ouvrard, at his house at Raincy, which became famous for its grotto, its iron bridge and its Russian House. He also worked for Carvillon de Tillière at his park at Pontchartrain, which he provided with waterfalls and grottoes. He had carried out his practical apprenticeship at the family property, Les Fontaines, near Chantilly, which he had gradually enlarged between 1792 and 1822. A few traces of the garden still exist, but some of its picturesque and neoclassical features (such as the fisherman's hut, the boat house, a sepulchre and an obelisk on an island) are more familiar through the series of drawings of it executed by C. Bourgeois and the mezzotint engravings by Louis-Martin's uncle, the well-known artist Pierre-Gabriel Berthault: *Suite de vingt-quatre vues de jardins anglais . . .* (Paris 1812).

Berthault was often required to transform French-style traditional gardens to the new style, but he also undertook restoration work, such as that for Watelet's Moulin-Joli and the park of the château of Prulay, near Tremblay, on the outskirts of Paris, which Abbé Delille had already redesigned. In 1820 Berthault was commissioned by Arrighi de Casanova, Duke of Padua and a cousin of Napoleon, to adapt the ancient park of Courson (originally laid out *c.* 1680). He did away with the eighteenth-century ditches and laid out a network of curvilinear avenues, planting a number of rare trees and decorative hedges. The work continued under the direction of the Bühler brothers in 1860, and between 1920 and 1950 the Comte de Caraman (to whom Courson had come by descent), a friend of Albert Kahn, completed the whole magnificent project.

Nominated in 1805 as chief architect to the Empress Josephine, Berthault succeeded Morel and took over the complex assignment of the park of La Malmaison, west of Paris, a 'little kingdom' covering more than 700 hectares (1730 acres). With the help of numerous botanists (Howatson, Delahaye and Bonpland among them), he laid out an impressive planting scheme. The park was crossed by a river and ornamented with a few buildings, the most famous perhaps being the Temple of Love designed by Alexandre Lenoir, and around these features Berthault set out a plant collection that was to become widely celebrated. It included 250 species of rose, which were painted by Redouté, hydrangeas, dahlias, camellias, peonies, hibiscus and many other flowering plants, as well as a magnificent variety of trees: cedar of Lebanon, ginkgo, beech, magnolia, larch, Mediterranean hackberry and white lime. The mania for *fabriques* gave way to a passion for botany, but not without some criticism; the landscape architect J. Lalos condemned the park for its 'excessive quantity of exotic trees', and maintained that 'indigenous trees combine much better to form large masses and perspectives'.

Berthault was not, however, a true innovator: the fashion for plant collections of this sort was not a new one if we are to believe the testimony of *Descriptions des nouveaux jardins de la France* (1808). This magnificent volume, influenced by the work of Humphry Repton, was written by Comte Alexandre de Laborde, son of the marquis-financier, who before being guillotined in 1794 had created, with Hubert Robert, the park of Méréville. He wrote that the change

took place forty years ago without the need of any foreign influence; it came about quite naturally, through the introduction of exotic trees: the multiplicity of their shapes and the variety of their foliage made it apparent that they were seen to greater advantage grouped together in clumps or planted singly than ranged in straight avenues. In this way they could develop more freely and form more beautiful compositions. Once this irregularity had been adopted, similar changes took place within the watercourses that were to irrigate them. For the paths that were made amid them, there was no longer any need to bring in from foreign parts masters of an art that nature could teach us just as well in our own country.

De Laborde, adopting the tone of a historian, felt the need to add a reflection on the change of attitude that had occurred and to draw a parallel between 'the regularity in the pattern of life' and the symmetry of the garden: 'Feelings themselves had their own gradations and, so to speak, their own ceremonial, just as the Court had its etiquette.' And further: 'It is certain that the imprecision that has pervaded all principles, and the freedom of action that has become a part of the way of life, would have been enough to abolish any regularity in the places in which peopled lived.'

Berthault, by now regularly employed by the imperial family, was commissioned to complete the park of St-Leu-Taverny, at that time in the possession of Louis Bonaparte and Queen Hortense (owner of the legendary eight thousand pots of hydrangeas), and also the park of Beauregard, near Villeneuve-St-George, for Prince Aldobrandini Borghese. After Berthault's death the work at Beauregard was carried on by Nicolas Vergnaud. At the same time Joseph Bonaparte acquired the estate of Mortefontaine and developed its vast series of landscaped lakes, which had been begun in the eighteenth century. In 1806 Berthault was appointed architect to the Palace of Compiègne and converted into an English-style park the garden designed by Gabriel, which had never been completed. Seventy thousand trees and shrubs were provided by the imperial nurseries and direct from Gabriel Thouin at the Jardin des Plantes. The Berceau de Fer, an enormously long pergola covered in climbing plants, was built along the side of the park. If it is difficult to define Berthault's style with any accuracy – it could perhaps be described as eclecticism or, alternatively, as a pragmatic response to the changing tastes of his clients – it is undoubtedly true that at Compiègne he created one of the first 'mixed' gardens, a formula that he was later to develop in major projects such as the garden of the King of Rome at Chaillot in Paris. A sure sign of a change in taste was provided by the refusal by A. F. Peyre, on behalf of the Council for Civic Buildings, to grant permission for the plans presented by Giuseppe Valadier for the gardens of the Campidoglio and for the Nuovo Giardino del Gran Cesare, between the Piazza del Popolo and the Pincio in Rome (1812); the English style in which they were designed was considered inappropriate for the times. Berthault and Alexandre de Gisors were commissioned to draw up alternative plans, which consisted of a regular, geometric layout and included an ingenious arrangement of ramps between terraces; their scheme was put forward and accepted in 1813.

Further indications of imminent change could be perceived in a new attitude towards the purpose and significance of the garden, as was the case with the English-style garden designed by Giuseppe Jappelli for Cavaliere Antonio Vigodarzere, at Saonara in the Veneto. It appeared to be traditional in reflecting its owner's social status and the principles and aims of his life – his philanthropic aid for the local population, in particular, demonstrated by his charitable work in 1816 – and the Masonic connections of both the client and the architect, which were expressed, for example, in the controversial statue of Baffometto in the Grotto of the Knights Templar (probably installed by Vigodarzere's adopted son, Andrea Cittadella, sometime after 1835). But it also signified an important change and reflected a shift towards greater political sensibility on the part of a new generation of the ruling class, one that was more enlightened, progressive and idealistic in its attitudes. It frequently bore the imprint of the Masonic movement, and was to be seen particularly clearly in the culture of Tuscany in, for example, the work of the architect Luigi de Cambray Digny: the Oricellari Gardens in Florence (begun in 1813), for Marchese Stiozzi Ridolfi; the garden of the great reformer Marchese Pietro Torrigiani (laid out in 1813–14); the park of the Puccini family at Scornio, Pistoia (1821–7). A few decades later, visitors flocked to this Tuscan park to see the Pantheon dedicated to the memory of virtuous men, and the Napoleon Bridge. Both these buildings were completed in 1838. On an island was a temple dedicated to Pythagoras, and, nearby, a Gothic castle designed by Alessandro Gherardesca, the author of *La casa di delizia, il giardino e la fattoria* (Pisa 1826). Gherardesca was also responsible for the silkworm house and spinning mill in the garden of the Villa Roncioni at Pugnano, near Pisa, whose design anticipated by several years Japelli's Gothic scenographical work. It also pre-dated the work of the architect Pelagio Palagi, whose Gothic tower, intended as a museum, was built between 1831 and 1836 in the romantic garden of the Villa Traversi at Desio, near Milan; Palagi also created the neo-Gothic fantasy of Margheria (c. 1832–42), a farmhouse with chapel and apartments, which he built for King Carlo Alberto of Savoy in the Racconigi park in Piedmont, working in collaboration with the garden designer Saverio Kurten. An example of an industrial application of the Gothic style of the period – a mixture of Venetian and Byzantine – was seen in the garden designed in 1859–64 by the architect Alessandro Negrin for Alessandro Rossi's wool mill at Schio, near Vicenza.

In the gardens laid out as a model estate for the philanthropist and agronomist François de la Rochefoucauld, Duc de Liancourt after 1799, a *Rond de la danse* was provided for the workers employed in the manufacture of ceramics and textiles. The architect-engineer Curten the Elder, a great traveller, agronomist and theoretician on the subject of gardens, took up an idea first proposed by Perrache in 1776 to develop the 'peninsula' of Lyons, between the Rhône and the Saône; he presented a design for the project which included a garden and an imperial palace, but Napoleon, deterred by the estimate of its cost, refused even to consider it. In his *Essai sur les jardins* (Lyons – Paris 1807), Curten put forward his first theory on the urban garden:

In the city, where land is precious and limited, it is necessary to use methods different from those suitable in the countryside . . . one should try to create, as far as the environment will permit, the impression of a site larger than it really is . . . This method involves enclosing the site by planting, and creating a large space at the centre.

With this proposal, Curten helped to disseminate theories already put into practice in the parks designed by Humphry Repton and John Nash. He also put forward the idea of an 'industrial garden' for an agricultural and industrial community:

Such a development, by means of its numerous buildings (*fabriques*) and hydraulic machinery, the water courses provided by the Rhône and the variety of crops and plantations laid out according to a plan for the entire project, would combine all the greatest advantages, particularly those of clean air and proper drainage of the marshland.

In his treatise, Curten also opened a discussion on the qualifications appropriate to a garden designer. The art of the garden was, in his words, the 'luxury of agriculture', so 'the term Garden (*Jardin*) seems to me inappropriate, as does the term Gardener (*Jardinier*). The man whom the English call a Gardener is something quite different from us; we call him a Garden Designer because he knows the art of the garden; in consequence, he knows how to make a garden.'

The park of *fabriques* of the Garenne Lemot at Clisson, laid out for the sculptor François-Frédérique Lemot between 1805 and 1827 by Mathurin Crucy, chief architect of Nantes, was intended as a sort of

deliverance from the devastation caused by the recent fighting in the Vendée, and as a symbol of moral and cultural uplift. It followed in every detail the doctrines of the brothers François and Pierre Cacault, founders of a museum-school in Clisson set up to provide the younger citizens of the town with a cultural education. One might say that Lemot and Crucy attempted on a small scale what Peter Joseph Lenné, a pupil of Thouin, and Karl Friedrich Schinkel had carried out on a large scale in the Berlin Tiergarten (1818–40) and in the Charlottenhof in Potsdam (1826).

In *L'Art de créer les jardins* (Paris 1835), the architect Nicolas Vergnaud, who had paid a long visit to England in 1835, proposed the introduction of watermills and industrial buildings in gardens: these (*les usines*) were, according to him, 'one of the elements that most enliven the scene, adding a picturesque aspect to any site . . . factories shrouded in steam effortlessly assume impressive lines and shapes.' The idea that the first visible effects on the landscape of the industrial revolution might consist of the creation of parks around factories is an indication of the extent to which the garden was considered by philanthropist and social reformers to be the most efficient means of introducing moral and sanitary improvement. It was no coincidence that Vergnaud, who worked at the château of La Perrine (Eure-et-Loir) and at Beauregard (Seine-et-Oise) was the author of *Projet d'amélioration et d'embellissemens pour Auteuil, Passy et communes voisines de la capitale* (Paris 1832), published after the cholera epidemic of 1832. His plan for improvements in urban cleanliness, and in slaughterhouses, the water and fire services, fountains, sewers, public baths, pavements, lighting and public transport in the areas surrounding Paris was entrusted to the banker Gabriel Delessert, the fourth son of a Swiss financier living in Lyons, Etienne Delessert, who had been a friend of Rousseau and Necker, and a disseminator of the ideas of Jeremy Bentham. The Delessert family had founded a sugar refinery at Passy, the city of which Gabriel was elected mayor in 1830. In the course of his long political career he strove to improve traffic conditions in Paris, and fought strenuously against noise and against the steady disintegration of many of the city's monuments.

In 1819 Vicomte Amédée de Viart, the owner and creator of the park of Brunehaut (Essonne), published *Le jardiniste moderne*, in which he endeavoured to coin the new terms of *jardinisme* and *jardiniste*, in order to distinguish the 'recognized artist who creates gardens' from 'the workman who cultivates them'. In the second edition of his treatise, which appeared in 1827, Viart used instead the neologism *jardinique*, which was taken up by the great English theoretician on eclecticism John Claudius Loudon, who wrote the following in the *Gardener's Magazine* (VIII, December 1832):

There are various other beauties besides those of the picturesque, which ought to engage the attention of the landscape-gardener; and one of the principal of these is, what may be called the botany of trees and shrubs . . . Mere picturesque improvement is not enough in these enlightened times: it is

Plan of the Perrache peninsula in the city of Lyons, at the confluence of the Rhône and the Saône rivers, by Curten the Elder. From Essai sur les jardins, 1807.

View of a valley in the park of Brunehaut (Essonne). From A. de Viart, Le jardiniste moderne, 1819.

necessary to understand that there is such a character of art as the gardenesque, as well as the picturesque.

Loudon was by no means preaching in the wilderness. In England the renewal of interest in the Baroque garden had led to the restoration of the topiary garden at Levens Hall in Cumbria, completed by the head gardener Archibald Forbes *c.* 1810. The Frenchman Pierre Boitard was to use a view of it as a frontispiece to his treatise (fourth ed. 1834). The fashion for eclecticism had already been reflected in the Earl of Shrewsbury's garden at Alton Towers in Staffordshire, which was the work of Robert Abraham. Loudon visited it and disapproved of its excesses; he preferred to wander in the garden created by Lady Broughton in the 1820s at Hoole House in Cheshire, where a lawn, punctuated by flowerbeds, was enclosed by a rock garden modelled on the Alps at Chamonix, where even the spaces between the rocks 'are filled up with . . . fragments of white marble, to look like snow.'

Loudon endeavoured to establish a theory in order to promulgate his idea of the recognizability of the art of the garden. A source of inspiration was provided for him by the *Essai sur la nature . . . de l'imitation* (1823) by Quatremère de Quincy, which strangely enough echoes Pindemonte's discourse on the non-imitative character of the art of landscape gardening (published in 1817). Quatremère's new argument, which was different from that propounded in 1788, was that in the informal garden 'the desired image of nature is simply nature itself. The medium of this art is reality. . . . Now, nothing can pretend to be at the same time reality and imitation'. Who can have served as intermediary between the Paduan theoretician and the brilliant writings of the Parisian academic-sculptor? Very probably a friend, the President of the Venetian Academy, Leopoldo Cicognara, who in 1817 had translated an extract of Quatremère's *Giove olimpico* (1814) and in 1824 was to publish an extract of his essay on imitation in the magazine *Antologia*, printed in Florence. It was Loudon himself, however, who asked the painter J. C. Kent to translate Quatremère's book into English (1837). Equipped with these confirmations of his theory, which emphasized the need for artifice in the garden, Loudon set out to achieve recognition for the aesthetic principles in which he believed, and to gain acceptance for the use of a wide variety of both native and exotic species, for a return to pure formality, and for the laying out of flowerbeds and the planting of isolated trees. At the same time the head gardener at Elvaston Castle in Derbyshire, William Baron, reintroduced topiary work and in the section of the garden called Mon Plaisir he based the design on a seventeenth-century plan by Daniel Marot. The architect Anthony Salvin laid out Elizabethan-style terraces at Harlaxton Manor in Lincolnshire between 1831 and 1838 for Gregory Gregory, a descendant of the Prince de Ligne. Between 1851 and 1854 Sir Charles Barry designed a garden at Shrubland Park in Suffolk, which included a staircase of 137 steps linking a series of Italian-style terraces.

An interpretation of the facts based on changing fashion and taste, or

on the recognition of the influence of a revival, seems, however, inadequate. The dominion of the picturesque garden, that splendid English invention of the first half of the eighteenth century, began to give way the moment the principle on which it had been based – the imitation of nature – revealed its limitations and weaknesses. Is it fair perhaps to suggest that a connection existed between the rejection of an established formula and the changes in attitude that took place at this time as a result of the scientific and industrial revolution?

Bibliography

GENERAL

C. Batteux, *Les Beaux-Arts réduits à un même principe* (1746), ed. by J.-R. Mantion (Paris 1989).
A. C. Quatremère de Quincy, *Encyclopédie Méthodique: Architecture*, 3 vols (Paris and Liège 1788–1825), reissued as *Dictionnaire historique d'Architecture* (Paris 1832); *idem, Essai sur la nature, le but et les moyens de l'imitation dans les beaux-arts* (1823; reprinted Brussels 1980).
G. L. Hersey, 'Associationism and Sensibility in Eighteenth-Century Architecture' in *Eighteenth-Century Studies*, Vol. 4, no. 1 (Autumn 1970) pp. 71–89.

FRANCE

G. Thouin, *Plans raisonnés de toutes les espèces de jardins* (1820; reprint Paris 1989).
E. de Ganay, *Bibliographie de l'art des jardins* (1944; reissued Paris 1989); *idem, Les Jardins en France et leur décor* (Paris 1949).
Jardins en France, 1760–1820. Pays d'illusion, terre d'expérience, exhib. cat., CNMHS (Paris 1977).
Mathurin Crucy (1749–1826). Architecte nantais néoclassique, exhib. cat. (Nantes 1986).
J. P. Babelon (ed.) *Le château en France* (Paris 1986).
P.-F.-L. Fontaine, *Journal (1799–1853)*, 2 vols (Paris 1987).
J. D. Devauges, 'Berthault, Louis-Martin' in *Encyclopedia Universalis* (Paris, in course of publication).

ITALY

S. Lange, *Ville della provincia di Milano* (Milan 1971).
E. Silva, *Dell'arte de' giardini inglesi*, ed. by G. Venturi (Milan 1976).
Pelagio Palagi, artista e collezionista, exhib. cat. (Bologna 1976).
L'arte del Settecento emiliano. Architettura, scenografia, pittura di paesaggio, exhib. cat. (Bologna 1979).
Il giardino storico italiano. Problemi di indagine. Fonti letterarie e storiche (Florence 1981).
G. Mazzi (ed.) *Japelli e il suo tempo*, 2 vols (Padua 1982).
F. Borsi and G. Pampaloni (ed.) *Monumenti d'Italia. Ville e giardini* (Novara 1984).
Alla scoperta della Toscana lorenese. Architettura e bonifiche, exhib. cat. (Florence 1984).
A. Maniglio Calcagno (ed.) *Giardini, parchi, paesaggio nella Genova dell'ottocento* (Genoa 1984, 2nd edn. 1985).

Valadier, segno e architettura, exhib. cat. (Rome 1985).
Forma. La città antica e il suo avvenire, exhib. cat., CNMHS (Rome 1985).
Il giardino romantico, exhib. cat., Parco di Pratolino (Florence 1986).
Racconigi. Il castello, il parco, il territorio, Sovrintendenza B. A. e Arch. del Piemonte (Racconigi 1987).
A. Tagliolini, *Storia del giardino italiano* (Florence 1988).
M. Azzi Visentini (ed.) *Il giardino Veneto. Dal tardo medioevo al Novecento* (Milan 1988).

GREAT BRITAIN

The Landscape Gardening . . . of Humphry Repton, ed. by J. C. Loudon (1840; reprinted Farnborough 1969).
H. I. Triggs, *Formal Gardens in England and Scotland* (1902; reprint London 1989).
C. Hussey, *The Picturesque, Studies in a Point of View* (1927; reissued London 1983).
J. Dixon Hunt, 'Emblem and Expressionism in the Eighteenth-Century Landscape Garden' in *Eighteenth-Century Studies*, Vol. 4, no. 3 (Spring 1971) pp. 294–317.
G. Hersey, *High Victorian Gothic. A Study in Associationism* (Baltimore 1972).
J. Harris, '"Gardenesque": the Case of Charles Greville's Garden at Gloucester' in *Journal of Garden History*, Vol. 1, no. 2 (1981).
John Claudius Loudon and the Early Nineteenth Century in Great Britain (Dumbarton Oaks 1980).
G. Carter, P. Goode, K. Laurie (eds.) *Humphry Repton, Landscape Gardener. 1752–1818* (Norwich and London 1982).
T. H. D. Turner, 'Loudon's Stylistic Development' in *Journal of Garden History*, Vol. 2, no. 2 (1982) pp. 175–88.
D. Watkin, *The English Vision. The Picturesque in Architecture, Landscape and Garden Design* (London 1982).
T. Carter, *The Victorian Garden* (London 1984).
B. Elliott, *Victorian Gardens* (London 1986).
K. L. Simo, *Loudon and the Landscape. From Country Seat to Metropolis, 1783–1843* (New Haven 1988).
E. Clarke, G. Wright, *English Topiary Gardens* (London 1988).
J. Brown, *The Art and Architecture of English Gardens. Designs for the Garden from the Collection of the RIBA. 1609 to the Present Day* (London and New York 1989).

Present-day view of the topiary in the garden of Levens Hall, Cumbria. (Photo Brigitte Thomas and Philippe Perdereau)

View of the garden of Alton Towers, Staffordshire. (Photo Daniele De Lonte)

Public Parks in Great Britain and the United States: From a 'Spirit of the Place' to a 'Spirit of Civilization'

Alessandra Ponte

It is possible, in a very simplified way, to summarize the majority of the arguments concerned with the creation of public parks in Great Britain in the early part of the nineteenth century by means of an analysis of the plans of two particular parks. The first, published in 1829 in *The Gardener's Magazine*, was by John Claudius Loudon, gardener and celebrated popularizer of the art of garden design. The second, which appeared five years later in the *Magazine of Botany*, was the work of Sir Joseph Paxton, garden designer and architect.[1]

Loudon's plan was presented against a background of the great debate surrounding the demand for Hampstead Heath to be enclosed and developed. This vast, uncultivated area, made up of fields and woodland, had until then been freely enjoyed by the whole community; craftsmen, clerks and working people of all sorts walked miles on their days off to enjoy its green spaces and clean air, and the threat of its disappearance as an area open to all came as a serious blow. London's population had doubled in three decades (there were a million and a half inhabitants in 1830) and its suburbs were expanding at an uncontrollable rate. The development of two hundred acres of Hampstead Heath represented another significant stage in the gradual erosion of London's open spaces, and the loss, according to contemporary comment, of one of the city's most vital 'lungs'.[2]

There is no intention to list here all the well-known ills that afflicted cities and industrial centres in the nineteenth century; it is enough to remember that the concept of a public park emerged as a response to problems of sanitation and urban growth. The public park was one of the principal means by which nineteenth-century reform endeavoured to improve the situation and thus the quality of life. Among the first to recognize the true scale of the problem was John Claudius Loudon. In adding his voice to the chorus of protest aroused by the proposal to develop Hampstead Heath, Loudon did not confine himself merely to demanding the conservation of an open space but also presented an elaborate plan for the whole capital, consisting of a series of concentric circles in which 'city' belts alternated with 'rural' belts. This proposition, described in an article entitled 'Breathing Places for the Metropolis' was illustrated by means of an ingeniously simple device: on a map of London and its outlying suburbs Loudon superimposed a diagrammatic overlay of white rings for built-up areas and grey rings for open spaces, centring on St Paul's cathedral. On the map the scheme appeared to be rigid in its definition of the borderlines between one area and another, but in fact in the 'urban' areas all the gardens were to be retained and in the 'rural' areas existing buildings were to be conserved. London would, according to this proposal, have become a homogeneous series of urban areas linked by green spaces. The plan was accompanied by a description of an ideal capital city – its application to London was implied – served by a network of radial concentric streets and provided with an efficient system of public transport, mains water and gas supplies, irrigation canals and drainage. It presented a scheme that made sense in terms of sanitation, economics and aesthetics, and that would require to be implemented by a city council capable of coordinating long- and short-term objectives and of working on a scale that embraced not only the heart of the capital but also the outlying districts.

Loudon's plan could be regarded as Utopian in that it depended on the enactment of laws and governmental procedures that did not exist at the time. It did, however, specify the technical operations required to put the scheme into practice and indicated, with remarkable clarity, what precisely would be needed to run it: this consisted above all of new political and administrative legislation to back up that of the existing city council and a close relationship between garden design and town planning.

This last factor did not apply simply to the design of the public parks or other green spaces in the city but rather to the planning of the entire capital as part of the landscape. The garden designers involved were perhaps the only professionals of their kind at the time to have the means to undertake a project on such a large scale and the tools to carry it out: in the eighteenth century special garden implements had been designed specifically for the maintenance of the vast landscaped parks then being laid out for many of England's great country houses.

Loudon laid out London as a homogeneous and varied succession of picturesque, pastoral, urban and formal scenes, using precisely the same criteria as were applied to the planning of a country park, where the landscape designer's task was to create a variety of different scenes and to achieve a natural transition from one to the other. A particularly interesting aspect of his proposal was the introduction into an urban setting of the concept of a 'belt', which Loudon had proposed as the solution to the problem of the outer perimeters of the parks. In the language of contemporary garden designers, these belts consisted of a dense, and sometimes broad, band of trees intersected by avenues that marked the confines of the territory and, at the same time, provided openings in the trees at strategic intervals, revealing views into the park itself or towards the city outside it. It should be remembered perhaps what an effect this proposal was to have on the concept of urban planning. Two early examples of its influence, to which we shall return later, are worth mentioning here: the ring of parks designed for Manchester in the 1840s and for Liverpool between 1862 and 1872.

Loudon was not the only one to present a proposal of this sort with great precision and clarity. For instance, in a scheme put forward around the middle of the nineteenth century, which recommended the formation of a series of parks in Liverpool, it was suggested that there should be 'a belt of garden or park land bounding the present extent of the town, and insuring the interposition of a stretch of comparative country between the existing buildings and any more of a town character'.[3] This quotation implies references both to the idea of the 'belt' and to the city as part of a landscaped scheme comprised of areas of a variety of different characters. Almost two decades later, and in more specific terms, William Robinson – celebrated above all as the creator of the wild garden – wrote an important book on the parks, walks and gardens of Paris, which was published in 1869: in it he

Proposals for 'Breathing Places for the Metropolis', by J. C. Loudon. From The Gardener's Magazine, *5, 1829. The Royal Horticultural Society, London.*

Plan of the Derby Arboretum by J. C. Loudon. From The Gardener's Magazine, *16, 1840. The Royal Horticultural Society, London.*

praised, with some reservations, the urban landscaping schemes undertaken in France and demanded that they should be imitated in Great Britain. In order to do so, it was essential that central government should accept the responsibility for devising an overall design programme. 'The real want', lamented Robinson, 'is a want of plan'.[4] Such a plan would have had to embrace the creation not only of public parks but also of tree-lined avenues, squares, places of recreation and 'breathing spaces' since, as Robinson pointed out, the parks only fulfilled the needs of the people to breathe and relax in the open air at the weekends, when they had time to walk to the nearest park, which for many people was some distance away. Robinson concluded by inviting the urban planners to concentrate available resources on 'city gardening', in other words on an overall plan for the city's development rather than putting them towards the useless embellishment of a single park. His article finished with a practical suggestion: that future laws on the development of open spaces should specify the retention of a certain percentage of the designated area as parkland. This was also to apply to the first attempts to regulate, by means of specific legislation, the development of commons and wastelands close to centres of urban density. It is worth recalling the proposals put forward by John Arthur Roebuck, a member of parliament and an active supporter of the Utilitarian Society, in which he stressed the importance of a number of factors: the city council's involvement in the conservation and maintenance of areas of common land in the immediate vicinity of the city; the observance of the law of 1836 which prohibited the development of commons within a radius of ten miles of London or three miles in the case of cities with 100,000 inhabitants, two and a half miles in the case of cities with 70,000 inhabitants, etc.; and the observance of the law of 1837 which stipulated that every development should include an area for 'recreation' and 'physical exercise' for those living in the neighbourhood.[5]

It was in 1833 that the subject of public parks was taken up by parliament, when the Select Committee on Public Walks and Places of Exercise presented its first report. The task of the committee was to establish the number of open spaces accessible to the public in all the major cities and to put forward proposals for appropriate action on a local and a national level. The report outlined the various factors that determined the need for green spaces and the necessity to provide healthier and cleaner conditions for the working classes. It concluded with the observation that in the previous fifty years nothing had been done to obviate the problems caused by urbanization, and recommended the creation of open spaces. The words 'open spaces' are particularly relevant because the subject of enquiry was never exclusively parks but included also areas of common land in general that were not built over. In fact, in calculating the availability of open spaces, the report included botanical gardens, walks, paths, cemeteries, sports fields, commons and the gardens belonging to a variety of public institutions.[6] This approach introduced one of the questions central to the early history of the nineteenth-century public park and, in a more

1. Finchley Common; in the zone of country.
2. Tottenham; in the zone of town.
3. Walthamstow; town.
4. Forrest House; town.
5. Stoke Newington; town.
6. Highgate; country.
7. Hampstead; country.
8. Kingsbury; country.
9. Wilsdon; town.
10. Kentish Town; town.
11. Clapton; town.
12. Hommerton; town.
13. Stratford; country.
14. West Ham; country.
15. West Ham Abbey; country.
16. East Ham; town.
17. Bethnal Green; country.
18. Hoxton; town.
19. Islington; country.
20. Somers Town; country.
21. Regent's Park; country.
22. Paddington; town.
23. Paddington canal; town.
24. Six Elms; town.
25. Bayswater; town.
26. Hyde Park; country.
27. Green Park; town.
28. Southwark; town.
29. London Docks; town.
30. West India Docks; town.
31. Woolwich; town.
32. Isle of Dogs; town.
33. Greenwich Park; country.
34. Deptford; town.
35. Walworth; town.
36. Brompton; town.
37. Kensington; town.
38. Hammersmith; town.
39. Lambeth; country.
40. Kennington; country.
41. Camberwell; country.
42. Peckham; town.
43. Dulwich; town.
44. Clapham; town.
45. Fulham; country.
46. Putney; town.
47. Roehampton; country.
48. Wandsworth; town.
49. Wimbledon Park; country.
50. Tooting; town.
51. Norwood; town.
52. Sydenham; town.

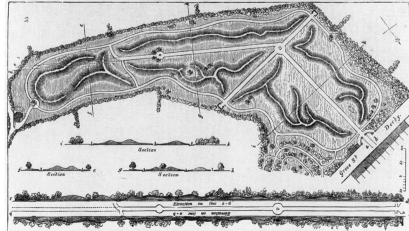

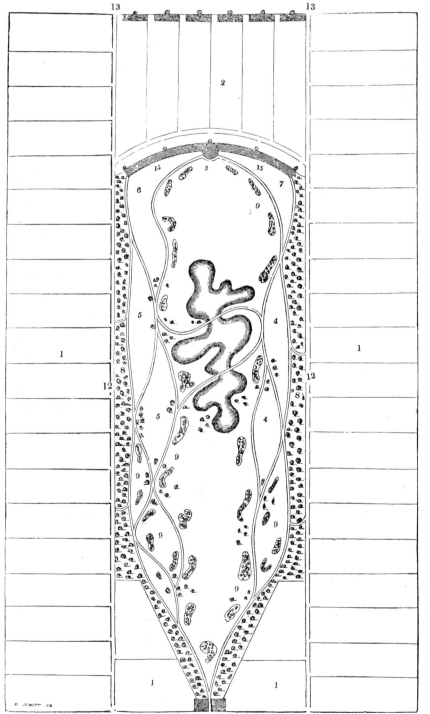

general way, the history of the art of garden design. Between the end of the eighteenth century and the beginning of the nineteenth, the evolution of the garden suffered, as did the architecture of the period, from a shift in emphasis from aesthetics to functionalism. A corresponding change occurred in the attitudes of those for whom the gardens were intended; in the past they had simply enjoyed them as observers, now they wished to make use of them, to organize them in such a way that they fulfilled their needs.

Clear signs of this revolution can be seen in the work of Humphry Repton, who, in the course of his celebrated debate with Richard Payne Knight and Uvedale Price on the nature of the picturesque, had defined a series of distinctions between painting and the art of gardening. Knight and Price had accused Repton, as a follower of Capability Brown, of employing the same scheme without variation or discrimination in gardens of very different character, with results of stultifying monotony. Brown's parks, like those of Repton, lacked poetry because they had ignored the lessons of the great landscape painters. Not least of the charges levelled at Repton and his colleagues (the 'professionals', who were drawn up on one side) by Knight and Price (the 'dilettanti', on the other) was the accusation that garden designers had transformed a means of artistic expression reflecting the taste and judgment of an individual into a scientific profession.[7]

The most important argument in Repton's defence was that the park or garden was designed for people's enjoyment. The landscapes depicted in the work of the painters, as Repton explained, was not; it might have suited gypsies or bandits (the work of Salvator Rosa was a case in point) but not civilized people. Nature had to be domesticated, tamed, made comfortable. Throughout his career Repton reiterated this belief, even to the extent of denying the links that he had earlier admitted between garden design and painting. He turned in the end to architecture, and in particular to domestic architecture and the definition of space according to its intended use, for a justification and an endorsement of the principles governing the art of gardening. In his last treatise, published in 1816, Repton wrote:

And while I have acceded to the combination of two words, Landscape and Gardening, yet they are as distinct objects as the picture and its frame. The Scenery of Nature, called Landscape, and that of a Garden, are as different as their uses; one is to please the eye, the other is for the comfort and occupation of man: one is wild, and may be adapted to animals in the wildest state of nature; while the other is appropriated to man in the highest state of civilization and refinement.[8]

This is an early reference to the 'civilized' garden of the nineteenth century. As will be discussed later, it was in the design of parks in the nineteenth century that the search for the Beautiful, the Sublime and the Picturesque, which were the main preoccupations of the treatise writers of the period, began to be replaced by an aesthetic ideal based on the changing, transient and complex concept of civilization. It was concerns such as these that were to lead Repton to lay out 'practical' gardens comprised of 'formal' elements in the vicinity of the houses to which they belonged rather than relegating them to the most distant corner of the park, as before. This accounts for the appearance on his plans and in his writings of gardens designed to fulfil a particular function: a kitchen garden laid out close to the house made the cutting of herbs and vegetables a simple operation while at the same time, if it was enclosed by walls, it provided a pleasant place for a walk; glasshouses, essential features of any large garden, were included in his schemes, as were menageries housing pheasants and other attractive game birds; rose arbours for the peaceful pleasures of the women of the house; sheltered areas for the protection of delicate species and to provide greenery in winter; gardens full of exotic plants to satisfy the desire for specimens of botanical interest . . .

For Repton, however, gardens designed for a particular use were simply part of a much wider concept: their relationship to each other and the actual purpose they fulfilled were unimportant in themselves compared to the overall design of the landscaped park of which they formed a part and to its value as a work of art. The shift from an aesthetic to a functional emphasis was marked by the publication, in 1820, of *Plans raisonnés de toutes les espèces de jardins* by Gabriel Thouin. The remarkable success of Thouin's collection is understandable only if we regard it as the first real attempt to classify the various types of garden according to their function. In celebrating certain sorts of garden, however, it diminished the art of garden design in general. It gave equal importance to the orderly rows of trees in an orchard and to the asymmetrical planting scheme of a 'garden of delights', to a gardener's hut and a pavilion designed for feasts and celebrations, to the geometric regularity of a kitchen garden and the sinuously curving lakes of a landscaped park (it is clear, incidentally, that for both Repton and Thouin, 'practical' corresponded to 'orderly and regular' and 'beautiful' to 'irregular'). As a result, Thouin removed the barriers separating practicality from beauty and art from technology. This did not, however, produce greater freedom; on the contrary, it caused disquiet. Loudon, for example, who was fascinated by Thouin's work, and by his idea of classification, was forced to seek some sort of compromise, placing garden design between the high arts and the practical arts and coining the term 'mixed' art to define it.[9] The principle of classification by function, and its corresponding effect on garden design did, however, remain the predominant influence on nineteenth-century gardening, as an analysis of the writings of the period make abundantly clear.

If the example of Loudon is an indication of the general trends in the art of gardening and of its relationship with the city, a study of the work of Paxton brings us back to an analysis of problems closely linked with the design of public parks. In a treatise published under the title of *A Plan for Forming Subscription Gardens*, Paxton proposed a scheme in which a rectangular area of land should be divided into fifty plots of a quarter of an acre (about a thousand square metres) each along the perimeter of a garden covering four acres (one and a half hectares). A

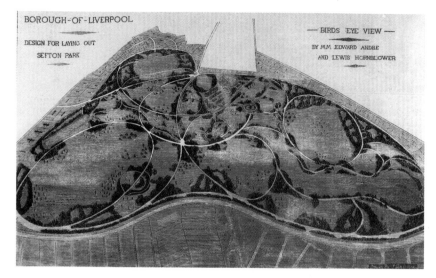

BOROUGH-OF-LIVERPOOL

DESIGN FOR LAYING OUT
SEFTON PARK

— BIRDS EYE VIEW —

BY M.M. EDWARD ANDRE
AND LEWIS HORNBLOWER

house would be built on each plot, which would be surrounded by its own private garden facing a central public garden. This proposal illustrates, if somewhat sketchily, the fundamental plan employed in the design of many public parks of the period. The perimeter was marked by a belt of trees and a carriageway. The park itself was crossed by a series of winding paths and consisted of wide areas of grass planted with beds of shrubs and isolated trees. The main element was a lake whose irregular outlines were carefully designed to appear as natural as possible. The scheme in no way represented an innovation in the history of gardening: at the end of the eighteenth century similar ideas – labelled 'belting, clumping and dotting' – were employed. It did, however, contain at least two original features: the idea of adopting the same overall system for the design of different types of garden, and the proposal to finance the enterprise by means of the subscribed plots around the perimeter.

In the article accompanying his plan, Paxton explained that the common central space could be laid out as a botanical garden, a suggestion born of the contemporary passion for rare plants and of the fact that public parks provided the perfect opportunity for education. Loudon was the first person to identify the characteristics of this style of gardening, which had grown from the introduction in Europe of new and exotic plant species. There was an increasing aesthetic and scientific interest in the idea of single rare specimens rather than massed planting, which underlined the distinction between the garden and the park as it demanded the planting of each specimen in such a way that it could be examined and appreciated for its particular characteristics.[10] It was, however, an expensive style of gardening in that these exotic rarities needed to be cared for by expert gardeners and to be provided with appropriate conditions, all of which involved considerable financial investment and maintenance. In general, this precluded such gardens from being incorporated into public parks, where one of the major considerations was, naturally, economics. On the other hand, it did offer fascinating possibilities in terms of education and garden development: what better method could there possibly be for improving the health of the working classes both morally and physically? So the exotic or botanical garden was adapted wherever possible to suit the constraints of the public park, and one of the most brilliant and influential solutions to the problem was the arboretum laid out by Loudon at Derby.

It was begun in 1839, and it represented one of the most important landmarks of Loudon's career. It was, as has already been said, a time when town and city councils had no legal or financial powers to buy and maintain areas of land for public parks, and the site in question – an area of eleven acres (four and a half hectares) – was offered to the city of Derby by the ex-mayor, Joseph Strutt. It consisted of a piece of flat land of irregular shape with such poor drainage that it was regarded as unhealthy, and unfortunately Strutt had not accompanied his gift with sufficient funds to cover the costs of drainage and future maintenance. Loudon's task was to overcome the problems it presented without

Philips Park, Manchester. (Photo Daniele De Lonte)

Sefton Park, Liverpool. (Photo Daniele De Lonte)

touching any of the existing features of the site – a belt of trees, a flower garden, a cottage, a hut covered in ivy and an oak tree near the main entrance. Loudon drew up a relatively simple plan based on two axes with a rotunda at their point of intersection. The line of the main axis, which began at the entrance, was bent to follow the shape of the site while a winding path followed a meandering course around the perimeter. The flatness of the terrain was relieved by the creation of a series of small hillocks. The most important aspect of the plan was, however, the planting scheme: Loudon chose shrubs and trees from all the major English nurseries and arranged them according to Jussieu's classification of plant species. Every specimen was numbered and labelled with its botanical name, its common name, its place of origin, the date of its introduction into Great Britain and the height of a mature specimen in its native land. More information was provided in a booklet written by Loudon and available at the arboretum. His planning of the arboretum was governed by economics: he believed that the park could be maintained by a head gardener and two assistants, and this would make it a viable proposition. It seems that he was right. According to various contemporary accounts, the arboretum was enormously successful, and the concept quickly took hold both in Great Britain and in the United States. To quote just one comment of the time, from a parliamentary commission reporting on conditions in the cities of the United Kingdom in 1845, 'The Arboretum . . . is much frequented, and has already produced a perceptible effect in improving the appearance and demeanour of the working classes, and it has, doubtless conferred an equal benefit upon their health'.[11]

It has been said many times that there were three principal influences on the design of public parks from the beginning: the eighteenth-century landscape park, the botanical garden, and pleasure-gardens of the sort made famous by Vauxhall Gardens in London.[12] In the Derby Arboretum the influence of the first two categories is clearly recognizable but no trace is to be found of the third; the arboretum remained a place principally intended for walking. Elements derived from pleasure-gardens are, however, detectable in the three parks laid out in Manchester in the 1840s: Peel Park, Queen's Park and Philips Park. The parks – one of whose functions was to offer a healthy alternative to the 'temptations of the inn and the tavern, with their frequent accompaniment of immorality and vice' – contained, apart from their ornamental features, various items of equipment for sporting and physical recreation and other leisure activities of a healthy nature. The local parks committee organized a competition for new designs, specifying that planners must include in their proposals for each park a gymnasium, one or more fountains of pure water, numerous seats and suitable spaces for archery, skittles and other games. The winner of the contest was Joshua Major, who was given the difficult task of providing, in a limited space, areas for a vast range of different activities without detracting from the fundamental concept of the park as a public garden.[13]

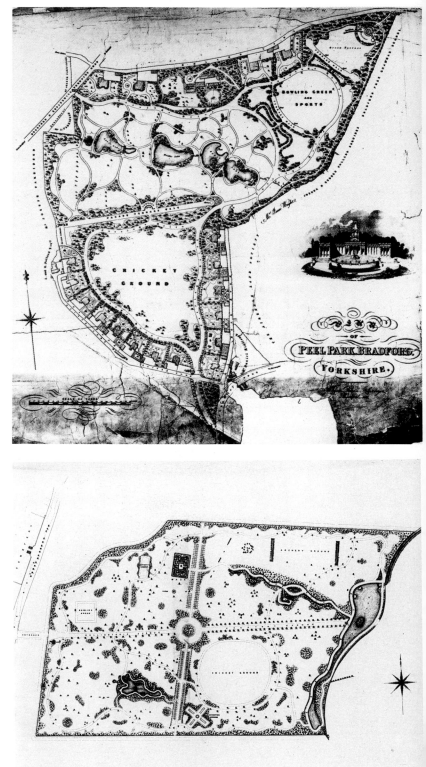

*Plan of Stamford Park, Altrincham, 1879.
Altrincham Library.*

Plan of Abbey Park, Leicester. From The
Gardener's Chronicle, *2, 1880. The Royal
Horticultural Society, London.*

PLAN OF STAMFORD PARK.
ALTRINCHAM.

In a recent article on the provision of games and sports facilities in nineteenth-century public parks, Hazel Conway singled out three different approaches to the problem: the first was a pragmatic solution involving the incorporation of the necessary facilities into an already existing design; the second proposed laying out the sports grounds in an area entirely separate from the gardens; the third proposed the integration of the sports and games areas into the design concept of the park as a whole. The first proposal was really a variation on the third in terms of the problems it presented to the designer, in other words the incorporation of the required facilities into the landscape of the park.[14] Here too, then, designers were confronted with the conflict between the useful/systematic concept applied to the sports fields and games areas, and the beautiful/irregular concept of the park itself. In Manchester, Major chose to lay out a series of small sports areas around the perimeter, separating them from the main central space by means of screens of shrubs and trees. These areas were equipped with facilities for archery, skittles, ninepins and bowls or provided with see saws and swings or gymnasium equipment. In the central area there was a large open space for public meetings or for cricket or football matches. Unfortunately the scheme was not wholly successful, and Major was harshly criticized, above all from the aesthetic point of view. It was clear that the problem of incorporating a wide range of facilities into a space intended to be botanically interesting and visually pleasing had still to be resolved. It was one that occupied garden designers for some time to come: some of them opted for the separatist solution, setting sports facilities apart from the park itself, others favoured the integrated approach, incorporating the required facilities into the overall design. One example of the latter was Peel Park, laid out at Bradford in about 1850, where a series of avenues and screens of trees linked the areas for walking with those, of various different dimensions, destined for sporting and recreational activities. By contrast, William Barratt's scheme for Albert Park (1868) at Middlesborough consisted of a completely unconnected and incoherent series of spaces, including labyrinths, cricket and croquet pitches and an archery field, laid out haphazardly around the two principal axes.

A rather different and interesting approach to the problem was made by the French garden designer Edouard André, who laid out the much praised Sefton Park in Liverpool, in collaboration with Lewis Hornblower. His plan, which dates from 1867, was not, however, without its critics. It consisted of a complex series of interlocking curves in a geometric layout, and was designed in such a way that the various different sections of the park were separated and at the same time connected. Its ellipses, half-moons and tear-drop shapes are clearly recognizable in two parks laid out shortly afterwards. Stamford Park in Altrincham, designed by John Shaw of Manchester in 1879; and Abbey Park in Leicester, the work of William Barron & Sons in 1878, who won the competition for the best park design. André's influence, although significant, was not, however, very far-reaching. Strangely enough, it was the geometry of his curves, which on the face of it

seemed to offer the best possible solution both on a practical and a theoretical level to the problems of linking regular and irregular shapes, that aroused great controversy and hostility among British designers. A typical reaction was that of Markham Nesfield, a well-known professional garden designer of the period, who described Sefton Park in the following words: 'The roads and walks, indeed, often run nearly parallel with each other, at short distances apart, and curving in the same direction; thus cutting up the ground into narrow and ugly strips, with very long acute corners, and presenting, as a whole, the appearance of a network of railways'.[15] A similar view was expressed by William Robinson in his book on the parks and gardens of Paris. Setting aside, for the time being, the question of the curve in the design of the public park – which does, however, warrant further study – let us turn our attention to the second aspect of the scheme proposed by Paxton, that of the plots of land around the perimeter of the park.

Putting Paxton's scheme into practice presented certain financial difficulties, already referred to, relating to the costs involved in actually acquiring the land and laying out and maintaining the park. In order to provide for these expenses, Paxton adopted the solution applied by John Nash to the redesigning of Regent's Park. Nash conceived the park as the focus of an affluent residential area consisting, both inside and outside the perimeter, of a series of crescents and terraces lined with elegant villas. The main object of the operation in fact was to provide a source of income which would cover the cost of the investment. The council's financial outlay would be confined to the provision of roads, railings and entrance buildings, and of course to the planting up of the park itself. The rest of the building work would be financed by private developers.[16] The successful outcome of the project, which was carried out between 1811 and 1826, was undoubtedly due very largely to the elegance of its design, which was clearly influenced, particularly in terms of the layout of the actual park, by the work of Humphry Repton. Although Repton did not collaborate with Nash on this particular venture, he had for many years worked in close conjunction with him on other projects, and certain features of Regent's Park are recognizably derived from his style: for example, the design of the great lake, whose extremities are concealed by groups of trees and by bridges, and the use of water and grass to create areas of different character, alternating wide open stretches with intimate corners enclosed by shrubs. Using landscaping techniques developed by Repton, each of the houses around Regent's Park was placed in such a way that it could enjoy a view of the gardens while at the same time being shielded from the public gaze by means of planting schemes devised to provide a degree of privacy. This device created the illusion for the owners of the houses that the entire park really belonged to them, thus increasing the value of the plots of land round its perimeter. This principle was to inform the work of garden designers, philanthropists and social reformers, county councils and speculators in their designs for new developments and public parks throughout the nineteenth century.[17]

Regent's Park, London. (Photo Daniele De Lonte)

Victoria Park, London. (Photo Daniele De Lonte)

Battersea Park, London. (Photo Daniele De Lonte)

Not all their projects were successful, however. Victoria Park in London, designed in 1841 by James Pennethorne, a pupil of Nash, was both an economic and an aesthetic disaster, partly as a result of incompetent administration by the Office of Woods and Forests which was responsible for funding the project, and partly because its position was unfashionable and it consequently failed to attract private developers and tenants. Pennethorne was forced to make drastic alterations to his original design, which only resulted in harsh criticism. He had equal difficulty with the planning and realization of Battersea Park, which he designed in 1845.[18] This is not, however, the place for a long list of all the parks financed by means of private investment of this sort, and one example will suffice as an instance of how well the system could work: Birkenhead Park, which was designed by Paxton and completed in 1847, and was praised and imitated perhaps more than any other of its day. The following extract from the diary of another great garden designer, Frederick Law Olmsted, who visited Birkenhead in 1850, conveys a clear idea of contemporary reactions to it:

The baker had begged us not to leave Birkenhead without seeing their *new park* . . . Five minutes of admiration, and a few more spent in studying the manner in which art had been employed to obtain from nature so much beauty, and I was ready to admit that in democratic America there was nothing to be thought of as comparable with this People's Garden. Indeed, gardening, had here reached a perfection that I had never dreamed of . . . we passed by winding paths, over acres and acres, with a constant varying surface, where on all sides were growing every variety of shrubs and flowers, with more than natural grace, all set in borders of greenest, closest turf, and all kept with most consummate neatness. At a distance of a quarter of a mile from the gate, we came to an open field of clean, bright, green-sward, closely mown, on which a large tent was pitched, and a party of boys in one part, and a party of gentleman in another, were playing cricket. Beyond this was a large meadow with rich groups of trees, under which a flock of sheep were reposing, and girls and women with children, were playing. While watching the cricketeers, we were threatened with a shower, and hastened back to look for shelter, which we found in a pagoda, on an island approached by a Chinese bridge. It was soon filled, as were the other ornamental buildings, by a crowd of those who, like ourselves, had been overtaken in the grounds by the rain; and I was glad to observe that the privileges of the garden were enjoyed about equally by all classes.[19]

It has often been said that, in planning the layout of roads and paths for Central Park in New York, Olmsted was inspired by Birkenhead, where Paxton had for the first time designed a system of separate routes for pedestrians, carriages and heavy traffic extraneous to the park.[20] It is perhaps equally important to note how, in the passage quoted, Olmsted stressed other aspects of Paxton's design: the pride of the residents of Birkenhead in possessing such a place of recreation; the democratic nature of the park; the fact that it offered innocent pleasures and activities in an idyllic situation; and, above all, the beauty of the whole scheme. The lyrical tones of Olmsted present a surprising contrast to the rather austere and prosaic style of many British garden designers in discussing the problems of the public park. Charles H. J. Smith, in his

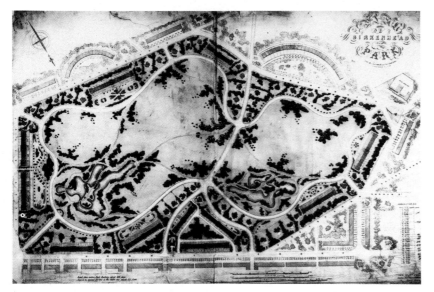

treatise on gardens published in 1852, is a significant example: in his
chapter on parks and public gardens he wrote,

It may be presumed . . . that the average taste of those who frequent suburban
parks (we refer more particularly to the working classes) is not highly
cultivated and severe, and consequently the expression of these localities need
not be so quiet, nor the style so strictly in harmony with the character of the
ground, as may be deemed necessary in the secluded retreats of men of much
cultivation and refinement.[21]

Should we read into this statement only the paternalism of an
aristocratic and reformist society, and attribute Olmsted's enthusiasm
to the egalitarianism of a republican? The matter is surely more
complex than that, and the exchange of ideas and influences between
the old world and the new is surely more subtle. The heart of the
question seems in fact to be the concept of 'civilization', which
appeared for the first time in the work of Repton and then in that of
Loudon.

As Loudon wrote in a paragraph devoted to parks and public
gardens in *An Encyclopaedia of Gardening*, 'Civilization . . . in this country
[England] has now nearly arrived at that point, when the higher classes
find that while they enjoy the luxuries and indulgencies of their station,
it is their duty, as well as their interest, to see that the whole mass of
society be rendered comfortable.'[22] And in another passage of the same
work, he observes,

Garden design, Gardening, in all its branches, will be most advantageously
displayed where the people enjoy a degree of freedom. The final tendency of
every liberal government or society is to conglomerate property in irregular
masses, as nature has distributed all her wealth; and this irregularity is the most
favourable for gardening as a necessary, convenient, and elegant art.[23]

The 1833 report of the Select Committee on Public Walks illustrates the
fact that public parks, which enabled people of different social classes to
come into contact, had a beneficial effect on the appearance and
behaviour of the working classes, who emulated their 'superiors'. The
desire 'to be properly clothed'. as the report says, 'but this desire duly
directed and controlled, is found by experience to be of the most
powerful effect in promoting Civilization and exciting Industry'.[24]
William Robinson invited the government to use public funds to
transform cities into places worthy of the times, reflecting the
awareness and civilization that were part of the new age, in other words
to lay out public parks and gardens.[25] Edward Kemp, a protégé of
Paxton and his collaborator at Birkenhead, wrote in his important
treatise *How to Lay Out a Garden: A General Guide in Choosing, Forming or
Improving an Estate*, published in 1850: 'A garden is for comfort and
convenience, and luxury, and use, as well as for making a beautiful
picture. It is to express civilization, and care, and design, and
refinement.'[26] Andrew Jackson Downing, the most important American garden designer of the first half of the nineteenth century, put
forward a proposal for financing the construction of public parks:
'That such a project, carefully planned and liberally and judiciously

carried out, would not only pay, in money, but largely civilise and refine the national character, foster the love of rural beauty and increase the knowledge of and taste for rare and beautiful trees and plants, we cannot entertain a reasonable doubt.'[27] Even in those books and treatises that do not specifically mention the world 'civilization' in listing the benefits of parks and gardens, or the criteria which should be applied to their planning, frequent reference is made by garden designers, reformers and social workers to those elements that contribute to a civilized environment: comfort, good behaviour, education, respectable dress, hygiene, and systems of government, of class relationship and of production.[28]

The fact that this concept was stressed by those involved with the subject of public parks is clearly connected to the shift described earlier, from an aesthetic to a practical, functional approach to the art of the garden. The recourse to the notion of civilization – which suggests pride in the technical achievements and the moral and political state of a society – seems to have been an attempt to revive a practice that had lost its hold on the world of the fine arts and fallen among the 'useful' arts. This development culminated in a work by Olmsted which celebrated the very concept of civilization, transforming it into a distinct aesthetic movement. In 1880, during a discussion held at the American Social Science Association, Olmsted told the story of the evolution of the public park in the United States, describing its progress as that of a 'common, spontaneous movement, of that sort which we conveniently refer to as the Genius of Civilization'.[29] Olmsted's parks, with their pastoral scenes, represent an essential part of urban life, or of the environment which has been made 'civilized'. Their domestic landscapes create an environment in which the tensions and contradictions of an industrial society are sublimated and transformed into an aesthetic ideal.

With Olmsted, the term 'landscape gardening', which had been coined by Repton and then discarded, gave way to 'landscape architecture'. The change seems to have indicated the end of a long period of unrest, whose principal features were perceived by, among others, Sir Walter Scott, who described landscape gardening thus:

The art . . . has been unfortunately named. The idea of its being, after all, a variety of the gardening art, with which it has little or nothing to do, has given a mechanical turn to the whole profession, and certainly encouraged many persons to practise it with no greater qualifications than ought to be found in a tolerably skilful gardener.[30]

[1] J. C. Loudon, 'Breathing Places for the Metropolis' in the Gardener's Magazine, 5 (1829) pp. 6–90. Loudon's plan was analysed and described in M. L. Simo's 'John Claudius Loudon on Planning and Design for the Garden Metropolis' in Garden History, Vol. 9, no. 2 (1981) pp. 184–201 and in M. L. Simo's Loudon and the Landscape. From Country Seat to Metropolis (New Haven/London 1988); see in particular the chapter 'Planning for London and the Ideal Capital', pp. 226–46. Paxton's plan was published in Paxton's Magazine of Botany, No. 1 (1834). On this aspect of Paxton's work see: G. F. Chadwick, The Works of Sir Joseph Paxton 1803–1865 (London 1961) pp. 46–7; G. F. Chadwick, The Park and the Town. Public Landscape in the 19th and 20th Centuries (New York/Washington 1966) p. 66. Chadwick mentions, however, an earlier article, in the Horticultural Register 'Design for Forming Subscription Gardens in the Vicinity of Large Commercial Towns' (1831) which has not been consulted.

[2] See G. F. Chadwick, The Park and the Town . . ., op. cit., and the numerous publications on the history of the birth of urban planning and the development of the nineteenth-century town.

[3] The quotation is taken from H. Conway, The Municipal Park. Design and Development, circa 1840–1880, doctoral thesis, School of Art History, Leicester Polytechnic (1985) p. 257.

[4] W. Robinson, The Parks, Promenades and Gardens of Paris (London 1869) p. XVIII.

[5] For information on the laws relating to the creation of parks, see G. F. Chadwick, The Park and the Town . . ., op. cit.; H. Conway, 'Victorian Parks', part 1, in Landscape Design, no. 183 (1989) pp. 21–3.

[6] The report was fully described and analysed in G. F. Chadwick's The Park and the Town . . ., op. cit.; H. Conway's The Municipal Park . . ., op. cit.

[7] On the works of Repton see; D. Stroud, Humphry Repton (London 1962); G. Carter, P. Goode, K. Laurie, Humphry Repton. Landscape Gardener 1752–1818 – exhibition catalogue (Norwich/London, 1982); A. Ponte, 'Paesaggi artificiali. Il caso di Humphry Repton' in Lotus International, no. 52 (1986) pp. 52–71.

[8] H. Repton, Fragments on the Theory and Practice of Landscape Gardening (1st ed. 1816; reprinted New York/London 1982) p. 141.

[9] G. Thouin, Plans raisonnés de toutes les espèces de jardins (1820, reprinted Paris 1989). On the influence of the work of Thouin on Loudon, see M. L. Simo's Loudon and the Landscape . . ., op. cit.

[10] For a more thorough study of the subject, apart from the works by Chadwick and Simo already mentioned, see: John Gloag, Mr Loudon's England (London 1970); E. B. MacDougall (editor) John Claudius Loudon and the Early Nineteenth Century in Britain (Dumbarton Oaks 1980); T. H. D. Turner, 'Loudon's Stylistic Development' in Journal of Garden History, Vol. 2, no. 2 (1982) pp. 175–88.

[11] The quotation is taken from M. L. Simo, Loudon and the Landscape . . ., op. cit., p. 201.

[12] This, for example, is the theory put forward by Chadwick in The Park and the Town, op. cit.

[13] For a thorough study of the parks of Manchester, see: H. Conway, 'The Manchester/Salford Parks: Their design and development' in Journal of Garden History, Vol. 5, no. 3 (1985) pp. 231–60; B. Elliott, 'The Manchester/Salford Parks: two additional notes' in Journal of Garden History, Vol. 6, no. 2 (1986) pp. 141–5; D. Baldwin, 'Joshua Major' in Journal of Garden History, Vol. 7, no. 2 (1987) pp. 131–50.

[14] See H. Conway, 'Sports and playgrounds and the problems of park design in the nineteenth century' in Journal of Garden History, Vol. 8, no. 1 (1988) pp. 31–41.

[15] The quotation is taken from B. Elliott, Victorian Gardens (London 1986) p. 170.

[16] On Regent's Park, see: G. F. Chadwick, The Park and the Town, op. cit.; J. N. Simpson, The Life and Work of John Nash, Architect (Cambridge, Mass., 1980).

[17] For more information on this subject, see H. Conway, 'Victorian Parks', op. cit.

[18] See G. F. Chadwick, The Park and the Town . . ., op. cit., in particular the chapter 'The Parks of London', pp. 111–36; H. Conway, The Municipal Park . . ., op. cit.

[19] F. L. Olmsted, Walks and Talks of an American Farmer in England (1st ed. 1852, 2nd ed. 1859. Ann Arbor) pp. 51–3.

[20] Among the innumerable publications on the works of Olmsted, particularly noteworthy is C. Capen McLaughlin (ed.), The Papers of Frederick Law Olmsted (Baltimore/London, 2 vols, 1977–88); I. D. Fisher, Frederick Law Olmsted and the City Planning Movement in the United States (Ann Arbor 1976).

[21] C. H. J. Smith, Landscape Gardening or Parks and Pleasure Grounds with practical notes on Country Residences, Villas, Public Parks and Gardens (1st ed. 1852 – New York 1853) p. 220.

[22] J. C. Loudon, An Encyclopaedia of Gardening (1st ed. 1822, and numerous others with revisions between 1824 and 1878), reprint of the 1835 edition published by Garland Publishing (New York/London 1982) 2 vols, Vol. I, p. 337.

[23] Ibid., p. 419.

[24] The quotations are taken from the long extract of the report transcribed by G. F. Chadwick in The Park and the Town . . ., op. cit., pp. 50–51.

[25] W. Robinson, op. cit., p. XIX.

[26] The quotation is taken from G. F. Chadwick, The Park and the Town . . ., p. 102. Note that in this case the reference is to private gardens.

[27] Ibid., p. 181.

[28] On the concept of Civilization see: N. Elias, The Civilizing Process. 1: The History of Manners (Oxford/New York 1978).

[29] The quotation is taken from I. D. Fisher, op. cit., p. 102.

[30] The extract is taken from C. H. J. Smith, op. cit., p. 288. It is interesting to note that Smith, while bearing in mind Scott's observation, does not infer from it Scott's intended implication, and defends his art by reiterating the distinction between painting and the art of garden design.

Haussmann's Paris: A Green Metropolis?

Thomas von Joest

'If only over the last hundred years our municipalities had had greater foresight, how many magnificent gardens we should enjoy today. For Paris formerly had all the necessary resources. . . .'[1] Was Haussmann's Paris a failure? Had not the capital of capitals, proud of its new tree-lined avenues, its flower-decked squares and verdant parks, invited the whole world to discover its splendour at the magnificent universal exhibition of 1867? Was the Paris of Nana – 'our table cloth is the grass' – still pastoral even in its worldly heyday, purely an illusion?[2]

In the early years of this century Eugène Hénard, author of the above quotation and Haussmann's true successor in the field of the written word, drew up some harsh figures: while Paris possessed 263 hectares (650 acres) of green open space, London, whose reputation as a city suffocated by lack of oxygen was legendary, had nearly three times as much.

The Haussmann heritage, often presented as the fulfilment of an ideal model, is here examined from quite a different point of view – critical, but at the same time fair. For the truth is that it never matched the scale of the growth of Paris after the fall of the second Empire in 1870. Haussmann's work had a fatal flaw – the realization of his vast projects tended to overshadow the underlying principle. How disappointed our author would have been had he lived a few generations later. Picturesque architecture lay exposed in all its frailty to the depradations of the elements, in a sylvan setting that had been abandoned to its fate, witness to an administration far too complaisant about its obligations. Fortunately the public authorities have recently gradually become aware of this scandalous neglect, and are concerned, at last, to create new parks and gardens.[3] But the days of large-scale schemes of urban improvement are gone, nevertheless. Green Paris, floral Paris, remains the creation of the nineteenth century. Its charm reflects the sensitivities of another age.

The introduction of green spaces into large towns in the nineteenth century was inherently bound up with contemporary developments in urban planning. The eighteenth century had already become aware of the idea of urban 'pathology' – hospitals and cemeteries were pushed outside the town walls, more fountains were installed and polluted water was carried away in drains, all with a view to improving public hygiene – but trees and other planting schemes were considered primarily as embellishments. The industrial revolution, however, brought about a population growth hitherto unknown, and atmospheric pollution in large towns increased to such an extent that the presence of greenery, sun and wind rapidly assumed more importance than health regulations. Demands for such improvements are found initially in the writings of the Utopians, of the followers of Saint-Simon and of other early Socialists who, from the beginning of the nineteenth century, never ceased to spell out the need for including green spaces in urban designs. Thus Robert Owen, Charles Fourier, Victor Considérant and Etienne Cabet spoke of groves of trees, of flowery lawns, indeed even of agricultural enclosures where their new idealized working man might relax from his toil. Whether they were envisaged as zones separating areas of housing from industrial workshops or forming their immediate surroundings, such gardens became an integral part of their model towns.[4]

In Paris, however, the problem took quite a different form from that posed in these idealistic plans, which were necessarily wholly artificial. Here there could be no phalanstery, no construction of a Socialist community. The town, in many respects still medieval in plan, already existed, and those of the working population who did not travel in daily from the inner suburbs often lived in the same neighbourhoods as the middle classes, but in attics and backyards. Paradoxically, or perhaps typically of the times, it was Haussmann's schemes which, despite their socially-motivated intentions, were to push the underprivileged masses out of the capital. These, the first victims of a boom in speculative housing, were obliged to find refuge far away from the new parks and squares, in unplanned suburbs, wholly unorganized on the level of town planning. And of course Paris, the Paris of the Empire, of the Restoration and of Louis-Philippe, already had its parks and gardens, though in limited numbers. Paris was even one of the first towns to throw its green spaces open to all its citizens. It is with justice that François Loyer has emphasized the importance of the Palais-Royal and the Tuileries as places of popular resort. Nevertheless, the new English parks which were being designed from the 1840s inspired the whole of Europe in their picturesque landscaping, and their development in the second half of the century far surpassed the French achievement.[5] Great admirer though he was of Haussmann, Eugène Hénard was not wrong.

The beginning: Jacques-Ignace Hittorff's Champs-Elysées

The first act of this play which transformed Paris into a theatre of greenery took place to the west of the Tuileries, along the axis constructed to create a monumental perspective from the Arc de Triomphe, completed in 1836. The woods planted half a century earlier by the Marquis de Marigny between the Cours de la Reine and the gardens of the town-houses in the Faubourg St Honoré were already a favourite meeting-place for the people of Paris, who thronged the avenues and glades in the summer months.[6] There they sauntered among the numerous pleasure-gardens, refreshment stalls, entertainments and travelling pedlars. In the eyes of the authorities, however, such an unsanctioned development was unacceptable. If the people of Paris were to take possession of the Champs-Elysées, it was the administration's responsibility to oversee them. As urban life spread, so its presence must be acknowledged in the form of properly laid out paths, boundaries and regulations. Moreover, criticisms were beginning to be heard. It was 'no longer a walk, but almost a forest – very pleasant, certainly, during the day and in the summer months, but dangerous after dark and particularly in winter,' accused the journal *L'Artiste* in 1835; and shortly afterwards Horeau, Bères and Dronsart, authors of an improvement plan, gave an even more damning indictment: 'By night, no one is unaware that this place is the shameful

Bird's-eye view of the Champs-Elysées in Paris. From Le Magasin Pittoresque, *1849–50.*

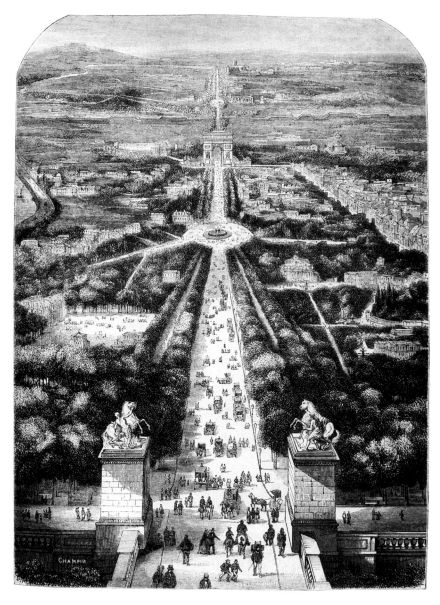

refuge of men and women of ill repute, and also of criminal elements. For the weary walker, the child, the old person, there is nowhere to sit, nor anything pleasing to take their fancy.'[7]

The first attempts to remedy this situation go back to the year 1828. Under the terms of the law of 20 August, the crown ceded to the town both the future Place de la Concorde and the Champs-Elysées, with the obligation to smarten them up within five years. This time limit was considerably exceeded, since it was not until the Comte de Rambuteau was nominated to the prefecture of Paris in 1833 that an architect, Jacques-Ignace Hittorff (1792–1867) was assigned to the task. In December of that year Hittorff submitted a detailed plan to the new prefect. He divided the work into two parts: one to be carried out at the expense of the town (fountains, lighting, carriageways) and the other to be privately funded (various buildings and concessions). In addition there would be an open-air theatre for 4000 spectators and 1000 musicians – Berlioz's dream – a circus, Panorama, a provisional racecourse which would also serve as a parade ground for official occasions and a museum of curiosities.[8] Hittorff's plans aimed to do away with the 'dirty hovels' – temporary kiosks and buildings – in order to endow Paris with 'architecture for leisure'. The skilful placing of such attractions seemed to him the best guarantee of success.

The 'squares' – the name of the clearings – of the Ambassadors and the Elysée-Bourbon 'could, if the restaurants, bars, ice cream stalls and dairies placed around them were well managed, become a meeting-place for those who frequented the Boulevard Italien', in other words the fashionable meeting-place. The 'great square' traditionally 'for use on occasions of public rejoicing' would be 'particularly attractive to the middle classes, who will find there everything to contribute to their enjoyment': the Panorama and numerous taverns, cafés, food stalls and wine-sellers. As for the Ledoyen square, its restaurant and reading room could 'draw together the different classes of society'.[9] As it turned out, only a part of these plans, including the Summer Circus, the Panorama, the Théâtre des Folies, the restaurants Laurent, Ledoyen and de l'Horloge, and the Café des Ambassadeurs, came to fruition. Hittorff designed all these buildings to be in polychrome, following the principles of his own theories.[10] Their neoclassical elegance was heightened by vivid paintwork – blue, yellow, red and green – which was intended to form a closer link between the worlds of town and country. For the architect the weak point in this development was that he was strictly bound to respect existing plantations. Rambuteau, the prefect who 'would rather have tooth pulled than pull out a tree', made it his motto 'to give to the people of Paris water, air and shade' without however possessing the means to put this policy into effect.[11] Unable to create new open spaces, he made the most of existing ones, increasing the number of benches and replanting the trees uprooted by the insurgents in 1830. But the citizens of the day did not complain. In the evening the Champs-Elysées seemed more spacious than ever with the sound of the fountains set in the greenery and their full extent now revealed by the light of the new street lamps.

Design for the Embellishment of the
Champs-Elysées. The Great
Hippodrome, *1834. Drawing by
J.-I. Hittorff. Wallraf-Richartz Museum,
Cologne.*

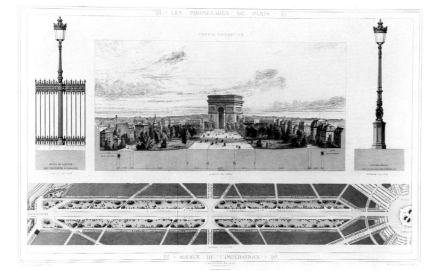

The Haussmann regime

'Parisians are like children, they must constantly be kept amused, and if they cannot be given battle bulletins monthly, or constitutions annually, they must daily be offered public works or improvements.'[12] Rambuteau did not realize how true his words were. Under Napoleon III, the prince-president elected emperor at the close of the Second Republic, Parisians had a front-row view of unprecedented building-works. Anxious to turn France into a modern state, Louis-Napoleon appointed a prefect without equal, Georges Eugène Haussmann, to establish the capital as a symbol and model of progress. Properties were expropriated, whole areas – formerly 'strongholds of insurrection' – demolished, new avenues created, enormous road junctions constructed, bridges and squares built, drains and drinking-water mains excavated. All these were the essentials of a town-planning policy without precedent.[13] No obstacle was great enough to deter Haussmann from the completion of his project, set out in a detailed plan drawn up in agreement with the Emperor.[14] In their eyes Paris was like an ailing body, which could be healed only by radical treatment: body fluids would be piped through new arteries, impurities would by systematically eliminated, and respiration aided by 'green lungs'. The uniqueness of the plan lies in the comprehensive nature of its approach, achieved by means of a road system which would give the city its structure. The function of the boulevards was to link key buildings. Drainpipes and mains connected domestic and municipal areas. As for parks and gardens, their role was to define the geography of Paris both in terms of the city as a whole and of individual neighbourhoods. The Bois de Boulogne in the west had as its counterpart the Bois de Vincennes in the east, just as the park of Buttes-Chaumont in the north had as its southern equivalent the Parc Montsouris. This layout was emphasized by the addition to the urban plan of twenty-four garden squares, between the boulevards and the blocks of dwellings.

At the heart of this newly organized Paris lay one axis of prime importance. Running from north to south, it signalled clearly to the lower and middle class areas of eastern Paris that they should take as their model the affluent new neighbourhoods of the west. It also – most importantly – shifted the centre of Paris towards the Hôtel de Ville (Place du Châtelet, St-Michel) from which the prefect held sway. Several theatres, meccas of public life, were to complete this new heart of the capital.[15] Haussmann, a designer of genius, had realized that no town-planning policy could succeed without the participation of the people. Whether taking the air on a park bench or going to the theatre, the people of Paris were allowed to play a walk-on part in the creation of the 'new Paris'.

The realization of such a vast project required considerable resources. Financial matters apart, Haussmann's principal instrument was a body of municipal officers established when he first went to the Hôtel de Ville (1853) and regrouped into several services, including that of Promenades et Plantations.[16] At its head was the Ponts et

Plan for the Redesigning of the Champs-Elysées and the Place Louis XVI, *1828. Drawing by J.-J. Ramée, Musée Carnavalet, Paris.*

Paris and its Environs. Café des
Ambassadeurs, in the Champs-Elysées:
*view of the two cafés designed by
J.-I. Hittorff around 1847. Lithograph
by G. Muller. Musée Carnavalet, Paris.*

Chaussées engineer Adolphe Alphand, assisted by the architect Gabriel Davioud (1824–1881) and the horticulturist Barrillet-Deschamps. Their first achievement was the Bois de Boulogne, which had been ceded to the city by the Emperor in 1851.[17] Initially its development had been entrusted to Hittorff and the landscape gardener Varé, both skilfully ousted by Haussmann, who wanted no further interference from independent architects.[18] The transformation of the Bois de Boulogne became a testing ground for the Promenades et Plantations service, which created a picturesque setting in the English style, in accordance with the ideas of Napoleon III. Straight avenues gave way to sinuous paths, while Alphand supervised the excavation of two serpentine lakes with curving shorelines, and of other water features adorned with grottoes and waterfalls. Barrillet-Deschamps laid out the groves of trees and the undulating lawns dotted with charming island beds of flowers and green plants, while Davioud designed numerous buildings. His kiosks, lodges, restaurants, bars, cafés, grandstands in the hippodrome, and aviaries and cages in the Jardin d'Acclimatation (zoo) made reference sometimes to Gothic architecture, sometimes to the vernacular style of Swiss chalets, then very fashionable and much publicized in anthologies of picturesque gardens.[19] Brick, glazed tiles, different coloured woods, ceramic and stone were all pressed into service to create a natural polychrome effect, quite different from that used by Hittorff in the Champs-Elysées. Allusions to the pastoral life were to be found in a wealth of stylized decorative motifs taken from the plant world to reappear on the balustrade of a bridge, on the back of a park bench, or in a shelter. For the Bois de Boulogne was also a testing ground for the street furniture which was to invade the boulevards and garden squares of Paris in the years to come.

In the Bois de Vincennes, a former military parade-ground converted into a park in 1860, architecture and landscape were conceived and created in unison. 'Here it was a question,' wrote Haussmann in his *Mémoires*, 'of creating to the east of Paris, in accordance with the Emperor's noble plans for the working classes. . . . a promenade to equal the one recently provided in the west for the wealthy, elegant neighbourhoods of our Capital.'[20] A praiseworthy initiative, indeed, but was this really a worthy counterpart to the Parc Monceau, the former *Folie* of the Duc de Chartres, dating from the end of the eighteenth century, which was being restored and completed at the same time? One has only to think of Davioud's superb wrought-iron railings, reminiscent of those in the Place Stanislas in Nancy.[21]

Of all the parks within the city walls, not including the woods on the outskirts of Paris, the Buttes-Chaumont (1864–7) is certainly the finest and the most exciting. The extremely uneven and 'naturally very picturesque' site – which was in fact a disused quarry – has been exploited to the full.[22] The lake, at the foot of a promontory crowned by a pillared temple, reflects the suspension bridge, the cliffs, and the banks of greenery rising from lawns intersected by winding paths; a succession of delightful images for strollers. Considerable embank-

The great lake with the Emperor's Kiosk
in the Bois de Boulogne. (Photo Fulvio
Ventura)

The artificial rock and the temple of Buttes-Chaumont. (Photo Fulvio Ventura)

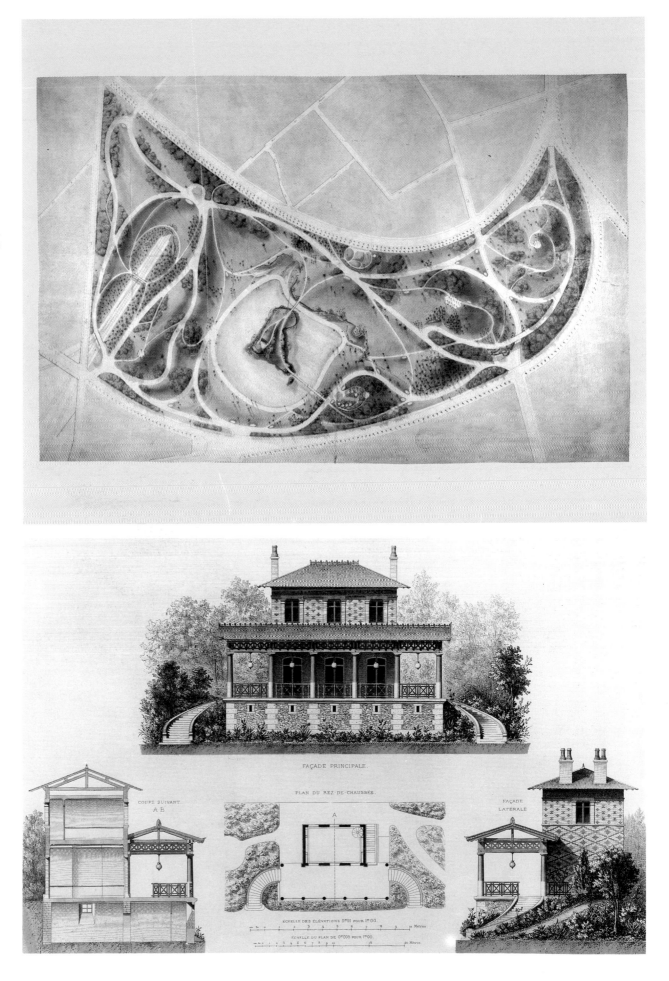

Plan of the park of Buttes-Chaumont.
Bibliothèque Nationale, Cartes et Plans,
Paris.

Restaurant in the park of Buttes-Chaumont.
From J. C. A. Alphand, Les promenades
de Paris, *Paris 1867–73.*

FAÇADE PRINCIPALE.

COUPE SUIVANT
A B

PLAN DU REZ-DE-CHAUSSÉE.

FAÇADE
LATÉRALE

Plan of the Square des Batignolles. From J. C. A. Alphand, Les promenades de Paris, *Paris 1867–73.*

Elements of urban design, Square des Batignolles. From J. C. A. Alphand, Les promenades de Paris, *Paris 1867–73.*

Square des Batignolles. (Photo Fulvio Ventura)

Plans of the Square St Jacques and the Square Louis XVI. From J. C. A. Alphand, Les promenades de Paris, *Paris 1867–73.*

ments were required, and grottoes and waterfalls of artificial rocks, for which Alphand, the gardener-engineer at whom everyone once scoffed, drew on all his civil engineering skills.[23] Davioud, always eclectic in his garden pavilions, here created whimsical concoctions of vaguely antique columns, capitals, pedestals and palmettes mixed with his usual rustic style.

The garden squares are a further example of the benefits of Napoleon III's patronage. Haussmann wrote:

During his lengthy stay in England the Emperor had been impressed by the contrast between the well-kept London squares and the sordid condition of the slums where the workers' families lived crowded together. . . . He therefore instructed me to avail myself of every opportunity to create as many garden squares as possible in every neighbourhood in Paris in order to make generous provision . . . of places for relaxation and amusement for all families and all children whether rich or poor.[24]

This was a novel idea, since English town squares were reserved for the use of residents. Twenty-four of these small 'green living rooms', designed after the manner of the new parks, and embellished with wrought-iron gates, fountains and Davioud's street lamps, have ever since brought a breath of fresh air to the different parts of Paris. Though they have a common origin, their natures and functions vary. Most of them are miniature parks, but some honour an ancient or symbolic monument, such as the St Jacques tower or the Chapelle Expiatoire consecrated to the memory of Louis XVI and Marie-Antoinette. The square of the Magasins-Réunis (1867) was unique. Situated in the forecourt of a large department store close to the Place de la République, it was considered as the counterpart of the gardens of the Palais-Royal – a further example of Napoleon III's obsessive desire to educate and improve the common people. A people's opera house for 10,000 spectators – a replica of the Palais Garnier, the new Imperial Academy of Music – was to complete this group of buildings.[25] Whether by means of ornamental embellishments or sanitary improvements, the ultimate aim of Haussmann's town planning was to stamp social expression with uniformity.

It was the tree-lined avenues which were the unifying element in the reorganization of open spaces in Paris. The Champs-Elysées, remodelled in the English style by Haussmann in 1858, was extended beyond the Arc de Triomphe towards the Bois du Boulogne. The prefect's wish was that these propylons should be grandiose: three times the width of a normal boulevard, flanked by lawns and paths, and punctuated with beds of rare plants – in short, an enormous arboretum. It is hardly surprising that even the most unforgiving critics, including César Daly, founder of the famous *Revue Générale de l'Architecture et des Travaux Publics*, should shower it with praises: 'Of all the improvements carried out in Paris during the Second Empire there is none more worthy of praise, of sincere admiration than those carried out by the service of the Promenades et Plantations. . . . Paris, formerly a quarry, has been transformed into a nosegay.'[26]

Plan of the Paris Exhibition of 1867,
Champ de Mars. From J. C. A. Alphand,
Les promenades de Paris, *Paris 1867–73.*

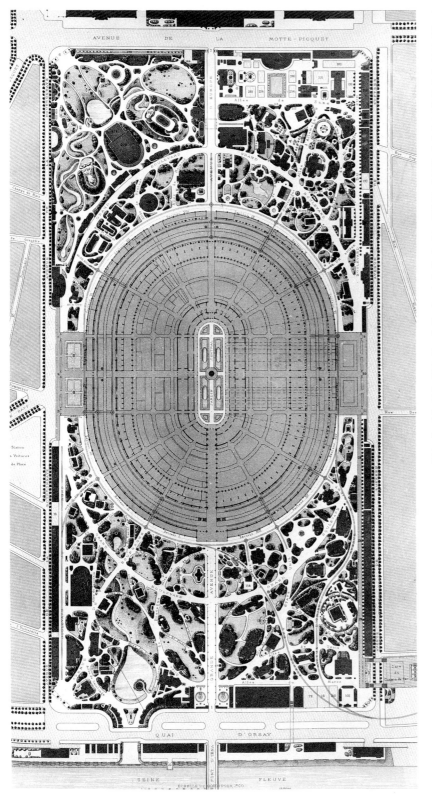

1 Eugène Hénard, *Etudes sur les transformations de Paris* (Paris 1903–9), 1982, pp. 72–3.

2 Emile Zola, *Les Rougon-Macquart, Nana* (La Pléiade edition, Paris 1962) Vol. 2, p. 1658.

3 See the parks developed in the former abattoirs in Vaugirard and La Villette. The Gabriel Davioud exhibition gave the opportunity to reveal the sorry state of the buildings in the Bois de Boulogne and particular of the Emperor's Kiosk which had fallen into total ruin. Today it once again adorns the island in the great lake.

4 Françoise Choay, *L'urbanisme, utopies et réalités. Une anthologie* (Paris 1979). This author has also written an excellent article entitled 'Haussmann et le système des espaces verts parisiens', in *Revue de l'Art* (Paris 1975) pp. 83–99.

5 François Loyer, *Le siècle de l'industrie, 1789–1914* (Paris 1983) pp. 14–15; and F. Choay, 'Haussmann . . .', *op. cit.*, pp. 84ff.

6 Quentin-Bauchert, 'Rapport présenté au nom du comité du budget et du contrôle sur les concessions des Champs-Elysées', *Conseil Municipal de Paris, Rapports et Documents* (Paris 1896) No. 160.

7 Thomas von Joest, 'Hittorff et les embellissements des Champs-Elysées', in *Hittorff, un architecte du XIXème* (Musée Carnavalet, Paris 1986) pp. 153ff.

8 Thomas von Joest, 'Hittorff . . .', *op. cit.*, pp. 155ff.

9 Thomas von Joest, 'Des restaurants, des cafés, du théâtre jadis célèbre, du géorama et de la grandeur de quelques projets', in *Hittorff . . .*, *op. cit.*, pp. 189ff.

10 Uwe Westfehling, 'Le Panorama', in *Hittorff . . .*, *op. cit.*, pp. 173ff. and Thomas von Joest, 'Le Cirque d'Eté', in *Hittorff . . .*, *op. cit.*, pp. 173ff.

11 *Mémoires du Comte Rambuteau* (Paris 1905) pp. 269, 377.

12 *Ibid.*, p. 269.

13 *Mémoires du Baron Haussmann. Grands travaux de Paris, 1853–1870* (Paris, reprinted 1979), 2 vols.

14 *Ibid.*, Vol. I, pp. 47ff.

15 Thomas von Joest, 'La place du Château d'Eau', in *La piazza e la città* (Istituto italiano di cultura di Parigi, Paris 1985) pp. 63, 64; and Thomas von Joest, 'L'Orphéon et la place du Château d'Eau', in *Gabriel Davioud, architecte (1824–1881)* (Paris 1982) pp. 77–87.

16 *Mémoires du Baron . . .*, *op. cit.*, Vol. I, p. 121.

17 *Ibid.*, p. 183; and Dominique Jarrassé, 'Les parcs et les squares', in *Gabriel Davioud . . .*, *op. cit.*, pp. 27ff.

18 Thomas von Joest, 'Les projets pour le Bois de Boulogne', in *Hittorff . . .*, *op. cit.*, pp. 213ff.

19 The sale catalogue of the library of 'the late M. Davioud' preserved in the Bibliothèque Nationale in Paris has provided an invaluable record of all the publications in his possession.

20 *Mémoires du Baron . . .*, *op. cit.*, Vol. I, p. 210.

21 D. Jarrassé, *op. cit.*, p. 38.

22 Darcel, 'Projet d'embellissement d'un square sur les Buttes-Chaumont', *Conseil Municipal* (Paris 1863).

23 *Mémoires du Baron . . .*, *op. cit.*, Vol. I, p. 126 – much pleasantry about the engineer who had just accepted a permanent post as 'gardener'.

24 *Mémoires du Baron . . .*, *op. cit.*, Vol. I, p. 240.

25 Thomas von Joest, 'L'Orphéon . . .', *op. cit.*, and Thomas von Joest, 'La place du . . .', *op. cit.*

26 *Revue Générale de l'Architecture et des Travaux Publics*, Vol. 21 (1863), col. 249.

The Beaux-Arts Garden

Ignasi de Solà Morales

The term 'Beaux-Arts' is rarely used to describe a specific school of gardening or a single style of garden design. The Beaux-Arts method or tradition is, as numerous studies in recent years have shown, a methodological attitude with reference to an architectural project which, being formal, is characterized by the hierarchical organization of its components and the pragmatic use of historical imitation.

Since there exists a Beaux-Arts architecture which characterizes a good part of European and American production from the French Revolution of 1789 to the Second World War in 1939 it is hardly surprising that there are also theories of garden and park design influenced by the same projected system and by the same methodology of design.

One of the first characteristics of what we shall call Beaux-Arts gardening is its formal continuity with such urban and architectural design as can be given a similar definition. Foremost amongst the ideological tenets of the Beaux-Arts system is unity of method, and following on from this, a common thread running through the criteria which are applied to the design of urban areas, buildings and natural spaces. The Beaux-Arts gardening tradition imitates architecture in advance of the immediate and visual imitation of nature. Beaux-Arts gardens are architectural in the most conventional sense of the term: that is, regular symmetrical constructions rationally composed in the first place from simple forms, arranged according to rigid geometric laws into a hierarchical visual order within a given space.

From this first premise, related to the architectural possibilities of gardening, a particular problem of Beaux-Arts design, it follows that the laws of composition which apply to the planning of buildings are much the same as those which apply to the planning of green spaces, parks and gardens. Symmetry, order and hierarchy are universal principles which stem from an appropriate re-working of the architecture of the classical age, which, from at least the time of Durand, could be adapted for any building programme.

Yet, accepting that Beaux-Arts gardens have an architectural nature, another important question is raised. Given that the gardens are by definition architectural, it will not come as a surprise that their development is intimately linked to architecture proper. In other words, whilst at other periods in the history of garden design gardens tend to develop their own models of order and meaning, Beaux-Arts gardens have an almost obligatory reference to actual architecture. Beaux-Arts gardens are almost always gardens attached to buildings, or when on a large scale, gardens and parks to the city seen as a huge edifice. In principle Beaux-Arts gardens do not immediately evoke nature in its primeval state, but rather the ordered surroundings and necessary introduction to the uniqueness and representation of a building or series of buildings, public or private, with which a park or garden establish relations of continuity, direction, focus and tricks of perspective.

But in the same way that the totality of Beaux-Arts forms is not defined by a limited vocabulary, the repertory of its possible forms is not subject to a previously established code. To the eclectic language of the Beaux-Arts tradition in architecture there is an equally evident corresponding eclecticism in the garden tradition. The polemicists of Beaux-Arts design tend to limit themselves to presenting historical examples, examining each, and drawing from them the nature of Beaux-Arts gardening theories. An academic treatise as seminal as *Le traité général de la composition des parcs et jardins* by Edouard André, published in Paris in 1879, is structured in a revealing way. Before the technical section on the various stages in the design of a garden, there is a historical section – gardens through the ages; styles and their national origins – and a theoretical section in which an attempt is made at defining the aesthetic principles behind the designs of parks and gardens.

But the historical eclecticism of the Beaux-Arts tradition does not imply a total indifference to the past. Similarly to architecture, the classical tradition had a special place for the garden designer trained in the discipline of the Ecole. The gardens of the ancient world (by which was understood the gardens of Greek and Roman monuments), the Renaissance and Baroque garden, and in particular the gardens of the French *Grand Siècle*, formed reference points common to those which inspired Beaux-Arts garden projects.

The Beaux-Arts gardener makes use of historical knowledge, in his case a knowledge of the history of gardens, principles of unity, variety, form, colour, verisimilitude and character, with a technique adapted to a particular garden problem. To him, a classification of the possible problems which might occur, and the sort of solutions which can solve these possible problems, is fundamental. The solution adopted will depend on whether he is dealing with parks or gardens, whether they are public or private, whether they serve a function or are simply decorative, whether formal or landscape. The key to each project will be found in suitable past solutions, in the relationship between the garden or park and surrounding architecture, or perhaps in the nature of the city itself.

Yet the central debate which recurs in the minds of those who confront the Beaux-Arts problem as applied to the gardens of the nineteenth or twentieth century, in theory or in practice, is in establishing which of two opposed traditions forms the model for the Beaux-Arts garden: the so called geometric and regular French garden, or the so-called English or picturesque garden.

From the Rousseauesque doubts of Watelet in his *Essai sur les jardins* (1774) to the eclectic recommendations of Gaudet in the fourth volume of his *Eléments et théorie de l'architecture* of 1904, the Beaux-Arts theorists adopt a syncretic attitude when faced by the alternatives which the diverse culture of the nineteenth century presented. A figure as central to the forming of opinions of Beaux-Arts as Charles Blanc in his *Grammaire des arts du dessin* (1867) does not come to a final conclusion, and although he does emphasize the modernity of the landscape garden, he sees this as the result of eclecticism. Gustave Umbdenstock (1930) Georges Gromort (1942) and Pierre de Lagarde (1954) were

The Temple of Fortune at Praeneste,
reconstructed by J. N. Huyot, 1811. Ecole
Nationale Supérieure des Beaux-Arts,
Paris.

Elevation of thermal baths and casino
designed by Paul Bigot, Prix de Rome 1900.
Ecole Nationale Supérieure des Beaux-Arts,
Paris.

discussing in the mid-twentieth century the difficulties of choosing as a source geometrical classicism or the picturesque landscape tradition.

What is clear is that this unresolved contradiction, the contrast between classicism as a historical tradition able to give credibility to the institution of architecture, and psychological empiricism as a modern reply to the open and unpredetermined problem of form, ends up becoming that which is most typical of what we here have decided to name the Beaux-Arts Garden Style. A composition with a sense of balance, the mixing and juxtaposition of natural spaces, the imitation of nature in its unspoilt state, together with the presence of hierarchical, geometric and perspective interventions, this, in the final analysis, is the best way of describing the majority of those gardens which we can define as 'Beaux-Arts'.

Garden architecture and the city

The need to incorporate vegetation in urban spaces is not alien to the Beaux-Arts development of gardens as an extension of city design. Alphand's treatise *Les promenades de Paris* (1863–1873) which should be seen as a mixture of encyclopedic primitivism and aesthetic eclecticism with classical roots, has in its introduction a theory typical of Beaux-Arts thinking: that the historical examples which are the basis of our knowledge of our present experience of Beaux-Arts gardens, and the grading of gardens in terms of scale and character defined by their relationship to the city, are an obvious example of the neutral critical attitude which a gardener bore towards his work. But one should point out the extent to which, in Alphand, discussions on large spaces and parks run parallel to the description and analysis of squares with gardens (*squares*) or without (*places*), boulevards and promenades whose relationship to gardening are not in question.

We know the various drawings in Schinkel's work of 1828 in which the Berlin architect studies in detail the organization of a garden in the large area between his new Altes Museum and the old royal palace, in the centre of Berlin. The not entirely symmetrical co-ordination of the visual axes of the four architectural elements (the museum, palace, new cathedral and the bridge which links up with the Unter den Linden) are treated with distinct garden designs, across which an ordered view of the buildings is achieved, by means of spaces planted with trees and shrubs. This is an obvious example of garden as architecture – with symmetry, hierarchy and perspective – its prime function being to establish the relationship between a building and its surroundings. However, the relationship can only be resolved by taking into account the problem posed by both traffic and vistas, in such a way that the simple square or piazza can truly be considered a garden.

When the students of the Ecole des Beaux-Arts were entering for the Grand Prix, most of the plans for the spectacular projects referred to gardens. These were the first projected visions of architecture submerged in gardens, reflected also in the imaginative bas-reliefs from

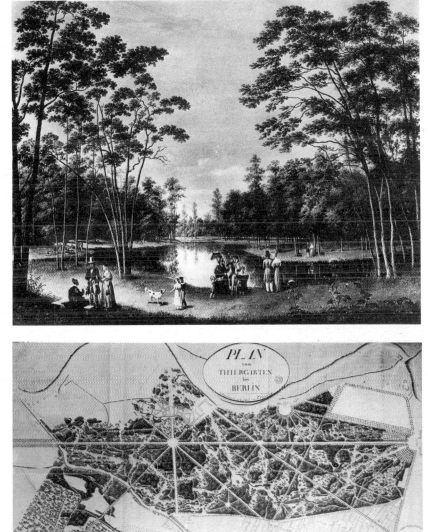

ancient monuments re-created for the art history courses, and in the *envois* of the Prix de Rome which were made during the academy's Italian summer school. The Roman forum, the Palatine Hill, Nero's house, Pompeii and Herculaneum served as models for designs which established a free relationship between architecture and open spaces; it was Greece however which provided the best examples – Mount Olympus, Eleusis, Delphi and the Ionian cities of Pergamon, Miletus and Priene – often not without a certain touch of the picturesque.

We find these same procedures, in a more developed form, in the Beaux-Arts designs entered for the diploma or the Grand Prix. The gardens surrounding the large buildings of Boullée; the plans of Percier and Fontaine and Vaudoyer; the great gardens of Emile Bernard which completed the Villa Madama (1871); the *Votive church in a place of pilgrimage* of S. E. A. Duquesne (1897); the *Thermal baths and casino* of Paul Bigot (1900): all these academic projects reflect a new relationship, peculiar to the Beaux-Arts system, between building and garden.

It is hardly surprising therefore, that in the collection of Alphand already mentioned, the great Parisian parks such as the Bois de Boulogne and Bois de Vincennes should be considered so important; or indeed that the entire organization of public space and gardens should play an important part in an overall urban planning scheme. Be it the simple gardens of the Place Grenelle or the Square des Invalides; the more complex designs of the Champs-Elysées, or the restructuring of the Jardin du Luxembourg, in all of these the design of the garden, the buildings incorporated, the surroundings, and the organization of city traffic are decisive components in the hierarchical composition and axial perspectives achieved by these green spaces.

Werner Hegemann is probably the most prominent theoretician who, in the context of urban renewal in the first third of the century, dedicated special attention to the compilation of the architecture of gardens with a Beaux-Arts vision. In his publication of 1911 on American parks, and while publications director of Wasmuth Verlag (his last job), and above all in his *Civic Art, an American Vitruvius* (1922) Hegemann gives significant attention to the design of parks and gardens in relation to architecture and the city.

Chapter 5 of *Civic Art* is dedicated to the theme of *The Garden as a Civic Art*, and in it, again, is reproduced the Beaux-Arts logic with which, with the study of the history of the movement and commentaries of various and dispersed examples, he tries to formulate a set of practical solutions to the problem of public space in the modern city. To the classical examples of Le Nôtre or *Vitruvius Britannicus* he adds the contemporary plans of Lutyens, Platt, Carrère and Hastings, or those of the firm of Hegemann and Peets, in different residential locations in the USA. But what is significant about his book is its attention to gardens which are linked to detached buildings. Formal Beaux-Arts logic (a consistent feature of this architect's work) is not treated separately from the requirement for specialized zoned areas in the modern city. A civic centre in a new American city, a university campus, a hospital, a cemetery and, of course, residential blocks are

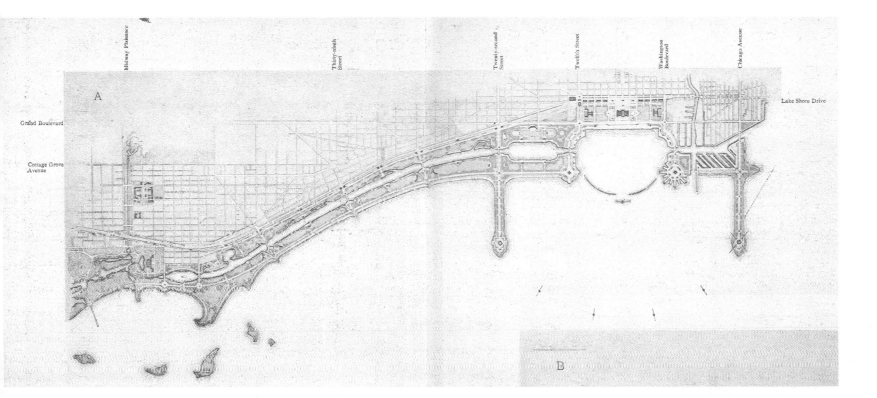

examples of the grouping of buildings for which the strict geometry of
Beaux-Arts composition acts as a binding force.

If in the European city the square was a privileged space in which the
grouping of buildings found its best figurative presentation, then, in
the modern city, which for Hegemann was the American city of the end
of the nineteenth century and beginning of the twentieth, it is the public
garden which acts as the organizing force, in the placing together of
autonomous units, linking them in a common function. The list of
examples is endless, but notable among American examples are the
campus designed by Jefferson for the University of Virginia, with its
modern additions by McKim, Mead and White, the campus at Johns
Hopkins University in Baltimore, and that of Berkeley in California,
where F. L. Olmsted, a convert from a landscape gardening background to that of a convinced designer of articulated geometric Beaux-
Arts structures, made a significant contribution.

But the system is at its best, not only in defining the limits of the
organization of gardened city areas, but also in considering the whole
city in terms of model schemes of gardens and parks conceived within
Beaux-Arts traditions. By the generic term 'The City Beautiful' is
understood the city planning movement which started after the
Chicago exhibition of 1892, developed in the USA, and which has also
been highly influential in Europe and colonial territories in other
continents.

The Chicago Plan, published in 1909 by Daniel H. Burnham and
Edward H. Bennett begins, in the best Beaux-Arts tradition, with an
introduction on the planning of cities and includes as one of the
fundamental principles in its discussion what the authors call 'The
Chicago Park System'. For our purposes in a book of the history of
gardens over the centuries, nothing could be more instructive than a
minute analysis of the pages of this treatise. In it we will see that the plan
of the city as architecture is inseparable from the plan of the city as
urban park. In any case the great process of establishing an urban
dynamic next to Lake Michigan is just like the planning of a huge park
in the manner of Versailles, in which certain areas are devoted to urban
spaces, some monumental, some for walking around, together with
smaller gardens and parks. The principles expressed by the analogies
suggested by the Beaux-Arts style are taken to their limits, in such a way
that the parks and gardens of the city are like a reduced section of a
global concept for the unlimited metropolis, and produced according
to the same principles.

If we look closely at the different parts of this plan we discover:
central squares laid out as gardens; on the axes leading to these, other
gardens which set off large public buildings; main thoroughfares
punctuated by gardens; and urban parks characterized by the meeting
of geometry and landscape.

The concept of 'The City Beautiful' – the Beaux-Arts garden city –
has spread throughout the world in the first three decades of the
twentieth century. Denver, St Louis, Madison, Cleveland, Rochester

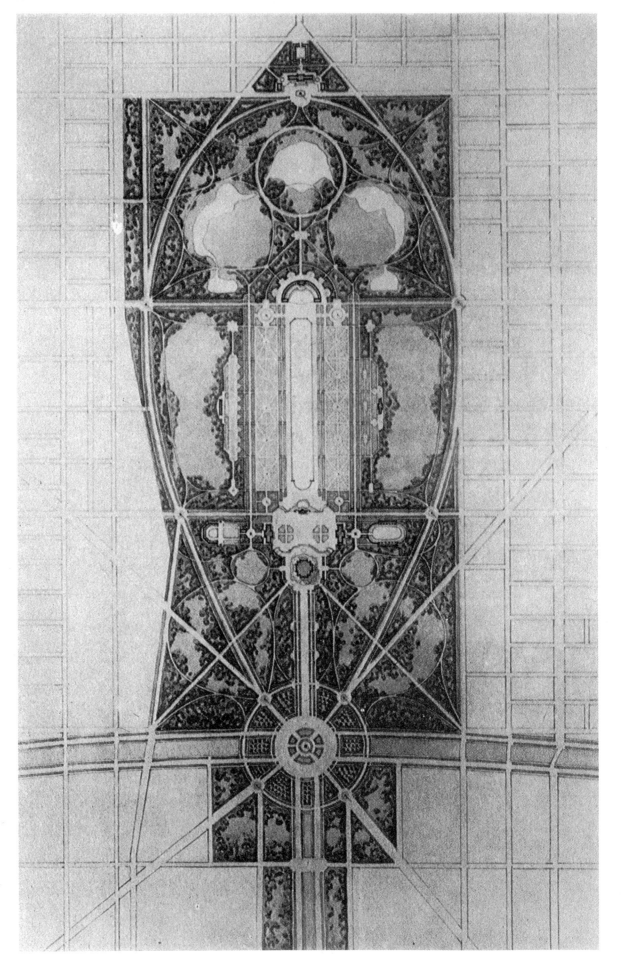

Gardens of the Hôtel del Léon, Pedralves:
the long pergola. From J.C.N. Forestier,
Jardins. Carnet de plans et de dessins,
July 1918.

The Black Yew in the Garden of Love.
From André Vera, Les jardins, *1919*.

The Chalices in the Garden of Love.
From André Vera, Les jardins, *1919*.

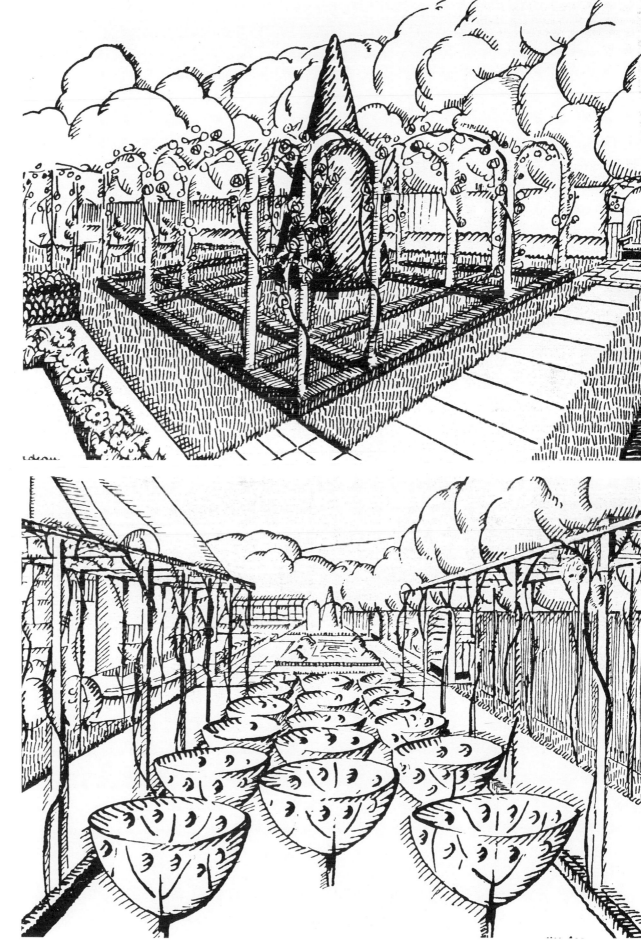

The Park of Montjuich. From J. C. N. *Forestier,* Jardins. Carnet de plans et de dessins, *October 1918.*

are typical, but most impressive are the remodelled hearts of older cities in the States such as Boston, Philadelphia and San Francisco, and above all Washington DC. All are examples of the inseparable relationship between concepts of gardens and parks and concepts of the city. The plan of the Park Commission of 1901 and the proposals of Cass Gilbert for the organization of buildings on the basis of L'Enfant's treatise are examples copied since hundreds of times, not only in the capitals of other states of the Union, but in Sydney, Canberra, Manila, New Delhi, Rabat and Saigon.

The gardens and parks which grew out of the Beaux-Arts tradition have thus become the most powerful tool in the modern control of the metropolitan phenomenon. When Le Corbusier tries to represent the modern metropolis as a logical arrangement of buildings and landscaped parks, he is in fact once more, together with other elements, undertaking an operation similar to that of the architects and landscape gardeners trained in the apparently rigid classical language. So not surprisingly this system appears as the first instrument of organization, encompassing both park and garden, of the complex elements of the modern city.

Bibliography

Paris, Rome, Athènes. Le voyage en Grèce des architectes français au XIX et XXe siècles. Exhibition catalogue, Ecole Nationale Supérieure des Beaux-Arts (Paris 1982).

Roma Antiqua. Forum, Colisée, Palatin. Exhibition catalogue, Académie de France à Rome (1985).

Adolphe Alphand, *Les promenades de Paris.* 2 vols (Paris 1867–1873).

Edouard André, *Traité général de la composition des parcs et jardins* (Paris 1879).

Charles Blanc, *Grammaire des arts du dessin. Architecture, Sculpture, Peinture* (Paris 1867).

M. Boitard, *L'architecture des jardins* (Paris 1854).

Daniel H. Burnham, *Plan of Chicago* (Chicago 1909).

Donald Drew Egbert, *The Beaux-Arts Tradition in French Architecture* (Princeton 1980).

A. Drexler, *The Architecture of the Ecole des Beaux-Arts.* Museum of Modern Art (New York 1977).

J. C. N. Forestier, *Gardens. A note-book of plans and sketches* – Eng. trans. (New York and London 1924).

Georges Gromort, *Essai sur la théorie de l'architecture* (Paris 1942).

Julien Guadet, *Eléments et théorie de l'architecture.* 4 vols (Paris 1901–1904).

Werner Hegemann, *Amerikanische Parkanlagen. Ein Parkbuch* (Berlin 1911).

Werner Hegemann, *Civic Art. An American Vitruvius* (New York 1922).

Pierre de Lagarde, *Cours d'Architecture* (Paris 1954).

Robin Middleton, *The Beaux-Arts and Nineteenth Century French Architecture* (London 1982).

Gustave Umbdenstock, *Cours d'architecture.* 2 vols (Paris 1930).

Folkin Wanland, *Berlins Gärten und Parke* (Berlin 1979).

The Green Revolution:
Leberecht Migge and the Reform
of the Garden in Modernist Germany

Marco De Michelis

The debate on the reform of the urban park which took place in Germany in the early years of the twentieth century was fuelled by arguments not dissimilar from those that, in the same period, helped to change the landscape of German cultural reform: the spread of new standards of hygiene and eugenetics, of better nourishment and medical facilities; criticism levelled at city housing conditions, and the conflict between the town and country which produced initiatives such as *Siedlung*, (new housing schemes and garden cities); the search for a 'third way' between capitalism and socialism, capable of alleviating the class war; the need for a 'new style' to give form and expression to the modern industrial world, which was dominated by the machine.

Ludwig Lesser, who in 1913 founded a German association for parks for the people (Deutscher Volksparkbund), outlined the principal elements of the new reform parks.

They must not in future be equipped mainly or only for walking, with few areas set aside for other activities. To fulfil their primary function they must provide large spaces for games of all sorts, which must be available to all. Only then will they become part of the life of the German people . . . Tree-lined avenues should enclose these sports grounds and lead to large areas of water. There, people of every social class will be able to gather to enjoy the delights of a place designed to compensate for the tracts of countryside eaten away by housing and industry, and to provide an oasis of peace in which to escape the pressures of the working week.[1]

Town planning developments and existing sanitary conditions were the main factors governing the increase in green spaces in urban environments in the following years, and in deciding their siting, accessibility and facilities.[2] Right from the beginning there had been lively discussion among garden designers and architects on the best layout and structure for a modern public park, throwing open for discussion the tradition, now a century old, of landscape gardening which had begun with Lenné and been disseminated, through the influence of the Potsdam School of Garden Design, throughout the whole of Germany.

These early years of development coincided with crucial events in the German reform movement, and brought together the main protagonists. The German Werkbund was founded in 1907, and the first German garden city, Hellerau, was begun in the same year. A little while before, in 1904, the first congress for the reform of the home had taken place in Frankfurt, and the Deutscher Bund für Heimatschutz, whose principal responsibility was the protection of the German countryside, was founded in Dresden. The first plans for public parks, in the sense defined by Lesser, were produced in 1906. One was Carl Heicke's design for the Ostpark in Frankfurt, consisting of a large triangular area of grass divided in two by a lake and enclosed by a dense screen of tall trees. Its winding paths and groups of trees in the grass and around the edge of the lake, together with the absence of any large buildings, seemed to indicate the continuation of the design tradition of Lenné, but the concept of the park as three distinct elements – a stretch of water, an island of grass and a shady screen of trees – was a step in a

new direction, and it presented a formula that was adopted for many years to come. The second plan was devised by Lesser for Berlin-Frohnau, and was entitled 'Park for games and sport'; its areas of green were largely devoted to athletics grounds, polo fields and tennis courts, which required rectangular spaces and a geometric layout, similar in general terms to the architectural schemes designed by Behrens, Läuger and Olbrich for the gardens laid out for the Düsseldorf Fair of 1904. Many other park designs quickly followed, among them the Berlin Schillerpark, created by Friedrich Bauer in 1908, and the Vorgebirgs-Park in Cologne, the work of Fritz Encke in 1909.[3]

The conflict between the heirs of the landscape tradition and the reformers, adherents of the new architectural movement, was concentrated on the competition for the realization of the great Stadtpark in Hamburg on an impressive stretch of land covering 180 hectares (445 acres). The competition was held in 1908 and was won by the city's chief architect, Fritz Schumacher.[4] A second prize was won by H. Foeth and the Röthe brothers (who did little more than bring up to date and simplify the meandering and tortuous lines of designs of the previous century), but it was contested by Max Läuger – an architect, not a garden designer – who put forward a scheme based on a much more rigorous approach, consisting of a straight axial line linking two main architectural features, a reservoir (designed by O. Menzel) and a restaurant building. Laid out between them were a small artificial lake, a large rectangular lawn, a flower garden and a straight avenue flanked by cascades and mature trees leading to a water tower. Equipment for various games and sports pavilions completed the plan, whose clear architectural associations confounded the old professionals who saw in it a return to the artifices of the French-style garden and a repudiation in aesthetic terms of the German tradition. The originality of Läuger's scheme did not, however, escape the supporters of the reform movements, who included the director of the Hamburg Kunsthalle, Alfred Lichtwark; Hermann Muthesius, one of the founders of the Werkbund; Ferdinand Avenarius, director of *Der Kunstwart* and a leading spirit behind the influential cultural association of the Dürerbund; and Leberecht Migge, a young garden architect who, as a result of his support for Läuger's project, was instrumental in encouraging a new attitude towards the reform of contemporary parks and gardens.[5]

Migge's arguments were typical of the modernist debate. He based his theories on the development of the domestic garden, and on the fact that its future was inextricably linked with the outcome of the controversy on the reform of the home, and an awareness that the one-family house as a solution for the mass of the people would bring with it radical reforms in the design of the garden. This was also true of the park, or 'extended garden', whose future depended on reforms in city planning. Migge wrote as follows:

The practical function of a park, its value to the people, is to provide a place for walking and relaxation in the sunshine and fresh air . . . its ideal function is as

M. Bromme, stadium in the Stadtwald, Frankfurt-am-Main. View of the Festival Square, 1923.

L. Migge, view of the German naval cemetery at Wilhelmshaven, 1916.

an environment in which plants and the natural world, and life itself, can be enjoyed to the full. The satisfaction to be derived from its ideal function is infinitely more important than its practical function. And it can happily live in concord with it.

The renewal of the aesthetic aspect of the public park coincided with the programme of reform: an ordered geometric scheme was better suited to the provision of sports facilities and other attractions, and did not in any way result in a stereotyped uniformity in the design of the landscape. On the contrary, it had a harmony and logic that was undeniably modern and that owed much to painters such as Klimt, Munch, Thoma and von Hoffmann, just as the gardens of the eighteenth century were clearly derived from the landscapes of Watteau, Boucher and Claude.

Migge worked as an employee of Ochs in Hamburg from 1904 to 1913, and later as a self-employed designer. The gardens he devised seem to have been based primarily on a conception that originated not only from the houses they surrounded but also from the notion of extending the functionality of the house into the spaces outside. They provided living areas beyond the house itself, in which children could play and adults take exercise and relax, and vegetables and herbs could be grown for the kitchen. The structural elements of the garden were all natural, consisting solely of plants which were chosen for the length of their flowering period or for their autumn colouring. But Migge's gardens were in no way miniature versions of an idealized landscape; theirs was a new 'modern landscape', designed to answer the demands of the times and employing all the technical and artistic means at their disposal.[6] The point from which Migge viewed the modern city, uniting the reform of town parks with reforms in town planning, gave his vision a remarkable originality. In 1913[7] he commented that every reactionary attitude was redundant in the face of the simple fact that large cities already existed, and that their very existence, with all their attendant ills, produced gardens which helped to attenuate the unhealthy conditions created by the sea of houses surrounding them. 'Large cities need gardens as a basic necessity, and I believe', wrote Migge, 'that the will and the desire exist, to create gardens for the sake of pure pleasure'.

The allotment gardens (*Schrebergärten*) that grew up in open areas of the city, on undeveloped plots of land, were for Migge clear proof of a 'great city, a mother of gardens'; they were 'the city's crown of laurels'. Their size – ranging from 200 to 500 square metres (2150–5382 square feet) – established the norm for domestic gardens. They grew up spontaneously in small groups, and were provided with facilities for children's games and for the community in general; over a period they became an established part of local life and a powerful influence on the development of the new *Siedlungen* housing programme and on the design of the urban park.[8]

It is worth remembering that in the Twenties the close relationship that existed between public parks and these community gardens was reflected in the city council's social policies; among the projects that

L. Migge, M. Wagner, design for a youth
park in Berlin, 1916. Plan and vignettes
showing the main features: entrance;
Siedlung for returning soldiers; field for
military exercises; sports garden; garden for
festivals; open-air theatre.

H. Maass, The City of the Happy Man,
1922.

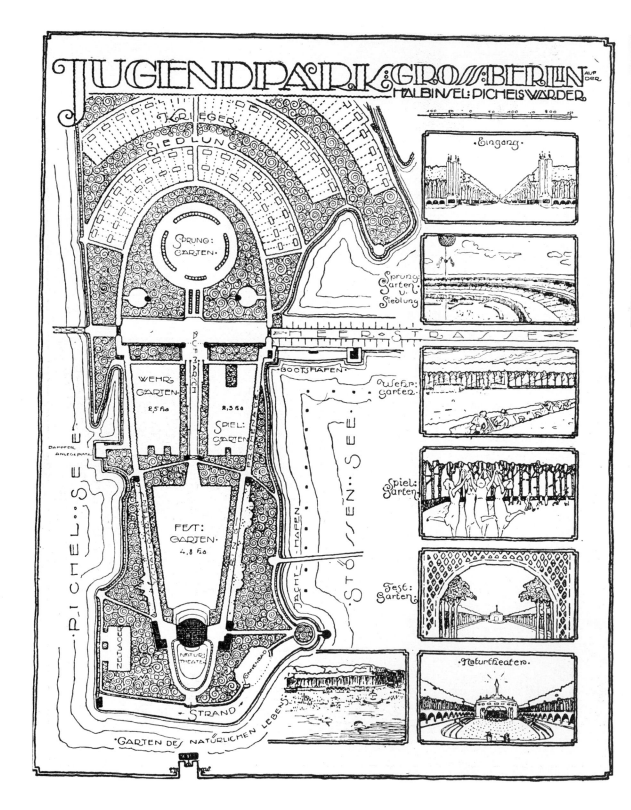

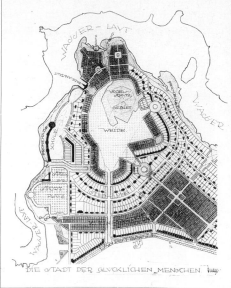

E. Barth (based on a design by R. Germer),
plan of the Volkspark Rehberge, Berlin-
Wedding, 1927.

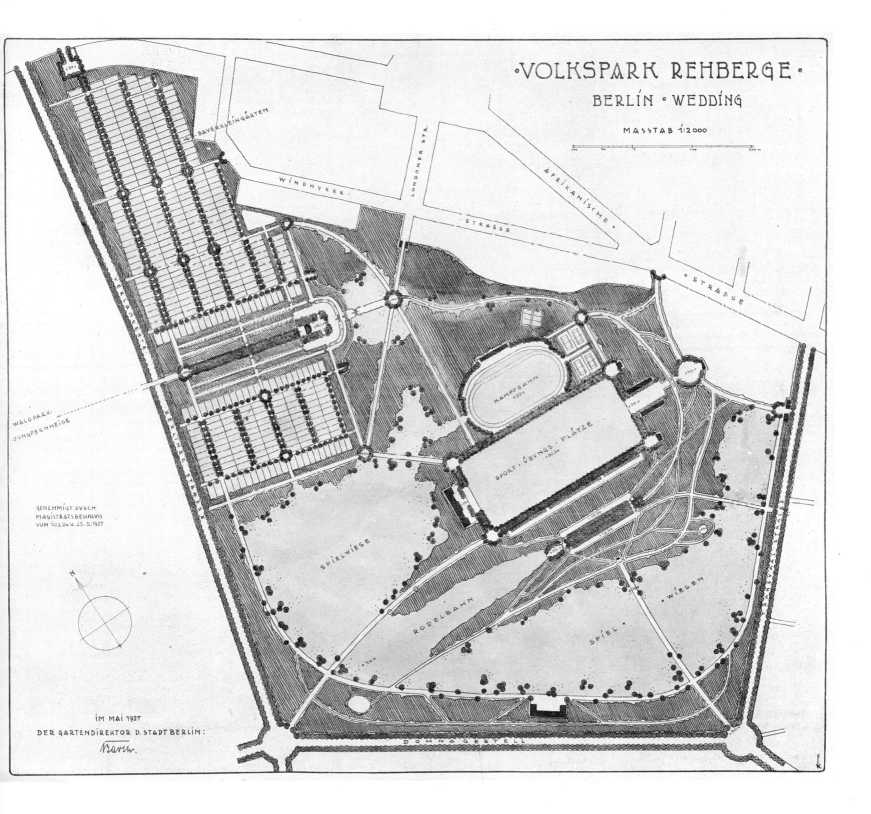

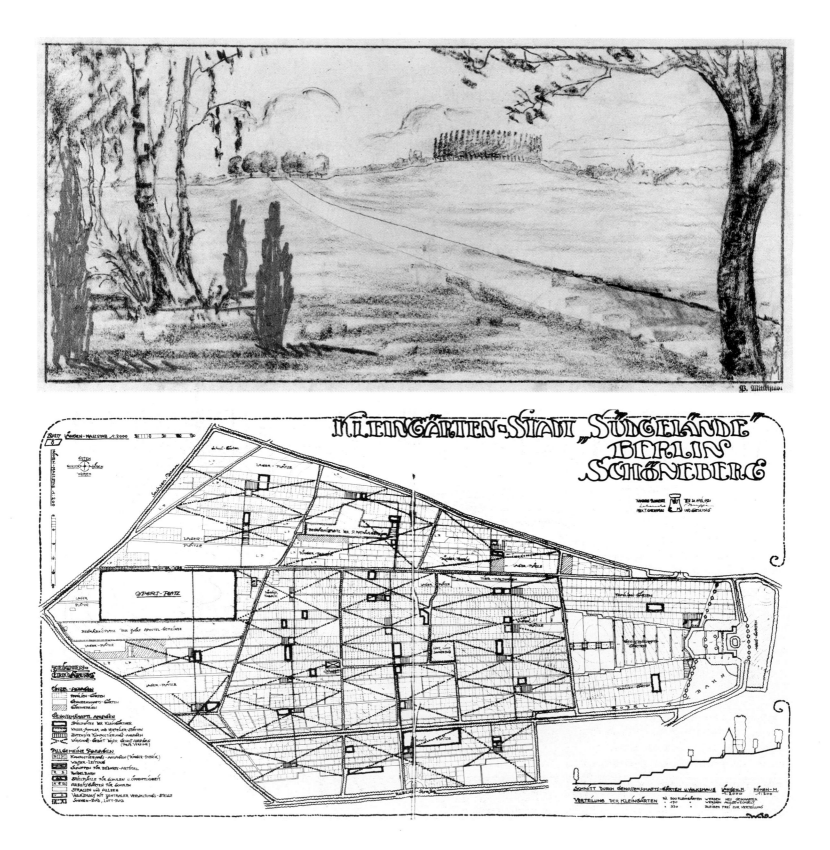

View of the Volkspark Rehberge, Berlin. Designed by Edwin Barth, 1927.

L. Migge, plan of the 'city of working gardens' in the Südgelände, Berlin-Schöneberg, 1920. The density of the plan, which included a thousand gardens, was interrupted by the provision of stables, sportsfields, air and sun baths, tennis courts, cooperative gardens and public housing.

414

demonstrated this connection were the Volkspark Rehberge in Berlin, designed by Erwin Barth in 1927, the Zeppelinfeld Park in Nuremberg, designed by Henfel in 1923, and the community gardens by Max Bromme, director of garden planning at Frankfurt-am-Main.

The First World War had the effect of disseminating Migge's arguments through a new and wider movement for reform that would bring about a change in the direction of modern civilization. The reforming zeal of the intellectuals of the time, and the 'new, young, vital' spirit that the post-war period brought with it, contributed to a renewed sense of national identity and unity.

Between 1915 and 1916, Migge laid out two great war cemeteries at Wilhelmshaven and Brussels,[9] in which the monumental theme of a memorial to the fallen was handled, as had already been the case in his public parks, with remarkable restraint, ignoring every temptation to arouse sentimental feeling or to indulge in affectation. Every grave was designed as a flowerbed and the overall scheme, as Migge said, 'formed a garden'. The colours of the flowers changed throughout the seasons, creating constant variety and a sense of continuous renewal. The critic Adolf Behne was full of admiration for Migge's rejection of a grander, more superficial solution, and above all for the way in which the purely natural elements had been treated; 'It is easy to work with heavy forms but difficult to do so with light ones.' Memorials to the fallen were combined with gardens in innumerable other projects during the immediate post-war years: one example was Bruno Taut's design for a 'garden of the dead' enclosed by a building in crystal, in which the corpses would serve to fertilize the soil,[10] and another was Willi Lange's proposal for a *Heldenhaine* (grove of heroes) to be planted in every German city, with an oak tree for every fallen soldier.[11]

Together with Martin Wagner, who was to be responsible for urban planning in Berlin – on which he had been involved since his collaboration on the public park at Rüstringen – Migge began in 1916 to work on a scheme for the creation of 'youth parks' as a memorial to the war.[12] His concept provided the perfect expression of a desire for reform and a means of creating healthier living conditions within the city, combining all the elements that Migge had been advocating for the urban park since 1913[13] – open-air facilities for sports and gymnastics, for dancing and swimming and other diversions (beer halls were naturally excluded) – with a spirit of nationalism and patriotism intended to inspire the younger generation to fight for the principles for which those who had fallen at the front had given up their lives. The concept of the pre-war *Volkspark* was extended in this 'youth park' (*Jugendpark*) to include certain new features: a central axial route for marching and parades, a field for military exercises, an open-air theatre, a camp site on the edge of the lake and, at the southernmost end of the park, residential quarters for soldiers returned from the war. It was a clear statement of recognition of those who had fought for their country and of the reuniting of the park and the *Siedlung* in the reformed Berlin of the post-war period.

Towards the end of the war Migge extended his vision of the reform

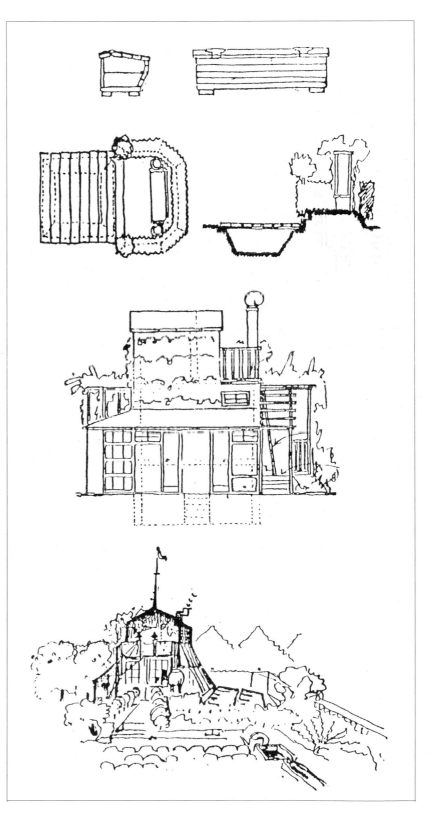

of the garden beyond the spheres of improved health and moral uplift to the point where it became the centre of a general economic plan for the reform of German society. And he remained dedicated to this concept for the rest of his life, a concept based, once more, on the *Schrebergarten* and its productive potential as a means of providing for the needs of the family. The Migge motto became 'Self-sufficiency for all!'[14] The domestic garden, properly equipped and laid out to the appropriate dimensions for its new purpose, was given the task of supplying food to the family nucleus. Closely connected to this aim was the frequently reiterated statement from the supporters of vegetarianism that it was economically nonsensical to pursue a programme in which food grown on the land was fed to animals, which were themselves raised to provide meat for people who could just as well live on a vegetarian diet. Another factor relevant to Migge's argument was a theory in circulation since the end of the nineteenth century, which favoured the widespread colonization of the German countryside by small family farming communities. His proposals were endorsed by the pressing need for a solution to Germany's economic plight in the postwar years. The originality of his scheme lay in his endeavour to base the reform programme on the cultivation of the garden. The city became more than ever the 'mother of gardens' when it shook off its dependence on the countryside, and could break the link which had attracted the criticism of the Darwinists and eugenicists. The catastrophe of the war did much to bring this about. The 'return to nature' seemed to be the only solution for a Germany reduced to poverty, and also an expiation for the war itself, which had been brought about by the imbalances resulting from an industrial and mechanized society.

Migge, under the pseudonym of 'Spartacus in Green', published his Green Manifesto in *Die Tat*,[15] announcing that a return to nature held the secret for the twentieth century, and that the countryside would provide the means of salvation for the city and of its transformation into a new *Stadtland* (country-city).

Towns must once more embrace the land. Hundreds of thousands of hectares today lie idle and uncultivated: land fit for building, for houses and roads has been abandoned. It should be tilled and planted with public gardens for the young who are chained to the cities, with small gardens for those who are chained to their city houses, with *Siedlungen* for those who are chained to their work in the cities.

Commissioned by Martin Wagner, by then *Stadtbaurat* of the Berlin suburb of Schöneberg, Migge designed the gardens of the Lindenhof *Siedlung*, not only those of the small one-family houses but also those redeemed from the private sector for co-operative apartment buildings. One of his most important schemes of this kind was the design of a large project in the Südgelände of Schöneberg, a major example of the means by which a collection of garden-orchards could be gradually transformed into a city, following the same laws as those governing the cultivation of the soil.[16] 'There exists only one natural way of building',

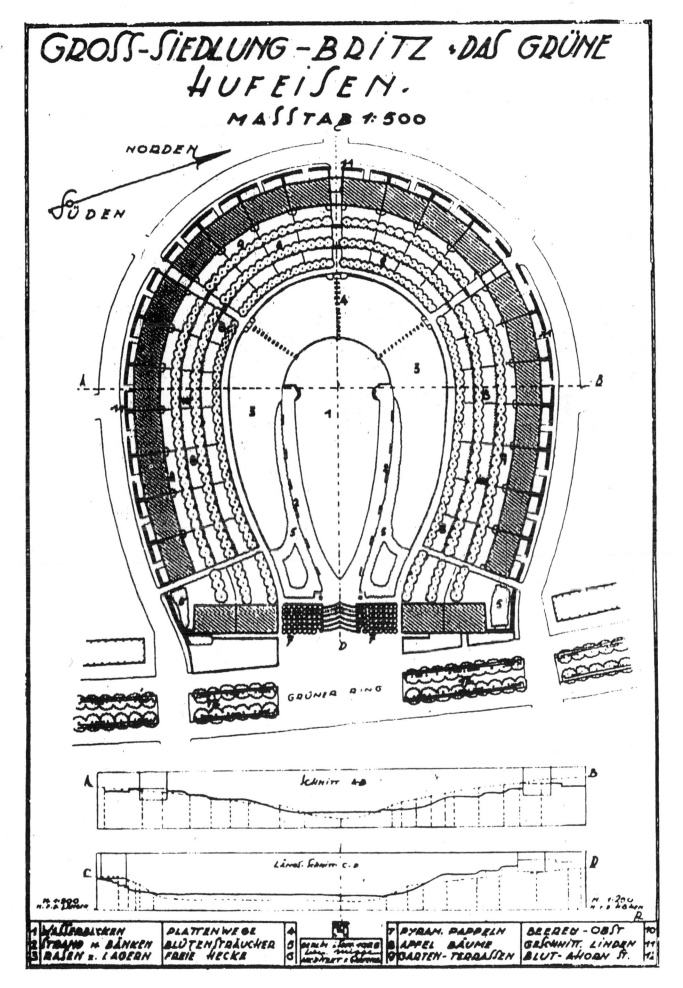

L. Migge, the 'green horseshoe' of the Siedlung Britz by B. Taut and M. Wagner, 1926. From the centre: the lake, the public lawns and the terraced gardens.

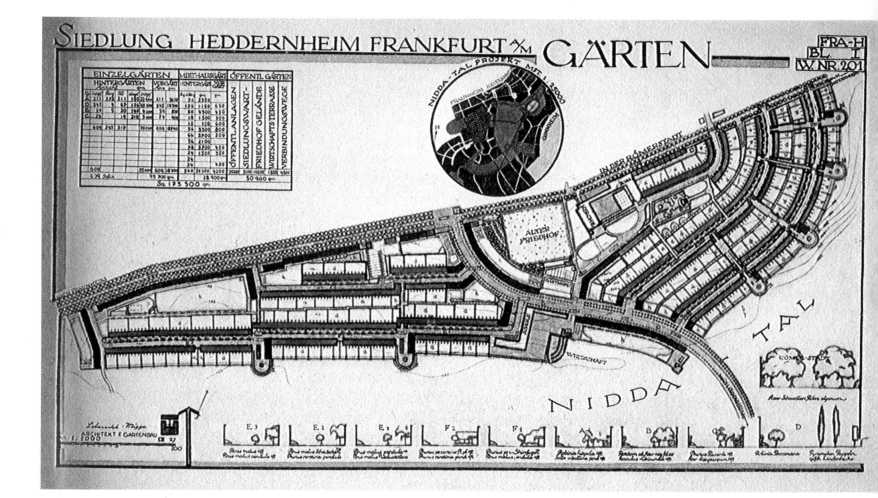

Colony of working gardens in the Siedlung Römerstadt at Frankfurt-am-Main. (Photo Gartenamt, Frankfurt-am-Main)

Model of a plan for a 'professional community'. The design for the house is by Leopold Fischer, c. 1926.

wrote Migge, 'with the help of the fruits of the earth and the materials of the site, and the direct involvement of the owner . . . Each man should be his own architect-builder: these are the guidelines for the solution to the problems of today.' The garden-city conceived by Migge was intended to be built in stages, regulated by the cultivation of the land, and culminating in the building of a hut that was gradually transformed into a house. The same system applied to the laying out of the garden, which in time acquired a more specialized function: nurseries were planted up, glasshouses were built along the external walls of the house, which improved its insulation, and areas were set aside for children's games.

In 1920 Migge and Martin Wagner founded the Stadtland-Kulturgesellschaft Gross-Hamburg und Gross-Berlin, whose objective was a new policy for the settlement of the land, to bring ten million city-dwellers back to their original country towns and villages in order to transform them into communities consisting of gardens and one-family units.[17] Similar appeals for an initiative of this sort in post-war Germany had been discussed in the socialist monthly *Sozialistische Monatshefte* and in Friedrich Naumann's social-nationalist paper *Die Hilfe*.[18] Migge engaged in correspondence, in the pages of *Neue Hamburger Zeitung*, with Walther Rathenau,[19] putting forward a counter proposal to the policy of an urban culture by outlining his vision of a future based on a new 'culture of the countryside' and a 'country-city' concept. The solution proposed by Rathenau to the problem of the traditional separation of intellectual from manual work remained unresolved by the reformists, who put their faith only in the fact that the policy of self-sufficiency they advocated would overcome every obstacle, bringing 'an end to every war, to every struggle for survival, to every conflict between men'. Rathenau's scepticism, which was evident from his response, was based entirely on his traditional view of agriculture, a view ignorant of technical innovations that had resulted in dramatically increased productivity.

The garden as a place in which to experiment with new techniques became the theme of Migge's programme of research; this included his Siedlerschule, founded in 1920 at Worpswede, a small town in the north of Germany where a colony of artists had settled, among them a contemporary of Migge, the painter Heinrich Vogeler, who started an experimental communist *Siedlung*. In 1924 Migge collaborated with Ernst May – the future chief architect of Frankfurt – on the founding of a society for the development of the cultivation of gardens in Silesia,[20] and from 1923 to 1927 he produced his own magazine, *Siedlungs-Wirtschaft*, which regularly published reports of his researches and experiments.[21]

His designs for the gardens of the major housing developments built by the architects of the Weimar period are a clear indication of the way in which his researches brought together the architecture of the house with the architecture of the garden, involving all the great masters of the Modern Movement, such as Adolf Loos, Bruno Taut, Otto Haesler and Ernst May.

Plans for the transformation of Frankfurt into a great 'community park', which were drawn up in 1928,[22] and for the resettlement of a million inhabitants of Berlin in self-supporting *Siedlungen* in 1932,[23] were the most extreme and coherent examples of the attempts by the 'green movement' to revolutionize productivity by exploiting the potential of the thousands of small city gardens throughout Germany. Only a few years later, in 1935, Migge died, isolated from the policies of the new Nazi regime and hostile to its aims.

[1] 'Die Volksparks der Zukunft (Vortrag von L. Lesser)' in *Der Städtebau*, no. 9, (1912) p. 60. See W. Richard, *Vom Naturideal zum Kulturideal, Ideologie und Praxis der Gartenkunst im deutschen Kaiserreich* (Berlin 1984).

[2] Most important of all is M. Wagner's thesis, *Das Sanitäre Grün der Städte. Ein Beitrag zur Freiflächentheorie* (Berlin 1915). On Wagner, see L. Scarpa, 'Quantificare il verde. Gli standard della felicità nella Berlino socialdemocratica' in *Lotus International*, no. 30 (1981) pp. 119–22.

[3] Apart from W. Richard's work referred to, the following may be singled out from the vast number of publications on this subject: L. Lesser, *Volksparks heute und morgen* (Berlin-Zehlendorf 1927); H. Wiegand, *Entwicklung des Stadtgrüns in Deutschland zwischen 1890 und 1925 am Beispiel der Arbeiten Fritz Enckes* (Berlin-Hanover 1975); *Stadtgrün*, edited by V. Hampf-Heinrich, G. Peschken (Berlin 1985); D. Hennebo, 'Der deutsche Stadtpark im 19. Jahrhundert' in *Gartenamt*, no. 8, (1971) pp. 382ff; I. Maass, 'Parchi per il popolo in Germania' in *Lotus International*, no. 30 (1981) pp. 123–8.

[4] F. Schumacher, *Ein Volkspark* (Munich 1928); M. Goecke, *Stadtparkanlagen im Industriezeitalter. Das Beispiel Hamburg* (Berlin-Hanover 1981); A. Venier, 'Il latte, il prato, l'acqua, il mattone. Storia dello Stadtpark di Amburgo' in *Lotus International*, no. 30 (1981) pp. 98–103.

[5] L. Migge, 'Der Hamburger Stadtpark, Läuger und Einiges' in *Die Raumkunst*, no. 17 (1908) pp. 257–67; L. Migge, *Der Hamburger Stadtpark und die Neuzeit* (Hamburg 1909).

[6] On Migge see I. Meta Hülbusch, '"Ciascuno è autosufficiente". Il verde coloniale di Leberecht Migge', in *Werkbund, Germania, Austria, Svizzera*, edited by L. Burckhardt (Venice 1977) pp. 66–71; M. De Michelis, 'Il verde e il rosso. Parco e città, Germania di Weimar' in *Lotus International*, no. 30 (1981) pp. 104–17; see also the monograph *Leberecht Migge. 1881–1935. Gartenkultur des 20. Jahrhunderts* (Worpswede 1981).

[7] L. Migge, *Die Gartenkultur des 20. Jahrhunderts* (Jena 1913) pp. 6ff.

[8] Migge was not alone in basing his premise for the reform of the urban park on the community garden scheme. It was also in 1913 that Harry Maass, the architect of the Lübeck gardens, published a short volume entitled *Der deutsche Volkspark der Zukunft* (Frankfurt-on-Oder 1913), in which he put forward a similar proposal.

[9] L. Migge, 'Der deutsche Ehrenfriedhof zu Brüssel-Evere' in *Der Städtebau*, Vol. 13, no. 8–9 (1916) pp. 83–5 and plates 48–50; 'Der Ehrengarten der deutschen Marine zu Wilhelmshaven. Der Deutsche Kriegerfriedhof zu Brüssel-Evere' in *Die Bauwelt*, no. 28 (1916) pp. 9–14; A. Behne, 'Zu den Soldatenfriedhöfen Leberecht Migges in Brüssel-Evere und Wilhelmshaven' in *Bau-Rundschau*, nos. 44–7 (1916) pp. 193–207; M. De Michelis, 'Riforma del monumento, riforma della città. Il dibattito degli architetti tedeschi negli anni della Grande Guerra' in *La grande guerra. Esperienza, memoria, immagini*, edited by D. Leoni and C. Zadra (Bologna 1986) pp. 671–84.

[10] B. Taut, 'Die Vererdung. Zum Problem des Totenkults' in *Die Tat*, Vol. 8, no. 10 (1917) pp. 917–22.

[11] W. Lange, *Deutsche Heldenhaine* (Leipzig 1915).

[12] Among the many articles on this subject, see L. Migge, 'Geistesschutzpark oder Jugendpark?' in *Die Tat*, Vol. 8, no. 9 (1916–17) pp. 869–70; L. Migge, 'Jugendparke als Kriegerdank' in *Der Kunstwart*, no. 6 (1917) pp. 188–91.

[13] L. Migge, *Die Gartenkultur . . .*, op. cit., pp. 24–5.

[14] This is the translation of the title of a short volume by Migge, published in 1918, *Jedermann Selbstversorger. Eine Lösung der Siedlungsfrage durch neuen Gartenbau* (Jena 1918). See also, by the same author, *Laubenkolonien und Kleingärten* (Munich 1917).

[15] Spartakus in Grün, 'Das grüne Manifest' in *Die Tat*, Vol. 10, no. 12 (1918–19) pp. 912–19.

[16] L. Migge, 'Die Kleingartenstadt "Südgelände" zu Berlin-Schöneberg' in *Sitzungsbericht des Arbeitsausschusses für sparsame Bauweise*, Vol. 2, no. 5 (1920) pp. 143–8; by the same author, 'Natürliche Architektur (Etappenbauweise)' in *Heim und Scholle*, Vol. 6, no. 2 (1921) pp. 17–20.

[17] L. Migge, 'Mehr Land, mehr fruchtbares Land! Zur Gründung der Stadtland-Kulturgesellschaften Gross-Hamburg und Gross-Berlin' in *Haus Wohnung Garten*, no. 20 (1920) pp. 253–4; no. 21, pp. 265–6; M. Wagner, 'Der Wiederaufbau der Wirtschaft als Bau- und Siedlungsproblem' in *Schlesisches Heim*, no. 5 (1921) pp. 138–42.

[18] M. Machler, 'Das Siedlungsproblem' in *Sozialistische Monatshefte*, XXVII, 4, 1921, pp. 182–7; by the same author, 'Wie ist das Siedlungsproblem zu lösen?' *ibid.*, 5–6, pp. 222–7; F. Landwehr, 'Siedlungswesen und Revolution' in *Die Hilfe*, 5 (1919), pp. 61–2; W. Heilig, 'Erreichbares der Gegenwart im Siedlerwerk', *ibid.* 31, pp. 408–9.

[19] L. Migge, 'Offener Brief an Herrn Walther Rathenau' in *Neue Hamburger Zeitung*, no. 630 (11 December 1919); *Stadt und Land. Ein Briefwechsel zwischen Walther Rathenau und Leberecht Migge, ibidem*, no. 13 (8 January 1920).

[20] E. May, L. Migge, 'Niederschlesische Gartenfürsorge m.b.H.' in *Schlesisches Heim*, no. 8 (1924) pp. 244–5.

[21] In the 1920s and 1930s Migge published two new books: *Deutsche Binnen= Kolonisation* (Berlin 1926) and *Die wachsende Siedlung* (Stuttgart 1932).

[22] L. Migge, *Grünpolitik der Stadt Frankfurt a.M.*, unpublished typescript, 1929; by the same author, 'Grünpolitik der Stadt Frankfurt am Main' in *Der Städtebau*, no. 2 (1929) pp. 37–47.

[23] L. Migge, M. Schemel, *Eine Weltstadt kolonisiert. Berlin versorgt sich selbst! Eine Million Berliner siedeln aus!*, unpublished typescript, 1932.

The Park at Klein-Glienicke, Berlin

Klaus von Krosigk

View of the schloss and the Kleine Neugierde (tea pavilion) in the park at Glienicke on the Havel, c. 1835. Gartendenkmalpflege, Berlin.

Casino at Klein-Glienicke, with Glienicke bridge, c. 1850. From H. Günther, Peter Joseph Lenné, Gärten Parke, Landschaften, Stuttgart 1985. Gartendenkmalpflege, Berlin.

The Glienicke gardens, situated near the Havel on the south-western edge of Berlin, and traditionally part of the Potsdam area, form an architectural, artistic and cultural ensemble of landscape gardens, parks and historic townscape of European significance. Created in several stages during the first half of the nineteenth century, the unity between the architecture and garden makes Glienicke an outstanding synthesis of the arts reflecting the spirit of Berlin neoclassicism and romanticism. In 1814 it was acquired by the Prussian State Chancellor, Karl August Fürst von Hardenberg, and in 1824 passed to Prince Carl of Prussia, the son of King Friedrich Wilhelm III and Queen Luise, who used it as his summer residence until his death in 1883, keeping a large part of his collection of antiquities there. He had considerable artistic discernment and such important architects as Karl Friedrich Schinkel and his pupils Ludwig Persius and Ferdinand von Arnim, as well as the most celebrated landscape gardeners of the period, Peter Joseph Lenné and Hermann Fürst von Pückler-Muskau, were all to be involved with Glienicke.

In 1934 and 1939 the city of Berlin acquired Glienicke Park from Prince Carl's heirs and opened the greater part of it to the public.

As early as the autumn of 1816, shortly after his appointment as assistant gardener at Potsdam, Lenné presented his first design for the alteration and remodelling of the Glienicke gardens to Fürst Hardenberg. He restricted himself at first to replanning the parts of the garden situated between the schloss and the Havel bridge. In this design the 'English garden areas', originally located only on the south side of the schloss, were combined with the rest of the garden, extensive geometric kitchen garden areas and the fruit terraces, to form a unified garden in the landscape style. The characteristic landmarks of this small landscape garden known as the Pleasureground and laid out near the schloss following English models, were three raised areas of ground, planted with deciduous copses and cleverly arranged so that the meadows descending from these hills to the Havel created an artificial effect of distance and grandeur by forming various vistas, which changed depending on the standpoint of the viewer.

Early in 1824, shortly after the death of Fürst Hardenberg, Prince Carl purchased Glienicke. In the same year Lenné prepared another design for the estate, which now covered more than 150 Prussian acres.

During the first great planting in 1824/25 over 25,000 trees were introduced, not only native deciduous trees, such as beeches, oaks, elms, limes, ashes, poplars and birches, but also foreign species such as Weymouth pines, American red oaks, robinia and several thousand ornamental shrubs.

In 1824 Schinkel was also working at Glienicke, beginning with the conversion of the old billiard house into a *casino*. For this the Crown Prince had provided a sketch for a lake-side 'Italian villa' flanked by pergolas, and it was on this that Schinkel based his conversion. The *casino* is the first evidence at Glienicke of the longing for Italy so characteristic of

View from the Stibadium looking towards the Havel and Potsdam. Beyond the Fountain of the Lions on the right can be seen the circular flowerbed, with its ornamental features enclosed within the perimeter, 1847. Gartendenkmalpflege, Berlin.

Plan of the park of Klein-Glienicke. Coloured lithograph by L. Kraatz, 1862. Gartendenkmalpflege, Berlin.

the culmination and the conclusion of the development of a garden extending over more than fifty years and extraordinary even in the context of Potsdam.

Conservation measures

After the death of Prince Carl in 1883 the maintenance of the park declined. In 1939 there were disruptive plantings and changes to the paths, then came war damage and alterations in the post-war period. The fountains and small lakes were drained, and the area divided among several municipal authorities. The relationship between the views within the park and to the outside was obscured by new plantings and overgrown foliage. These vicissitudes resulted in a considerable reduction of the variety of experiences and a disfigurement of the historic state of the park.

The objectives of the conservation work were the recovery of the park's former state, its long-term care as a monument, and suitable use for Glienicke as a unified combination of architecture and park, bound up with the cultural landscape of Potsdam. The reconstruction of the park grounds – as a *Gesamtkunstwerk* – is thus as important as the restoration of the architectural features.

The reconstruction work in Glienicke Park has been going on for eight years under the direction of the Gartendenkmalpflege (Department III of the Senator for City Development and the Protection of the Environment). It aims to restore the park to the state reached by 1840, after which there were no important alterations.

the period, and of the desire to construct the ideal southern landscape and architecture in the March of Brandenburg.

Begun in 1825 and also by Schinkel was the remodelling of the schloss in austere neoclassical style with a flat roof emphasizing the rural and private character of the estate.

The basic form of the Pleasureground had already been established in the 1816 design. It was now much refined and completed with the construction and conversion of garden buildings, an increasingly rich embellishment with foreign trees, exotic plants, rare flowers, valuable works of art, fountains and pergolas. A network of paths carefully planned by Lenné opened up this area in a very subtle way, creating the maximum number of impressions and sensations within a relatively restricted area by the

reshaping of the terrain and delightful, ever-changing main sight-lines.

In 1839 Glienicke acquired modern orangeries and greenhouses designed by Ludwig Persius which were urgently needed for the maintenance of the Pleasureground with its wealth of flowers and tub plants. These were destroyed in the Second World War but have since been rebuilt.

In 1840 Persius replaced an earlier greenhouse on the eastern edge of the Pleasureground with the Stibadium, a raised seat in the form of a semi-circular bench with a view over Potsdam. Lastly, next to the already existing Kleine Neugierde, a classical tea pavilion now moved near the road, stands the Grosse Neugierde or Rotunda. It was built in 1835–37 from a design by Schinkel on a prominent site at the Havel bridgehead. It

served as a belvedere giving the visitor a magnificent panorama extending from Babelsberg to the south as far as Sakrow to the north, and including the town of Potsdam and Pfingstberg to the west.

Together with the 'Venetian' monastery courtyard build in 1850 by Ferdinand von Arnim, a highly picturesque and rhythmically composed ensemble of buildings extending from the schloss to the *casino* marks the northern limit of the Pleasureground.

In the mid-nineteenth century the whole park was once more recorded in a colour lithograph printed in 1862 by Leopold Kraatz. Beside the park on Böttcherberg, this plan also shows the garden of the old hunting lodge, dating from the seventeenth century and later altered, which was acquired for Prince Carl's son in 1859. It thus illustrates both

Bibliography

K. v. Krosigk, 'Anmerkungen zum Pleasureground', in *Das Gartenamt*, no. 28 (1979).

K. v. Krosigk, 'Gartendenkmalpflegerische Aspekte bei der Behandlung der Wiesen und Grasflächen in historischen Parkanlagen', in *Das Gartenamt*, no. 29 (1980).

K. v. Krosigk, 'Schinkel als Gartenkünstler', in *Das Gartenamt*, no. 31 (1982).

G. Meyer, *Lehrbuch der schönen Gartenkunst* (Berlin 1860).

H. Fürst v. Pückler, *Andeutungen über Landschaftsgärtenerei* (Stuttgart 1977, reprint of the 1833/1834 edition).

Karoline v. Rochow and Marie de la Motte-Fouque, *Vom Leben am preussischen Hofe 1815–1852* (Berlin 1908).

J. Sievers, *Bauten für den Prinzen Karl von Preussen* (Berlin 1942).

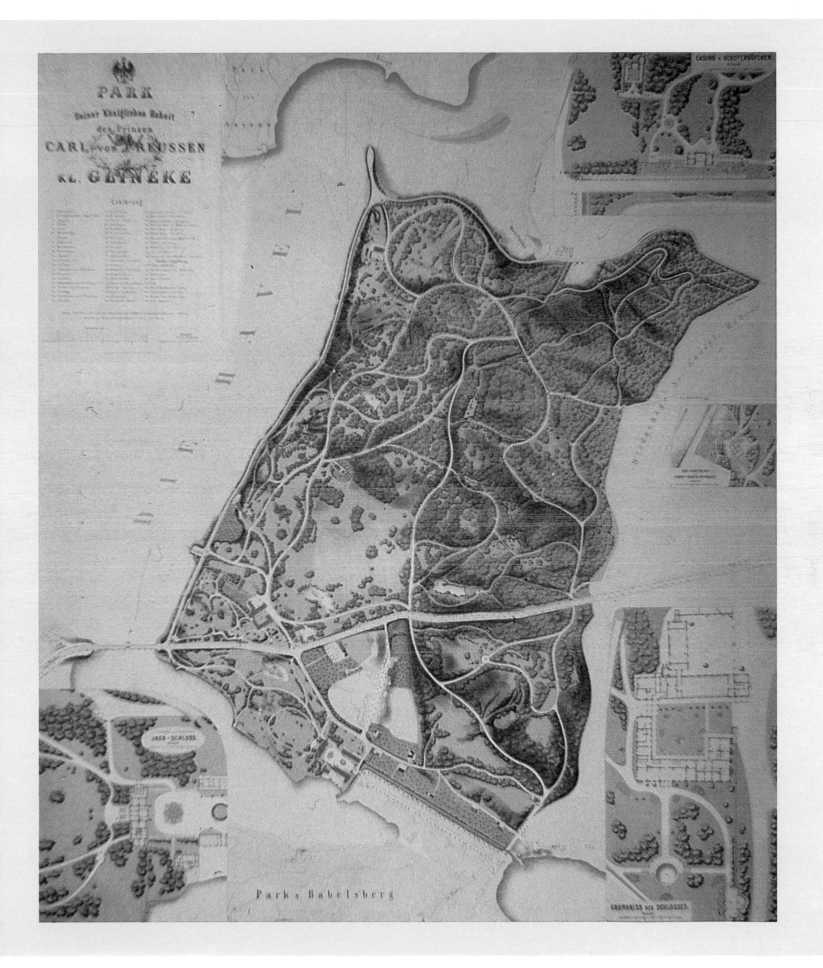

The English Cottage Garden
Gillian Darley

The English cottage garden seen from a late twentieth-century perspective appears to be a nineteenth-century creation. It was not, of course, but it was in the Victorian era that it assumed such enormous importance.

The Victorians chose it as a symbol, which, in a dramatically urbanized and often rootless society, stood as a repository of rustic values and rural simplicity. As an image, it did not have to contend with the realities of poverty; as a picturesque scene the cottage garden became a favourite subject for watercolourists and photographers, as well as a popular setting for scenes in literature. In fiction, the tension between traditional countryside and the development of the cities could be illustrated, on the one hand in the sweet smelling cottage garden, and on the other in the foul back streets of the exploding cities.

A sophisticated interest in the cottage garden was already evident in Georgian England. Humphry Repton, the eminent landscape gardener bought his cottage near Romford, east of London, in 1786. In his 1816 *Fragments*, he showed the process of change. Somehow he had taken over the village green, and, in his words

by this appropriation of twenty-five yards of garden, I have obtained a frame to my landscape; the frame is composed of flowering shrubs and evergreens; beyond which are seen, the cheerful village, the high road, and that constant moving scene, which I would not exchange for any of the lonely parks that I have improved for others.

His objective may have been the formal setting-up of a landscape, but nevertheless here was one of the first self-conscious cottage gardens.

It was only a short step from here to the *cottage ornée*. Here high society, following the unsuitable example of Marie Antoinette, could play at cottage life – though the 'cottage' was a villa and its garden usually a sizeable affair with more concern for the decorative than the practical.

On a smaller scale however, the appeal of the cottage garden was obvious. Landowners in the late eighteenth and early nineteenth century were often engaged in rebuilding their estate villages – sometimes as a result of improvements to the landscape around the great house which often included the razing to the ground of older cottages which stood in the way of the grand scheme.

This was not the case, however, at Blaise Hamlet, outside Bristol, where a Quaker banker named Harford decided to build a hamlet of almshouses for retired estate workers. John Nash and George Stanley Repton (Humphry's son) designed the cottages with careful attention to their gardens, abundantly planted with the traditional cottage flowers. Over the thatched roofs and wooden verandahs trailed roses, jasmine, honeysuckles, and each cottage bore the name of a plant.

The hamlet, completed in 1811, was to be the inspiration for many another early nineteenth-century picturesque model village and it enshrined the garden as a feature as important as any architectural detail. It seemed appropriate that these elderly people should end their days in a setting designed to conjure up the traditions of an ostensibly unchanged rural society. Within a few years Blaise became a stopping place on the picturesque tour which both English and Continental visitors followed in search of inspiring landscape or pleasing architecture. The inclusion of Blaise on such journeys, as well as the production of lithographs showing each cottage, demonstrated what a hold the notion of rural simplicity – even if it was entirely reconstructed – had taken on the early-nineteenth-century romantic imagination.

Later on in the nineteenth century, the cottage garden was to become the model, even the justification, for those gardeners who rebelled against the formality and the rigidities of either the suburban garden or the grand garden, with, in the former, dank shrubberies and in the latter, bedding out and elaborate parterres. The writings of William Robinson, in *The Wild Garden* and *The English Flower Garden* heralded a sea-change; the late Victorian and Edwardian gardeners, especially Gertrude Jekyll, began from a

The Old Place: *cottage garden. Watercolour by Helen Allingham (1848–1926). Private collection.*

Laverstoke, Hampshire: gardener's cottage designed by P. C. Hardwick for Mr Portal. Watercolour, c. 1854. Drawings Collection, Royal Institute of British Architects, London.

premise in which a delight of the natural sets the scene. Following those meadows scattered with spring bulbs and summer flowers was a well-deserved admiration for the cottage gardener who was guided by practical considerations (growing flowers, herbs, fruit and vegetables for household consumption) as much as by an innate sense of beauty. In the same way that the Arts and Crafts architects looked to traditional techniques and materials for inspiration, so the new gardeners were guided by the wisdom of generations of country people who both needed and delighted in their patch of ground.

The cottage garden may have been caught in a wash of romantic tints, but it was also a productive place. Like medieval town gardens, when there was still space to spare, flowers and vegetables grew together, as well as herbs and fruit trees. By the nineteenth century the old traditions were being passed on in printed form, as the vogue for gardening magazines and manuals gathered momentum. Guidelines were laid down. The distinction between the work of man and woman for example; the man tended the vegetables, the woman the flowers and herbs. This collaboration, one author thought, was a perfect metaphor for marriage.

One of the attractions of the cottage garden for the new generation of romantic gardeners was the fact that many old-fashioned plants lingered on there, having long gone from more sophisticated gardens. While the fashion was for hard, bright colours and rigid display, the traditional cottage garden plants, perennials or annuals, were gentler – both in growth and colouring. The florists' flowers, a select number of species grown competitively and bred for excellence – such as pinks or ranunculus – were generally the quiet blooms of the garden while the climbers, such as old roses, clematis, jasmine or honeysuckle, accen-

tuated the abundance and informality of the cottage garden.

Nor should it be forgotten that the cottage garden had a political resonance. As common lands were being lost in the enclosures, so country people were losing their rights to the major landowners. Those who supported the idea of generous cottage gardens or allotments (plots of ground, generally in another part of the village), were often radically inclined, or philanthropists who saw the inequities of the redistribution of land. It was also good for the soul; F.D. Maurice, a late Victorian social reformer wrote that 'small unit cultivation elicited moral

Cottage garden with beehives in the foreground: late nineteenth century. Museum of English Rural Life, University of Reading.

Cottage garden in North Devon.

values which fostered political independence.' The independence of the English working classes, he felt, could be guaranteed 'when they are working upon ground attached to their homes, upon which they are not hirelings.'

So, the English cottage garden passed on into the twentieth century as the more contrived garden suburb, and currently enjóying a revival, has been a vehicle for aspirations of many sorts. That happiest combination of the practical and the aesthetic has been made to stand for visions political, picturesque, horticultural or merely romantic. The English cottage garden has achieved a resonance few other approaches to gardening can claim.

Bibliography

Anne Scott-James, *The Cottage Garden* (Harmondsworth 1981).
The Cottage Garden and the Old-fashioned Flowers (London 1969) [gives useful information on plant history, dates of introduction, etc.]
The Garden. Catalogue from the exhibition held at the Victoria and Albert Museum (London 1979). Various useful essays, including Gillian Darley, 'Cottage and Suburban Gardens'.
William Robinson, *The English Flower Garden* (1883, reissued in 1984). Introduction by Deborah Nevins.

426

Glasshouses
and Winter Gardens
Renzo Dubbini

Palm house in the Botanical Gardens, Berlin, designed by K. F. Schinkel, 1821.

Design for a glass house at Romainville (Seine-St-Denis) by A. T. Brongniart, August 1803: section and elevation. Private collection, Paris.

The origins of the great glasshouses of the nineteenth century lie in the expeditions of Bougainville, Cook, Bonpland and von Humboldt, and in the eagerness of western scientists both to discover more about the natural world, which was still largely unexplored, and to make collections of exotic new plants. Glasshouses already existed, as places in which tender specimens could be protected in winter, but only in the nineteenth century did the technical advances in architecture and engineering make it possible to construct large hothouses, with sophisticated heating and ventilation systems.

Initially, large glasshouses were all privately owned, and belonged almost exclusively to grand houses such as La Malmaison; Wilhelmshöhe; and Syon House and Alton Towers. Loudon also built one for himself in his relatively modest house in Bayswater. Gradually, however, they began to appear in town parks, botanical gardens and other public places devoted to the study and conservation of plant life.

The technology involved in the building of glasshouses was largely developed by Loudon, who was responsible for analysing the inherent physical problems and defining the type of construction best able to provide the appropriate biological environment. He was the first person to study in depth the question of how glass should be angled in relation to the rays of the sun under different conditions. The fundamental principle on which his architectural designs were based was that the walls must have both strength and flexibility. They were made of fine but extremely strong wrought-iron ribs, which formed the structural 'cage' of the building. Later on, Joseph Paxton chose to use cast iron for the load-bearing interior framework and wood for the external connecting structure in order to achieve greater adaptability to heat variation and resistance to weather; in time industrial production methods were adopted in order to reduce the cost of both manufacture and assembly.

Continuous research and experimentation eventually produced a glasshouse capable of sustaining the weight of its own structure and at the same time sufficiently flexible to withstand the force of the prevailing wind, following in many respects the principles of shipbuilding. It was also equipped with thermostats and pressure gauges so that the inside atmosphere could respond to weather conditions outside.

With later contributions by Richard Turner, Hector Horeau, Charles Rohault de Fleury, August von Voit and Roland Mawson Ordish, the design of the glasshouse reached new heights of originality and inventiveness. It was undoubtedly the technical daring as much as the aesthetic genius of the schemes they devised that earned the glasshouse a place among the greatest architectural achievements of the nineteenth century. But it must also be said that it was soon to lose its elegance and grace, and that the relationship between the glasshouse and the plants it contained was to become extravagant to the point of absurdity: elaborate cast-iron capitals, ornate sculptures and even fake ruins began to emerge from the surrounding greenery in such an

C. D. Bouché and J. Bouché, *Bau und Einrichtung von Gewächshäusern* (Bonn 1886).

G. F. Chadwick, *The Works of Sir Joseph Paxton* (London 1961).

A. Corbin, *Le miasme et la jonquille* (Aubier Montaigne, 1982) pp. 269ff on the spread of the greenhouse in the 1880s.

J. Gloag, *Mr Loudon's England; The Life and Work of J. C. Loudon* (Newcastle upon Tyne 1970).

J. Harris (editor), *The Garden. A Celebration of One Thousand Years of British Gardening* (London 1979) in particular pp. 92–110.

J. Hix, *The Glass Houses* (London 1974).

G. Kohlmaier and B. von Sartory, *Das Glashaus. Ein Bautypus des 19. Jahrhunderts* (Munich 1981); English edition *Houses of Glass* (Cambridge, Mass. and London 1986).

J. C. Loudon, *Remarks on the construction of Hothouses* (1817), and *Sketches of Curvilinear Hothouses* (1818).

B. Marrey and J. P. Monnet, *La grande histoire des serres et des jardins d'hiver, France 1780–1900* (Turin. n d.)

H. E. Milner, *The Art and Practice of Landscape Gardening* (London 1890), chapter on hothouses.

Neumann, *Art de construire et de gouverner les serres* (Paris 1846 – second edn).

N. Pevsner, *A History of Building Types* (London 1976).

P. Scheerbart, *Glasarchitektur* (1914), in particular pp. 17, 27, 51, 53, 77 and 126.

Hector Horeau, architecte de la transparence (1801–1872), catalogue of the exhibition at the Musée des Arts Décoratifs, Paris. A supplement to 'Cahiers de la recherche architecturale', No. 3.

Jardins en France, 1760–1820, Pays d'illusion, terre d'expériences, Catalogue of the exhibition 18 May – 11 September 1977, Caisse Nationale des Monuments Historiques et des Sites (Paris 1977).

excess of exoticism that the delights of the hothouse frequently degenerated into a display of the worst possible taste.

Around the middle of the nineteenth century, however, the glasshouse was in its heyday: in the great botanical gardens and at horticultural exhibitions – and eventually at the international exhibitions – it became an object of wonder, offering a glimpse of the exotic and infinitely fascinating plant life of countries that, for most people, there was a little hope of visiting. The glasshouse of the Musée d'Histoire Naturelle drew enormous crowds, who were thrilled by the brilliance of its design and entranced by the profusion of rare species on display. Its success prompted the building of the sumptuous Winter Gardens in the Champs Elysées in 1846, where one could admire unusual plants, buy flowers, and even have breakfast in a comfortable salon. Public response was so enthusiastic that the entrepreneurs responsible for its construction put up a second, much larger, building the following year, complete with ballroom, billiard room, art gallery and aviary.

By this time the future of the glasshouse was assured, and demand spread rapidly among the middle classes who saw it as a symbol of refinement and social distinction. It took on many different roles – orangery, hothouse, winter garden, conservatory – becoming part of the house and a place for rest and relaxation. As its popularity grew, so the variety of shapes and styles increased. Glasshouses were soon being mass-produced: smaller models were designed to lean against a wall of a house or even to stand on a terrace or balcony. They were also used inside to safeguard plants from the harmful effects of gas lighting, though no such measures were taken to protect people.

Apart from its variety of uses, the glasshouse appealed above all to the imagination. The painter Rousseau might well have invented his luxuriant jungles without ever travelling to West Indian islands; he had only to visit the glasshouse in the Jardin des Plantes. And Zola, Maupassant and the Goncourt brothers saw the symptoms of social change in the dripping, steamy atmosphere of the glasshouse. Perhaps the character who most clearly personified its decadance, however, was Huysman's des Esseintes (in *A rebours*, 1884), who had a bizarre dream in which he created a collection of imitation plants that mimicked real ones and a collection of real plants that reproduced the colours and textures of inanimate materials – the softness of velvet, the streaks and flecks of minerals and the dull, dark tones of metals. It was the sort of surrealistic invention that could only have been born of an imagination overheated by the heavy, fetid atmosphere of the glasshouse.

But whether it inspired wild imaginings or offered a place for peaceful relaxation or scientific research, it did provide an opportunity to explore a new relationship with nature. Walter Benjamin was right to count it, together with the railway station, among the nineteenth-century architectural inventions in which the worlds of fantasy and reality succeeded in finding a meeting point.

Bibliography

G. Barthélemy, *Les jardiniers du Roi. Petite histoire du Jardin des Plantes de Paris* (Paris 1979).

Portrait of A. J. Downing. Engraving from a daguerreotype c. 1852.

'A planted elm of fifty years . . . let us take it then as the type of all true art in landscape gardening'[1]

Eight months before his death in a steamboat accident, Andrew Jackson Downing offered 'A Few Hints on Landscape Gardening' to readers of *The Horticulturist*, the Journal of Rural Art and Rural Taste that he had edited since 1846. This brief essay is the most mature statement of the man who had become in the ten years following the 1841 publication of *A Treatise on the Theory and Practice of Landscape Gardening* America's pre-eminent practitioner and author in the field. Although Downing revised the treatise twice in his lifetime, first in 1844, the last time in 1849, his more thoughtful responses to American conditions can be discovered in his later editorials.[2]

'In what manner is nature to be imitated in Landscape Gardening?'queried Downing in the first edition of his treatise.[3] Initially reliant for the answer on the theory of imitation espoused by John Claudius Loudon in Britain (1783–1843), Downing gradually reformulated his ideas. The most significant changes in Downing's theory of landscape gardening concerned this issue of imitation.

The relationship of art to nature had been debated since antiquity. Theories of imitation were formulated in ancient times to define the nature of poetry, i.e. Aristotle's *Poetics* and Horace's *Ars poetica*, and subsequent efforts were made to invest other arts with the dignity of poetry.[4] Arguments over the nature of imitation have vacillated between whether it should result in a simple copy of the original, or be modelled on a judicious selection of an object's best attributes. Some thought that the artist should turn from a direct experience of nature to an *a priori* idea of perfection in the person's mind. Others turned to origins and looked to the primitive hut or the human body for imitation; yet others to the ancients, who had accomplished in art everything to which they could aspire.[5]

At various times and in various treatises, painting, sculpture, music, dance, eloquence, and architecture have been included in the ranks of the imitative arts. However, attempts to secure a place for landscape gardening within this ranking were met with scepticism by such critics

as A. C. Quatremère de Quincy (1755–1849), a Frenchman who devoted his life to formulating a coherent philosophical system of the arts. Quatremère disputed neither the gratification yielded by this art of forming gardens, nor the kind of skill that it required, but every element that he considered necessary to constitute imitation was absent. What pretended to be an image of nature was nothing more nor less than nature herself; this was especially so when the artifice of the designer was well concealed in irregular or natural style landscapes.[6]

A review of the competing ideas of imitation and particularly of Quatremère's contribution to the debate is important if one is to understand Downing's theory of landscape gardening. In his early work, Downing borrowed heavily from Loudon, and this prolific writer and editor provided the link between the

young American author and the prominent French theoretician.[7]

It was in direct response to Quatremère's exclusion of garden making from the ranks of the imitative arts that Loudon formulated his theory of landscape gardening. Writing in *The Suburban Gardener*, Loudon revealed the elevated status which the designation 'fine art' held in his mind and the reason he wanted to associate the term with his profession. It was a synonym for 'elegant art, art of imagination, art of taste.' The two essential qualities of fine art were to create and to please, and the work produced had to be a creation of an artist and, most importantly in Loudon's eyes, had to be acknowledged as such. Landscape gardening was not just a matter of taste for him – Loudon endeavoured to make a living from design commissions and publications, and his concern for the visibility

and status of his art was clearly revealed in this passage: 'To imitate nature in such a way as that the object produced should be mistaken for nature, could never excite much approbation for the artist.'[8]

Loudon searched for a means of conveying a high character of art to a scene without resorting to the geometrical style. His solution of Quatremère's objections to the natural style was to plant foreign trees and shrubs totally different from the material in a given locality. While Loudon had a specific theoretical basis for his selection of plant materials, to fully understand his position one also needs to recognize the general eighteenth- and nineteenth-century fascination with rare and bizarre foreign plants. As new accessions and overseas trade treaties opened up unknown areas of the world, there was a great influx of new plants into Britain.[9] One of Loudon's major publications was devoted to the dissemination of information about these plants and to the encouragement of their use.[10] It is not surprising that this botanical craze was reflected in Loudon's theory.

Loudon sought standing as an imaginative artist by basing his theory on the substitution of foreign plants for indigenous materials, and developed a new style based on the recognition of art which he named 'gardenesque'. He expounded on two modes of 'artistical imitation': the picturesque and the gardenesque – the first being the imitation of nature in a wild state, and the second the imitation of nature 'subjected to a certain degree of cultivation or improvement suitable to the wants and wishes of man'.[11] For picturesque effect, no tree or shrub was to stand isolated, but rather form part of a group or mass; in contrast, for gardenesque effect the beauty of every individual tree and shrub – as a single object – was to be taken into consideration. A third mode, which Loudon called rustic, indigenous, or fac-simile imitation, was considered to have no design merit.[12]

In his first edition of *Landscape Gardening*, Downing echoed Loudon's theory of imitation, with a reference to Quatremère.[13] For an 'artistical imitation' of nature, Downing concurred, one had to use materials different from those in nature herself – hence, the necessity of introducing largely exotic ornamental plant material.[14] He introduced his

readers to Loudon's gardenesque style with a long quotation from that author. Downing differed on one point; he added the category of 'beautiful' imitation to Loudon's fac-simile, picturesque, and gardenesque. Fac-simile was ranked lowest, geometric and gardenesque next, and highest on the scale picturesque and beautiful, because they joined 'to fine forms, and elegance in arrangement, the higher beauty of sentiment of expression'.[15] When Downing recapitulated his main principles, Loudon's 'recognition of art' headed the list; the imitation of the beauty of expression was third.[16]

In the final revision of his treatise (1849), however, Downing underplayed the principle of the recognition of art to concentrate on the creation of scenery full of expression. The 'imitation of the beauty of expression' was ranked first, and Downing devoted many pages to a discussion of the Beautiful and the Picturesque 'the two most forcible and complete expressions to be found in that kind of natural scenery which may be reproduced in Landscape Gardening.'[17] Downing's vision of the ideal had come to be embodied in a 'natural' landscape whose true expression, whether beautiful or picturesque, had been detected and heightened. He described and illustrated both of these scenes. The ideal Beautiful vision had flowing and gradual curves, soft surfaces, and rich and luxuriant growth, expressive of infinity, grace, and willing obedience. The ideal Picturesque vision had a spirited irregularity, with surfaces comparatively abrupt and broken, and wild and bold growth, expressive of violence, abrupt action, and partial disobedience.[18]

Downing reported in his 1849 edition of *Landscape Gardening* that the picturesque was beginning to be preferred in the United States because in a suitable locality it had great advantages – namely that the raw materials of wood, water, and surface could be appropriated with so much effect and so little art – in other words, so little money.[19] The identification of this American preference was one of the factors in the maturation of Downing's theory of imitation in landscape gardening. A recognition of the existing raw materials unique to his native landscape and a concern for economy became more apparent about this time; his theory and practice became more truly adapted

to North America.[20] Going beyond the final revision of *Landscape Gardening,* one finds in Downing's *Horticulturist* editorials indications that he came to temper his ideals concerning this art. His readers' comments on his books and monthly editorials, and his own ever expanding practical experience surely contributed to these changes.

Downing began *The Horticulturist's* new year of 1849 with a statement on 'the true philosophy of living in America'. It was to be found in 'moderate desires, a moderate establishment, and moderate expenditures'.[21] He warned his readers against trying to realize 'the perfect model of beauty and convenience' floating dimly in their heads, because everyone tended to underrate the cost of improvements. Beautiful parks, pleasure-grounds, and flower gardens did not constitute the highest and most expressive kind of rural beauty, Downing advised, although they were certainly the most expensive.[22]

In the following years, Downing continued to make concessions to his young nation, admitting that a perfect taste in the arts could not be expected when his countrymen were mainly occupied with the practical wants of life.[23] He was content, his readers learned, to work toward 'the largest amount of comfort, convenience, and beauty, for the moderate sum which an American landholder [had] to spend.[24]

Downing's landscape ideal still embraced a scene which, through a selection of nature's finest features, had reached a more perfect expression, but the recognition of art so important to Loudon came to be relegated simply to the need for a well-kept appearance. The extent to which Downing changed his views concerning this once sacred principle can be seen in his late editorials. His former encouragement of the use of exotics became rather an embarrassment to him as he realized that the adoption of Loudon's thinking in this regard made little practical and aesthetic sense in a country so rich in indigenous materials. He found it necessary to explain his former stance in an editorial devoted to the subject: 'We had always, indeed, excused ourselves for the well-known neglect of the richest of our native Flora, by saying that what we can see any day in the woods, is not the thing by which to

make a garden distinguished.'[25] He admitted that no new shrub, 'whether from the Himmalayas or the Andes', surpassed the American laurel when in perfection.[26]

Thus, in his final hints on landscape gardening, Downing tried to re-educate his readers to use their native landscape as the basis for the ideal. He reminded them that the real lessons in the beautiful and picturesque were to be taken from their beautiful woodland slopes, broad river meadows, steep hills sprinkled with picturesque pines and firs, and deep valleys dark with hemlocks and cedars. The object of imitation should be nature rather than gardens, Downing pro-

claimed, and 'the fields and woods [were] full of instruction'.[27]

Downing stipulated, however, that there should be no precise resemblance between a portion of the woods and fields and the scenery of the finest pleasure-ground. Selection and recomposition were essential – a selection 'from the finest sylvan features of nature', and a recomposition of the materials 'in a choicer manner'.[28] These ideas had been repeated many times by other landscape theorists, but the image that Downing chose to reinforce his point is significant.[29]

He painted a picture of a planted American elm standing gracefully in the

midst of a smooth lawn, and contrasted its refinement and perfection of symmetry with what would be found in a wild elm in the woods. Downing proclaimed this common American tree 'the type of all true art in landscape gardening', and in doing so, bowed to the American context in which he worked and wrote.[30] His beau ideal in 1841 had been a lawn arranged with groups of limes, horse-chestnuts, and magnolias; these trees would be exotic ornamentals where the native forests were filled with oak and ash. In addition to this variety of foliage and blossoms, which would immediately suggest the recognition of art, Downing required for his 'artistical imitation' in landscape gardening, borders of rare flowers and climbing plants, gravel walks, smooth turf, and elegant accessories such as vases and architectural ornaments.[31]

When, in 1851, Downing suggested a type which was meant to inspire a work of landscape gardening in his readers' imaginations, the image he presented was the elm – one of the neglected American plants. He suggested a technique of imitation, and these words constitute Downing's final advice to the 'rising generation of planters' in America: 'Study landscape in nature more, and the gardens and their catalogues less.'[32]

Although Downing resigned himself to a more practical vision, he never completely abandoned his highest aspirations, in which he saw his countrymen with enough money, time, and taste to live amidst perfect pleasure-grounds. Downing could do nothing about the money and time available to his readers, but as America progressed from the wilderness to civilization, Downing's inspirational prose on the tasteful in architecture, grounds, and gardens had something for everyone.

1 A. J. Downing, 'A Few Hints on Landscape Gardening', in *The Horticulturist* 6 (November 1851), p. 491.
2 Downing, *A Treatise on the Theory and Practice of Landscape Gardening adapted to North America; with a view to the Improvement of Country Residences* (New York, London and Boston 1841); 2nd edn (New York and London 1844); 4th edn (New York and London 1849). No third edition has been located.

Most of the *Horticulturist* editorials were republished in a memorial volume after Down-

Blithewood, the home of R. Donaldson at Barrytown on the Hudson River: the picture was used as the frontispiece for Landscape Gardening *by A. J. Downing.*

ing's death, but significantly not in chronological order; see *Rural Essays* ((New York 1853). In the 'Memoir' that prefaced *Rural Essays* (p. xxiv), George William Curtis pointed out that 'Hints on Landscape Gardening' contained 'the most concise and comprehensive definition of Landscape Gardening' that could be found in Downing's works.

Downing's other major works were *Cottage Residences* (New York and London 1842); *The Fruits and Fruit Trees of America* (New York and London 1845); and *The Architecture of Country Houses* (New York 1850).

[3] Downing, *Landscape Gardening* (1841), p. 33.

[4] For example, on the relationship of painting and poetry, see Rensselaer W. Lee, *Ut Pictura Poesis* (New York 1967).

[5] The literature on mimesis/imitation is growing: *Lotus International* 32 (1981) is devoted to the topic; see also R. Wittkower, 'Imitation, Eclecticism, and Genius', in *Aspects of the Eighteenth Century*, ed. by Earl R. Wasserman (Baltimore 1965), and Wladyslaw Tatarkiewicz, *A History of Six Ideas: An Essay in Aesthetics* (Warsaw 1980).

[6] Quatremère de Quincy, *An Essay on the Nature, the End, and the Means of Imitation in the Fine Arts.* Translated by J. C. Kent (London 1837), pp. 170-1.

[7] In the preface to his treatise, Downing publicly acknowledged Loudon as 'the most distinguished gardening author of the age'; they also had a close personal relationship as is evident in this letter: 'In him I lost not only the most intelligent of friends but one whose place as a critic in the arts of tasteful gardening and rural architecture neither England nor the continent is at the present moment able to supply'. A. J. Downing to Joel Rathbone, 17 June 1845, Historical Society of Pennsylvania.

In addition to such works as Loudon's *Encyclopaedia of Gardening* (1822) and *The Suburban Gardener* (1838), to which he referred in his books and articles, Downing was familiar with Loudon's two journals: *The Gardener's Magazine* and *The Architectural Magazine*. See A. J. Downing to John Jay Smith, 15 November 1841, Smith Papers, The Library Company of Philadelphia: 'I perceive by Loudon's Mag. . . .'

Starting in January 1835 and running for two years in *The Architectural Magazine*, Loudon published translated excerpts from Quatremère de Quincy's *Essay on Imitation*; and in January 1837, Loudon reviewed the English edition of this book which Loudon claimed had just been translated by Mr Kent at his request.

[8] J. C. Loudon, *The Suburban Gardener, and Villa Companion* (London 1838), pp. 136-7.

[9] See Nicolette Scourse, *The Victorians and Their Flowers* (Portland, Oregon 1983).

[10] J. C. Loudon, *Arboretum et Fruiticetum Britannicum*, 8 vols. (London 1838). Vol. 1, p. v: 'The main object . . . was the hope of diffusing more generally, among gentlemen of landed property, a taste for introducing a greater variety of trees and shrubs in their plantations and pleasure-grounds.'

[11] Loudon, *Suburban Gardener*, p. 164.

[12] *Ibid.*, p. 166.

[13] Downing gave no hint of Quatremère's conclusions about landscape gardening in the lone excerpt that he selected for his readers: 'M. Quatremère de Quincy, has defined the end of imitation to be, "to present to the senses and the mind, through the intervention of the fine arts, images which, in all the different forms of imitation, shall furnish an aggregate of perfection and ideal beauty to which particular models afford no equal." In this sentence may be found the true nature of imitation in Landscape Gardening.' Downing, *Landscape Gardening* (1841), p. 33.

[14] *Ibid.*, p. 35.

[15] *Ibid.*, p. 39. Downing gleaned his ideas concerning the superiority of the beauty of expression from Archibald Alison, *Essays on the Nature and Principles of Taste* (Dublin 1790). Alison proposed that a distinctive emotion was inspired by a scene or object with a particular expression; for example, the scenery of spring suggested ideas productive of emotions of cheerfulness or tenderness. Dependent upon the exercise of the imagination, the emotions of taste were distinguished from the emotions of simple pleasure; one could be *pleased* with the gratification of any appetite; one was *delighted* with the prospect of a beautiful landscape.

[16] *Ibid.*, p. 43.

[17] Downing, *Landscape Gardening* (1849), p. 67.

[18] *Ibid.*, pp. 73-5. See Sir Uvedale Price, *An Essay on the Picturesque as Compared with the Sublime and the Beautiful* (2nd edn London 1796) for his precise definitions of this aesthetic trinity. Downing considered Price to be the master of the Picturesque school; see his footnote in *Landscape Gardening* (1844), p. 55.

[19] Downing, *Landscape Gardening* (1849), p. 78.

[20] By 1849, Downing had been editor of *The Horticulturist* for two and a half years. Freed from the heavy burden of his nursery business (he sold his interest in February 1847), Downing had devoted himself to his practice and literary pursuits.

For a discussion of the high cost of labour in America (as opposed to Britain) and the advisability of selecting a site 'where nature has done as much as possible for you', see Downing, 'Citizens Retiring to the Country' in *The Horticulturist* 7 (February 1852) p. 60.

[21] Downing, 'On the Mistakes of Citizens in Country Life' in *The Horticulturist* 3 (January 1849) p. 307.

[22] *Ibid.*, p. 309. Downing's statements in *Landscape Gardening* were in opposition to this good advice. He wrote in the 1849 treatise (p. 19): 'we should convey a false impression, were we to state that [landscape gardening] may be applied with equal success to residences of every class and size. . . . In the case of large landed estates, its capabilities may be displayed to their full extent, as from fifty to five hundred acres may be devoted to a park or pleasure grounds.'

[23] In the opening lines of the 1841 preface to *Landscape Gardening* (p. v), Downing had recognized the extremes of living conditions existing in America: 'While yet in the far west the pioneer constructs his rude hut of logs for a dwelling, and sweeps away with his axe the lofty trees that encumber the ground, in the older portions of the Union, bordering the Atlantic, we are surrounded by all the luxuries and refinements that belong to an old and long cultivated country.' It was in 1841 that 48 wagons in the first large group to emigrate to California reached Sacramento. Downing realized that these homesteaders who faced life in log or sod houses did not have the time or energy to cultivate a taste for 'rural embellishment'.

His acknowledgment of these enterprising spirits in the far west was done more as a comparison with the cultivated gentlemen who could be found in the older portions of the union, and to disabuse Old World notions of a general state of savagery in the country. One year after its publication, Downing could

humorously report to a friend: 'the Landscape Gardening treatise . . . seems to have startled the Europeans, who can hardly believe that we have any thing but log houses.' Downing to John Jay Smith, 21 May 1842, Smith papers, The Library Company of Philadelphia.

24 Downing, 'A Few Words on Rural Architecture' in *The Horticulturist* 5 (July 1850), p. 9.
25 Downing, 'The Neglected American Plants' in *The Horticulturist* 6 (May 1851), p. 202. By seeing American plants away from home on his trip to Europe in 1850, Downing may have realized what his native country's gardens had lost.
26 *Ibid.*, p. 203.
27 Downing, 'A Few Hints on Landscape Gardening' in *The Horticulturist* 6 (November 1851), p. 491. Although Downing would write eight additional editorials before his death, the November one was the last to deal with 'landscape gardening'.
28 *Ibid.*
29 Just two examples are: Thomas Whately, *Observations on Modern Gardening* (London 1770) and Archibald Alison, *Essays on the Nature and Principles of Taste* (Dublin 1790).
30 Downing, 'A Few Hints on Landscape Gardening,' *op. cit.*, p. 491. Quatremère had defined 'type' and 'model' in his essay in *Encyclopédie Méthodique: Architecture*, Vol. 3, pt. II (Paris 1825): 'The word "type" presents less the image of a thing to copy or imitate completely than the idea of an element which ought itself to serve as a rule for the model . . . when a fragment, a sketch, the thought of a master, a more or less vague description has given birth to a work of art in the imagination of an artist, one will say that the type has been furnished for him. . . . The model, as understood in the practical execution of the art, is an object that should be repeated as it is; the type, on the contrary, is an object after which each [artist] can conceive works of art that may have no resemblance.' *Oppositions* 8 (Spring 1977) p. 148.
31 Downing, *Landscape Gardening* (1841), p. 35.
32 Downing, 'A Few Hints on Landscape Gardening', *op. cit.,*, p. 491.

Bibliography

Brenda Bullion, 'Hawthorns and Hemlocks: The Return of the Sacred Grove' in *Landscape Journal*, 2 (Fall 1983), pp. 114–24.
James T. Callow, *Kindred Spirits* (Chapel Hill 1967).
Walter L. Creese, *The Crowning of the American Landscape* (Princeton 1985).
Arthur Channing Downs, 'Downing's Newburgh Villa' in *APT*, 4 (1972), pp. 1–113.
David P. Handlin, *The American Home* (Boston 1979).
Neil Harris, *The Artist in American Society* (Chicago 1982).
U. P. Hedrick, *A History of Horticulture in America to 1860* (Oxford 1950).
Catherine M. Howett, 'Crying "Taste" in the

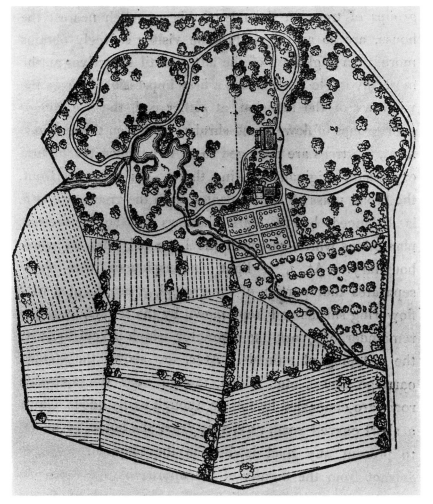

Plan of an estate in the 'natural' style. In a considerably enlarged version, it was illustrated in Landscape Gardening.

Wilderness: The Disciples of Andrew Jackson Downing in Georgia' in *Landscape Journal*, 1 (Spring 1982), pp. 15–22.
Kenneth T. Jackson, *Crabgrass Frontier: The Suburbanization of the United States* (New York and Oxford 1985).
W. G. Jackson, 'First Interpreter of American Beauty: A. J. Downing and the Planned Landscape' in *Landscape*, 1 (Winter 1952), pp. 11–18.
Ann Leighton, *American Gardens of the Nineteenth Century* (Amherst 1987).
James L. Machor, *Pastoral Cities* (Madison 1987).
Charles Capen McLaughlin (ed.), *The Papers of Frederick Law Olmsted*, Vol. I: *The Formative Years: 1822 to 1852* (Baltimore 1977).
Judith K. Major, 'The Downing Letters' in *Landscape Architecture*, 76 (Jan./Feb. 1986), pp. 50–7.
Ross L. Miller, 'The Landscaper's Utopia Versus the City: A Mismatch' in *The New England Quarterly*, 49 (June 1976), pp. 179–93.

Keith N. Morgan, 'The Emergence of the American Landscape Professional: John Notman and the Design of Rural Cemeteries' in *Journal of Garden History*, 4 (July/Sept. 1984), pp. 269–89.
Blake Nevius, *Cooper's Landscapes: An Essay on the Picturesque Vision* (Berkeley 1976).
John W. Reps, 'Downing and the Washington Mall' in *Landscape*, 16 (Spring 1967), pp. 6–11.
David Schuyler, *The New Urban Landscape* (Baltimore 1986).
J. E. Spingarn, 'Henry Winthrop Sargent and the Landscape Tradition at Wodenethe: An English Inheritance Becomes an American Influence' in *Landscape Architecture*, 29 (October 1938), pp. 24–39.
Roger B. Stein, *John Ruskin and Aesthetic Thought in America, 1840–1900* (Cambridge, Mass. 1967).
George Bishop Tatum, 'A. J. Downing: Arbiter of American Taste, 1815–1852', Ph.D. dissertation (Princeton 1950).
George Bishop Tatum, 'The Emergence of an

American School of Landscape Design' in *Historic Preservation*, 25 (Apr.–June 1973), pp. 34–41.
George Bishop Tatum, 'New Introduction' in *Andrew Jackson Downing: Rural Essays* (New York 1974).
John William Ward, 'The Politics of Design' in *Who Designs America?* (New York 1966).

434

The Viktoriapark in Berlin

Vroni Heinrich

Plan of Viktoriapark, Berlin, designed by H. Mächtig, 1888–94. A Baroque cascade had also been planned but was never built.

Plan of Viktoriapark, Berlin, designed by H. Mächtig; note the waterfall redesigned in naturalistic fashion.

he king to his people,
ho at his call nobly gave their goods and
 blood to the fatherland,
 memory of the fallen,
 recognition of the survivors,
or the emulation of future generations.

o runs the dedicatory inscription of he monument on the Kreuzberg. Its nhappy history has meanwhile been rgely forgotten.

Napoleon's progress through Europe ecame a march of conquest. It did not ring the equality and fraternity that had cen hoped for. The revolution, above all he freeing of the peasants without com-ensation, was restricted to the areas west f the Rhine. Disappointment and indig ation grew in occupied Prussia, which ad traditionally been Francophile. In 799, shortly after his accession, King riedrich Wilhelm III had already freed he peasants on his domains from serf om, and after 1806 he was able through

his minister Freiherr von Stein at least to begin implementing further reforms against the aristocracy, thereby streng-thening popular resistance to Napoleon. By the promise of a constitution he was finally able to raise a resolute army which in 1813–15 fought the Wars of Liberation against enemy rule as well as for its own political maturity and national unity. Napoleon was defeated and driven out. In gratitude and joy a great national Cathed-ral of Liberation was to be built in the centre of Berlin to the designs of Karl Friedrich Schinkel in the Gothic (also called the 'altdeutsch') style symbolizing civil liberty (the French origins of Gothic were not known). But after the Congress of Vienna in 1815, when the power of the princes and small states was once again established, a meagre cross was substi-tuted as a monument.

The state purchased a former vineyard some distance outside the Hallesches Tor

(the south gate of Berlin), on a site that had originally belonged to the city, but then became the property first of the electors and finally of the citizens. It had been damaged in 1813 by the construc-tion of military fortifications. The foun-dation stone for the monument was laid in 1818 on the site of a fieldwork with a view far over the city. Its construction of cast iron, famous far beyond Prussia as *fer de Berlin*, was very symbolic: the citizens had exchanged iron for gold to pay for the war, and also the iron cross at the top of the monument was in the shape of the military Iron Cross, which, in accordance with democratic trends, had been awarded both to generals and to soldiers in the ranks. This cross is the origin of the name Kreuzberg which was later applied to a whole district. However, the allegori-cal figures on the monument, represent-ing the victorious battles and designed by Rauch, Tieck and Wichmann, bear only

the names of princes and generals; there is no representative of the people. In 1819, while the monument was still under construction, Friedrich Wilhelm III under pressure from Metternich, broke his word and suppressed any mention of his promise of a constitution. Disregard of this prohibition led to the notorious persecution of the demagogues.

The monument was provided with a railing in 1823 to protect it from being damaged and to make it more substantial. In 1824 Peter Joseph Lenné suggested laying out the sandy hill of the Kreuzberg as a garden and improving the road that linked it to the city to make it pleasanter. As this recommendation came from a royal official the state was unwilling to provide any funds for it, and the city had no interest in enhancing a royal monu-ment. Lenné's scheme of 1861 also seems to have foundered on the reluctance of either side to pay for its execution. In the

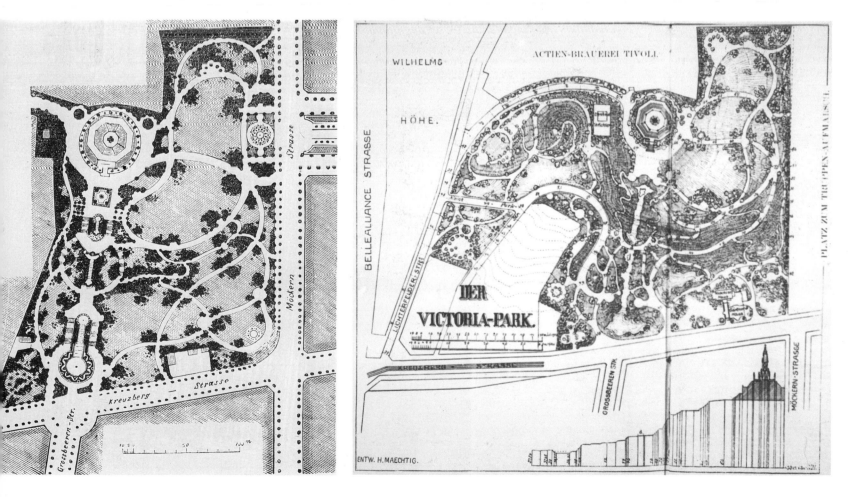

meantime tenements had spread closer and closer to the Kreuzberg and threatened to obscure the view of the monument almost completely. However, the state under Bismarck's chancellorship had a great interest in preserving the national monument from further obliteration by buildings. At Emperor Wilhelm I's command it was raised hydraulically eight metres, moved into the line of view of the Grossbeerenstrasse (the road leading to the city), and placed on a great terrace designed by Heinrich Strack. To enable the city to lay out an ornamental park worthy of the monument, the treasury donated the area of 5.5 ha (13.5 acres) around the monument, as well as making a contribution towards construction costs. The city still had to purchase a further three hectares (seven acres) at enormous cost. After lengthy debates the city council finally approved the park design by the municipal director of gardens Hermann Mächtig. Viktoriapark – named after the Crown Princess Victoria (but also signifying victory) – is designed in the plush historicist style and is undoubtedly a work of art. Along cleverly laid out winding paths the stroller makes an effortless ascent to the monument and hardly notices how dense the network of paths is. Native and foreign flowering shrubs, climbing plants and above all the wealth of evergreen trees and shrubs give the park even in winter an unusual lushness not found elsewhere in Berlin. Particularly romantic and exotic is the steep Wolfschlucht (Wolf's Chasm) created from the former sand and clay quarries on the eastern slope. So as not to lose face completely the city ornamented the park in a bourgeois, national-liberal manner – not with statues of the Hohenzollerns, as Mächtig had suggested, but with herms of poets of the Wars of Liberation: Arndt, Kleist, Körner, Rückert, Schenkendorf and Uhland. After 1893 the main attraction was the artificial waterfall which fell 24 metres (79 ft) in several steps from beneath the monument towards the Grossbeerenstrasse, and later was even

View of the cascade and the Kreuzbergdenkmal in the formal version, designed by H. Mächtig.

View of the waterfall and the monument, 1904. (Photo Landesbildstelle, Berlin)

flood-lit. Instead of the Baroque cascades originally planned but rejected as too French, the waterfall was built in a naturalistic style out of granite boulders and limestone – the monument was supposed to look as if it were built on rock. And the mountain scenery was intended to provide servant girls with a substitute for holiday travel. This was a macabre social and humanist regression, since Gustav Meyer, Mächtig's predecessor from 1845 to 1877, with the support of the physician Dr Virschow and Oberbürgermeister Seydel, had laid out three large public parks with extensive playing fields and information about natural history for recreation and general education. In this period the liberal city authorities sought to bridge the gulf between themselves and the proletariat,

who had flooded into Berlin and who, because of the way in which the reparcelling of land and the liberation of the peasants had been implemented, were now deprived of the basic essentials of life and recreation. Around 1910, in a period of mass unemployment, the creation of new public parks was again linked with a social policy. The Viktoriapark was extended by the inclusion of five hectares (twelve acres) of military land to the west, landscaped in a slightly *art nouveau* style by the director of gardens, Albert Broderson, in 1911–16, and provided with areas for playing and relaxing as well as sports fields. In 1925 a menagerie at the old gardener's house was added.

During the Third Reich the monument remained a centre of nationalist activities, but Albert Speer's scheme to link it by a

great architectural axis with Tempelhof airport as part of his megalomaniac replanning of Berlin was not realized.

Provided with all the attributes of a public park – albeit a very small one – the Kreuzberg (the name Viktoriapark is not used by Berliners) is today an oasis in the Bronx of Berlin.

Bibliography

E. Böttcher, 'Die öffentlichen Park-, Garten- und Baumanlagen der Stadt Berlin – IV. Der Viktoriapark' in *Zeitschrift für Gartenbau und Gartenkunst* (1895).

E. Clemen, 'Landschaftsbilder aus dem Viktoriapark zu Berlin' in *Zeitschrift für Gartenbau und Gartenkunst* (1895).

G. Peschken, 'Die ersten kommunalen Parkanlagen Berlins' in *Das Gartenamt* (1975).

I. Maass, 'Die kommunale Parkpolitik Berlins Ende des 19. Jahrhunderts' in *Gustav Meyer zum 100. Todestag 27.5.1977*, ed. V. Heinrich and G. Peschken (Berlin 1978).

F. Wendland, *Berlins Gärten und Parke* (Frankfurt am Main, Berlin, Vienna, 1979).

G. Peschken, 'Spielwiesen für die arbeitende Bevölkerung' in *Exerzierfeld der Moderne, Industriekultur in Berlin im 19. Jahrhundert* (Munich 1984).

G. Peschken and W. Richard, 'Der Viktoriapark' in *Stadtgrün*, ed. V. Hampf-Heinrich and G. Peschken (Berlin 1985).

M. Nungesser, *Das Denkmal auf dem Kreuzberg* (Berlin 1987).

The Park Güell, Barcelona
(1900–1914)
Ignasi de Solà Morales

Eusebio Güell y Bacigalupi (1846–1914), founder of the Park Güell, was a well-known member of Barcelonan society in the last century, a sort of Maecenas-cum-industrialist. He was an important businessman, with interests in shipping, textiles, cement, tobacco, and the wine trade, but also a patron of composers, poets, painters and architects. One of the many artists who benefited from his patronage was Gaudí (1852–1926), who practised in Barcelona although he had been born in Reus, and was supported by Güell from the age of seventeen.

A knowledge of both the modern and traditional atmosphere of Barcelona towards the end of the nineteenth century is essential if the nature of Park Güell is to be fully understood. It was a time of urban renewal, promoted by a bourgeoisie who saw that a social consciousness had to go hand in hand with industrialization. Inspiration was drawn from stereotyped Catalan images, from Catalonia's medieval past, from Mediterranean imagery, from artisanal traditions, and from the virtues of pre-industrial society. Underlying this interpretation of Catalonia's traditional past was a strident new regionalism.

Güell's excellent education was primarily scientific. He read engineering, biology and applied science; he even published a monograph in Paris in 1889 on microbiology. In addition he studied law and economics, both of which shaped his interest in business and politics. For a while Güell was one of the leading lights in *Lliga Regionalista*, a pressure group representing the interests of the emerging class of Catalan industrialists. The group's political philosophy involved a distinct regionalism, and a desire to break the bureaucratic constraints of central government. Its social beliefs centred on the organization of a burgeoning capitalist society. This was reflected in Güell's ideas on city planning; influenced by a study of France and England he favoured organized cities, with distinct zones, in which residential areas were integrated in a new way.

In 1891 Güell established a large factory at Sta Coloma de Cervelló, a village some 30 kilometres (20 miles) from Barcelona on an independent industrial estate in which manufacturing, accommodation, education and leisure zones were carefully demarcated. Gaudí

Park Güell in Barcelona, designed by Antoni Gaudí: the interior of the pillared hall. (Photo F. Català-Roca)

*Park Güell in Barcelona, designed by
Antoni Gaudí: detail of a section of the
viaduct redesigned by the architects E. Torres
and E. Martinez la Peña, 1988.*

and his collaborators helped design the Güell Colony. The unfinished church, houses, schools and communal centres can still be seen.

Park Güell was a different initiative, and yet one which was born of the neo-traditionalist thinking which Güell and Gaudí derived in part from Ruskin, Whitman and Morris and later from Howard, Geddes and Unwin. Güell first became interested in creating a residential park some years before the garden city movement became influential in Barcelona; the Museu Social and the Societat Cívica la Ciutat Jardí were not founded until 1912. The result was Park Güell, which the future count commissioned from Gaudí, and the design of which bore Güell's influence. It was conceived from the start as a garden city, a residential zone which was to be a model for future 'implants' of simple family housing in a park setting.

Already the hillsides north of the plain, which Cerdá planned should carry the expansion of Barcelona, had become a sought-after area by private developers, intent on promoting the garden-city idea. Between 1890 and 1917 there were to be, in addition to Park Güell, several such developments in Barcelona: Tibidabo, San Pedro Martir, Torre Baró, La Floresta and La Florida being examples.

The site for Park Güell was a field of some 20 hectares (50 acres) situated on the southern flank of the so-called Montaña Pelada (the Treeless Mountain), a hill 400 metres (1300 ft) above sea-level and overlooking the plain of Barcelona and the neighbouring villages of Gracia, Sants, Sant Andreu, with, on the horizon, views of the Mediterranean.

The plan which Gaudí put forward, and on which he worked intermittently from 1900 to 1914, was the enclosure of the field with a wall more than 2 m (6½ ft) high behind which the park would be laid in triangular building plots. There would be one house per plot, and up to sixty plots. The main access to the park was to be from the lower part of the field through a gatehouse, with separate lodges for the porters and caretakers. From here, two carriage drives would make concentric circles around a raised central precinct which would include a market and open-air performance space, which was initially conceived in the form of an amphitheatre. The structural com-

position would be complete with the construction of two equally singular buildings: a temple, which would serve as the church for the Park community, and a hillock in a pious imitation of Calvary. The church was to be sited on a spur at the most westerly point of the park, whilst 'Calvary' was conceived at the highest point of the field, linked by a footpath which followed the course of the Roman road and which joined Barcino (Barcelona) with Castrum Octavium (San Cugat del Vallés).

The plants chosen for Park Güell were a far cry from the exotic plants found in northern European parks. Instead, the Mediterranean was evoked by plantations of pines, carobs and palm trees, and great clumps of oleander. The cultural impact of this arrangement on garden design of the early twentieth century has not been given its true worth. It was the Mediterranean in fact which was to be the central aesthetic principle in Park Güell. The irregular topography of the hills was used as a setting for aqueduct-like bridges for the park roads, and is an example of the clear references to the Mediterranean region.

In addition to what we might call Park Güell's Mediterraneanism, other strands of symbolism are part of the fundamental design. The first is the evocation of Greece and Antiquity. A popular misconception about the late-nineteenth-century decadent culture is that it never sought to evoke the ancient world. Indeed Güell was probably, as a result of his deep interest in Plato and Greek literature in general, the instigator of Gaudí's essentially Greek-inspired centre for the garden city. The precinct has obvious, if distorted, Doric resonances; the attention given to the course of the old Roman road is a case in point. In short, the design of the park had the effect of evoking the Mediterranean civilizations which had existed for centuries previously. What is curious about the design, however, is the way in which these classical references were superimposed on an aesthetic derived from the more militant elements of the Roman Catholic Church, of which both Gaudí and Güell were energetic advocates.

The modernistic tendencies of civilized society at the start of the twentieth century were not accepted without reserve. Gaudí's neo-Catholicism is ever-

Park Güell in Barcelona, designed by Antoni Gaudí: view of the viaduct with the city in the background.

present in the park's religious symbolism. The whole conception – the church which was never built, 'Calvary' on the highest hill, the Via Crucis which led to it, the numerous crucifixes, and the names inspired by the Virgin – was derived from a cosmic conception of liturgical symbols.

Financially Park Güell was a failure. With the exception of Güell, who spent the last years of his life in the old house on the estate, and Gaudí, who lived in the show-house (the only one built), not one plot of land was sold, nor was there built a single *torre* (the name used in Catalonia for middle-class country and suburban villas).

In 1914 Park Güell was bought by the town council of Barcelona so that it could be incorporated within the Sistema de Parques de la Ciudad de Barcelona. All plans to build Gaudí's designs were scrapped. What had been intended as a residential area, instead became a municipal city park.

Bibliography

Juan Bassegoda Nonell, *El Parque Güell.* ICOMOS (Barcelona 1979).
Juan Bassegoda Nonell, *Antoni Gaudí, Vida y Arquitectura* (Barcelona 1977).

Carlos Flores, *Gaudí, Jujol y el modernismo catalán* (Madrid 1982).
Xavier Güell, *Antoni Gaudí* (Barcelona 1986).
Cesar Martinell, *Gaudí, su vida, su teoria, su obra* (Barcelona 1967).
Francesc Roca, *Política económica i territori a Catalunya, 1901–1939* (Barcelona 1979).
Eduardo Rojo Albarrán, *El Park Güell* (Barcelona 1986).
Salvador Selles, 'Park Güell', in *Anuario de la Asociación de Arquitectos de Cataluña para 1903* (Barcelona 1903).
Ignasi de Solà Morales, *Antoni Gaudí* (Barcelona 1983).
Salvador Tarragó Cid, *Gaudí* (Barcelona 1974).
Manuel Torres Capell, *El planejament urbà i la crisi de 1917 a Barcelona* (Barcelona 1987).

*Park Güell in Barcelona, designed by
Antoni Gaudí: aerial view. (Photo TAF,
Barcelona)*

The Parc Léopold: The Home of Scientific Imagination

Annick Brauman

Plan of the estate of Dubois de Bianco, destined to become in 1851 the Parc Léopold. Designed by J. G. Druaert, 1847. Archives de la Ville de Bruxelles.

The reason for including in this book the public park created in Brussels in 1851 – the Parc Léopold[1] – is to examine the application on the ground of a specifically nineteenth-century pattern of thought, linking Nature, Science and Progress. We shall examine it over a historically adequate period of time (1850–1920) with a view to drawing firm conclusions about the project, including any mistakes that were made.

Stage one – the public meeting-place of a new district

The creation of the park was linked to the construction of a new neighbourhood, an undertaking of financial importance and itself connected with Brussel's new role as capital of an independent country. The district was intended for a mixed social group – aristocrats, members of the upper middle classes and liberal professionals – who were invited to move out from the town centre in order to take their chance in a modern, grid-plan part of the town 'outside the walls'. In all the confusion surrounding the project – the policy of social decentralization, over-investment in grandiose schemes such as a race course, exhibition centre, circus – only one scheme, not mentioned in the plan, saw the light of day, and this was the park which concerns us.

How did this come about? Since in the nineteenth century Nature was said to be 'lost' (a favourite theme of journalists), what could be more meaningful than to offer a heightened reflection of it in an all-purpose garden: hence the first appearance of the park as a *Zoological, Horticultural and Pleasure Garden*. This effectively meant a zoo, with a promenade for which there was a charge, an amusement park managed in a chaotic and highly unbusinesslike way, both scientifically and financially, and which went bankrupt after thirty years of legal quibbling, excessive payouts to shareholders and incompetence among those who looked after the animals. Apart from some rather amateurish private attempts to find new ways of making money, the idea of creating a picturesque promenade which would take advantage of the fashion for zoos to bridge the gap between middle class leisure and scientific interest was not out of touch with the preoccupations of the time. For the park[2] was indeed aimed at couples, families, the new middle classes, who had to be provided with something to look at. In their honour the great open spaces of the countryside and the feelings of nostalgia they aroused were condensed into a prescribed route with fixed stopping places. Man was no longer lost and found in the bosom of nature, but rather a passive visitor gaping at the sights of nature, which were now endowed with a purpose. For this was a walk with a function, spelling out conscientiously the words 'order', 'progress' and 'prosperity'.

Stage two – the Museum of Natural History

It took the new urban middle classes some time to forsake this ideal of a place of public amusement, at once educational and expensive, and to return to the idea of specialized institutions which would adopt a scientific attitude towards this thirst for knowledge which was presumed to exist. In 1891 a Museum of Natural History opened its doors at the park's highest point. The arguments in its favour paid lipservice to the former purpose of the park, but was there really any logical plan or rational continuity in the idea? It could be claimed that the new select district beside it imposed on the park, which was otherwise unremarkable in size, in its design or in its planting, the need to fulfil a civic and institutional role – in short to make national pride part of its programme. The Museum of Natural History was even more suited to this purpose since it immediately became unique in the world for its collection of iguanodons.[3] Moreover, through the theories of its founder Edouard Dupont, it became associated with the novel concept of museums as tools of research, and not simply as centres of accumulation. Dupont, following the well-defined national ideal, was persuaded to accept the centralist idea of a museum which would house all the natural sciences together – botany, geology and zoology. The museum, which was to be impersonal, autonomous, centralized and conservative, then underwent a sort of palace revolution, after which notions such as 'public utility' and 'collective interest' gave way to the passive idea of a museum as a reservoir for individual scientific work by 'free officials'. The commission on 'Scientific Progress through the Success of the Institution' came to an end in 1889, decentralization for the sake of personal convenience triumphed, and in its wake classified sections, like so many small, isolated museums, regained their role in the concept of national research. What remains is an unusual museum with an open-plan industrial design laid out according to the main geological classifications, culminating in the Bernissart collection of iguanodons, upright or recumbent, like a tableau illustrating the passage of time.

Stage three – the 'scientific city'

In 1892, still mindful of the philosophy of classification which was the predestined

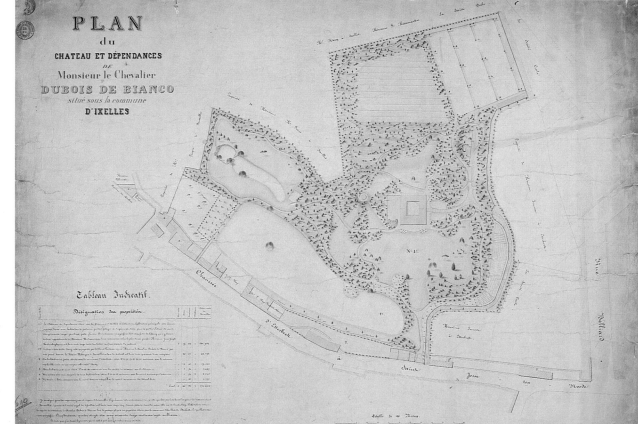

Museum of Natural History, Department of Comparative Sciences and Colonial Exploration. Archives d' Architecture Moderne, Brussels.

The Scientific City: the Great Auditorium of the Institute of Physiology. Interior design by A. Crespin, 1902. Archives d' Architecture Moderne, Brussels.

purpose of the park, the municipality, which had taken it over after the bankruptcy of the zoological enterprise, signed an agreement with the industrialist Ernest Solvay, under the terms of which the park was to be given over to the establishment of a scientific city. Solvay dedicated this para-university centre, financed with Belgian assets, to the methodical interpretation of the standard liberal ideals, 'knowledge' and 'progress'. In the imagination of the capitalist pioneer, it was in the bosom of this symbolic 'city', sheltering in the noble surroundings of a park under the shade of mature trees, that the quest should be pursued to reconcile the ideas of 'capitalism' and 'progress'; to formulate a system of ethics, a philosophy, a scientific framework and a system of laws for an equitable industrial society. Meanwhile the parallel creation of a permanent international organization for scientific debate (the celebrated International Council on Physics and Chemistry, set up

in 1911 and 1913 and based in the Parc Léopold) may be considered even today as a fundamental constituent element in scientific communication and a revolutionary step in the history of science. As for the scientific city, how would it relate to the park? Its establishment posed no problems: the annexation of a public park by heavy building equipment was a difficulty that the politicians of the time faced without qualms, and the architectural intrusion on the space was viewed only as a plus on the aesthetic side. But unlike the pioneering plans and achievements of garden-cities or artist-cities which were taking place at this time in various countries, the scientific city did not fulfil the role of standard bearer for a cultural manifesto. On the contrary, it was simply the product of a pragmatic accretion of buildings, laboratories, as it were, for the improvement of the human condition, secular temples of learning, recalling the architecture of certain 'houses of the people',[4] set in the leafy intimacy of the park

Epilogue – the 'world city'

Since it could not expand, the scientific city fell out of use in 1919. One last occupant, in 1941, returned to the triple theme of Nature-Science-Progress. Paul Otlet, turned out of more spacious premises, set up in the disused Institute of Anatomy the remains of his great Mundaneum project. His major work, the completion and publication of his Universal Decimal Classification, is internationally known. Concealed within it, however, is a more obscure aspect of documentary classification, the Mundaneum, in which Otlet elaborated the idea of a new Babel – the world city.[5] The object of the Mundaneum is formulated in a few aims which are as precise as they are far-reaching: the setting up of a world-wide system of documentation by the centralization of scientific publications and works; the creation of a centre for international associations; and working towards the establishment of a world-city in an area free from territorial jurisdiction, in which the Mundaneum would be one of the institutions. Like Solvay, Otlet planned an integrated scheme, an organized system of institutions for the parallel study of learning and social progress. But Otlet's proposal for dealing with the question of world peace by constructing

View of the Zoological Garden: the bear pit, designed by A. Canelle, c. 1856. Archives de la Ville de Bruxelles.

L. Becker, mounting of the Natural History Museum's first iguanodon in the Nassau chapel, 1884. Musée des Sciences Naturelles, Brussels.

one enormous city leaves behind the familiar territory of the exchange of ideas in the heart of the space held in common in a traditional town. Instead it invents a radical no-man's land of urban culture and political thought, uprooting democracy from the confusion of the real town, and projecting it into the clarity of a perfectly ordered metropolis, designs for which had provided between 1927 and 1933 an excellent theme for two major figures in functional town planning – Le Corbusier and Victor Bourgeois.

Today the Parc Léopold lies next door to the administrative sector of the EEC, and has been virtually annexed by it. This final assault by the executive of a political

and cultural institution, might be seen as no more than the continued expression of the conventions of a particular age, if it were not for the fact that this time, however splendid the supranational cultural intentions of the European Community, there has been an unacceptable breach: the fact is that this acquisition runs the risk of being nothing more than a property deal pure and simple, with no trace of planning or consultation, an act of wanton vandalism. And this, it must be acknowledged, is what the Parc, as a concept embodying the spirit of the nineteenth century and the encouragement of discussion and planning, had always managed to avoid.

[1] The history of the Parc Léopold and particularly the stages summarized in this article are the subject of a book detailing the various aspects linking the park with the development of a specifically nineteenth-century urban culture. This book was compiled by Annick Brauman in collaboration with Marie Demanet and edited by Les Archives d'Architecture Moderne in 1985: *Le Zoo, la Cité Scientifique et la Ville* (Brussels 1985).
[2] *Le Zoo, la Cité Scientifique et la Ville, op. cit.*, p. 87.
[3] This refers to the remarkable collection of twenty-nine prehistoric iguanodons discovered in 1877 in the Barbe coalfield in Bernissart, Belgium, 350 metres (1150 feet) underground.
[4] On this subject see Marco De Michelis and others, *Case del Popolo. Un'architettura monumentale del moderno* (Venice 1986) for the Italian version and Archives d'Architecture Moderne (Brussels 1984) for the French edition. See in particular the articles on Vienna, Germany, and Holland which refer to plans for domestic dwellings inspired by the idea of a secular temple and envisaged as a complete work of art.
[5] The history of the World City plan in relation to urban culture and architecture has been recounted in the book by Giuliano Gresleri and Dario Matteoni, *La Città Mondiale, Andersen, Hébrard, Otlet, Le Corbusier* (Venice 1982).

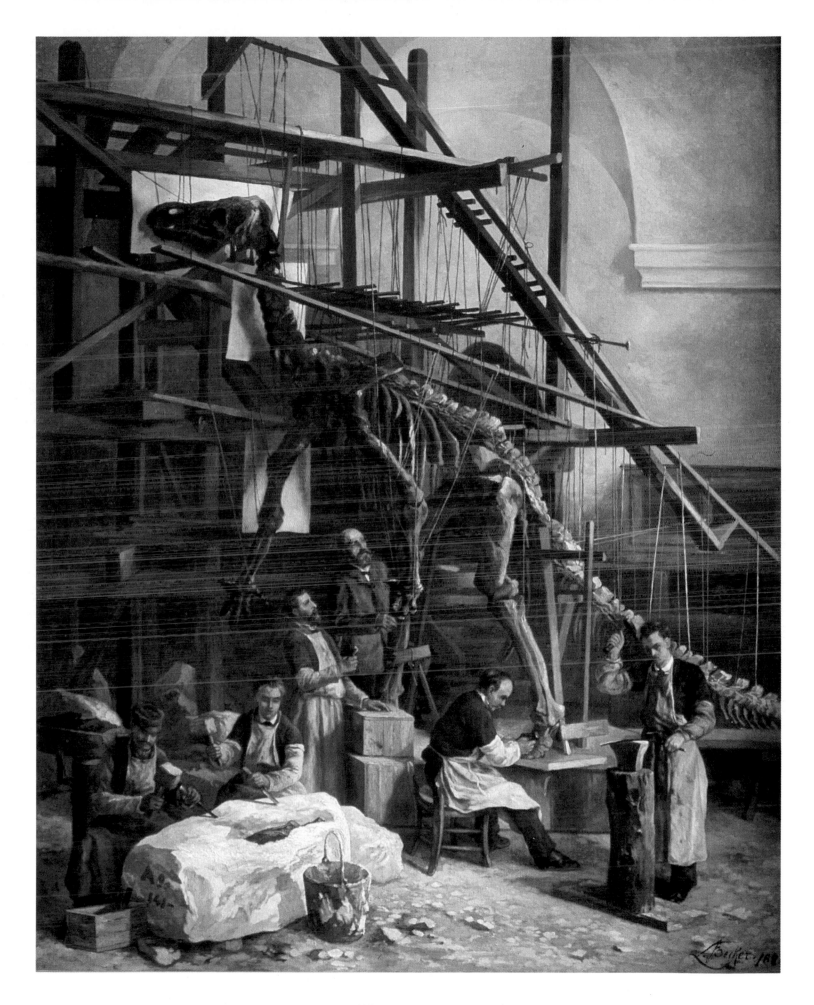

Henri and Achille Duchêne and the Reinvention of Le Nôtre

Monique Mosser

It is a *topos* to try to establish to what extent garden aesthetics are a reliable indication of fashion, and further, whether they are a concrete reflection of a particular period's view of the world: whence the facile but seductive equation: garden = microcosm. Michel Le Bris goes further when he writes, in a book of essays on the ideas of the eighteenth century, 'Gardens are not innocent playthings: they are the landscapes within us, constantly registering our relationships with our fellow men, with the world and with God. Disagreements between gardeners should be studied as if they were metaphysical debates.'[1] We can take this argument even further and state that gardens – like all forms of artistic expression, and however peculiar it may seem – are an ideological domain in the modern sense, even a realm where polemic may become heated. For example, it was shown some time ago that the birth of the informal garden in Great Britain was very closely linked to a contemporary dispute over royal power, and John Dixon Hunt has analysed the way in which the political emblems on the garden *fabriques* at Stowe are an anti-Stuart, anti-Catholic, pro-British statement.[2] It would be an exaggeration to try to identify the landscape garden automatically with a more or less liberal movement of thought, but it is indisputable that for many lovers and owners of English-style gardens in the Europe of the Enlightenment only a Nature freed from all shackles was capable of reflecting a new perception of the individual and his place in the social system.[3] Thus in the *Guide des Jardins de Franconville-la-Garenne* (1784) we read:

The uniformity [of classical gardens] soon wearies the attention . . . which turns to the simplicity of the fields. The random patterns created by the different crops are much more pleasing to the imagination and the eye than the tiresome symmetry of older parks. Our forefathers' bad taste is fortunately disappearing, and soon we shall have the satisfaction of seeing the whole of France as a single garden: then it will be difficult to conceive that man, born free, born to abhor slavery, used to take pleasure in being enclosed at the centre of his estate like a criminal locked up in prison.

If we accept the cyclical theory of the history of design or more simply the logic of reaction, it could have been foreseen that the very prolonged development of landscape style and its impoverishment at

the hands of the *petite bourgeoisie*, excellently caricatured by Gustave Flaubert in *Bouvard et Pécuchet*,[4] would involve not only radical stylistic changes but, more than that, a veritable adopting of doctrinal positions. To consider the exact nature of the French problem, we should look at a parallel situation in Great Britain.[5] Here, as early as the 1820s there could be discerned the first signs of the eclecticism which was to triumph in architecture, as in the art of gardens, during the reign of Victoria. Brent Elliott has shown how a renewal of interest combined with a growth in historical knowledge led to the foundation of a series of new aesthetic standards.[6] Thus, the continuance of a moderated form of 'Picturesque' did not exclude a re-interpretation of 'Gothic, Tudor or Jacobean' gardens, while at the same time Charles Barry was delving into Italian Renaissance sources and William Andrews Nesfield was seeking 'official' models in the French classical repertory. There was no such movement in France, where the 'mixed' style of the Second Empire gave place chiefly to mosaiculture and to horticultural experiment, but without altering the general design of gardens. Thus it is not until after the Franco-Prussian War of 1870 that we see the

return to favour of Le Nôtre, and the development of the cult surrounding him. This interesting episode not only reflects the history of taste but also provides considerable insight into a very precise moment in French history.

In the warlike, vengeful, deeply nationalistic atmosphere which was to pervade France until the First World War, there were many who strove to identify in French tradition – both literary and artistic – the fundamental characteristics of 'national genius'. If in the realm of music the enemy was necessarily 'Germany, the symphony and morbid hypertrophy of a certain sentimentality typical of Beethoven',[7] as far as the art of gardens was concerned it was without doubt England and its informal landscape style which were to serve as the foil. Le Nôtre paragon of all that was French, would henceforth sit enthroned in the pantheon of this triumphant *ars gallica*, 'which would be characterized by the intellectual satisfaction of developing in a majestic framework, solidly built, well aired, where everything pays homage to the soundest laws of logic, stability and reason, and the moral and philosophical atmosphere is healthy and reassuring'.[8] For gardens, 'professions of faith' were equally numerous. But one book above

all others became a 'manifesto'. In the preface to *Les Jardins de l'intelligence. Parcs et jardins de France*,[9] published in 1912, Lucien Corpechot wrote:

If the French language ceased to be heard, if our literature ceased to be understood, if the names of Corneille, Bossuet, Racine, Molière, Voltaire, Montesquieu no longer inspired in minds their divine *frisson*. . . . and if Le Nôtre's park had meanwhile continued to be traditionally maintained, the essence and quality of the spirit of France, the purity and perfection of the intellectual power of the greatest geniuses of our lineage would be revealed at Versailles in all their glory. That is why the terraces at Versailles are a choice place to contemplate the spirit of France. Here our history is revealed, is unfolded before our eyes like a clear and logical campaign. All the endeavours of our race in all directions, all its toil and even its setbacks here make sense and fall into place according to an apparently concerted plan.

In the early days two artists were to give expression to this ideological sentimentalism, later refining it by developing a Louis XIV 'revival' so perfect that even to this day it influences our perception of a certain historical reality: these two men were the landscape architects Henri and Achille Duchêne.[10] The recent discovery of the records of their practice, together with analysis of previously known documents (Collection in the Musée des Arts

Décoratifs, articles in the *Gazette Illustrée des Amateurs de Jardins*),[11] gives a comprehensive picture of the enormous extent of their work. Indeed, the total number of original creations and works of restoration or reconstruction with which their name was linked, both in France and abroad as far as Russia, the United States, Argentina and Australia, comes to over 380. Henri Duchêne, after working in the town planning offices in Paris, founded his own practice in 1877. His son Achille, born in 1866, soon joined his father's business, and from the age of twelve his education consisted of taking part in all aspects of his father's work. On his father's death in 1907 Achille took over the business, and for almost half a century (he died in 1947) diversified the work undertaken. Almost symbolically, it was the restoration of the parterres and cascades at Vaux-le-Vicomte (begun by the architect Laîné) which marked the beginning of their activities.[12] For the wealthy industrialist Alfred Sommier, who had acquired the estate in 1875, they reconstructed the borders of the Great Parterre in all their magnificence. It must be remembered that at the time this was a real 'innovation' for, as Ernest de Ganay recalls,

After some tentative explorations, during which were uncovered traces of the formal gardens of the Second Empire (mosaiculture, raised flowerbeds, vases and groups in the centre of lawns, and so on) their art became more refined, returning to strictly classical sources, and even exaggerating tradition, since their *parterres de broderie* were made to conform to the strictest levelling of surfaces, while Le Nôtre liked to give them some relief, some movement', by means of a variety of shrubs and topiary, introducing a feeling of rhythm into his compositions, and embellishing them in order to avoid monotony.[13]

This ability to interpret and modify the accepted aims of the art of the Grand Siècle, to adapt them to a new and contemporary socio-economic climate, is seen again in their second great enterprise – the château of Champs-sur-Marne, where the park had practically disappeared.[14] Ernest de Ganay analysed to perfection the inspiration which always guided the Duchênes in their many undertakings, whether at Courances, Baillon, Breteuil, Bizy, Maintenon, Balleroy, Rosny, Langeais or Hautefort, when he wrote:

The Past cannot be remade. If it is brought back to life, it can never, despite science, good taste and the advice of those of experience and discrimination, resume *exactly* its original form. A restoration, and even more a reconstruction or remaking, can always be detected. It is therefore vain to attempt it. True artists, if asked to attempt a restoration, know this. They discreetly *interpret* the Past. And the best way to honour it is not to seek to replace it with a Present which can never be its exact image. On the other hand, what we must do is seek to re-create the atmosphere of the Past. . . . If by good fortune an original plan exists, that is the idea to be interpreted.

In many cases, however, the Duchênes' 'interventions' were works of pure imagination: if certain of them appear as 'true successes', others seem today to be mistaken interpretations of the 'spirit of the place'. This can be explained however, by the pervasive influence of the classical revival of 1900. Thus the restoration 'in the French style' of the park of Le Marais – a great neo-classical building constructed by Barré in about 1770 – was a complete misunderstanding by Achille Duchêne of the aesthetic balances of the Enlightenment, a subtle accord between line and curve, between the strict austerity of the building and the abundant 'naturalness' in the garden. On the other hand, the impressive skill of the Duchênes can be seen in the water parterre at Blenheim, a direct inspiration from Versailles; in the successful treatment of the park at Nordkirchen in Westphalia;[15] and especially in the design for the whole estate at Voisins (Yvelines). As Molinier writes, "The manuscripts relating to their reading bear witness to the extent of their library. A profound erudition is the source of their technical expertise, enriched by the enlargement, since the seventeenth century, of the palette of available materials.'[16]

In the early years of the twentieth century, when wealth made possible even more ambitious dreams, the Comte de Fels charged Duchêne with an enormous commission which was carried out between 1903 and 1925. This was the construction of the park at Voisins. He was instructed to surround the château (architecturally directly inspired by Gabriel) 'with a frame of French art, and to extend this frame as far as the foot of the hills, without making the transition too abrupt and contrary to the rules of art'.[17] Thus the Comte de Fels, who to serve his own purposes appointed himself Gabriel's historian, set forth the strange theory of a 'Louis XVII' style in gardens, a sort of post-classicism which took no account of the 'overturning of the English style by the unfortunate queen Marie-Antionette'. Relying on St-Hubert's forgotten theory, Fels conceived a formal style, refined to the point of abstraction, even in the decorative areas. This is the same impression that one often receives from the very fine projects produced by the many draughtsmen in the Duchêne practice. Their bird's-eye views, taken from a very high viewpoint, and with geometric treatment of wooded areas and exaggeratedly diagrammatic parterres, seem to our eyes to contain the signs of a latent 'modernism'.

But it would be wrong to reduce the Duchêne aesthetic to this harsh classicism. He himself explained that he permitted the use of the landscape style in very large open spaces, to form the

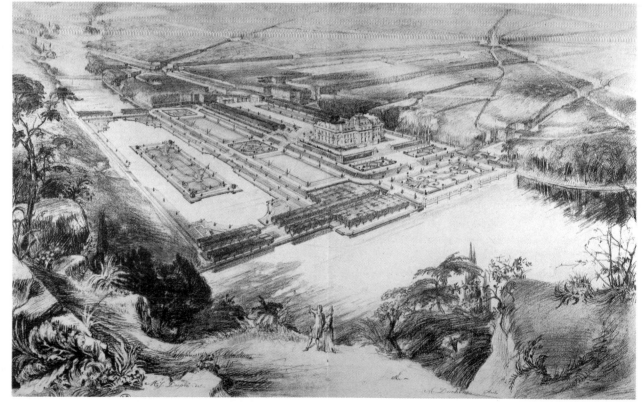

'wings' of a more formal arrangement, as at Bois-Boudran, Chambly, La Francport, Laversine, La Boissière or Vaux-le-Pénil. But Duchêne's extraordinary imaginative ability embraced a wide range of projects, and in his designs and executed projects for American millionaires seems virtually unlimited.[18] Here the classical vocabulary served merely as a vast framework, into which he inserted a panoply of unusual devices (fountains, sculptures, 'sacred woods') more like a grandiose Hollywood set (for instance for D. W. Griffith's *Intolerance* in 1916) than a Dezallier d'Argenville engraving! The designs for Mrs Carolus-Pulmann in California seem as fanciful as the most ingenious of our contemporary strip cartoons. In these New World gardens, with their vast spaces, their profusion of plants and their multiplicity of references, all combining to make extraordinarily original landscapes, there is an eclecticism pushed to extravagant limits, bordering on a sort of poetic delirium.

Achille Duchêne also enjoyed designing town gardens of extreme elegance; for Madame Porgès in the Avenue Montaigne; for the Hôtel Matignon; and also the strange Roman style composition on the terrace of the town house belonging to Gulbenkian. There were also numerous 'small'[19] gardens, both in the fashionable suburbs of Paris and on the Côte d'Azur, for instance 'Lou Sueil' at Eze. However, the aftermath of the Great War, and the radical changes in general circumstances that followed, as well as the violent onslaught of new techniques in the realms of radio, aviation, cars and so on, were to give a completely different direction to the last twenty-five years of Achille Duchêne's career. Only urban planning and public schemes could henceforth provide commissions of the scale he required. In his book *Les Jardins d'hier, d'aujourd'hui et de demain*, published in 1935, Duchêne explains the theories underlying an intensive series of projects, which moreover influenced theories throughout Europe in the thirties: 'I have endeavoured to foresee future social changes, already implicit in the present, together with the new forms of art they will engender.' In this avowed desire to 'create order in the soul of the individual through the influence of the environment' there is a recognizable echo of a certain 'national socialism'. Ernest de

Ganay's review of the book, published in the same year, is quite explicit on this point:

The author [Duchêne] deserves praise for having studied with such passion, with such desire for the good, and with such good intentions the role that gardens should play in the 'social life' of a future when everything is anticipated: ornate gardens surrounding a school, a public park for the town, with a splendidly impressive plan for a 'house for social activities', a sports ground, and this astonishing 'park for education, recreation and repose', in which are drawn and stated ideas of beauty and progress, as well as of festivities intended to form the minds of the people, and to lead them to happiness through beauty, healthy living and sport, by offering festivities and rejoicings which will help the soul to blossom in spheres of both ideals and action.[20]

This system, which culminated in the highly representative Musée du Progrès, the design of which resembles almost exactly the architecture of the new Palais de Chaillot and the pavilions of the 1937 exhibition,[21] is also reminiscent of experiments being carried out at that time in Berlin, Rome and Moscow. One of the most interesting of Achille Duchêne's projects at this time, however, was the development of Le Tréport, with its terraces, seaside promenade and sports ground.

Ernest de Ganay has written a discerning critique of the role of the Duchênes:

They had indicated the way forward, or rather had set French gardens on the road that they should take, the traditional road, returning to old models in order to re-create gardens around ancient dwellings which had been despoiled of theirs. Once these gardens had been restored, the lesson was clear and vital, and the style would evolve naturally, since it was founded on the correct principles. This is an essential condition if new art is not to be still-born. There is nothing paradoxical in the

assertion that it is to this reaction that we owe our present progress in the art of gardens, progress which has been obvious now for many years. Today a whole new school of gardening comprises both the most creative and the most imaginative of modern gardens.[22]

Among Duchêne's successors, some of whom quickly established their independence, were Louis Decorges, the brothers Vera,[23] J. C. Moreux,[24] Jacques Greber and above all F. Duprat,[25] Duchêne's 'spiritual son', to whom we owe the superb 'restoration' of the gardens at La Roche-Courbon (Charente).

But it is possible to go further and state that the 'eloquence' of Duchêne's art, the strength of his own vision of history, have endured for almost three-quarters of a century, and that the view that many of our contemporaries take of Le Nôtre is to some extent influenced by that of Duchêne. It is as if, in historical perspective, the two men have become superimposed. It must, however, be appreciated that Duchêne used historical models to develop a 'creed' for his own purposes and his own application. This he states very clearly, for example in the preface to M. Fouquier's book *De l'art des jardins du XVe au XXe siècle* (1911):

Thus the art of architectural gardens in France will continue to develop naturally according to our inherited national characteristics: everything will be regular, symmetrical, co-ordinated, clear, logical, carefully planned with the overall effect in mind. . . . Is there not a certain analogy in the seventeenth century between literary and metaphysical ideas and the art of gardens, which gave rise to rather artificial parks, clearly laid out, with everything clipped, straight, exact and stylized to create an effect of beauty?

This remorseless hyper-classicism, this demand for the 'imperialism of reason'[26] are indeed signs of 'a time of inevitable combat', according to Corpechot himself. Today, however, we remain unconvinced by this too rigid interpretation, which fails to take account of many aspects of Le Nôtre's art or his time, particularly of his astonishing mastery of the most advanced techniques,[27] or of his comprehensive interest in every aspect of the work.

[1] Michel Le Bris, *Le paradis perdu* (Paris 1981).
[2] John Dixon Hunt, 'Emblème et expression-

nisme dans les jardins paysagers du XVIIIe siècle', in *URBI*, no. 8 (1983) pp. 16–32.

[3] See in this volume the article 'Paradox in the Garden' (p. 263) and the role of the Freemason aristocracy.

[4] Gustave Flaubert left this novel unfinished and it was not published until a year after his death in 1881. See M. Mosser 'Le texte mis en espace ou la littérature dans le jardin', in *Eidos* (1989).

[5] There is a general lack of a history of the history of gardens, which is still to be written. For an Anglo-French parallel it would be interesting to study the effect of Reginald Blomfield's *The Formal Garden in England*, (1892) and H. Inigo Triggs, *Formal Gardens in England and Scotland* (1902) with reference to the role of the Duchênes.

[6] Brent Elliott, *Victorian Gardens* (London 1986). See Chapter 3: 'The uses of the past', pp. 55–78.

[7] Catalogue of the exhibition *Gustav Mahler, un homme, une oeuvre, une époque*, Musée Moderne, Paris (24 Jan. – 3 Mar. 1985) Chapter X: 'Mahler et la France', Yves Simon: 'Les premières tribulations de Mahler en France ou Germania contre les enfants de Descartes', pp. 162–87.

[8] Emile Vuillermoz, 'La symphonie', *Cinquante ans de musique française de 1874 à 1925* (Paris 1925) Vol. 1, p. 323.

[9] Lucien Corpechot, *Les jardins de l'intelligence. Parcs et jardins de France*, the first edition dated 1911 was a 'theoretical basis' for many garden historians and practitioners. It is interesting to read the preface to the second edition in 1937 in which the author seeks to 'relativize' the effect of his work.

[10] These artists are currently the subject of a State thesis by Jean-Christophe Molinier at the University of Paris-Sorbonne under the direc-

tion of Prof. Bruno Foucart. See J.C. Molinier, 'Une dynastie de jardiniers: Henri et Achille Duchêne', in *Monuments Historiques*, no. 142 (Jan. 1986) pp. 24–9; also 'Les Duchêne ou les jardins réinventés', in *Vieilles Maisons Françaises*, no. 120 (Dec. 1987) pp. 50–7; and 'Duchêne à Chambord', in *Monuments Historiques*, no. 164 (July-Aug. 1989) pp. 76–80.

[11] The finest drawings of the Duchêne collection have been given to the Museé des Arts Décoratifs in Paris. The rediscovery of the archives of the Duchêne practice has led his descendants to form the 'Henri and Achille Duchêne Association', 124 Boulevard Auguste Blanqui, 75013 Paris. These archives include the drawings from the Duchêne workshops and also an extremely valuable collection of old photographs showing the sites before, during and after the work.

[12] See Edmé Sommier, 'Vaux-le-Vicomte', in *Gazette des Amateurs de Jardins* (1931–2).

[13] Ernest de Ganay, *Les jardins de France* (Paris 1949) p. 296. The author moreover dedicated this book of essays 'To the memory of my much missed and admired master of gardens Achille Duchêne'.

[14] Ernest de Ganay, 'Le château de Champs', in *Gazette des Amateurs de jardins* (1933–4).

[15] Achille Duchêne, 'Le parc de Nordkirchen (Westphalie)', in *La Gazette illustrée des Amateurs de Jardins* (Winter 1914) pp. 26ff.

[16] J.C. Molinier, *op. cit.*, note 10.

[17] Comte de Fels, 'Le château de Voisins', in *Gazette des Amateurs de Jardins* (1929).

[18] Raymond de Passillé, 'Les jardins français aux Etats-Unis', in *Gazette des Amateurs de Jardins* (special edition 1923).

[19] Achille Duchêne had before his death in 1947 put together material for a book which was published posthumously: *Petites et grandes*

résidences, preface by Ernest de Ganay.

[20] Ernest de Ganay, 'Les Jardins d'Achille Duchêne', in *Art et Industrie* (Aug.-Sept. 1935) pp. 31–4.

[21] Catalogue of the exhibition *Paris 1937, Cinquantenaire de l'exposition internationale des arts et des techniques dans la vie moderne*. Musée d'Art Moderne de la Ville de Paris (May-Aug. 1987).

[22] Ernest de Ganay, 'Les jardins de Jacques de Wailly', in *L'Architecture*, 15 (January 1935) pp. 21–36.

[23] The career of the Vera brothers was the subject of a Mastership in History of Art at the University of Paris-Sorbonne by Catherine Gueissaz, under the direction of Prof. Bruno Foucart.

[24] The work of the landscape painter Jean-Charles Moreux is the subject of a thesis in History of Art at the University of Paris-Sorbonne under the direction of Prof. Bruno Foucart. See also by the same author Jean-Marie Dubois, 'Jean-Charles Moreux (1889–1956)', in *Monuments Historiques*, no. 142 (Jan. 1986) pp. 30–5.

[25] See Jean-Pierre Bériac, 'Ferdinand Duprat, architecte-paysagiste, 1887–1976', in *P. & A. Paysage et Aménagement*, no. 1 (Oct. 1984); no. 2 (Jan. 1985).

[26] See note 9. Corpechot uses as title p. 75: 'La création de Versailles ou l'impérialisme de la raison'.

[27] See in this volume Hélène Vérin's article, p. 135. The most recent Anglo-Saxon and American historians of Le Nôtre have also given another dimension to their studies; for example: F. Hamilton Hazlehurst, *Gardens of Illusion, The Genius of André Le Nôtre* (Nashville 1980); and Kenneth Woodbridge, *Princely Gardens, The Origins and Development of the French Formal Style* (London 1986).

Allotments and Schrebergärten in Germany

Birgit Wahmann

Scheme for permanent colony of allotments at Königsheide, Berlin-Treptow, designed by E. Barth. Technische Universität, Plansammlung, Berlin.

The development of allotments in Germany took place against the background of the technological, economic and social transformations of the nineteenth century, and by now they have undergone many changes both in their significance to society and to the individual, and in their outward appearance.

The beginnings of the allotment movement were connected with campaigns for public welfare when municipalities provided the poor sections of the population not with financial support but with plots of land situated outside the residential areas for growing fruit and vegetables. These were intended to improve the poor nutrition of families, and were laid out as simple kitchen gardens with rows of vegetable beds and fruit trees.

The demand for these gardens for the poor grew with the advance of industrialization in the second half of the nineteenth century, when the male population of the countryside moved to the cities in large numbers to find work. At first they lived in makeshift hostels, then, from about 1870 onwards, when their families followed them, they filled the densely built speculative tenement blocks in the residential districts which were springing up in the big cities. The poor living conditions, the prevailing working conditions and the food shortages which resulted from the decline in agriculture caused considerable social problems for the emergent working class. A section of this previously rural population, accustomed as it was to self-sufficiency, could thus alleviate hunger and hardship to some extent by cultivating fruit and vegetables on small allotments outside the cities.

Further encouragement for the spread of the allotment movement came from an educational association founded in the mid-nineteenth century to promote the ideas of Dr Schreber. It aimed to improve the health and education of the people through sport and play in the open air, particularly for children and adolescents. As the director of the orthopaedic home in Leipzig Dr Schreber saw the physiological and psychological damage caused by the working conditions which even those age groups suffered at that time. He therefore recommended local authorities to create public playgrounds and organize regular games there under pedagogical supervision. Dr Schreber's objectives were continued after his death by Dr Hauschild, who started the idea of introducing gardening as a means of education for school children. Beds were laid out along the borders of the playgrounds, which were at first intended for children, but were later transformed into family gardens.

These two developments – the gardens for the poor, which were mainly allocated to industrial workers; and what later became known as *Schrebergärten* (Schreber gardens), which also had an impact on the lower middle-classes outside the purely industrial districts – came together in 1910 to form the 'Zentralverband der Arbeiter- und Schrebergärtner' (Central Association of Worker and Schreber Gardeners). Up to that time allotments had been connected with such basic necessities as the production of food and the provision of a minimum of open space, which meant that they were equipped simply to fulfil these functions. The allotment holders, the great majority of whom came from the proletarian classes, had a straightforward, unromantic need for and understanding of nature. They were not concerned with gardening as an art, but it is nevertheless possible to speak of a proletarian garden culture which had as its aim the improvement of living conditions.

Allotments and Schreber gardens were systematically planned by cities and local authorities from the beginning of the twentieth century onwards and were often introduced in conjunction with public parks. At that time this meant above all the people's parks (*Volksparke*), which were the first green areas to be open to all sections of the population, and were created in the changed political climate that followed the foundation of the Weimar Republic. Consequently allotments too were associated with democratic ideas such as independent government and individual responsibility, and these were reflected in the passing of the Allotments and Smallholdings Act in 1919, and the recognition of their public utility in 1924.

During and after the First World War the number and importance of allotments greatly increased because of food shortages, and only declined after the National Socialists came to power. At the beginning of the Second World War the socio-political aspects of allotments were overshadowed by the militaristic objective of self-sufficiency, but the allotment was also given an ideological significance: it was to help bring about 'direct attachment to the soil'. Towards the end of the Second World War and during the

Hut-shelter, garden shed and garden house for
Magdeburg, designed by B. Taut and Schütz,
1921. Büro der Stadtarchitekten, Magdeburg.

Design for allotment hut by E. May, 1920s.

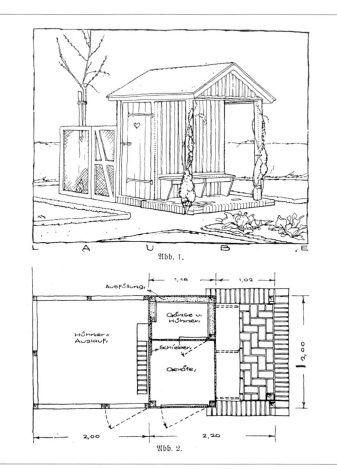

Abb. 1.

Abb. 2.

post-war period allotments were often given over to residential use, to provide accommodation for the homeless and refugees. Some groups of allotments were developed with support of the authorities as small-holdings for soldiers (*Laubenkolonien*), a large number of which were founded in Berlin, for example. In 1948, because of the shortage of housing and food, allotment holding in Germany reached a peak with 800,000 registered members of associations, as well as an unknown number of unregistered allotment holders.

Beside the economic reasons for acquiring additional land, there were other motives which became increasingly important in the 1950s, such as relaxation, recreation, leisure and a desire for contact with nature. In the following years economic considerations were pushed further into the background. The allotment

became a substitute for the house garden the whole plot of land with a summe house even made it possible to realiz one's dream of having a house and garde of one's own – albeit on a small scal Allotments were laid out along the lin of house gardens and ornamental ga dens, with carefully tended lawns, deco ative flower beds, summerhouses an garden seats. In this way a type of garde design, projected on to a narrowly cor fined space, was developed by a broa cross-section of society. The proportio of working-class allotment-holders wa still large in the 1970s, but since the 195c it had been steadily reduced by the influ of middle-class, professional people.

The allotment associations limit th size of allotments to a maximum of 40 square metres (4000 square feet) and la down rules about how they can be use and altered, which often severely restri the freedom of the individual, and fr quently result in a uniform, standardize appearance. Even today a certain portio of the allotment must be used for grow ing fruit and vegetables. However, th principal motives behind this – apar from the demand for home-grown foo because of a change in nutritional aware ness and an interest in gardening an physical activity – are the contemplativ enjoyment of nature through the obser vation of the world of plants and animal and a restful time spent in the open ai Nature and garden assume the function c a better 'alternative world', a contrast t life in high-density housing and th routine of work.

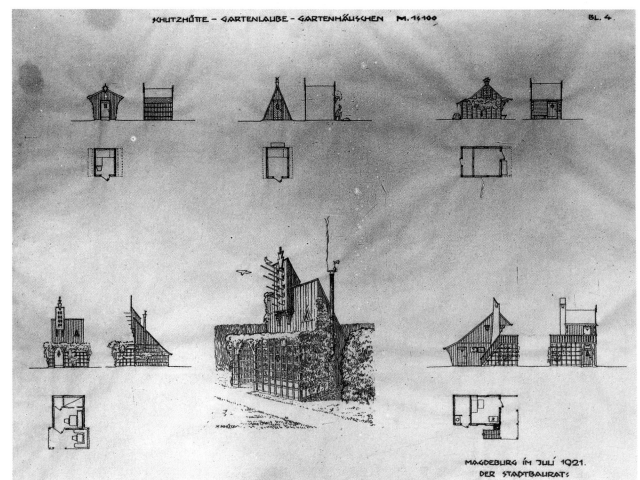

SCHUTZHÜTTE - GARTENLAUBE - GARTENHÄUSCHEN M. 1:100   BL. 4.

MAGDEBURG IM JULI 1921.
DER STADTBAURAT:

Bibliography

G. Gröning and J. Wolschke-Bulmahn, *Ei Rückblick auf 100 Jahre DGGL* (Berlin 1987

G. Gröning, *Tendenzen im Kleingartenwese* (Stuttgart 1974).

K. R. Schmidt, 'Das Kleingartenwesen in heu tiger Zeit,' in *Das Gartenamt*, no. 31 (1982 pp. 405–10.

M. Spitthöver, *Freiraumansprüche und Freiraum bedarf* (Munich 1982).

B. Wahmann, *Freizeitgärten, eine neue For privat nutzbarer wohnungsferner Freiräun* (Darmstadt 1987).

Colony of allotments at Marienthal, Neukölln, Berlin, 1912. Landesbildstelle, Berlin.

Allotment at Siedlung Neue Zeit at Reinickendorf/Wittenau, Berlin, 1931. Landesbildstelle, Berlin.

453

The Jugendstil Garden in Germany and Austria

Birgit Wahmann

A. Lilienfein, garden for a villa in Stuttgart. From Skizzen und Entwürfe aus dem Wettbewerb der Woche, *1908.*

Design by J. M. Olbrich for the garden of his house at Darmstadt. Kunstbibliothek, Staatliche Museen Preussischer Kulturbesitz, Berlin.

J. Lepelmann, garden near Düsseldorf. From Skizzen und Entwürfe aus dem Wettbewerb der Woche, *1908.*

The reform movement at the turn of the century reached garden design by way of the middle-class artistic and architectural circles which were seeking to develop a new unified philosophy of life and a formal language that was in tune with the times. Changing social and economic conditions led to a growing self-awareness in the middle classes. The new standards associated with this extended to all cultural fields, partly because of new industrial techniques of production.

Historicist stylistic elements from the late nineteenth century had still survived in garden design, which had continued to take the landscape garden of the Lenné and Meyer school as its model. A contrast to the features of artificial landscaping which even the smallest gardens attempted to imitate and so to idealize nature, was provided by the 'architectural' garden.

From about 1900 the architectural garden was taken as a model by the followers of various ideological tendencies, of which only those connected with the art movement known in Germany and Austria as 'Jugendstil' will be discussed here. Its first supporters were the young middle-class intelligentsia, often encouraged and employed by the upper middle classes and the aristocracy.

The garden was to fit in with the concept of a *Gesamtwerk*, a total work, as a synthesis of art, nature and way of life. Hence, both functionally and formally, the enclosed space in the garden was regarded as an extended living-room, while the garden was brought into the house in the form of winter gardens, loggias, and flowers displayed in rooms and at windows. In this way nature was to be drawn into the man-made living space and at the same time was a means of supplementing the architectural designs. The model for the organic ornaments which make up the character of Jugendstil, and are also found in the garden, can be seen both as the humanizing of nature and the denaturing of man.

This new form of garden had as its aim the movement away from the receptive enjoyment of nature, which no longer fitted the commercially-orientated progressive consciousness of the age, and instead emphasized the objective, functional aspects of the garden. Architectural gardens were based on clear spatial articulation which often subdivided even the

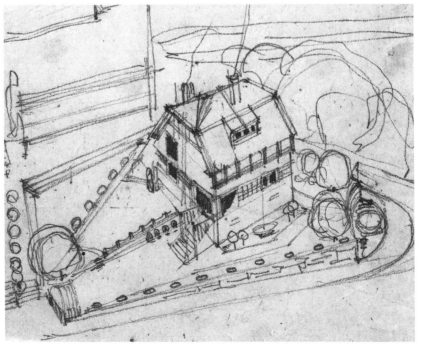

smallest spaces into decorative and functional areas: the garden for living in and the vegetable or kitchen garden. Despite the desire for simplicity, practicality and functionalism, attention was also given to decoration in accordance with the aesthetic ideals of this movement, though it was not to be the guiding principle.

One result of these ideals was an emphasis on three-dimensionality; for example, axial perspectives, geometric paths widening into open spaces, and severe compositions based on terrace walls and flower beds were broken up by delicate forms and tall, slender trees. Trees were used as accents in vistas or to close off spaces. The preferred trees were ones with thin trunks – ashes, birches, willows or limes – evoking the idea of indigenous trees rooted in their native soil, and showing a naturalistic approach. Yet there was also borrowing from Italian Renaissance gardens, and thujas, Italian poplars, and cypresses were planted. Other typical features which

should be mentioned are tubs planted with long-stemmed shrubs bordering the paths or marking an entrance or the passage from one part of the garden to another. Also characteristic are creeper-covered pergolas and arbours, and the rose borders or herbaceous borders in which great importance was attached to the coordination of the colours of the flowers. One purpose of the emphasis on three-dimensionality, both in the planting and the accentuation of differences of level by architectural means, was to make what are often very small gardens appear larger and more extensive.

All in all, the strict geometric division of some sections, often arranged symmetrically, together with the stylized, artificial treatment of plants, recalls the French style of the seventeenth century. These elements are found contrasted with a rounded, vegetative ornamental style, and a use of plants based on the rules of floristics. There is also the appearance of terms such as *Heimatliebe* (love of home)

and *Heimatverbundenheit* (attachment to home) which were later to be perverted to the *Blut-und-Boden* theory of race and territory in National Socialism, and were even ideologically misused by some garden architects.

An example of a Jugendstil design is the garden of the Olbrich House built in 1900 at the artists' colony on the Mathildenhöhe in Darmstadt. The structure of the garden is derived mainly from the triangular shape of the building plot. This meant that basically only residual areas were left. The visible area in front of the house was laid out as a 'representative' arrangement of lawn, flower garden and trees. Behind the house lies the vegetable garden, the kitchen yard and a sheltered seating area. Olbrich positioned a few trees and shrubs as eye-catchers and borders to paths. The geometrical composition is interrupted by single trees and a group of birches to the north, as well as the ornamental paving at the entrance and on the paths running beside the house.

Less well known is the garden laid out by Lepelmann at Düsseldorf in 1908 for a competition. It is situated in the Neander valley near Düsseldorf and rises in terraces towards the north-east. The ornamental garden is located near the entrance, while behind the house is the kitchen garden. The fruit and vegetable gardens are separated by a sunken path leading out of the garden through a gate, and the kitchen garden is divided from the ornamental garden by a pergola linked to the house.

A garden in Stuttgart designed for the same competition by Lilienfein brings together all the characteristic features of a villa garden of the period. The illustration shows a view from the lower terrace towards the two upper terraces. All the flower beds and borders are linked by coordinated colours with roses predominating. Yew and privet hedges with a row of small long-stemmed shrubs line the terraces. Over the steps are trellis arches with climbing roses.

The new style of garden was first employed in private gardens, but soon became influential in the design of gardens for public use. In a number of towns, parks and squares were laid out as architectural gardens in this way.

The town squares, such as the Viktoria-Luise-Platz in Berlin-Schöneberg with its geometric arrangement of paths and ornamental beds show the features typical of the period. While a strong emphasis on the ornamental is evident in the parks, the aesthetic ideas of the time are combined with a functional approach to their active use.

An example of this is the city park in Hamburg-Winterhude, one of the largest parks in the new style. The central area consists of a lake for boating and a rectangular playing field arranged in a symmetrical composition, the axis of which is marked by the main building on the lake and a water tower on the opposite side of the park. This zone is surrounded by geometrically arranged playing and

F. Encke, *plan of Viktoria-Luise-Platz, Berlin-Schöneberg, 1899.*

Viktoria-Luise-Platz, Berlin-Schöneberg, 1903. Landesbildstelle, Berlin.

sports fields as well as ornamental areas articulated with strict rows of trees.

The parks should be seen as forerunners of the people's parks (*Volksparke*), which introduced a new development. In contrast to the landscape parks originally laid out by the aristocracy and upper middle class which were connected with a schloss or villa, these parks marked the beginning of the municipal planning of green open spaces for the public.

Although the Jugendstil originated from the upper strata of society it was later employed for all groups of the population in both the public and the private sectors.

Bibliography

Exhibition Catalogue, Mathildenhöhe Darmstadt, 22 Oct. 1976–30 Jan. 1977, *Ein Dokument deutscher Kunst 1901–1976*, Vol. 5 (Darmstadt).
Exhibition Catalogue, Mathildenhöhe Darmstadt, 18 Sept. 1983–27 Nov. 1983, *Olbrich, J. M. 1867–1908* (Darmstadt).
Peter Behrens, 'Neue Sachlichkeit in der Gartenformung', in *Jahrbuch der Arbeitsgemeinschaft für deutsche Gartenkultur*, no. 1 (Berlin 1930) pp. 15–19.
Jürgen Milchert, 'Architektonischer Stil kontra Landschaftsgarten 1905–1910', in *Garten und Landschaft*, no. 1, (Munich 1987) p. 97.
Paul Schultze-Naumburg, *Kulturarbeiten*, Vol. 2, *Gärten* (Munich 1902).
Skizzen und Entwürfe aus dem Wettbewerb der Woche, Hausgärten (Berlin 1908).
Viktor Zobel, *Über Gärten und Gartengestaltung* (Munich 1905).

Gardens of the Côte d'Azur

Michel Racine

Plan of Charles Garnier's villa and garden at Bordighera, from a survey by the garden designer Edouard André. Drawing by J. P. Olive.

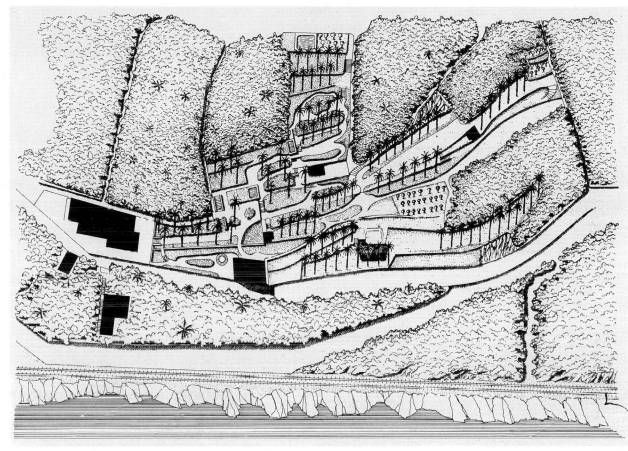

Trial gardens of the pioneers

The *pays des orangers* (land of the orange trees),[1] a landscape of discovery for lovers of the picturesque, was also an ideal terrain for European botanists wanting to set up trial gardens or attempting to acclimatize plants from overseas. But it remained difficult of access until the mid-nineteenth century: this was the age of the pioneers, intrepid souls who were prepared 'to brave the weariness of the stage-coach and uncongenial rooms in the hope of finding beauty', as Stendhal wrote in Toulon in 1837. Around the towns stretched a coastal area which seemed to be one continuous expanse of citrus groves, flower gardens, orchards and vegetable plots. The innovations which took place here at the beginning of this century can be seen on the one hand in the attempts to naturalize exotic plants in trial gardens, and on the other in the creation of landscaped parks, with a strong botanical bias, around the hotels and the first villas of the English colonies in Nice and Cannes.

Winter gardens and temperate tropical landscapes

With the advent of the railway, European high society discovered the Riviera. As it penetrated eastwards (Cannes in 1861, Ventimiglia in 1872) the train opened up all the small towns to tourism. Municipalities created public parks and organized festivals for the 'season'. The coast became a winter meeting-place.

People of private means in search of eternal spring and invalids seeking a cure came down daily from the palaces, Moorish villas or other buildings of eclectic styles, all painted a uniform white. Everyone was there, enjoying walks along the winding paths of the landscaped parks, admiring the skill of the gardeners, marvelling at the exotic plants growing in the open ground. Palm trees were particularly sought after by collectors because of their size and evocative power. Among the five thousand plant species at his villa Les Cocotiers at Golfe Juan, the Comte d'Eprémesnil possessed sixty-two varieties of palm. In his garden at Les Tropiques in Nice, Dr Robertson-Prochovski had made a collection of 120. The *Phoenix canariensis* (the date palm) was acclimatized in Nice in 1864 and then spread along the whole coast up to Hyères. It is now the symbol of the Riviera, symbol of

a landscape hardly more than a century old. Gazing out over the glassy Mediterranean, people dreamed of oriental shores, which they reconstructed in Westernized images. For the tropics that were offered to the stroller remained sedately restrained. Plant life was kept at a distance, behind balustrades and rock-work borders. There was much coming and going among the plots. Some proprietors admitted carriages to the main walks. The garden gates were often open. Winter visitors were like a large family, and visiting gardens formed part of their way of life. In his book *La Côte d'Azur*,[2] a sort of guide book, Stephen Liegeard noted the permanent opening in 1887 of many gardens, in particular the one at the Villa Bermond in Nice, where the orange and lemon groves 'can be visited freely at any time, without any irritating supervision', and the Bennet garden in Menton where 'each morning the gates are open until one o'clock. No permission to be sought,

no tiresome keepers. A Carrara marble plaque welcomes you in the universal language: *Salvete amici* [Greetings, friends].'

In their design nineteenth-century gardens on the Côte d'Azur juxtaposed formal and English-style elements. A very wide terrace would encircle the villa, often with more terraces rising above it, a greenhouse, a rustic grotto, a chalet, a Gothic or Moorish pavilion, and a few ponds or pools kept as small as possible because of the scarcity of water. Terracing was imposed by the terrain, as Edouard André remarks:

The gardens in this region have a layout quite different from that to be found on level or regularly sloping ground. On this steep terrain there was no choice but to adopt a system of steps, with ascending rows of terraces, thus giving the gardens the appearance of a construction. Sometimes the terraces are wide enough to be treated as formal parterres; sometimes there will be paths winding down

the slopes, with here and there terraced resting places.[3]

As plants were collected, so was stone. Caroline Miolan Carvalho had 'forty three fragments from the Tuileries' at villa Magali at St Raphaël, and Charles Garnier[4] himself had another collection in his villa at Bordighera. At the beginning of the twentieth century the Italian painter Raffaele Maïnella scattered authentic medieval fragments around his creations,[5] but his mixed layouts and grand flights of steps sweeping down to the sea reveal a quite different interpretation of the landscape.

The 'Mediterranean' garden

The English, faced earlier than their neighbours with the disappearance of the rural landscape had, from the end of the nineteenth century, designed a new form of garden. Country house architecture, local materials and wild flowers were all

Perspective view of the Villa Sylvia at Villefranche, Alpes-Maritimes, built by the architect Harold Peto, 1902. From L'Illustration, *Christmas 1922.*

The loggia of the Villa Fiorentina at Cap Ferrat, Alpes-Maritimes, from a drawing by Ferdinand Bac. From L'Illustration, *Christmas 1922.*

set off to best advantage and enhanced by the use of designs and settings from the Italian Renaissance or from Andalusian gardens.

This new way of seeing, of integrating and displaying the local landscape, was transported from England in the pages of journals, by members of the English colony, and in particular by the architect Harold Peto who worked on the Côte d'Azur from 1893 to 1910. In his designs for the Villa Sylvia, inspired by the Villa Medici in Fiesole, and for Maryland, Rosemary, Les Cèdres, Isola Bella, and Bella Vista, he skilfully combined very elaborate areas with formal, flower-filled parterres and orchards.

This interpretation of the Côte d'Azur landscape was enriched by another development – the *jardin-encyclopédie*. While some landscape artists were publishing various histories of gardens in Europe and throughout the world,[6] others were offering world tours in the gardens they created. At the Villa Ile-de-France (1905) and at Champfleuri (1912), as in the Albert Khahn garden in Boulogne or at Compton Acres near Poole, a visit to the garden was like turning the pages of a book on gardens, travelling by way of the Florentine garden to the Spanish, Dutch, Moorish or Japanese. This was also the beginning of the theme garden, of the colour garden, of a return to geometry and of the creation of Mediterranean gardens.

The Côte d'Azur was without doubt one of the world's most richly cultivated areas between the wars. After the English, the Russians and the Germans, came the Americans, Greek shipowners, and the great French fortunes. Now more than ever, the Mediterranean was the fashionable place to be. The cypress usurped the supremacy of the palm. With the advent of the motor car more places became accessible, sea bathing and the sun were discovered and the gardens became spring, summer and autumn gardens.

J. C. N. Forestier and Ferdinand Bac both proposed their own models of gardens where shapes, colours, materials and themes were inspired by their travels in Mediterranean countries. J. C. N. Forestier accompanied the publication of his executed garden designs in Spain, Morocco and France with a history of Mediterranean gardens.[7] From 1912 he created in Béziers, halfway between his winter residence on the Côte d'Azur and his workshops in Spain, a garden of a refined design, in which he combined formal parterres, brick pergolas covered in blue woodwork, and ceramics and a watercourse of Andalusian inspiration. In 1927 he designed the garden of the Bastide du Roy at Biot, notable for its geometric parterre, planted in subtle colours, flowering in the midst of an olive grove.

Ferdinand Bac meanwhile, having created the Italian and Spanish-inspired garden at the Villa Croisset in Grasse (1912), and having transformed La Fiorentina at Cap-Ferrat, achieved his masterpiece at Les Colombières in Menton. This was an excursion-garden, 'a nosegay of all the memories of his travels', and it contained countless surprises: on the one hand there were evocative visions of colour contained in geometric plots within an olive grove, on the other skilfully arranged perspectives designed to frame views of the surrounding landscape. Bac was a talented designer, writer and journalist, who defined the aesthetic principles of his Mediterranean garden in several articles and books.[8]

The demand for gardens on the Côte d'Azur was such that some landscape gardeners settled there permanently. Among them was Octave Godard, a pupil of Edouard André, who was to publish

The *Art of Gardening in the South of France*.[9] Others, such as Achille Duchêne, Jacques Greber, Léon Lebel and André Riousse, only came down from Paris to supervise the construction of a garden. Very detailed in design, these gardens are characterized by a strong architectural element, coloured materials, terraces, patios, pergolas, axes marked by avenues, monumental flights of steps, and watercourses bordered by cypresses.

There were, however, a few amateurs who equalled or surpassed the professionals. Among the great designers were two authors – Edith Wharton in her Parc Sainte Claire at Hyères (1927), and Blasco Ibañez in his Jardin des Romanciers at Menton (1922), inspired by one of Forestier's designs in Valencia. Above all, there was Lawrence Johnston, at Serre de la Madone at Menton (1919). A celebrated plant hunter and the creator of Hidcote Manor – a model for the new English garden – Johnston transformed a few terraces into a succession of green arbours, arranged along a deliberately unobtrusive main axis, which afforded a view across the landscape at each level.

Breaking with cultural trends the garden that Gabriel Guévrékian made for Charles de Noailles at Hyères in 1926 was part of the avant-garde movement of the '*années folles*'. Today it is known as the Cubist Garden, because of the vitality of its shape, its geometry, the zig-zag design of the jardinières, and Lipchitz's moving sculpture.

Trompe-l'oeil painting by Ferdinand Bac in the garden of Les Colombières, Menton, Alpes-Maritimes.

Plan of the Cubist Garden of the Villa Noailles at Hyères, Var, by G. Guévrékian. Drawing by C. Briolle and J. P. Olive.

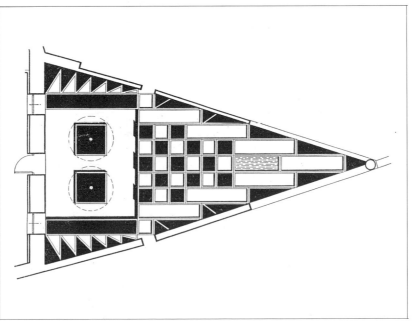

1   The coast between Hyères and Nice.
2   S. Liegeard, *La Côte d'Azur* (1887).
3   E. André, *Traité général de la composition des parcs et jardins* (Paris 1859).
4   Charles Garnier was the architect in charge of the demolition of the Tuileries.
5   Villa Cypris and Villa Roquebrune.
6   A. Maumène and A. Duchêne, *Quatre siècles de jardins à la française* (1910).
7   J. C. N. Forestier, *Gardens. A note-book of plans and sketches* – Eng. trans. (New York and London 1924).
8   F. Bac, 'Villas et jardins méditerranéens', in *L'Illustration* (Christmas 1922); F. Bac, *Les Colombières, ses jardins et ses décors* (Paris 1925).
9   O. Godard, 'L'art des jardins dans le Midi', in *Bulletin de la Société d'Horticulture pratique de Nice et des Alpes Maritimes*; O. Godard, *Les jardins de la Côte d'Azur* (Paris 1927).

Art Deco Gardens in France
Catherine Royer

Modern Garden: *drawing by Franz Lebitsch. From J. C. N. Forestier*, Carnet de plans et de dessins, *Paris.*

The 'garden of water and light': *watercolour by G. Guévrékian. From J. Marrast,* Jardins, *Paris 1925.*

Art Deco parterre: *watercolour by A. Laprade. From J. Marrast,* Jardins, *Paris 1925.*

For four centuries the art of gardens in France was dominated by the classical tradition, then for a further century by the landscape school and mixed gardening. What new aesthetic of gardening would emerge at the dawn of the twentieth century? A synthesis evolving from several different currents in contemporary art was to become the Art Deco movement.

Art Deco
This new aesthetic, which advocated purity of line and the use of geometric forms and bright colours, influenced architecture and the decorative arts from 1910, whereas the art of gardens was touched by it only from 1920–25.

One of the reasons why ideas were so slow to change in the gardening world was the renewal of interest in the great classical designs of the sixteenth and seventeenth centuries. From 1880 the French classical style returned to favour: garden designers of that time were more concerned to rediscover the guiding principles of Le Nôtre and to adapt them to the needs of a new era than to break with tradition like other contemporary artists in order to define the principles of a new aesthetic.

Economic conditions also favoured the development of designs on a grand scale, for between 1880 and 1914 the art of garden design was the prerogative of a traditionally-minded and wealthy private clientele, who resisted the modern and functional ideas that the avant-garde were then attempting to define. Thus it was not until the break-up of the large estates, caused by post-war economic uncertainty, that a vision and concept of garden design developed that were more attuned to contemporary needs and tastes.

From the aesthetic point of view, this abrupt change of scale from large gardens to much smaller ones inspired for a brief time between the wars the creation of two types of garden, both of which may be considered as part of the Art Deco tradition: the Architectural Garden, traditional in feeling; and the Cubist Garden, directly inspired by the Fauve and Cubist schools of painting.

The architectural garden
The architectural garden, which was espoused by the more conservative designers, went back to the principles of classical seventeenth-century design. The layout of these gardens was perfectly symmetrical, arranged round a main axis with the house at its centre. With their straight lines, regular plots, level ground and perspective effects, these small enclosed areas remained in the mainstream of the traditional ethos. Nevertheless, in their concern to adapt such gardens to limited areas and to the new way of life engendered by the economic difficulties of the industrial age, the designers had simplified layouts and introduced functional, easily-maintained arrangements. This resulted in clear and compact schemes, sometimes of a rather extreme regularity, but which were quick and easy to understand and therefore appealed to the rational outlook which typified the early years of this century.

Although in their reliance on models from the past these designers remained traditional, they were not unaware of contemporary artistic movements, or of the new materials becoming available as a result of recent industrial discoveries. New models for gardens displayed at the Exposition des Arts Décoratifs in Paris in 1925 showed an awareness of recent trends to revitalize garden design. Every aspect of the plans had been completely reworked to show the influence of Art Deco, and never had there been such a desire for colour harmony.

Some designers, more in touch than others with movements in the arts, produced plans in the manner of painters, interior decorators or goldsmiths. The architect André Vera and the engraver Paul Vera, both very sympathetic to the geometric Art Deco style, gave their plans the decorative quality of the fabrics, ornaments or jewellery of the period. This quality was emphasized in their chequered designs, where the space was divided into a series of square or rectangular compartments, by the use of bright, warm colours regularly interspersed with splashes of a single colour in clearly defined spaces.

Although they were directly inspired by contemporary abstract geometric design, they nevertheless still respected the traditional classical principles, and continued to plan their compositions on a central axis.

The Cubist garden
By absorbing more thoroughly the rules of composition of the abstract paintings derived from Cubism, the more modernist designers succeeded in completely revolutionizing the concept of space in garden design.

The architect Gabriel Guévrékian had provided the first intimations of this in his plans for a garden 'of water and light' for the Exposition des Arts Décoratifs in 1925. This design, based on triangular geometric form, broke away from the architectural nature of traditional gardens, and became instead an abstract picture composed of natural living elements.

Conceived as a purely decorative parterre, the garden was a three-dimensional reproduction of a pictorial work, based on Chevreul's theories of colour. According to these, geometric areas of monochrome should be enlivened by being placed in positions of mutual contrast, thus

The 'garden of love' designed by André Vera. From A. Vera, Les jardins, *Paris 1919.*

P. Legrain, design for an abstract garden on the outskirts of Paris. From J. Marrast, Jardins, *Paris 1925.*

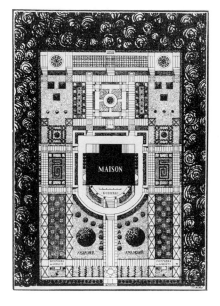

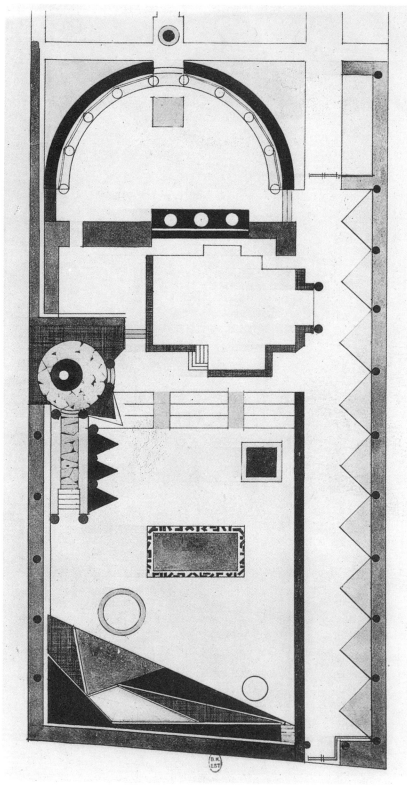

giving an impression of relief purely from the intensity of the colours; an optical illusion which demonstrated the three-dimensional application of the principles of modern painting.

Other designers attempted to modify the traditional composition of classical gardens by designing asymmetrical plots within which they arranged contrasting effects on large flat areas, opposing empty spaces with planted areas, rocks with vegetation, and geometric shapes with colours. These abstract compositions could be reduced to a collection of geometric shapes and monochrome areas, each enhancing the others. A new style of garden design had arrived. It was not to last long, but the few attempts that were made proved that the aesthetic of gardening was able to evolve in other ways than by the simple improvement of design or continuance of earlier styles.

Bibliography

André Vera, *Le nouveau jardin* (Paris 1911).
André Vera, *Les jardins* (Paris 1919).
J. C. N. Forestier, *Gardens. A note-book of plans and sketches* – Eng. trans. (London and New York 1924).
J. Marrast, *Jardins* (Paris 1925).
S. N. H. F., *Jardins d'aujourd'hui* (Paris 1932).
William McCance and H. F. Clark, 'The influence of Cubism on garden design' in *Architectural Design* (March 1960) pp. 112–17.
Richard Wesley, 'Gabriel Guévrékian e il giardino Cubista', in *Rasegna*, no. 8 (Oct. 1981) pp. 17–24.

The Heimatschutz Movement and the Monumentalization of the Landscape

Marco Pogačnik

The word 'fatherland' translates in two different ways in German: *Vaterland* and *Heimat*. This duality indicates that the fatherland is the place where a German feels at home (*Heim*) and that his home is the land of his fathers.

The word *Land* is a synecdoche in this context inasmuch as it refers only to a specific part of the fatherland – that part which is defined by the phrases *plattes Land* or *gerodetes Land* (flat unwooded terrain). The *Land* referred to is therefore that part of the country in which the German is established as a farmworker (*Bauer*); he is both a builder and a worker in that what he builds (*bauen*) consists either of the construction of an actual building (*erbauen*) or the tilling of the land (*bebauen*). It is this peasant settler (*Siedler*) who, in taking possession of the land, defines the form of a settlement, which becomes a *Stammesland* in the territory settled by its populace. He is the true founder of the *Land* and his work is *Landbau*, the old word for agriculture.

The Germans appeared on the historical scene not as nomads nor as city-dwellers but as a nation of farmworkers. They built their houses in the middle of their own property, and they had neither country villas not city palaces for relaxation or diversion. The German city is exclusively a place for commerce and trading, and it in no way belongs to the surrounding territory. It is, as Carlo Cattaneo wrote around the middle of the last century, anchored to its own site like a ship moored in a foreign harbour. It is not the city that is fundamental to the history of Germany but the *Land*. The ways in which work on the land is directed and the physical conformations that result from this direction constitute the landscape of the country, its *Landschaft*.

The peasant and the king (*Landesherr*) both live on the land, and it is these two figures that Julius Langbehn endeavours to bring to life in his book *Rembrandt als Erzieher* (1890). They are the German fatherland: '*Bauerngeist ist Heimatgeist*', the spirit of the peasant is the spirit of the nation. In the king there is something of the rustic and in the peasant something of the monarch. This peasant-king combination is known in German as *ländlich* and is essentially what characterizes the architecture of Heimatschutz.

Among the architects of Rembrandt-deutsche is Paul Schmitthenner. His work is *ländlich*: isolated buildings enveloped in light, their interior spaces part of the heavens in that the house is like a roof open to the four cardinal points and to every angle of the surrounding landscape of which it is an integral part. The work of Schmitthenner reflects all the principal concepts of Langbehn's theories: (1) the fugue as a form characteristic of the spirit of German music, which is composed (*fügen*) according to a formula of 'articulation and modulation'; (2) regionalism as a sign of a culture rooted in the soil and composed of the influences of neighbouring states, which are central to the German heartland (Rembrandt was Dutch, Schmitthenner Alsatian); (3) the artist conceived as a *Bauernkönig* (peasant-king) whose mission is to mediate between the aims of political theory (the Bismarckian myth) and those of his own *Land*. To regard these factors as the essential elements of the German culture is to accept the concept of Heimatgeist, and its defence as the ultimate symbol of an end to the search for the fatherland.

As has already been said, the *Bauer* is the settler (*Siedler*) and his territory is the *Siedlung*. This premise must be accepted by anyone embracing their ancient fatherland as a new *Heimat*, and it is from this point of view that the defence of the old values associated with patriotism (*Heimatschutz*) represent a *Siedlungswerk*, a process of colonization for which the organization Bund Deutscher Heimatschutz was founded in 1904.

The Bund was set up in Dresden on 30 March 1904 on the initiative of Ernst Rudorff and Hugo Conwentz. During the preparatory work involved in structuring the organization they were joined by the architect Paul Schultze-Naumberg and the economist Carl Johannes Fuchs from Freiburg. The league's organ was the *Mitteilungen des Bundes Heimatschutz*.

The first paragraph of the statute reads: 'The aim of the Bund is the defence of the German fatherland's natural and historical heritage'. The field of activity covered by the Bund was divided for this purpose into six sectors, and a leader was appointed to run each division. Fischer was given responsibility for the protection of national monuments; Schultze-Naumberg was put in charge of rural and urban building standards; Fuchs was made responsible for the environment; Conwentz for the preservation of the country's botanical, zoological and geological heritage; Brinkmann for traditional crafts; Frank for costumes, customs and festivals.

Among the first active participants in the work of the league were Ferdinand Avenarius, Fritz Schumacher and Cornelius Gurlitt, whose names also appear in the list of founder members of the Dürerbund in 1902 and of the Werkbund in 1907, testament to the fact that the German movement towards reform at this time manifested itself in the establishment of a variety of interconnected associations.

The Bund developed as the organizing body of a highly fragmented and complex movement comprising groups for the protection of concerns as diverse as the nation's historical heritage, its environment and its birds. But above all it was involved with the Denkmalpflegetagungen (the Congress for the Protection of National Monuments), in association with which the Bund held an annual conference from 1911 onwards. Conwentz regarded the Bund, of which he

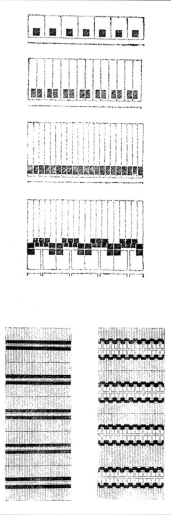

an object worthy of study and conservation, invested with a significance that, through links with the applied arts, is involved with 'the aesthetics of daily life', a theory of which Ferdinand Avenarius was one of the principal proponents in his magazine *Der Kunstwart*, founded in Dresden in 1887. It was mainly concerned with a programme to overcome those degenerative elements that had been introduced into German culture through nineteenth-century eclecticism and the spirit of the Vienna Secession. Both these influences were in contrast to the Biedermeier concept of the focus of domestic life and its intention to make the home (by which was meant of course both the house and the garden) the basis of the new reformed society.

Kunstwart and Heimatschutz together attempted to unite the two words that, as we have seen, comprise the notion of fatherland: *Heim* and *Land*. The aesthetics of daily life and the 'monumentalization' of the landscape were to be the two pivots on which a newly reformed global concept of life was to turn.

The whole history of the Bund is characterized by the wish to transform its own passive position as the defender and protector of the *Land* (*Schutz*) into a concrete programme for its transformation according to the values of the past (*Pflege*). From Heimatschutz to Heimatpflege. The rationale behind this objective coincided with that of the dissolution of the Bund. What Avenarius called the Partei der Sachlichen (the Party of Apolitics) succeeded in articulating its own beliefs only within the new conditions imposed by the war, with two manifestos that represent a final attempt to find a political solution to the conflict: Mitteleuropa and Ostpreussen. The first was an ambitious project set out by F. Neumann within the Werkbund, which defined the limits of the colonizing programme assigned to the central powers. The second, on the other hand, was an initiative sponsored by the Bund Heimatschutz with the intention of preparing the ground for the reconstruction of the eastern provinces of Prussia, which were the states – the only ones in the whole territory of the Reich – that had seen cruel fighting in the course of which entire cities had been razed to the ground and vast areas of agricultural land had been devastated. Taken together, the two

projects provide a picture of the Heimatschutz movement as a whole, in its twin aspects of external and internal colonization of German territory.

Together with the Vereinigung für Deutsche Siedlung und Wanderung (the Association for German Settlement and Emigration), the Bund prepared a programme of reconstruction which would, after the war, have served as the basis of the reorganization of German settlement policy throughout the territory of the Reich. The Ostpreussen project – based on Georg Steinmetz's *Die Grundlagen für das Bauen* – was presented and published in several volumes devoted to the ancient art of building, the *Siedlungskunst*. This work, which bears the title of *Siedlungs-*

was a founding father, as essential to the programme of the Congress, particularly after the major changes that had occurred in the previous decade with regard to the concept of national monuments. As Alois Riegl observed, the contemporary attitude towards monuments was to consider them not as works of man but as works of nature. The monument was regarded as no longer having an artistic and historical value but only a sentimental or emotional one. Whether referring to a painting or a tree, what moves one is not their past (*Vergangenheit*) but their transience (*Vergänglichkeit*), a factor that enables us to recognize in the monument 'a part of our own being'. In the debate between Riegl and Dehio, the Heimatschutz movement

favoured the views of the latter, who held that what moves us about a monument is not so much a 'feeling of being part of it' as a 'feeling of nationhood' in that the embodiment of all values is really the nation. A monument is therefore not necessarily simply a building of architectural merit but may also be a wood, a lake, a traditional costume or building technique, and the impetus that persuades us to concern ourselves with every aspect of the land is the clear indication that the landscape is a *Kulturarbeit*, the result of a long and habitual association with the land that it is possible to revive and maintain only through cultivation of the soil (*Pflege*).

The entire country therefore becomes

B. Möhring, design for ideal urban project with tower blocks, 1920. Each of the 320 homes in the tower blocks has its own garden.

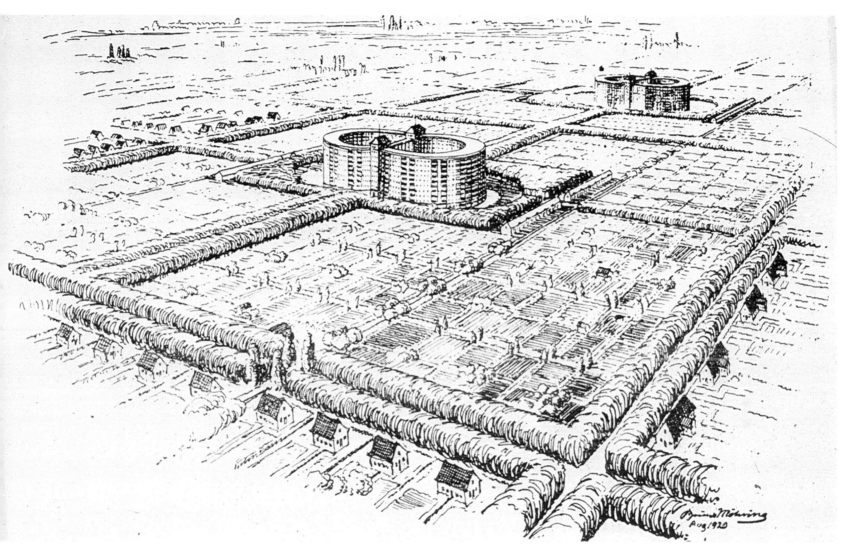

verk, sets out in detail the principles of the colonization plan, of which the Bund had been the main promoter; in it, spanning two historical eras, is to be found the final evidence of that sympathy between Heimatschutz and Sachlichkeit which, in the period of the Reformbewegung, had found common ground.

Bibliography

D. Brunner, *Land und Herrschaft. Grundfragen der territorialen Verfassungsgeschichte Süddeutschlands im Mittelalter* (Brno – Munich – Vienna 1943).

C. Cattaneo, *La città come principio* (Padua 1972).

Georg Dehio and Alois Riegl. *Konservieren nicht restaurieren. Streitschriften zur Denkmalpflege um 1900*, Vol. 80 (Brunswick 1988).

C. J. Fuchs (ed.) *Die Wohnungs- und Siedlungsfrage nach dem Kriege. Ein Programm des Kleinwohnungs- und Siedlungswesens* (Stuttgart 1918).

G. Kratzsch, *Kunstwart und Dürerbund. Ein Beitrag zur Geschichte der Gebildeten* (Göttingen 1969).

W. Kuhn, *Kleinbürgerliche Siedlungen in Stadt und Land. Eine Untersuchung der Siedlungsformen an Hand von Beispielen aus der Zeit von 1500–1850* (Munich 1921).

J. A. Langbehn, *Rembrandt als Erzieher* (Leipzig 1890).

G. Langen, *Die halbländliche und städtische Kleinsiedlung* (Munich 1925).

P. Mebes, *Um 1800. Architektur und Handwerk im letzten Jahrhundert ihrer Entwicklung* (Munich 1908).

W. H. Riehl, *Land und Leute* (Stuttgart 1883; 1st edn 1853).

P. Schmitthenner, *Baugestaltung* (1st ser.): *Das Dt Wohnhaus* (Stuttgart 1932). *Die gebaute Form* (Leinfelden-Echterdingen 1984).

W. Schönichen, *Naturschutz und Heimatschutz. Ihre Begründung durch E. Rudorff, H. Conwentz und ihre Vorläufer* (Stuttgart 1954).

G. Steinmetz, *Die Grundlagen für das Bauen in Stadt und Land*, 3 vols. (Munich 1917, 1922, 1928).

P. Schultze-Naumburg, *Kulturarbeiten*, Vol. 1–9 (Munich 1901–17).

The Reform Park in the United States (1900–1930)

Galen Cranz

Park history does not end with the nineteenth-century pleasure-ground. Many urbanists, planners, garden and environmental historians have written on the significance of the nineteenth-century park movement in American cities, but few have followed the line of continuity that runs through the turn of the century into the twentieth. To be sure, the differences between the nineteenth-century pleasure-ground and the early twentieth-century reform park are the sharpest in municipal park history, but the reform park and the ensuing recreation facility and open space system are part of a continuing social experiment with ways to solve social and urban problems as each era defined them.

Before 1900 most citizens saw cities as a necessary evil to which an antidote – the pleasure-ground – was necessary. Between 1900 and 1930 progressives recognized that however chaotic cities were, they were here to stay – so they should be reformed. The park that would bring the needed order was a combination of twin movements – the small park advocates who wanted to bring parks into tenement districts close to the working classes, on the one hand – and the playground advocates who wanted an alternative to the street for children's play, on the other.

Programming the reform park

Unlike the pleasure-ground, which encouraged family excursions and recreation, the reform park segregated ages and sexes. For the first time children became a distinct and important focus of park planning. The playground movement came into being several years before it was institutionalized in municipal park service in the decades around 1900. Originally championed as a place other than the street for children to go for spontaneous play or athletics, such parks came to be seen first and foremost as places for organized play. Games were regarded as an improvement on simple play, since they involved a definite programme and conclusion. The care of the playground was entrusted only to play leaders who understood that the significance of the play instinct was its relation to the physical and social development of young people. The emphasis on leadership grew, and the area over which leadership was meant to hold sway

expanded. The 1909 textbook for professional play leaders, *The Normal Course in Play*, was renamed *Introduction to Community Recreation* in 1925. Playgrounds, in fact, became recreative centres, combining playground features with some of the social aims of the settlement house. In organizing activities like music weeks, community days, singsongs in factories and streets etc., they sought to ensure a wholesome expression of community life and the socialization of residents to a common core of American values. Nevertheless,

by the Depression park service had lost any pretensions to being an agent of social change.

The pleasure-ground imitated nature, and its use was curtailed by nightfall and in rough weather. In contrast, the focus of the reform park on organized activity led to its use during times when it would previously have gone unused, and to the strict scheduling of its use. The day was broken into parts according to temperature changes and the schedules of school children, mothers, and workers. The modern city was on a seven-day week,

and even Sunday, the day of rest, was opened for active recreation. Chicago kept eleven centres open year-round beginning in 1912, which increased the popularity of winter sports – skiing, tobogganing and ice-skating.

Athletics were a primary focus. German immigrants had set up turnvereins (athletics associations) in the early nineteenth century, and the YMCA integrated the gymnasium into the culture at large in the decade from 1886 to 1896: park departments merely adopted the already existing form. Tennis courts, golf courses, archery, football and ice-hockey were more like extensions of the gymnasium than pieces of landscape. Swimming baths were introduced to encourage working class people, many without private baths, to be clean. But soon swimming became a sport, and swimming pools became necessary recreational and social equipment. Athletics were organized into communitywide tournaments. To turn sports to the purpose of community integration, Chicago developed a system of points that rewarded team spirit and cooperation as much as athletic achievement.

By the first decade of the twentieth century, folk-dancing had been assimilated into park programmes as a form of athletics and was taught in gym classes. Folk-dancing was the lesser of two evils, being relatively wholesome compared with the social dancing and practices of the dance halls. But in time, in the hope of competing more effectively with the dance hall, park programmers offered social dancing. By 1920 the national literature reported that dance pavilions were very popular; a small fee, seating for those not dancing, and male and female chaperones, converted the questionable activity into a manageable one.

Crafts were geared to the working class, and welcomed into the reform park as a further expansion of its base of participation. During the pleasure-ground era, crafts were considered inappropriate because of their similarity to factory work, and for the first few years of the reform era crafts such as sewing, basketry and carpentry were excluded, in part because crafts were considered an additional evil to the unhygienic ills of factory life and schooling of children. By the late 1920s park departments everywhere justified 'ingenuity work' as a

Plan for the Sherman games park in Chicago, designed by Olmsted Bros. and Burnham and Co., from Plan of Chicago . . ., *edited by C. Moore, Chicago 1909.*

Mark White Square, Chicago: in the background is the field house. From Plan of Chicago . . ., *1909.*

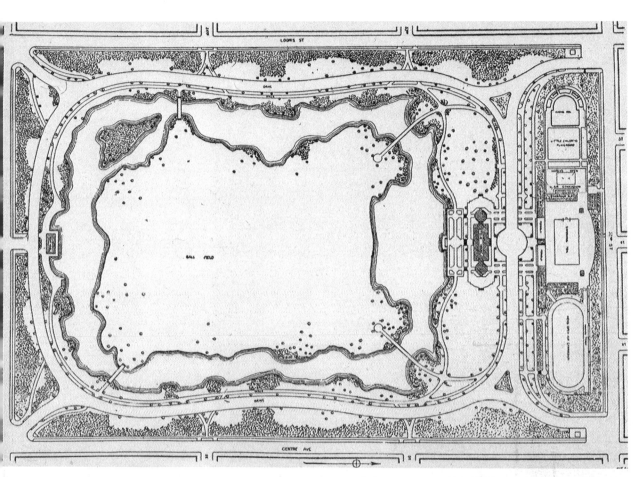

medium for personal expression and as a way to build up park attendance.

Vegetable gardening, somewhat similar in appeal to handicrafts, first became a recreational activity in New York's DeWitt Clinton Park in 1902, when it was divided into miniscule farms, each assigned to an individual child. Schools began to sponsor such farm programmes in parks shortly thereafter, and these gardens became Victory Gardens during the First World War. As a response to wartime shortages, the Chicago Parks Department itself raised vegetable plants for distribution to the public. Demonstration gardens showed adults how to grow fresh vegetables in city-owned gardens, both before and for a few years after the First World War.

Strictly educational activity considered inappropriate to the pleasure-ground was welcomed in the reform park. Thus public libraries installed branches in the small parks, and lectures on civic issues were allowed. The new smaller park type was idealized because it could be tucked in almost anywhere. In time the issue of whether a city should invest in small or large parks was superseded by the general theory that a park system consisted of two kinds of park: the local neighbourhood park for frequent and regular use and the rural park for holidays. By the 1920s the more abstract inference emerged that the park system was composed of areas increasing in size as one moved away from the city centre, the area of highest land value and density. Administrators attempted to formulate standard guidelines for determining playground size. Ideally, a playground would be located near cheap and quick transportation systems. But topographical considerations of all aspects of the character of the land were also considered rational and legitimate criteria for site selection. In the ensuing era of the recreation facility, these criteria became formal standards, in turn eroded by open space ideology that justified taking available land no matter what its size or shape.

The form of reform

In 1894 C. S. Sargent, the staunchest defender of the pleasure-ground, was horrified when a Philadelphia city officer recommended that cities provide more playgrounds and fewer ornamental parks. After the turn of the century park

Cabrillo playground, San Francisco. One of the reform parks around the Golden Gate Park, with a field house and an informal adventure playground opposite.

designers, who were increasingly employees of park departments rather than consultants, shifted from artistry as a design priority to utility. This changing perspective is apparent in the official reports, as the length of landscape reports diminished while the playground and gym director's reports increased.

Ideally, the playground could be both beautiful and serviceable, since most modern facilities could be decorated with trees, shrubs, and flowers without their interfering with the play space; as such, the City Beautiful and settlement house mentalities, which seemed to be at cross purposes in questions of site selection, could actually be reconciled in the design of parks themselves.

The designers' handling of landscape elements and details of construction shows how the tension between utility and appearance was resolved in practice. The overall layout of the park was symmetrical and formal, and paths and roadways were minimized to save space for games and direct use. Spatial sequence was not particularly important; no illusion of more space than existed was called for, nor were the kinesthetic experiences of moving through different volumes or meandering along serpentine paths sought after. If anything, the pedestrian was offered a feeling of order and civic importance through the formal, central, and axial array. Views were no longer carefully controlled, except inasmuch as shrubs and trees might screen out the immediate environs of the city though obviously not the skyline of industrial areas and tenements beyond. Buildings dominated the landscape, their location, size, and style making them important.

The rationale of reform park design was as highly evolved and consistent as that of pleasure-ground design, but virtually antithetical to it; it represented much more than an erosion of the older ideal. Thus water was not used for psychic effects but for practical ones: it filled wading and swimming pools and showered people before and after swimming. Just as the showers were usually adjacent or linked to the swimming pools, the gymnasium lockers were linked to the shower baths and to the indoor and outdoor gymnasiums. Such requirements for adjacencies locked the reform park into a characteristic sequence of functions in layout. The grounds were no longer undulating but flat to accommodate baseball diamonds, running tracks and other equipment, and grass was abandoned in favour of hard surfaces for games. One of the first things done to a small park or playground was to fence it. In part an indicator of care and concern, a fence was also an instrument of social control. The proliferation of wire meshing was largely a response to the hazards of baseball, but while baseball was eventually severely restricted in reform parks, wire mesh fencing was not. It is one of the living legacies of the 1920s.

Buildings had been accepted only as a necessary evil in the pleasure-ground but proliferated in the reform park, and the field house was the characteristic building type of the era. A coherent field house style was not achieved, but rather remained a composite of rustic and classical conventions.

Conclusion

The quality of experience in a reform park was markedly different from that in a pleasure-ground. Rather than quiet and serene, it was noisy and organized, both visually and in terms of activity. During the early twentieth century the pressure and rigidity of industrial production were maintained or increased, and labour gains mainly took the form of compensation for them: a shorter working week, earlier retirement, longer vacations, and higher pay. Ironically, however, the reform park offered urban populations leisure experience to fill the newly available time that was nearly as rigid in its organization. Parks, like business firms and schools, followed an industrial model: age segregation, specialization of function, and a horror of waste. This industrial top-down style of leisure-time organization in the reform era had some virtue, namely the careful programming of local playgrounds by social workers. The benefits of this control were lost in the 1930s when the desire to give everybody a playground nearby went beyond staffing abilities. Playgrounds could be built quickly using both skilled and unskilled labour, but committment to paying for trained leadership eroded in the next era whose spokesmen viewed reform as 'absurd' and turned instead to meeting the 'demand' for recreation.

Bibliography

G. F. Chadwick, *The Park and the Town. Public Landscape in the Nineteenth and Twentieth Centuries* (London 1966).

N. T. Newton, *Design on the Land. The Development of Landscape Architecture* (Cambridge, Mass. 1971).

G. Cranz, *The Politics of Park Design. A History of Urban Parks in America* (Cambridge, Mass. 1982).

PART FIVE

Aspects of the Contemporary Garden:
From the Leisure Park to Artistic Experimentation

Part title: Parque del Este, Caracas (Photo Giovanni Chiaramonte)

Gardens and Photography

Tony Mott

Our experience of a garden often begins with seeing a photograph. The photograph may encourage us to go and see this garden for ourselves, although we are unsure if the carefully chosen view is representative of the entire garden.[1] Conversely we may use photographs as a reminder of a garden that we have seen; here, we use the camera to try and record our own experiences, and to communicate and conserve visual ideas and details. At present the photograph is the most convenient and common way of communicating ideas about landscape and the garden, and we have become used to the idea of this two-dimensional medium representing space and volume.

This short review of the relationship between the landscape garden and photography is concerned with the still image only, and the way that photography relates to other two-dimensional means of representing a garden. The purpose of photographing gardens is also considered, and how far the medium can be objective. Does the photographer need to be involved in presenting an image which incorporates his own aesthetic decisions, or can the photograph act simply as record?

The depiction of gardens using two-dimensional means

Before the first photographic images on paper were made in the 1830s,[2] gardens and landscapes were painted, engraved, drawn, woven and embroidered. In each case, the artist or craftworker had complete control over the contents of their image. In some cases, elements of the composition have been included which were not complete or even created within the garden. Often a garden was depicted in its future state, with the planting matured, and unbuilt architectural features complete. If the artist wants to depict the garden at its best, he may have to make some adjustments to the planting, or perhaps change the scale of some elements. Engravings and paintings were usually made to cause a pleasurable response, rather than point out deficiencies. Photographs have added another concept to the portrayal of gardens; the images might show that the photographer is purposely highlighting decay or neglect. It may be a photograph which is unlikely to impress an owner, and may displease or perhaps anger the specialist viewer, who generally has faith in the reality or objectivity of a photograph and is likely to be more concerned about the conservation of gardens. A photograph can only represent a garden retrospectively, whereas the artist can become a designer by altering what is seen by the naked eye. The extra freedom that a photographer has over the artist is to multiply and diversify his range of images. Hundreds of photographs can be taken in quick succession; black and white or coloured images can be simultaneously offered, and the use of different cameras, lenses or filters add more diversity to even one viewing position. Given this freedom of choice, garden literature does not need to be encumbered with long written descriptions of scenes which can be shown by a photograph.

In the eighteenth century there was some debate as to whether landscape painting had a relationship with garden design. Humphry Repton decided that there was no question of the two arts having a definite relationship, and he presented some practical differences. In his work, *Sketches and Hints on Landscape Gardening* published in 1795, he wrote, 'the spot from whence the view is taken is in a fixed state to the painter; but the gardener surveys his scenery whilst in motion'. Repton also pointed to another problem in the relationship between reality and the two-dimensional depiction of a scene, 'the quantity of view, or field of vision, is much greater than any picture will admit'. Any two-dimensional image of a garden has to have a finite boundary, and this is not the way that our eyes function in that we are always aware of peripheral information although it may not be in focus.

The landscape through a viewfinder

The composition of photographs and that of painting and drawing have been linked for centuries because of optical viewing devices that artists have used. The camera obscura was used for drawing from the sixteenth century, and was a type of viewfinder used for composing pictures. Sir Joshua Reynolds regarded the camera obscura with some contempt:

> If we suppose a view of nature represented with all the truth of the camera obscura, and the same scene represented by a great Artist, how little and mean will the one appear in comparison with the other, where no superiority is supposed from the choice of subject. The scene shall be the same, the difference will only be in the manner in which it is represented to the eye. With what additional superiority then will the same Artist appear when he has the power of selecting his materials, as well as elevating his style?[3]

One advantage of the camera obscura was the way that the landscape could be viewed in miniature. Another device which had a similar effect was the Claude glass: a convex mirror with a darkened ground. William Gilpin (1724–1804) used this to help form his opinions on picturesque scenery. Essentially he was concerned with ordering natural scenes into a more pleasing composition, and said that 'the exact copies can scarcely ever be entirely beautiful'.[4]

Reactions towards the invention of photography

When William Henry Fox Talbot addressed the Royal Society on 'The Act of Photogenic Drawing' in 1839 he pointed out the possibilities that photography would give for topographical records. He said,

> now nothing prevents him (i.e. the traveller) from simultaneously disposing in different positions, any number of the little camerae, it is evident that their collective results, when examined afterwards, may furnish him with a large body of interesting memorials, and with numerous details for which he had not himself time either to note down or delineate.

Photography had many effects on the work of artists, and to a large extend the country house and its occupants came to be portrayed in photographs rather than paintings.[5] J. M. W. Turner said 'this is the end of Art. I am glad I have had my day'. John Ruskin was exited by the detail contained in a daguerreotype, and brought this new invention in to his five volume work *Modern Painters* (1843–60): 'I have seen Daguerreotypes in which every figure and rosette, and crack and stain, and fissure are given on a scale of an inch to Canaletto's three feet'. One effect which photography had on painting was to create new imagery dependent on the camera's own technical limitations. In work dating from the mid nineteenth century the painter Jean Baptiste Camille Corot seems to have created the effects of halation or objects being out of focus. 'Corot tried to portray the spirit of nature in a sublime fashion and consciously evoked a feeling of wind currents blowing through the leaves. He had seen leaves recorded in a sketchy way by the camera and their appearance must have suggested a pantheistic connotation consistent with his aims.'[6]

By the end of the nineteenth century, photography had established itself as an objective means of portraying gardens and landscapes. The American architect Charles Platt in his introduction to *Italian Gardens* (published in 1894) was critical of the engravings of Roman villas by Percier and Fontaine (*Choix des plus célèbres maisons de plaisance de Rome et de ses environs*, 2nd edition Paris 1824). He complained that 'the views from different points are so freely treated as to leave one familiar with them in much doubt as to their having looked as they are represented, and they are misleading, to say the least, to one who has never seen the gardens'. He continued by saying that

the art of photography has been perfected since their treatment of the subject, and the object of the present writer has been by its means to illustrate, as far as possible, the existing states of the more important gardens of Italy, leaving out the matter of research altogether, since a more profitable study of the subject can be made as a result of these reproductions of nature, and it is quite possible (by making a careful study of all the gardens as a whole) to come to certain conclusions as to the fundamental principles which guided the original designers.[7]

It is not clear whether Platt sees the photographer as being a highly informed or casual observer. It does seem however that some knowledge of a garden is required to make a photograph say something about the design concept. As yet no one has advocated an ideal way to record a garden in photographs, whether for archival or any other purposes. However, it does seem that without any background knowledge, important images might be missed, new planting or building might take on far too much importance. In effect, the person looking at the photographs could be shown a series of images which totally ignored the ideas of the original plan.

In his book on the photographer Eugène Atget, William Howard Adams makes an interesting comparison between photography and the work of the seventeenth-century engraver Israel Silvestre. He gives the

Harewood House, *photograph by Roger Fenton. The Royal Photographic Society, Bath.*

The Temple of Philosophy at Ermenonville, photograph by Geoffrey James. From M. Mosser, Morbid Symptoms. Arcadia and the French Revolution, *Princeton 1987.*

impression that the artist has every advantage over the photographer in creating an ideal image of a garden, unimpeded by the effects of time or decay.

Silvestre was the photographer for the court and the nobility, recording the châteaux, fêtes, gardens, and the countryside of that Golden Age. His views encompassed all there was to see, or so it appears, and if this was the garden as at Vaux, that meant that his wide angle focus included not only the green palisade walls that framed the vast layout but the far horizon as well and everything in between.

His drawings of the gardens at Vaux and of the Tuileries prepared for the engravings have a morning freshness to them that one can fairly breathe: the masses of new foliage on either side of the avenue, the clipped and squared parterres, the beds of flowers newly set out, the central axis running majestically to the horizon. It was still a moment when the whole thing could be taken in and reduced to a piece of paper not much larger than Atget's negative plate.[8]

Two purposes of photography – The work of Eugène Atget and Maxfield Parrish

In 1897 at the age of forty Eugène Atget ended his career as an actor, and became totally involved in photography. There were commercial possibilities in making detailed photographic records of aspects of Paris, owing to a programme initiated by the Commission des Monuments Historiques. Paris was undergoing rapid changes with Haussmann's grandiose plans.[9] At the same time Atget was able to record the melancholy grandeur of the decaying gardens of the seventeenth century. William Howard Adams says in his introduction to Atget's work, 'in the 1880s, when Atget first came to Paris, the black ruins of the (Tuileries) palace were still there facing the gardens before they were finally removed and scattered around France to other parks as souvenirs. Like the ruins of St Cloud to the west, new flower beds took their place'.[10] Watteau and Fragonard were inspired by the same scenes, although Atget's images were without people emphasizing the fact that these gardens were abandoned. Atget worked alone and the images reflect his isolation and non-involvement with the current trends in photography.[11] 'The painterly photograph celebrating the cult of art or the ritual portrait, both fashionable, even dominant at the time, did not interest him.' Atget did keep close contact with some of the notable artists of the period, and sometimes as with Derain the photographs were used as reference material.[12]

An artist who made use of his own photographs was the American illustrator Maxfield Parrish (1870–1966). For his paintings for *Italian Gardens*, Parrish contact printed the 5 by 4 in (13 × 10 cm) negatives to make positive transparencies. He then projected the image using a large 'magic lantern' projector and traced round the image relying on the photograph for composition and field of vision. Parrish used a plate camera with bellows extension. The maximum aperture was f6.8 and so with the slow photographic emulsions it was necessary to use a large

Villa d'Este at Tivoli. Painting by M. Parrish, 1903. From E. Wharton, Italian Villas and Their Gardens, New York 1904.

tripod to cope with slow shutter speeds. Parrish was working at a time when colour photography was just becoming a reality – although it was not until 1907 that the Lumière brothers began commercial manufacture of 'Autochrome' plates.

The sketches and photographs for the *Italian Gardens* illustrations were made in 1903 when Parrish made a three month trip to Italy with his wife. Parrish sought advice from his neighbour Charles Platt who was an expert on Italian architecture and landscape gardening. The author of *Italian Gardens*, Edith Wharton, was always working a few weeks ahead of Parrish in another part of Italy, so he must have had some freedom in his choice of image or composition.

The colours of the Italian landscape were beautifully captured in his work. In a letter written to Spencer Penrose on 15 September 1919 he confirms his technique.

Should I ever be able to come out there and paint the place, I would do just as I did on the series on the *Italian Gardens*, make my photographs and studies on the spot and then paint the actual picture at my home. In some ways this is better, for with a certain temperament, a literal rendering of the material facts can be avoided, and the part that stays in the mind can the better be brought out, the spirit and the atmosphere of the place.[13]

Garden designers as photographers

The garden designer Gertrude Jekyll used photographs to document the progress of her work and to add to her working notebooks.[14] She concentrated on details such as flower specimens, and when photographing the landscape around her home in Surrey she recorded the local craftsmen at work. Gertrude Jekyll had her own darkroom although little record has been kept to reveal her technical approach to the medium and the sort of equipment she used. A large proportion of the photographs in *Wood and Garden* are her own, although she was very modest about her technical abilities. In her introduction to *Wood and Garden* she says,

the greater part of the photographs from which the illustrations have been prepared were done on my own ground – a space of some fifteen acres. Some of them, owing to my want of technical ability as a photographer, were very weak, and have only been rendered available by the skill of the reproducer, for whose careful work my thanks are due.[15]

Jekyll also mentioned that some of her photographs were made for reproduction in wood engraving for publications by William Robinson – such as *The English Flower Garden*. The first edition of this appeared in 1883, just after the half-tone process for reproducing photographs had been used commercially.

Once it was possible to reproduce photographs in books on gardens new types of garden books could appear. Illustrations could be provided more readily, and as said before, a wealth of material to choose from could be more easily provided.

Photographic archives

An historic garden is now recognized as being an element of a nation's heritage which warrants conservation as does for example a building. The most important gardens are listed on a register which grades them according to their importance.[16] As yet there is no coordination of photographic records past and present although there are important photographic archives which include gardens. The Royal Commission on Historical Monuments holds the National Monuments Record, which is primarily a large photographic collection of over a million items and was established in 1941. Another large collection of architectural and landscape photographs is held by the journal Country Life which began in 1897. In his introduction to a book displaying a selection of photographs from the National Monuments Record, Alastair Forsyth wrote, 'many of the photographs are valuable in their own right, either because of their age or because they are the only records we now possess of buildings, or even whole environments which have now disappeared'. He concedes that a photograph has a value in itself if its subject no longer exists and that it gives us 'a better record than is available from earlier centuries to work from in studying gardens and those who planned, cared for and paid for them'.[17]

An unexpected bonus for garden researchers has been the information yielded by aerial photography. Some aerial photographs – particularly those taken in extreme weather conditions such as drought or snow – have made images of parterres reappear in a ghost-like fashion. The planting of the original parterres has become evident on areas of lawn, and these temporary images would be impossible to see from the ground. In most conditions, the contour of lost features such as earthworks, terraces, raised walks, mounts, canals, basins, ponds, and sunken gardens have shown up clearly from the air. Christopher Taylor of the Royal Commission on Historical Monuments identified forty-one 'lost gardens' dating from 1540 to 1725 and estimates that there may be up to a thousand sites with some remains still visible.[18]

The photography of gardens in the future

It may be possible that national photographic archives will be established, that are devoted solely to recording gardens. A recognized system for portraying the garden may be devised so that all aspects of its horticultural, architectural and spatial elements are considered. Other media such as film, video and even holography may contribute towards giving the impression of works of art which are impossible to conserve in a static state of existence, and difficult to shield from the effects of contemporary culture and civilization.

View of the Gothic Tower at Painshill Park, 1958. (Photo Country Life).

Aerial view taken in 1956 of the remains of the embankment in the gardens of Harrington Hall, demolished in 1740. (Crown copyright reserved)

*Villa Gamberaia, photograph by Mrs
Aubrey Le Blond. From I. Triggs,* The
Art of Garden Design in Italy, *1906.*

[1] Before the invention of photography, travellers expected to find the images that they had seen in engravings – 'the English visitor to Italy brought back prints as modern travellers brought photographs'. Elizabeth Wheeler Manwaring, *Italian Landscape in 18th Century England* (London 1965, second impression).

[2] A detailed study of the early history of photography is given in Helmut Gernsheim, *The Origins of Photography* (London 1982). Gernsheim suggests that photographic images on paper might have appeared as early as 1827. He discusses some important discoveries in *Photographic Journal*, Section A, January 1951. Details of early photographic processes are given in Bruce Barnard and Valerie Lloyd, *Photodiscovery* (London and New York 1980). A more complete history of photography is given by Ian Jeffrey, *A Concise History of Photography* (London 1981).

[3] Quoted from Aaron Scharf, *Art and Photography* (London 1968). The statement is taken from the thirteenth Discourse of Sir Joshua Reynolds (the fifteen Discourses covered the period 1769–1790). Scharf also describes variations of the camera obscura. The camera obscura was an instrument which was originally used to observe solar eclipses. It existed as early as the eleventh century. In the Renaissance it was used as a drawing instrument and in 1550 Girolamo Cardano added a lens. The Neapolitan scientist Giovanni Battista della Porta gave a full description of the camera obscura in *Magiae Naturalis* (1558). He also described an elaborate trick where a theatrical production was organized outside a darkened room. From within, the spectators could see a projected image of the performance by the use of the camera obscura – in effect an early concept of a cinema.

[4] William Gilpin, *Observations, chiefly related to the picturesque beauty of the mountains and lakes of Cumberland and Westmorland* (1786).

[5] 'The portrait of the House and Garden was becoming less popular by the second half of the nineteenth century. By 1850 itinerant painters belonged to the past, and it was becoming difficult for country house portraiture to be a tangible form of income for the artist. Between 1870 and 1890 photographers took on a new importance and landed families were photographed in front of their houses.' John Harris, *The Artist and the Country House* (London 1979). A fascinating series of country house photographs is gathered in Christopher Sykes, *A Country House Camera*.

[6] John Ruskin, *Modern Painters* (1856).

[7] Charles A. Platt, *Italian Gardens* (New York 1894).

[8] William Howard Adams, *Atget's Gardens* (London 1979).

[9] Georges Eugène Haussmann was Préfet de la Seine to Napoleon III from 1853 to 1869. His plans helped improve communications in the city and also a system of public parks was created. See George F. Chadwick, *The Park and the Town* (London 1966) and the article in this book on Haussmann on p. 387.

[10] Adams, *ibid.*

[11] Photographs which might quite easily have been mistaken for lithographs and etchings were reproduced in *La Photographie est-elle un art?* by Robert Gizerame (1899). The gum bichromate process, where gum acacia and a pigment are mixed with the light sensitive potassium bichromate, is particularly suitable for creating photographic images with a painterly effect.

[12] Adams, *ibid.*

[13] Coy Ludwig, *Maxfield Parrish* (New York 1973).

[14] 'The Flower Gardens of Gertrude Jekyll' in *Design Quarterly* 137 (1987).

[15] Gertrude Jekyll, *Wood and Garden* (London 1899).

[16] English Heritage has prepared a register of gardens in England and has appointed an Inspector of Historic Parks and Gardens. The register was submitted to a Select Committee on Historic Buildings and Monuments, with the assistance of the Garden History Society, ICOMOS UK Gardens Committee and the Centre for the Conservation of Parks and Gardens (University of York). Recommendations were made that the Department of the Environment should make more funds available to grant-aid historic gardens.

[17] Alastair Forsyth, *Yesterday's Gardens* (London 1983).

[18] Christopher Taylor, *The Archaeology of Gardens* (Aylesbury 1983). See also Marcus Binney and Anne Hills, *Elysian Gardens*, Save Britain's Heritage, 1979, in which a number of interesting aerial images are illustrated.

The park of Fontainebleau. (Photo Fulvio Ventura)

Leisure Parks in Europe: Entertainment and Escapism

Isabelle Auricoste

Elsewhere is always paradise. To escape from our everyday surroundings is to experience the feeling of entering 'another world'. The desire to encounter the duality of existence, ever-present in the history of humanity, sends us in search of a world different from our own, rich with possibilities. In this sense, the association between gardens and paradise is not only the perpetuation of a universal myth (supported by the etymology of the word 'paradise' – the carefully cultivated parks of the rulers of ancient Persia, luxuriant and cool under the burning sun of the Euphrates). It is also an affirmation that gardens, or parks, are a favoured setting for rewarding encounters between the world of desires and the world of experience.

The term 'park' has been unhesitatingly adopted virtually throughout the world to imply a formula, and apparently a novel one, for places dedicated to amusement. The use of this word draws attention to the essential qualities supposed to belong to this sort of place. A park is first of all an enclosure, an area defined by limits; it is also a place in some way connected with a garden, and to an image of paradise in the collective imagination. There is no question here of pronouncing on whether contemporary amusement parks should be included among gardens in the naturalistic sense. Nor do we intend to consider the relation of man to nature, or even the plants used to embellish them. The question is simply: to what extent we may hope to feel, to live, the experience of 'another world'? This, the yardstick by which the success of any garden may be measured, is the fundamental question. These are the conditions which lead to the encounter with 'elsewhere' with which we are concerned, and the means by which they are produced are, as we know, many and ever-changing.

'Here' and 'elsewhere' are two territories belonging to different spheres, and they represent two ways of life between which there is a constant state of tension. Curiously, words denoting the pleasure arising from this tension take no account of the satisfaction of the desire, but instead describe actions. Diversion (*divertere*) is precisely the action of turning away, departing from the norm, just as distraction (*distrahere*) is to pull in the opposite direction. These terms indicate the essential duality of two opposing directions. They are also metaphors, couched in terms of concrete experience, which connect 'elsewhere' with the idea of a known place. The feeling of strangeness depends on the knowledge we have acquired of the differences and limits between the territories. 'Here' and 'elsewhere', taken together, introduce the possibility of entertainment. If we are amusing ourselves it is not because a space is devoted to this precise function, but because there is a corresponding territory where other preoccupations dominate. It is not a question of fixed areas being assigned a particular character, but of the bond between that territory and another, between a familiar country and another world.

This hypothesis will serve to take us into the recent and somewhat confused discussion aroused by the massive creation in Europe since 1950 of a new generation of parks designed on the model of American amusement parks, particularly the archetypal Disneyland.

Europe has known these leisure and amusement parks since the 1950s. The phenomenon is most widespread in West Germany, Belgium and Holland; Great Britain, France and the southern European countries have begun to build them only in the last few years. What best characterizes their novelty is that they are vast and permanent installations, intended to accommodate the populations of entire regions, and that they are to some extent delocalized, being situated away from towns, and without any obvious connections with them. They are carefully sited according to measurable criteria of efficiency, and to formulae designed to offer the maximum attraction. From the zoo park to the amusement park via the theme park, the means vary but the objective and formulae remain almost the same. Federal Germany has some thirty of them, the most important of which are Europa Park, Holiday Park and Phantasia Land. Altogether they receive more than twenty million visitors a year, even though some of them are open only in high season. In Holland, thirteen leisure parks form a tight network spread over the whole of the country. The largest, De Efteling, receives annually more than two million visitors, and Flevohof more than a million. In Belgium, the parks at Walibi, Bellewaerde and Meli Park have considerably more than two million visitors annually. These are therefore enormous enterprises, which compel their promoters to rationalize the running of them more and more. The financial investment required to accommodate large numbers of visitors; the choice of geographical situation which will provide a large enough clientele; the nature of the attractions: none of these can be left to chance. A new generation of recreational areas is appearing which seems foreign to all our traditional ideas of entertainment. Enterprises devoted exclusively to occupying the extensive leisure time of modern society now offer structures, schedules and programmes which reflect the familiar pattern of everyday life so accurately that we seem to see all the most spectacular aspects reproduced before our eyes in a concentrated and idealized form.

However, the popular success of these new formulae for places of amusement leads us to believe that they create a real sense of another world; a world more real than might be imagined from the scornful and disdainful initial reaction provoked by the lack of imagination in the design, the cultural poverty of the attractions, and the effortless dispensing of pleasure. Moralizing journalists and affronted designers mistake their target when they deplore the artificiality of this 'world turned upside-down' to be found in amusement parks, for in this world we may find the authentic existential experience now lost to our planet, undermined by the advance of technology.

The decorations, the painted canvas, the illusion of an enchanted place in and through which the ordinary course of life is overturned and momentarily eclipsed, are not an unhappy sign of our times.

We tend to forget rather quickly that these parks, apparently new inventions, inherit a long tradition of quarters devoted to pleasure in European towns, and that entertainment, when well done, is often a

Cemetery of the Innocents, Paris, 21 February 1786. Bibliothèque Nationale, Cabinet des Estampes, Paris.

Alfresco banquet in the forest of Isle-Adam, given by the Prince de Conti in 1766. Painting by M.-B. Ollivier. Château de Versailles. (Photo Bulloz)

Design for a game with rings, with a figure of Neptune, by A. T. Brongniart. Private collection, Paris.

source of renewal of social and urban mores. We have become accustomed, on the model of the analytical methods used by the life sciences, to dissociate life as it is lived in public spaces from the shape and form of the spaces themselves. The habit of reducing important forms of human activity to convenient categories, and of considering spaces only from the point of view of the type of remarkable objects they contain, has been developed to such a point that we have completely lost sight of the right of public places to belong to the world of the mind as well as to the physical world.

By considering only the outward appearances of things we risk seeing in amusement parks only a collection of equipment, of operational plans and financial procedures, or the acrimonious inventory of their shortcomings, when the possibility for entertainment is found mainly in the relationship the amusement parks maintain with the whole system of urban space.

In European towns the medieval cemetery was the first acknowledged form of a place of public entertainment. Cemeteries have for a long time been more than places of burial. Until the eighteenth century they fulfilled the role of a free, extraterritorial zone, a meeting place and a place of freedom. In this enclosure beyond the reach of lay law, all matters spiritual and temporal could be discussed at leisure, and amorous encounters and games of all sorts could take place, under cover of the crowds attracted by such opportunities and titillated by the proximity of death.

A paradise on earth in more senses than one, cemeteries for a long time united all the characteristics we still find today in places of amusement, and in particular they possessed the duality which makes entertainment possible – that is, the existence of two territories, forming part of a system and subject to opposing rules. It is useful to note that this dual relationship which is propitious for entertainment, exists not only in space but also in time. All festivals, pre-eminently times of entertainment, have an episodic nature, and their duration is well defined. In this way they concentrate all the effectiveness of inverting the normal time in which they operate. Thus Carnival is a perfect example of a festival which overturns the normal order and instigates a new and limited form of time in the social sphere, during which roles are exchanged and new relationships and habits emerge.

A fragmentation of estates and authorities in towns allows free movement between places of amusement but is damaging to the integrity of social customs and the maintenance of civic order. The uncertainty it creates is of course uncontrollable, but it is also quite naturally the target of every attempt to rationalize urban and also political space. The strengthening of centralized power and its identification with the modern form of towns will tend steadily to eradicate the complexities of landownership and the resulting dualities, replacing it with a unified concept of municipal, and then of national territory. Good management and order are the principles which will continue, with varying success, to guide all planning policy in modern times.

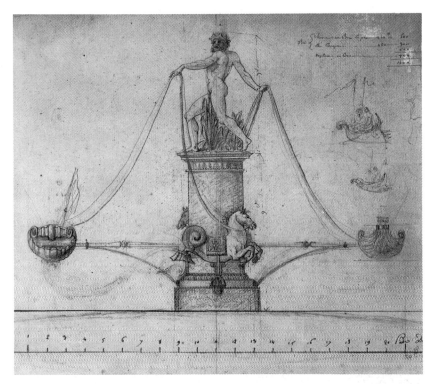

When the first fiscal cordon round Paris imposed a barrier beyond which merchandise entering the town was taxed, there immediately sprang up places outside the walls where goods could be obtained tax-free. The notion of consuming produce outside the toll house and then bringing it back into town so to speak fraudulently certainly added spice to the wines and other victuals offered by shrewd innkeepers in bars set up at the gates of the noisy, overcrowded city. For if these inns offered tax-free wine, they also offered a fleeting and precious return to the world outside the city, a perfect place of escape. Soon long tree-lined avenues would be thrust across the fields, giving concrete form to the city dwellers' country walks. The sole purpose of these avenues and their trees was to represent the town outside the town, to give form to the contradiction of urban entertainment outside the walls. They mark the confrontation of territories.

It was therefore the planted areas which gave form to new types of places of entertainment, as the land was divided up into areas combining commerce and a part of 'nature in the city', a double invitation to an imaginary journey. Taking advantage of the unlimited licence enjoyed by landowners, the public admitted to these private gardens could indulge in an unusual freedom of behaviour and opinion. The gardens of the Palais-Royal are an example of this. The original nature of these pleasure-grounds, a direct result of the speculators' spirit of enterprise, prescribed open spaces where the public could escape the constraints of city life. The essential characteristic of these gardens, and the reason for their attraction, was the difference in their juridical status. Already some of the essential characteristics of contemporary amusement parks were emerging.

A new style was also developing in these places, a style deliberately designed to draw customers, to win their attention, and to hold them in attractive surroundings. It was an enterprise requiring the allocation to specific purposes. The enclosed space was hemmed in by small lots; access was limited to a few easily controlled entrances; and variety and novelty in the attractions becomes the rule, along with an irregular plan designed to encourage people to stroll around and to facilitate the arrangement of surprises. The very specialized role of entertainment, which can no longer take place on the municipal ground that was once urban public space, is now fulfilled elsewhere, by other means and with new methods.

The second half of the eighteenth century saw a tremendous increase in the numbers of these new pleasure-gardens: Vauxhall and Ranelagh

The Tower of Aeolus. Flights through the air in the Tivoli gardens, Paris. Lithograph by C. Motte, after 1800. Musée Carnavalet, Paris.

View of the switchback in the Tivoli gardens. Lithograph by C. de Last.

in London; Tivoli, Ruggieri, Turkish gardens and switchbacks in Paris; and the famous Prater constructed in Vienna in 1767. Balls, musical entertainments, menageries, equestrian circuses, exotic plants, shady groves and fountains combined to offer escape and oblivion, duly planned and financed. The mingling of social classes and the relaxed behaviour in these pleasure-gardens encouraged the new ideals of equality and liberty.

The growing specialization of the amusement parks together with the promoters' concern to make a good profit on their investments, encouraged the development of new ideas. There was at this time in the nineteenth century an indisputable surge of creative energy, without which wonders such as the Crystal Palace in London or the English seaside piers, the cultivation of exotic plants in greenhouses, the great fairground Ferris wheels, universal exhibitions, zoos, and Tivoli in Copenhagen, among others, would have been neither conceived nor financed. Yet the impetus given by financiers, and the proliferation of specialized amusement grounds seemed to wane at the turn of the century. The only notable creation of any size was the American park at Coney Island.

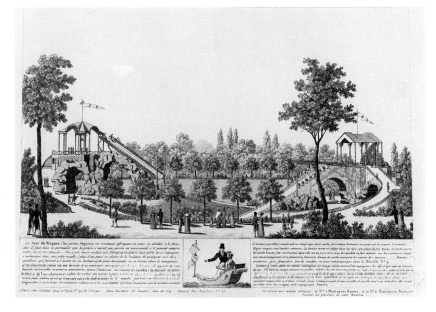

It was not until the second half of this century that theme parks, a new generation of amusement grounds, appeared. The idea was born in California in 1955 with the opening of Disneyland. This new formula was not a completely original idea; it was the outcome of a process of development and the product of close analysis of previous commercial ventures of the sort. Its special characteristic is the way it links the attraction of a landscaped park, evoking the purity of virgin nature, with the largely fictional heroes of Walt Disney films, and totally subordinating the usual fairground attractions, spectacles and services to these two dominant themes. The shrewdness of the concept, demonstrated by enormous popular success, relies on the strict submission of activities in the park to particular and specific rules of conduct, with no equivalent outside, which allow the visitor to enter into an obviously different world and there to participate in a way of life foreign to his everyday experience.

Nothing is left to chance. The success of a park, according to the numerous sociological, marketing and behavioural studies which nowadays precede any new undertaking, depends on 'choice of site, choice of theme, and organization of space'. The optimum surface area seems to be about 100 hectares (250 acres), divided into three parts – the park proper, parking space, and space reserved for extensions or new equipment. A flat treeless site is not suitable since terracing and planting would strain the budget. On the other hand ground which is very undulating or forested is too restricting for the promoter. The ideal site must be in a densely populated area within reach of large urban conglomerations. Attendance figures are calculated according to classifications established on existing lines. The theme, or themes, which characterize each park are the means, when served by adequate organization and space, of conditioning the visitor and ensuring his wholehearted belief in the proposed world of fantasy.

489

The organization of the park must be perfectly worked out in order to achieve this aim. The overall plan reflects the purpose, which is to assume complete responsibility for the visitor. For the most part the entertainment area is in the form of a flower, of which each petal is a magnetic pole linked to a particular theme. The areas which are to attract the greatest number of visitors are distributed around the park to avoid causing crowds which could upset the required peaceful atmosphere. Cultural areas are inserted between spaces for games or performances, and the distance between each zone is designed to allow the visitor to relax and prepare himself for the next new experience. It is in these intervening spaces that shops, services, restaurants and planted areas are installed. The whole park is designed like a cocoon to enfold the visitor completely.

It is designed quite deliberately to be a self-sufficient world. The illusion must be perfect. Nothing must remind the visitor of the ups and downs of everyday life. The directors of Disneyland are so aware of this that they have set up a completely original system of management, as described by a reporter on the spot. It is 'inside the Disney University that is hidden one of the keys to the extraordinary success of the business. Thousands of permanent or seasonal employees are systematically poured into the house mould. From the first half-hour, the tone is set. "Henceforward you have the honour of being part of the Disney team," they are told. "You are therefore part of the marketing of a multi-dimensional spectacle in which, whatever your job, you play a part. Never forget that you are on display." But employees who live on site must remain totally invisible. The Disney world is a dream which must never be broken. Employees arrive at work by car, but by special roads, and they park in concealed parking areas. From there they are taken by minibus to the many service entrances behind the scenes. They enter the "Magic Kingdom" by an underground passage, put on their costumes and reach their posts by underground corridors. Cleanliness is also one of the Disneyland managers' obsessions. The streets are constantly swept, hosed, and cleaned, the sanded areas round the lake are raked each morning at dawn and the lawns are mown. As soon as a bed of flowers loses its petals a team of gardeners replaces it that very night.' (Report by Marc-Ambroise Rendu, in *Le Monde*, 2 October 1987).

This first-hand description gives a clear account of the essential characteristics of the Disneyland model, which is now a reference point for all promoters of amusement parks throughout the world. The originality of the idea rests on the fact that the main emphasis is on the way it functions, on employee and visitor relations and on the visitor's experience rather than on the content of the attractions. This does not, of course, ignore the design and quality of the enterprise, but one is well aware that it is a secondary aspect in relation to the intrinsic perfection of the functioning, on which depends that escape from reality which is the aim of the parks. It is equally apparent that the difficulties experienced by some European enterprises are caused by inadequate understanding of this essential factor. With too much importance

490

The Trône Fair in Paris.

The 'Dijn' labyrinth in the Walibi Park in Belgium.

The 'Kinemax' in the Futuroscope park in Poitiers, France, built by D. Laming in 1987. (Photo De Sazo-Rapho)

accorded to 'cultural' activities or to anecdotal wonders, there has been a tendency to underestimate the role and importance of taking complete responsibility for the visitor, who must be convincingly transported 'elsewhere'.

It in the case of modern parks the feeling of being in 'another world' no longer stems from a feeling of breaking the rules stimulated by a real feeling of going 'beyond the bounds', they must now appeal to the visitor's credulity, making him believe he is shut up in an unlikely world exempt from the normal stresses of existence. This idea is applicable generally to all modern leisure centres, and is perhaps even more valid in other forms less bound by a preconceived notion of attractions. There is little fundamental difference between the formula used by holiday clubs and that of leisure parks. It is the same experience of a supranormal world that is being offered. The 'principle of reality' is systematically banished in a highly symbolic fashion. Money is replaced in one case by multicoloured beads and in the other by an entry payment after which all the amusements are free. In the same way aqua-centres, an idea that is still novel, offer a pseudo-tropical climate and ambiance, protected under glass, for an all-inclusive weekend.

Here we enter a new phase of entertainment. The extreme efficiency produced by planning and the setting of economic targets has carried entertainment further and further away from the social scene, and seems to be taking it into the universal realm of games. Within its walls a pleasure park is a sort of dematerialized world. Nothing of what happens beyond its frontiers matters. As Roger Caillois wrote: 'The domaine of the game is always a reserved, closed, protected world, a pure space,' where the rules are 'exact, arbitrary and unchallengeable'. Play makes an abstraction of the reality of territories and social situations. The isolation of specific places to provide momentary escape is not incompatible with the general move towards the separation of functions, with the planning and total urbanization which characterizes modern social space. This specialization disconnects the accomplish-ment of a function from the territory where it takes place. A subtle strategy is required: the territorial complex is given over to the profit of the introverted system of the game, a game which has spread to the whole area of social and spatial functioning, where the entertainment gamble can find a place. But the game being played in the amusement parks is in its turn a victim of the rationality of the programmes and techniques of management. It is a game with its essential parts removed: uncertainty, and the risk of failure without which 'the game would cease to amuse'. The minimization of risks, as ensured by the promoters, is a major drawback for these new places of escape. If the search for perfection is a very effective way to experience 'another world' and if it comes very close to what must be the abstract area of the game, it also carries the contradiction of setting up the principles of a perfect system, forcibly controlled. A development known in advance is incompatible with the nature of the game, which for its existence needs constant and unforeseeable change. The game must create nothing, neither wealth nor definitively organized space: it must be only the opportunity for pure expenditure, and it is thus that it generates another dimension to life.

The economic rationale and good intentions of the planners seem to weigh too heavily to be countermanded in the present state of affairs. Henceforth we must rely on the inventors' and visitors' imagination to perpetuate the entertainment. The imposed elements of the programme are only inevitable constraints and, when all is said and done, are comparable to the usual restraints imposed by instructions. It is new solutions for this apparently fixed situation which will change the present model and hasten its disappearance. Putting into perspective the different methods adopted by the entertainment world encourages the thought that invention in this area is always possible, and that it is nurtured by an unlimited capacity for renewal. There are weaknesses in the most perfect of systems, but entertainment always manages to survive.

Bibliography

Tableau de Paris en 1797 par Madame S.S (Paris 1797).
Promenade à tous les bals publics de Paris, barrières et guinguettes de cette capitale (Paris 1830).
Guide du promeneur aux barrières et dans les environs de Paris, indiquant les bons endroits pour boire et manger . . . (Paris 1855).

E. d'Auriac, *Essai historique sur les spectacles forains* (Paris 1878).
G. Capon, *Monographies parisiennes: les Tivolis* (Paris 1901).
M. Poëte, *Une vie de cité. Paris de sa naissance à nos jours* (Paris 1924).
J. Garnier, *Forains d'hier et d'aujourd'hui*

(Orléans 1968).
P. Ariès, *L'homme devant la mort* (Paris 1977).
M. A. Rendu, 'Parcs de loisirs: Disney et la vitrine magique' in *Le Moniteur des Travaux Publics* (Feb. 1986).
C. Bouclet, *Les parcs de loisirs et d'attraction à thème*, thesis, University of the Sorbonne

(Paris 1987).
M. A. Rendu, 'Disneyworld côté coulisses' in *Le Monde* (2 Oct. 1987).
'Parcs urbains et suburbains' in *Cahiers du CCI*, 4 (1988).

The Garden and the Visual Arts in the Contemporary Period: Arcadians, Post-classicists and Land Artists

Stephen Bann

This brief survey starts from a simple proposition. It is well recognized that the connection between garden design and the visual arts in the period from the Renaissance to the end of the eighteenth century was a particularly close one.[1] One only has to mention the capital effect of the landscape paintings of Poussin and Claude upon the elaboration of the English gardens of the century following them. It is equally clear that, with the onset of the nineteenth century, garden design and landscape painting began to go their separate ways. Despite the occasional exception, like Monet's garden at Giverny, the provinces of gardening and painting became progressively estranged from one another, and the apparent atrophy of the landscape genre under the impact of Modernism only hastened this process.

I have written elsewhere about the broader implications of this development.[2] Kenneth Clark's well-known study, *Landscape into Art* (first published in 1949), forms a valediction to the great tradition of landscape painting which had reached its peak in the nineteenth century. From the threshold of our contemporary period, Clark testifies to the fact that the genre is virtually dead, without any prospect of resuscitation. Whether he wishes to recognize it or not, he is acknowledging the potency of the Modernist ideology which forged a close alliance between the plastic arts and the new architecture, but relegated the study of nature to a relatively minor and retrogressive role.

My proposition is that the partial eclipse of Modernism which has been a feature of the arts in the last quarter-century, has disclosed other possibilities latent in the artistic tradition. To take one incontestable fact, the burgeoning of what is rather flatly called 'Land art' in areas like America, Britain and the Netherlands from the late 1960s onwards is a sure sign that artists can thrive on the medium of landscape without regressing to pre-modern paradigms. But I would wish to go further than this. It seems to me that by far the most interesting aspect of 'Land art' – one which indeed conflicts with its more spectacular and often meretricious side – is the fact that it facilitates a connection, once again, with the practices of landscape design and gardening.

By this I do not mean, of course, that Land artists are usually, or in some significant sense, gardeners. In the strict sense, the interfusion of garden design and the contemporary visual arts has not yet got very far, and the unique example of Ian Hamilton Finlay itself demonstrates what a subtle blend of artistic and cultural influences has been required to bring about a genuine renewal of the tradition of the 'Poet's Garden'.[3] But I would claim, nonetheless, that there now exists a continuum of mediations between art, on the one hand, and landscape and garden design on the other. For artists like Richard Long and Hamish Fulton, the representation of landscape becomes an interactive process, in which the signs of human intervention are carefully recorded, and the supremacy of the idealized 'vista' is systematically denied. For the sculptor David Nash, the fashioning of trees into art works is no longer a matter of estranging them from their native context, but of allowing them to reinvigorate and reinterpret the forest environment. In both of these examples, the crucial factor is that nature is no longer a neutral, pre-existent domain from which the artefact is set apart. Nature is herself already invested with meanings which must be investigated and conserved.

In a rather different way, the interdisciplinary group known as the New Arcadians works through traditional media like water-colour painting and photography to create a composite act of homage to the great landscape gardens of the past. This could appear merely retrospective, if it were not for the fact that their collaborative activity has a strong polemical thrust. They align themselves with the critique of contemporary cultural values which is implicit in the planning of Finlay's 'Little Sparta'. Thus the garden features which they commemorate – often in a decayed or ruinous state – become powerful emblems of a cultural and philosophical seriousness which is conspicuously lacking in the majority of contemporary works of art.

The more detailed discussion which follows is therefore not aimed at providing a summary of the history of 'Land art', or any other contemporary movement. It is intended to show that, once again, the interchange of models and concepts between artists and garden designers has become an exciting possibility. In this process, we can observe not merely the emergence of garden designs which are securely rooted in the history of the visual arts, but also the incipient mutation of display areas like the 'sculpture park' into something more akin to the great landscape gardens of the past.

Land art in Britain: Richard Long, Hamish Fulton

Despite the international resonance of the movement, it is in Britain that the clearest signs of the mutation are to be seen. In America, the compelling feature of the new landscape art is its sheer scale: the audacity of the ventures of artists like Christo and Robert Smithson has resulted in a new perception of the wildness of nature, while at the same time reanimating (in Smithson's case) the myths of an aboriginal non-Western culture lying beneath the earth's surface. In the Netherlands, on the other hand, the refined art of Jan Dibbets reflects the continual Dutch concern with horizon lines, and the accommodation of minimal landscape differences to the expanded pictorial format (in much of his recent work, the preoccupation with landscape and panoramic vision has been superseded by an interest in architecture and the vertical dimension, which is no less reminiscent of the traditions of Dutch art). In Britain, the landscape presents neither an untamed wildness, nor an almost irrecoverable mythic layer; nor is it subject to the necessarily rigid structuring found in the art of the Netherlands. It is both a garden and a palimpsest – cultivated intensively over a long period, and traversed by innumerable, ancient ways.[4]

Both Richard Long and Hamish Fulton offset their work on British landscape with adventurous forays into the remote and sublime regions of the wider world. The basic code of their approach to landscape can, however, be seen clearly in the British projects with which they began.

Long's *A Line Made by Walking* (1967) illustrates the point at which the new art of landscape started to diverge from the dematerialized sculptural idiom of Anthony Caro and the artists associated with the St Martin's School of Art. Just as Caro had negated Moore in striving to reduce the 'graspability' of sculpture, so Long outdoes Caro in the creation of an ephemeral imprint, barely differentiated from the context in which it is set, and at the same time given an enduring quality by the relentless perspectivism which the photograph frames and perpetuates. The meadow is bedecked with flowers, which cluster like tiny points of light where the image slips out of focus, and we sense that the bruised grasses on which the 'line' is registered will slowly but surely spring back into place.

Long's art thus depends on creating a kind of rhetorical antithesis between the dominance of the artist and the submission of the landscape, with the effect that we ourselves are impelled to reverse the terms, and reinstate the landscape's primacy. In *A Hundred Tors in a Hundred Hours – A Walk on Dartmoor* (1976), the walk is condensed in an immemorial feature of the moor landscape. Its methodical and disciplined parameters – a hundred tors in a hundred hours – cannot fail to have an ironic resonance if we reflect that the artist has had to submit himself to this punishing and precise schedule! The tor will not disappear, like the 'line made by walking', but its massive presence is asserted as a kind of counterweight to the artist's systematic constructions.

In Hamish Fulton's work, the antithesis is not so stark, but the landscape is still enabled to tip the balance against any too intrusive presence of the artist. Fulton is finely aware of the semiotic possibilities of an art based for the most part on photography, and allows the artifices of the print to underscore the ambiguities of his own role. *A Dew Pond on the South Downs Way* (from *Skyline Ridge*, 1975) marks the equivalence between the grain of the black and white printing and the uniform texture of downland grasses forming a broad band between water and sky: the concentric ripples on the pond itself suggest, even more than Long's ephemeral line, the evanescence of human traces on the landscape, even though the 'South Downs Way' is a path taken by countrymen over many centuries, and the 'Dew Pond' itself is likely to be a man-made receptacle with a clay bottom that has been periodically renewed.

For Fulton, line is a privileged index, whether of the artist's own manual activity (as in the line drawings of the *Horizon to Horizon* booklet of 1983), or of his peregrinations throughout the country. The print *Coast to Coast Walks* (1987) simply records, across the outline map of Great Britain and Ireland, a series of walks undertaken over the last fifteen years.[5] But the straying lines which trace his movements across the countryside can occasionally acquire a lyrical character of their own, by juxtaposition with an image that interprets the world of landscape, photographically, in terms of a linear patterning. In *Skyline Ridge*, the schematic map of a number of walks in Southern England is close by an untitled image of two birds perched in a gauntly outlined

tree. The intensity of a landscape experience is here refined in a way that suggests the broad effects of Japanese wood-block printing.

Recovery of Nature: David Nash, Chris Welsby

Both Long and Fulton hold an attitude to landscape which is, in the broad sense, ecological. Yet this concern to make the artist, in some respects, a counterweight to the tendency of modern technological man to dominate and despoil the natural world, is itself compatible with an attentive reading of the prior history of landscape art. In Cézanne's case, above all, there is a powerful precedent for the view that art is 'a harmony parallel to nature', and must not force natural phenomena into patterns that are preconceived. What Merleau-Ponty described as 'Cézanne's doubt' was in part a passionate search for a means of accommodation between the bewildering and seductive appearances of the natural world, on the one hand, and the specific limitations of the square canvas, on the other.

It is therefore particularly interesting to find a young British film-maker, Chris Welsby, devoting himself to landscape, with basic premises that recall Long and Fulton, though their technical application is necessarily quite different. Welsby has stated that it is 'the constantly shifting interface [between 'mind' and 'nature'] which lies at the core of [his] attitude towards landscape in art.'[6] If a work like Long's *A Line Made by Walking* perpetuates the artist's intervention through an ephemeral trace, Welsby uses the possibilities of cinematography to link the recording of the image with the very processes of nature which would have been bypassed in a strictly instantaneous 'vista'. He has used an anemometer to govern the speed of the film according to the speed of the wind, and he frequently makes use of the time-lapse mechanism to condense long periods of time (in one film, *Seven Days*) into an absorbing visual record. The production still from *Stream Line* shows the camera mounted in the midst of a stream, activated by remote control. Wherever possible, Welsby allows the structure of his films to be determined to some extent by the 'interface' of nature and technology, as in *Seven Days* where the camera device pointed towards the sky, when the sun was in, and towards the ground when it emerged, setting up a strong effect of counterpoint.

Chris Welsby's approach makes it possible to envisage an art of landscape where (in the words of Peter Wollen) 'observation is separated from surveillance and technology from domination': in short, a future for the genre as it 'enters a new post-painterly phase.'[7] David Nash's work, by contrast, retains the intimate contact with traditional materials that has been a feature of much Modernist sculpture in Britain. His chosen medium is wood, but it is wood encountered in a dynamic process of mutation 'from tree to wood to vessel': that is, from a living part of nature to a material which can be 'worked to retain the echo' of its earlier life.[8] No less than Welsby, Nash works for a non-masterful relationship with the natural world. As he

David Nash, Running Table *in Grizedale Forest, 1978.*

puts it: 'The objects I make are vessels for the presence of the human being, aware and surrendering to the realities of nature.'

It is in the pursuit of this ecological goal for art that David Nash creates a significant mutation in the relationship between the work and its context – a mutation which has also affected a number of other sculptors who hold similar ideas. *Running Table* (1978) is pictured beside a rough track in Grizedale Forest in Lancashire, where Nash spent a year. Like the other sculptures which have now been installed there, often as a result of similar residencies, it hardly intrudes upon the natural environment. Indeed some later work has utilized still living trees, which are trained in traditional ways to form interlocking figures. As opposed to the customary 'sculpture park', where smooth lawns and a background of mature trees are used to set off works of art as if in an outdoor gallery, Grizedale Forest points towards a type of environment in which 'sculpture' is almost a form of husbandry, continuous with the traditional crafts which are necessary to the maintenance of the woodland.

Return to the garden: New Arcadians, Ian Hamilton Finlay, Bernard Lassus

Of the examples already given, many suggest that an artist has chosen to work with a particular type of landscape: Long with the moors of Dartmoor, Fulton with the Southern Downland, Welsby with the upland streams of Wales, Nash with the forest of Grizedale on the edge of the Lake District. Yet none is specifically concerned with garden landscape, in the strict sense of the term. The interest of the New Arcadians is that they have concentrated their efforts on recording, researching and, in a sense, reviving some of the great gardens of the past. But they do so not merely because the Arcadian theme is a congenial and pleasant one. By choosing to bring out the political and cultural implications of the English gardens established in the nineteenth century, and by working as an interdisciplinary team, they are commenting sharply on the triviality and individualism of the dominant tendencies of contemporary art.

In over a decade of activity, the New Arcadians have ranged widely over different types of garden landscape. One of their most original early publications was a folio of prints, typographical presentations and historical commentary on the 'Happy Valley' of Culzean Castle, on the West coast of Scotland. More recently, their periodic journal, which is issued by subscription, has featured William Kent's unique Augustan garden of Rousham, near Oxford: the publication included 'The Way to View Rousham' (a letter of 1750 by John MacClary), articles by Patrick Eyres and Simon Pugh, and illustrations and vignettes by Howard Eaglestone, Ian Gardner and Andrew Griffiths. At present, they are turning their attention to industrial 'New Arcadias' – the model towns of New Lanark and New Harmony established by the nineteenth-century Utopian philosopher Robert Owen.

Some of their most successful work, however, has been devoted to the gardens and landscape of Yorkshire, where the majority of the

Richard Long, ring in the turf. Park at Celle, Pistoia, Tuscany.

Ian Hamilton Finlay, Virgilian olive grove in the park at Celle, Pistoia, Tuscany.

group live. The work of the Aislabie family at the great gardens of Studley Royal and Hackfall has been evoked with particular effect, partly because the fate of these two estates has been so dramatically different. Ian Gardner's beautifully restrained watercolours (themselves based on a careful study of eighteenth-century technique) celebrate the Temple of Fame at Studley Royal – a garden which is now undergoing massive restoration by its new proprietors, the National Trust. Hackfall, by contrast, is in the words of Patrick Eyres a 'Secret Garden', set apart from any habitation and now in the last stages of dilapidation. Nevertheless, Grahame Jones can record its waterfalls in his fastidious pen sketches, and John Tetley can show with his coloured drawings the desolate and overgrown situation of the Fisher's Lodge.

Perhaps the most important point of reference in contemporary gardening for the New Arcadians is the work of Ian Hamilton Finlay at Stonypath. Finlay indeed has often benefited from the collaboration of members of the group, who chose their title in acknowledgement of his publications on the Arcadian theme,[9] and have loyally supported him in the different stages of the 'Little Spartan War'.[10] Finlay's achievement as a gardener is discussed in more detail elsewhere in this book. But it is important to mention at this point the crucial importance of his example in the process which I have been describing.

The essence of Finlay's position is that our culture has evacuated all the serious political and philosophical content which great gardens like Stowe and Ermenonville undoubtedly possessed at the time of their creation. Such gardens are viewed, for the most part, as pleasant recreational spaces, and not as the symbolic middle ground between human institutions and the shifting concepts of Nature that they undoubtedly formed in the eighteenth century. And, as a consequence, present-day gardens are seen exclusively as the province of the landscape architect who (in Britain at any rate) is usually a professional without a single idea in his head. It is remarkable that Finlay has started to shift this burden of ignorance. Not only has he established the ever more influential prototype of Little Sparta, but he has also carried the message into the very citadel of the avant-garde. At the 1987 Documenta exhibition in Kassel, he exhibited the awesome *A View to the Temple*, in which one of the pre-existing temples from Kessel's palace gardens was revealed in the interstices of a sequence of inscribed guillotines.

It is rare indeed to find a professional garden architect who measures up to the richness and urgency of Finlay's vision. Yet one person who has arrived at a similar position by a very different route is the French garden designer Bernard Lassus. As a pupil of Léger, who exhibited in shows of kinetic art in the 1960s, Lassus had benefited from an artist's training when he became Professor of Architecture at the Ecole des Beaux-Arts in 1968. His course of research, which had already resulted in the foundation of the Centre de Recherche d'Ambiances in 1962, led him subsequently to document and analyse the phenomenon of suburban gardens of the *habitants-paysagistes* throughout France. In 1975, however, his detailed plan of the Jardin de l'Antérieur for the

Richard Serra, installation (stone monoliths)
in the park at Celle, Pistoia, Tuscany.

Anne and Patrick Poirier, installation of May 1987 (commemoration of the death of a titan) in the park at Celle, Pistoia, Tuscany.

French new town of L'Isle d'Abeau inaugurated a series of garden designs which derived from careful consideration of their fundamental principles: the differences between 'visual' and 'tactile' scales, the presence of myth, legend and history as a sub-stratum of the physical arrangement of the garden, and so on.[11]

Lassus' most ambitious garden scheme, in many ways, was his Jardin des Planètes of 1980, which reached the short list in the competition for the new Parc de la Villette, in the outskirts of Paris. His decision to open up a vertical dimension to the landscape, with an underground planetarium, while at the same time keeping the horizontal stretch as a gently sloping meadow land, was a bold and imaginative gesture, which did not prevail against the fashionable Post-Modern pavilions of the architect Bernard Tschumi. Lassus' most recent garden design, the Jardin des Retours, is however in the process of construction at the Corderie Royale, Rochefort. His decision to break up the lines of sight on to the eighteenth-century façade of the Corderie, to divide the intervening space adjacent to the town by means of a ramp, and to create special gardens dedicated to the botanical finds of local worthies like Bégon and La Galissonnière, testifies to the originality of his conception. This is not a revivalist eighteenth-century garden, but a contemporary creation involving highly sophisticated 'poetics of space', as well as a respect for the historical character and associations of the site.

Art in the garden: the Villa Celle at Pistoia

There exist innumerable 'sculpture parks' at the present day. But very few of them escape the fate of being (as I expressed it earlier) mere 'outdoor galleries', where the vegetation is no more than a backdrop. Of course it is possible to undermine this system from within, as Ian Hamilton Finlay did in his *Sacred Grove* at the Kröller-Müller Museum, Otterlo. In contrast to the large pieces by Moore, Dubuffet, Oldenburg and others, which simply occupy their designated spaces, the *Sacred Grove* is a reinterpretation of the very landscape, utilizing the trees themselves with discreetly attached 'column bases'.

For an entire park to be replanned in the way that Finlay proposes would be a large-scale enterprise. Nevertheless, the exceptional ambiance created over the last few years at the Villa and Parco di Celle, under the patronage of Giuliano Gori, deserves mention here as the boldest venture of its kind. It is important to note that the Parco di Celle was already a *jardin à l'anglaise*, magnificently situated behind an eighteenth-century villa. There can be no doubt that some artists have responded to the challenge of this environment more resourcefully than others, and in many cases the 'sculpture park' conception is quite reasonably followed. What marks out Celle as exceptional is the opportunity to incorporate and express a whole feature of the landscape, in the way that the monumental features of the classical garden succeeded in doing. Hence Richard Serra peoples a whole meadow with his sober monoliths of stone; Joseph Kosuth screens off an island in his Nietzschean meditation on appearance and reality; Anne and Patrick Poirier commemorate the death of a titan in their grandiloquent investment of a river-bed, comparable to the water features of the Baroque. Richard Long, by contrast, deliberately underplays his hand with a simple ring in the turf, while Ian Hamilton Finlay puts the whole 'Forest of the Avant-Garde' inhabited by the other artists behind him, and colonizes a Virgilian olive grove.

1 See, for example, John Dixon Hunt on the tradition of 'Ut pictura poesis', in *Word & Image*, Vol. 1, No. 1 (Jan. 1985).
2 See contributions by Stephen Bann in J. C. Eade (ed.), *Projecting the Landscape* (Canberra: Humanities Research Centre, 1987), pp. 1–35, 78–91.
3 *Rivista di Estetica* No. 8 (1981) pp. 160–7.

4 See Oliver Rackham, *Trees and Woods in the British Landscape* (London 1976) for a recent account of this development.
5 See Stephen Bann, 'The Truth of Mapping', in *Word & Image* (April 1988).
6 David Curtis (ed.), *Chris Welsby – Films – Photographs – Writings* (London 1980), p. 6.
7 *Ibid.*, p. 3.

8 See *Tree to Vessel – David Nash Sculpture* (Annely Juda Gallery: London 1986), unpaginated.
9 See Finlay's act of homage to Poussin's *Et in Arcadia Ego*, in *Ian Hamilton Finlay*, Arts Council catalogue (London 1977), pp. 37–47.
10 See 'Despatches from the Little Spartan War', in *New Arcadians Journal* No. 23 (Autumn 1986).
11 See 'The Landscape Approach of Bernard Lassus' (texts translated and introduced by Stephen Bann), in *Journal of Garden History*, Vol. 3, No. 2, pp. 79–107. This covers the period 1975–1980.

The Bos Park, Amsterdam, and Urban Development in Holland

Sergio Polano

Official plan for the expansion of Amsterdam (1935), showing the extent of the Amsterdam Bos Park.

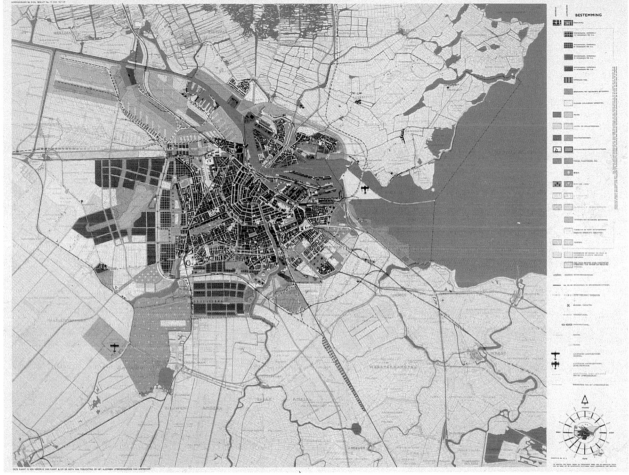

ALGEMEEN UITBREIDINGSPLAN VAN AMSTERDAM. SCHAAL 1 : 50000

Controversy over plans for the Amsterdam Park began around the turn of the nineteenth century when two particular historical events in the Low Countries coincided: one was the instrumentation of controls on urban growth, which emerged from discussions at Woningwet in 1901, and was to lead to fundamental changes in the laws on house-building and land usage. The other was a debate on improvements in the quality of life, a cause close to the hearts of those who wanted to see a change in standards of environmental health. In the last decade of the nineteenth century many similar debates had taken place in nearby Germany, and Holland was becoming increasingly eager to follow its neighbour's lead. In 1908, for example, the 'biologist' Jacob P. Thijsse, who had championed a scheme for rural recreation parks for city-dwellers in the mid-1890s, appealed in the columns of *Algemeen Handelsblad* for a properly organized system of walks and public gardens to be laid out in Amsterdam. One of his proposals – for a landscape area of parkland around Nieuwe Meer, the long, meandering stretch of water to the south of the city – anticipated both the site and the character of the future Bos Park.

In 1909 the theme of open-air recreation was raised again in a report on the parks and public gardens of Amsterdam, *De Amsterdamsche parken en plantsoenen*, edited by the Amsterdamsche Woningraad commission, which included leading figures in Dutch urban planning such as Dirk Hudig and Hendrik Petrus Berlage, as well as Thijsse himself. It was clear that the problem of urban parks, a matter which had also preoccupied those responsible for the expansion of nineteenth-century Amsterdam, was one of the principal concerns – and weaknesses – of both of the very different proposals for the area to the south of the city put forward by Berlage in 1900 and 1914–15, in other words significantly earlier and later than the Woningwet scheme.

It was not until 1921 that two events essential to the control of urban growth occurred: one was a series of changes to the Woningwet law, which meant that any plans drawn up by the city council were no longer confined simply to the laying out of a network of streets and waterways but could also specify the use of the spaces in between. At the same

time, the annexation of the neighbouring councils of Watergraafsmeer and Sloten quadrupled the size of Amsterdam, with the result that Berlage's scheme – which incorporated areas, such as the park, that had until then lain outside the city boundary – was now viable in its entirety. It also created a whole range of new planning problems.

At the congress on urban development held in Amsterdam in July 1924, the major topics under discussion included the provision of public open spaces, and among the main speakers was Fritz Schumacher, Baudirektor of the city of Hamburg. From then until 1928, the year in which the Stadsontwikkeling dei Publieke Werken was founded (this was an autonomous sub-division of the department of public works, whose principal task was the drawing up of plans devised

by the engineer L. S. P. Scheffer), numerous planning proposals for the city were presented, including various schemes for the Amsterdam Park. The Schemaplan Groot Amsterdam, a plan for Greater Amsterdam drawn up in stages between 1924 and 1926 by A. W. Bos, Director of Public Works, incorporated, in accordance with the new 'green policy', the creation of parks in three areas (as opposed to the 'garden quarters' proposed by his opponents, among whom was the powerful director of the Woningdienst, Arie Keppler); these would extend in a belt around the city, running from south-east to south-west. The plan was derived from the design for the great city park proposed by Berlage but never carried out, and in Bos's hands it became a vital element of the entire scheme for the development of the city. In the debate

that followed the presentation of the Schemaplan it became clear that it solved various problems relating to the expansion programme but also that it lacked any very specific statement of scientific intent. Dirk Hudig, Director of the Dutch Institute of Urban Housing, demanded from the Stedebouw that a wider and more comprehensive view of the problem should be adopted than that implicit in the Schemaplan's intention to 'create beautiful squares' and to 'decide on the sites most suitable for the erection of major buildings'.

A number of alternative proposals, such as that put forward by Keppler and Witteveen, were presented in the course of these discussions, indicating the liveliness of the controversy that surrounded Bos's plan and the urgency of finding an acceptable solution. In the end the Sche-

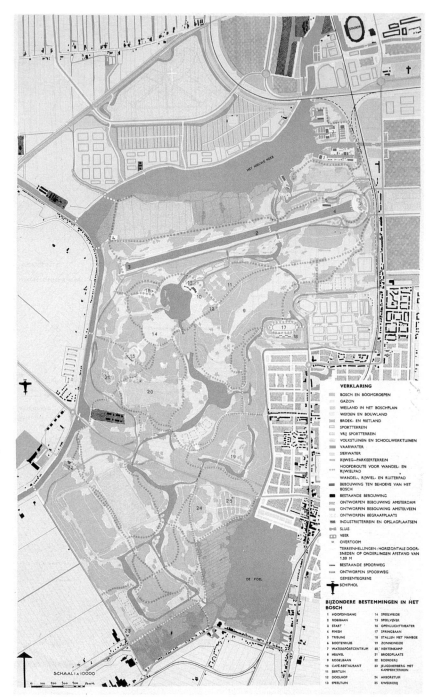

maplan Groot Amsterdam was rejected by the council, but it did provide the launchpad for a series of studies on which the scheme finally adopted in 1935 was based, and it also brought about the reorganization of the city council planning departments. Bos's design for a public park, on the other hand, found instant approval, partly by virtue of the fact that it covered a considerable area, and the spaces available for recreation in the Amsterdam of the mid-Twenties were decidedly limited. In this initial scheme, known as the Boschplan, an area immediately south of the Nieuwe Meer was designated for the Amsterdam Park, and, though Bos himself had resigned as Director of Public Works in 1926, his proposal became the foundation on which the final plan was based.

A series of legal and administrative procedures took place between the end of 1925 and the middle of 1927, and it was not until 28 November 1928 that the Amsterdam city council eventually approved the plans for the park, which it was agreed should extend from the Amstelveenschenweg to the Haarlemmeerpolder ringroad and the Nieuwe Meer, and appointed a commission to oversee its creation. The 'Boschcommissie', established at the end of January 1929, worked long and hard to produce a detailed study of all aspects of the scheme, setting up sub-committees responsible for flora and fauna, sport and recreation and technical operations. In May 1931 the commission presented the results of two and a half years' work in a detailed document entitled *Rapport van de Commissie voor het Boschplan*. Around the same time, the Woningwet law introduced certain changes which facilitated the expropriation of the 895 hectares (2211 acres) designated for the park. The Boschplan was ratified in its entirety in 1935, and it constituted the first officially accepted initiative in the programme for the expansion of the city, the Algemeene Uitbreidingsplan Amsterdam. Published as the *Toelichting Boschplan* in 1937, it represented in certain respects the role of Amsterdam itself within its surrounding conurbation.

Work on the park had in fact already begun in 1934 with the drainage of the marshland, a complex operation organized by a highly skilled team including not only engineers and landscape archi-

tects but also geologists, biologists, botanists and sociologists employed by the Boschcommissie. Their first task was to lay about 300 kilometres (186 miles) of underground pipes, since the normal method of land drainage – by means of a network of canals – was clearly unacceptable in the context of the park. After about a decade, in the course of which these pipes steadily drained off all surplus water from the ground, trees were planted, and their root systems gradually helped to absorb the remaining moisture and to bind together the soil. This system of drainage permitted great freedom in the landscaping of the whole area, making it possible to plant not simply an area of wooded parkland but a stretch of

forest of European significance. More than 300 hectares (740 acres), almost a third of the entire park, were planted with about a hundred different species of trees, including oaks, limes, beeches, birches, ashes, maples, poplars, willows and alders, the latter to form a windbreak. A vast nursery was laid out to provide new specimens for the park itself and to supply other city parks and gardens, and a botanical garden to the south was filled with a wide range of exotic plants. To the north of the wooded area was a sports complex covering a total of 36 hectares (89 acres), two-thirds of which was occupied by a football pitch, and on the banks of the Nieuwe Meer was a small marina with moorings for pleasure boats. The

lake itself, which was more than 2 kilometres (1.2 miles) long and 65 metres (210 feet) wide, had facilities for a variety of water sports, including rowing, sailing and cruising. It formed the lateral axis of the park and was one of the first features to be completed; it was opened in 1937. The only building in this area was a covered grandstand with seats for 2400 people; set at a slight angle to the lake, it allowed the audience to watch any one of a number of sporting activities going on around them. To the north-east were covered and open-air horse-racing tracks; a stadium; and football, hockey and cricket pitches.

Forest and open land combined with areas devoted to recreation and sport to create an entirely natural-looking landscape of remarkable variety, particularly in the central section of the park. To the east was a small artificial hill crowned with a restaurant with panoramic views, to the south a deer park, to the west a 'natural' theatre created by skilful planting, to the north a small lake with an island bird sanctuary, and right at the heart of the park a great open space, almost circular and about 300 metres (980 feet) across, which formed the gravitational point of a network of paths, avenues and tracks linking the various features around the perimeter to the central axis. This network was made up of over 150 kilometres (90 miles) of walks, 50 kilometres (30 miles) of bicycle tracks (cycling being a traditional means of transport as well as a popular sport in the Low Countries), 16 kilometres (10 miles) of avenues and paths for horse riding and only 13 kilometres (8 miles) of roads for motor traffic. Apart from the axial route crossing the park and linking it with Schiphol airport, in the newly expanded southern section of the city, cars and other motor vehicles were in fact limited to the outskirts of the park, to the banks of the Nieuwe Meer to the north, and to the area around the sports complex to the east.

The evident attention to detail in the planning of the park demonstrates the skill of its designers not only in creating a picturesque landscape in an urban context but in adapting it so ingeniously to the sporting and recreational needs of the people. Extensive studies had already been carried out in Germany to establish precisely what sort of outdoor facilities

Poster of the exhibition organized for the presentation of the Amsterdam Boschplan, 1937.

Maquette of the Boschplan made for the presentation exhibition, Amsterdam 1937.

Aerial view of the Bos Park, 1950s.

were required by the people, and how best to provide them, and the results of these studies were borrowed by the Amsterdam planners and modified to suit the milder nature of the Dutch national character. As a publicity slogan proclaimed, 'the free enjoyment of nature' had become a reality: the park made it possible to enjoy many of the benefits of a natural environment in the heart of an urban development, where nature owed almost everything to man. For the people of Amsterdam it was a remarkable and infinitely valuable achievement.

Bibliography

Historical literature on the subject of the Amsterdam Park is extremely scarce, although there is a good deal of official documentation, above all the *Rapport van de Commissie voor het Boschplan* (Amsterdam 1931) and the *Toelichting Boschplan* (Amsterdam 1937). Two essays by Gerrie Andela, art historian and lecturer at the Landbouw Hogeschool of Wageningen, are however significant: 'Ontspanning in het groen' and 'Het Boschplan', which appeared as part of a collection of works published to mark the fiftieth anniversary of the Amsterdam city planning development, *1935–1985 Algemeene Uitbreidingsplan Amsterdam 50 jaar* (Amsterdam 1985), pp. 173–87, complete with references to official documentation, to which this article owes much.

Among the few titles in languages other than Dutch are 'The Amsterdam Boschplan', published in the *Journal of the Royal Institute of British Architects*, Vol. 45, Series III (23 May 1938 – also in extract), and the invaluable if now dated contribution by Antonio Cederna, 'Attrezzature verdi di Amsterdam' in *Casabella continuità*, no. 277 (July 1963) pp. 34–49.

*City of Brooklyn. Plan of part of the
parkway planned for the eastern section of
the city, 1868. (Parks Photo Archive)*

The tumultuous years of the Great Depression – from the stock market crash late in 1929 until America's entry into World War II – created circumstances that actually contributed to a period of remarkable achievement in the development of recreational resources. The collapse of the nation's economy and attendant social upheaval precipitated an unprecedented scale of intervention by the federal government, especially through programmes aimed at creating jobs for legions of unemployed workers. Since the administration of Franklin Delano Roosevelt was also committed to the cause of conservation of natural and cultural resources, agencies such as the Works Progress Administration (WPA), Civilian Conservation Corps (CCC), and Soil Conservation Service (SCS) were established to provide a labour force for a wide range of public works projects, including many under the supervision of the National Park Service or the U.S. Forest Service, and often in cooperation with state, county, and municipal governments. During the New Deal era, federal spending for recreation constituted the third largest amount among all categories of construction spending. These initiatives at national level fostered growing popular acceptance of a new philosophy of recreation, one that saw the provision of well-designed recreational landscapes and facilities as an essential, rather than an optional, responsibility of good government.

Additional pressures for more and better recreational facilities were occasioned by shifting demographic patterns, dramatic increase in automobile ownership, and steady decrease in the number of hours in the average working week. Whereas almost sixty-five percent of the U.S. population had lived in rural areas in 1890, by 1930 well over half was urban and suburban. This new population in cities and towns, with more leisure time at its disposal, demanded more opportunities for both active and passive recreation – for parks, campgrounds, and nature trails as well as playgrounds, athletic facilities, and community arts and crafts programmes. The mobility afforded by the automobile and expanding public transport networks brought many previously inaccessible rural and wilderness areas within reasonable range for outings or vacations, while the late-nineteenth-century concept of the 'parkway' – a road designed to provide recreational opportunities and scenic vistas along its corridor – achieved new importance in regional as well as metropolitan planning. The Blue Ridge Parkway, traversing almost five hundred miles (eight hundred kilometres) of spectacular mountain terrain between Shenandoah National Park in Virginia and the Great Smoky Mountains National Park in Tennessee, epitomizes the vision of its era: many agencies cooperated in its planning and construction, as did the landscape architects, engineers, and other professionals hired to do the work; and the design of the road and other man-made features was sensitive to both the existing natural environment and historic human settlements.

Indeed, the ideal of preserving nature and at the same time celebrating the hardy pioneer traditions of America contributed to the development of a distinctive style identified with the burgeoning state park movement of this period. The layout of the parks and the design of recreational and service structures reflected an aesthetic of rustic simplicity, good craftsmanship, and naturalism; rough-cut stone and hewn timbers were used to complement picturesque woods and lakes, many of which were painstakingly brought into being on sites that initially lacked significant natural features. Four hundred thousand acres (162,000 ha) of submarginal land were transformed into Recreation Demonstration Areas (RDA's) under a programme initiated by the Resettlement Administration, the aim of which was to create campgrounds and recreational complexes close enough to major population centres to serve the special needs of the urban poor.

The character of many metropolitan recreational systems changed dramatically during this period as well, under the impetus of federal funding and advisory support. The example of the New York metropolitan area furnished a model that cities in all regions of the country strove to emulate; 166 million dollars were spent on parks and parkways in just three years during the tenure of Robert Moses as Chairman of the State Council of Parks, of the Long Island State Park Commission, and finally in the salaried office of Commissioner of Parks for New York City. Aquatic facilities were key elements in Moses's bold planning. Jones Beach, Rockaway Beach, and Orchard Beach represented state-of-the-art recreational complexes linked to the city by handsome parkways; in addition, ten large swimming pool complexes were developed within the city – the largest, Astoria Pool in Queens, accommodating six thousand people.

From the far-reaching impact of the CCC's 1937 survey of the nation's seacoasts that first awakened popular support for the cause of bringing more coastal land within the public domain, to the more modest scale of roadside picnic shelters or neighbourhood tot lots, the decade of the Thirties left a legacy of enlightened public planning for the recreational needs of Americans of every region and of every class that has not since been equalled.

PROPOSED PLAN.

Bibliography

George D. Butler, *Introduction to Community Recreation* (New York 1940).
Galen Cranz, *The Politics of Park Design* (Cambridge, Mass. 1982).
Phoebe Cutler, *The Public Landscape of the New Deal* (New Haven 1985).
Norman Newton, *Design on the Land: The*

Map indicating the recreational areas of
Linville Falls along the Blue Ridge Parkway
in Virginia, 1930. National Park Service,
National Archives, Washington DC.

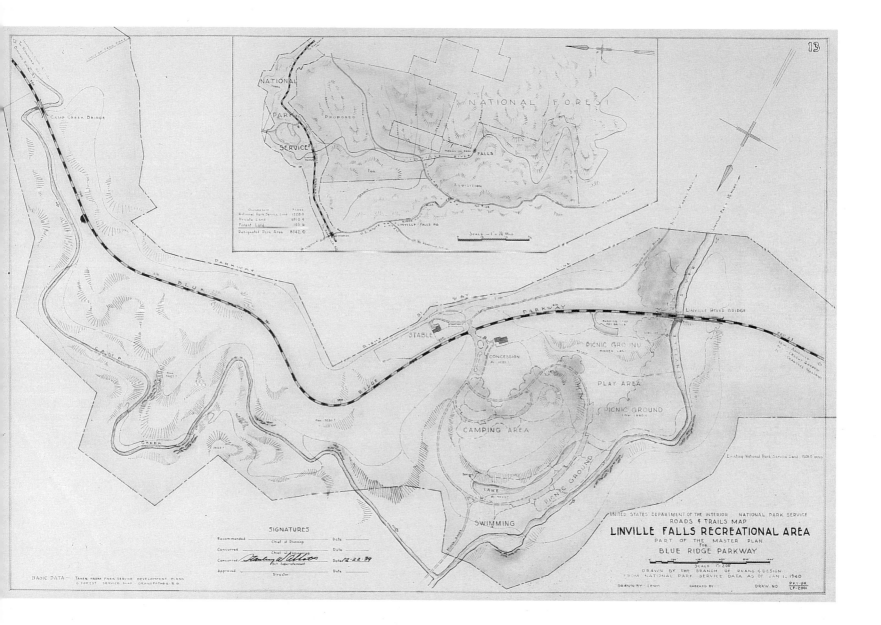

Development of Landscape Architecture (Cambridge, Mass. 1971).

Jesse F. Steiner, 'Challenge of the New Leisure' in *New York Times Magazine* (24 Sept. 1933).

Freeman Tilden, *The State Parks: Their Meaning in American Life* (New York 1962).

U.S. Dept, of the Interior, National Park Service. *The CCC and the National Park Service, 1933–42: An Administrative History,* by John C. Craige (Washington DC 1985).

Idem. Park and Recreation Structures, ed. Albert H. Good. 3 vols. (Washington DC 1938).

Idem. A Study of the Park and Recreation Problem of the U.S. (Washington DC 1941).

Idem. Yearbook: Park and Recreation Progress. 4 vols. (Washington DC 1937–41).

Greenbelt, Maryland

Christian Zapatka

Greenbelt, Maryland: design model, 1936(?).
US Department of Agriculture, Farm
Security Administration.

The town of Greenbelt, Maryland, was one of the manifestations of Franklin Roosevelt's 'New Deal' programme for fighting the Great Depression. Produced through the efforts of the Resettlement Administration, Greenbelt was built 'to employ the unemployed, to demonstrate the soundness of town planning and to provide low-rent housing'.[1]

When Roosevelt appointed Rexford Tugwell, who had previously taught economics at Columbia University, to direct the Resettlement Administration, he was able to realize one of his favourite ideas, the building of new towns on the model of the recent English garden cities. Tugwell shared the President's belief that the country should make use of its natural resources, and he was eager to find ways of resettling the countryside in order to alleviate the congestion of the cities.[2]

The announcement made, however, by the Resettlement Administration in 1935 of its plans for three new government-owned towns was met by the public with great scepticism. It appeared to many that the administration might be interfering with the progress of private development. Tugwell was immediately labelled a radical and the Resettlement Administration did not receive congressional sanction for its plan. It was popularly believed that 'putting Tugwell in charge of the resettlement administration was like putting "Typhoid Mary" in charge of the public health service'.[3]

Despite strong public sentiment against the idea, three new towns were eventually built outside cities that badly needed new housing. The towns were Green Hills, Ohio; Greendale, Wisconsin; and Greenbelt, Maryland. A report in *The Baltimore Sun* on the progress of Greenbelt helped salvage Tugwell's reputation:

The village, in spite of its associations with the idea of low incomes, . . . will closely approach deluxe standards. . . . If as they anticipate, the demonstration of what can be done in the low-cost housing field, of what can be done in the way of town planning, have a nation-wide influence on private and public enterprise, scepticism will be laid, criticism will be hushed and Dr Tugwell, the dreamer, will become Dr Tugwell, the prophet.[4]

The building of Greenbelt began in 1936 when the Resettlement Administration bought land twelve miles outside Washington, in Berwyn, Maryland.[5] Iso-lated from major arterial highways, the site, a slightly elevated, crescent-shaped ridge, was insulated from the encroachment of private development by a broad band of woods – the 'greenbelt'.

The initial town plan, in the form of a grid, was rejected when the architects and planners decided that they could simply segment the crescent-shaped ridge into 'super-blocks' (blocks five to six times the size of an average city block) that followed the contour and size of the land.[6] This way they only needed to construct six miles of road instead of sixty (nine km instead of ninety).

The accepted plan had one main road following the inner curve of the crescent, with residential super-blocks on the outer side and a village green in the hollow of the crescent. Pedestrians did not have to cross the main road since there was a set of underpasses between the superblocks and the green. The super-blocks were, in turn, segmented by garden paths. The residential units (over one hundred per super-block) were placed on the edges wherever possible so as to leave as much open parkland as possible. The village green encompassed a commercial centre, recreational facilities, civic building, and a school/community centre, all within walking distance of each other.

The architecture of Greenbelt was disarmingly simple. In 1941, O. Kline Fulmer, resident architect and assistant community manager of Greenbelt, commented that if the style of the buildings had to be labelled it would be 'functional' and not 'modernistic' or 'continental'. The architects drew up ten residential plans, through discussion among themselves, since the results of surveys were being returned too slowly. They generally provided one large space rather than attempting to divide restricted space into tiny rooms and narrow corridors, a solution that allowed breezes to travel through from front to back in the hot Maryland summer months. The service sides (including kitchen door, tool shed and dustbin area) were reached by a small court that separated the house from the street, while the living areas faced inwards on to the parks. The façades were uniformly painted white over cinder-block or brick. The Farm Security Administration, which was responsible for running the town, provided inexpensive, sturdy furniture on credit.[7]

The commercial centre of Greenbelt consisted of a central square flanked by low-lying colonnaded buildings. The square, containing grass plots, small trees and tables and benches, was dominated at one end by a monumental, roughly-cut stone statue of a mother and child.

The elementary school/community centre displayed a series of sandstone bas-reliefs at the base of its façade representing the tenets of the preamble to the constitution: 'Provide for the Common Defense, Promote the General Welfare, Insure Domestic Tranquillity, Establish Justice, to Form a More Perfect Union.' Carved in smooth, broad surfaces, the bas-reliefs depicted bulky figures engaged in acts of goodwill and labour celebrating the New Deal ethic. This building was the hub of the town's cooperative society in 1937. The building was used at night for a great number of clubs and organizations, each assigned a classroom, while the auditorium was usually filled with a meeting or a church service.

Commerce in Greenbelt was established as a cooperative. Initiated and

operated at first by the Consumer Distribution Corporation of New York (a non-profit-making organization founded by Edward Filene of Boston), the cooperative permitted only one shop of each kind in order to eliminate competition. All the residents, in effect, became shareholders of a corporation known as 'Greenbelt Consumer Services, Inc.' Eventually, a 'Cooperative Organizing Committee', formed by the citizens, took over the responsibilities of the corporation.[8]

There was also a cooperative health plan and clinic, and a swimming pool, both open to the county (Prince George's) at large. The free town newspaper was called *The Cooperator*. Government in the town was in the form of a council-manager.[9]

If there was a problem in Greenbelt, it was the lack of an indigenous industry. While the spirit of cooperation was strong, the town could never be completely autonomous if it had to derive its economic sustainment from a larger city outside the bounds of its protective greenbelt. In 1947, this predicament was made clear in *The Magazine of Art*:

Located beyond reasonable commuting distance from its central city, the source of most employment, the community has never been permitted to develop that cornerstone of true garden cities – local industries within walking distance of homes. Such industries were originally planned, but selfish interests prevented their location in Greenbelt. The community remains a 'dormitory town'.[10]

The Resettlement Administration did not, in fact, have enough money to initiate industry in any of its new towns, and in Greenbelt the soil was no longer arable.

If lack of an industry made Greenbelt seem like a commuter town, the decision made by the Federal Government to build one thousand units of defence housing there in 1941 confirmed this impression. Apart from increasing the mass daily commuting to Washington, the arrival of the defence workers congested the town's facilities to a point where enthusiasm and activity gave way to frustration and apathy among the original settlers. The commercial cooperative was preserved but the community suffered a physical and spiritual decline.

In 1952, after some debate over the possibility of liquidating the town, the Veterans' Corporation bought Greenbelt from the government. With this transaction, Greenbelt was launched into the world of private development. The woods surrounding the town were slowly thinned out as private speculators began to acquire the land from the Veterans' Corporation. The completion of the Capital Beltway in 1964 led the way for subdivisions and shopping malls to continue eroding the formerly dense 'greenbelt'.

In 1967, Albert Mayer, Director of the National Housing Conference, made an evaluation of Greenbelt in the *Journal of Housing*. The report was favourable but acknowledged the obvious drawback of the lack of industry. He concluded, in light of the successful English garden cities, that industry, however light, is a necessary stimulant to a new town for achieving self-sufficiency.

If Greenbelt never had the chance to exist independently as a town due to this inadequacy, it is remarkable nonetheless, that, in spite of the bulldozer effect of private development and highway building over the past forty years, the town has managed to retain its core of 'super-

Greenbelt, Maryland: present-day view of a pathway in a residential area.

Greenbelt, Maryland: Insure Domestic Tranquillity. *Bas relief.*

blocks', village green and pedestrian paths. There have been some minor changes to outward appearances: the once white walls of the commercial centre now have a brick veneer; the neon 'Greenbelt' theatre sign has been replaced with plastic letters that spell 'Utopia Theatre'; underpasses are covered with graffiti; some residential buildings have acquired solar panel roofs.

But overall, Greenbelt, as a community, still recommends itself as a successful example of the work of Franklin Roosevelt's New Deal Administration, and more specifically, Rexford Tugwell's Resettlement Administration, for it is still appropriate to call this place a town . . .

[1] The Works Progress Administration provided the labour for the building of Greenbelt and the low-cost housing was intended primarily for government workers who could not afford District rents. Leslie Gene Hunter, 'Greenbelt, MD: A City on a Hill', in *Maryland Historical Magazine*, No. 63 (June 1968) p. 106.

[2] As an undergraduate at the University of Pennsylvania, Tugwell had written in a poem that he would 'Roll up his sleeves, bend the forces untameable, harness the powers irresistible and make America over.' (*Ibid.*, p. 110.)

[3] *Ibid.*, p. 110.

[4] Clark S. Hobbs, 'Resettlement Administration Presents: Greenbelt,' in *The Baltimore Sun* (26 August 1936).

[5] This land was largely owned by individuals and families, some of the deeds going back to original grants from the King of England with never a change in title. O. Kline Fulmer, *Greenbelt*, American Council on Public Affairs (Washington, DC 1941) p. 16.

[6] *Ibid.*, p. 7.

[7] Mary Lou Williamson, *Greenbelt, History of a New Town 1937–1987* (Virginia 1987) p. 72.

[8] *Ibid.*, p. 77.

[9] *Ibid.*, p. 74.

[10] Frederick Guthrim, 'Greenbelt Revisited', in *Magazine of Art* (January 1947) p. 3.

INSURE DOMESTIC TRANQUILLITY

The Gardens of Geoffrey Jellicoe at Sutton Place, Surrey

George Plumptre

Sutton Place is an outstanding early-Tudor house built during the 1520s by Sir Richard Weston, an important courtier in the reign of Henry VIII. As well as being an early example of an unfortified manor-house with Renaissance influence, Sutton Place has remained remarkably unaltered since it was originally built.

Sutton Place remained in the ownership of the Weston family and their descendants until the end of the nineteenth century. Since then it has been owned by a series of wealthy magnates: the newspaper baron Lord Northcliffe, whose wife was responsible for extensive alterations in the garden; the Duke of Sutherland; J. Paul Getty and finally Stanley J. Seegar – like Mr Getty an American whose fortune was founded in oil.

Stanley Seegar purchased Sutton Place in 1980. The various rooms of the house were used to display his collection of modern art. At the time Sutton Place was surrounded by parkland and the main garden features were the remains of a formal lime avenue leading up to the north entrance front of the house, the complementary avenue of clipped yew domes leading from the south front of the house to where the ground drops away to the valley of the River Wey, and the old walled kitchen gardens to the west of the house.

Seegar had ambitious ideas about developing the gardens in a manner which would be sympathetic to the house's long history and yet be contemporary rather than just restoration of an old style. He invited Sir Geoffrey Jellicoe to give his thoughts on a possible project and it was on the basis of Jellicoe's preliminary drawings that he was commissioned to undertake the redesigning of the gardens.

For Jellicoe it was the most exciting private commission of his career, not only because of the scale on which Stanley Seegar envisaged the project but also because of the affinity between Seegar's aspirations and Jellicoe's own ideas which he had been evolving over many years. At Sutton Place he was given the opportunity to put these ideas into practice.

Drawing upon the example of the gardens of the Italian Renaissance and in particular the inspiration of the Villa Gamberaia at Settignano, Jellicoe evolved a design which was classical in its firm stress upon retaining historical continuity at Sutton Place, building upon the past to project the house and its gardens into the future. In the true Italian tradition Jellicoe envisaged something which would be both mentally and physically stimulating. As well as being beautiful to look at, the gardens are full of important symbolism and the progression from one area to another represents an allegory on human existence, from creation, through life to final aspiration.

Creation is represented in the twelve-acre (five-hectare) lake which was dug to the north of the house. Life itself is represented in the gardens around the house and eventually one comes to the point of aspiration, the wall of white Carrara marble sculpted by Ben Nicholson. Formal in shape, abstract in its austere carving, the wall is the climax of the gardens, representing the close relationship between the landscape, the human mind and modern art.

While all the important existing garden features were retained, many new ones were added, especially to the east of the house where Jellicoe planned a journey through the gardens to begin. To balance the existing walled gardens to the west of the house two new walled gardens were created on the east side, the walls built of specially fired bricks. Closest to the house is the Paradise Garden and beyond the Moss or Secret Garden. From the house the Paradise Garden is approached across a formal rectangular lily pool or moat, with modern sculptures at either end and balconies overlooking the water. The path leads from the house to a series of stepping-stones across the pool which represent the necessary hazards incurred when approaching paradise.

In the Paradise Garden paths wind between conversation bowers each with its own central bubbling fountain. The perpetual sound of water is added to by spouting stone masks set into the surrounding walls. The encircling metal frames of the bowers are hung with climbing roses, clematis and honeysuckle and along both sides of the garden straight paths lead beneath metalwork arches hung with laburnum and honeysuckle. The planting in the Paradise Garden, as in the rest of the gardens at Sutton Place, was devised by Jellicoe's wife, Susan.

Through the thick yew hedge on the far side of the Paradise Garden from the house is the Moss Garden, secluded and shaded by the canopy of a great plane tree. Around the base of the tree is a circle of moss. On one side, grille windows set in the brick wall provide glimpses of the countryside beyond – a reminder that

fantasy is never completely detached from reality.

At the south-east corner of the Moss Garden is a new octagonal pavilion, built in patterned brickwork sympathetic to that of the house and making a pair with an old gazebo in the same style in the west walled garden. A curving flight of steps down out of the pavilion leads to the South Walk, the long terrace with a paved path which stretches for 350 yards (380 metres) along the wall of the Moss and Paradise Gardens, across the south front of the house and beyond. The axial strength of the South Walk provides important continuity to the varied parts of the gardens and heightens the sense of progress which Jellicoe wished to evoke.

Both close to the octagonal pavilion and further along, beyond the house, the path is covered in by pergolas of pleached limes. As one approaches the house the path is flanked by a deep herbaceous border beneath the south-facing wall of the Paradise Garden, filled with plants that recall the age of Gertrude Jekyll who advised Lady Northcliffe in her development of the garden at the beginning of the century. As the border ends the cross-axis of yew domes comes into view, striding away across a large expanse of open lawn. Sadly one of the major features of Jellicoe's original design, a grand cascade of water down the yew avenue leading to a fountain and grotto, has never been carried out. The avenue leads to a curving stone seat and the path down the wooded slope above the River Wey.

Where the façade of the house extends to form a small enclosure is the Impressionist Garden, a warm intimate corner sheltered on three sides by brick walls and planted with brightly coloured summer flowers such as poppies, penstemons, lilies and iris. The medley of colours provides fleeting, momentary pleasure before one passes on along the terrace to the Surrealist Garden, inspired by the artist Magritte. Between the path and the brick wall of the old kitchen garden to the east of the house is a line of five giant Roman vases. Although the vases are in an orderly line they do not appear in order of size and with the rest of the Surrealist Garden, the small window in the far boundary wall, flanked by columnar cypress trees and giving a glimpse of a magnolia beyond, they promote a confused, surrealist idea of scale.

517

Gardens of Sutton Place: the wall by Ben Nicholson and the Surrealist Garden.

A doorway leads from the South Walk into the east walled garden, in the first part of which is the swimming-pool garden. Here the balance between planting and modern design which is integral throughout the gardens is clearly evident. The paths around the pool are covered by pergolas of vines such as would have been familiar to Sir Richard Weston. Immediately around the pool beds of white 'Iceberg' roses mix with domes of santolina and other silver-foliage plants. The pool itself has been transformed into a humorous picture suggested to Jellicoe by the work of the artist Miró. A series of fixed stepping stones leads out to a raft which the unsuspecting visitor also expects to be fixed, but which is actually floating and only secured by a chain, allowing it to tilt alarmingly. Beyond, the main area of the east walled garden is taken up with the kitchen garden, re-planted in traditional style with squares of

vegetables divided by rows of espalier fruit trees.

A second doorway in the boundary wall leads back out into the Surrealist Garden on the far side of which a dark, leafy tunnel beckons and leads to the garden's finale, the Nicholson Wall. The hidden path opens out at an area of lawn enclosed by yew hedges with a central formal lily pool whose water reflects the awe-inspiring picture of Nicholson's wall. Raised off the ground, the wall appears to be suspended in space, its meaning uncertain as it was to Nicholson himself. When he remarked, 'It is interesting that had the smaller circle been two inches higher the design would have been without meaning', and was asked what he meant by meaning, he replied, 'How should I know?'

The measure of Jellicoe's achievement at Sutton Place is that he succeeded in creating something original and contemporary which also perpetuates the historical continuity of the place, creating harmony between a classical tradition and modern art. On this basis Sutton Place may prove to be the most significant garden to have been made in England during the second half of the twentieth century.

It was fortunate that Jellicoe was able to work at the remarkable speed which he did, for by 1986 Stanley Seegar had decided to sell Sutton Place. The major parts of Jellicoe's original plans which never materialized were the great water cascade; a huge bronze sculpture by Henry Moore, *Divided Oval*, (of which Seegar owns the white marble original), planned to overlook the lake; and the Garden Music Room, an outdoor concert theatre. The amount which was achieved in the space of a few years was greatly assisted by modern machinery and technology, and certainly Jellicoe achieved his ambition of creating a complete garden scheme on a grand scale.

Bibliography

J. C. Shepherd and G. A. Jellicoe, *Italian Gardens of the Renaissance* (New York 1966; 1st edn 1925).
G. A. and S. Jellicoe, *Modern Private Gardens* (New York 1968).
G. A. and S. Jellicoe, *Water. The Use of Water in Landscape Architecture* (London 1971).
G. A. and S. Jellicoe, *The Landscape of Man* (revised and enlarged edn London 1987; 1st edn 1975).

The Pictorial Technique of 'Ecological Painting': The Gardens of Roberto Burle Marx

Fernando Aliata

General plan of the Parque del Este in Caracas, Venezuela, designed by Roberto Burle Marx, 1957.

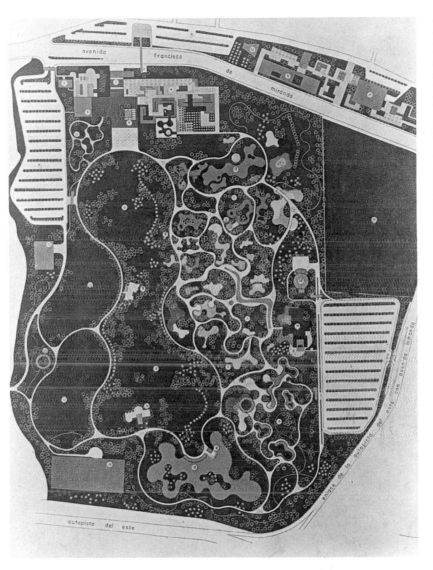

The clearly stated aim of the Brazilian avant-garde to incorporate local flora and fauna into modern planning is widely documented in the early Modernist houses of Gregori Warchavchik and in the revolutionary project by Flávio de Carvalho for the Government Palace in São Paulo. The garden of the house in Rua Itapolis (1930) and the tropical terraces along the main façade of the Government Palace (1927) are early examples of the desire to join the specifically local aspects of flora and fauna to the fundamental tenets of Brazilian national art.

These aims were not divorced from the important association of the local avant-garde with German Expressionism, both of which sought, in the first decades of this century, to expand the sources of western culture to include the primitive. In this sense Brazil was a fathomless store of resources for an art which sought to link the primitive to the modern without the stifling mediation of European traditions. This process led, in Brazil, to an individual pattern of the search for, break-up and re-assertion of tradition within a context of renewal which was distinct from similar developments in the rest of Latin America.

From this perspective, the aims of regional art lay in adopting the most noticeable peculiarities of its 'national condition'. Paradoxically it was the centralist view which was in large measure to serve as a guide to what was specific to each region. It was thus that the manifestations of the avant-garde endeavoured to combine the primitive art of the native Indians of Brazil, the complex contributions of African culture, the cosmopolitan forms and inventions of the Baroque, and the exuberance of tropical vegetation into one peaceful whole.

It was during this intensely cultural period, during the 1920s, that Burle Marx's art matured. A pupil of Leo Putz and Cândido Portinari, he spent 1928 in Germany, where he studied painting and discovered, not accidentally, the exoticism of Brazilian flora in the greenhouses of the Dahlem Botanic Gardens in Berlin. Together with his thorough knowledge of the ecological gardens of Adolf Engler and the theories being developed in Germany for evoking the national landscape in the planning of new parks, the formation of Burle Marx's complex vision was complete.

Burle Marx's discovery by Lúcio Costa in 1932, and his invitation to design a garden in a project with Warchavchik, was thus not accidental. It is after Costa's invitation, later repeated for the series of experimental works at Recife, that Burle Marx began to play a part in the avant-garde in exploring the possibilities of bringing together natural surroundings as a basis for the development of Brazilian Modernism.

The wish for 'total art' revealed in the work of the partnership of Portinari, Costa and their group on the Ministry of Education in Rio de Janeiro serves further to illustrate this tendency in Burle Marx, and is the product of an artist seeking to use in plastic forms the resources of figurative art as a means of organization. For Burle Marx these were 'general principles of art', to which the design of gardens must adhere. It was thus that in his dual role as painter and landscape artist he brought a new vocabulary to the figurative treatment of green space, in a way which was totally new to contemporary culture.

As well as similarities with the French avant-garde sculptor Jean Arp, the interpretation of Burle Marx's gardens is linked to the reading of the procedure of composition. The distribution of masses, the rhythmic frequencies of colour and shape, the use of repetition and juxtaposition, the contrasting differences in mass, these are the elements which single out his best work, and which form part of the avant-garde buildings constructed in the forties and fifties, such as the Park of Pampulha (1942) and the gardens of the Museum of Modern Art in Rio (1955).

Other problems, besides that of composition, arose when the garden, defined by Burle Marx as 'ordered impulse', confronted nature. Given that his art sought an ideal of Brazilian flora and fauna, the problem was to establish carefully the distinction between what was natural in art and what was natural in its own surroundings. If the aim was not simply to copy the exotic, and if the model – nature – surrounded one, how and where should the limits be set? The use of trees as fences and artistically treated walls became part of the repertory of 'total art' and define the early stage in the garden work for Olivo Gomes (1951) amongst others, where the problem is approached from the establishment of clearly defined limits, to the point where the boundaries are imperceptible.

Notwithstanding Burle Marx's deep knowledge of Brazilian flora, the result of rigorous work over several decades in the search for and classification of plants, the development of his work shows a great change in his attitude to nature, leaving aside its role as an artistic work and becoming instead part of a plan of total art, and by extension a global problem requiring solutions.

On the one hand, a deepening botanical knowledge brings with it the acknowledgment of landscape techniques as a pursuit not wholly part of the world of figurative art, now that the three-dimensionality, temporality and dynamics of living creatures should be considered part of the composition; laws beyond those which apply to the static character of pictorial techniques are thus required. On the other hand, a knowledge of Brazilian flora also implies a knowledge of its destruction, which, during the last few decades of economic growth, has taken place at an alarming rate.

It was as a result of both these factors that Burle Marx's output underwent important changes. The problem established by the analogy between the arts of painting and creating gardens resulted in Burle Marx breaking the frontiers of the problem, and his vision of the integration

*Views of the Parque del Este, Caracas.
(Photos Giovanni Chiaramonte)*

of landscape into a greater whole, involving all green spaces and the problems of conservation. This position was consciously militant in its defence of nature, and was reflected in the speech which Burle Marx read before the Federal Senate in 1976, in which he denounced the superficiality with which both the state and individuals approached the problem.

His stance in this speech is reflected in Burle Marx's more recent parks, gardens and green urban spaces. These are usually, and not surprisingly, large-scale commissions, which serve not only to fulfil the functions required by the programme providing for recreation in large cities, but also to instruct. The idea of the 'teaching park' was already established in the unfinished Park of Araxá (1944), and expanded in the Zoobotanical Park of Brasilia (1961), which set out passionately to show the degree to which nature is threatened. Burle Marx wished it to be a place where 'town dwellers can understand the values of nature' from the didactic ordering of phyto-geographic regions showing real 'ecological paintings' at the edges of the organized park and nature reserve. In this case the function of the landscape artist is limited to showing Brazilian flora. The need for boundaries or gradations between nature and the 'ordering impulse' of the garden ceases to exist. The limits of real nature are instead defined by the degree of economic expansion and the distortions which this creates in its environment.

The didactic park, and Burle Marx's dramatic search for a collective acknowledgment of the values of nature, is a direct result of the paradox inherent in the development of Brazilian Modernism: while it celebrates the syntheses revealed in the great manifestations of its culture, it has to start concerning itself with the processes of destruction, considered at one time a major source for its ideas.

Bibliography

Aracy Amaral (ed.), *Arte y arquitectura del Modernismo brasileña (1971–1930)* (Caracas 1978).

P. M. Bardi, *The Tropical Gardens of Burle Marx* (New York 1964).

Damián Bayón and Graziano Gasparini, *Panorama de la arquitectura latinoamericana* (Barcelona 1977).

Views of the Parque del Este, Caracas.
(Photos Giovanni Chiaramonte)

Roberto Burle Marx, *Arte e paisagem, conferencias escolhidas* (São Paulo 1987).
'Cadernos Brasileiros de Arquitectura', in *Paisagismo I y II*, Vols. 5 and 11 (São Paulo 1986).
Carlos Eduardo Dias Comas, 'Una cierta arquitectura moderna brasileña: experiencia por reconocer' in *Summa* no. 243 (Nov. 1987).
Flavio Motta, *Roberto Burle Marx e la nova visao da paisagem* (São Paulo 1985).
Jorge F. Liernur, *Arquitectura latinoamericana contemporanea (1967–87)*. In preparation.
Enrico Tedeschi, 'El medio ambiente natural' in *América Latina en su arquitectura* (Mexico City 1975).

The Gardens of
Ian Hamilton Finlay

Stephen Bann

Ian Hamilton Finlay, the Sacred Grove;
detail. Kröller-Müller Museum, Otterlo.

Ian Hamilton Finlay and J. R. Thrope,
Nuclear Sail *monolith, 1971. (Photo*
Lindsey Stewart)

Ian Hamilton Finlay's development as a poet, artist and gardener over the past twenty years has an exemplary significance. In 1966, he and his wife Sue made their home at the small farm of Stonypath, on the edge of the Pentland Hills in the Lowlands of Scotland. Finlay already had a wide reputation as a concrete poet and as the enterprising editor of the Wild Hawthorn Press. He had therefore experimented to a certain extent with the visual and typographic possibilities of the printed word, and even constructed some poems for display out of doors at a previous home in Ardgay, Ross-shire. But the farm of Stonypath offered a much greater potential. Despite its dilapidated state at the outset, it was a promising site, with a cluster of farm buildings at the centre and a variety of different terrains ranging from rough moorland to a small cultivated area adjacent to the cottage; the hill-side on which it was set offered splendid views, and was fed by a small stream whose waters could be dammed to form a series of ponds. Finlay's achievement over the next two decades was to transform this area into a poet's garden, in the tradition of the English poet/gardeners of the eighteenth century, Alexander Pope and William Shenstone.

In the initial stages of this work, the garden features and the inscribed stones placed within them were fairly modest in scale. Finlay began with two projects: the Top Pond, which was full enough for his small son to sail on it by May 1967, and the Sunken Garden in front of the cottage, which was inlaid with stones bearing poetic texts. It rapidly became apparent that gardening was a long-term activity, which could not be rushed.[1] The plants needed time to get established, and the strong prevailing winds made it necessary to introduce trees and trellises for their protection. By the early 1970s, it was however possible to glimpse the character of the main features of the garden. In front of the cottage, a small gate led into the most enclosed area, with fruit and vegetables as well as a profusion of flowers, inscribed stones and small benches accompanying sundials and other traditional features. On the other side of the farm courtyard, the sequence of ponds had culminated in the creation of Lochan Eck, a stretch of water made possible by the clearing of the site by bulldozers in September 1970. In the

miniaturized scale of the garden, Lochan Eck had become the Ocean, signalled as such by the placing (in 1973) of the slate monolith *Nuclear Sail*, derived from the conning tower of a nuclear submarine.

This use of the imagery of modern warfare points to the fact that, by 1973, Finlay had launched into the programme of 'neoclassical rearmament' which was to transform the meaning of the garden, and necessitate its change of name from Stonypath to Little Sparta. As the vegetation became more profuse, and Finlay's ambition to recreate the features associated with the great gardens of the past became more evident, it also became increasingly clear that a didactic message was embodied in his work. Little Sparta became not simply an implicit critique of the shallowness and ephemeral nature of much contemporary art, but also the embodiment of what Yves Abrioux has called a 'polemological poetics'.[2] The clearest demonstration of the seriousness of this claim was to come in 1983, when

Finlay and his 'Saint-Just Vigilantes' defended the Temple of Apollo in the farm courtyard against the depredations of the local rating authority, which wished to raise taxes on it as a commercial gallery. Little Sparta had inevitably come into conflict with the instruments of the secular state.

The maturity of the garden can now be seen clearly from a series of views of the inner courtyard, adjacent to the Temple of Apollo. A stone shell reminiscent of the *Birth of Venus* (and inscribed with a punning identification between the 'Goddess' and the 'Caddis', an insect of the pond) marks the point at which the waters of the small stream enter the pond. At the other side, rock plants and ivy frame the *Aircraft-Carrier Birdbath*, an example of a traditional feature of the cottage garden which has been given a new urgency by the choice of the modern warship for the birds (like fighter planes) to refresh themselves. In the northerly direction, the entrance to a recently

installed Grotto, let into the hillside, can be glimpsed beyond the stretch of water with its tranquil inscriptions. To the east of the cottage, a small agricultural building has been imaginatively transformed, by the addition of a rustic portico, into the Temple of Baucis and Philemon. The flash of gold on the roof, caught by the sun, signals the moment at which the hospitality of the old couple is rewarded by Jupiter, and the humble cottage is metamorphosed (according to Ovid) into a temple: *stramina flavescunt* – the straw thatching turns yellow-gold.[3]

Although the garden of Little Sparta remains Finlay's most complex and challenging achievement, he has also worked on a number of other projects. Originally these were conceived as comparatively simple installations, like the *Land/Sea Sundial*, commissioned by the University of Kent at Canterbury in 1972, and carried out (like many of his larger commissions) with the aid of the stone-carver Michael Harvey. Of a more am-

Little Sparta, Scotland: the Grotto, seen across the pond. (Photo Antonia Reeve)

Little Sparta: Aircraft-Carrier Birdbath *by Ian Hamilton Finlay. (Photo Antonia Reeve)*

bitious scale was the *Wave Wall* completed with Denis Barns and Ron Costley at Livingston New Town, Scotland, in 1976, which formed a self-contained area adjacent to the new shopping centre. In the same year, he completed his first garden away from Stonypath at the Max Planck Institute in Stuttgart, West Germany. In collaboration with the architects Brenner and Partner, and utilizing the lettering of Ron Costley once again, Finlay created a small formal garden with poems inscribed on marble, concrete and steel; the unity of conception derived from the fact that these were all simple, elemental texts, inspired by his readings in pre-Socratic philosophy and appropriate to the theme of a scientific institute named after a pioneer of modern physics.

There can be no doubt, however, that Finlay's most striking and successful new garden is the Sacred Grove established in 1982 at the Sculpture Park of the Kröller-Müller Museum, near Otterlo in Holland. Although it forms part of the park, it is surrounded by bushes and trees, and approached by a winding, paved path which effectively insulates it from the other works. Here Finlay has utilized a system originally used at Little Sparta with good results; a number of trees (in this case, mature trees already existing in the park) have been supplied with column bases which do not inhibit their growth, but supply a neoclassical reference and, in a sense, transform the living tree into a column. Each base is inscribed with a dedication to a hero associated with the French Revolution: Lycurgus, its Spartan precursor; Rousseau, its philosophical inspiration; Michelet, its historian; Robespierre, its defender and victim — and finally Corot, whose own neoclassical style is envisaged as a tribute to the classical ideals of the revolutionary heroes. Finlay's Sacred Grove belongs to the long tradition of celebrating heroes in garden features, as with the Temple of British Worthies at Stowe and the Temple of Philosophy at Ermenonville. It is a historical point of reference, both in its form and in its subject matter. But it is also a vital contemporary statement, which vindicates the practice of landscape design as a polemical insertion into the present-day context of the visual arts.

[1] For a fuller account of the different stages of development of the 'Little Sparta' garden, see Stephen Bann, 'A Description of Stonypath' in *Journal of Garden History*, Vol. 1, No. 2, pp. 113–34.

[2] For the 'polemological' aspect of Finlay's work, see Yves Abrioux, *Ian Hamilton Finlay: A visual primer* (Edinburgh 1985), pp. 168–85.

[3] See Stephen Bann, 'Finlay's Fane' in *PN Review* 42 (Vol. 11, No. 4), pp. 21–25.

The Impossible Quest for the Past: Thoughts on the Restoration of Gardens

Monique Mosser

Sceaux: headless statue in the park. (Photo Fulvio Ventura)

Shortly after the last war, Ernest de Ganay, reflecting on the terrible fate of one of the finest classical gardens in France, wrote

It is beyond question that the fine embroidered box parterres, the gushing fountains, the superb terraces of Louis XIV's reign no longer embellish the gardens at Harcourt, but the past, once gone, must be the past. Let us not seek to resuscitate defunct gardens when we are ignorant of the details of the original design. Let us restore order to gardens that have been defaced: there are problems enough in this undertaking. And it is precisely in using discretion in the restoration of these shattered gardens that we show the greatest respect for the past.[1]

It has taken a considerable time for us to accept that, faced with irreparable losses or damage caused by more specific causes (disease that has struck certain species of tree, or pollution of various sorts) we must be prepared to view gardens in a way that is simply different. Their close links with the 'noble art' of architecture have in fact for a long time relegated them to the ill-defined category of 'surroundings' a vague area derived from a concept in western thinking that is traditionally restrictive. Gardens are viewed as a setting, as the means of creating a mood or atmosphere, or more recently as the 'green' factor in modern planning jargon: but rarely are they considered as designs in their own right, as an independent art form.

In matters of gardening, the English were often pioneers. Thus it was that shortly after the last war, they defined the first principles of a specific policy. Later, international authorities in the field of culture followed suit. In 1971 the IFLA (International Federation of Landscape Architects) and ICOMOS (International Council on Monuments and Sites) organized at Fontainebleau an initial conference on historic gardens[2] which was the basis for the creation of a permanent international Committee. Ten years later this committee was to draw up a seminal document, the Florence Charter (21 May 1981), setting out a few basic definitions as well as strict regulations concerning the maintenance, conservation, restoration and reconstruction of gardens. Essentially the Florence Charter defines a 'historic garden' as a *living monument*, in so far as 'its appearance reflects the perpetual balance between the

cycle of the seasons, the growth and decay of nature, and the desire of the artist and craftsman to keep it permanently unchanged'. The entire text is outstanding both for its subtlety and its relevance.[3] But there is no doubt that its authors, writing in an international context, had in mind outstanding examples of 'showpiece' gardens: Versailles, Caprarola, the Alhambra as well as celebrated oriental sites. However, as concern for gardens has become widespread, so it has diversified, an attitude which is indicative of the intense interest currently being shown in the concept of 'heritage'. In France, for example, within the framework of regional inventories organized in 1980 by the Direction de l'Urbanisme et des Paysages, the wider definition of 'parks and gardens of landscape, historical and

botanical interest'[4] was preferred. And the Italians sum up all these ideas in one striking phrase: '*Il verde storico*'.

Thus the conceptual, ethical and political vacuum surrounding gardens has been succeeded, as often happens in such cases, by a variety of projects inspired by very different ambitions and interests, and not always independent of the concerns of big business and high finance. Now the debate is wide open. Specialists argue about matters of principle – restoration, reconstruction or rehabilitation?[5]

In 1932, in a little-known text which she dedicated to the Désert de Retz, Colette, who loved walled gardens and arbours of russet vines, pleaded for the preservation of 'this garden lovely as a poem', while at the same time musing,

'Since I saw the Désert on a stormy day in June, I tremble at the thought of seeing it changed, cleared of all its debris, and faced with the shining glory of its own renewal.' Sadly the Désert was not restored, and it has taken a great deal of devotion and determination to prevent its disappearance forever. Is this nostalgic desire to save the ineffable a purely 'literary' preoccupation? Not really, since the premises of a similar attitude were to be found towards the end of the eighteenth century, as can be seen in this observation by the landscape architect Pierre-Adrien Pâris: 'What adds further to the great charm of Roman gardens is the impression of dignity imposed by the hand of time.'[6] We should recall too the tremendous controversy surrounding the felling of virtually all the trees in the park

Chantilly: the water parterre. (Photo Fulvio Ventura)

Claremont: the Belvedere by Sir John Vanbrugh. (Photo Daniele De Lonte)

...reaux: the cascade, restored c. 1930. (Photo ...ulvio Ventura)

527

at Versailles, ordered – very judiciously – by Louis XVI shortly after his accession.[7] Confronted by the extensive 'restorations' carried out in the first quarter of the twentieth century in the great gardens of France, the historian de Ganay also noted,

It is important to state here that no one more than ourselves admires French-style gardens. But we recognize also the art of the English approach to gardens, which is superior in certain situations. Concerning certain gardens restored in recent years, moreover, the future will tell whether it would not have been better to leave these glorious dead to their eternal sleep, rather than condemning them to a sort of invalid existence, while splendid and beautiful estates such as Méréville are abandoned to a pitiful and unjust death agony.[8]

It is not the intention here to fuel a debate almost as old as gardens themselves, a debate which is fruitful because it transcends their creation, like any vision of nature. But, oddly enough, it is a debate which has echoes in current attitudes towards historic gardens. Thus Jean Feray, at the eighth assembly of the International Committee for Gardens and Historic Sites in 1985, gave a paper on *Versailles, the archetypal historic garden.*[9] Archetype is a strong word. It means 'an original model from which copies are made'. An historic garden, but which historic garden? Versailles, but which Versailles? It has long been demonstrated that in gardens, as in architecture, there was never *one*, but *several* Versailles. Here we have, explains B. Teyssèdre,[10] 'a living organism which evolves, is profligate in growth, achieves wisdom with age. None of its successive appearances is a mere extension of what has gone before, nor is the preceding state eliminated in favour of a more perfect creation.' The early gardens of Versailles – picturesque, playful and garish, with their painted porcelain pagoda, their marshes with reeds made of tin plate, their statues gleaming with gold or blazing with colour – do not accord with the accepted idea of classicism. It is this same 'frozen' vision, for example in the gardens of the châteaux of the Loire, which is denounced by Isa Belli Barsali, an Italian specialist in this area. Analysing the risks inherent in any attempt at systematic reconstruction, she illustrates the point perfectly with the prestigious example of the gardens of the Villa d'Este in Tivoli:[11]

In these gardens little was done during the nineteenth century. Neglect and lack of maintenance have at different times been the reason for the exuberant plant growth. Today Tivoli is no longer the place which delighted its original creators, the cardinals of the House of Este. It is an altogether different garden, a romantic wood where you stumble across architectural fragments like islands, with fountains gushing from them. . . . The Tivoli gardens today have a special beauty made up of different layers laid down over the course of time. It is true that the overgrown vegetation means that the main axes of the design can no longer be distinguished, but it seems to me that any intervention should be limited to cutting back the plant life where it covers the paths and fountains too thickly. Uprooting and replanting would be equally absurd. . . . The problem with our inheritance of gardens with a composite Renaissance appearance – Baroque or nineteenth century – is the preservation of these features, rather than the 'restoration' of

them. We should not make the mistake – so common in certain historic monuments and archeological sites – of obliterating the most recent states in order to restore false ones.

Here we have two points of view at opposite ends of the spectrum: on the one hand 'immutable Versailles', an historic fiction nurtured on the interpretation of documents which, whatever their value, were originally no more than idealized images; and on the other 'minimal' intervention, incapable of coping with certain medium or long-term problems.

When Achille Duchêne removed all traces of the informal gardens surrounding certain neoclassical châteaux (at Le Marais, for example) – revealing in this case a failure to understand the Age of Enlightenment's paradoxical balance between architectural order and the

'wildness' of the garden – he was conforming to a certain ideological doctrine of Classicism.[12] When Dr Carvallo designed the wonderful gardens at Villandry, marrying 'post-Troubadour' Renaissance and *fin de siècle* symbolism, he created an inspired work of art.[13] One mistake, one stroke of genius, two perfect creations perpetrated to a greater or lesser degree in the name of history.

Restoring, rehabilitating, bringing back to life a symbolic or significant fragment, re-creating 'in the spirit of . . .' daring to create, purely and simply: there are as many attitudes, and as many risks, as there are arguments. Here it is no longer a question of choice between 'gardens of the intelligence' and 'gardens of the emotions', but of close analysis, allowing time for understanding. Between the permanence (however rela-

View of the Bosquet d'Apollon During the Felling of the Trees. *Painting by H. Robert, 1777. Musée de Versailles. (Photo Bulloz)*

tive) of stone and the transience of flowers, time in the garden demands ambition and modesty, patience and passion. Here we return to Michel Tournier's subtle approach to the garden:

As soon as we start talking of gardens we must go beyond the geometric plane and introduce a third dimension into our thinking. For the man whose vocation is the garden digs the ground and examines the sky. To have complete understanding it is not enough to design and rake. We must learn the hidden secrets of the humus, and know the passage of the clouds. But for the man-gardener there is a fourth dimension, by which I mean metaphysics.[14]

This is the dimension that the 'restorer' cannot afford to ignore.[15]

[1] Ernest de Ganay, 'Les jardins d'Harcourt', in *Revue de l'Art Ancien et Moderne* (Jan. 1923) pp. 60–64.

[2] International Conference on Monuments and Sites (Colloque International des Monuments et des Sites), Fontainebleau, 13–18 September 1971. Since that time the Gardens Section of ICOMOS has met regularly, publishing the results of its deliberations and appointing members, who are garden specialists, in a number of countries. In 1988 Mme Carmen Añón assumed the presidency of this international section from its founder, M. René Pechère. The International Committee for Historic Gardens also regularly publishes a bibliography with particular reference to the problems of restoration.

[3] The Florence Charter should be cited in its entirety in a work on the history of gardens. It therefore figures as an appendix.

[4] For a complete summary of work being currently undertaken in France in this respect, see the catalogue of the exhibition 'Et les Jardins en France?', Institut Français d'Architecture, Paris, 20 April–14 May 1988.

We know, from another source, that certain European countries are very active in this area. See, for England, the researches of the Centre for the Conservation of Historic Parks and Gardens of the University of York, directed by Peter Goodchild. This centre has published a very useful *Conservation reading list* compiled by Janette Gallagher and Peter Goodchild. Italy, Spain, Holland and Germany are beginning to fund similar organizations for cataloguing, documentation, and specialist training. In certain eastern European countries such as Poland and the USSR the work being done towards a genuine policy on gardens must not be overlooked.

[5] The relevant bibliography is increasing considerably and it would be of great benefit if an organization such as ICOMOS would undertake the compilation of a comprehensive inventory within the framework of Europe, and beyond.

[6] See note 1 to 'The Gardens of Hubert Robert' (this volume p. 342).

[7] *Ibid.* As it happens, more than two hundred years later the problem at Versailles is almost identical. See *Régénérer les jardins classiques* Deliberations of the French section of ICOMOS, Versailles, 2–4 Oct. 1985.

[8] Ernest de Ganay, preface to the new edition of *Coup d'oeil sur Beloeil* by the Prince de Ligne (Paris 1922) p. 19.

[9] See above, note 7 pp. 9–11.

[10] Bernard Teyssèdre, *L'Art au siècle de Louis XIV* (Paris 1967) p. 128.

[11] Isa Belli Barsali, 'Quale Giardino? Ipotesi di restauro per giardini storici romani' in *Giardino, Storia e Conservazione* (Rome 1985) pp. 33–41.

[12] See, in this volume, M. Mosser 'The Duchênes and the Reinvention of Le Nôtre'.

[13] See, with reference to Villandry, Dr Carvallo's introduction to Prosper Péan's *Jardins de France* (Paris 1925) and also Kenneth Woodbridge, 'Doctor Carvallo and the absolute' in *Garden History*, Vol. 6, no. 2 (Summer 1978) pp. 46–68.

[14] Michel Tournier, *Le vent paraclet* (Paris 1977) p. 293.

[15] We think it of interest to quote here some useful titles on the specific subject of garden archaeology:

Audrey Noël Hume, *Archeology and the Colonial Gardener*, Colonial Williamsburg Archaeological Series No. 7 (Williamsburg 1974).

Christopher Taylor, *The Archaeology of Gardens* (Aylesbury 1983).

Other important sources worth consulting:

Il Giardino storico italiano. Problemi di indagine, fonti letterarie e storiche, Proceedings of the convention in Siena, 6–8 Oct. 1978 (Florence 1981).

Tom Wright, *Large Gardens and Parks, Maintenance, Management and Design* (London 1982).

Recreating the Period Garden, under the direction of Graham Stuart Thomas (London 1984).

Mario Catalano and Franco Panzini, *Giardini storici, teoria e techniche di conservazione e restauro* (Rome 1985).

Il Giardino storico. Protezione e restauro, ICOMOS, Regione Toscana (Florence 1987).

John Harvey, *Restoring Period Gardens* (Aylesbury 1988).

ICOMOS:
Florence Charter

ICOMOS
International Council on Monuments and Sites

*International Committee on
Historic Gardens and Sites*
ICOMOS-IFLA

FLORENCE CHARTER
21 May 1981

The ICOMOS-IFLA International Committee for Historic Gardens, meeting in Florence on 21 May 1981, decided to draw up a charter on the preservation of historic gardens which would bear the name of that town. The present Charter was drafted by the Committee and registered by ICOMOS on 15 December 1982 as an addendum to the Venice Charter covering the specific field concerned.

Definitions and objectives
Art. 1. 'An historic garden is an architectural and horticultural composition of interest to the public from the historical or artistic point of view.' As such, it is to be considered as a *monument*.
Art. 2. 'The historic garden is an architectural composition whose constituents are primarily vegetal and therefore living, which means that they are perishable and renewable.' Thus its appearance reflects the perpetual balance between the cycle of the seasons, the growth and decay of nature and the desire of the artist and craftsman to keep it permanently unchanged.
Art. 3. As a monument, the historic garden must be preserved in accordance with the spirit of the Venice Charter. However, since it is a *living monument*, its preservation must be governed by specific rules which are the subject of the present charter.
Art. 4. The architectural composition of the historic garden includes:
— Its plan and its topography.
— Its vegetation, including its species, proportions, colour schemes, spacing and respective heights.
— Its structural and decorative features.
— Its water, running or still, reflecting the sky.
Art. 5. As the expression of the direct affinity between civilization and nature, and as a place of enjoyment suited to meditation or repose, the garden thus acquires the cosmic significance of an idealized image of the world, a 'paradise' in the etymological sense of the term, and yet a testimony to a culture, a style, an age, and often to the originality of a creative artist.
Art. 6. The term, 'historic garden', is equally applicable to small gardens and to large parks, whether formal or 'landscape'.
Art. 7. Whether or not it is associated with a building – in which case it is an inseparable complement – the historic garden cannot be isolated from its own particular environment, whether urban or rural, artificial or natural.
Art. 8. An historic site is a specific landscape associated with a memorable act, as, for example, a major historic event; a well-known

myth; an epic combat; or the subject of a famous picture.
Art. 9. The preservation of historic gardens depends on their identification and listing. They require several kinds of action, namely maintenance, conservation and restoration. In certain cases, reconstruction may be recommended. The *authenticity* of an historic garden depends as much on the design and scale of its various parts as on its decorative features and on the choice of plant or inorganic materials adopted for each of its parts.

Maintenance, conservation, restoration, reconstruction
Art. 10. In any work of maintenance, conservation, restoration or reconstruction of an historic garden, or of any part of it, all its constituent features must be dealt with simultaneously. To isolate the various operations would damage the unity of the whole.

Maintenance and conservation
Art. 11. Continuous maintenance of historic gardens is of paramount importance. Since the principal material is vegetal, the preservation of the garden in an unchanged condition requires both prompt replacements when required and a long-term programme of periodic renewal (clear felling and replanting with mature specimens).
Art. 12. Those species of trees, shrubs, plants and flowers to be replaced periodically must be selected with regard for established and recognized practice in each botanical and horticultural region, and with the aim to determine the species initially grown and to preserve them.
Art. 13. The permanent or movable architectural, sculptural or decorative features which form an integral part of the historic garden must be removed or displaced only insofar as this is essential for their conservation or restoration. The replacement or restoration of any such jeopardized features must be effected in accordance with the principles of the Venice Charter, and the date of any complete replacement must be indicated.
Art. 14. The historic garden must be preserved in appropriate surroundings. Any alteration to the physical environment which will endanger the ecological equilibrium must be prohibited. These applications are applicable to all aspects of the infrastructure, whether internal or external (drainage works, irrigation systems, roads, car parks, fences, care-taking facilities, visitors' amenities, etc).

Restoration and reconstruction
Art. 15. No restoration work and, above all, no reconstruction work on an historic garden shall be undertaken without thorough prior research to ensure that such work is scientifically executed, and which will involve everything from excavation to the assembling of records relating to the garden in question and to similar gardens. Before any practical work starts, a project must be prepared on the basis of said research and must be submitted to a

group of experts for joint examination and approval.
Art. 16. Restoration work must respect the successive stages of evolution of the garden concerned. In principle, no one period should be given precedence over any other, except in exceptional cases where the degree of damage or destruction affecting certain parts of a garden may be such that it is decided to reconstruct it on the basis of the traces that survive or of unimpeachable documentary evidence. Such reconstruction work might be undertaken more particularly on the parts of the garden nearest to the building it contains in order to bring out their significance in the design.
Art. 17. Where a garden has completely disappeared or there exists no more than conjectural evidence of its successive stages a reconstruction could not be considered an historic garden.

Use
Art. 18. While any historic garden is designed to be seen and walked about in, access to it must be restricted to the extent demanded by its size and vulnerability, so that its physical fabric and cultural message may be preserved.
Art. 19. By reason of its nature and purpose, an historic garden is a peaceful place conducive to human contacts, silence and awareness of nature. This conception of its everyday use must contrast with its role on those rare occasions when it accommodates a festivity. Thus, the conditions of such occasional use of an historic garden should be clearly defined, in order that any such festivity may itself serve to enhance the visual effect of the garden instead of perverting or damaging it.
Art. 20. While historic gardens may be suitable for quiet games as a daily occurrence, separate areas appropriate for active and lively games and sports should also be laid out adjacent to the historic garden, so that the needs of the public may be satisfied in this respect without prejudice to the conservation of the gardens and landscapes.
Art. 21. The work of maintenance and conservation, the timing of which is determined by season, and brief operations which serve to restore the garden's authenticity, must always take precedence over the requirements of public use. All arrangements for visits to historic gardens must be subjected to regulations that ensure the spirit of the place is preserved.
Art. 22. If a garden is walled, its walls may not be removed without prior examination of all the possible consequences liable to lead to changes in its atmosphere and to affect its preservation.

Legal and administrative protection
Art. 23. It is the task of the responsible authorities to adopt, on the advice of qualified experts, the appropriate legal and administrative measures for the identification, listing and protection of historic gardens. The preservation of such gardens must be provided for

within the framework of land-use plans and such provision must be duly mentioned in documents relating to regional and local planning. It is also the task of the responsible authorities to adopt, with the advice of qualified experts, the financial measures which will facilitate the maintenance, conservation and restoration, and, where necessary, the reconstruction of historic gardens.
Art. 24. The historic garden is one of the features of the patrimony whose survival, by reason of its nature, requires intensive, continuous care by trained experts. Suitable provision should therefore be made for the training of such persons, whether historians, architects, landscape architects, gardeners or botanists.
Care should also be taken to ensure that there is regular propagation of the plant varieties necessary for maintenance or restoration.
Art. 25. Interest in historic gardens should be stimulated by every kind of activity capable of emphasizing their true value as part of the patrimony and making for improved knowledge and appreciation of them: promotion of scientific research; international exchange and circulation of information; publications, including works designed for the general public; the encouragement of public access under suitable control and use of the media to develop awareness of the need for due respect for nature and the historic heritage. The most outstanding of the historic gardens shall be proposed for inclusion in the World Heritage List.

Nota bene
The above recommendations are applicable to all the historic gardens in the world.

Additional clauses applicable to specific types of gardens may be subsequently appended to the present Charter with brief descriptions of the said types.

Index of people and places

541